STUDIES IN LABOUR AND SOCIAL LAW

GENERAL EDITORS

B.A.HEPPLE
Sometime Fellow of Clare College, Cambridge

PAUL O'HIGGINS
Fellow of Christ's College, Cambridge
University Lecturer in Law

VOL. 2

Fair Wages Resolutions

BRIAN BERCUSSON

Fellow of Christ's College, Cambridge

Fair Wages Resolutions

MANSELL 1978

© Brian Bercusson 1978

Mansell/Information Publishing Limited
3 Bloomsbury Place London WC1A 2QA

International Standard Book Number: 0 7201 0709 1

British Library Cataloguing in Publication Data

    Bercusson, Brian
        Fair wages resolutions. — (Studies in labour and social law; vol. 2)
        1. Great Britain. Parliament. House of Commons — Resolutions
        2. Wages — Great Britain
        3. Public contracts — Great Britain
        I. Title   II. Series
        331.2'3   HD4932.F/

    ISBN 0–7201–0709–1

Printed in Great Britain by
Ebenezer Baylis and Son, Limited,
The Trinity Press, Worcester, and London

This book is as much
from, as to
my parents
Libby and Joe Bercusson

CONTENTS

vii

PART III

THE THIRD FAIR WAGES POLICY
1946–1976

PART IV

SCHEDULE 11 AND THE FUTURE OF
FAIR WAGES POLICY

PREFACE

The origins of this book lie in a doctoral dissertation submitted to the University of Cambridge in October 1973. It comprised a comparative analysis of early attempts at regulation of wages on government contracts in the United Kingdom and the United States. In the United Kingdom, regulation was attempted through the Fair Wages Resolutions of 1891, 1909 and 1946.

These Resolutions are not legislation passed by Parliament. Only very rarely have they been subjected to judicial interpretation and analysis in the courts. They are not, therefore, 'law' in the sense of that word as defined by lawyers. Nonetheless, as Professor Sir Otto Kahn-Freund commented in 1948:

> Those most interested in the fair wages resolutions adopted by the House of Commons and by local authorities were, of course, the unions and their members. From their point of view these clauses were, whatever the lawyer may say, one of the corner-stones of British labour 'law'. (*Modern Law Review*, **11,** p.274.)

For his appreciation of a wider perspective on labour law, I am most grateful to Dr. Paul O'Higgins, Fellow of Christ's College, Cambridge, who encouraged me in the preparation of the thesis and the completion of this book.

The writing of the dissertation was made possible by a Doctoral Fellowship provided by the Canada Council, and its continuation into the present book by my election as a Research Fellow of Christ's College. I am grateful to both these institutions for their generosity.

Doctoral dissertations are not easily converted into readable books. The first half of this book, originally part of the dissertation, certainly resisted my strenuous endeavours. Still, it was completely re-written. Throughout the book, an attempt has been made to ease the burden on the reader by limiting the number of footnotes to the absolute minimum. The principal method has been to accumulate the citation of sources into long footnotes at the conclusion of each chapter. It is possible to trace the source of quotations in this way, without unduly disturbing the reader by constant interruptions requiring referral to footnotes.

Finally, the primary aim of this book is to examine the Fair Wages Resolutions in the context of industrial relations. As will quickly be realized, the dearth of secondary literature on the Resolutions has meant that most of the sources referred to in the notes are primary— Reports of and Evidence to Committees of the House of Commons, other Parliamentary papers, records of government departments and other bodies, awards of arbitration tribunals. In contrast, for information on the state of industrial relations from the end of the last century to date, I have relied primarily on secondary sources, inadequate though these are. It is for the synthesis between the two that I am responsible.

BRIAN BERCUSSON

May 1977

LIST OF ABBREVIATIONS

A.C.A.S.   Advisory, Conciliation and Arbitration Service
A.C.T.A.T.   Association of Cinematograph, Television and Allied
                Technicians
A.E.U.   Amalgamated Engineering Union
A.S.S.E.T.   Association of Supervisory Staff, Executives and
                Technicians
A.S.T.M.S.   Association of Scientific, Technical and Managerial
                Staffs
A.U.B.T.W.   Amalgamated Union of Building Trade Workers
A.U.E.W.   Amalgamated Union of Engineering Workers
A.U.T.   Association of University Teachers

B.A.L.P.A.   British Air Line Pilots Association
B.E.A.   British European Airways
B.E.C.   British Employers' Confederation
B.R.S.   British Road Services
B.S.C.   British Sugar Corporation
B.U.A.   British United Airways

C.A.C.   Central Arbitration Committee
C.A.G.   Cleaners' Action Group
C.A.W.U.   Clerical and Administrative Workers Union
C.B.I.   Confederation of British Industry
C.E.G.B.   Central Electricity Generating Board
C.C.M.A.   Contract Cleaning and Maintenance Association
C.S.E.U.   Confederation of Shipbuilding and Engineering
                Unions
C.S.U.   Civil Service Union

D.A.T.A.   Draughtsmen's and Allied Technicians' Union
D.H.S.S.   Department of Health and Social Security

E.E.F.	Engineering Employers' Federation
E.E.T.P.U.	Electrical, Electronic, Telecommunication, and Plumbing Union
E.T.U.	Electrical Trades Union
G.L.C.	Greater London Council
G.M.W.U.	General and Municipal Workers Union
H.S.A.	Hawker Siddeley Aviation Ltd.
I.A.B.	Industrial Arbitration Board
I.D.T.	Industrial Disputes Tribunal
I.L.O.	International Labour Organization
J.I.C.	Joint Industrial Council
J.S.S.C.	Joint Shop Stewards Committee
L.C.C.	London County Council
L.E.A.	Local Education Authorities
NAAFI	Navy, Army and Air Force Institutes
N.A.L.G.O.	National Association of Local Government Officers
N.A.T.	{ National Arbitration Tribunal { National Association of Toolmakers
N.B.P.I.	National Board for Prices and Incomes
N.C.B.	National Coal Board
N.C.E.O.	National Confederation of Employers' Organizations
N.F.B.T.E.	National Federation of Building Trade Employers
N.G.A.	National Graphical Association
N.J.C.	National Joint Council
N.J.I.C.	National Joint Industrial Council
N.S.M.M.	National Society of Metal Mechanics
N.U.B.E.	National Union of Bank Employees
N.U.G.M.W.	National Union of General and Municipal Workers
N.U.J.	National Union of Journalists
N.U.M.	National Union of Mineworkers
N.U.P.E.	National Union of Public Employees
N.U.V.B.	National Union of Vehicle Builders
P.A.C.	Public Accounts Committee
P.O.E.U.	Post Office Engineering Union
R.H.A.	Road Haulage Association

| R.I.B.A. | Royal Institute of British Architects |
| R.I.C.S. | Royal Institute of Chartered Surveyors |

S.B.A.C.	Society of British Aerospace Contractors
S.E.T.	Selective Employment Tax
S.L.A.D.E.	Society of Lithographic Artists, Designers and Engravers

T.A.S.S.	Technical, Administrative and Supervisory Section
T.G.W.U.	Transport and General Workers' Union
T.U.C.	Trades Union Congress
T.U.L.R.A.	Trade Union and Labour Relations Act 1974

U.P.W.	Union of Post Office Workers
U.R.T.W.A.E.	United Road Transport Workers Association of England
U.S.D.A.W.	Union of Shop, Distributive and Allied Workers

INTRODUCTION

This book comprises an historical analysis of the Fair Wages Resolutions. These Resolutions—administrative directives to government departments—were passed by the House of Commons of the United Kingdom Parliament in 1891, 1909 and 1946. So the book is arranged chronologically, taking in turn each of these Resolutions, and concluding with the current state of what will henceforth be called the 'Fair Wages policy'. The analysis is developed on a number of different planes. First, there is a straightforward historical account of the origins, evolution and application of the Fair Wages policy—initially a policy on wage rates to be paid by government contractors to their employees. Secondly, it is a case study of the inter-relationship between law and society in the field of industrial relations. The development of collective bargaining is traced from the end of the nineteenth century to its present state. A key element of the study is the description of how legal institutions and formulae have trailed behind these developments. By failing to keep pace, their influence has been severely limited, or worse, they have become obstructions to further development. Finally, the book is an analysis of the evolution of government policy on industrial relations. With documents from the Public Record Office, the Department of Employment Library, the Library of the Trades Union Congress and others, it has been possible to construct the record of the development of the Fair Wages policy from its origins in trade union agitation, to its endorsement by the House of Commons, through to the various degrees of acceptance and modes of implementation by the contracting departments of government. The evolution of government policy on fair wages was a fascinating exercise, replete with inter-departmental conflicts, committee infighting and battles for the control of Ministerial initiative by the bureaucracy. It reached a peak in the crucial period of the 1930s when the tendency towards the statutory recognition of collective agreements was at its height.

For notes see p. xxvi

An analysis of the Fair Wages policy experience has become necessary today because of two recent developments which will be the subject of detailed analysis later. First, the Fair Wages policy has come into open conflict with the incomes policy objectives of governments. This was the subject of a lengthy series of Awards by the Industrial Arbitration Board—now the Central Arbitration Committee—which led to an appeal by the Pay Board to the High Court in the case of *Racal Communications Ltd.* v. *Pay Board* (1974). Secondly, the Fair Wages policy has appeared in a new form in the provisions of section 98 of and Schedule 11 to the Employment Protection Act 1975. *The Times* of 22 April 1975 quoted the C.B.I.'s description of the new policy, while still at the Bill stage, as 'the most dangerous and potentially most inflationary proposal in the whole document'. In order to anticipate the future of the Fair Wages policy, it is necessary to understand its past.

The account of the Fair Wages policy during its first two decades, 1891–1909, which is the term of the first Fair Wages Resolution, consists of the treatment of three major themes. First, the Fair Wages policy, being concerned with the fixing of terms and conditions of employment, in particular rates of wages, naturally affects and is affected by the industrial relations situation currently prevailing, which also regulates these terms of employment. It is necessary, therefore, to examine on broad lines the system of industrial relations, particularly collective bargaining, which existed during the period 1891–1909. The result of this investigation reveals that the Resolution passed in 1891 was formulated with a view of the *then* current system of industrial relations based on the experience of previous years. This view became completely inappropriate after significant changes occurred in collective bargaining in the years immediately following its passage.

Secondly, the meaning of the actual wording of the 1891 Resolution needs to be analysed. Here, however, one is faced with a difficulty resulting from the peculiar legal status of the Fair Wages Resolution as a mere resolution of the House of Commons. There are three possible approaches: (a) standard linguistic analysis of the text, as is done by lawyers in interpretating more ordinary legal materials—judicial decisions or legislation. Yet the Resolution is not of such a status; (b) discover the Resolution's meaning by ascertaining the intention of the House of Commons which passed it regardless of the ambiguities of the actual text. The difficulties of such an approach are well known and may be equally well illustrated through the Fair Wages Resolution; and (c) since the Resolution is in practice an administrative instruction to government departments, its 'meaning' might be discovered by examining the implementation of it in practice by these departments. Various problems will arise here as well. The result of this analysis reveals that the wording of the 1891 Resolution was so ambiguous as to preclude its effective and uniform enforcement.

Finally, in the light of the above two factors, the enforcement in practice of the 1891 Resolution by the government departments will be examined. What did the persons and organizations involved consider to be its impact on them and its success in achieving its stated aims? Then, from what may be deduced from the evidence available, an evaluation of its worth will be attempted. The result of this assessment reveals that for this, as for subsequent periods, the Fair Wages Resolution has been a dead letter—a useless prop to the defences maintained by workers' autonomous collective action.

The analysis of the Fair Wages Resolution of 1909 which replaced that of 1891 continues the development of the three principal themes: (a) the discrepancy between the industrial relations system upon which the 1909 Resolution was based and the developing reality of collective bargaining during the 1920s and 1930s with which it had to come to terms; (b) the conflicting interpretations of the Resolution; and (c) its enforcement in practice. Study of the period 1909–46, during which the second Fair Wages Resolution was in force, reveals that the evolution of the system of collective bargaining is of such significance that it overshadows the questions of interpretation and enforcement and, in effect, the latter two themes are integrated into the first.

During the period 1891–1909, the industrial relations scene in the United Kingdom had undergone a fundamental transformation with the widespread emergence of collective bargaining on a district basis in various trades. This process of change, however, had produced a confused situation where the 1891 Resolution, vague and indefinite in meaning, was allowed to succumb to ineffectiveness through the distaste or indifference of the administering bureaucracy and the animosity and self-interest of employer-contractors. The Fair Wages Resolution of 1909 followed a remarkably similar course. The period 1909–46 was one which experienced profound changes in industrial relations, but constantly accompanied by this fixed and unchanging formula. The First World War was a traumatic interruption, and its impact reached beyond the immediate emergency and transformed the industrial relations situation fundamentally. It is not argued that the changes would never have occurred but for it, nor that the seeds of the change were not already sprouting before. Nevertheless, it marks a significant watershed. The subsequent conflict which emerged between a rigid Resolution and a dynamic industrial relations system will be described.

The 1909 Resolution was worded totally differently from its predecessor. This presumes an intention of the House of Commons to instruct the administrative departments to follow a new policy with

regard to wage rates payable on government contracts. Apart from this
presumed certainty of some change, however, it is necessary to be
cautious in advancing a definitive interpretation of the new Resolution.
The lessons of the past indicated that vagueness of phraseology plus a
rapidly changing industrial relations environment resulted in administrative policies which varied widely among different departments
despite the universal reliance for authority on the same Resolution.
The setting up of a Fair Wages Advisory Committee shortly after the
1909 Resolution was passed was a move against this tendency. The
Committee, however, consisted exclusively of departmental representatives, and moreover, was purely advisory to the contracting departments who retained the power of final decision-making. Its meetings
appear to have been very sporadic: by early 1914 it had held a total
of thirty-three. From then until 1920, however, only four more meetings
were held. Another ten meetings took place over the following two
years, but between 1923 and 1936 an average of only one per year was
held—hardly adequate for effective co-ordination or supervision. Nor
were its interpretations of the Resolution, as those of the departments
it represented, regarded favourably by the trade union movement.
The Committee performed in its first years a useful function in supporting
the uniform implementation of the new Fair Wages policy across
departmental lines. Its role in the further development of the policy
was essentially conservative and obstructive.[1]

Another source for what purports to be authoritative interpretation
of the 1909 Resolution is the decisions of the Industrial Court, set up
as an independent industrial arbitration tribunal under the Industrial
Court Act 1919. However, no exhaustive analysis of the judgments of
the Court will be undertaken here. The number of cases actually
concerned with government contractors is miniscule, though there was
a small number on the disputes between government departments and
their employees, whose rates of wages were governed by the Fair Wages
Resolution. A few other decisions are to be found on the Fair Wages
Clauses of local authorities and on those contained in legislation
relating to certain special industries. But the Court was usually very
careful to restrict its observations to the facts of the cases before it and
very rarely expressed a more general view of Fair Wages policy.
Where it did do so, a review of the judgments shows that they did not
provide any useful guide to the implementation of the policy.

The crucial question throughout the period of the second Fair Wages
Resolution was the one perceived during the term of its predecessor—
the relation of collective bargaining agreements to Fair Wages standards.
The consequence of the upsurge in union organization and industrial
mobilization during the First World War was to place collective

bargaining on a basis that could no longer be disputed; the question was whether it could be ignored. The inter-war period experience of the Resolution revolved around that question. Thus, those cases which did come before the Industrial Court were most often brought by trade unions arguing that their collective agreements should be observed by government departments or by their contractors or those of local authorities, all of whom were subject to Fair Wages policies of one kind or another. Unfortunately, the Court's response to these pleas was most often in the negative. In one case the Court ignored provisions in a London building trades' agreement relating to lodging allowances and travelling expenses on the grounds that 'it does not appear from the evidence submitted to be the practice in the industry to pay' such allowances and expenses. In other cases the Court ignored collective agreements and relied instead on wages and conditions 'which in practice prevail amongst good employers'. In another case the company complained and urged the Court to ignore a collective agreement on the grounds that it 'could not be regarded as an agreement commonly recognized by employers and trade societies in the district having regard to the number of workpeople employed on other terms than those set out in that agreement', and the Court accordingly ignored it. In other cases the Court gave neither reason nor explanation for its determination of rates. Otherwise, the most common response was simply to reject the union's complaint.[2]

These Industrial Court cases, which cover only an infinitesimal sample of experience under the Fair Wages Resolution and which were of little practical guidance to contracting departments, are the most 'legal' of all aspects of the Resolution. But they are not the best way to understand the phenomenon. Rather it is the inter-relationship between collective bargaining and the Fair Wages policy which is the key to understanding it during this period. Consequently, the investigation will concentrate on this aspect.

Finally, as to the actual enforcement of the 1909 Resolution, the familiar litany is once again encountered: of accusations and complaints from trade unions, accompanied by government prevarication, reassurance, sometimes capitulation, but most often abrupt rejection. As collective bargaining developed, and the wording of the 1909 Resolution had appeared to recognize this, the quality of the official negativism became more sophisticated as demands were couched in terms of an industrial reality which had at least formally left the master-servant era and entered that of collective negotiation. The new terminology and more comprehensive demands, however, do not disguise the harsh reality of life for those workers undergoing the suffering and deprivation of the unemployment-ridden 1920s and the depression

1930s. They remained the victims of an economic system whose wage-competition bore fruit also for the government in its contracting requirements.

To explain the performance of the third Fair Wages Resolution of 1946, analysis of the fair wages formula and examination of the machinery of its enforcement are insufficient. Again, the key to understanding the impact of the Resolution is through its relationship to the system of industrial relations which emerged with it after the Second World War. This relationship was crucial for the understanding of the Resolutions of 1891 and 1909. The vague Resolution of 1891 was emasculated by the confusion engendered by volatile forces of collective bargaining emerging for the first time at the turn of the century. The inter-war period of the 1909 Resolution was characterized by collective bargaining at the national level, whereas the Resolution was interpreted as imposing district rates and was not considered by government departments as setting up national agreements as the standards to be observed. The 1946 Resolution was intended to remedy this defect in the 1909 Resolution by making as explicit as possible that national agreements should be the standards setting fair wages. The particularly confused draftsmanship of the Resolution resulted in a residue of misunderstanding about the extent to which the district-local element was to remain, but there was no doubt as to the intention of the Trades Union Congress which had campaigned for the new Resolution—national, not district or local rates or agreements were to be the standards of fair wages.

Three decades later, there is no need to emphasize the irony entailed in the T.U.C.'s insistence on national agreements as the post-war fair wages standards. The unions had been in conflict with government departments for decades over the question of whether national agreements were to be imposed on contractors. Now, at last, they appeared to have had their view embodied, albeit obscurely, in the Fair Wages Resolution itself. Yet few are today unaware of the secondary role national agreements have taken in the determination of wages since the War. The Donovan Commission Report of 1968 set the seal of official recognition on the industrial relations situation which had developed with the changed economic conditions following the War:

> Britain has two systems of industrial relations. The one is the formal system embodied in the official institutions. The other is the informal system created by the actual behaviour of trade unions and employers' associations, or managers, shop stewards and workers. (para. 46)

The maintenance of a previously unheard-of high level of employment had given rise to a phenomenon soon noticed by the economists—wage drift. This economic phenomenon became institutionalized with the growth of the shop stewards movement. The result was, as the Donovan Report put it, 'a remarkable transfer of authority in collective bargaining':

> Before the war it was generally assumed that industry-wide agreements could provide almost all the joint regulation that was needed, leaving only minor issues to be settled by individual managers. Today the consequences of bargaining within the factory can be more momentous than those of industry-wide agreements. (para. 57)

The consequences of these changes in the economic position and in industrial relations for the Fair Wages Resolution are obvious. The high level of employment and the economic boom which persisted through the post-war decades were accompanied by the steady maintenance of trade union strength and the superior bargaining power of workers. The depression of the inter-war period disappeared as the chief threat to the wage standards of workers. Those employed on government contracts enjoyed the respite granted workers generally, though by no means universally. That hardy annual of pre-war years, the T.U.C. resolution condemning the implementation of the Fair Wages policy, faded into intermittent outbursts at particular areas of dissatisfaction with the current Resolution. Much of the need for protection, though again by no means all, had been met through general economic measures. For the purposes of this study, however, it is interesting to note that once again the legal instrument of protection was at variance with what it sought to achieve. As will be illustrated in detail later, cases in which the Fair Wages Resolution of 1946 was invoked before the Industrial Court (later the Industrial Arbitration Board) showed up its inappropriateness to the new system of industrial relations. The nemesis of incompatibility with the industrial relations system was to dog the Fair Wages Resolutions to the end.

The consequences of this incompatibility of the Resolution with the industrial relations system is of the first importance to this study. In addition, however, certain specific provisions of the 1946 Resolution will be examined: clause 4 relating to the safeguarding of trade union rights, and clause 6 which regulated the sub-contracting arrangements of the main government contractors. Both these were the subject of much debate.

The 1946 Resolution was significantly involved in two other areas. First, the use of the Resolution as the standard for the wage rates of the employees of government contractors (as well as the industrial employees of the government) created certain conflicts with successive attempts by governments to impose incomes policies. Contractors found themselves subject to severe pressures from rising wage rates while tied to fixed-price contracts and forced the government to consider the inclusion of variation clauses in contracts allowing for such rises. The exemption of wage increases attributable to the Resolution from the pay freeze imposed by the succession of statutory instruments promulgated in the early 1970s led to a direct confrontation between contractors and the unions on the one side and the government in the shape of the Pay Board on the other.

The second major area of involvement took the form of the most determined attempt to utilize the Resolution as an instrument for the safe-guarding of standards in the post-war period. This was the effort made by the Civil Service Union to combat the low wages and poor conditions of women cleaners employed by contractors to the government to clean its buildings. This was always considered to be the classically effective area of operation of the Fair Wages Resolutions. The Union's effort can be traced back more than two decades, and the past ten years have witnessed a campaign of ceaseless agitation aimed at extending the protection of the Resolution to contract cleaners. Yet it was only on the 1 April 1975 that the Union and the Civil Service Department finally agreed that all contractors involved in cleaning government offices must provide at least local authority pay rates and holidays, similar to those of the Civil Service, for their workers, and thus prevented the undercutting of directly-employed cleaners' pay rates. That it should have taken so long to carry out this elementary function of the Fair Wages policy is the most damning indictment of its effectiveness.

In concluding this introduction, a few words should be said about the legal aspects of the Fair Wages Resolutions. In two articles published in the Modern Law Review in 1948, Professor Sir Otto Kahn-Freund examined these legal aspects in great detail. He asked:

Are these resolutions 'law'? If 'law' is a body of norms safeguarded by sanctions administered by the courts, the answer must surely be in the negative. The passing of a Fair Wages Resolution by the House of Commons was not an act of legislation, the resolution not an Act of Parliament. At best it imposed a disciplinary duty upon the civil servants charged with the making of Government contracts. An official who adopted a policy which flouted the principle of the resolution might have been taken to task by his Minister, the Minister might have been exposed to a vote of censure by the House of Commons to which he was responsible, in the last resort the House might have refused to grant a Government unwilling to act on the resolution the financial means on which it depended. But all this is not, in the legal sense, 'enforcement', or a 'sanction'.[3]

From the legal perspective, therefore, the Resolutions, not falling within the legally defined territory of legislation, could not be called law. Insofar as the Resolutions were included in the contracts entered into by the Government with its contractors as a binding term, and thus enforceable, the Fair Wages policy did acquire the status of 'law'. But, as Kahn-Freund quickly points out: 'But the lawyer must insist that what would then have been enforced would have been the contract, not the resolution' (p. 274).

As is evident from this introduction, the study of the Fair Wages Resolutions in this book will not be confined by this legal perspective. As Kahn-Freund himself states:

> Those most interested in the fair wages resolutions adopted by the House of Commons and by local authorities were, of course, the unions and their members. From their point of view these clauses were, whatever the lawyer may say, one of the corner-stones of British labour 'law'. (p. 274)

But the influence of the legal perspective has had the consequence that the Fair Wages Resolutions and their sphere of operation have not been the subject of any detailed historical analysis. Most commentators have deemed it sufficient to mention the Fair Wages policy only in passing—a reference to its origins, quotation of the clauses of the Resolution itself, and a vague generalization as to its probable objectives and success. Legal commentators tend to concentrate on peripheral questions: the jurisdiction of the Industrial Court, or the *locus standi* of parties appearing before it when complaints of violation of the Resolution are made. These rather scanty reviews of the policy have left the impression that the Fair Wages Resolutions were a genuine, and even successful attempt by Governments to protect workers from 'unfair' employers. In particular, it is emphasized that Governments sought to achieve this by supporting collectively agreed standards, which were designated as 'fair'. Kahn-Freund even goes so far as to assert that: 'It can be said with confidence that, to some extent, it is this system of fair wages clauses which accounts for the functioning in this country of voluntary collective bargaining without legal sanctions' (p. 278). This claim will be examined more closely in chapter 5. But experience of the effects of labour law in other spheres should arouse an initial degree of scepticism. It may be doubted that Governments—whether Conservative in 1891, Liberal in 1909, or Labour in 1946—even if they so desired, could dictate the development of class struggle at the point of production in an economy dominated by private capital. When the instrument adopted consists of a single short Resolution of the House of Commons, considerable evidence is required before accepting the claims of Government benevolence, let alone control.

This book, then, is the first attempt to study this peculiar instrument of public policy. In the course of my research, I have attempted to analyse some of the mysteries which surround the formulation of policy, its implementation through legal means, and the administration of the legal policy. The Fair Wages policy is distinguished from the normal phenomenon of attempts at legal regulation of industrial relations matters through statutory legislation. Its embodiment in a Resolution of the House of Commons—an administrative directive—throws into relief aspects of the normal phenomenon which might otherwise remain undiscovered. The analysis is not diverted into paths dictated by the legal perspective—judicial interpretation of the legal instruments is not the focus of attention. Rather, it is necessary to enter into those relatively unexplored realms of departmental administration of legal policy. The emphasis on policy and administration, rather than text and procedure, requires the investigator to consider the wider industrial relations context. And this wider perspective reduces the legalistic approach to insignificance. This is not legal research as lawyers conventionally define it. But if the end result is greater understanding, then other points of view may be preferable. The perspective of this study is not, therefore, legalistic. The Fair Wages Resolutions will be examined in the context of history, industrial relations and the administration of public policy.

NOTES

1. For details of the Fair Wages Advisory Committee, see Parl. Deb., H. of C. (Fifth Series); 14 March 1910, vol. XV, col. 9. For an attempt to get a worker on to the Committee, see Parl. Deb., H. of C. (Fifth Series); 23 June 1910, vol. XVIII, col. 504. That the Committee acted in a purely advisory capacity was confirmed in the House of Commons by Sydney Buxton on 28 July 1910, vol. XIX, col. 2335. While there is no complete record of the meetings of the Fair Wages Advisory Committee, various documents in the Public Record Office and in the Department of Employment Library refer to specific meetings and reports, and it is from these that the above record is compiled.

2. The cases referred to here are the following: Industrial Court Case No. 1216 (4 June 1926): Constructional Engineering Union and Nortons (Tividale) Ltd.; in vol. VIII of the Court Reports, pp. 144–8, at paras. 16, 17; Industrial Court Case No. 1544 (28 October 1932): Complaint under the Road Traffic Act, 1930; in vol. XIV, pp. 109–13, at para. 8. See also Case No.

1569 (18 July 1933) for another example, in vol. XV, pp. 74–8; Industrial Court Case No. 1546 (28 October 1932); in vol. XIV, pp. 117–20, at para. 6. See also Case No. 1605 (5 December 1934); in vol. XVI, pp. 118–22; and Case No. 1661 (28 September 1936); in vol. XVIII, pp. 98–100. For an example of the equivocal position adopted by the Industrial Court, see Case No. 967 (1 August 1924): the Trade Union Side of the Shipbuilding Trade Joint Council for Government Departments and the Official Side; in vol. VI, pp. 239–42, at para. 7. The case concerned a claim by the trade unions for an increase in wages.

3. O. Kahn-Freund, 'Legislation Through Adjudication. The Legal Aspect of Fair Wages Clauses and Recognised Conditions'. *Modern Law Review* **11** (1948), p. 274.

PART I

The First Fair Wages Policy
1891—1909

I

Origins of the Fair Wages Resolution of 1891

In 1883, the 16th Annual Trades Union Congress had instructed its Parliamentary Committee 'to induce the Government to bring in a Bill to regulate the hours of all the workers in the employ of the State and by all public bodies and companies requiring Act, or concession of, by Parliament, and that eight hours be the maximum time of the working day in all their establishments'. The Webbs attribute to Mr. C. J. Drummond, then Secretary to the London Society of Compositors, and a friend of the Parliamentary Committee, the credit for having taken the first step towards the enforcement through the government of a standard minimum wage. When the government's printing contracts came up for revision in 1884, an attempt was made by Drummond and the Parliamentary Committee to induce the Stationery Office to adopt the trade union rates of London compositors as the basis of the contract. The Parliamentary Committee reported to the Congress of 1885 how, at the request of the London Society of Compositors, it had, by questions to and correspondence with the Financial Secretary to the Treasury and the Controller of the Stationery Office, called attention to the unsatisfactory manner in which the printing contracts had been disposed of. It was asserted that the schedules of prices had been framed by 'non-practical men' in an incomprehensible fashion based on a system known only to the Stationery Office. This resulted in preventing union firms from competing for tenders and, consequently, a very large proportion of the work had been done by unfair labour. To remedy this state of affairs, the Parliamentary Committee suggested that the new schedules of prices be based on the London Scale of Prices.

In the end, the new contract was nevertheless given to a 'closed' house, in which no members of the union could work. The Parliamentary Committee reported optimistically, however, that:

For notes see p. 9

3

Although our efforts were not crowned with that success we could have wished, considerable improvement has, nevertheless, been made in the new schedules just issued, the prices, as a matter of fact being based on the London Scale, which, for the first time, is thus officially recognized and mentioned in the Schedules issued by the Stationary Office. Some very important extras have, however, been ignored.

Keen interest in these efforts was shown by other trade unions at the Congress of 1885. One delegate demanded whether it was the printing trade alone which deserved inquiry as a result of workers suffering hardships by reason of government contracts: 'He could show that one thousand families were on the verge of starvation, owing to the wretched prices paid to them for the making of army and navy clothing by contractors of the Government'. He was assured by the Parliamentary Committee that any complaints would receive attention to the same extent as the printers.

Despite the result of their first efforts, the London compositors continued their agitation and in early 1886 Mr. Drummond, in reply to a government circular, explicitly demanded the recognition of the standard wage in all government dealings. A general demand was started that public authorities should present a good example as employers by themselves paying trade union rates and insisting on their contractors doing the same. A circular of the London Society of Compositors of June 1886 urged that candidates for the General Election of that year be interrogated on their willingness to insist on 'Fair Wages'. The next few years coincided with the detailed investigations of a Select Committee of the House of Lords on the Sweating System which resulted in a series of reports. The conclusions drawn by the Select Committee were by no means universally welcomed. One clothing workers' union leader commented: 'That commission of noble lords knew nothing about trade and its practices and ways, and therefore, their recommendations were quite useless'. Nevertheless, the stream of revelations about the terrible conditions of labour prevalent among workers in various sweated trades appears to have had some impact on certain sections of the public, notably the members of the Fabian Society. It was pointed out by the same union leader that it was a mistake, however, to say that the reports were 'in the hands of the public when they cost from 25s. to 30s.' The expense clearly limited their circulation to particular circles.

The Parliamentary Committee of the T.U.C. gave evidence to the Lords' Committee, and saw the opportunity to press the government for reforms on this issue. One witness, for example, referred to a government contract for 400 coats where sweated wages were paid, only 2s. per coat. Another mentioned a firm of government contractors in London whom he described as sweaters of the most confirmed of description. Twenty-five per cent of the work done for the government was given out to 'slop shops' and done by non-society men, and the price paid for it was 30 per cent less than the contractors to the government themselves paid. In his address to the Congress in 1888, the President of the T.U.C. pinpointed the dilemma: the system of obtaining goods from sweaters with consequent demoralization of the trades would continue, 'unless the State steps in with drastic remedies. The State, otherwise the legislative body, will be loth to do this, seeing that so many so-called representatives benefit either directly or indirectly from the system.' Nor were these 'leaders of public opinion' the only ones to benefit. The Parliamentary Committee reported:

> The religious teachers of the country, who might have done, and in some cases have done, much to protect the poor, are not all free from reproach in this matter, as they are frequently guilty of using the lives of men and women to produce cheap articles. We have it on authority—an authority from our own ranks— that many religious publications that are presumed to have for their object the elevation of the people and the advocacy of their cause, are produced in printing offices where fair wages and other equitable conditions of labour are ignored for the sake of obtaining extra profit.

The Report of the 1888 Congress included a 'List of Religious and Temperance Weekly Newspapers, showing those printed Fairly, and those printed Unfairly'. Among those included on the Unfair list were the *Catholic Times*, the *Jewish Chronicle* and the *Protestant Standard*. This particular segment of the elite does not appear to have heeded the warnings. Ten years later Sir Charles Dilke was to be found pointing out the low wages paid by the Bible Board of Scotland to the printers of their Bibles.[1]

The obstacles to effective government intervention in the area were raised in the debate on a resolution put to the 1888 Trades Union Congress:

> That provision be made whereby the Board of Trade, or other Government Department, shall have full power to prevent any contract for articles required by Governmental Departments, or by any municipality where such articles are provided out of either Imperial or local taxes, being carried out by sub-contractors or sweaters.

Speaking on the resolution, a trade unionist pointed out that in fact the government already had full power to prevent the sweating system by means of a clause in their contracts providing that no work must be done at the homes of the people under a penalty of £100. It was admitted, however, that that regulation had been violated and the penalty had not been enforced. Government officials were lax in enforcing the regulation, although the Government ought to set an example in paying a fair wage to those who laboured for them. Consequently, there was added to the resolution a clause asking the government to exercise this Factory Clause of their contracts, and urging them to enforce the penalty for its infringement. The resolution was carried unanimously.

Meanwhile, the London Society of Compositors had continued its agitation. The action of the London School Board in October 1886 giving its printing contract to an 'unfair' house aroused bitter resentment and led to a futile deputation from the London Trades Council. At the same time the Secretary of the United Committee of Carpenters and Joiners, Mr. G. Dew, began to take an interest in the low wages paid by government contractors for the repair and maintenance of government buildings. He submitted a plan to the Secretary of the T.U.C. Committee who advised him to obtain the co-operation of other trades. Accordingly, a conference of delegates from the building trades was convened on 5 April 1888, at which a scheme was unanimously endorsed 'that the workman's wages and his recognized limit of working hours should form a part of every contract, and to be strictly observed by any person who may obtain a contract'. A deputation was appointed to bring the matter before the government and a circular letter was also addressed to various Members of Parliament, asking for their support.

The deputation was received by Mr. D. R. Plunkett, First Commissioner of Works, on behalf of the government. To him were submitted the following suggestions in the form of a 'Memorial':

> That clauses shall be inserted in all Government contracts to the following effect:
> (1) That all contractors be required to pay the Trade Union or standard rate of wages.
> (2) The working hours to be in accordance with the rules and customs of the various trades.
> (3) That as far as possible overtime should be abolished.
> (4) Sub-letting to be strictly prohibited.

Four months later the government replied to the suggestions in what was called 'a marvellous piece of circumlocution, occupying no fewer than nine pages of foolscap'. The proposals were rejected as infringing the principle of Freedom of Contract: the government's sole duty was to look at the solvency of the contractor; the question of the payment of Fair Wages was a matter in which they had no concern. Another deputation was dispatched by the delegates, who had meanwhile formed themselves into a Committee to promote the campaign—known as the London Building Trades' Committee. This time the main plea of the government was that it had to be guided by public opinion. The Committee thereupon resolved to get the question tested by a Resolution in the House of Commons.

The contracting policies of the London School Board aroused not only the resentment of the Compositors, but also that of the Building Trades Committee. At the School Board election in November 1888 the issue of 'Fair Contracts' was prominent, with many candidates pledged to support the principle if returned. Two of the successful candidates, Mr. A. G. Cook, a member of the Compositors' Society, and Mrs. A. Besant, led the School Board to declare in early 1889 that it would henceforth insist on the payment of 'Fair Wages' by all its contractors. The second public body to adopt the principle was the Nottingham Corporation, and shortly afterwards the London County Council in March 1889. The significance of these developments may be seen from the fact that Sydney Buxton, who initiated the debate which produced the first Fair Wages Resolution of 1891, referred as examples of local authority Fair Wages Clauses to that of the London School Board: the contractor must sign: 'I hereby declare that I pay to the workmen employed by me not less than the minimum standard of wages in each branch of the trade'; and that of the London County Council: 'We hereby declare that we pay such rates of wages and observe such hours of labour as are generally accepted as fair in our trade'.

The successful result of this local London campaign was a spur to action by the trade union movement as a whole. At the annual Trades Union Congress in September 1890, the subversive influence of government contracts which led to intense competition among contractors resulting in wage-cutting was remarked upon, and the following resolution moved:

That this Congress instructs the Parliamentary Committee to take such steps as it may deem most effective to secure at the earliest moment, in all Government works and municipalities, and all contracts for the same, the full payment of the *current rates of wages recognized by the organized industries* of the United Kingdom. (My italics.)

In the somewhat confused debate that followed, the following addendum was accepted: 'that a contract should not be accepted from any firm which does not pay the *recognized rate of wages of the town or district;* and that this Congress pledges itself to oppose all candidates for Parliamentary and local bodies who do not pledge themselves to do all in their power to support the above resolution'. (My italics.) Another trade unionist raised an objection to the whole procedure, claiming that 'no resolution on this subject would be of use; so long as employers could get non-society men they would avail themselves of their services so as to save wages'. The movement should put its trust in self-reliant organizing of the unorganized, rather than in the beneficence of the State. A delegate who had had experience with the policy of the London County Council stated that the resolution moved 'would improve matters slightly, but not to the extent this Congress would believe'. He suggested that the words 'trade union rate of wages' should be inserted in the motion, and this too was assented to. As a result of further claims, however, the motion was temporarily withdrawn and, in company with Tom Mann and others, the mover of the resolution retired to redraft it. The remodelled resolution submitted to Congress was carried almost unanimously and read as follows:

> That this Congress condemns the system of contracting by schedule adopted by the Government and other public bodies, as it conduces to low wages, scamped work, and inferior materials, which are pernicious to the public interest. The Parliamentary Committee is hereby instructed to take such steps as may be most effective to secure the insertion of a clause in all contracts prohibiting subletting; that no contract shall be given to any firm that does not pay to all its workpeople the *recognized trade union rates of wages in the respective localities where any work may be done,* either by those directly employed by Government and municipalities, or contractors taking contracts from these bodies; also demands that where the factory clause is inserted and violated the penalty shall be rigidly enforced' (My italics.)

With the success of campaigns at the local level and the backing of the trade union movement, the time had arrived to bring the matter to a head in the House of Commons. Under pressure the government had appointed a departmental committee of enquiry, composed of representatives from the Mint, the Board of Trade, the Office of Works and the Treasury. The Building Trades Committee gave evidence before this committee and a favourable report was presented to the government in November 1890. Due to the illness of Mr. H. Broadhurst, M.P., Secretary of the Parliamentary Committee of the T.U.C., it was decided to place the matter in the hands of a London M.P. The Liberal Member for Tower Hamlets, Poplar, Mr. Sydney Buxton, had previously exhibited interest in the problems resulting from sweating and the subversive contribution made to this system by the government's contracting process. This was evinced in numerous complaints he addressed to representatives of government departments in the House of Commons on behalf of trade unionists. Together with a group of trade unionists, he drafted a resolution which he introduced into the House on 13 February 1891:

> Clauses to be inserted in all Government contracts, requiring that the contractor shall, under penalty, observe the recognized customs and conditions as to rates of wages and working hours that prevail in each particular trade; and that the contractor should, under penalty, be prohibited from sub-letting any portion of his contract, except where the Department concerned specifically allow the sub-letting of such special portions of the work as would not be produced or carried out by the contractor in the ordinary course of his business.[2]

After some debate, the government, represented by the First Commissioner of Works, rejected this formulation and substituted the final Resolution:

> That, in the opinion of this House it is the duty of the Government in all Government contracts to make provision against the evils which have recently been disclosed before the House of Lords' Sweating Committee, and to insert such conditions as may prevent the abuses arising from subletting, and make every effort to secure the payment of the rate of wages generally accepted as current for a competent workman in his trade.

Somewhat prematurely, as will be seen later, the Parliamentary Committee of the T.U.C. reported in September of that year that it regarded 'with satisfaction the progress which has thus been made in the direction of securing trade rates of wages for those employed on Government contracts'.[3]

NOTES

1. Parl. Deb., H. of C. (Fourth Series); 4 August 1898, vol. LXIV, col. 130.

2. Parl. Deb., H. of C. (Third Series); 13 February 1891, vol. CCCL, cols. 622ff. For examples of Buxton's previous activity, see Parl. Deb., H. of C. (Third Series);
23 June 1890, vol. CCXLV, col. 1630; 8 December 1890, vol. CCCXLIX, col. 701; and 6 February 1891, vol. CCCL, col. 147.

3. The above account is principally derived from the following sources:

—Sidney and Beatrice Webb, *The History of Trade Unionism* (revised edition), London, 1920; pp. 398–9.

—Fabian Tract No. 37, *A Labour Policy for Public Authorities* (undated).

—Fabian Tract No. 50, *Sweating: Its Cause and Remedy*, published by the Fabian Society, London, February 1894.

—Pamphlet by Geo. Dew, District Organiser, Amalgamated Carpenters and Joiners, entitled *Fair Wages Movement—A Brief History*, printed in London by Fredk. Tarrant & Sons, May 1896 (14 pp.).

—*Sweating System*, Verbatim Report of the Trades Union Conference for the Abolition of the Middleman Sweater; published by the Executive of the International Tailors', Machinists', and Pressers' Union, 14 April 1891 (14 pp.).

—Report of the 16th Annual Trades Union Congress, Nottingham, 1883, p. 47.

—Report of the Parliamentary Committee to the 18th Annual T.U.C., Southport, 1885, pp. 13–14.

—Report of the 18th Annual T.U.C., Southport, 1885, p. 22.

—Report of the Parliamentary Committee to the 21st Annual T.U.C., Bradford, 1888, p. 14.

—Report of the 21st Annual T.U.C., Bradford, 1888, pp. 16, 39.

—Report of the 23rd Annual T.U.C., Liverpool, 1890, pp. 34, 39–40.

—Report of the Parliamentary Committee to the 24th Annual T.U.C., Newcastle, 1891, p. 29.

—Evidence of Mr. H. T. Foster, father of the chapel at a branch of Eyre & Spottiswood, printers, given on 24 March 1896, to the Committee on Stationery Contracts, 1896; Minutes of Evidence, Qs. 2649ff., at Qs. 2676–80. House of Commons Papers of 1896, vol. XIII, at pp. 445ff.

2

Industrial Relations and the Fair Wages Resolution of 1891

The Rise of Collective Bargaining, 1891–1909

The Fair Wages Resolution which was finally adopted by the House of Commons on the 13 February 1891 read as follows:

> That in the opinion of this House it is the duty of the Government in all Government contracts to make provision against the evils which have recently been disclosed before the House of Lords' Sweating Committee, and to insert such conditions as may prevent the abuses arising from subletting, and make every effort to secure the payment of the rate of wages generally accepted as current for a competent workman in his trade.

The Resolution was formulated in very broad terms and made no specific reference to terms of employment arrived at through collective bargaining. The closest it could be said to come to this was in requiring payment of rates of wages 'generally accepted as current'. This was the Resolution that was to remain in force until 1909. Yet since the beginning of the latter half of the nineteenth century the evolutionary pace of the collective organization of workers had quickened noticeably. Recognition of the strength and demands of certain craft unions by employers and their organizations was a well-marked phenomenon of these years. An I.L.O. study of 1938 stated that: 'Especially during the last three decades of the century there was a rapid extension of collective bargaining, and well-organized industries frequently set up joint machinery for the settlement of differences'. Only two years prior to the 1891 Resolution there had occurred an extraordinary eruption of industrial militancy, culminating in what has been called the most famous strike of the nineteenth century—the London dock strike of 1889. Ben Tillet's Tea Operatives' and General Labourers' Union, formed in 1887, jumped from two to thirty thousand members

For notes see p. 32

almost overnight, comprising mostly casual and unskilled workers untouched by the craft unions. A number of other new unions were set up during the flush of this 'new Unionism'. In writing about the craft unions at about this time, the Webbs concluded: 'that in all skilled trades, where men work in concert, on the employers' premises, ninety per cent of the workmen find, either their rate of wages or their hours of work, and often many other details, predetermined by a collective bargain'. An authoritative study of British trade unionism in the period 1889–1910, which is almost exactly the period of the first Fair Wages Resolution (1891–1909), concludes:

> The development of collective bargaining was the outstanding feature of this period. In 1889 only cotton weaving had a national agreement. By 1910 national agreements had also been signed by the unions and the employers' federations in engineering, ship-building, cotton spinning, building, printing, iron and steel and footwear. Moreover, almost every other well-organized industry, except the railways, had evolved its own system of collective bargaining, even if not yet on a fully national basis.

An illustration of the development of collective bargaining in Britain during the latter half of the nineteenth century is to be found in the British printing industry. Prior to 1890, regulation of terms of employment in the printing industry appears to have been done on a unilateral basis by the printing craft unions. These union rules amounted almost to a code which sought to prevent unfair competition among employers at the expense of the unions' members, yet benefited the employers as well in providing them with reasonably stable labour costs. Employers were generally not prepared to meet with trade unionists to discuss these matters on equal terms, and some militant unionists reciprocated by considering that employers had no right to be consulted in the formulation of union rules. The period 1848 to 1890 saw the evolution from a few simple union rules relating to minimum conditions of labour, to more complicated provisions designed to counter certain 'sharp practices' on the part of employers, to rules governing the introduction of new machinery and novel methods of working. The employers were totally excluded from this rule-making process and, with the growing power of the craft unions, gradually saw their control of working conditions within their shops being diluted. These two factors resulted eventually in the organization of the employers to conduct collective bargaining with the unions. This development reached its climax in the years following 1890. As summarized in one study of the industry:

In 1890 there was hardly one effective written agreement in the printing industry. By 1914 there were more than eighty, involving all of the major unions and employers' associations, and covering more than 50,000 workers. This change in the regulation of terms of employment from unilateral enforcement of Union Rule to bilateral agreement was the dominant feature of the period.

A survey of the progress made by collective bargaining during this period may be found in the *Report on Collective Agreements between Employers and Workpeople in the United Kingdom,* 1910, compiled by the Labour Department of the Board of Trade. The Report listed a total of 1,696 trade or district agreements. The number of workers estimated to be covered by these agreements was 2,400,000, which was still less than one quarter of the total number of industrial workers. However, this list excluded most agreements concerning terms of employment which had been negotiated by a single firm with its employees. The distribution by industry of these agreements is given in Table 1.

TABLE 1

	No. of Agreements	No. of Workpeople
Mining and Quarrying	56	900,000
Textile Trades	113	460,000
Railway Service	2	420,000
Metal, Engineering and Shipbuilding	163	230,000
Building Trades	803	200,000
Other Transport	90	80,000
Printing Trades	79	40,000
Boot and Shoe Manufacture	122	30,000
Other Trades	268	40,000

The Report clearly demonstrated that by the end of the term of the first Fair Wages Resolution collective bargaining had become a significant force in industrial relations, one which could not be denied. And even more importantly, *it identified the chief characteristic of the collective bargaining process as it had grown since 1890—that it was of a basically local character; it took place on a district, or in some trades on a single establishment basis.* To what extent, then, was a connection established between this new phenomenon and the Fair Wages policy of the House of Commons?

These developments and their importance as regards the effective functioning of the Fair Wages policy were recognized by Sydney Buxton, the initiator of the debate on the Fair Wages Resolution of 1891. They were provided for expressly in his own draft resolution subsequently rejected by the House of Commons: 'Clauses to be inserted in all Government Contracts, requiring that the contractor shall, under penalty, observe the recognized customs and conditions as to rates of wages and working hours that prevail in each particular trade'. This connection between such a policy and collective bargaining had been understood already by at least one of those who would be responsible for the implementation of such a policy. In 1890, the then Director of Contracts of the War Office, a Mr. Nepean, in giving his evidence to the Committee inquiring into the Sweated Industries, was reported to have said:

> I propose to put the workmen and the masters in conference, and that they shall concur in something they can present to me as a clear agreement in the trade as to the prices to be paid. I do not want to regulate them myself, but, if possible, to induce masters and men to regulate them for themselves.

Here there is a clear recognition of the role a government agency can play in encouraging collective bargaining, and ensuring that the rates of wages paid by employers are scrutinized by the government through its control of prices to be paid to the contractor under the contract. A little later the Fifth (and final) Report of the Royal Commission on Labour of 1894 favoured the system of collective bargaining and negotiated agreements. The Minority Report of that Commission went to the length of suggesting that, where a scale of trade union rates existed which was current in the district, legal facilities should be afforded for enforcing it at law. This recommendation was signed by various important persons, including a future President of the Privy Council, a future Chancellor of the Exchequer and the future Chairman of the Committee on Stationery Contracts, 1896, which reported on the application of the Fair Wages Resolution in the Stationery Office.

The Fair Wages Resolution adopted ·by the House of Commons in 1891 failed to make explicit this connection between the policy and collective bargaining. This failure, and the generally unsettled industrial relations situation resulting from the development of collective bargaining, had for its result an enormous confusion in the interpretation and application of the Fair Wages policy, a confusion to be examined later.[1]

Recognition of Collective Bargaining by Local Authorities' Fair Wages Clauses

The evolutionary pattern during this period, however, is clear, and as the reality of collective bargaining moves more and more to the forefront of industrial relations, the views of the administrative authorities come to reflect it. The principal evidence for this is derived from the changes in their Fair Wages policies instituted by various local authorities during this period. Following the successful campaign in the House of Commons, the policy came to be advocated with renewed fervour in the country at large. Thus, during the years that followed, a series of Fabian Tracts was published entitled 'Questions For' various candidates to elected bodies—the London School Board, Poor Law Guardians, London Vestrymen, London County Councillors and Town and County Councillors generally, as well as Parliamentary candidates. The list of questions invariably included one or more asking the candidate's views on the Fair Wages policy. For example, Fabian Tract No. 28, *Questions for Candidates for County Councils (outside London and County Boroughs)*, revised in February 1895, enquires:

> *II.11* – Whenever it is found necessary to employ a contractor, will you insist upon the insertion, in all contracts for supplies, as well as for works, of clauses stipulating (a) against sub-contracting; (b) for the payment of the trade union rate of wages, if any, fixed for that trade; (c) that the working hours shall be those recognized as fair in that trade; (d) that all clothing or other similar supplies be made in the contractors' own factory and not put out?

Already in 1893 a Return to an Order of the House of Commons concerning the conditions of contracts of Urban Sanitary Districts contained very detailed lists of their contractual Fair Wages Clauses. Of all the authorities considered at that time, the great majority (872) had no conditions at all inserted into their contracts. Only 148 authorities had conditions of some kind. And of these 148, only 83 had regulations concerning wages, hours, etc. The other 65 had other miscellaneous conditions relating to, for example, the power to sack incompetent workers, or quotas of local labour which must be hired. Despite the preponderance of authorities not fixing any conditions at all, it is curious to note that the larger the authority concerned, i.e. the more populous its district, the more likely it was to have such conditions (a Fair Wages policy). Thus, there is a steady progression upwards: at the level of Local Boards, 625 had no conditions at all while only 15 had; on the level of Improvement Districts, none of the authorities had conditions in their contracts. But on the level of non-County Boroughs, although 195 had none, 33 had conditions, while on County Borough level, only 23 had no conditions, while fully 40 County Boroughs had Fair Wages policies of some sort.

Even at this early date, however, the trend was away from the ambiguous formula of the 1891 Resolution towards one more explicitly recognizing collective bargaining as a force. In the County Borough of Liverpool, the Fair Wages Clause of the Sanitary Authority provided for the payment of rates of wages 'recognized and agreed upon between the trades unions and the employers respectively in the locality'. Similarly, in the County Borough of Wolverhampton, the phrase used was: rates of wages 'recognized and agreed upon between the trades unions and the employers'. The County Boroughs of Ipswich, Northampton, Oxford, Swansea and West Ham all provided for the payment of trade union rates, as did the non-County Boroughs of Rochester and West Hartlepool. Other interesting examples of Fair Wages Clauses were those of Cardiff: 'mutually accepted between employer and employed as fair', and Manchester: 'the regular standard of wages'.

By 1898 there had been an enormous proliferation of Fair Wages clauses of all varieties, many of which were clearly indicative of the emerging system of collective bargaining on a district basis. A Return to the House of Commons of that year gives details of each of the conditions inserted into contracts for the execution of works by 48 County Boroughs, 54 non-County Boroughs and 116 other Urban Districts (though, on the other hand, a total of 16 County Boroughs, 188 non-County Boroughs and 666 other Urban Districts used contracts which did not specify any conditions as to wages to be paid by their contractors). The astonishing diversity exhibited by these clauses is an indication of the failure of the Fair Wages Resolution of the House of Commons to have any influence on the Fair Wages policies of local government. Among the forty-eight County Boroughs, only those of Bristol and Dudley had clauses parallel to that of the House of Commons. The following list illustrates the variety of provisions relating to wages and/or hours in the contracts of County Boroughs in England and Wales:

Barrow-in-Furness, Wolverhampton	'recognized and agreed upon between the trades unions and the employers respectively, in the locality'.
Birmingham	'recognized minimum standard rate of wages current in the district or districts'.
Bolton	'the standard rate of wages for the time being payable in respect of such like employment within the town or other place'.

Bootle	'recognized standard of wages for competent workmen and hours of labour respectively in the particular trade or trades'.
Bradford, Burnley, South Shields, York	'the minimum standard rate of wages'.
Brighton	'the standard rate of wages in force in the borough of Brighton in their several trades . . . such standard to mean the rate agreed upon by the masters' and workmen's associations in Brighton'. (This clause also gave a right of recovery to the Corporation of underpaid wages, and contained an arbitration clause for use in the event of disputes with contractors.)
Cardiff	'recognized by the respective trades unions and the employers in the town and district'.
Chester	'minimum standard of wages paid in the district'.
Derby	'standard rate of wages applicable to the respective classes of workpeople recognized by the respective workpeople's trade societies in the borough of Derby, and in practice obtained by them at the date of the contract'.
Exeter	'generally accepted by competent workmen as current in Exeter for work of this class'.
Gateshead	'generally accepted in the trade as current for workmen where such work is carried out'.
Gloucester	'minimum standard rate of wages paid in the city of Gloucester for the time being in each branch of the trade'.
Grimsby	'current rate of wages paid in the district'.
Halifax	'minimum standard rate of wages in each branch of the trade in the district . . . understood to mean such wages and hours as have been mutually agreed upon by the associations of employers and employés in such trade, or such wages and hours as having been formerly claimed by the employés have been accepted by the majority of the employers in such trade in the district concerned'.
Hastings	'minimum standard rate of wages . . . in force in the borough of Hastings'.
Ipswich	'recognized by the trades unions in this district'.

Kingston-upon-Hull	'a minimum wage of "one guinea per week of 53 hours". Generally: "minimum standard rate of wages in the district for each class of labour respectively'.
Leeds	'recognized in the district . . . as the standard rate of wages in such workman's trade'.
Leicester	'current local standard rate of wages'.
Lincoln	'regular standard rate of wages in the district'.
Liverpool	'recognized and agreed upon between the trades unions and the employers respectively in the locality'.
Manchester	'regular standard wages obtaining in the city of Manchester or the district'.
Middlesbrough	'recognized standard rate of wages in their respective trades'.
Newport (Mon.)	'trade union rate of wages current in such person's trade'.
Northampton	'the trades' union rate of wages in Northampton'.
Norwich	'the full rate of wages customarily paid at the date to workmen engaged in the trade in Norwich and the district'.
Nottingham	'local standard rate of wages'.
Oldham, Plymouth	'standard rate of wages'.
Oxford	'present recognized trades' union wages in the city of Oxford'.
Portsmouth	'trade union rate of wages . . . recognized and in practice obtained by the trades unionists in the place or places'.
Rochdale	'recognized rate of wages adopted in the town'.
Salford	'regular standard rate of wages for the time being enforced within the district'.
Sheffield	'the standard rate of wages recognized by trade societies in Sheffield, in each branch of the trade'.
Southampton	'the minimum local standard rate of wages, as settled from time to time between the Masters' Association and trades unions respectively in each branch of the trade'.
Stockport	'the standard rate of wages payable in the district'.
Swansea	'the trades' union rate of wages'.
Walsall	'standard rate of wages current in the district'.

West Ham	'recognized by the workmen's trade unions, and in force'.
Wigan	'minimum standard rate of wages in the district'.
Worcester	'minimum standard rate of wages current in the district'.

The continuing progress of the Fair Wages policy at the local level may be monitored through numerous returns to Orders of the House of Commons setting out such information. Thus, full particulars of the clauses specifying conditions as to wages, conditions, etc., inserted by the various local authorities of the United Kingdom in the contracts let by them were given in a Return to the House of Commons of 1906. Cumulative tables given showed that 169 boroughs (county and non-county) in England and Wales specify conditions as to wages in their contracts. Of these, ninety-six state that the rates are to be those 'current', 'prevailing', 'recognized', and so on; forty that they are to be those agreed upon between employers and trade unions; and twenty-nine those recognized by trade unions. Four (plus the London County Council) fix the rates in the contract itself. In Scotland, twenty-one boroughs specify conditions as to wages, eighteen being rates 'current', 'prevailing' and so on; two specify rates agreed upon between employers and trade unions; and one specifies rates recognized by trade unions. In Ireland, eleven town councils specify conditions as to wages, eight being 'current' rates; two specify rates agreed between employers and trade unions; and one specifies rates recognized by the trades unions.

These statistics demonstrate clearly the growing recognition of the role which collective bargaining was beginning to play in the determination of rates of wages. A few examples on the local level will illustrate this evolution even more graphically. In the city of Bradford, Yorkshire, a Fair Wages Resolution was first passed by the City Council on 13 December 1898. It provided for the payment of the 'minimum standard rate of wages'. In July 1903, however, the old resolution was changed to a new form. The main reasons advanced for the change were the ambiguity of the old resolution where, for example, neither side of the industry was organized; doubt had been expressed as to what the 'standard rate' was; and also that the effectiveness of its enforcement was questionable. In the new Fair Wages Resolution the standard rate of wages was:

deemed to be the rate mutually agreed upon by the Masters' Association and the Trade Unions respectively concerned, or in case there should at any relevant time be no such rate as aforesaid, then such rate of wages to be deemed to be that last mutually agreed upon by the Masters' Association and the Trade Unions respectively concerned. Provided that in the case of engineers, founders, and metal workers the rate of wages and conditions of employment last agreed upon as between the Federated Engineering Employers and the Allied Trade Unions shall be observed.

By 1903, therefore, the rise of collective bargaining had been recognized sufficiently to be incorporated here. The local scene was close enough to industrial reality to make specific provision for arrangements in the engineering industry.

The history of the Fair Wages policy of the London Borough of West Ham illustrates the difficulties encountered during the growing pains of collective bargaining. The Fair Wages Clause first introduced by the City Council on 24 February 1891 (only eleven days after the House of Commons passed its own Resolution) required all firms tendering 'to make a declaration that they will pay such rate of wages and observe such hours of labour as are recognized and determined by the London Trades Council'. It was subsequently discovered, however, that the London Trades Council rates were not applicable to the provinces, and as a result the Resolution was revised on 12 January 1892 and another substituted which required payment of wages and observance of such hours 'as are recognized by the workmen's Trade Unions and in force at the time of signing the contract'. The next significant change came in a Resolution of 26 April 1898. This laid down the following: (1) the rates as determined by the Council were to be inserted as a schedule in all contracts and that they were to be paid by the contractor; (2) that the agreed rates and hours for the London building trade be adopted in all building contracts as a schedule. On 10 January 1899 yet another clause was added requiring the contractor to pay 'to the whole of his workmen such rate of wages (etc.) as are recognized by the Workmen's Trade Unions in the several localities where his work is done'. The contracts let by West Ham spelt out in great detail the rates of wages and hours of labour of the different grades of workmen employed by the contractor, these being attached in a schedule which was part of the contract. It should be noted that West Ham, in 1898, became the first local authority to be controlled by Labour.

In conclusion, there is the testimony of a member of the Council of the Wolverhampton Corporation. He reported that the Corporation had a Fair Wages Resolution similar to that passed by the House of Commons, but that it was found that employers were evading it and and that it was impossible to prevent them. As a result of this

Councillor's efforts, the Corporation passed a new resolution which read as follows: 'The contractor shall pay the rate of wages and observe the hours of labour recognized and agreed upon between the Trades Unions and the employers respectively'. This resolution, the Councillor claimed, 'prevented the employers from evading our Fair Wages Resolution as they did when it was similar to the Government one. We could not prevent them from doing that at first, but under this resolution we have prevented them.' The development of collective bargaining through organization of workers was recognized as being an essential component of an effective Fair Wages policy.[2]

The Relation of Collective Bargaining to the Fair Wages Resolution as considered by the Committee on Stationery Contracts, 1896

A similar evolution of ideas is apparent from the views of and evidence to various committees which considered the Fair Wages policy and its enforcement between 1891 and 1909. Perhaps the best example of the conflict between the acceptance of the developing reality of collective bargaining and the old concepts embodied in the 1891 Resolution is seen in the prolonged dispute which took place during the Proceedings of the Select Committee on Stationery Contracts of 1896.[3] The dispute arose during a consideration of the practical question of whether the London scale of prices, mutually agreed by representatives of probably a majority of the workmen (estimates were between 50–65 per cent) and those of 90 per cent of the employers, could be considered to be the 'current rate' in London, within the terms of the 1891 Resolution. In fact, the Controller of the Stationery Office had admitted that the London scale was the most general scale of prices in that no other scale was accepted by so many compositors, and that consequently he treated it as the standard or test by comparison with which he would decide the question whether the wages paid in any case corresponded to those wages which could be said to be accepted as current in the trade (p. vi). In his actual evidence before the Committee, however, the Controller had been much more cautious in his acceptance of the London scale than the later categorical statement by the Committee represented. He refused there to agree that the scale represented the 'current rates', since he claimed many (perhaps half) of the compositors did not belong to the trade union and, therefore, it would be wrong to impose it. He did, however, say he would approve of it if it could be shown that it was the current rate, but that it would be very difficult to do this (Qs. 201–18).

The problem arose from the fact that several government contractors, and one in particular, did not observe all the particulars of the London scale, though their wages were, they argued, in total not inferior. The question thus posed was formulated as follows:

Is this scale to be recognized not merely as the standard by which wages are to be judged, but also as the scale to which the wages of compositors doing Government contracts must in all particulars conform? The question may be restated in the following manner: assuming that two-thirds of the compositors of London work under the London scale, and that two-thirds of the work done are so paid for, does the Resolution of the House of Commons require that all Government printing contracts should be executed in accordance with this scale, or is it satisfied if it can be shown that the wages realized by workmen doing Government work are as good as would be realized under the scale? (p. vii)

The answer finally given by the Committee to this question was firm:

Your Committee believe that the intention of the House of Commons in the third part of its Resolution did not go beyond securing to workmen engaged on Government contracts the payment of wages equivalent to the wages current in the trade in the circumstances of his work, and that *the House had no wish to interfere with the organization of labour beyond what might be necessary to obtain this result. As long as the wages paid are of this normal character the method of calculating them is comparatively immaterial.* There are, indeed, obvious objections to any attempt to give quasi-legislative sanction to particular details of doing work. It is sufficient that the State, so far as it requires work to be done for itself, should secure that the workmen engaged in it should receive remuneration equal to the wages generally accepted as current in the trade. (p. viii) (My italics.)

It is interesting that the Chairman of the Committee which arrived at this conclusion should have expounded an exactly opposite viewpoint only two years before, as mentioned above, in the Minority Report to the Fifth Report of the Royal Commission on Labour of 1894. Indeed, he played the crucial role in determining the Committee's final position.

The paragraph quoted above formed the nub of the internal division within the Committee as it was obviously bound to do, presenting as it did a very contentious view of the Fair Wages Resolution. Indeed, the Draft Report debated by the Committee in its Proceedings presented a very different interpretation of the Resolution.

As was normal, the Chairman of the Committee had presented a Draft Report to the Committee for discussion. However, in this case his draft had been rejected by the close vote of five to four, and a Draft Report submitted by a member of the Committee, Mr. Lough, had been adopted for discussion (p. xxiii). The position taken by this draft report on the vital question of the London scale was very different from that of the Final Report, and it reflected a totally different approach to the Fair Wages policy. Mr. Lough considered the question on broad lines:

> The point relied on was, that the amount of total earnings per week was satisfactory, and that if this were so the Resolution of the House of Commons was sufficiently complied with, and there was no necessity to inquire into the system by which the result was obtained. In most of the skilled technical trades throughout this country the efforts of the general body of workmen have been devoted for many years to the settlement of a system of fair remuneration for each part of the work, no less than to the amount of the total wages earned. Great assistance has been given to bodies of employers by bodies representing working men, in the settlement of difficult questions, possibly small in themselves, but which, if left open, would have created great disruptions, and in the elaboration, in the textile and other industries, of complete scales of wages for every portion of the work. No better example can be found of the progress of this great movement than in the particular instance before your Committee, whether it is measured by the length of time that the mutual arrangement between the employers and employed has continued, or by the extent to which it is observed by both parties. Your Committee therefore hesitate to take any step which will impugn the authority or lessen the influence of such a salutary arrangement. (p. xxi)

The Draft Report went on therefore to recommend that the words of the Resolution, 'such wages as are generally accepted as current', be taken to mean the London scale of prices for all work executed in London, and for work executed in the provinces that it should be remunerated 'in accordance with the system generally adopted wherever the work is done'; i.e., where scales are widely recognized, remuneration should be in accordance with the scale; but where there are no such agreed rates, 'then it should be the duty of the Stationery Department to see that such wages were paid to men carrying out the Government work as were in practice obtained by other workmen of the same grade in the district in which the work was carried out' (p. xxii).

The position taken by the Chairman's Draft Report, which had been rejected in favour of discussion of Mr. Lough's draft, took a very dim view of the latter's opinion. Such an interpretation 'would be going beyond the letter, and the question presents itself whether it would be carrying out the spirit, of the Resolution' (p. xiv). The substance of the Final Report quoted above was contained in the Chairman's Draft Report in paragraph 19. What had happened was that in the course of the Proceedings of the Committee discussing Mr. Lough's Draft Report, the alternative view of the Fair Wages Resolution as embodied in that draft came to be voted upon. The result was a deadlock of five votes in favour and five against. As was standard practice, the deadlock was broken by the Chairman's casting vote, which, as might be expected, was against this view of the Resolution. The view adopted by the Final Report, which was substantially that of the Chairman's Draft Report, was then proposed. It was bitterly disputed by the proponents of the alternative view, who put forward three separate amendments seeking to dilute it as much as possible. Each of these amendments was defeated in turn, twice by the Chairman casting his decisive vote against them to break the 5–5 tie, and once by a vote of 6–4 (pp. xxviii–xxix).

The importance of these details lies in the very real ideological divisions they disclose which existed among those who at least accepted the Resolution, both as to what its meaning was and how it was to be implemented. The view adopted by this first Committee to consider the working of the Fair Wages Resolution appears to have influenced the future implementation of the Resolution and thus has wide ramifications. It is important to note that this view, as expressed in the Final Report, was only reached after very strong opposition which strove to put across an alternative view, and which was only defeated by the very narrowest of majorities. In what appears to have been a consolation prize to the opposition view, the following paragraph was included in the Final Report:

> The conclusion thus arrived at is not inconsistent with the opinion, that, if within any district an agreement was established between all employers and all workmen, the task of supervising the execution of a contract in respect of wages would be considerably lightened, if it did not disappear. Where such an agreement has been established, the duty of the Controller would be simply to see that wages were paid in accordance with the agreement. (pp. viii–ix)

The inadequacy of this is clear—the reference to 'all' employers and workers makes it almost impossible to achieve in practice.

To sum up: there are here two views of the Fair Wages Resolution. First is that adopted by the Final Report. This view had its partial fulfilment in the evolution of the 'not less favourable' doctrine of later Resolutions. It regarded the enforcement of the Resolution as being the function exclusively of the government departments concerned, an aspect to be examined in greater detail later. This view was based on what was regarded as the 'meaning' of the Resolution as seen by the House of Commons at the time. Any other interpretation was regarded as a distortion of the intention of the House. The second view was that of Mr. Lough's Draft Report and the minority of the Committee. It saw a direct link between the Fair Wages policy and collective bargaining. The Fair Wages Resolution was to be enforced through utilization of the collective bargaining process where it resulted in agreements. These were to be the standards set up by the Resolution. Enforcement would be greatly facilitated when concrete standards were available, and the machinery of organized labour would be actively concerned with the maintenance of these standards, and not of some amorphous and uncertain formula. So the Resolution was to benefit from collective bargaining. But the Resolution itself was seen as another means, and a very important one, of encouraging the growth of collective bargaining. This was regarded by many as a fundamental aim to be achieved. This second group did not see anything in the Resolution which could be construed as prohibiting such a view. Nevertheless, they were defeated, with adverse consequences for the future of the Fair Wages policy. The disappointment of the trade union movement was expressed in a resolution of the Typographical Association:

> That the recent inquiry by the Select Committee of the House of Commons appointed to inquire and report with reference to the placing and working of Stationery Office Contracts in regard to Government printing and bookbinding has been most unsatisfactory, both with reference to the narrow interpretation placed upon their instructions by the Committee and the limitation of essential evidence and witnesses necessary to enable the Select Committee to elicit the grievances of the workers and prove the non-observance of fair wages conditions by various contractors.[4]

District Bargaining and the 1897 Committee on Government Contracts

The Select Committee on Government Contracts set up in 1896 to inquire into the workings of the Fair Wages Resolution of 1891 displayed a rather different attitude.[5] In giving evidence before it one major contracting department admitted that collective bargaining was utilized by it in implementing the Fair Wages policy. The representative of the Office of Works declared that the reason why complaints concerning the Resolution were rarely made was that 'we practically adopt the rates of wages which have been agreed to between the Master Builders' Association and the workmen' (Q. 6). The trade unions' witnesses almost invariably regarded the Resolution as referring to collective bargaining arrangements. Thus the General Secretary of the Amalgamated Society of Home Decorators and Painters held that: 'The rate that is agreed to between the trade union and the employers must be the current rate of the particular district' (Q. 241). Similarly, the representative of the Carpenters and Joiners union declared that the 'current rate' cannot be other than the trade union rate as understood by trade unionists in his trade (Qs. 639–42). Finally, the Liverpool representative of the Plumbers' union declared that in Liverpool 'the current rate is the rate agreed on between masters and workmen' (Q. 2596).

The Committee itself in its Report recognized implicitly both the existence of collective bargaining on a district basis and its relevance for the Fair Wages policy. It concluded that in practice the government departments interpreted the phrase 'current' wages as being applicable on a district basis, and this practice it stated:

> is the natural interpretation of the Resolution. In no single trade is there a general current rate of wages prevailing throughout the country; while in nearly every trade, there are more or less defined, recognized, and agreed-on rates of wages prevailing in particular districts. There are many rates of wages 'current in the district', there is no one rate 'current in the trade'. Unless, therefore, the definition adopted by the departments is upheld, it would not be possible, in any given case, to decide with equity whether the current rate of wages was being paid in accordance with the terms of the contract and the spirit of the Resolution. (p. iv)

In other words, the government departments concerned with a practical application of the Fair Wages policy transformed the 1891 view of the House of Commons on the industrial relations situation into a workable formula. The Report of the Committee upheld the departments' action on strictly practical grounds. This is interesting in view of the ideological differences revealed here, as in the 1896 Committee on Stationery Contracts, in the Committee's Proceedings.

A Draft Report was proposed by the Chairman of the Committee, Sir Matthew White Ridley. An alternative Draft Report was proposed by Sydney Buxton, the originator of the 1891 debate on the Fair

Wages Resolution, who was a member of the Committee. The two reports were similar in some areas, but contained significant differences. The Chairman's Draft was adopted by the Committee for discussion, and voted on paragraph by paragraph, with Buxton proposing amendments where his own Draft differed. His amendments were consistently voted down, invariably with the Committee split by a 6–4 majority against, the same members voting together each time. Consequently, the Chairman's Draft Report, with very minor changes, became the Report of the Committee as a whole. Buxton's Draft Report is of interest inasmuch as it allows a view of how a liberal M.P. saw the Fair Wages Resolution, and how this interpretation differed from that of conservative members as reflected in the Final Report of the Committee. Still, even these latter members recognized the need for recognition of district rates if the Fair Wages Resolution was to be practicable at all.

An instance of this ideological division may be seen in Buxton's attempt to assimilate the definition of 'current rate' in the Resolution with the much reviled 'trade union rate'. On the one hand he understood the meaning of 'current rate' to be that rate of wages recognized and paid by the good employers in a given district, recognized and accepted as, for the time being, fair wages by the representatives of the workmen. 'In other words, a rate of wages that the men are willing to work at and the masters are willing to pay'. On the other hand, he defined the trade union rate as being, 'not necessarily the rate which a particular trade union would like their men to receive, but the rate at which they will allow their men to work'. He concluded, therefore, that: 'the term "current rate" and "trade union rate" (as above defined) are substantially the same thing' (p. xvii). This view was completely rejected by the Committee during the Proceedings and omitted from the Final Report.

Even after the Committee's recognition of district bargaining, the problems of applying such a loose formula to the very fluid situation of collective bargaining development were by no means resolved. These may be illustrated by the difficulties experienced by Buxton, who, while also declaring the district rate to be the only practical method (p. xvii), found some difficulty in defining how this formula was to be applied in various situations. For example, he posed the following problem:

That where within a given district in which a certain rate of wages prevails, there is included a small area in which a local contractor alleges that a lower rate prevails; the decision, in case of dispute, should largely depend on the question of whether other employers within the area pay the higher rate, and whether, if an outside contractor took a contract to be fulfilled within the area in question, he would pay the higher or the lower rate. If these questions are decided in the affirmative, the local contractor should be expected also to pay the higher general rate. (p. xviii)

This is by no means a clear-cut answer to the problem posed, and, indeed, it shows the intractability of the problem of defining a 'district'. If, as here, there is a 'given district', then why does the possibility arise of an 'area rate'—unless this 'area rate' is also a 'district' rate itself? There cannot be a district within a district, otherwise every factory or two would establish a 'district' or 'area' rate for its own immediate vicinity.

Fair Wages, Collective Bargaining and the 1908 Fair Wages Committee

The changes in the industrial relations situation which had occurred since 1891 were reflected in the evidence given to the Fair Wages Committee of 1908 and in the deliberations of the Committee itself.[6] Various local authorities' Fair Wages policies were examined and the trend towards recognition of collective bargaining reality was clearly shown. For example, in the city of Leicester, the Corporation's original Resolution of 28 July 1891 has been changed three times, in 1895, 1900 and finally on 30 September 1902, and it now read:

(the contractor) pays such rates of wages and observes such hours of labour and conditions of employment as are then recognized and practised by the employers and the trade unions of the town or district in which the work tendered for is to be done; and if no such organization or organizations exists or exist, that he pays the rate of wages and observes the hours of labour and conditions of employment which are accepted for similar work by the employers and the organized trades in the town or district nearest to the place where the said work is to be done. (Appendix VI)

A number of government departments had displayed a considerable degree of administrative independence in adapting the 1891 Resolution to the new reality. Evidence before the Committee showed that the contracts let by the War Office, Admiralty, Office of Works and the General Post Office all contained Fair Wages Clauses not as proposed by the House of Commons but more or less as follows: 'The wages paid for all work performed under the contract shall be those generally accepted as current in each trade for competent workmen *in the district where the work is carried out*' (Appendix I) (My italics). The term 'district' has thus been introduced to accommodate the development of collective bargaining on a district basis.

Various trade union representatives appeared before the Committee and testified as to the existence of collective bargaining in their industries on a district basis. The representative from the Parliamentary Committee of the T.U.C. spoke of the division of the country into districts, each of which had a different rate of pay prevailing throughout the district, and used as an example the boilermaking part of the ship-building trade (Q. 27). Another representative of metalworkers spoke of a minimum list of rates in addition to the local rates: 'We let every district fix its own price according to the conditions of its work, but we have a minimum list under which no district must work' (Q. 432). Here are the beginnings of national regulation. Even one or two employers were prepared publicly to recognize collective bargaining, which they saw at times as the lesser of two evils. Witness the statement of a building employer: 'I think it is essential that the rate should be agreed upon, because we do not recognize the rules a trade union may impose upon its men in any way, except so far as they are agreed upon between our Association and the workmen's Union' (Q. 4834). One employer, however, went so far as to advocate that the 'trade union rate' be substituted for the 'current rate' in the Resolution, and thus be made mandatory on government contractors—to the shocked surprise and horror of the Committee. This exchange between the President of the Saddlers' and Harness Makers' Association and the Committee shows a neat contrast between the shocked questions asked unbelievingly by the Committee and the witness's calm replies, e.g.:

Q. 5800 – But would that be fair? Would not you be enforcing on a contractor there a rate which neither he nor other employers in his district had ever agreed to pay to their men?———That might be so.

Q. 5801 – Would a provision of that kind be well received in the trade, do you think?———I think the members of my Association would like to see a fixed rate applying generally.

Q. 5802 – Would they be content to pay it?———Yes.

Q. 5806 – By the trade union rate you do not mean the rate demanded by the trade union, but the rate actually paid in practice, I suppose?———That usually is the rate demanded, I think.

Q. 5807 – Do you always pay what the workers demand?———If their Union has a fixed rate.

Q. 5809 – Would you see no objection in the contract which compelled you to pay the rate demanded by the trade union of the trade, whatever it was?————If it were a fair rate, and if it affected us all equally, we should pay it. We wish to see the condition of the workers better, if possible. In some branches of our trade the condition at present is very good; in some branches it is not so, and we should like to see an improvement in the lesser-priced branches.

The evidence of this witness must be considered in the light of his previous admission that he had little experience of the Fair Wages Resolution in practice (Q. 5784).

By 1908 the Committee could not avoid becoming aware of how collective bargaining was affecting the application of the Fair Wages policy:

We may also point out that the resolution does not contain the word 'district', but that the phrase 'wages current in each trade for competent workmen' is in practice (and, we think, rightly) interpreted as wages current in the district in which the work is carried out. (para. 8)

Recognition of the district basis of bargaining was necessary 'in view of the fact that wages in the same trade generally vary in different parts of the country' (para. 115). The view of this Committee on the relation between collective agreements and the rates required to be paid under the Fair Wages Resolution differed significantly from that of the 1896 Committee on Stationery Contracts which required an agreement between all employers and all workmen before its rates would be considered 'current'. This Committee held that, 'where in a given district the trade union has succeeded in establishing a rate which is so far accepted by the employers that the majority of the workpeople in that district do in fact obtain the rate, the trade union rate is of course the "current rate" of the district' (para. 21). The burden of establishing such 'current rates', however, lay wholly on the workers concerned (Q. 3575).

That in the face of departmental intransigence this burden was no light one is indicated by a case of 1905. A meeting had taken place between Army contractors and workers' representatives in June 1904, which resulted in an agreement being signed by both sides setting up a scale of wages for boot contracts. On 30 March 1905, a complaint was presented in the House of Commons that the wages stipulated by this agreement were being undercut by some contractors. The Secretary of State for War, however, was far from encouraging this experiment in collective bargaining. Although he admitted that 'a statement was agreed to by certain of the contractors and signed by their representatives', he asserted that it did not represent the whole of the contractors in the district, and furthermore had been afterwards partially repudiated. Certainly, 'it was never accepted by this Department as a statement of wages to be paid. It was merely regarded as some evidence of a desire to arrive at a uniform scale.' When the continued refusal of some contractors to observe the agreement eventually precipitated a strike by the men, he put forward the following ingenious justification for his department's attitude: 'So far as concern the men who are on strike, it would appear to be impossible for the Department to insist upon a particular rate being paid as current at a moment when such a rate is precisely the matter in dispute'. In other words, the strike was an indication not that current rates were being evaded, but rather that the agreed scale was not representative of current rates.[7]

Thus, despite this recognition, the Committee was still unable and unwilling to break away from the original orthodoxy governing Fair Wages policy. Government contracting policy was not to stray from the dictates of *laissez-faire* economics: 'If the Government is to have its work executed at the ordinary market price it cannot require the contractor to pay more than the market rate of wages' (para. 22). This reveals the Committee's basic misunderstanding of the aims of a Fair Wages policy, which is precisely to avoid the pure market rate. The Committee realized that the Resolution was intended 'to prevent Government contracts from falling into the hands of employers who were able to quote lower prices by undercutting their competitors in the rate of wages paid' (para. 7). The Committee failed to appreciate the incompatibility of maintaining a pure market rate, while at the same time excluding 'competitive employers'.

Accordingly, it recommended that no changes be made in the original wording of the Fair Wages Resolution of 1891 (para. 125(a)). Even the inclusion of trade union conditions within the framework of a Fair Wages policy was rejected as not being 'proper' in government contracts, and the reasons given were obviously partisan:

> Some employers consider the conditions unduly restrictive of their freedom of management, and, although they quite willingly pay the trade union rate of wages, decline to recognize all the trade union conditions. To enforce the observance of trade union conditions would prevent many non-Union houses from taking Government contracts, although they paid the trade union wages, and the proposed form of clause would therefore give a distinct preference to Union houses. (para. 25)

The Committee's final conclusion contained some small consolation, if only verbal:

> While we do not *recommend* that words intended to enforce the observance of 'trade union conditions' should be inserted in Government contracts, we *think* that such conditions of employment as are generally accepted in the district in the trade concerned must be taken into account when considering the question whether a particular contractor is observing the Fair Wages Clauses. (para. 125(b)) (My italics.)

The Committee's animus towards trade unions and their functions evinced here appeared in a number of other passages during their taking of evidence from various parties. The objection of the Committee to the formulation of the Fair Wages standards on the terms recognized by trade unions derived from the well-worn prejudice that this would enable the trade unions to fix any price they liked and force it on the government contractors who would have to abide by the Resolution: 'It would make the Trade Unions masters of the situation' (Q. 496). Or witness the general statement of a member of the Committee in an exchange with a trade unionist: 'The Fair Wages Clause may be used, and I believe has been used or was intended to be used, in order to secure fair rates of wages to the men employed on Government work, and not to further general Trade Union principles' (Q. 1791). To such a mind, even the simple request for a condition of labour such as one limiting the number of apprentices appeared as a 'general Trade Union principle', and as such was to be abhorred (Q. 1792). Fortunately, this Committee's attitudes were not those of the proponents of the Fair Wages Resolution passed in the following year, 1909.

NOTES

1. This account of collective bargaining between 1891 and 1909 is principally derived from the following sources:
—J. Henry Richardson, *Industrial Relations in Great Britain*, I.L.O. Studies and Reports, Series A (Industrial Relations), No. 36; Geneva, 1938.
—Alan Bullock, *The Life and Times of Ernest Bevin, vol. I, Trade Union Leader, 1881–1940*; Heinemann Ltd., London, 1960.
—A. Flanders, 'Collective Bargaining', in A. Flanders and H. A. Clegg (eds.), *Industrial Relations in Great Britain;* Blackwell, Oxford, 1954.

—H. A. Clegg, A. Fox and A. F. Thompson, *A History of British Trade Unionism Since 1889, vol. I: 1889–1910;* Clarendon Press, Oxford, 1964.
—John Child, *Industrial Relations in the British Printing Industry;* Geo. Allen & Unwin Ltd., London, 1967.
—*Report on Collective Agreements between Employers and Workpeople in the United Kingdom*, 1910; Cd. 5366.
—Evidence of Mr. J. T. Morrison, Secretary, London Saddle and Harness Makers' Trade Protection Society, and Secretary, Military Harness and Accoutrements Makers' Trade Union,

to the Departmental Committee appointed to consider the Working of the Fair Wages Resolution of the House of Commons of 1891; given on 20 February 1908. See Report of the Fair Wages Committee, 1908, Minutes of Evidence, Q. 3831, at Q. 3841, Cd. 4422.

—Proceedings of the Select Committee on Stationery Contracts, 1896, at pp. xxi–xxii (paras. 23–4); House of Commons Papers, 1896, vol. XIII, at p. 413.

2. The information on local authority Fair Wages policies is derived from the following sources:

—Circular addressed to Candidates for the London School Board, November 18, 1891, and their replies on the fair wages question.

—London Society of Compositors, *Government Printing Contracts*, pamphlet published in 1894 (19 pp.).

—Fabian Tract No. 11, *The Workers' Political Programme*, 1891.

—Fabian Tract No. 20, *Questions for Poor Law Guardians*, (Revised, March 1900).

—Fabian Tract No. 21, *Questions for London Vestrymen*, (Revised, September 1894).

—Fabian Tract No. 24, *Questions for Parliamentary Candidates*, (Revised, July 1895).

—Fabian Tract No. 25, *Questions for School Board Candidates*, (Revised, October 1894).

—Fabian Tract No. 26, *Questions for London County Councillors*, (Revised, February 1898).

—Fabian Tract No. 27, *Questions for Town Councillors*, (Revised, May 1899).

—Fabian Tract No. 28, *Questions for Candidates For County Councils* (outside London and County Boroughs), (Revised, February 1895).

—*Urban Sanitary Districts (Conditions of Contracts)*. Return to an Order of the Honourable the House of Commons, dated 31 May 1893: Return 'showing in respect of each Urban Sanitary District, whether the Contracts entered into by the Authority for the execution of Works specify any Conditions as to the Wages to be paid by the Contractor, or other Conditions with respect to the Persons employed by him; and if so, what are the conditions so specified'.

(3 November 1893) House of Commons Papers, 1893–4, vol. LXXVII, p. 573.

—Return to an Order of the Honourable the House of Commons, dated 4 August 1897. Urban Sanitary Districts (Conditions of Contracts), in continuation of Parliamentary Paper No. 435 of Session 1893. House of Commons Papers of 1898, vol. LXXIX, p. 647.

—Scottish Local Authorities. Return to an Order of the Honourable the House of Commons, dated 28 July 1898. Urban Sanitary Districts (Conditions of Contracts). House of Commons Papers of 1898, vol. LXXX, p. 773.

—*Contracts for Local Authorities (Wages)*. Return to an Order of the Honourable the House of Commons, dated 9 April 1900: Return 'showing in respect of each Administrative County and each Poor Law Union in England and Wales, whether the Contracts entered into by the Authority for the execution of works specify any conditions as to the Wages to be paid by the Contractor, or other conditions with regard to persons employed by him; and, if so, what are the conditions so specified'. Ordered to be printed 24 July 1900. (16 pp.)

—*Contracts for School Boards (Wages)*. Return to an Order of the Honourable the House of Commons, dated 26 April 1900. Printed 3 August 1900. (47 pp.)

—*Contracts of Local Authorities (Wages)*. Return to an Address of the Honourable the House of Commons, dated 22 February 1905; Return 'showing (1) for England and Wales as regards each County Council, Town Council, Metropolitan Borough Council, Urban and Rural District Council, and Board of Guardians; (2) for Scotland, as regards each County Council, Town Council, Parish Council, and District Committee; and (3) for Ireland, as regards each County Council, Town Council, Urban District Council (not being a Town Council), Rural District Council, and Board of Guardians; whether the Contracts entered into by the Authority for the execution of works specify any conditions as to the Wages to be paid by the Contractor, or other conditions with regard to the Persons employed by him; and, if so, what are the conditions so specified'. Ordered to be printed 7 August 1905. (105 pp.)

—*Report of the Fair Wages Committee, 1908.* Cd. 4422. Appendix VI: 'Fair Wages Clauses in the Contracts of Certain Corporations'; and Appendix VII: 'Fair Wages Clauses Entered into by Local Authorities (1905)'.

—Evidence of Mr. W. Sharrocks, of the Staffordshire district of the Boilermakers and Iron and Steel Shipbuilders' Society, given on 27 February 1908, to the Fair Wages Committee, 1908. Minutes of Evidence, Qs. 4278ff. Cd. 4422.

3. The following account is derived from the Report of the Select Committee on Stationery Contracts, 1896, its Proceedings and Minutes of Evidence. House of Commons Papers, 1896, vol. XIII, p. 413. In the remainder of this book, statements and quotations from this source will be accompanied by the page number in the Report and Proceedings, or question number in the Minutes of Evidence, where they may be found. For the background to the setting up of this Committee, see the debate in Parl. Deb., H. of C. (Fourth Series); 18 August 1894, vol. XXVIII, cols. 1559–80.

4. Parliamentary Committee of the Trades Union Congress, Agenda for the 29th Annual Congress, Edinburgh, 1896, at p. 19.

5. The following account is derived from the Report of the Select Committee on Government Contracts (Fair Wages Resolution), 1897, its Proceedings and Minutes of Evidence. House of Commons Papers, 1897, vol. X, pp. 1, 299, 473. In the remainder of this book, statements and quotations from this source will be accompanied by the page number in the Report and Proceedings, or question number in the Minutes of Evidence, where they may be found. For the background to the setting up of this Committee, see the debate in Parl. Deb., H. of C. (Fourth Series); 24 March 1896, vol. XXXIX, cols. 66–84. Sydney Buxton described at length the dissatisfactions with the existing situation: that the Resolution was indefinite was repeatedly emphasized; that there was a lack of conformity in its administration by departments; that contracts went to unfair houses; and that departmental investigations of complaints were unsatisfactory or so protracted as to be useless.

6. The following account is principally derived from the *Report of the Fair Wages Committee, 1908*, its Appendices and Minutes of Evidence. Cd. 4422. In the remainder of this book, statements and quotations from this source will be accompanied by the paragraph number in the Report, the number of the Appendix or the question number in the Minutes of Evidence, where they may be found.

7. The quotations are to be found in Parl. Deb., H. of C. (Fourth Series); 30 March 1905, vol. 143, cols. 1709–10; and 13 April 1905, vol. 145, cols. 65–6.

3

The Interpretation of the 1891 Resolution

Having analysed the changing situation of industrial relations in the period between 1891 and 1909, the performance of the Fair Wages Resolution of 1891 under these circumstances must now be examined. How was it applied during a time of such unforeseen changes? To do this, however, it is necessary first to scrutinize exactly what was embodied in the terms of the 1891 Resolution. Hence the second major theme of this section: analysis of the meaning of the actual wording of the Resolution.

Given the approach adopted by the House of Commons towards regulation of the terms and conditions of employment of employees of Government contractors—that of a single, short resolution—the comment of the Chairman of the 1908 Fair Wages Committee is only to be expected: 'If you have to provide in clear and concise language a formula which will apply to an immense number of transactions, a large variety of contracts, and a very big business all over the country, ambiguities and imperfections must necessarily arise in the wording' (Q. 3). The question of ambiguity is of particular legal interest. In the usual case the Fair Wages Resolution was inserted in government contracts as a term of those contracts. It is a basic principle of the common law of contract that a contract is void if its terms are insufficiently clear and precise. In the instance of a term of such importance as the Fair Wages Clause, which in cases of breach appeared to give the government the right to repudiate the contract, often expressly, the contract might prove to be void should the Fair Wages Clause be considered to be too vague. This very point was raised by an American commentator who complained about the 'frequently poor and meaningless draftsmanship' of certain Federal government contract clauses which aimed to implement government policies. He gave as an example military contracts which contained a clause entitled 'Utilization of

For notes see p. 49

Small Business Concerns', whereby the contractor bound himself to employ small business concerns to the greatest extent consistent with efficient performance of his contract. Of such a clause he said: 'The enforceability of such a covenant is doubtful to say the least'.[1] The following analysis shows that a similar conclusion may be reached concerning the Fair Wages Resolution of 1891.

For, despite the cautious warning of the Chairman quoted above, one may inquire whether it is justifiable to expect some degree of accuracy and clarity, and whether the adoption of such a method of regulation necessarily leads to the failure of the policy. A number of examples illustrate some very broad and significant difficulties which arose from the ambiguity of the Resolution. Some employers were prepared to argue that the Resolution did not apply to skilled labour at all. They pointed to the reference in the Resolution to the Sweating Committee, and claimed that the House of Commons had distinctly limited itself to remedying the evils which had been disclosed to that Committee. In other words, the injunctions of the Resolution referred only to employers of sweated labour. In their evidence to the 1908 Committee, representatives of the Engineering Employers' and Ship-building Employers' Federations were able to quote from the Report of the Sweating Committee in support of this view: 'As a rule, however, it must be remembered that the observations made with respect to sweating apply in the main to unskilled or only partially skilled workers, as the thoroughly skilled workers can always obtain adequate wages' (Qs. 5420–2). To their mind the protection of the Resolution did not apply to a large section of the industrial work force, a quite legitimate interpretation in the light of the Resolution's vagueness.

Again, doubt was expressed in various quarters as to whether the Resolution applied to women workers at all. Reference was made to the fact that the Resolution referred only to the wages of a 'workman'. In reply to a question from the 1908 Committee about the operation of the Fair Wages Clause on women's labour, the Secretary of the Manchester and Salford Women's Trades and Labour Council stated: 'As far as I know anything about it, women are not taken into consideration at all in the work. If the wages are all right for the men it does not seem to matter very much about the women' (Q. 6226). One M.P. asserted bluntly that: 'The Fair Wages Resolution says nothing as to the standard rate of wages for women'.[2] The 1908 Committee noted that the General Post Office apparently felt it necessary to make express provision that the Fair Wages Clause in its contracts applied to women workers employed on the government contract: 'This clause shall apply to all women and girls (not being learners) employed either wholly or partly on the contract' (Appendix

I). Even where the Resolution was accepted as perhaps applying to women, it was interpreted to their detriment; viz. the opinion of the 1908 Committee: 'we do not think that it was the intention of the resolution to enforce the payment to women of the rate "current" for men employed on the same class of work' (para. 70). This appeared to reflect accurately the departmental point of view, as stated by the Financial Secretary to the Treasury, in 1902: 'If a particular rate of wages in a particular district is paid for men, I cannot say that in all such cases I will enforce the same wages for women. If a case is made out that women are being underpaid, then I will give it my most careful consideration.'[3] Following this review of two substantial problems—the exclusion of skilled labour and of women workers from coverage of the Resolution—it is possible to begin to form an opinion as to the quality of its draftsmanship. But first, more details.

The detailed examination of the 'meaning' of the Fair Wages Resolution of 1891 proceeds as follows: first, some of the overall general views of the Resolution held by various parties—members of Parliament, trade unionists, employers and government departments—are presented. Then the interpretation of certain of the key phrases of the Resolution is given, followed by some examples of particularly thorny problems which arose; and finally, the conclusions arrived at concerning the effects of the wording on its efficacy.

General Views

In 1893, the Trades Union Congress adopted the following resolution at its annual meeting: 'That in the opinion of this Congress, the expression "fair wages" in the House of Commons resolution of 13th February, 1891, *re* Government contracts, should be interpreted and construed to mean the usual trade union rate paid and conditions of employment in force in each trade in the locality in which any Government contract is executed for the time being'.[4] By 1907 the view was widely expressed by trade unionists that the Fair Wages Resolution was too vague; that so many interpretations could be made of it that its intention was frustrated. Representatives of the Vellum (Account Book) Binders' Trade Society complained to the 1908 Committee that they could not get a definite idea of what the Resolution meant so as to be useful to them (Q. 1163). The trade union point of view was reiterated to the 1908 Committee by the T.U.C. representative: 'When that Resolution was passed in 1891, the trade union world had the impression that it meant the trade union rate; and after all we consider the current rate should be the rate that has been generally agreed upon between the employers and the workmen's associations' (Q. 165). In their view, from watching the course of the debate on the Resolution, that was the correct view of the Fair Wages policy, and only faulty wording had given rise to the subsequent difficulties.

This interpretation of the Resolution was clearly not acceptable to many government departments charged with its enforcement. Rejection was not the only response. In one case there was a blank refusal to offer any other interpretation. The Secretary of the National Amalgamated Lock and Key Smiths' Society testified to the 1908 Committee as to the efforts of his member of Parliament to get the Admiralty to define what was meant by the Resolution. All that could be obtained from them was the statement quoted by this witness: 'We have the Resolution passed by the House of Commons, but we have to leave you to define it and interpret it yourselves. We are not here to define it or to interpret it' (Q. 3576). In an early attempt, the Secretary of the Treasury was asked in Parliament whether the Resolution referred to trade union rates. In a stonewall reply he repeated the text of the Resolution and added: 'I have no authority to limit or add to this definition'.[5] This basic disagreement over what constituted a 'current rate' and the inability to come to a definite and clear understanding with the departments continued. The General Secretary of the Galvanised Hollow Ware Sheet Metal Workers and Braziers' Association summed up to the 1908 Committee his experience of complaining to departments about infringements of the Resolution: 'What we recognize as the current rate it appears that the officials who investigate these matters will not understand in the same way' (Q. 2986). The Webbs recognized the seriousness of this problem when, in 1897, they wrote:

> Finally, we have the fact that the present generation of the higher civil servants—our real rulers in points of administrative detail— are, for the most part, invincibly ignorant both of industrial organization and modern economics, and are usually imbued with the crudest prejudices of the Manchester School. It is in vain that Ministry after Ministry avows its intention of abandoning competition wages, and of making the Government a 'model employer'. The permanent heads of departments have no intention of departing from the 'sound' principles which they brought into the service in 1860 or 1870. Hence a trade union secretary will often declare that the Government, instead of being the best, is one of the very worst employers with whom he has to deal.[6]

An interesting insight into the views of the House of Commons which passed the Resolution of 1891 is gained from the remarks of a compositor who claimed to have been one of the trade unionists who drafted the Resolution together with Sydney Buxton. The meaning of that Resolution was, he stated to the 1896 Committee on Stationery Contracts: 'that all Government contracts should be given out according to the scale of the trade unions of the country'. When questioned closely as to why these very words were not inserted, he declared that it had been thought a matter of policy to avoid a reference specifically to unions, but that the phrase 'current rate' was still meant to be the trade union wage. Pressed even further as to why these words were omitted, however, he finally admitted, 'that being the case we might not perhaps have got the House to take the matter so readily into consideration', and seeing the reaction of his questioners, he went on, 'I do not wonder at your smiling. As we go along we are obliged to use a little tactical judgment over these matters.' But he refused to retract his former interpretation, 'but that is really the meaning of (the Resolution) as we take it' (Qs. 2676–80). The Committee on Stationery Contracts was clearly not very receptive to this view of the intention of the House. However, the conclusion drawn by the Chairman in his Draft Report may be thought to go to the opposite extreme. He stated: 'A conclusion withheld from the House for this reason cannot be said to have been within its mind when the Resolution was adopted' (p. xiv). Both these views can only indicate the various currents of opinion on the meaning of the Resolution which existed in the House at the time. Any assertion of a single unified interpretation must be erroneous. The closest approach to such an interpretation would perhaps be that expressed to the 1908 Committee by a trade unionist who was present in the House of Commons on the night of the debate when the Resolution was passed: 'if I understood the feeling of the House at that time, it was that Government work should only be done by fair employers' (Q. 2219). This is not very helpful in interpreting the Resolution actually passed.

'Current Rates'

The phrase, the meaning of which was most frequently debated in the course of the years 1891–1909, was: 'generally accepted as current for a competent workman in his trade'. Concerning the first part of this phrase, 'generally accepted as current', it appears to have been understood that the general reference to 'make provision against the evils which have recently been disclosed before the House of Lords'

Sweating Committee', was complementary to the subsequent admonition to 'make every effort to secure the payment of the rate of wages generally accepted as current'. The reference to sweating in the Resolution was rarely mentioned independently of this latter question. As it was put by the Controller of the Stationery Office to the 1896 Committee on Stationery Contracts: 'If it could be shown that the firm was paying less than the wages current, I should consider that so far sweating. It seems to me the two inquiries are one and the same' (Q. 183).

The Controller went on to explain, however, that in the printing trades at least, the current rate was not the trade union rate, and could not be as long as a large number of workers in the trade did not belong to the union or work in union houses (Qs. 201–18). Before the Committee on Government Contracts of 1897, a representative of the carpenters' union defined the 'current rate' as the trade union rate, but failed to elaborate exactly what he meant by this (Qs. 639–42). Representatives of the Amalgamated Society of House Decorators and Painters and of the Plumbers' Association explained the term to the Committee as operating within a collective bargaining framework, thus excluding the idea of unilateral regulation by unions (Qs. 241; 2596). The confusion over the term 'current rate' resulting from developments in collective bargaining was reflected, as was described above, in the bitter disputes during the Proceedings of the Committee on Stationery Contracts of 1896. The question was whether the collective agreement was to be adhered to in all its details, or that merely to abide by the general standard prevailing because of it was adequate compliance with the Resolution. In view of the appointment of the Committee, the London Society of Compositors prepared a pamphlet explaining why the London Scale of Prices should be paid on government work within the metropolitan area. It urged that the following condition be inserted in the form of tender of the Stationery Office specifically with reference to the Fair Wages Resolution:

> In this contract the words 'such wages as are generally accepted as current' shall be taken to mean, for all work executed in London, the wages fixed in the London Scale of Prices, signed and mutually agreed upon at Stationers' Hall between representatives of the London employers and the London workmen.[7]

The Committee nonetheless refused to accept collective bargaining as the norm-fixing mechanism. This rejection was maintained by the Committee on Government Contracts of 1897, though the developments were recognized. Buxton drafted a minority Report which proposed a definition of 'current rate' closely adhering to the views of trade unionists, and upholding the role of collective bargaining in determining the 'current rate'. But this view was decisively rejected by the Committee.

With the mass of differing rates that existed in the same industry, trade or district, the determination of a 'current rate' which could be applied as the standard stipulated by the Fair Wages Resolution was almost impossible. The only element of uniformity was to be found in the efforts of trade unions to regularize wages. At this stage in the development of industrial relations, however, the ruling classes in government were not prepared to accept collective bargaining as the standard of a Fair Wages policy. The alternative being no standard at all—no standard at all was chosen.

Ten years after the 1897 Committee reported, however, such had been the changes in the industrial relations situation regarding the cognizance, if not the widespread acceptance, of collective bargaining that the Fair Wages Committee of 1908 felt able to declare that the current rate of a district would be the trade union rate, provided the majority of the workers in that district received the trade union rate, due to its acceptance by their employers (para. 21). The requirement that there be a numerical majority of workers receiving the trade union rate before it could be called a 'current rate' did not go unchallenged by trade unionists. One trade union M.P., the Organizing Secretary of the National Amalgamated Furnishing Trades, declared to the 1908 Committee that where a small percentage of employers had formed an association and had agreed with their workmen on trade union rates, these rates should be enforced on the other non-associated employers. He went so far as to say that if only one employer out of twenty in a district accepted the trade union rate, this rate should be enforced as the current rate on other employers; though he admitted that at least one employer must be prepared to accept it (Qs. 1763–8). The London District Secretary of the Electrical Trades Union agreed, and maintained his opinion regardless, he stated, of the number of employees employed by the employers in question. It was pointed out that the single employer accepting the trade union rate might employ only two employees, while each of the nineteen others might employ twenty employees. In the face of the irrefutable logic of this mathematical proof, the trade unionist could only reply with such irrelevancies as: 'In the specific case you put, do you not think it would be a pity to have only two men working in a good-wage firm and twenty men working in a bad-wage firm?' Or: 'Because there are only two men out of three hundred odd who are getting a living wage, that is no reason why the remainder should not get it' (Qs. 1873–9). The

1908 Committee was not moved by such obvious appeals to sentiment and maintained stolidly its 'democratic' formula. As to what was to be the 'current rate' in the event of there being no majority, several solutions were mentioned by the Committee (paras. 33; 125(d)). But in practice the problem of determination of the current rate in a work force unorganized for the most part remained unresolved.

Other difficulties arose concerning the interpretation of the very short phrase which supposedly formed an adequate standard. The point was raised whether an employer who demanded very long hours, but paid the union rate of wages, was in breach of the Fair Wages Clause. The employer would pay, say, the union rate of thirty-nine shillings a week, but exacted a greater number of hours than the union would recognize. The General Secretary of the London Society of Compositors asserted to the 1908 Committee that he thought the employer would get away with this, for he would not be violating the letter of the present Resolution, though he might be violating the spirit (Qs. 234–5).

Another logical consequence of the ambiguity of 'current rate' is in a case pointed out by the 1908 Committee. If the work done by employees is facilitated appreciably because of the large amount of work made available through a government contract, on the irreproachable ground that new conditions of work have been created, it would seem that the ordinary 'current rate' does not apply, and a reduction in ordinary wages is justified (para. 118). A similar logical deduction was made by a War Office official. He argued that if a manufacturer introduced the least little thing into his method of construction or working, and there was no other firm who offered an analogy to that, it would be necessary to regard his rate of wages as the current rate, inasmuch as there was nobody else to make a comparison with. Again, if there was a single isolated firm in a little village who paid a much lower rate of wages than anybody near him, this same official maintained that his rate of wages was the current rate of the particular district. Representatives of the National Amalgamated Tin and Iron Plate, Sheet and Metal Workers' and Braziers' Union who presented these examples objected strongly to such interpretations, calling them 'a deliberate evasion of the terms of the contract' (Q. 426) They are, however, the inevitable result of applying strictly logical legal interpretations to a very ambiguous formula. The question is, of course, whether this excessively legalistic approach will achieve the results the Fair Wages policy was intended to obtain, or whether it will give rise to exactly the opposite—drive down wages on the slightest excuse.

'In His Trade'

The latter part of the section of the Fair Wages Resolution presently being discussed—specifically the words 'in his trade'—was also a source of much difficulty and confusion. It gave rise to two principal problems. First, the reference to rates of wages current in the trade demonstrated an astounding ignorance of industrial relations in 1891. As described above, the determination of rates of wages was not a process regulated by collective bargaining or otherwise, and to speak of uniform rates in a trade was blatantly illusory. It was therefore necessary that some administrative means be found to circumvent the unreality of the Resolution and apply it to existing industrial conditions.

There is some evidence of the efforts of government departments to find their way towards a solution. Thus, the Stationery Office informed the 1896 Committee of its endeavour to narrow down the area required by uniformity by concluding that the phrase 'in his trade' referred not to a whole trade, but to 'branches of a trade' (Qs. 105–10). Even so the difficulties of varying and fluctuating rates of wages proved insuperable obstacles if the strict application of the Resolution was desired. In 1894 the Treasury was asked if the Resolution could be improved by annexing to all specifications for tenders a 'schedule setting out the rate of wages paid to the various trades to be employed in and about the execution of the contract'. The reply of the Secretary of the Treasury showed he was aware of the meaninglessness of 'trade rates': 'I do not consider that that Resolution authorizes the issue of a hard-and-fast schedule of wages and hours, *nor do I see how this could be done seeing that they vary in different localities in the country*'. (My italics.) The precedent of the London County Council was discounted on the grounds that it was not applicable to the country generally.[8]

The solution adopted by those responsible for implementing the Resolution was described in the Report of the Committee on Government Contracts of 1897: 'Practically each Department interprets this to mean the rate of wages generally accepted as current in each trade for competent workmen *in the district where the work is carried out*, and these words, with slight variations, are now inserted in nearly all Government contracts' (p. v). (My italics.) The criterion of wages current in the trade was transformed into wages current in the district, a change dictated by practical considerations. Sydney Buxton justified this interpretation by referring to the speeches on the Resolution in 1891: 'what was in the speakers' minds was not a general current rate, but the different district rates applicable in different places'.[9]

This interpretation of 'trade' remained dominant at least until 1909. In 1908 the London District Secretary of the Electrical Trades

Union testified to the 1908 Fair Wages Committee of the Resolution's use of the term wages current in the trade as having 'been reproduced in the contracts in the form of "the rate current in the district where the work is performed" ' (Q. 1840). By this time, however, there was a growing desire and inclination in the trade union movement towards the extension of collective bargaining on a district basis into national negotiations. A sign of this is to be found in the testimony of the President of the Union of Weavers and Textile Workers to the 1908 Committee. He contended that 'district' should be much larger than it was then interpreted as being. He desired in effect a re-interpretation of 'trade' away from the narrow geographical district basis to a wider 'trade area' idea (Q. 1271). This trend will be examined more closely when the industrial relations situation affecting the 1909 Fair Wages Resolution is discussed.

Even the reduction of the unreal view of rates current over an entire trade to the level of rates current in a district was inadequate in view of the unorganized state of collective bargaining. A realistic working definition of 'district' was required, but the efforts of various parties to obtain one were shattered against the industrial realities. The problem was described in 1896 by the First Lord of the Admiralty:

> Then there is the great question of area, of district; and according as we draw the district there you will find whether wages are paid as current in the district or not. To reconstruct the areas for trade union purposes would be as difficult as the redistribution of political power in the representation of this House. Every difference of area would certainly make a variation in the rate which, according to the views of some persons, ought to be paid.[10]

Thus, for example, having outlined the departments' solution to the problem of a 'trade' rate of wages, the 1897 Committee on Government Contracts endeavoured to explain what a 'district' rate would be, and came up immediately against the problems posed by the splintered nature of such collective bargaining as existed (p. xviii). In December 1907, the Secretary of the National Hosiery Federation, representing a total of 3,000 members out of a labour force of 30,000–40,000 workers in the trade, was still pleading with the government before the 1908 Fair Wages Committee:

> Could they see their way clear to define what they mean by a district? It is so vague, so indefinite now, that it is not a bit of good, and the Fair Wages Clause is really no good at all, because manufacturers can go and make their own arrangements, they can pay their own price. ... If the Government would simply

describe a kind of radius, a given number of miles, even that
would help. (Qs. 1562; 1592; 1622)

One paragraph in the Report of the 1908 Committee indicated a
solution to this problem at least insofar as organized workers were
concerned. It proposed that the definition of district for the purposes
of the Resolution be given over to collective bargaining: 'The area
agreed upon by the organized employers and workpeople might be
regarded as the "district" for the purposes of the Fair Wages Clause'
(para. 61). At the same moment, the First Commissioner of Works was
refusing to accept that collectively agreed rates applied in certain
districts where employers refused to recognize them.[11]

The second problem concerning the word 'trade' in the Fair Wages
Resolution is one which was not of major significance at a time when
collective bargaining existed only at a very local level. It concerned
the difficulty of determining whether a particular worker or group of
workers, whose wages were the subject of a dispute, was engaged in
one or another trade. Thus, it only became of practical importance at
a time when rates were determined reasonably steadily for a particular
trade as distinguished from another trade, a development which was
somewhat later in coming than the period of the first Resolution. Still,
there was evidence that in its latter years this problem did arise. Two
examples are present in the evidence of a trade unionist to the 1908
Committee. This representative of carpenters and joiners in the building trade discussed the question of whether his members who worked
at their professions in the engineering industry were still to be regarded
as being in the building trade. As regards the hours of their work, he
conceded that it would be unreasonable to require that an engineering
firm adapt their hours to those of the builders. But as far as wages
were concerned, he maintained that, in so far as the engineering
industry employed building workers, they should pay them at an
equal rate to what a builder would give them, and he was prepared
to uphold this view even where his members might be in a small
minority in the industry (Q. 2330).

The second example mentioned by this witness concerned the
problem of the distinctions between joiners and cabinet-makers. These
two professions had separate unions and different rates of wages, but
the men possess similar skills and could transfer without much difficulty
from one trade to the other; for example, they could move from building work, which was paid hourly, to cabinet-making, which was paid
on a piece-rate basis. At first the witness seemed to say that a joiner
going into a cabinet-maker's shop would have to be paid at building
rates. However, he later stated: 'No man in the one trade will ever

take advantage of the other, and whichever trade the work belonged to, of course the rules of that trade would govern' (Qs. 2332–9). This appears to be a different principle from that maintained by the witness in the first example; however, it may be understood by taking it that in cabinet-making the joiners would not be working in building-construction, while in the engineering industry they would be, though in another industry. There is apparent here an enormous potential for disputes over the distinction between one trade and another, or a trade and an industry. In general, however, this issue is overshadowed in importance by the issue of recognition of collectively agreed rates, whatever the trade or industry.[12]

Particular Problems

It would hardly seem necessary to speak of any particularly thorny problem raised by the difficulties of interpreting the Fair Wages Resolution of 1891. Its terms are so vague and so general that, in the context of an industrial situation where a rate 'generally accepted as current in a trade' was a rarity, the problem was not one of interpreting the Resolution in those situations where it applied, but of finding situations where it could be said to apply at all. For even in 1910, at the end of the period under discussion, there were only two million trade unionists in the country: this being no more than one in five even of the men engaged in manual labour, without taking into account the women. In certain areas and industries (the industrial North and South Wales; mining, printing, engineering and ship-building) the proportion was much higher than the national average, but in others (London and the agricultural areas; transport, agriculture, shop-workers) it was still lower. Again, most of these members were in small, often entirely local societies numbering only from a few hundred to a few thousand with little organization, few funds and limited interest. Of the 669 unions which divided these members, only eighteen numbered more than 20,000 members.[13] It is no wonder that in 1908 the Fair Wages Committee still raised as one of the major complaints made by trade unionists, 'the difficulty of providing protection by means of the Fair Wages Clause to the workers in unorganized trades in which a variety of rates of wages is found and no standard rate exists' (para. 12(a)).

To point to one particular problem would seem a superfluous gesture. However, to illustrate a difficulty of interpretation inherent in the 1891 Resolution there is an example which appeared very frequently in the complaints of trade unionists before the various

Committees. It was, as defined by the 1908 Committee, 'The difficulty of applying the clause in those cases where the establishment at which the work is carried out is the only one in the trade in the district in which it is situated', known as the 'isolated factory' problem (para. 12(b)). As it was later put by the Committee:

> The factory being isolated and not surrounded by others with which it can be compared, the phrase 'current rate of wages', so far as it means anything at all, can refer only to the rate paid at that factory, so that the clause gives no independent standard with which to compare the wages paid. (para. 60)

Two examples of specific cases where the failure of the Resolution to provide for this situation had detrimental effects are found in the evidence to the 1908 Fair Wages Committee. The first concerned a firm in the hosiery trade which moved twenty miles from the city of Leicester with the result that they were the only firm in the locality to which they had moved which was doing hosiery. They subsequently fixed their rates at nearly 50 per cent less than the recognized rates at Leicester, and then called their rate the 'current rate' of that locality. As the witness stated, it was impossible for the people who were isolated in that district to protest. He regarded this lacuna as 'one of the biggest evils of the faulty wording of the present Resolution' (Q. 21). A second instance concerned government printing contractors, who were accused of having put up branch establishments in districts that had either a low rate or no rate at all. Consequently, they could determine unilaterally what they should pay their operatives, and that became the current rate of the district, there being no other printers in the district (Q. 191). Other cases went as far as the House of Commons. In 1894 a complaint was made that in a country district, joiners were paid 6½d. for a 52-hour week as compared to trade union rates of 8d. for a 50-hour week in Leeds; and in 1902 it was said that a firm 'were the only employers of women in that locality, and were thus enabled to set up a standard rate of wages themselves, and by paying that rate were able to show that they were entitled to have nothing said to them by the Government'.[14]

Given these concrete examples, it might be expected that the 1908 Committee would give the problem some serious consideration. Their conclusion, however, was quite the reverse: 'Although the case of the isolated factory may theoretically present some difficulty, we do not find that it is at all of frequent occurrence in practice' (para. 67). Perhaps for this reason the solution they proposed was also very theoretical and abstract given the concrete situation existing with regard to the enforcement of the Resolution: 'A solution . . . might perhaps be found in comparing the wages paid in other trades in the same district, or with those paid in the same trade in other districts, taking into account the cost of living' (para. 66). As will be seen, the frequent occurrence of this solution in practice was unlikely, to say the least.

Conclusions

In view of the failure of the wording of the Resolution to come to terms with either the objectives of the Fair Wages policy or with the industrial realities prevailing at the time, what consequences can be attributed to this failure? The General Secretary of the United Society of Brushmakers gave a bitter critique of the administration of the Fair Wages policy to the 1908 Committee. He stated that in his trade 'conditions, so far as Government work is concerned, show no improvement when comparing the present times with the periods previous to the Resolution'. And when asked to what he ascribed this failure, he replied: 'We ascribe it to its indefiniteness' (Qs. 1931–4). In calling for an inquiry in 1896, one M.P., a long-time supporter of the Fair Wages policy, stated: 'The vague and indefinite terms in which the Resolution of 1891 was framed had led to confusion in its administration'. The chief difficulties were concerned with the 'current rate' formula, where differences of opinion existed as to whether it meant the wages demanded by trade unions, the average wages of the district, or the wages which individual contractors had been accustomed to paying for similar work. He called for a Committee of Inquiry to define the term.[15]

It is questionable whether, given the chaotic industrial situation, any brief formula could have served to fulfil the broad objectives of a Fair Wages policy. In reply to criticisms, the First Lord of the Admiralty commented in 1896: 'It was said that the Resolution was vague. It was vague because the subject matter with which it deals must leave it vague. There is only one way in which this Resolution, in my judgment, can be made fairly to work—namely, the existence of a disposition on both sides to work it fairly according to its general spirit'.[16] Unfortunately, this lack of definition also served as an excuse for bureaucratic procrastination. So in reply to a deputation from the T.U.C., a Treasury representative could protest: 'it would be unbecoming for me, at any rate, to put any strict interpretation upon a resolution which the House of Commons had, perhaps purposely, left in somewhat vague terms'.[17]

It is not in its specific wording that the 1891 Resolution stands condemned, but in the use of such a brief formula as an administrative mechanism to implement such a far-reaching policy. Given a sincere desire to implement the policy expressed in the brief formula, one would have to abandon the actual wording and turn to the administrative implementation of the Resolution for hope of its success. Such, at least, was the view taken by the Scottish Organizer of the National Amalgamated Society of Enginemen, Cranemen, Boilerman, Firemen and Electrical Workers. When asked by the 1908 Committee to suggest an alternative formula of words which might improve the 1891 Resolution, he replied in the negative: 'It is not so much in the wording as in the actual practice—the compelling of the thing to be carried out' (Q. 4030). It remains, therefore, to examine the enforcement in practice of the Resolution of 1891.

NOTES

1. P. M. Risik, 'Federal Government Contract Clauses and Forms', *George Washington Law Review*, **23** (December 1954), at p. 134.

2. Parl. Deb., H. of C. (Fourth Series); 14 February 1902, vol. CIII, col. 84; per Mr. Nannetti.

3. Ibid., at col. 75, per Mr. Austen Chamberlain.

4. Report of the 26th Annual Trades Union Congress, Belfast, 1893, at p. 71; moved by Mr. Collins.

5. Parl. Deb., H. of C. (Fourth Series); 24 May 1894, vol. XXIV, cols. 1182–3; per Sir J. T. Hibbert.

6. Sidney and Beatrice Webb, *Industrial Democracy*, Volume II, London: 1897; at p. 555.

7. Pamphlet by C. W. Bowerman, Secretary, London Society of Compositors, *Government Printing Contracts*, February 1896, 8 pp.

8. Parl. Deb., H. of C. (Fourth Series); 6 July 1894, vol. XXVI, col. 1068.

9. Parl. Deb., H. of C. (Fourth Series); 24 March 1896, vol. XXXIX, col. 71.

10. Ibid., at col. 81; per Mr. G. J. Goschen.

11. Parl. Deb., H. of C. (Fourth Series); 27 November 1908, vol. 197, cols. 940–1.

12. For a detailed analysis of this problem as undertaken by the Industrial Court in deciding cases under the 1909 Fair Wages Resolution, see M. T. Rankin, *Arbitration Principles and the Industrial Court*, P. S. King & Son, Ltd., London: 1931. Chapter V, 'The Craft Principle and the Industrial Principle', and chapter VII, 'The Industrial Principle and Monopolies—Government and Municipal Services'. She concludes that 'the Court had no clear or analytical view of the nature of these principles or their relation to each other'; at p. 111.

13. This description is taken from Alan Bullock, *The Life and Times of Ernest Bevin*, *vol. I, Trade Union Leader 1881–1940*, Heinemann Ltd., London: 1960; at pp. 25–6.

14. Parl. Deb., H. of C. (Fourth Series); 19 February 1894, vol. XXI, cols. 729–30; 14 February 1902, vol. CIII, cols. 81–2.

15. Mr. C. Fenwick, who had seconded Sydney Buxton's original motion in 1891, in Parl. Deb., H. of C. (Fourth Series); 24 March 1896, vol. XXXIX, at col. 74.

16. Ibid., at col. 81; per Mr. G. J. Goschen.

17. Per Mr. Hanbury, Parliamentary Secretary to the Treasury, to a deputation from the Parliamentary Committee of the T.U.C. See *Report of Important Delegations to Cabinet Ministers*, published by the T.U.C. Parliamentary Committee, London, 13, 14 and 15 November 1895; pp. 34ff., and p. 38.

4

The Administration of the 1891 Resolution

Against the background of an industrial relations situation at variance with the new Resolution's emphasis on rates current in the trade, and with conflicting interpretations of its wording advanced by interested parties, how was the new policy administered by the government departments given this task by the House of Commons? The account of the first two decades of experience of the Fair Wages policy proceeds as follows: first, those general concepts of implementation, administration and enforcement which could have been anticipated after the passage of the Resolution of 1891 are considered. Next, the steps taken by various government departments to implement the policy are described in detail, followed by a summary of the principal kinds of complaints made by various parties concerning their administration. Then the views of various parties—trade unionists, employers, members of Parliament, Parliamentary Committees, etc.—on the enforcement of the Resolution are put forward, together with their suggestions and proposals for its improvement during the period 1891–1909. Finally, the views of these various parties concerned on the value and efficacy of the Fair Wages Resolution will be summed up in light of its stated objectives, and otherwise.

General Conceptions of Fair Wages Policy Administration

What general ideas concerning the implementation, administration and enforcement of the Fair Wages policy were envisaged in 1891? The wording of the Resolution was in very general terms. Nevertheless, there are three principal specific demands made by the House of Commons: (1) the government has a duty in all its contracts *to make provision* against the evils of sweating; (2) *to insert such conditions* as may prevent

For notes see p. 99

the abuses arising from subletting; and (3) *to make every effort* to secure the payment of current rates of wages. Apart from the specific instruction to insert conditions in government contracts relating to subletting, there does not appear to be any specified means of implementation or enforcement laid down by the House of Commons in relation to its Fair Wages policy. It is quite possible to understand the injunction 'to make provision' against the evils of sweating as not limiting the government departments to the insertion of contractual conditions. Certainly the requirement 'to make every effort' is wide enough to include almost any administrative measures to secure the objectives of the policy.

Such a liberal interpretation of the 1891 Resolution derives support from a comparison with the Draft Resolution submitted by Sydney Buxton in initiating the debate, which was eventually rejected in favour of the final Resolution adopted. Buxton's draft began with the specific instruction: 'Clauses to be inserted in all Government Contracts'. No other means of implementation appear to have been foreseen. The 1891 Resolution, however, seems deliberately to leave other options open. And in fact other means of enforcement of a Fair Wages policy were available. Buxton himself gave an example of a government department, the Office of Works, which prior to 1891 was already enforcing a Fair Wages policy by means of including schedules of wages within the contract itself. Realizing that the prevailing political temperament of the House would not be amenable towards a step of this magnitude towards governmental regulation of wages, he declared that he himself regarded this method as more than was required by his own more modest resolution. In light of the fact that even Buxton's more modest resolution was rejected in favour of the government's, it is perhaps understandable that to have expected an even more interventionist enforcement policy than Buxton's proposed insertion of contractual conditions would be illusory. It is very likely that the vagueness of the final Resolution was intended to soften and thus weaken the practical impact of the policy. Even so, however, the actual demands put in the wording of the Resolution were still capable of transformation into a vigorous policy of enforcement— given the will so to apply them.

What, then, was the means of enforcement envisaged by the House of Commons when it passed the Fair Wages Resolution? An insight into the principal currents of opinion in the House may be gained, once again, from the views expressed in the Proceedings of the Select Committee on Stationery Contracts, 1896, the first Parliamentary Committee to consider the Resolution in any depth. The view of the administration of the Fair Wages policy which may be classified as 'conservative' is presented by the Chairman of the Committee in his Draft Report to the Committee. The point of departure as regards implementation of the Resolution is the insertion in government contracts of the full Resolution passed by the House, as an express contractual covenant. In this way, the contractor is seen as being legally bound to observe each branch of the Resolution. In addition, the head of the government department (in the case of this Committee, the Controller of the Stationery Office) is held to be the sole judge of any doubts which may arise in the interpretation of the contract. The contract thus gives the Controller the power to unilaterally terminate the agreement for what he may consider a breach of it. The contractor is considered to be bound by his decision without the possibility of appeal. Since the Controller is an officer of the Treasury, his actions are subject to the concurrence and approbation of the Treasury. The Treasury itself, like the other government departments, is responsible to and under the direct control of the House of Commons. The House, so this view maintains, can thus itself ensure that its own Resolution is obeyed to the letter (p. xiv).

There is here a formalist approach to the administration of the Fair Wages policy, an approach taking absolutely no account of the realities of the exercise of bureaucratic and Parliamentary powers relative to each other. It calls for a very active departmental enforcement policy—one which will supervise closely the rates of wages actually paid by the contractor to his employees and will impose sanctions for violations of the Resolution where these occur. Some machinery for the determination of disputes over the interpretation of the Fair Wages Clause in the contract is also envisaged. The assertion that the House of Commons itself both would and could supervise the administration of its own Resolution is in line with this same idealistic conception. This last point exposes the unreality underlying the whole of the proposed enforcement machinery. In practice the passivity of the proposed administration ensured that the Resolution remained a dead letter.

An indication of the attitudes of mind which produced such an administrative framework may be seen in an exchange between the Chairman of the Committee on Stationery Contracts and the Controller of the Stationery Office. After outlining his view of the Resolution's enforcement, as described above, the Chairman continued:

Q. 85 – Do you think that that would therefore be a complete
security for carrying out the wish of the House of
Commons?———I think so; I do not know any better
way of doing it.

Q. 86 – It becomes then not a question of machinery, but a question of the competence of the agents to work the machinery?——Yes.

Q. 87 – And you do not need to give any opinion upon that?—— No.

Q. 88 – You recommend nothing more?——On the whole I know no better basis to work upon than the old contracts with such improvements as you suggest.

The self-satisfied air of the parties to this exchange is disturbing. Including the preceding statements, there is an atmosphere of very leading questions. The Controller is at first not entirely sure where the Chairman is leading him, but, finally seeing the light, though not quite believing the Chairman's faith in the powers of supervision exercised by the House, nevertheless agrees wholeheartedly with the theory, secure in his awareness that in practice his autonomy is assured.[1]

The alternative approach to the administration of the Fair Wages policy was that put forward by Mr. Lough in his Draft Report to the 1896 Committee. This emphasized the connection between the policy and collective bargaining. The standards of the Resolution were to be those embodied in collective agreements. Enforcement would be greatly reinforced by the active co-operation of organized labour. Collective bargaining and trade unions thus being essential components of a successful administration of the policy, both were to be encouraged as much as possible (pp. xviff.). This view was regarded without much enthusiasm by the Controller of the Stationery Office. The evidence for this is to be seen in the argument as to whether the Resolution's requirement that the government is 'to make every effort to secure the payment of current wages' is satisfied by mere insertion of the Resolution into contracts; or whether reference should be made to a required adherence to the London Scale (a collective agreement) (Qs. 201–18).

Sydney Buxton, the initiator of the Resolution, was clearly associated with this latter view of its administration. This appears from the opinions he expressed in his Draft Report to the 1897 Committee on Government Contracts. His first general principle for guidance in administering the policy was: 'That where, in any given district, rates of wages have been mutually agreed upon by a considerable number of the employers and the representatives of the workmen, these rates should be recognized and enforced'. Again, one of the criteria he proposed for judging whether an act of a contractor constituted a legitimate grievance which should be remedied was whether the action tended 'to break down any mutual agreement come to between masters and men' (pp. xv–xx). The idea of collective agreements serving as standards for a Fair Wages policy was neither unrealistic nor abstract at the time, though it was limited by the relative scarcity of such agreements.

The only government department with experience of a Fair Wages policy prior to 1891 was the Office of Works. Even before the 1891 Resolution, contractors for ordinary works and repairs had to fulfil certain conditions. They had to submit with their two tenders two schedules. The first was to specify the rates of wages for various categories of labour (twenty-four categories) which they considered to be generally accepted as current in the district. There were to be two rates for each category: a minimum rate per hour for 'efficient workmen', and a maximum rate for 'leading men, and for special works'. Contractors were warned, however, that the margin between the maximum and minimum rates should be a moderate one. The second schedule submitted was to specify the regulations as to overtime observed in the district. Before the conclusion of the contract, these schedules were carefully examined and, if necessary, discussed with the builder-contractor whose tender was to be accepted, with such changes made as were felt to be required. It was also possible to make further changes from time to time during the running of the contract, but for such change conclusive evidence was required that the change was justified by 'a general and accepted alteration in the trade'. The contractor was required to give to each man sent to work a card stating his trade and the rate of his wage.[2]

Up to now, no mention has been made in the procedure of the Office of Works of standards agreed collectively by organizations of workers and employers' associations. However, in giving evidence to the 1897 Committee, the Senior Surveyor of the Office admitted that 'we practically adopt the rates of wages which have been agreed to between the Master Builders' Association and the workmen' (Q. 6). The force of the collective agreements as the sole standards for judging wages was emphasized by his insistence that his Office would refuse to reimburse a contractor who agreed with a group of workers on a project to raise wages. Such a wage increase concerning only a particular contract could not be considered part of a generally accepted rate, 'unless the increase had been agreed to generally by the master builders and the workmen in London. They agree to an alteration as a general arrangement, not upon one contract' (Q. 176). Strangely enough, however, in the event of underpayment of wages by a contractor, the Office's course of action appeared to be less insistent. They did not insist that the employer raise the wages of workers on government work, but only concede that 'we should at once assent to an increase if demanded by the workpeople of that firm who were then being paid below the current rates of wages in the district' (Q. 178).

There is here, therefore, such an example of collectively agreed standards of fair wages as were advocated by those who took a liberal view of the Fair Wages Resolution. They went on to advocate that organizations of workers should be actively involved in enforcing these standards. But it must be emphasized that, while the liberal wing desired collective bargaining as contributing to the enforcement machinery, they were aware of its weakness due to the limited extent of workers' organization. Thus, although they were consistent in demanding the encouragement of collective bargaining and organization, they were aware that this did not obviate the need for other enforcement procedures.

The example of the action of the Office of Works in the event of a contractor underpaying his employees is significant. For such a breach of the Resolution would only be remedied where workers were organized sufficiently to present a demand that fair wages be paid, a condition fulfilled in only a minority of cases in those days. Thus the importance of alternative enforcement measures is obvious. Even if the Resolution was interpreted as desired by the liberal wing, and set up the standards negotiated by collective bargaining as fair wages standards, it would still be necessary to ensure the enforcement of those standards, especially where trade unionism was weak. For, in practice, the Fair Wages Resolution only fulfils a need where trade unions and collective bargaining are weak. As it was put by representatives of the metalworkers' union to the 1908 Committee: 'But if we were strong enough to do it, there would be no occasion to have a fair wage inserted in the contract at all from a trade union point of view' (Q. 507).

Departmental Administration of the 1891 Resolution

In this section, the steps taken by the various government departments to comply with the Fair Wages Resolution of 1891 will be considered. The Resolution was in effect an instruction to these departments from the House of Commons. There exist conflicting accounts of the zeal with which the wishes of the House were carried out. Some five weeks after the Resolution had been passed, Sydney Buxton asked the First Lord of the Treasury what steps the Government had taken to carry out the Resolution. In reply, the Treasury representative stated: 'I have conferred with my Colleagues at the head of the several Departments with whom the responsibility of making contracts rests, and it is arranged that they will take such steps as are practicable to give effect to the Resolution of the House in entering into any contracts for works'.[3] Yet in a letter from the Treasury to the Committee on Government Contracts, 1897, dated 13 June 1896, concerning the steps taken by it as to communicating to the other government departments the Resolution of 1891, it emerged that the Treasury had *not* in fact bothered to communicate the Resolution to the other departments—an administrative action normally undertaken in the event of new policies being introduced. The Treasury explained itself as follows:

> that the Resolution of the House of Commons of 13th February 1891, respecting Government contracts (Wages) was within the knowledge of every Government Department, and that, consequently, the Treasury did not think it necessary to communicate it to any of them. (Appendix 23 to the Report of the 1897 Committee)

This explanation is belied by the experience of an 1893 addition to the Resolution. In a debate on 3 August 1893 in the House of Commons, Sydney Buxton, then Under-Secretary for the Colonies, speaking on behalf of the Government, stated that: 'the Government would consider that any preference given to a non-unionist against a unionist in regard to Government printing would be, to a large extent, against the principle' of the Resolution of 1891. He added with regard to a particular complaint under discussion, that 'one of the terms and conditions of the renewal of the contract, if it were renewed, or in giving it out to another contractor would be the insertion of a clause that no preference should be given as between unionists and non-unionists'. It appeared, therefore, that the Government of the day had given an undertaking that in all future government contracts a clause would be inserted stating that no preference should be given as regards the employment of workers on these contracts as between unionists and non-unionists. Of the compliance of the government departments with this instruction, the Committee on Government Contracts of 1897 had this to say:

> It appears that, for some reason, this point and pledge has not been brought to the attention of most of the Departments, though it is carried out in all stationery and some other contracts. Your Committee consider that, in accordance with the undertaking of 1893, this additional point should be assumed to have been

incorporated by the House in the Fair Wages Resolution, and that in every contract the words which already appear in all stationery contracts should be inserted, namely, that 'the contractor ... shall undertake that, in the engagement and employment of workmen and others required for the execution of the work, no preference shall be given as between "unionists" and "non-unionists" ' (p. vii)

This conclusion was reached after the Committee had interrogated representatives of various government departments. Thus, the Assistant Secretary of the Post Office admitted to the Committee that no information had been given to the Post Office by the Treasury as to employment of unionists or non-unionists by contractors to date (29 April 1897) (Q. 2238). The Treasury's opinion as to the awareness of departments seems rather optimistic in light of this same witness's admission that the 1897 Committee's inquiry was the first the Post Office had heard of the 1893 addition (Q. 2259).

Even more ominously, however, it appears that after this enquiry once again no steps were taken by government departments or the Treasury to ensure that the wish of the House of Commons was enforced. This may be deduced from the fact that the 1908 Committee again singled out the Stationery Office contracts as containing, in addition to the usual Fair Wages clause, also the above clause on the subject of union and non-union labour (para. 9). The Committee failed to mention any other government department as complying with the 1893 instruction. Only one explanation for the behaviour of the Treasury in this instance has been uncovered. It is a remarkable example of how effectively the policies of the House of Commons could be frustrated by a recalcitrant bureaucracy. In reply to a question in the Commons concerning the Stationery Office's implementation of the Resolution that contractors be forbidden to discriminate between unionists and non-unionists, it was stated:

The Controller of the Stationery Office informs me that, although this condition has been inserted in all Stationery Office contracts since 1893, and no objection has been taken to it by contractors, it has, in the majority of cases, been practically inoperative owing to the action of the men themselves. *Such a condition, if enforced, must shut out, for instance, firms which engaged trades unionists only,* which is not, I think, the desire of the hon. Member. What Sir John Hibbert stated on the 3rd August, 1893, was that the Government would be justified in refusing to enter into contracts with contractors who were shown to have dismissed certain men while, as I understand, the contract was running because they had become trades unionists—*a promise which must also be held to apply to dismissing men because they have ceased to be unionists*. The Treasury have been in communication with the other Departments on the subject, and the conclusion at which they have arrived is not favourable to the adoption of such a condition'[4] (My italics.)

The question is whether this interpretation which renders the Resolution 'practically inoperative' can possibly be justified. It would be grotesque to resort to the assertion that such was the intent of the House of Commons. Rather, it seems that a contractual condition upon which the departments looked with disfavour, was discarded on the flimsiest of grounds. The problem of contractors discriminating against non-unionists was again discussed in a committee of departmental representatives who concluded in a Memorandum of 1 December 1910 that:

> A clause of this nature may involve the Department in very difficult questions relating to the treatment of individual workpeople, such as, for example, deciding between the allegation of a trade union that a workman has been discharged because of his activity on behalf of the union and the allegation of the employer that the man's work was unsatisfactory or that he was discharged through slackness of employment.

Since it was declared to be the policy of the departments 'to take serious notice of cases in which contractors are clearly showing a preference for non-union men without any justifiable cause, and such action as may be necessary can be taken without the insertion of a clause in the contracts', the departmental representatives recommended against the inclusion of any anti-trade union discrimination clause. In their view: 'Having fully considered the question, the Committee regard it as undesirable to lay down a rule that Departments should not deal with employers who exercise a preference for workpeople who are not members of a trade union'. This administrative defiance was to prevail over the policy expressed by the Government of the day in 1893 and the Select Committee of the House of Commons of 1897.[5] As a consequence of departmental inaction, this anti-trade union discrimination clause disappeared from government contracts and did not re-emerge until its inclusion in the third Fair Wages Resolution of 1946.

There will now be described the steps taken by the various government departments to comply with the Resolution of 1891.[6]

Office of Works

The process of compliance in this department varied according to the different types of contract. The very thorough procedure as regards contracts for ordinary works and repairs was described earlier in this chapter—an application of a Fair Wages policy which dated from before the 1891 Resolution was passed. The only additional step undertaken by the department after 1891 was to circularize the contractors advising them of their duty to comply. The circular provided as follows:

> 2. It is the intention of the Commissioners that men employed in day-work should be competent workmen, who should be paid wages at rates such as are generally accepted as current in each trade for competent workmen, and persons tendering should take care that the Schedule of Rates submitted by them should conform to this requirement, and that the margin between the maximum and minimum rate should be a moderate one.
> 3. Every person tendering is to sign the Tender, and the Schedules referred to in it, first duly filling up that relating to the rates of wages in day-work; and any Tender which is not upon this form, or which is not properly filled up and signed, will be rejected.[7]

The form of tender contained the following declaration to be signed: 'The rates of wages which (X tenderer) propose to pay to the men employed in day-work under this Contract are as shown in the accompanying Schedule which *in (X's) opinion* represents the range of wages generally accepted as current in each trade for competent workmen' (p. 6). (My italics.) There is, of course, all the difference in the world between an obligation to specify in a Schedule the rates in practice current in the trade, and the obligation merely to specify rates which, in the tenderer's opinion, represent these rates. All this is, anyway, only relevant in the pre-contract stage. In the actual 'General Terms of Contract', as opposed to the 'Particulars for the Information of Persons Disposed to Tender' just described, the principal provision relating to wages was clause 20, which, however, merely stated:

> The contractor shall provide a sufficient number of competent workmen for day-work, who shall be paid by him at such rate of wages or rates of wages as the surveyor may from time to time approve, being not more than the maximum nor less than the minimum of the rates quoted in the Schedule for each trade respectively, and the amount so paid by the contractor shall be repaid to him by the Commissioners on their being satisfied, as

hereinafter provided, that the payments have been duly made by
the contractor in compliance with the provisions of this condition.
(pp. 3–4)

Clause 23 provided for the contractor to furnish such evidence of these
payments to the Commissioners 'as may be required from time to time'.
Unfortunately, it seems it was not unknown for the Office of Works to
allow the contractor to pay even less than the minimum stipulated in
the Schedule after the contract had been made.[8]

This perhaps adequate compliance of the department was not to
be found, however, in the case of contracts for new buildings at an
agreed sum (called Special Works). The procedure as described to
the 1897 Committee by the Senior Surveyor in the Office of Works
was simply to include in the contract a clause forbidding subletting or
piecework without the consent of the department: 'The contracts
contain, however, no clause controlling the rates of wages to be paid
by the contractor' (Q. 4). It was apparently thought that the sending
of a circular to the contractors warning them to comply with the
Resolution would be adequate compliance, this being done prior to
acceptance of the tender, and thus not being considered a contractual
condition. The view of the department was well summarized by a
member of the 1897 Committee:

> I take it your position in regard to (payment of current rates)
> is this: you deal with reputable firms; you assume that they will
> carry out the contract into which they have entered, and in that
> contract you insist, not only by them but under the sub-contract,
> the recognized current rate will be paid. (Q. 285)

As regards the setting up of Fair Wages standards, the department
would seem to have succeeded to some extent in respect of contracts
for ordinary works and repairs, but much less so in the case of special
works. The situation was even less satisfactory in connection with the
enforcement of these standards. As was previously pointed out, the
department did not insist on payment of current rates where the
contractor was known to be underpaying his workers until those
workers actually demanded that their wages be increased. The
position of the department as regards enforcement generally was as
follows:

> Q. 286 – When complaint is made you inquire, but it is not your
> business before any complaint is made to follow it up
> and see whether they do or do not pay the current
> rate?————That is the course we take.

As to the number of complaints received on behalf of the workers regarding violations of the Resolution, this was estimated to be very small, whether relative to the amount of work done by the department, or absolutely (Qs. 6; 33; 203). In the rare instance of a complaint being made, a representative of the department would be sent to make enquiries as to what the men were being paid. The process of enquiry as described by the Senior Surveyor is not very thorough: in the normal event he would go straight to the contractor and enquire from him as to whether he was complying. Should the men persist and a dispute develop between them and the employer as to whether a certain rate was being paid, and complications as to deductions arise, he would act as follows: 'I should have to get the information in the best way I could *from the contractor* and if necessary I should require to see his pay sheets for the week' (Q. 43). (My italics.). The point to emphasize is that it does not appear to have occurred to him to make enquiries from the men or their representatives as to what wages were actually being paid. In the unlikely event that the contractor's word was not accepted, the ultimate authority was seen as being the pay sheets prepared by him. The Surveyor was questioned closely, but his faith in the objectivity and accuracy of the employer's pay sheets could not be shaken. He claimed he could not think of any better 'system of arriving at the true facts of the case' (Qs. 236–43; 44–5). If he did happen to discover that the employer was not paying current rates, the department would insist upon the employer at once paying the current rate. Even this sanction, which did nothing to reimburse the men previously underpaid, was qualified by the ominous phrase: 'as far as I might be able' (Q. 40). In sum, one may understand the dissatisfaction of workers with this method of enforcement.

Stationery Office

In 1896, the Select Committee on Stationery Contracts requested the Stationery Office to produce a summary of its action to date on the Resolution of 1891. In evidence to the Committee, the Office submitted what might be termed a classic bureaucratic response concerning its action immediately following the passage of the Resolution:

> Its bearing on the Stationery Office contracts was fully considered; but as no contracts of any great importance were about to be granted, and no complaints of the action of contractors with regard to their workmen had, at least for some time past, been received, and as, moreover, it was felt desirable that Departments

should, as far as possible, act on the same lines, it was not judged
necessary to take any immediate action. (Appendix 2 to the
Minutes of Evidence to the 1896 Committee)

It appears that action on the same lines as other departments amounted
to taking no action at all. It may be noted that at the time of the 1896
Committee's Report, there were forty-nine existing contracts let by the
Stationery Office and these amounted to an annual expense of
£322,440: this only five years after the decision to take no immediate
action was made, so even then the outlays were serious.

On 29 January 1892, almost one year after the Resolution had
been passed, a complaint was finally received, somewhat surprisingly,
perhaps, in view of the secrecy which had been maintained. At any
rate, following what appear to have been hurried consultations with
the Treasury, the department issued a circular, dated 9 February 1892,
to all firms holding running contracts, calling attention to the Resolution and stating that non-compliance with the 'spirit of the Resolution'
might entail being struck from the list of eligible contractors (Appendix
2; 1892 Return, pp. 12–13). In addition, the Resolution was to be
printed on the face of all contracts issued from that date, with a large-
type note calling attention to it. Such notice to the contractor did not,
however, constitute a binding contractual condition. The Resolution
was not inserted in the contract itself, and was not made a specific
condition of the contract until a general revision carried out in 1896.[9]
A year after the Resolution's passage, Sydney Buxton questioned
whether merely seeking an assurance from the contractor that he
would comply with the Resolution was adequate without a contractual
obligation. The Secretary to the Treasury, however, refused point
blank to accept that such an obligation be included in Stationery
Office contracts: 'It is not expedient to insert the Resolution as a
condition of contract'.[10] Strangely, the next change occurred following the statement in the House of Commons on 3 August 1893 concerning the employment of unionists on government contracts.
Accordingly, on 22 September 1893, the order was given that in all
future contracts it should be an express condition that the contractor,
'in the engagement and employment of workmen and others required
in the execution of the work', should give 'no preference as between
unionists and non-unionists'. There was thus the peculiar situation
where the original Resolution was not binding on the contractor, but
the later addition was.

The 1896 Committee on Stationery Contracts was appointed to
enquire: 'whether the present system of issuing invitations for tenders,
and of making contracts for Government printing and binding, suffici-

ently secures compliance with the terms and spirit of the Resolution of the House of Commons of the 13th day of February 1891; and whether any, and, if so, what improvements on the system are called for'. The Report of the Committee gave a brief description of the system under which contracts were issued by the Office (p. iii). Tenders were invited, sometimes generally, sometimes from a select list. These tenders were to be based on a Schedule issued by the Controller of the Stationery Office giving prices for the different work required. This Schedule itself was based on a scale known as the London scale and the bids were to quote a specific percentage of the prices in the Schedule. In the contract itself there were included provisions regulating sub-letting. Also, that the Controller had 'power at any time to close the contract on failure of compliance with any condition', and:

> should any question or questions arise in regard to the inter-
> pretation of this contract, or of the statements in any one or more
> of the subjoined schedule, memoranda, or notes, or as to the
> execution of any order or work arising out of the same, such
> question or questions is, or are, to be settled by the award of the
> Controller without appeal from his decision. (p. iv)

As to the enforcement of these standards, the method adopted appears to have been that described above of the Office of Works, viz., enforcement by complaint. Thus the Controller was quoted as having said: 'that if a man came to him and said that he was not being paid a fair rate of wage on the work that he was doing for the Government he would take very serious steps to see that the contractor was dealt with'. The response of trade unionists familiar with the realities of power and organization on the shop floor was one of barely concealed derision. As put by representatives of the Vellum (Account Book) Binders' Trade Society, to the 1908 Committee:

> We would like to place before you the difficulty of an individual's
> position in attempting to carry out such a thing. I do not believe
> that in the whole history of the Fair Wages Resolution it has
> been done. No individual has gone to him personally and said
> he was not receiving the fair rate of wage. (Q. 1161; also
> 1260–3)

Whether received from individuals or representatives of organized labour or other sources, the Controller was unable to deny to the 1896 Committee that there had been complaints 'in many instances' that contractors were not paying such wages as were generally current (Qs. 27–8). It subsequently emerged that, despite these many complaints, not one contract had been annulled by the Controller for breach of

the Resolution by a contractor (Q. 116). Here, too, the workers'
dismay was understandable.

Having digested the evidence presented to it, the Committee of
1896 delivered its views on what it saw as the three divisions of the
Resolution. As regards the injunction on the evils of sweating, the
Committee considered three specific complaints against the Stationery
Office on this count, without reaching any general conclusions (pp.
iv–v). On the problem of sub-letting, the Committee concluded: 'So
far as sub-letting has arisen, it appears to have been effectively dealt
with by the Stationery Office, and the provisions of the Resolution of
the House of Commons upon this subject are, on the whole, fairly
complied with' (p. v). Concerning payment of current rates, the fundamental debate among the members of the Committee has been discussed
in chapter 3. The Committee refused to adopt collective agreements
as the standards of a Fair Wages policy, and refused to encourage the
growth of collective bargaining as a means of enforcement of the
policy. It preferred to rely entirely on theoretical control and administration by the House of Commons itself through its servants in the
government departments. The most radical recommendation the
Committee could make was that the Resolution be made an express
covenant in the contract, instead of being merely printed on its face,
and that the Controller reserve the right to recover damages from the
contractor when a contract was terminated by him through a violation
of the Resolution (p. ix). Even reimbursement of the cheated worker,
as opposed to the Office itself, was not thought of as a possibility.

The revision in the contract methods followed by the Stationery
Office as a result of the 1896 enquiry may have had even more ominous
consequences. In the opinion of the Committee of Inquiry into
Government Printing Establishments of 1927, this revision had been
undertaken 'with a view to dividing the printing work amongst a
greater number of contractors and to give provincial contractors
opportunities of competing on equal terms with the London printing
houses' (para. 20). This opinion coincides with the sharp attack of the
Committee on collectively negotiated standards, which in practice
meant an attack on the use of the London Scale of Prices as a basis
for drawing up the Controller's Schedule of prices, upon which tenders
were based. The Committee appears to have attempted to substitute
the insertion of the Resolution as an express covenant for the previous
Fair Wages standards based on the London scale. By employing a
much vaguer formula as a standard for Fair Wages, the provincial
firms no longer had to base their prices on the London scale, which was
naturally higher than those of the provinces, and thus could compete
more easily in tendering for government contracts. The result of the

Committee's recommendation, therefore, was precisely what the Fair Wages policy had been designed to prevent—namely, competition among government contractors based on the undercutting of wage rates.

War Office

From the evidence of the Director of Army Contracts to the 1897 Committee, it seems that the War Office maintained a list of contractors permitted to tender. Following the passage of the 1891 Resolution, persons on the list were required to sign a pledge that they accept the terms of the Resolution. The pledge, however, referred only to wages, not to sub-letting. In addition, a paragraph was inserted in all contracts which read as follows:

> No portion of this contract shall be transferred without the written permission of the Director of Army Contracts. Sub-letting, other than that which may be customary in the trades concerned, is prohibited. The wages paid in the execution of this contract shall be those generally accepted as current in each trade for competent workmen in the district where the work is carried out. (Qs. 299–303; also 1892 Return, pp. 13–14)

Up to this point the practice of the War Office was normal. In the course of taking evidence, the 1897 Committee discovered a serious deviation, however, from the purposes of the policy. The Director of Army Contracts was confronted with a form of contract for gas fittings which contained a schedule headed 'Schedule of Rates and Wages considered as current in the Woolwich district on the date hereof'. In the course of questioning, it emerged that the amounts put under that Schedule were nominal and did not necessarily signify that they were the actual wages current. When asked whether it was not misleading to put in a figure which bore no relation to actual current rates, under a heading stating that they were such rates, the Director could only reply: 'We do not consider in the War Office we have the means of determining the rates in all cases that are current all over the country', and 'They are examined so far as our information goes in the War Office' (Qs. 526–9). The opportunities for evasion of the Resolution offered by such a practice need not be elaborated. It vitiates any effect an insertion of the Resolution into contracts might have had. One year after the Resolution had been introduced, army contracts for socks were described by the men employed in making them as 'a curse to the trade'. Since 1885, prices had fallen nearly 17 per cent.[11]

Enforcement of the Resolution by the War Office also followed the normal pattern. In the Director's words:

> We do not initiate inquiries in these cases; as a general rule we wait for representations from some quarter or other, and if, on inquiry, those representations are substantiated, that is to say, if a charge is made that a man is not paying the current rates, we have terminated the contract in some cases, and where the contract has already been completed, we should remove him from the list of future contractors. (Q. 316)

Once the complaint was made, it went through the hands of several officers until it reached the local officer who made the enquiry. After some argument it was agreed that this officer usually would see both sides—the contractor and the workmen—before reaching a decision, but that this would depend on the circumstances of the case (Q. 481). As with the Office of Works, there appeared to be a tendency to accept the contractor's version of the case as adequate. In one example, the War Office accepted the contractors' assurances that wages were adequate and 'that their men were perfectly satisfied. The Secretary of State does not consider that further inquiry is necessary'.[12] The Director estimated the average delay in dealing with a complaint was from four to six weeks (Q. 500).

The utility of this complaints procedure and subsequent enquiries is revealed by the Director's remarks. To his mind, most of the complaints 'had very little or no foundation in fact' and were of 'a very flimsy character'. He calculated that of about ninety cases reported since 1891, seventy were baseless and required no action on the part of the Department (Q. 317). Despite his earlier casual remark that the Office had terminated contracts 'in some cases', it turned out that he was aware of only one case where a contract was terminated. As regards the other sanction, removal from the list of eligible contractors, again only one contractor's name had been removed following a complaint. As for other complaints, 'in some cases the contractor has admitted the complaint, and has conformed to the Resolution by paying the current rate', but 'he has suffered no penalty' (Qs. 606–12). In other words, despite the department's investigation, it appeared that only when the contractor practically admitted his violation was a complaint upheld, and then sanctions were only applied if the contractor refused to comply in the future. In one case where a contractor had sub-let a contract to a black-listed firm, the Secretary of State for War replied to the complaint as follows: 'I am very anxious to enforce the Factory Clause; but in this case there was no deliberate intention to violate the Clause. They acted honestly, but under a misapprehension; therefore, I do not think it necessary to prosecute the matter further'.[13] Such mild-mannered enforcement would hardly inspire confidence in the Fair Wages policy on the part of workers, individually or in unions.

The Committee's examination appears to have had some effect on the practice of the War Office. During the course of taking evidence, Sydney Buxton had asked the Director whether it would not be better to have some minor penalty in addition to termination and removal from the list (Q. 605). Although he demurred at the time, by 1908, in addition to the 1891 formula, provisions were included in various contracts relating to sanctions for infringement—including fines and termination with damages recoverable. In addition to these there were provisions inserted regulating home-work, the posting of notices, methods of wage payment (direct only), and providing for the inspection of wage records (Appendix I to the 1908 Committee's Report). Whether these changes in form had any effect on the more important aspect of departmental attitudes to enforcement of the Resolution is questionable. Thus, in 1902, the Financial Secretary to the War Office could still declare in the House of Commons: 'Provided a contractor pays the current rate of wages when warned, he is not held to be disqualified for future tendering; the circumstances, however, are noted against him'. An earlier reply by the Secretary of State for War to a complaint of infringement of the Resolution lodged with the War Office provides an illustration of this policy in practice:

> My attention was called to this case (in about 1900). An official was sent to investigate the case. The firm stated in defence that they used machinery to a larger extent than usual, and that therefore skilled labour was not so essential. The War Office considered that the wages clause had been infringed, and warned the firm that very serious notice would be taken of any future infringement of the clause. A second case having arisen in 1901, the firm was struck off the list for six months.[14]

A debarment of only six months after two successive complaints and two investigations was unlikely to be much of a deterrent to contractors or a protection to workers.

Admiralty

Evidence of the Director of Dockyards to the 1897 Committee shows the response of the Admiralty to the passage of the 1891 Resolution to have been similar to that of the War Office. A general circular was issued to all contractors advising them of the Resolution's terms and requiring that they comply on pain of their being removed from the official list of contractors. This circular was also sent to all parties when they were invited to tender (Q. 774; 1892 Return, p. 3). Nothing appears to have been done, however, as regards the inclusion of the Resolution as an express clause of the contract. In February 1893, a revised circular letter was issued requiring that 'no contract or any portion thereof should be transferred without the written consent of the Admiralty'. The following words were also added to the end of the 'current rate of wages' section of the Resolution: 'in the district where the work is carried out'. This, as shown above, was only to be expected in light of the development of collective bargaining on a district basis.

Surprisingly, however, there appears to have been some indecision in the Admiralty as to the recognition of the industrial realities. For, just prior to 1896, the First Lord of the Admiralty again revised the conditions of tendering to the extent of deleting the words 'in the district where the work is carried out'. The origin of this change of policy is to be found in the controversy over the future of the Thames shipyards, which will be discussed later in this chapter.[15] At any rate, by 1908 the Admiralty had reinstated this phrase. The practice of the Admiralty had become very similar to that of the War Office by this time. In addition, provision had been made for the insertion of a Fair Wages Clause in the contracts of sub-contractors, instead of relying only on the legal responsibility of the main contractors (Appendix I to the Report of the 1908 Committee).

Enforcement of the Resolution involved a very lengthy process of investigation, much of it involving the writing of letters of complaint and the submission of written evidence. The content of some of this correspondence indicates that Admiralty officials shared common attitudes with War Office officials on the enforcement of the policy. A letter printed in *The Star* newspaper of 15 December 1893 contained the response of the Admiralty to a complaint lodged by the London Trades Council on 26 May, some six and a half months earlier. The letter stated: 'My Lords find upon investigation that the facts stated in your letter are substantially correct, and being unable to accept the explanation offered in justification, have intimated their views to Messrs. Waterman Brothers (the contractors) as a warning to comply with the spirit of the House of Commons Resolution'. A warning was thus the only sanction the Admiralty were prepared to apply. In a similar case a few months later, the Admiralty again upheld the complaint, but asserted: 'It is not possible to impose any penalty'. They would only write to the offending contractor as follows:

My Lords are of opinion that you have infringed the Resolution of the House of Commons of the 13th February, 1891. They trust that this communication will be a warning to you strictly to observe the Resolution in future, both in letter and spirit. Business relations with your firm can only be resumed on that understanding.[16]

Regarding this formal procedure of complaint, Sydney Buxton pointed out to the Admiralty representatives before the 1897 Committee that perhaps the most satisfactory way of enquiring into a dispute 'was not to deal with written documents, especially as coming from somewhat uneducated men, but to see the persons concerned personally'. To this he received a typical administrator's reply: 'the practice of asking them to put their complaints in writing has answered very well so far as the Admiralty is concerned' (Q. 990). The question was, however, how well it had served the needs of the men for whom the Fair Wages policy was instituted. An indication of the answer to this question may be had from the comment of this same administrator that complaints as to the Resolution in the Shipbuilding and Marine Engineering Department of the Admiralty had been 'singularly few on the whole. I think there are not more than 18 cases over the whole time' (Q. 910). An average of only three complaints per year on the quantity of government work done in the dockyards would at least suggest that the requirement of written complaints, etc., may have had a discouraging effect on workers who felt they were being underpaid in contravention of the Resolution. Rather, where organization made this possible, they were more likely to resort to independent industrial action. Thus, shortly after the Resolution was passed, the Amalgamated Society of Engineers struck an Admiralty contractor who had declined to comply with the ordinary trade conditions of work in force among the engineers and joiners. When Sydney Buxton raised the dispute in the House of Commons, the First Lord of the Admiralty, while acknowledging the existence of the dispute, would only state: 'I am not in a position to say whether these demands are reasonable or not, for I have no information on the subject'. When pressed to investigate the matter, he refused: 'It is no part of my duty to do so'.[17]

Home Office

At the Home Office, implementation of the Resolution differed in the Prisons Department and that concerned with the Police. In the Prisons Department, apparently nothing was done until the Order of the

House of Commons of 15 February 1892, requesting a Return concerning the compliance of the Department with the 1891 Resolution,
finally spurred the Office into action. As a result, on 31 March 1892,
a circular was issued to all contractors calling their attention to the
Resolution and requiring compliance. In addition, the forms of contract were altered and all future contracts contained a clause forbidding sub-letting and requiring the current rate 'in the district
where the work is carried out' to be paid. The single exception to this
rule was contracts for purchase of materials for building. The Resolution
was not inserted in these contracts, no reason being given for this
omission (Evidence to the 1897 Committee, Qs. 1403–9; 1585–7; 1892
Return, pp. 6–8).

As regards enforcement of the Resolution, it appeared that, since
the passage of the Resolution in 1891 and up to June 1896, there had
not been one single complaint by either workmen or unions as to a
violation of the Resolution by contractors. This was explained as
being the result of a very much smaller amount of work than other
departments (Qs. 1466–9; 1591). When asked what steps he would take
should such an allegation be made, the Surveyor of Prisons replied:
'I should probably go to the place where the complaint had been
made, and ascertain from the workmen what wages they had received,
and ask the contractor to give an explanation' (Q. 1494). What
promises to be a swift, personal investigation involving the workers
affected was, however, a purely hypothetical reaction. The Home
Office practice would probably be different. This conclusion may be
drawn from the description of action taken by another departmental
official, the Comptroller of Prison Industries, following an actual complaint of a violation of the Resolution, made by rival contractors.
What happened was as follows:

> Q. 1594 – We saw the contractor and put the question to him,
> and the contractor, a large employer of labour in
> London, emphatically assured us that he paid the
> union rate of wages.
> Q. 1595 – Did you satisfy yourself that that was the fact?———
> Beyond that we did not go, because we did not see
> what further action we could take.

It seems that consultation with workers affected as to what their wages
are is simply not considered: their evidence is not on a par with the
statements of a large and respectable employer.

In the Police Department of the Home Office, the clauses put in
by the Receiver of Police varied from contract to contract. For example,
a contract for carpets stipulated that: 'The contractor shall in carrying

out this contract employ skilled workmen only, who shall be paid by him such wages as are generally accepted as current in each trade for skilled workmen' (1892 Return, pp. 6–8). A contract for ankle-boots required payment of wages 'as shall from time to time be current in the trade for competent workmen'. Yet the Secretary of State for the Home Department could still assert that as regards the contract for police boots, there was no recognized rate in the trade and consequently only 3½d. per pair was paid; and that that bane of sweating, home work, was allowed 'according to the custom of the trade'.[18] One wonders what was considered to be left of the substance of the Resolution once these practices were permitted.

Contracts for repairs and contracts for new buildings were also treated on different systems. As described to the 1897 Committee by the Receiver for the Metropolitan Police District, the latter contained some very advanced provisions. The Department itself prescribed for the successful contractor the minimum rate of wages which he was obliged to pay his men. In practice that minimum rate was based upon the trade union rate. Another clause reserved to the Department the power to raise the wages due to that minimum should the contractor fail to pay it, and this out of monies due to the contractor under the contract. Again, if there should occur an unexpected increase in wages, the contractor was bound to pay that increase to his workers, even though he was not entitled to claim compensation from the Department:

> Should the rate of wages mentioned be increased by any subsequent arrangement which may be made between the contractor and his workmen, then the contractor shall not consider that the provisions of this clause exempt him from paying the workmen engaged on his contract the increased rates which are being paid to other workmen in the contractor's employ. (Qs. 1697–8; 1723–8)

This clause thus ensured that the contractor paid the current rate, and was not able to pay less relying on the minimum specified in the contract.

On reading this evidence, the impression is gained that these clauses are largely an expression of paternalism. While the Receiver stated, to the Department's credit, that they had 'in every case inspected more than once the factory where the work is done, and we have always entered into friendly conversation with those who were employed', still he concluded: 'I am glad to say that in every case the officer who has been down has reported that the labourers have been quite satisfied, and appeared very happy and contented' (Qs. 1756–9). This rather sanguine view was immediately challenged as follows:

But is there not a conceivable case in which both the contractor and the workmen may be satisfied, but which yet from the general point of view of the trade itself and trade unionists is not satisfactory; the representative of the trades unions may make a complaint that the recognized rate is not paid? (Q. 1814)

In his answer to this and following questions, the Receiver revealed on the one hand an unbecoming reluctance to deal with trade unionists, and on the other, a rather authoritarian attitude towards the question of what were current rates. He tried to avoid answering the question by claiming that it involved larger issues which were for the Government and not himself to determine. When asked what he himself would do were he in the Government's position, he replied: 'That case is a very good illustration of the danger there is in the Government trying to interfere between the master and his servants' (Q. 1818). By this he meant, as he later explained, that 'there is a danger in these matters, because the men feel in a Government contract that they have got their Member (of Parliament) on their side, and they can bring pressure to bear upon the Government of the day by their vote, and in other ways' (Q. 1833). And finally, 'I do not recognize that, in every instance, the trade union has got the right to interfere in the case of our Government contracts' (Q. 1886).

With regard to the Resolution's reference to current rates, he stated categorically that he constituted himself as the authority as to what were minimum rates to be paid in a contract, and by minimum rates he clearly intended those rates which were to be paid under the contract. He was incredulous at the idea that trades unions might have some role to play in the determination of current rates (Qs. 1928–33). In light of these attitudes, it is not surprising that since the Resolution of 1891 was passed there had been no complaints by individual workmen of violations. The Receiver, in character, expressed astonishment that the Committee should have expected that workers would even know of the Fair Wages Resolution, let alone have complained of its violation (Q. 1700). Even complaints from trade unionists had been very few, estimated at perhaps half a dozen in the first five years, 1891–6 (Q. 1701).

In sum, there is here a type of enforcement policy which would not have been welcomed, and was probably not foreseen, by either conservative or liberal commentators on the Fair Wages Resolution. On the one hand, there appears to be a tough, thorough and effective policy which, however, is unacceptable to conservatives inasmuch as it derives these qualities necessarily from the dictation of standards in the contract itself in the form of wage schedules. On the other, there is a paternalistic and authoritarian attitude towards enforcement which refuses to recognize the functions of trade unions in either representing their members or in determining current rates, a position unacceptable to those liberals who saw the Fair Wages policy as encouraging those trends. It typified a new enterprising bureaucracy, increasingly free of the restraints of *laissez-faire* dogma, and anxious to exploit its powers of governmental intervention to the full. It was an anomaly in its period.

General Post Office

When apprised of the Order of the House of Commons concerning a Return of Forms indicating compliance with its Resolution of 1891, the General Post Office replied on 15 March 1892 that, 'No forms have been issued by the Post Office, but it is proposed to insert in future contracts the following clause' (1892 Return, p. 10). This clause forbade sub-letting 'other than such sub-letting as may be customary in the trades concerned', and provided for all work to be remunerated in accordance with rates of wages 'generally accepted as current in each trade for competent workmen in the district where the work is carried out'. It appeared from the evidence of the Secretary to the Post Office to the 1897 Committee that the clause was not inserted in contracts for the conveyance of mails by steam packet and by railway companies, though no reason for this was given (Q. 1974). Another exception to the general practice illustrates the problems posed by the development of district bargaining during this period, and the difficulties of defining the word 'district' when it appeared in the Fair Wages clauses of some government departments. It was decided by the Post Office that, in the mail-cart contracts let by it, the words 'in the district' normally included in the clause would be omitted. The reason given for this was 'that the mail-cart runs very often through a very large district, and the wages at one part of the district might be different from the wages in another part of the district' (Qs. 1981–3). In other words, a single rate had not been established covering this large district, and it was felt not to be possible to divide it into smaller 'districts' each with its local rate. Wages were not stable enough for it to be said that a 'current' rate existed, and so the Resolution was not normally applied.

The sort of enforcement policy adopted was the normal one of enforcement by complaint. It appears to have been thought perfectly successful by virtue of the fact that since 1891 no complaints had been made up to 1896 (Q. 1998). As one exchange had it:

Q. 5052 – May I take it that the result of putting in the Fair
Wages Clause has been to avoid those complaints,
because the contractors practically carried out the
Resolution?————I think that is the fair inference.

This seems surprising in light of the admitted fact that immediately
prior to 1891 there had been 'a considerable number' of complaints
concerning contracts currently running relating mainly to excessive
hours of labour and underpayment of wages (Qs. 2045–9). It may be
supposed therefore that either the workers were now all entirely
content as regards their wages and hours, or that other reasons existed
for their failure to complain. The latter possibility is investigated in
the next chapter.

In addition to the normal Fair Wages Clause, between 1896 and
1908 the Post Office adopted as part of its Fair Wages policy a clause
to be included in its contracts which stipulated minimum rates of
wages to be paid, with special provision for certain cases. Thus, the
clause read by 1908:

> The Postmaster-General will not consider that Clause 14 is being
> properly complied with unless: (a) Piecework rates are so paid
> that the wages which an average female worker can earn shall be
> not less than 13s. 6d. per week of 54 hours, free of all deductions.
> (b) The average wage actually earned in any few consecutive
> weeks, by any person working on the contract, are at a rate not
> less than 3d. per hour. (Appendix I to the Report of the 1908
> Committee)

It should be pointed out that in 1908 Sydney Buxton, M.P., was
Postmaster-General.

Board of Trade

By June 1891, the Board of Trade had issued General Conditions of
Contract prohibiting sub-letting, but these made no mention of conditions as to rates of wages payable. It appears that the Board refused to
apply the full terms of the Resolution to any but clothing contracts.
As stated to the 1897 Committee by the Assistant Secretary of the
Financial Department of the Board, it was their view that their building
and repairing contracts were too insignificant to render such application necessary (Qs. 2187–93). It may be replied that however insignificant the contract's provisions may have been to the Board of Trade,
they were of critical importance to the workers on these small contracts,
and it was for their benefit that the Resolution was passed. In addition,

the General Conditions provided for a fine of up to £100 for an offence, a rare provision in those days (1892 Return, pp. 3–4). Unfortunately, it was probably never used as no complaints appear to have been made during the most important first five years of the Resolution (Q. 2182).

Board of Customs

The Board of Customs issued a General Order to their officers on 24 April 1891, notifying them of the Fair Wages Resolution and requiring that the tenders invited contain 'a clause providing that the contractor shall pay for whatever labour is employed in the fulfilment of his engagement to the Crown at the rate of wages current in the district in which his business is carried on'. This was not apparently regarded as absolutely binding, at least in its strict terminology, for an example was given of a clothing contract let which contained a clause requiring payment of wages current 'where the work is carried out'. It was precisely these slight deviations in terminology and meaning which caused much of the confusion surrounding the Fair Wages Resolution. Finally, the Board also provided for a fine of £100 for infringement, but, as in the case of the Board of Trade, never suffered the bother of any complaint (Qs. 2245ff.; 1892 Return, pp. 4–5).

Scottish Office

In the reply of the Scottish Office to the 1892 Order of the House of Commons, most of the Public Authorities concerned stated that they had not entered into any contracts and so measures to comply had not been taken. Only the Prison Commission for Scotland submitted a clause which is interesting in that they stated that it, 'in their opinion, meets the requirements of the Resolution of the House of Commons of 13th February, 1891'. The clause read:

> The Surveyor may at any time forbid or cancel any arrangements for sub-letting any portion of the work under this contract, and the contractor shall not be entitled to receive any payment under this contract for work done by the sub-contractor after such order. (1892 Return, pp. 10–12)

A clause which neglects even to mention wages cannot be said to adequately comply with the Resolution. It reflects adversely on the 'strict control' which it was hoped the House of Commons would exercise in itself enforcing the Resolution.

This inadequacy was soon remedied: on 13 August 1893 the Secretary for Scotland asserted that 'in issuing contracts the Scottish Office has taken full precautions for acting in accordance with the Resolution'.[19] In evidence to the 1897 Committee, the Permanent Secretary at the Scotch Office testified that the contractor was required to specify in the contract the wages he meant to give to each class of his men (Qs. 2303ff.). In smaller contracts there was no such schedule of wages, but it was stated that the officials did not invariably take the lowest tender, but had regard to other matters as well, including presumably matters relative to the Resolution (Qs. 2306–7). Other small contracts contained a very interesting innovation, namely, a clause which provided for some sort of arbitration proceeding in the event of disputes: 'The main contractor shall be bound to see that fair wages are paid to his workmen; and in the event of any question or dispute arising under this head it shall be referred to——or such other person'. This was to take the place of the schedule of wages in other contracts (Qs. 2317–19). Whether it was used or not is questionable, as here again there were no complaints made as to violation (Q. 2316).

Irish Government

The reply of the Irish Government to the Order of the House of Commons of 1892 stated: 'no forms of the nature indicated have been issued by any of the Departments of the Irish Government' (1892 Return, p. 10). There was neither explanation nor remorse; only a flat refusal to comply. The reply of the Irish Board of Works, given separately, was: 'Nil, so far as rate of wages is concerned, but the Board's contracts contain clauses against sub-letting'. There was a futile debate in Parliament over this departmental insubordination.[20] By 1896, there was a return to normal means of enforcement. However, after five years, it was stated to the 1897 Committee by the Commissioner of Public Works (Ireland) that no or few complaints had been made, and that the Board had never had to withdraw any contract on account of non-compliance with the Resolution (Qs. 2372ff.; 2495; 2546).

Weaknesses in Departmental Administration of the Resolution

From the above survey, several weaknesses in departmental administration of the Fair Wages policy became obvious, and were duly noted by various concerned parties. There was the very clear lack of uniformity in both the wording and the implementation of Fair Wages clauses. It was pointed out by representatives of metalworkers to the 1908 Committee that: 'Each department has to interpret that Resolution and to make certain clauses to put into its own contracts, and it does not necessarily follow that they all observe the same wording' (Q. 492). The 1897 Committee observed that there was an absence of uniformity 'both as regards the terms of tender and the clause in the contract, and in other ways' (p. iii). The 1908 Committee thought 'some saving to the State and diminution of trouble to contractors might ensue from greater co-operation among the Departments', in order to evolve one uniform list of eligible contractors 'in place of the present Departmental lists' (para. 120). It is a sad comment on the administration that this minimal requirement for efficient enforcement should still be lacking eighteen years after the policy was introduced.

The problem of sanctions for violation of a Fair Wages clause was analysed by the 1897 Committee:

> A word must be said in reference to the penalty which at present prevails for breach of the conditions of the Resolution clauses. It appears, generally speaking, that no specific penalty is attached for breach; and that the only penalties that can be enforced are to put an end to the contract, or to strike the offender off the list of contractors. Such a punishment is far too severe, except under aggravated circumstances; and, indeed, in the case of some of the more important contractors, it could only be enforced with damage to the public service. Some lesser penalty, by way of fine, should be provided. This is especially important in those cases where, by the time that the examination into an alleged grievance has led to its substantiation, the contract in question has almost, or altogether, terminated. In such cases, though the contractor is proved to have been violating the Resolution, and in his labour bill, has been benefiting from his laches, he escapes scotfree; the contract is over before the increased scale of wages can be enforced. (p. vi)

The Committee went on to recommend a moderate penalty be imposed in proven cases, and that the workers be reimbursed wherever possible. Despite this analysis, warning and recommendation, specific complaints were still being made to the 1908 Committee by, for example, the Amalgamated Society of Carpenters and Joiners, that Departments would only warn contractors who had been proved to have violated the Resolution. No penalty was exacted, let alone reimbursement of the workers involved (Qs. 2304–6; 2370–6). The bitterness of workers at this lack of teeth in the Fair Wages policy is understandable. In 1908 the Fair Wages Committee could still say that provision in the contract for a pecuniary penalty was exceptional and 'the usual penalty is temporary suspension from the list of contractors invited to tender, or, in more serious cases, permanent removal from the list' (para. 10).

The 1908 Committee made mention in passing of departmental inspection of the premises of new contractors, and even of surprise visits to old contractors, to ensure that sweating conditions did not exist (para. 10). Despite the fact that departments did maintain lists of eligible contractors, mention was hardly ever made of such inspections of premises, and certainly nothing of surprise visits, for the purposes mentioned by the Committee. Indeed, the General Secretary of the Scientific Instrument Makers' Trade Society complained to the 1908 Committee precisely about the lack of inspection over government work (Q. 718). In the words of the woodworkers' representative, inspection was carried out 'only when a complaint has been made and it is never done otherwise. I want that done automatically, not that you should only go and inspect when you receive a complaint and make your investigation then' (Q. 2364).

A number of examples will illustrate the extreme unevenness and unpredictability in the administration of the Resolution. For instance, several public authorities, including the War Office, refused to act on complaints on the grounds that the contracts concerned were only for the purchase of goods. The General Secretary of the United French Polishers' London Society complained to the 1908 Committee that certain purchasing contracts were apparently regarded as inappropriate for enforcement of the Fair Wages policy (Q. 583).

A clear illustration of the licence taken by the departments in applying the Resolution is to be found in the debate over the shipbuilding industry on the Thames (Report and Proceedings of the 1897 Committee, pp. v; xvii). The problem concerned the application of the Resolution as interpreted by government departments, in this case the Admiralty, to certain shipbuilding contracts given to the Thames shipyards. According to this interpretation the rates of wages payable under this contract would be the rates current in London. It was discovered, however, that if London rates were enforced, the Thames shipyards would be unable to compete with Northern shipyards in tendering for these contracts. As a result the Admiralty argued that, in this case, the omission of the word 'district' from their ordinary Fair Wages clause was justifiable.

The Report of the 1897 Committee supported this view. They thought it would be undesirable to insist on an interpretation which might injure or destroy a great local industry. Sydney Buxton, in his Draft Report to the Committee, pointed out that by allowing the owners of the Thames shipyards to pay wages below the rates otherwise required, the object of getting them the Admiralty contracts would still not be achieved. Rather their competitors would also be forced to reduce wages in order to maintain their competitive position of superiority. The sole result of the Admiralty's policy would be to 'get back to the position that prevailed before 1891, and the Government would again become instrumental in forcing down the rate of wages'.

As an alternative course to the Admiralty's action, Buxton suggested that they modify their absolute rule regarding acceptance of the lowest tender. In order to enable the Thames yards to obtain contracts, consideration should be given to the relative labour costs of different tenderers. In the Committee's view, this was simply to allow for artificially higher wages in Admiralty contracts, and as such was rejected out of hand. In brief, the Committee accepted the Admiralty's unilateral decision not to comply with the direction of the House of Commons in the Resolution with regard to a particular contract—a decision based on political reasoning. In an earlier debate over this decision, Buxton had commented: 'if all Government Departments put upon the Resolution the interpretation put on it by the Admiralty, the Resolution would practically be a dead letter altogether'.[21]

Another case concerned a complaint by representatives of the Anvil and Vice Trades Association to the 1908 Committee that a government contractor was not paying the rate of wages required by the contract, which included a Fair Wages clause. The department concerned, the India Office, appears to have refused to do anything at all. They stated flatly that they ought to be allowed to buy in the cheapest market, and they did not see the Fair Wages Resolution as calling on them to interfere in the case (Qs. 1459–69). In a similar outburst, the Financial Secretary to the War Office replied to a complaint of low wages some eleven years after the Resolution had been passed as follows:

> as a Government, we have to look at these matters rather as if we were managers of a business on behalf of the country, and to see that we do not set up a standard which will end, although there is a pecuniary advantage to the labourers, in a loss to the State. In all these matters our object must be to get the cheapest material and the cheapest form of labour combined, as it must be, in both cases, with the best class of material and the best form of labour.[22]

This after he had been pressed with details of the malnutrition suffered by the families of the workers concerned, of women workers resorting to prostitution to feed themselves and their families, and other consequences of the low wage policy.

A general outburst was delivered by representatives of the London Clothiers' Cutters' Trade Union to the 1908 Committee against the implementation by the General Post Office of the Fair Wages Resolution:

> The Post Office contracts as a whole have a most deplorable name, and they are absolutely paid at the worst rate of any, and have been for years. There is no party question about it, if I may use the term. It was done through a simple free competition, and the lowest prices, of course, got the tender, and the rest, as it were, was left to chance, the Fair Wages Clause being in no ways adhered to. (Q. 939)

A remark by Sydney Buxton in the Proceedings of the 1897 Committee on the impact of the Resolution on government departments reveals much about the class character of the Civil Service and how this influenced its attitudes towards implementation:

> The novel duties cast upon the Departments . . . have been considerably more arduous, *and probably more distasteful*, than the old simpler process of acceptance of the lowest tender with no responsibility for the conditions of employment that might subsequently prevail under the contract. (p. xvi) (My italics.)

Five years later he commented: 'He knew from personal experience in office in many Departments what an extraordinary amount of deadweight there was in regard to this question; there was a tendency to take the lowest contract, and not to inquire too closely into the wages paid'.[23] It is not surprising that trade unionists often preferred to turn for aid and advice to sympathetic M.P.s when faced with a blatant violation of the Resolution. The evidence of the 1908 Committee contained numerous references to enquiries by Sydney Buxton alone into problems concerning the policy (e.g. Qs. 1977; 2046; 2065; 2074). The alternative was to face an indifferent, if not positively hostile, government department.

The Enforcement Mechanism: Complaint and Investigation

Most government departments considered they had complied with the instructions of the House of Commons in the Fair Wages Resolution by inserting, to a greater or less extent and with more or less precision, the words of the Resolution into their contracts. With this, the great majority of the departments exhausted their initiative in this area— and enforcement of the policy was given over into the hands of interested parties, in particular, to the workers supposedly aided by it. The machinery of enforcement was to be one of complaint by workers or their representatives to the department concerned, which would then undertake, in the ordinary case, to investigate the accuracy of the allegation. The 1908 Committee described the procedure as follows:

> In the investigation of complaints the Departments necessarily require some reasonably definite statements to enable them to determine whether the Fair Wages and Sub-letting clauses of some specific Government contract may have been infringed. On receipt of specific information, the complaint is brought to the notice of the firm and their observations obtained, the name of the informant not being disclosed where such a course would be undesirable. When further inquiry is necessary, it is a very usual practice to send an Inspector to investigate matters on the spot, to see the parties to the dispute, and examine books and other evidence. (para. 10)

In that enforcement was to be entirely by means of complaint, the first requirement is to discover to what extent it was utilized. On this there is some information to be garnered from the above review of departmental administration. Up to the year 1897, the War Office led the field with ninety complaints (seventy of which were stated to be unfounded), together with the Stationery Office which claimed complaints in 'many instances' of violations by contractors. This is understandable as these are both large contracting departments, though even so in the case of the War Office this averaged out at only about eighteen per year (only four of which were justifiable). What is less comprehensible is that the Office of Works should have had only 'very few' complaints during these years. The Dockyards too had 'singularly few' complaints (eighteen in all); the Police had a few from trades unionists (half a dozen in five years), and the Irish Board of Works had none or few complaints. As to the General Post Office, the Department of Prisons, the Board of Trade, the Board of Customs and the Scottish Office—none of these ever received a complaint that the Fair Wages Resolution was being violated during the whole of this period.

The only other statistical information available covers the period 1903 to 1907 inclusive. The Fair Wages Committee of 1908 stated that taking the five major contracting departments in the government—War Office, Admiralty, Office of Works, Post Office and Stationery Office—the number of cases of *alleged* infringement of the Fair Wages Resolution brought to the notice of these departments during the five-year period averaged roughly one per week. The contract expenditure

of these departments at the time was estimated at £25 million (para.
13). If divided up among the departments, this comes to just over
ten allegations of infringement being made to each department each
year. In the case of the War Office this would mean a reduction from
an average of fourteen per year between 1891–6. Taking the War
Office's average rate of complaints proven (twenty out of ninety
alleged violations), it may be concluded that during this period
between two and three infringements of the Resolution were proved
to the satisfaction of each of the major contracting departments each
year. It was only from this point on, of course, that the question of
what sanctions were applicable became relevant.

The trade union view of this policy of enforcement by complaint
was dictated by their intimate knowledge of industrial realities—their
estimate of an individual worker's ability to respond to an abstract
Resolution of the House of Commons in the economic, social and
industrial conditions prevalent among the working class at the turn
of the century. A forceful expression of this view to the 1908 Committee
has already been quoted: 'We would like to place before you the
difficulty of an individual's position in attempting to carry out such
a thing. I do not believe that in the whole history of the Fair Wages
Resolution it has been done' (Q. 1163). By 1897, the Committee on
Government Contracts was prepared to recognize 'that complaints can
hardly be made by individual workmen, but must necessarily come
through their accredited representatives' (p. iii). In the debate which
led to the setting up of the Committee it had been stated: 'At present
everything was left to the vigilance and energy of the trade union
officials'. Yet the First Lord of the Admiralty actually complained
suspiciously about the fact that it was trade unions which usually
presented complaints under the Resolution, whereas he could recall
only one case where an individual worker had complained. To this
a trade union M.P. replied: 'It had always been asserted by the anti-
trade-union section of the community that each person aggrieved
should go direct to the employer; but if those who so argued were
workmen themselves they would tell a very different tale'.[24] The
idealized conception of enforcement by complaint persisted, however,
and it was still possible for the 1908 Committee to ask: 'Do you think
that their own power of seeing to their own interests is not enough?'
The reply to this by the President of the Women's Industrial Council,
London, referred specifically to women workers, but is indicative of
the situation in general:

In the first place, they are not organized, so that they do not
know to whom to complain; in the second place, they are extremely

unaware—partly also because they have no organization to bring
it before them—of the fact that there is any such Clause—most
of them do not know it; and in the third place, women are much
more afraid of losing employment than men, for the very reason
that they are lower paid. The worse you are paid the more afraid
you are of losing half a day. (Qs. 6487–8)

Despite this, the Report of the 1908 Committee appeared to regard it
as adequate: 'if it is left to the workers to see that the employer carries
out his obligations' (para. 93).

The impact of the Fair Wages Resolution can probably best be
appreciated by looking at a specific case of its working in a factory.
The evidence to the 1908 Committee of members of the Staffordshire
Potteries Manufacturers' Association described the situation in the
pottery industry:

Q. 4882 – What is your impression of the effect of the Fair Wages
Clause in your contracts?———We look upon the
present Fair Wages Clause as a matter of form, as it
has never been acted upon or taken any notice of at
all. . . . We have supplied the Government with many
thousands of pounds worth of goods, and we have never
been called upon to show our books or anything of the
kind; so we have looked upon the Clause as a matter
of form.

Q. 4883 – There has been no complaint made by your workmen
as a matter of fact, then?———Not the slightest.

Q. 4884 – And yet there is not anything which could be called a
current rate in your trade?———There are many rates
of wages; indeed, there is an enormous number. I may
say that the conditions vary very much.

Q. 4893 – But practically the Fair Wages Clause is inoperative as
far as your trade is concerned?———That is absolutely
so.

Q. 4894 – It is rather curious there has never been any complaint,
or any question raised in your trade. Are all your people
quite contented; do they never grumble?———I do
not say they are contented. . . . (Qs. 4877ff.)

In contrast, a case of a completely unionized firm was presented by
the employer as follows: 'As far as the present Fair Wages Resolution
is concerned, we find it acts admirably. It is fully comprehensive, and
any objections that the men make at any time have, of course, to be
met, and they are soon arranged' (Q. 4624).

If trade unions were to be relied on to enforce the Resolution, it meant that unorganized workers, who comprised over 80 per cent of all male industrial workers, were left totally unprotected. As far as these were concerned, the effect of the policy on them may be gauged from the response of a Post Office contractor when informed of the Resolution of 1893 concerning discrimination between unionists and non-unionists. He denied first that he interfered with the liberty of his workmen by refusing to employ unionists: 'if the workman wants to join a trades union he can go into somebody else's service, that is all. It is simply a question of terms.' 'I have got a right to arrange with my workmen on what terms they shall be in my service.' He was asked by the 1897 Committee: 'the promise given by the Government to the House of Commons will have to be enforced. Do you not think you had better take the initiative yourself?' To which he replied: 'Why should I? Things work very comfortably as they are now, and any change would be for the worse, and not for the better' (Qs. 2009; 2005; 1997).

The theory of enforcement by complaint among these workers was based on a psychological assumption which appeared to be widely accepted. As formulated by Sheffield employers before the 1908 Committee:

> If they do not know it, that is perfectly plain evidence on the surface that that work is not being worse paid than the average work the men are working on. If it goes through unobserved, it must be paid for at the current rate of wage or it would soon be observed. So the question answers itself from that point of view, that where there is nothing known it must be because there is no grievance, for if there was a grievance, it would soon become known. (Q. 5593)

The validity of this assumption is questionable indeed. The factors enumerated above all went to discourage individual workers from making complaints, and in addition there was the threat of employer vengeance. Cases were reported where employees were discharged for giving information leading to a complaint and no redress could be obtained (e.g. to the 1897 Committee, Qs. 595ff.). In 1902 a complaint was lodged that a painting contractor had discharged men who had complained to the War Office over his failure to pay current rates of wages. To this the Financial Secretary to the War Office would only reply: 'The question of the selection of workmen rests with the discretion of the contractor. So long as he pays the current rate, when warned, he is not held to be disqualified for future tendering. The circumstances are, however, noted against him.'[25] This was small comfort to the now unemployed men under the 'protection' of the Fair Wages Resolution.

Even when a complaint was brought, the same factors went to work so as to make proof of the offence virtually impossible. For example, the Secretary of the Bone Brush Makers' Trade Protection Society spoke to the 1908 Committee of the difficulty of proving complaints. He concluded: 'The people who worked at the place were so frightened to speak that we gave it up, and did not make any further complaint' (Qs. 3781–3). Another trade unionist in the harness-making trade complained that for want of evidence he had been unable to complain since the Sweating Inquiry had finished its work in 1889. Apparently, he had previously been able to obtain the workers' wage books, which showed the weekly amount of work done and the wages received. Since then the companies, having discovered this, had declared the wage books company property, and would not let them be taken off company premises. Consequently, he declared to the 1908 Committee: 'we had such difficulty in getting evidence to establish our case, though we knew it was correct, that we could not push the matter more forward' (Qs. 3877–81).

It was for reasons such as the above that trade unionists could assert to the 1908 Committee that government contractors could evade the Resolution with impunity (United French Polishers' London Society, Q. 609). 'It is a noticeable fact that the worst houses in the trade get hold of Government work. That is our experience, and not only is it our experience, but it is the experience in most trades, not only in London, but in the country' (Vellum (Account Book) Binders' Trade Society, Q. 1122). It reached a point where precisely the aim which was sought was that which was most obviously not being attained: 'What we term the unfair employer of labour was able to tender for Government work, and for public work generally; and it got to such a pitch that ultimately the fair employer, as we call him, would not attempt to tender—he was obviously out of it' (National Amalgamated Furnishing Trades, Q. 1704).

Apart from this general critique of enforcement by complaint, there was much criticism by workers, usually trade union officials, of the departments' treatment of cases which were finally brought before them. The principal criticism was over the delay in investigating and responding to complaints. The 1897 Committee on Government Contracts emphasized this:

> Further, it is alleged that, in every case, there is great delay and much circumlocution in dealing with complaints; that, thus it frequently happens, that in cases in which the Department

concerned ultimately admits the justice of the complaint and instructs the contractor to remedy the grievance, the inquiry has covered such a long period of time that, by then, the contract is almost or altogether completed. The men are not benefited, and the contractor escapes all penalty or charge. (p. iv)

Over a decade later the 1908 Committee was still putting forward delays in dealing with complaints as being one of the workers' chief criticisms (para. 12(g)). In evidence before that Committee the General Secretary of the Scientific Instrument Makers' Trade Society complained as to 'the time that elapses between your making a complaint and hearing anything more about it' (Q. 718). The representative of the Amalgamated Society of Carpenters and Joiners referred to a complaint to the War Office that was only settled after six months' correspondence (Qs. 548–64). He estimated the average time of correspondence over a complaint at five months (Q. 778). Further complaints were referred to by representatives of metalworkers who had encountered substantial delay (Q. 2991).

In addition to complaints about delay, there were numerous criticisms about the action taken by the departments. It was alleged to the 1897 Committee:

> that where inquiry takes place it is often very perfunctorily made: that information is frequently only sought from one side, that of the employer; while the complainants are not consulted or kept informed of what is taking place: that the decision is thus too often not in accordance with the true facts of the case. (p. iv)

In one case of a complaint against a contractor to the Office of Works, the official investigating the dispute had, in the words of Sydney Buxton, 'declined, in the exercise of his discretion, no doubt quite wisely, to meet the representatives of the men to discuss the matter, while he did so meet representatives of the employers interested, Messrs. Holland and Hannen; and it was after an interview with them ... that the rate was fixed'. Buxton requested that 'in the endeavour to arrive at a conclusion, the Department shall not proceed upon information derived from only one side, but should take the representations of parties on both sides'.[26] Trade unionists testifying to the 1908 Committee tended to regard the government inspectors sent out to investigate complaints as being inexperienced, not 'practical men', and thus easily fooled by employers (Qs. 771–2). Few workers felt satisfied with the way the investigation of complaints was conducted. They did not go so far as to challenge the integrity of the inspector; they merely suggested 'that anybody sent from a Department should be accompanied by some practical person who would be able to point out to him the glaring, misleading statements that are given to him. He cannot correct them himself, because he does not know exactly where the sore lies' (Q. 3903).

Problems also arose over the government departments' attitudes towards piece-work remuneration. One trade unionist told the 1908 Committee of a firm which did not pay the recognized minimum rate of the district, but which had introduced piece-work which enabled the men to earn just a trifle more than this minimum rate. On complaining to the War Office, the workers had received in answer that this practice complied with the strict requirements of the Resolution (Q. 718). It seems that the 1908 Committee also accepted the view that as long as piece-work earnings for a given period exceeded the standard time rates for the same period on similar work, the contractors could not be said to be in breach (para. 125(c)). One questions whether this interpretation is in line with the injunction against sweating, but here again such an argument is defeated by the ambiguity and vagueness of the Resolution.

Many examples may be given of disputes between the departments and the unions over the interpretation and application of the Resolution. Thus, a complaint was made to the 1908 Committee that the War Office had recognized a small area of sweat shops within London as a separate district, and so wages paid in it as the current rate of that district were not a breach of the Resolution. This occurred despite the union's claim that there was a clearly laid down rate for London as a whole (Q. 1706). There was also a complaint made to the 1897 Committee by the Vellum Binders' Society against the Stationery Office that a clause had been put into a contract let by them for the printing of Debates which read as follows: 'the contractors might obtain the report of the Debates in the best way they could be got' (Qs. 2350–3). In the eyes of the trade union, this was tantamount to ignoring the injunction concerning the regulation of sub-letting in the Resolution, and the matter was taken as far as a question in the House of Commons.[27]

Then there were the criticisms that many complaints were altogether ignored, and no inquiry made into them; that, on occasion, departmental promises of remedial action were not fulfilled, and the general attack on the lack of effective sanctions. These criticisms were voiced from every quarter in the trade union movement and in the country. Complaints on these and other matters were made in evidence to the 1897 Committee by the London United Society of Drillers: Iron Drillers (Qs. 278ff.), Amalgamated Society of House Painters and Decorators, Plymouth Branch (Qs. 447ff.), Cork Head-dress Trade

Union (Qs. 1568ff.), Belfast Operative House and Ship Painters and Decorators Union (Qs. 2014ff.), Amalgamated Society of Tailors of Dublin (Qs. 2125ff.) and London Building Trades Federation and Amalgamated Society of Carpenters and Joiners (Qs. 3057ff.), among others. An M.P. representing the National Amalgamated Furnishing Trades stated to the 1908 Committee that he felt safe in saying that in 95 per cent of the cases in which he had complained, he had received 'absolutely unsatisfactory replies' (Q. 1818). Another trade unionist testified to the 1897 Committee:

> Our executive council . . . had already made complaints innumerable in reference to other firms in London and other districts, and they either got no reply, in some cases, or where they did get a reply the reply was unsatisfactory, and therefore they thought it was needless to make any further complaints. (Q. 2581)

Similar statements of refusal or failure to register complaints for this reason were forthcoming from representatives of the Amalgamated Society of Engineers (Qs. 2826–7; 2830; 2446ff.). The 1897 Committee itself summed up the feeling:

> Finally, it is stated, that so great is the want of confidence in the ability or desire of the Department to remedy these grievances, that trades unions and other representatives of the men, despairing of obtaining proper consideration and redress, have allowed grievances to continue, being convinced of the futility of taking action in respect to them. (p. iv)

Evidence to the 1908 Committee from the General Secretary of the Labour Protection League, an unskilled labour union, indicated that even complaints to the House of Commons were abandoned for these reasons (Q. 389). This, together with the fact that over 80 per cent of the labour force was unorganized with all that implies as to the ability of the individual worker to react against exploitation, amount to an alternative and very plausible explanation for the very small number of complaints received by departments concerned with enforcement of the Resolution.

A very similar situation obtained concerning enforcement of the Fair Wages policies of various local authorities. An illustration is provided by an early dispute over the award by the London County Council of a printing contract to a non-union firm. Attempts by the London Society of Compositors to get the contractor to accept the London Scale failed, and its complaints culminated in a meeting of the General Purposes Committee of the L.C.C. attended by a deputation from the Society and the contractor himself. Only at that stage did the Society learn that the contractor had signed a declaration in his tender providing that 'the Contractor shall pay such rates of wages and observe such hours of labour as are generally accepted as fair in the respective trades required in this contract'. In explanation of having signed this condition the contractor claimed:

> that it was vague; that while his composing room was unfair, his machine and press rooms were fair, although he couldn't say the same for his warehouse; that taking the printing trade of the country as a whole, the majority of the workers were non-unionists; that there was nothing to show that the declaration applied to the Metropolis only; that the wages of the Firm were recognised as fair by non-union houses, but that some employers and workmen might, and doubtless did, consider his an unfair house.[28]

The General Purposes Committee reported recommending that the contractor be rejected, and after debate, the recommendation was accepted by the L.C.C.

Despite experiences such as these, the Clerk of the L.C.C. could still testify to the 1908 Committee that he made no investigation as to whether contractors were fair employers either before acceptance of tenders, or whether they adhered to the wage schedules included in the contract after it was granted them. In his words, 'we leave it to the Unions and the workpeople to make complaint if the firm is not carrying out its contract' (Q. 6822). He concluded that the system of dealing with complaints was quite satisfactory, and in fact complaints were rarely received. Indeed, a Fabian Tract of 1895 compared the L.C.C. favourably with the government: 'Nor is the Government yet as strict as it should be about payment of Trade Union wages by contractors. The London County Council enforces in all its contracts a rigid adherence to Trade Union wages and conditions, but the Government asks only for "fair wages", and scarcely insists on them'.[29] The 1908 Committee itself noted, however, how contractors tied to schedules requiring high rates of wages managed to evade the Council's policy. Apparently, by employing their workers for part of their time on Council work and part on other work, the contractors had been able to get the latter done at a very low rate of wages with the result that the total earnings were up to the 'normal' (below scheduled rates) level for weekly wages. The low rates on the private work made up for the higher wages demanded for Council work. It was stated that, 'The Clerk to the Council, however, had no information that this was the case' (para. 34).

In other local authorities, the position as reported to the 1908 Committee was much the same. In the Corporation of Bradford, out of some hundreds of contracts, only two complaints were made from the adoption of a Fair Wages Clause in July 1903, and in neither case were the allegations proven (Appendix VI). In Glasgow, enforcement was also by complaint, but these were declared not to have been numerous. If a violation was discovered, the Corporation could repudiate the contract, but as was stated: 'I do not think, however, that any case has actually occurred where such a course has been followed'. In Leicester, complaints had arisen in only nine cases since the introduction of the Clause into contracts in July 1891, while in Sheffield only one or two cases had arisen. In Liverpool, only one case was said to have been complained of in recent years. The following exchange between the 1908 Committee and a representative of the National Federation of Merchant Tailors concerning the Liverpool clause is indicative of the general situation:

> Q. 4955 – What is your clause in Liverpool; is it like the Government Clause?————It is very much the same, but I think I am right in saying that we do little to see that it is enforced. I think it is always a pity to put clauses in a contract where there is not what I call a reasonable attempt to follow it up and see that there is something done.

> Q. 4956 – I suppose you would get a complaint if it was not being carried out?————We do get complaints, and there are many questions in the Council Chamber and a certain amount of answering and all that sort of thing. I will tell you the way it operates—it operates against the fair employer, the man who would be a contractor and who really would be anxious to keep to fair conditions. I do not think he is getting a fair chance unless the authorities do something to try and see that the thing is carried out in practice. That is my view of it.

Proposals for Improvement of the Fair Wages Policy

Consequent on the dissatisfaction of many workers, trade unionists and sympathizers with the Fair Wages policy, proposals were frequently advanced with a view to its amelioration. Most of these were practical and well thought out ideas as to how the policy could be more efficiently applied. Occasionally, indeed, more fundamental challenges to the current practice were voiced, as in one exchange between printing trade unionists and the 1908 Committee over the definition of 'current rate':

> Q. 1196 – The accepted rate between the masters and the men is the trade union rate, is it not?————That may be your interpretation; I have my own opinion, of course.
>
> Q. 1197 – Is that not the rule?————I would not like to say.
>
> Q. 1198 – If the employers and the employed agree, what more do you want?————I should go a great deal further than any employer would. I should claim that labour has a right to all it produces.
>
> Q. 1199 – If labour agrees with capital there is an end of it? ————The labourer does agree with capital because he has got no alternative. If I have to work on a job, whoever likes to employ me, I have got no alternative. But I would go much further than 'the trade union rate'.
>
> Q. 1200 – Have you not got the market value?————Wages are not paid for value.

As to the proposed changes in enforcement procedure, however, it is interesting that most of them could easily have been accommodated within the broad phrasing of the 1891 Resolution. Indeed, in some cases it is difficult to understand not only why they were not conceded immediately by government departments as being necessary for effective implementation of the policy, but why they were not utilized from the very beginning. A number of the more important of these proposals will be examined.

Given that the machinery of enforcement of the Resolution was to be by complaint, it would seem the most elementary step that the names of contractors obtaining government contracts be made available to parties concerned, if not to the public generally. Otherwise, the opportunities for subterfuge and deceit by sweating employers would be greatly increased. This, however, does not appear to have been the view of the authorities. Already in 1896, the first inquiry into the Resolution, limited to the Stationery Office, had to make the specific recommendation that, 'the names of contractors and subjects of contract be made quickly and generally accessible to inquiry' (p. ix). In the following year, the Committee on Government Contracts also felt obligated to propose the self-evident, in view of the failure of the departments to do so. This Committee proposed that a list of government contractors *and their contracts* should be published from time to time (p. vi). Inexplicably, however, it appears that even in the face of such an authoritative proposal, the departments were still not prepared to accede. Thus, in 1908, the Fair Wages Committee was obliged to point out that it was still not the practice of the departments to disclose the names of the successful tenderers. Instead, facilities were given to authorised trade union officials to inspect the list of contractors from time to time (para. 11). It is not clear and even doubtful whether the officials were given a list of contracts actually let; rather they may only have been allowed to see the lengthy list of contractors eligible to tender. The Committee pointed out that 'many local authorities publish the names of contractors, and in Canada the names of Government contractors, brief particulars of the nature of the work and amount of the tender, and schedules of the wages to be paid to the workpeople engaged are published in the Canadian Labour Gazette' (para. 96). They were therefore prepared to make the very cautious recommendation that 'so far as practicable and at the discretion of the Departments concerned, the names and addresses of all firms obtaining Government contracts should be published in the "Board of Trade Journal" or "Board of Trade Labour Gazette" ' (para. 125(g)). The reaction of some employers even to this recommendation was outrage: 'Then the object is to let them know when they are on Government work instead of commercial work, in order that they may put the screw on us, and get something that they could not get on commercial work, in consequence of this agreement with you' (Q. 5583).

Another proposal was also aimed at ensuring that wherever possible workers would be able to inform themselves as to their rights under the Resolution. It need hardly be emphasized how important this was, since they were themselves to be the chief guardians of these rights through their own initiative in complaining of violations. It was proposed to create a schedule setting out those conditions of labour— especially rates of wages—required to be observed by an employer complying with the Resolution and, in addition, to have it publicly exhibited at the place of work. There were precedents for such actions. Prior to 1891, the Office of Works required tenders to include two schedules specifying rates of wages for various categories of labour and remuneration for overtime. Again, in the Police Department of the Home Office, contracts for new buildings contained minimum rates of wages prescribed by the department which the contractor was obliged to pay. As a result of a Committee Report to the London County Council in 1890, a 'log' or scale of prices to be paid on Council work was adopted in their contracts for clothing (1908 Committee Report, para. 34). Generally, the Council fixed its own rates for contracts—a fixed schedule of wages applied to places wholly or partly within a 20-mile radius. Beyond this, contractors would submit schedules with their own rates, usually drawn up on the same basis. Complaints of incorrect statement of wages would be investigated. If proven, after acceptance of the tender, payment would be enforced throughout the contract period, from its beginning. (1908 Committee, Qs. 6674ff.). Both Sheffield and West Ham had schedules of rates of wages. In the case of Sheffield the list was drawn up and published by a committee of the Council (1908 Committee, Appendix VI). Even the system in Canada was referred to the 1908 Committee, where a special official of the Labour Department fixed wage rates, not only for government contracts, but for all work paid from public funds (Qs. 6216–17).

It was, therefore, proposed to the 1908 Committee by the representative of the T.U.C. that a schedule of rates of wages, both time and piece rates, be posted publicly at the place of work where the government contracts was being carried out. Also, that this schedule be amended when and if changes in the current rate took place, as they were bound to do in a contract continuing over a number of years (para. 90; Qs. 172–4). The Committee recognized that such a schedule would probably help prevent evasion of the Resolution by informing the workers that contract work was being done and what rates of pay they were entitled to. The only objection the Committee posed was that 'a schedule of the rate of wages actually being paid would be of no use in preventing evasion of the Fair Wages Clause, as it would set up no independent standard' (para. 92). It is not clear what the Committee meant by this. But whatever its intention, it could not detract from the most important contribution—informing workers of their rights and so preventing evasion. Nonetheless, the Committee concluded that: 'On the whole we are of the opinion that it will be sufficient if the "Fair Wages Clauses" of the contract are posted' (para. 93). This was translated somewhat misleadingly into the list of recommendations at the end of the Report: 'We recommend that in all works where Government contracts are being executed, a copy of all the labour conditions of the contract should be prominently exhibited for the information of the workpeople' (para. 125(f)). One is left at a loss to understand the Committee's rejection.

Fundamentally, a system of enforcement by complaint was obviously all too weak and ineffective even among organized workers, let alone among the unorganized. Consequently, trade unionists realized that alternative methods of enforcement would be necessary. The one most often proposed was inspection by government officials of the compliance of government contractors with the Fair Wages policy. Such proposals fell into two groups: first there were those who advocated what came to be called a 'Fair Houses' policy. So, for example, the National Federation of Merchant Tailors and the Electrical Trades Union called before the 1908 Committee for the inspection of contractors' premises and terms of employment prior to the granting of a contract or even of his being placed on a list of eligible contractors (Qs. 4957; 1912–26). Such select lists of contractors eligible to tender did exist in various departments—the 1908 Committee even recommended one uniform list instead of departmental ones (para. 120). Compliance with the Resolution was often made a criterion for eligibility—the War Office required a signed pledge from every person applying to be listed. Most departments were satisfied to circularize the contractors on the list as to the Resolution's existence without any effort to ascertain whether there was actual compliance. Only the Police Department of the Home Office made mention of inspections not specifically tied to complaints; but this was an exceptional case. In any event, the 1908 Committee felt unable to recommend the adoption of a 'Fair Houses' policy. To adopt such a policy would, it considered, put the government:

> under the obligation of seeing that fair wages were paid and proper conditions observed not only on the Government work, but on all other work carried out by the firm, an obligation which might necessitate an enormous amount of inquiry to which employers would decline to submit. (para. 86)

Whatever obligation the government may have had to ensure that fair wages and conditions existed for workers on its projects did not extend to the benefit of other workers, sweated though they may have been. It was regrettable that these others prevented their more fortunate brethren from enjoying the benefits of government inspection.

The second proposal concerning inspection was much more radical. It regarded as perfectly feasible the possibility of government inspection of compliance with the Resolution during the course of the contract's running. As was stated by the General Secretary of the Scientific Instrument Makers' Trade Society to the 1908 Committee, just as machinery of inspection existed to ensure the quality of the goods produced for the government under contract was adequate, so such machinery should be applied to the problems of labour standards (Qs. 916–18). Such machinery was by no means unknown at the time. There were very thorough methods of checking the wage rates of men employed on shipbuilding in government dockyards, so as to ensure that overpayment did not result in exceeding previously budgeted estimates—this dated from 1889.[30] The proposal relating to the Resolution was spelt out to the 1908 Committee by the representative of the Amalgamated Society of Carpenters and Joiners:

> Wherever you have got work going on under the Office of Works, you have always got a clerk of works on the spot—that is, you have got a man looking after matters for the Government. While that man is looking after work on behalf of the Government, there would be no difficulty at all in his saying to the contractor now and again, 'Just let me have a look at your wages sheets and see what you are paying'. He can always see them, and the contractor could show them to him when he was going about there getting information if he liked. For instance, every Saturday when they are paying the men he could say, 'What rates do you pay? Just let me have a look at your sheet'. If it was in the contract that the clerk of works should have a right to look at the pay-sheet, he would have it shown to him, and you would not have to call in the officialism of headquarters over these matters. You could simply say to this man, 'You must see what wages are being paid; they are part of the conditions of the contract, just as much as to see that the contractors give good timber, good stone, good brickwork, and generally carry out a good sound job'. You simply hand the duty over to him, and ask him to look at it. I can assure you that unless you do something like that, you will never get the Resolution carried out. (Qs. 2362–6)

The Committee was not receptive to this idea. The process was thought to consume too much time and effort of the departments, despite the witness's insistence that if the Committee would talk to the clerks of works and inspectors in charge they would find that there was no difficulty involved in taking these minor steps. He was not insistent that an official be appointed for every little contract, 'but I think the very knowledge that it might be done would have a very good effect upon the contractors'. The suggestion was not taken up.

Another expression of this desire to bolster the effectiveness of the complaint machinery, without going as far as to demand an inspectorate, is to be seen in the proposal to set up some co-ordinating body which would specialize in the administration and settlement of disputes concerning the Resolution. The most notable contribution was that made by Sydney Buxton in his Draft Report to the 1897 Committee on Government Contracts (p. xix). He proposed that the services and knowledge of the Labour Department of the Board of Trade (the predecessor of the Ministry of Labour, set up in 1916) be utilized in cases of dispute under the Resolution. He pointed out that the Labour Department was already being consulted on this matter in some cases, and that he thought both the departments and representatives of workers were prepared to see this consultation placed on a more formal level. Accordingly, he proposed that the Labour Department be given the task of deciding two crucial questions: first, what was in practice the current rate of wages in the district; and secondly, whether a particular contractor was or was not paying this rate. He did not specify whether the character of the decision was to be purely administrative or with some judicial tinge, but his emphasis appears to have been on the former type. He claimed that the Department's duties, to acquire adequate knowledge in respect to the rate of wages prevailing in different parts of the country, to keep itself informed of any variations that might take place, and to obtain general information concerning all labour questions, put it in a much better position than any other department to deal 'expeditiously, impartially, justly and adequately' with these questions. Such a change would relieve the departments of their 'thankless and distasteful task', one which they were not especially fitted to perform. On the other hand, more efficient dealing with workers' complaints would inspire their confidence, and generally give greater uniformity to the administration of the policy. Buxton's proposal was very far-reaching: not only to determine whether a breach of the Resolution had occurred, but also to fix district rates where these were disputed. Even the future Industrial Court did not undertake that task in its dealings with the Resolution.

Buxton's idea of centralizing the administration and enforcement of the Fair Wages policy in the Labour Department of the Board of Trade was decisively rejected in the Final Report of the 1897 Committee (p. vi). The Committee considered his argument that to have complaints investigated by a central authority would lessen delays—one of the worst aspects of the present administration. It felt, however, that these delays were mostly the result of the newness of the measures, and as proof of this they emphasized that the complaints considered were mainly from the early days of the Resolution. Alternative explanations, relating to workers' disillusionment with the policy, have been described above for this falling off of complaints. By far the most important reason for the Committee's rejection was, however, that the making of the Board of Trade a central authority would derogate from the authority and responsibility of the individual contracting departments. Buxton had insisted that the nature of the Labour Department's intervention would be strictly limited to questions on the Resolution and it would not interfere in any way between the department and its contractor nor weaken the direct relations between the two. Nevertheless, the Committee felt that the interdepartmental conflict which would inevitably be engendered between the two would merely create even greater delays in enforcement. Thus, the jealously guarded prerogatives of individual bureaucracies were permitted to triumph.

The Fair Wages Committee of 1908 also considered the question of centralization and made proposals about this, although their proposals were much less ambitious than those just discussed (paras. 123–4). Thus, it did not even contemplate the establishment of an arbitration body, but merely suggested the setting up of an advisory committee, formed of representatives of the contracting departments. It was emphasized that the settlement of disputes or questions involving the Resolution was the task first and foremost of the individual contracting departments. If the contracting department met with difficulty, it was entirely at the department's discretion whether to call in the aid of the advisory committee. It would be expected to do so only in questions 'involving wider issues and affecting other Departments as well'. Whatever the advice of this advisory committee, however, it was clear that the final responsibility lay with the individual department concerned as to what action or decision was to be taken. Any trend towards centralization was strictly limited.

Finally, there were calls to widen the substantive content of the Resolution. The most frequent of these, as for example was advocated to the 1908 Committee by the Union of Weavers and Textile Workers, demanded the extension of the Resolution to cover conditions of labour as well as wages and, in particular, trade union conditions (Qs. 1407–8). Examples were given by the Amalgamated Society of Carpenters and Joiners, such as 'walking time and extra for overtime and a certain amount of payment given on discharge. Two hours, as a rule, is given on discharge' (Q. 2268). The reaction to such proposals was often hostile, with the 1908 Committee accusing the proposers of 'using the Fair Wages Clause for something beyond that which the Fair Wages Clause has been intended to secure. ... I want to ask you whether you are not trying to secure certain conditions which may embody excellent trade union principles, but which may be going a good deal beyond what has hitherto been the object and purpose of the Fair Wages Clause' (Q. 1787).

Yet it was not unknown for trade union conditions to be officially included in Fair Wages policies—thus the city of Glasgow had a clause as amended by 1908, which provided that only firms recognizing, *inter alia*, Trades Union conditions would be eligible to tender and receive contracts (Appendix VI to the 1908 Committee Report). The idea was obviously disliked by the 1908 Committee which saw it as restricting management's freedom of action, and also as indirectly opening the door to a 'Fair Houses' policy, which it had also opposed (para. 25). Consequently, the insertion of trade union conditions into the Resolution was specifically rejected by the Committee. Instead, it conceded a formula similar in its uncertainty to that of the Fair Wages formula: 'we think that such conditions of employment as are generally accepted in the district in the trade concerned must be taken into account when considering the question whether a particular contractor is observing the Fair Wages Clauses' (para. 125(b)). The disadvantages of such a formula have already been spelled out with regard to a relatively determinate factor such as wage rates. With regard to the multiplicity of conditions of labour prevailing among different factories, it was absurd to expect that such a vaguely defined standard could be realistically enforceable.

The perennial problem of the worker's right to belong to a trade union was also raised several times, despite the expectation that it would be resolved by the 1893 addition to the Resolution. In fact, that had been simply ignored in practice. In any event, trade unionists usually took the view that a simple declaration that contractors should give no preference to non-unionists was inadequate and probably impossible to enforce. Employers, said the representative of the Coventry Engineers and Allied Trades Federation, would not refuse to hire trade unionists, but would subsequently be able to find ways of ridding themselves of such workers without much difficulty (1908 Committee, Q. 4221). Some advance on this policy might be observed in a resolution accepted by the Government on 8 March 1906: 'That in the opinion of this House, the conditions of labour in the Arsenal should be, as regards wages and rights of combination, equal to the best Trade Union private firm'. This, it was pointed out, referred to government employees, not those of government contractors (Q. 270). Even that would not have satisfied one Scottish trade unionist, who demanded a contractual clause requiring an employer to recognize a union organized by his employees (Q. 4039).

The effort to implement a 'Fair Houses' policy can be, and was, seen by the 1908 Committee as an attempt to spread the benefits of the Fair Wages policy to all the employees of a government contractor, and not only to limit them to those employed on the actual contract work. It is interesting to compare the policies of various local authorities on this particular matter. As described to the 1908 Committee, some local authority Fair Wages clauses provided that all the employees of the contractor be paid fair wages (Appendix VI). Thus, in Bradford, the contractor was obliged to give an assurance that 'he has paid the whole of his workmen not less . . .'; in Glasgow, 'The contractor shall pay to all competent workmen employed by him not less . . .'; in Sheffield liability is imposed on 'any contractor who does not carry out and observe the conditions of this Standing Order with reference to all other work which he may be executing and carrying out in Sheffield or within a radius of 10 miles from the Town Hall' (clause 7). Others provide, sometimes vaguely, only for workmen employed on contract work, or are silent on the question. Thus, in West Ham, 'The contractor shall pay all workmen employed by him in and about the execution of this contract . . .'; in Leicester, the Fair Wages Resolutions of 1895 and 1900 referred to 'all the workmen employed by him (the contractor) in the execution of the contract . . .'. But the 1902 Resolution in force in 1908 did not stipulate to whom the rates should be paid. Liverpool's clause was also silent on this matter.

A proposal similar in character was made by the President of the Yorkshire Textile Workers' Union. He suggested to the 1908 Committee that the Fair Wages principle be applied also to the manufacture of the materials used by the contractor; e.g., a contractor making cloth would be responsible for the conditions under which the yarn he used was manufactured. The proposal was rejected by the Committee on the same grounds as the former proposal: 'the ultimate result would be practically to make Government contractors responsible for the payment of current rates of wages on all work in every industry in the country' (para. 116).

NOTES

1. I am, of course, aware that this is hardly an objectively verifiable opinion of the exchange.

2. This account is derived from: (a) a Return Ordered by the House of Commons on 15 February 1892, concerning compliance with the Terms of the 1891 Resolution by various government departments (16 May 1892); Office of Works, pp. 14–17. House of Commons Papers, 1892, vol. LXIV, p. 293; (b) Evidence of Mr. J. Taylor, C.B., Senior Surveyor in the Office of Works to the 1897 Committee on Government Contracts, at Q. 5.

3. Parl. Deb., H. of C. (Third Series); 20 March 1891, vol. CCCLI, col. 1538; per Mr. W. H. Smith.

4. Parl. Deb., H. of C. (Fourth Series); 4 April 1898, vol. LVI, cols. 39–40; per Mr. Hanbury.

5. The departmental views quoted here are to be found in Fair Wages Advisory Committee, Memorandum of Recommendations (No. 2), dated 1st December, 1910, at

paras. 9–12. In the Department of Employment Library, Box GP.331.215.

6. The principal sources of information for the following account are as follows: (a) Return Ordered by the House of Commons, 15 February 1892, of the Forms issued by the War Office, Admiralty, Board of Works, and other Departments of the Government, in compliance with the Terms of the Resolution of the House of 13 February 1891, (May 16, 1892); House of Commons Papers, 1892, vol. LXIV, p. 293. Thirteen Departments reported back to the Treasury: Admiralty, Board of Trade, Board of Customs, Home Office, Inland Revenue Department, Irish Government, Irish Board of Works, Post Office, Science and Art Department, Scottish Office, Stationery Office, War Office, Office of Works. (b) Minutes of Evidence to the Committee on Government Contracts, 1897; House of Commons Papers, vol. X, p. 1. See also Appendix I to the Report of the Committee, 1897, at pp. 123–37, for statements

by the various government departments of the conditions inserted by them in notices and contracts under the Fair Wages Resolution. (c) *Report of the Committee on Fair Wages, 1908*, Appendix I, 'Present Fair Wages Clauses in Government Contracts'. Cd. 4422. Source (a) will henceforth be referred to in the text as the '1892 Return'.

7. See Return 'of the Conditions of the New Contract of Her Majesty's Office of Works, for Works and Repairs in the London District', Return to an Order of the Honourable the House of Commons, dated 16 February 1891, at p. 5. House of Commons Papers of 1890–1, vol. LXIII, at p. 831.

8. For an example, see Parl Deb., H. of C. (Third Series); 13 July 1891, vol. CCCLV, cols. 1052–3; 20 July 1891, cols. 1746–7.

9. Evidence of the Controller of the Stationery Office to the 1896 Committee, Q. 26. Also Report of a Committee of Inquiry into Government Printing Establishments, 1927, at para. 20. Cmnd. 2828. House of Commons Papers, 1927, vol. IX, p. 353.

10. Parl. Deb., H. of C. (Fourth Series); 29 February 1892, vol. I, col. 1516.

11. Parl. Deb., H. of C. (Fourth Series); 18 February 1892, vol. I, col. 677.

12. Parl. Deb., H. of C. (Fourth Series); 16 May 1892, vol. IV, cols. 54–5.

13. Parl. Deb., H. of C. (Fourth Series); 18 February 1892, vol. I, col. 696.

14. Respectively, Parl. Deb., H. of C. (Fourth Series); 20 March 1902, vol. CIV, col. 540; 20 February 1902, vol. CIII, cols. 578–9.

15. For details of the controversy, see the discussion in Parl. Deb., H. of C. (Fourth Series); 24 March 1896, vol. XXXIX, at cols. 69–80.

16. Parl. Deb., H. of C. (Fourth Series); 9 January 1894, vol. XX, cols. 1147–8; for the earlier complaint, see the debate on 22 December 1893, vol. XX, at col. 208.

17. Parl. Deb., H. of C. (Third Series); 5 June 1891, vol. CCCLIII, col. 1714.

18. Parl. Deb., H. of C. (Fourth Series); May 1892, vol. V, cols. 40–1.

19. Parl. Deb., H. of C. (Fourth Series); 18 August 1893, vol. XVI, cols. 515–16.

20. Parl. Deb., H. of C. (Fourth Series); 30 May 1892, vol. V, cols. 199–201.

21. Parl. Deb., H. of C. (Fourth Series); 24 March 1896, vol. XXXIX, col. 70.

22. Parl. Deb., H. of C. (Fourth Series); 10 March 1902, vol. CIV, cols. 899–900.

23. Parl. Deb., H. of C. (Fourth Series); 14 February 1902, vol. CIII, col. 79.

24. Parl. Deb., H. of C. (Fourth Series); 24 March 1896, vol. XXXIX, cols. 74; 81; 84.

25. Parl. Deb., H. of C. (Fourth Series); 6 March 1902, vol. CIV, cols. 583–4.

26. Parl. Deb., H. of C. (Fourth Series); 10 February 1892, vol. I, at col. 131. The debate on this complaint was relatively lengthy (cols. 124–32), and in it references were made to the effect that the 1891 Resolution 'has not been faithfully interpreted, not been put in practice with all the trades concerned in Government contracts' (col. 125, per Mr. Broadhurst); or 'has not been satisfactorily carried out, so far, by any of the Departments' (col. 129, per Mr. Buxton). See too the comment of Mr. Cuninghame Graham at col. 132: 'I congratulate the House upon having, for the first time, a labour question introduced upon such an occasion. It is a new departure the House is taking in now discussing the subject of painters' wages. We generally, in these debates, deal with subjects of far less interest—matters of foreign policy, the balance of power, and such matters—which, of course, are of far less interest to the people we represent than the question of a half-penny more or less in the rate of wages.'

27. Parl. Deb., H. of C. (Fourth Series); 28 March 1895, vol. 32, cols. 337–8.

28. Pamphlet published by C. J. Drummond, Secretary, London Society of Compositors, *The London County Council Printing Contract*, (June 5, 1891) (8 pp.), at pp. 5–6.

29. Fabian Tract No. 65, *Trade Unionists and Politics*, (July 1895).

30. See Public Accounts Committee, Fourth Report, 1889, House of Commons Papers 259, of 1889; Appendix, paras. 10–15. Treasury Minutes of 11 December 1889 and 6 January 1890, in Epitome of the Reports from the Committees of Public Accounts, vol. I (1857–1937), at pp. 238–40. House of Commons Papers of 1938, No. 154.

5

Assessment and Conclusion

The results of the experience of the Fair Wages policy during the years 1891–1909 may be summed up in two respects. First, an assessment may be made of its impact in terms of the objectives it was created to achieve. In its own words, these were to prevent the evils of sweating and the abuses arising from sub-letting and to ensure the payment of current rates of wages. It was designed to eliminate wage competition among government contractors: to prevent contractors reducing wage rates to unacceptable levels in order to submit to lower bids in response to government tenders. Secondly, an attempt may be made to conclude whether the Fair Wages Resolution had an impact on the industrial relations situation generally, and, in particular, on the development of union organization and collective bargaining. For it had been a tacit hope on the part of supporters of the policy that its indirect effects in this way would perhaps be of even greater significance than its effects in achieving its direct objectives.

It is not difficult to find clear, firm, if sometimes vividly expressed opinions about the success of the Fair Wages Resolution in achieving its stated objectives. It is not surprising to hear, however, after reading the above account of the enforcement procedure, that the great majority of opinions expressed by those whom the Resolution was designed to aid—the workers and their representatives—were extremely unfavourable as regards the contribution made by the policy. Thus, the London District Secretary of the Electrical Trades Union stated to the 1908 Committee: 'Generally speaking, we are strongly of opinion that the Fair Wages Clause as it stands now is more or less a farce as far as Government contracts are concerned' (Q. 1829). The view of the representatives of the London Clothiers' Cutters' Trade Union was: 'this current wage clause, although it is very good possibly in its intentions, yet, when it comes out in theory, it means nothing, and it is evaded

For notes see p. 108

every day, every hour, and in every industry' (Q. 964). The Secretary
of the Sheffield United Cutlery Trades Council said: 'the process is so
slow and the difficulties of proving a complaint are so great, that it has
not been anything like as beneficial as it might be if it were amended'
(Q. 2464). Scottish printers considered that the Clause had done
them no good at all (Q. 2878); and brushmakers that it had been
ineffectual (Q. 1931). The representative of the Birmingham branch
of the Union of Saddlers and Harness Makers found that, 'The object
of the Fair Wages Clause is defeated as far as Birmingham and district
is concerned'. The result was that 'wages have gradually dropped down
until it is really a starvation existence' (Q. 4361). And when asked
whether he had found the Clause of any use to him, the representative
of the Staffordshire district of the Boilermakers and Iron and Steel
Shipbuilders' Society replied: 'Not at all. It is a dead letter in my
district' (Q. 4279).

Employers, as in the pottery industry, tended to regard the Resolution as a matter of form as it was never acted on and thus they took
no notice of it (Qs. 4877ff.). Employers in the cutlery trades paid the
Resolution a backhanded compliment, saying: 'It really means, not
that your present Clause is not good enough, but that your present
Clause is not put in force, surely?' (Q. 5637). Others reacted to the
complaints of trade unionists by claiming that they were frivolous or
false, that the witnesses before Committees were either ignorant or
malicious, and that their evidence did not represent the feeling of
workers generally (e.g. Qs. 3349ff.). The conventional view held by
employers was that the Fair Wages Resolution was unworkable, that
its tendency was only to raise wages, and not to maintain 'fair' rates
of wages, and that employers should retain the right to reduce wages
whenever they liked. There was a basic inability or unwillingness to
accept the ideological premises underlying the policy. One contractor
complained of by the Amalgamated Society of Engineers summed up
his position as follows: 'I maintain that employers of labour have the
right to manage their business in their own way, but there gradually
seems to be an idea that we are to be governed as to all sorts of regulations'. As to this he could only say: 'The remark I have to make is
that I cannot for the life of me see what the Board of Trade has to do
with our business' (Q. 3374; also others at Qs. 3652; 3726).

Whenever praise was extended to the Fair Wages Resolution by
workers, it was usually very heavily qualified. For example, a woodworkers' representative would say: 'It has done a great deal of good
. . . of course with some rather bad evasions and exceptions' (Q. 2184).
Or a London harness makers' representative: 'It has stopped in a
measure the cutting down prices that have been existing for some

considerable time; but, unfortunately, at very quiet times, the contractors for Government work utterly ignore the Fair Wages Clause,
and do not comply with it. We only know at the present time of one
instance of an employer in London complying with it' (Q. 3838). In
the words of an organizer of unskilled labour: 'Under the Fair Wages
Clause, the skilled trades probably would, through their organizations,
be able to get the rate which their Unions had fixed in the district;
but in regard to the unskilled man, employers seem to pay him whatever they like' (Q. 311). Writing over seven years after the Resolution
was passed, a trade unionist could still optimistically predict that it
would 'prove a powerful weapon in the hands of the Trade Unions
when they have mastered its economic possibilities, and so learned
the best way to use it'. It is difficult to perceive the basis of this optimism
from his subsequent description of the achievements of the policy
during seven years of existence:

> The Resolution seemed to promise so much, and has effected so
> little. The various Government Departments have been slow in
> grasping and slower still in applying a principle that was to them
> so new and strange. Before its passing there had been no one but
> the contractor to think about in the distribution of public work.
> Theoretically, work done for the State is work done for the benefit
> of the whole community, and not for that of any special class
> therein.
>
> It may have been that the Departmental heads knew the
> theory; it is certain that they never thought of putting it into
> practice. If Government work satisfied officials, and paid con-
> tractors, that was enough; and workmen by whose aid it was
> produced did not count. And when the Resolution became a
> part of all Government contracts the fact that he was thereafter
> to count was of so startling a character that it has taken the
> heads of the Departments seven years to learn the mere pothooks
> and hangers of the principles involved.[1]

The above statements present a rather pessimistic outlook. And yet,
despite this barrage of criticism and bitter disillusionment with the
Fair Wages Resolution, the Committees set up to inquire into the
workings of the Fair Wages policy were generally optimistic in their
conclusions. Thus, the 1897 Committee on Government Contracts
gave what can only be described as a whitewash to the government
departments' record of enforcement of the Resolution up to then:

> broadly speaking, your Committee have come to the conclusion
> that the Departments, as a whole, have loyally endeavoured to

interpret and carry out its provisions. . . . On the other hand it cannot be denied that, in certain quarters, there exists a great lack of confidence in the ability or in the desire of some of the Departments to enforce the spirit and the letter of the Resolution. . . . While, as already stated, the Committee do not consider that this lack of confidence is well-founded, they think it is very important that the feeling should be removed. And they are of the opinion that in some ways, there is room for improvement in administration and that there might be greater promptitude and uniformity in the working of the Resolution. (p. iv)

Similarly, the Fair Wages Committee of 1908 concluded that, 'On the whole, however, neither the evidence submitted to us, nor the number of cases brought to the notice of the Departments . . . seems to indicate any widespread defects in the working of the Fair Wages Clause' (para. 13).

The Fair Wages Resolution of 1891 was found, therefore, to be satisfactory in the eyes of employers and Committees of the House of Commons, but was thoroughly disliked by the workers and their representatives. Yet it had been expected that it would be the latter who would most probably benefit, and at the expense of the former. It may be concluded then, that between the years 1891–1909, the Fair Wages Resolution was a total and miserable failure in achieving its stated objectives.

The impact of the Fair Wages policy on trade union organization and collective bargaining is very difficult to assess. There are the statements of some of those intimately concerned with the policy that it was their hope that collective bargaining and the Fair Wages Resolution would go hand in hand; indeed, that the one would depend largely on the success of the other: without the development of collective bargaining it would be almost impossible to achieve an effective implementation of the Fair Wages Resolution. Does the failure of the Resolution in practice, therefore, imply that it failed to give rise to collective bargaining machinery sufficiently developed and powerful to effectively enforce it?

It is not easy to answer this question. There is the evidence of a large number of complaints made usually by trade union officials representing workers affected by the Fair Wages Resolution. It would be absurd, however, to deduce that their status as representatives of these men and women was owed to the right of complaint granted by that Resolution. Any intelligent reading of industrial relations history shows that in the United Kingdom the mere granting of a legal right as vague, innocuous and ill-protected as was the Resolution would not be adequate to raise up an organization of workers where none previously existed. It takes much more than this to raise the consciousness of the worker to the level of struggle against the conditions imposed upon him by the rulers of society. And particularly when one considers the terrible social and economic conditions of the working class during those two decades, portrayed so vividly in Robert Tressell's *The Ragged-Trousered Philanthropists*. One can scarcely imagine the passage of the Resolution by the House of Commons having any impact on the workers described in that book.

The opinion has been expressed, however, that the Fair Wages Clause did have some, even a considerable impact on the development of collective bargaining in the United Kingdom and, more particularly, was responsible to some extent for the development of a purely voluntary system of collective negotiation. The full statement by Professor Sir Otto Kahn-Freund is as follows:

> It is believed—though it is impossible to prove the point—that this extension of the fair wages clauses to sub-contractors (which was reproduced in the clauses passed by local authorities) was an especially powerful lever in establishing the habit of obedience to collective standards, far beyond the immediate field of operation of the resolutions. The fair wages clauses mobilized the employers' self-interest in the service of these standards. They thus obviated the need for 'direct' action either in the courts or on the battlefield of industrial relations. It can be said with confidence that, to some extent, it is this system of fair wages clauses which accounts for the functioning in this country of voluntary collective bargaining without legal sanctions.[2]

In the course of the research for this study, some evidence was uncovered supporting this assertion. Thus, the Secretary of the Basket, Skip and Hampermakers' Federation testified to the 1908 Committee that the work of his organization was mainly to organize in regard to government work, and that it was largely the result of the large amount of this work that five separate unions of workers in the industry had got together to form the Federation (Q. 2064). More specifically, the Secretary of the London Society of Compositors stated to the 1896 Committee that:

> within the past few years, I might say since the Resolution was passed by the House of Commons, we have had a great many applications from firms hitherto holding aloof from us, to go on our list. I think that in tendering for public work they have found it of considerable advantage to have their names upon the recognized list of fair employers. (Q. 669)

Again, the General Secretary of the National Glass Bottle Makers' Society admitted to the 1908 Committee that the Fair Wages Clause had assisted them, but without specifying how. The 1897 Committee on Government Contracts summarized:

> The Resolution has been in force for six years. So far as regards the relations between employers and employed, its working does not appear to have had any adverse effect. Indeed, it seems probable that it has done something to promote agreements between masters and men, in reference to the rate of wages and conditions of employment. (p. iii)

Even taking this evidence into consideration, Kahn-Freund's conclusion is correct only in a certain sense. The introduction of the Fair Wages Resolution did undoubtedly avoid any confrontation in the courts of law between unions and government contractors over the issue of compliance with collectively agreed standards. But this was *not* the result of the success of the Resolution in inducing compliance with its standards which were certainly not those of collective agreements. *Nor* was the absence of litigation a consequence of the growth of collective bargaining and trade union strength, neither of which were due to the Fair Wages policy. The reason for the lack of legal confrontation was inherent in the means chosen for the implementation of the Fair Wages policy: regulation of the terms of employment of the employees of government contractors was to be accomplished through a Resolution of the House of Commons. This was a mechanism which gave no opportunity to trade unionists to confront contractors in court. Instead, they were forced to rely on informal channels of complaint through government departments. It is a moot point whether, given the legal right to complain to the courts over a violation of the policy by a contractor, the organized craft unions of the time might not have utilized it, to the end that the policy might have had more of an impact in practice than it in fact did. This legal opportunity was not given to them. And so, as Kahn-Freund says, the need for direct action in the courts was obviated.

The second proposition advanced by Kahn-Freund was that the need for direct action on the battlefield of industrial relations was obviated because of the Fair Wages clauses. The history of working class struggle does not justify attaching such momentous weight to this government policy. For as the resort to government departments for redress proved to be unavailing, trade unions and workers turned to the only means available to them—industrial warfare. G.D.H. Cole characterized the industrial conflict of 1911–14, two decades after the Resolution, as 'a mass movement of sheer reaction against the

failure of either orthodox trade unionism or modern paraliamentari-
anism to secure any improvement in the working-class standard of
life'.[3] Between 1900 and 1909 the average number of working days
lost each year through strikes and lock-outs had averaged three and
a half million. In 1910, the figure shot up to twelve million and in
1912 to over thirty-eight million. The trade unions had rapidly
increased their numbers during the previous two decades and they
now threw over their previous defensive attitudes, inspired by weakness, for militant and highly class-conscious policies. As described by
Alan Bullock:

> The parliamentary reformism of the Labour Party, collective
> bargaining and the cautious building up of trade-union reserves
> were abandoned for the slogans of syndicalism and the class war—
> 'Direct Action', the general strike, the use of industrial power
> for revolutionary purposes and the overthrow of the capitalist
> system. If the new ideas and the new slogans did not produce the
> unrest, they fitted well with the angry mood which was taking
> hold of large sections of the working class in these years.[4]

There is some truth to Kahn-Freund's last conclusion, 'that to some
extent, it is this system of fair wages clauses which accounts for the
functioning in this country of voluntary collective bargaining without
legal sanctions'. The precedent established by the Fair Wages Resolution of 1891 was to remain the norm for governmental regulation
of the terms of employment of employees of government contractors.
Despite harsh criticism of it, this 'non-legal' means was endorsed
again in 1909 and once more in 1946. The government refused to
accede to demands for a different method of enforcement of its Fair
Wages policy. It would be erroneous, however, to conclude from this
that it was the Resolution itself which gave rise to the voluntary
system, to a certain extent, through its contribution to the development of collective bargaining. What it did do was to pre-empt this
area of governmental regulation and, by so doing, it prevented any
other form of 'legal' regulation being introduced. By its very presence
it forced the trade union movement to rely on its own strength and
organization to attain its objectives. Not being able to rely on the
Fair Wages Resolution, and in the knowledge that they would not
receive any other help in this area, the trade unions took the hard
road to self-reliant collective bargaining, independent of any legal
protection or privilege through government intervention. It is this
which may be said to be the 'contribution' of the Fair Wages Resolution to collective bargaining and industrial relations in the United
Kingdom.

NOTES

1. Extract from *The Trade Unionist*, dated October 1898, entitled 'The "Fair Wages Resolution" and Bookbinding', by Frederick Rogers (Vellum Binders' Society). Found in the Public Record Office, Files of the Ministry of Labour: LAB 10/12 (1935–7); I.R. 1080/1935.

2. O. Kahn-Freund, 'Legislation Through Adjudication. The Legal Aspect of Fair Wages Clauses and Recognised Conditions', *Modern Law Review*, **11** (1948), at p. 278.

3. Quoted in H. Pelling, *Popular Politics and Society in Late Victorian Britain*, Macmillan, London, 1968, at p. 148. And see generally, chapter 9, 'The Labour Unrest 1911–14', pp. 147–64.

4. A. Bullock, *The Life and Times of Ernest Bevin, vol. I, Trade Union Leader, 1881–1940*, Heinemann Ltd., London 1960, at p. 34. See generally, pp. 33–5.

PART II

The Second Fair Wages Policy
1909–1946

6

Origins of the Fair Wages Resolution of 1909

The Fair Wages Resolution of 10 March 1909 was moved on behalf of the Government by the Postmaster-General, Sydney Buxton, who had initiated the debate which had produced the first Resolution of 1891. The 1909 Resolution passed by the House read as follows:

> Clauses in Government contracts should be so amended as to provide as follows: The contractor shall, under the penalty of a fine or otherwise, pay rates of wages and observe hours of labour not less favourable than those commonly recognized by employers and trade societies (or, in the absence of such recognized wages and hours, those which in practice prevail amongst good employers) in the trade in the district where the work is carried out. Where there are no such wages and hours recognized or prevailing in the district, those recognized or prevailing in the nearest district in which the general industrial circumstances are similar shall be adopted. Further the conditions of employment generally accepted in the district in the trade concerned shall be taken into account in considering how far the terms of the fair wages clauses are being observed. The contractor shall be prohibited from transferring or assigning, directly or indirectly, to any person or persons whatever, any portion of his contract without the written permission of the department. Sub-letting, other than that which may be customary in the trade concerned, shall be prohibited. The contractor shall be responsible for the observance of the fair wages clauses by the sub-contractor instead thereof.[1]

Widespread dissatisfaction with the substance and administration of the 1891 Resolution had been voiced for years in complaints by trade unionists to government departments and M.P.s. The year 1906 was marked by two events which served to focus attention on the problems

For notes see p. 117

associated with sweated industries: the Sweated Industries Exhibition at the Queen's Hall and the undertaking of an Enquiry by the Board of Trade into the Earnings and Hours of Labour. Following the exhibition the National Anti-Sweating League was founded, and carried on a vigorous campaign, culminating in the appointment of a Select Committee of the House of Commons on Home Work in 1909, and the passage of the first Trade Boards Act in the same year. More significantly, however, the year 1906 saw the emergence of the new 'Labour Party' from the January election. The Parliamentary Committee of the T.U.C. itself found that of its thirteen committee members, nine were M.P.s, six as members of the Labour Party. B.C. Roberts states that the victorious Liberal Party was significantly more sympathetic to the demands of workers' respresentatives:

> With R.B. Haldane at the War Office, Lord Tweedmouth at the Admiralty and Sydney Buxton at the Post Office, the relations between the trade unions and these Government departments showed a notable improvement under the Liberal administration. The employment practices of these departments were still by no means to the satisfaction of the trade unions, but the new ministers did not treat union representatives with the aristocratic indiffer- ence that had been usual with their Conservative predecessors. (p. 204)

This was particularly important as the wages and conditions of govern- ment employees were subject to the same standards as those required by the Fair Wages Resolution.

The annual Trades Union Congress in September 1906 passed the following resolution, which was forwarded to the Labour Members of Parliament with a request to ballot for it:

> In the opinion of this Congress it is essential that the Fair Wages Resolution of February, 1891, should be amended by the sub- stitution of the words 'Trade Union rate' in the place of the words 'current rate', and that it be an instruction to the Parliamentary Committee to draft a Trade Union resolution and have it brought before the House of Commons with a view of its being inserted in all Government contracts. That a firm shall be deemed unfair that employs any workman or woman below such Trade Union rates. Where a Trade Union does not exist the Trade Union rate of the nearest town shall be accepted.

In the meantime, pressure was exerted on those Ministers who were thought to be the most amenable: thus, deputations from the Clothier Cutters' Union and the Amalgamated Society of Tailors, on 10

December 1906 and 15 July 1907 respectively, approached Sydney Buxton to protest against the sweating conditions under which the Post Office uniform was made. It was suggested as a remedy that the policy of the London County Council be followed and a log of prices be established.

Finally, on 15 August 1907, the Treasury appointed a Committee to consider the working of the Fair Wages Resolution as embodied in government contracts. On 20 August, the Prime Minister stated in the House of Commons that: 'The Committee has been instructed to report whether any changes are desirable in the administration of the Fair Wages Resolution in order to enable its objects to be more effectively attained. *It is not intended to amend the terms of the Resolution or enlarge its scope*' (My italics). It had been hoped to have a Select Committee rather than a Departmental Committee appointed, but the government had refused this.[2] Although, in the opinion of the T.U.C., the terms of reference were found to be 'most unsatisfactory', they appointed a representative to give evidence on their behalf.

Their principal objection to the 'current rates of wages' formula of 1891 was that, ' "Current" may, in fact, mean anything, and may be interpreted according to the inclination of those at the head of Government Departments, and it is this ambiguity which it is now sought on your behalf to satisfactorily remove, not by an inquiry into the working of the House of Commons' resolution, but by an alteration of the resolution as given above'. Consequently, the 1907 Congress passed a resolution suggesting the alteration of the Resolution on the following lines:

> That, in the opinion of this House, all Government contracts should contain a clause stating that the contractor shall observe the conditions, hours of labour, and pay the wages recognized and agreed upon between the employers and Trade Unions of the districts (the rate to be paid irrespective of piecework earnings) in which the work is carried on, and a schedule of wages paid shall be posted in some conspicuous place in the works where the work is done.
>
> Failing such agreement as to conditions, hours or wages, those in operation in the nearest town or district in which the work is carried on, under such agreement, shall be taken to apply.
>
> Any firm which does not recognize the above-mentioned conditions on all their work, whether Government or otherwise, shall be deemed an 'unfair' house, and not eligible to contract for Government work.
>
> Facilities shall be given by which Trade Union officials can learn to whom contracts are given in the trades they represent.

In its Report, the Fair Wages Committee of 1908 rejected the T.U.C.'s proposals for amendment of the Resolution:

> It is only in those cases in which the Trade Union rate is not the current rate that any change would be effected by the proposed amendment; but these are cases in which it is at least open to doubt whether the Government would be justified in enforcing the payment of the Trade Union rate by its contractors. ... It might be found on inquiry that such a rate was so high that its enforcement would render it commercially impossible to carry on the trade. If the Government is to have its work executed at the ordinary market price it cannot require the contractor to pay more than the market rate of wages' (para. 22)

As has already been shown, to equate the market rate with the Fair Wages policy reveals a basic misunderstanding of its objectives. Its recommendation was '*that the present wording of the Fair Wages Clause,* which obliges the contractor to pay the current rates of wages for competent workmen in the district where the work is carried out, *should be retained*' (para. 125(a)) (my italics). This decision of the Committee to accept the *status quo* was rejected by the T.U.C. and at the Annual Congress in September 1908 the view was reiterated that 'it is essential that the Fair Wages Resolution should be amended by the substitution of the words "Trade Union rates and prices" in the place of the words "current rate" '. The T.U.C. went on to instruct the Parliamentary Committee 'to act with the Labour Party in drafting a resolution to this effect and have it brought before the House of Commons with a view to its insertion in all Government contracts'.

On 10 March 1909, John Hodge, M.P., Secretary of the Steel Smelters Union, who was later appointed the first Secretary of Labour when he joined Lloyd George's War Cabinet in December 1916, presented the following motion to the House of Commons:

> That: the Fair Wages Clause in Government contracts should be so amended as to provide that the contractor shall, under penalty, pay to all the workmen in his employ not less than the minimum standard rate of wages recognized by trade societies in the district where such men are employed, and shall observe the recognized hours and proper conditions of labour; and if there shall be no such standard rate of wages or recognized hours and proper conditions of labour in such district the contractor shall pay to such workmen not less than the minimum standard rate of wages recognized by trade societies customarily executing such class of work in the nearest district, and observe the recognized hours

and proper conditions of labour prevailing in respect of the particular trade in the nearest district in which such men are employed; also, that the contractor shall be prohibited from sub-letting any portion of his contract, except where the Department concerned specially allows the sub-letting of such special portions of the work as could not be produced or carried out by the contractor in the ordinary course of his business; and any such sub-contractor shall be subject to the same conditions as the contractor.[3]

The government's amendment to this motion replaced the formula, 'minimum standard rate of wages recognized by trade societies in the district', with wages and hours 'commonly recognized by employers and trade societies (or, in the absence of such recognized wages and hours, those which in practice prevail amongst good employers) in the trade in the district'. Sydney Buxton, moving the government's amendment, declared:

> The objection I find to the motion is that it is not as specific as it might otherwise be, because it speaks only of the minimum rate of wages recognized by trade societies customarily executing such class of work in the nearest district. If there is only one or two employers out of a large number the rate of wages paid by them could not be regarded as the recognized rate. I gather from my Hon. Friend that the recognized rates are the rates agreed upon by the employer and the employed. (col. 430)

The government changed the emphasis, therefore, from trade union rates—'recognized by trade societies'—to negotiated rates—'agreed upon by the employer and the employed'. To a degree, this reflected the 1907 T.U.C. resolution which stipulated wages 'recognized and agreed upon between the employers and Trade Unions'. The government's secondary standard, however, that of rates prevailing amongst 'good employers' was not considered adequate by the T.U.C. But in one sense, the government's motion was clearly preferable to Hodge's. As was pointed out by one M.P. during the debate:

> I would like to draw the attention of the hon. Members who brought this motion before the House to the fact that the word 'minimum', although it is qualified by 'recognized by trade societies', and so on, 'in the district', is against the interests which he so ably advocated. I do not advise him to insist on that word, because it is a word which may be fastened on by the subordinates in a Department for the purpose of carrying out a contract at the lowest rate which would be accepted in a time of depression and slackness of employment. (col. 438)

Whatever the relation of Hodge's motion or the T.U.C. resolution to the 1909 Resolution, one thing is clear beyond doubt: the formula of that Resolution directly contradicted the position of the 1908 Fair Wages Committee, which had recommended that the wording of the 1891 Resolution be retained. It is perhaps surprising, therefore, to find that the predominant conception among departmental administrators of the 1909 Resolution *does not register the fact* of this rejection of the view of the departmental committee. Thus, in a letter of 24 March 1909 transmitting a copy of the new Resolution to government departments, the Treasury added: 'that His Majesty's Government approve generally of the recommendations made in the Report of the Treasury Committee appointed to consider the working of the Fair Wages Resolution of the 13th February 1891 (Cd. 4422)'. In subsequent years, officials concerned with implementation of the policy continually reiterated the view that: 'it is important to remember that the Resolution was introduced into the House of Commons to carry into effect the recommendations of the Fair Wages Committee appointed in 1907'; or 'Since the Resolution of 1909 arose out of the Report of the (1908) Committee, and was based on recommendations contained in that Report . . .'. Even the Ministry of Labour's 1961 *Industrial Relations Handbook* ignores the history, and even the logic. Immediately after stating that the 1908 Committee's 'main conclusion was that the wording of the Fair Wages Clause in Government contracts . . . should be retained', it goes on to say, 'The Resolution of 1909, based on these recommendations, prescribed . . . (wages and hours) . . . commonly recognized by employers and trade societies', as though there was no inconsistency between the Committee's conclusion and the subsequent Resolution, so different in character and wording from its predecessor. Yet a fundamental change had occurred: from 'current' rates to an express recognition of negotiated rates 'commonly recognized by employers and trade societies'.

The real danger in this departmental misconception of the new Resolution lay in the prospect that the assumptions of the 1908 Committee, a departmental committee, would become the foundation of future administration of the new policy. The 'market rate of wages' theory of the 1908 Committee (para. 22) would prevail over the new Resolution's recognition of collective bargaining. This might occur, despite the fact that the principal recommendation of the Committee —retention of the old Resolution—was not accepted. The principal contradiction that emerged in the period 1909–46 did indeed focus on the relation between collective agreements and fair wages, and this will be examined fully in the following chapters. But a different kind of example will serve here to illustrate how this misconception continually manifested itself in the course of departmental administration. A running controversy developed between the T.U.C. and the departments over the question of extending the Fair Wages policy to materials used by contractors. The T.U.C.'s demand was always treated as a request to extend the scope of the Resolution beyond its intended area of operation. The grounds for this response to the T.U.C. were stated as follows in one instance of 1933:

> The question of the extension of the Fair Wages principle to materials used by contractors was considered by the Fair Wages Committee, constituted in 1907 under the Chairmanship of Sir G.H. Murray, K.C.B., to consider the working of the Fair Wages Resolution of 1891. *It was as a result of the Report of this Committee that the Resolution of 1909 was passed and the present practice in Fair Wages cases established.* (My italics.)

The response went on to quote paragraph 116 of the Report of the Committee which held the proposal to be 'quite impracticable to enforce generally' on the grounds that 'the ultimate result would be practically to make Government contractors responsible for the payment of current rates of wages on all work in every industry throughout the country'. In this way the views of the Committee, rejected through the substance of the 1909 Resolution, were perpetuated in administrative practice.[4]

NOTES

1. Parl. Deb., H. of C. (Fourth Series); 10 March 1909, vol. II, col. 425.

2. Parl. Deb., H. of C. (Fourth Series); 20 August 1907, vol. 181, cols. 481–2; 18 March 1907, vol. 171, at col. 487.

3. Parl. Deb., H. of C. (Fourth Series); 10 March 1909, vol. II, cols. 415–16.

4. The above account is principally derived from the following sources:
—Pamphlet published by the Trades Union Congress and the Labour Party *Trade Boards and the Cave Report*, 1922, (23 pp.)
—Henry Pelling, *A History of British Trade Unionism*, 2nd ed., Macmillan, London, 1972; p. 125.
—B. C. Roberts, *The Trades Union Congress 1868–1921*, Geo. Allen & Unwin, London, 1958; p. 204.
—Report of the 40th Annual Trades Union Congress, Bath, 1907, at pp. 77–9.
—Report of the 41st Annual Trades Union Congress, Nottingham 1908, at pp. 81–3; 187.
—Document dated 1 March 1934, which appears to be a memorandum by officials in the Labour Department, entitled 'Fair Wages Resolution—Re-Draft Suggested by the General Council of the Trades Union Congress', at p. 11, Appendix C, para. 1. This document may be found in the Public Record Office, Files of the Ministry of Labour: LAB 10/12; I.R. 1080 (1935).
—Document dated 24 April 1933, entitled 'Fair Wages Clause—Making and Fixing of Materials Used in Connection with Government or Municipal Contracts', at p. 10, para. 12. In the Public Record Office, Files of the Ministry of Labour: LAB 10/12; I.R. 333/33.
—Ministry of Labour, *Industrial Relations Handbook*, H.M.S.O., 1961; at pp. 149–50.

—Papers of the Fair Wages Advisory Committee, Department of Employment Library, Box GP.331.215. Opinion of the Law Officers on the Enforcement of Fair Wages Clauses in Government Contracts; 12 May 1910. (8 pp.) Letter dated 24 March 1909 from the Treasury to the First Commissioner of Works on p. 4.

7

The Development of Collective Bargaining
after 1909

The development during the period 1891–1909 of collective bargaining
on a 'district' or 'local' basis, and the conflict between this growth
and the formula contained in the Fair Wages Resolution of 1891 have
been described above. The 1909 Resolution, in providing a new
formula, 'rates of wages and . . . hours of labour not less favourable
than those commonly recognized by employers and trade societies . . .
in the trade in the district where the work is carried out', was a belated
recognition of the industrial relations situation. A striking contemporary example of *legislative* recognition of collective bargaining on a
district basis was the Coal Mines (Minimum Wage) Act of 1912.
Following a demand by the Miners' Federation for minimum
guaranteed time rates for all grades of underground workers, negotiations with the coal owners broke down and in March 1912 the
Federation called for an unprecedented national strike. Following
Ministerial intervention led by the Prime Minister, legislation was
rushed through for the purpose of terminating the dispute. The Act
provided for minimum wages to be determined by joint district
boards. Such boards were to be representative of owners and workers
in the district, with an independent chairman appointed by agreement
between the parties or, in default of agreement, by the Board of
Trade. Workers' representatives on the board were to be those who,
in the opinion of the Board of Trade 'fairly and adequately' represented the workmen in the coal mines in the district (section 2(2)).
The Act provided that 'in setting any minimum rate of wages the
joint district board shall have regard to the average daily rate of wages
paid to the workmen of the class for which the minimum rate is to be
settled'. Wages were to be 'settled separately for each of the districts
named in the Schedule to this Act' (section 2(1)). The problem of
determining the boundaries of the districts was resolved by the listing

For notes see p. 131

of twenty-two districts in the Schedule. The fate of this experiment did not augur well for the future of its contemporaries. A comment in a Ministry of Labour document of 1934 is indicative of much else that went wrong in State attempts to determine wages: 'The machinery set up under the Coal Mines (Minimum Wage) Act is still in existence and is still used, but the resulting minimum rates have been effective only to a limited extent owing to their having been fixed generally at a lower level than the operative rates arranged from time to time as the result of collective bargaining'.

With the benefit of hindsight, it may be said that the belated official recognition of district arrangements by the 1909 Fair Wages Resolution was indicative more of past ignorance than of the ability to meet new contingencies. Flanders states that, despite the district basis of collective bargaining procedure at this time, provision had already been made in a number of industries for ultimate reference to *national* bodies or *national* conferences for the settlement of disputes. Pelling mentions that the national lock-outs in the boot and shoe industry in 1895 and in the engineering industry in 1897–8 were both concluded with national agreements between the parties and with the establishment of machinery to deal with disputes which arose in the operation of the agreements. J. Hallsworth noted in 1925 that although there was the power to do so under the Trade Boards Act of 1909, only a small minority of Trade Boards in Great Britain had established District Committees to recommend minimum rates applicable to the trades in their areas. A departmental memorandum of 1913 outlined the extent to which trade union organization had expanded among workers in the first four trades to be covered by the 1909 Act: tailoring, paper box, lace finishing and the chain trade industries. It noted 'that the Act has had a similar effect in the case of employers. The powerful federations of the paper box manufacturers and the wholesale clothiers have come into existence as a direct result of the Act, and the associations of lace finishers and chain manufacturers have received important accessions of strength owing to the same cause.' In contrast with this powerful organization on the employers' sides, it was estimated that of a workforce of 196,200 in these four trades, only 26,836 were in trade unions. As to the rates actually established by the Trade Boards, R.H. Tawney commented that 'the real criticism to be brought against the proceedings of the Box-making, as of the Tailoring Trade Board is, not that it has fixed the minimum rates too high, but that it has fixed them considerably below what many employers were already paying without difficulty before the Trade Board was established'. A memorandum published by the Garton Foundation in January 1919 makes the illuminating observation that 'Experience has shown that the fixing of minimum rates under this (Trade Boards) Act has had a beneficial effect on the wages paid, and that the increases so secured have raised the workers affected just above that margin where they become capable of organizing and securing fair conditions of employment for themselves'. Overall, the legislation tended towards a uniform national rate structure, rather than one varying from district to district. Organizations of employers and workers were encouraged to adopt a structure consonant with the policy.

The years immediately preceding the First World War appeared to augur great changes in the system of industrial relations. Table 2, compiled by Henry Pelling, indicates the strains to which the system was being subjected: giant increases in union membership, in the number of industrial disputes and their duration, a sudden rise in the cost of living (between 1902 and 1908 it rose by 4–5 per cent, and between 1909 and 1913 by another 9 per cent) and a relatively low level of unemployment.

TABLE 2

Year	Total Union Membership (000's)	No. of stoppages beginning in year	Total No. of working days lost by stoppages in progress (000's)	Average retail prices (1850=100)	Average Money Wages (1850=100)	Percentage unemployed
1907	2,513	585	2,150	95	182	3.7
1908	2,485	389	10,790	97	181	7.8
1909	2,477	422	2,690	97	179	7.7
1910	2,565	521	9,870	98	179½	4.7
1911	3,139	872	10,160	99	179	3.0
1912	3,416	834	40,890	103	184	3.2
1913	4,135	1,459	9,800	103	188½	2.1
1914	4,145	972	9,880	102	189½	3.3

SOURCE: Henry Pelling, *Popular Politics and Society in Late Victorian Britain*, Macmillan, London, 1968, at p. 149.

The outburst of industrial militancy which characterized this period was accompanied by spectacular gains in trade union membership, a trend that continued despite the outbreak of the First World War. After a short set-back in the early months, according to an account published by the Labour Research Department in 1923, membership steadily increased, reaching a total of 6,664,000 in December 1918. The increase was greatest in those industries which were largely developed to meet war-time needs. Thus in the metal, engineering and shipbuilding group, the membership rose from 547,000 in 1913 to 962,000 in 1918, and in the general labour group, in which the less skilled munitions workers were organized, from 375,000 to 1,081,000. The cotton industry, on the other hand, only increased from 372,000 to 403,000, and the male membership in this group showed an actual decrease from 158,000 to 142,000. The number of women organized in trade unions rose from 442,000 in 1913 to 1,228,000 in 1918, or from 10.5 per cent to over 18 per cent of the whole.

Richardson, in his study for the I.L.O. in 1938, described how industrial conditions during the war, particularly the growth of organization on both sides of industry between 1915 and 1920, led to many changes in the relations between organizations of employers and of workers, and to the development of further machinery for negotiation. Among others, he noted, 'the almost universal recognition of the Trade Unions, a great increase in nation-wide negotiations and agreements, and an extension of organized collective bargaining to many branches of industry in which, before the war, methods of regulating conditions of labour had been extremely chaotic' (p. 102). Flanders points out how, after the outbreak of war, 'one of the inevitable consequences of military and industrial mobilization was a greater degree of government intervention'. Most significantly, however, he adds:

> The change of enduring importance which resulted from such intervention and other war-time conditions was the *shift from local to national bargaining*. After the war, national, centralized negotiations between the headquarters of trade unions and employers' associations, or between federations of these bodies, became the predominant form of collective bargaining. (p. 276) (My italics.)

Richardson attributed the 'great extension during the war and in post-war years of national machinery for collective bargaining' to various factors: the consolidation of local into national organizations in many industries; and the fact that wages and other conditions in different localities became increasingly influenced by factors that were nation-wide in their operation. Thus, when the cost-of-living was rising throughout the war and up to 1920, nation-wide demands were made by workers for increases and 'it was found more expeditious and effective to deal with them nationally than to conduct a large number of isolated local negotiations' (p. 105).

A good illustration of this development occurred in the British printing industry when, during 1919, a lengthy series of negotiations ended in a comprehensive set of National Agreements covering the basic terms of employment. John Child points out that the centralization of authority on both sides of the industry, on the workers side due in part to the need for a central body to represent their interests to the government and employers on national issues arising during the war, 'was the result of the need for a more efficient method of regulating wage rates than the slow pre-war process of local negotiation' (p. 230). Consequently, throughout the inter-war period, the regulation of contractual relations was mainly effected by the 1919 series of national agreements: 'Apart from a brief suspension during and after the General Strike, and occasional disruption due to disputes, the terms of these agreements settled the basic terms of employment of the great majority of workers in the industry' (p. 268).

In the engineering industry, Arthur Marsh has asserted that only one national event, the war of 1914–18, brought any major change of a formal character in the system of industrial relations: the growth of national agreements of an *ad hoc* character outside the normal working of Procedure designed only to produce standardized conditions on a limited number of subjects. Up to the war, neither wages nor working conditions outside a limited range came to the joint notice of the national parties in engineering but were subject only to local or domestic arrangements. The war brought wage settlements for adult male workers into the scope of national negotiations and these became firmly established in the later 1920s. In addition, a demand was produced for greater uniformity of working conditions, and this led to continuous national negotiations on the subject between 1918 and the early 1920s. Marsh sums up:

> The period after the first World War therefore gave rise to the original national agreements covering the establishment of a national standard working week (November 1918), uniform overtime and shift arrangements (April, Stepember and December 1920), and regulations covering the payment of work done on holidays (December 1922), which were the forerunners of present day agreements on these subjects. (pp. 144–5)

Close examination of detailed arrangements in these and other industries reveals that simple generalizations as to the trend from local to national negotiations are inadequate to describe the highly complex reality of wage regulation. A survey published by the Labour Party and T.U.C. in 1923 gave the following analysis:

> In setting out the present position, three types of agreement have been distinguished, viz., local, district and national. Few Unions are confined to one or other of these types, of course, and those

Unions which insist most on national agreements are quite willing to enter into more restricted settlements if circumstances necessitate such a course. As far as wages, hours and other of the more important working conditions are concerned, however, an attempt is made always to keep negotiations on a national or, if that is impossible, a district basis. Where national agreements are secured it does not follow that wages, etc., are identical for all parts of the country, though an approximate equality is aimed at in most cases. . . . It is probable that there would be general agreement to the proposition that there should be a flat rate of *real wages* for all workers of the same grade all over the country, provided reliable cost of living statistics were available. As it is, some Unions negotiate for, and obtain, flat rates of nominal wages, some have two rates (London and Provincial) and some have more or less elaborate classification schemes, grading towns and rural areas in a number of classes, according to their estimated position as regards the cost of living. Such classification schemes almost invariably lead to dissatisfaction and to the demand for a national rate. The tendency seems to be to make the number of areas fewer and fewer, though it is probable that London will always be considered as a special case. . . .

Information received from Trade Unions indicates that local agreements dealing with the most important working conditions are now comparatively rare, and that national negotiations (including in the term negotiations covering practically the whole of a localized industry), with or without uniform rates and conditions, are common' (pp. 33–4)

Using this pamphlet, *Industrial Negotiations and Agreements*, and Richardson's I.L.O. Report, there will now be described briefly the collective bargaining arrangements in a number of industries which were likely more than others to be affected by the placing of government contracts.

In the Boot and Shoe Industry in 1923 there were both national agreements covering general conditions and local agreements fixing prices. Rates, consequently, varied from place to place. For example, the Rossendale Boot, Shoe and Slipper Operatives had agreements covering their own localized industry. By 1938, however, Richardson could state that wages, hours, overtime rates and other general questions were dealt with in a National Conference between the Federated Associations of Boot and Shoe Manufacturers and the National Union of Boot and Shoe Operatives, where they were discussed directly and adjusted uniformly on a national basis. On the other hand, the detailed application of the national agreements and the establishment of piece rates to give an earning capacity 25 per cent above the minimum weekly rates fixed in the agreements were undertaken by local boards of arbitration and conciliation.

In the building industry, the National Wages and Conditions Council for the Building Trades was set up in 1921 and consisted of representatives of several employers' organizations and of trade unions: the Amalgamated Union of Building Trade Workers, the Amalgamated Society of Woodworkers, the National Amalgamated Society of Operative House and Ship Painters and Decorators, the National Association of Plasterers, Granolithic and Cement Workers, and the Amalgamated Slaters' Society of Scotland. Major questions of wage rates, hours and conditions of labour involving money payments were regarded as national issues, but wages varied, the country being divided into districts and the districts into grades. In cases where employers were members of a local Employers' Association and/or not members of the National Federation of Building Trade Employers, and not otherwise parties to the National Wages and Conditions Council, wages were determined by local or district negotiation.

In the metal trades, the Amalgamated Engineering Union conducted both national and district negotiations, and wages varied in different parts of the country, owing to basic rates being different. The Ironmoulders, Machine Engine and Iron Grinders and Glaziers, and Stove, Grate, and General Metal Workers also had national agreements, and in the last-named section uniform rates obtained all over England and Wales. The Blastfurnacemen, Ore Miners, Coke Workers, and Kindred Trades Workers had national negotiations on week-end and holiday payments. On the other hand, the Iron and Steel Trades Confederation conducted negotiations mainly on a district basis, though in some cases they were equivalent to national negotiations, as certain parts of the industry were localized; e.g., Tinplate Trade in South Wales. The National Union of Blastfurnacemen, etc., negotiated on a district basis in most cases, but while district rates varied attempts were made to keep them as nearly equal as possible. The Northants district having only been organized since 1916, wages were lower there than elsewhere. The National Union of Gold, Silver and Allied Trades also conducted district negotiations and rates varied slightly in different areas. Thus, in the metal trades, the district basis was still predominant, though tending towards uniformity; in engineering, however, general alterations in wages, in the length of the working week and in some other general conditions of work, were considered nationally by direct conference between the Engineering and Allied Employers' National Federation and the various unions.

Finally, in textiles, the Woollen Industry negotiations were generally on a national basis through the National Wool and Allied Textile Industrial Council. Wales and the West of England, however, had their own district committees and arrived at their own decisions regarding wages in their districts, with confirmation by the Industrial Council. In Dyeing, Bleaching and Finishing, district agreements were in force in 1923, though general agreements had also been concluded through a Joint Board. In Cotton, which was almost entirely confined to the Lancashire district, while certain sections still favoured district negotiations for piece rate lists, generally the industry was covered by agreements applying to all districts. War increases had been made on a 'national' basis. The severe depression in the industry during the early thirties resulted in many breaches of agreed conditions as workers accepted lower wages and longer hours rather than risk losing their jobs. Undercutting threatened the entire basis of collective agreements. As a result both sides of the industry succeeded in prevailing on the government to pass the Cotton Manufacturing (Temporary Provisions) Act, 1934, which enabled statutory effect to be given to rates of wages agreed between representative organizations in the industry.

The trend towards national organization and negotiations and standardized conditions was emphasized by two other developments during the war and early post-war years: the Whitley Committee's proposals for Joint Industrial Councils, and the Trade Boards Act of 1918.

Following the experimental first four Trade Boards set up in 1910, an additional four sweated trades were added (sugar confectionery and food preserving, shirt making, metal hollow-ware and linen and cotton embroidery) and empowered to fix minimum time or piece rates throughout part or the whole of the trade. The Whitley Committee, set up in October 1916 to make suggestions for securing a permanent improvement in the relations between employers and employed, recommended the extension of the scope and purpose of the trade boards. The criterion for the setting up of a Trade Board was changed by the Trade Boards Act of 1918 from industries with 'exceptionally low wages' to those where 'no adequate machinery exists for the effective regulation of wages throughout the trade, and that accordingly, having regard to the rates of wages prevailing in the trade or any part of the trade, it is expedient that the Acts should apply to that trade'. A sudden impetus was given to the whole system by these recommendations. Hallsworth's study gives details of how by the end of 1919, fourteen additional Boards had been established, by the end of 1920 another thirty-four, and three more in February, July and November 1921 respectively making at that date a total of sixty-three, nineteen being in Ireland and forty-four in Great Britain, covering over 3,000,000 workers.

With the onset of the post-war depression in 1921, however, a determined campaign was begun by employers against the entire system, to which the government contributed by dismissing, in the spring of 1921, two-thirds of the investigating staff of the Trade Boards Department. A committee under the chairmanship of Lord Cave was set up to enquire into the system and reported in April 1922 recommending a reversion to the 1909 basis, a move characterized by the 1923 T.U.C./Labour Party pamphlet as 'part of the consistent policy of employers to invoke either State or joint machinery for fixing wages, at a time when Labour is in a strong bargaining position, and to repudiate and abandon all such "interference" at a time when Labour is comparatively weak'. A distinct tendency became noticeable for employers to utilize the low Trade Board rates against workers' organizations in negotiations or arbitration proceedings. Hallsworth concluded his survey in 1925 with this comment on what he termed a 'means of modifying the excesses of capitalism':

> To the extent that, first, the grosser forms of sweating have been eliminated and, second, their reinstitution has been prevented, a useful work has been done, and in doing it the Trade Boards have fulfilled part of the purpose they were intended to serve. But they have not up to the present, as the statistics clearly demonstrate, ensured, for ordinary time-workers at any rate, a minimum 'living' wage—that is, a wage adequate to procure the elementary necessities of a civilized life. (p. 62)

In 1936, Richardson could number only forty-seven trade boards in trades or branches of trades, covering over 1,000,000 workers, approximately 70 per cent of whom were women.

The Whitley Committee was set up, as the T.U.C./Labour Party pamphlet put it, partly because 'the feeling in favour of workers' control had so grown in the ranks of Labour that some verbal concession was necessary'. The Committee proposed that all industries be provided with machinery for joint discussion with employers of all questions affecting the workers, the exact constitution and scope of each Joint Council being determined by the two parties in the industry. The pamphlet again neatly summarizes the successful result of this manoeuvre: 'Labour, on the whole, welcomed the report; there was a section which really believed in a new dawn on the mountain tops, etc., a section which was thoroughly sceptical and would not touch the project, and a section which was also sceptical, but thought it might get something out of the situation'.

During the first four years of the scheme's operation (1918 to 1921 inclusive) seventy-three Joint Industrial Councils were formed, while in less organized industries thirty-three Interim Industrial Councils were set up, fourteen of which were soon reconstituted as J.I.C.s. The total number of workers covered was estimated at about 3.5 million. An indication of the activity of Whitley Councils on wages questions is seen in the fact that, between December 1919 and May 1920, forty-six national wage agreements were concluded by National Joint Industrial Councils. Richardson noted that a considerable number of J.I.C.s ceased to function, especially during the early years, and attributed this to 'wage conflicts, weakness of organization of employers and workpeople, and divergence of interests between different localities, between different sections of an industry and between large and small undertakings'. Labour's view, as expressed in the pamphlet, was the following:

> The basic fact, after all, is that whereas there was formerly, in some instances at least, a genuine desire to discuss matters frankly and amicably, there is now no such desire, for while the workers were then in a strong bargaining position, they are now much less powerful. Whitley Councils are therefore degenerating into standing negotiating committees which may indeed be of service but which cannot carry out the aims of those who enthusiastically supported Whitleyism in 1918–19.

Writing in 1938, Richardson numbered about fifty national Joint Industrial Councils, twenty of which had district or local joint bodies associated with them. The Labour Research Department described the Whitley experiment in 1923 as having been simply 'to stimulate the creation of central negotiating bodies in a number of the less organized industries'.

As described above, the inter-war record of achievement by the trade unions of formal bargaining arrangements at national and industry level is one of considerable unevenness. Its fluctuations reflect the trials of the movement during the 1920s and 1930s after the successes of 1909–20. The war-time boom in union membership had continued during the two post-war years. During 1919 the total membership leapt up from 6,664,000 to 8,081,000, and during 1920 there was a further increase to 8,493,000, fairly well distributed over the majority of industries and groups. The general labour group rose by a further quarter of a million to 1,353,000, while the building industry added about a quarter of a million, rising from 326,000 in 1918 to 572,000 in 1920. Increases of more than 150,000 in each case were recorded in the mining, metal, clerical and commercial, and general transport groups, while the groups organizing railway workers, the public administration services and agricultural workers showed in each case a rise of nearly 100,000. In 1921, however, the post-war demand for industrial goods broke and that one year wiped out practically the whole of the gains of 1919 and 1920. The total trade union membership fell from nearly 8.5 millions to 6,793,000, or only 129,000 above the total for 1918. The largest decrease occurred in the general labour group which fell by almost half a million, from 1,353,000 to 863,000. The miners, following the disaster of Black Friday in 1921 lost over 200,000 members, and five other groups—metal, building, railway, general transport, and clerical and commercial—each lost over 100,000 members during the year. This period of 1914–22, therefore, saw both the greatest expansion of trade union membership—from just over four million in 1914 to twice that in 1920—and also the heaviest loss of members that ever occurred in so short a time—over 2.5 millions in 1921–2.

The heavy set-backs in terms of union membership during these post-war years were accompanied by equally disastrous defeats over the maintenance of wages and conditions won during the war years. The pace-setters here, as in many instances in the future, were the miners. Negotiations between the unions and the mine owners were disrupted by the government's sudden announcement on 15 February that the war-time State control of the mines would end on 31 March 1921. The owners promptly announced their intention to enforce drastic reductions in wages and, while the Decontrol Bill was still before Parliament, lock-out notices were posted. The Triple Alliance of miners, railwaymen and transport workers at first stood solid, but on 'Black Friday', 15 April the latter two withdrew their support. By the end of June the miners were defeated and forced to accept the district basis for wages, though negotiated nationally, and an agreement under which wages fell rapidly to a point ranging from 20 to 40 per cent above the pre-war level. In 1923, the Labour Research Department described how this defeat marked the beginning of a general offensive by employers against the wages and conditions secured since the war:

The demand for wage reductions now spread rapidly from industry to industry, and the general fall in wage rates . . . began. Already, on April 19th, the shipyard workers, faced with serious unemployment, had accepted reductions. The engineers attempted to resist, but in July they were compelled to agree to similar terms. The building trade workers accepted reductions in May, and the seamen at the same time; the ships' cooks and stewards, who attempted to resist by means of a strike, being defeated in face of the surrender of the other sections. On June 4th the wages question led to a general lock-out in the cotton industry, but this was ended on the 24th by the acceptance of substantial reductions by the workers. In one industry after another wages came tumbling down.

The next eleven years, from 1923–33, witnessed the slow decline and stagnation of the movement: membership losses continued without a break from a total of 5,544,000 in 1924 to 4,392,000 in 1933. Beginning in 1934 a slow resurgence began with membership increasing by a few hundred thousand a year until the outbreak of the Second World War sparked off a new boom. Richard Hyman, in his account of the spectacular collapse of the Workers' Union in the early 1920s, provides this capsule summary of the decade:

> This disastrous record is largely explained by the drastic change in economic circumstances. At the end of 1920 the post-war boom suddenly collapsed, prices tumbled, and unemployment soared to unprecedented levels. Official returns showed 17.8 per cent of insured workers unemployed by the summer of 1921; for over a decade it was rare for the proportion out of work to fall below 10 per cent. The economic crisis led to a wholesale attack on workers' conditions, and in many areas of industry mass unemployment was accompanied by the disintegration of established bargaining procedures.

Unemployment reached new heights during the years of the worldwide depression beginning in 1929, and still amounted to more than one million workers at the outbreak of the Second World War.

The importance to this study of the above brief description of the weakness of the trade union movement and of workers *vis-à-vis* their employers lies in its providing the background for an understanding of how collective bargaining arrangements in industry operated in practice. The key point is to comprehend that the difficulties of organized labour constantly promoted the practice of undercutting wage rates and conditions of labour, despite the formal predominance of institutional arrangements. The existence of mass unemployment encouraged employers to decline to adhere to established standards, and forced workers into the position of continually defending their standards against the competition of others prepared to disregard them. The increasing futility of such attempts at self-defence is seen in the declining level of industrial militancy. Pelling points out that in the years 1934–9 the number of working days lost as a result of disputes only once exceeded two million, whereas between 1919 and 1926 it had never been less than seven million. It was this feature of the inter-war period—the contrast between the formal and actual systems of wage determination; the tendency of the latter to undermine the former—that became the battleground over which the struggle concerning the application and interpretation of the Fair Wages Resolution of 1909 was fought. The battle was between those who sought to utilize the Resolution to promote institutional arrangements to protect workers in these hard times, and those who, through a different interpretation, saw the Resolution as simply following contemporary developments—wage-cutting included. The progress of this struggle is described in the following chapters.[1]

NOTES

1. The above account is derived principally from the following sources:
—J. Henry Richardson, *Industrial Relations in Great Britain*, I.L.O., Studies and Reports, Series A (Industrial Relations), No. 36, Geneva, 1938; pp. 149–50, 102, 105, 110–32, 143, 132ff.
—Henry Pelling, *A History of British Trade Unionism*, 2nd ed., Macmillan, London, 1972; pp. 136, 119, 180, 210–11, 288–91.
—Henry Pelling, *Popular Politics and Society in Late Victorian Britain*, Macmillan, London, 1968; chapter 9, 'The Labour Unrest, 1911–1914'.
—A. Flanders, 'Collective Bargaining', in A. Flanders and H. A. Clegg (eds.), *Industrial Relations in Great Britain*, Blackwell, Oxford, 1954; pp. 275, 276.
—J. Hallsworth, *The Legal Minimum*, The Labour Publishing Company, London, 1925; pp. 23, 50, 9–10, 55–6, 62, 89–90.
—Alan G. B. Fisher, *Some Problems of Wages and Their Regulation in Great Britain Since 1918*, London, 1926; p. 193.
—The Garton Foundation, *Memorandum on the Industrial Situation After the War*, (revised edition), London, January 1919; p. 70.
—*The Workers' Register of Labour and Capital 1923*, prepared by the Labour Research Department, London, 1923; pp. 53,

112–13, 53–5, 37–8.
—John Child, *Industrial Relations in the British Printing Industry*, G. Allen & Unwin, London, 1967; pp. 226, 230, 268.
—A. Marsh, *Industrial Relations in Engineering*, Pergamon Press, 1965; pp. 213, 144–5.
—*Industrial Negotiations and Agreements*, pamphlet published by the Trades Union Congress and the Labour Party, London, 1923 (76 pp.).
—*Trade Boards and the Cave Report*, pamphlet published by the Trades Union Congress and the Labour Party, 1922 (23 pp.).
—Richard Hyman, *The Workers' Union*, Clarendon Press, Oxford, 1971; p. 129.
—Committee Paper No. 1 of the Committee on the Regulation of Road Transport Wages entitled: 'State Intervention in Industrial Relations', paras. 11–15, at pp. 5–6. Public Record Office, Files of the Ministry of Labour: LAB 10/72; I.R. 538/1934.
—Document entitled: 'Trades Boards—Memoranda—Extent to which Trade Unionism existed at the time of the passing of the Trade Boards Act; and its growth since operation of the Act, in Tailoring, Paper Box, Lace Finishing and Chain Trade Industries'. Public Record Office, Files of the Ministry of Labour: LAB 11/223 (1913).

8

Fair Wages Policy and Collective Bargaining:
1909–1922

In the years between the passage of the Fair Wages Resolution of 1909 and the outbreak of the First World War the problem of which wage rates were applicable to government contractors' employees appears to have continued along the well-worn path of uncertainty and confusion. The concept of encouraging certain collective institutional arrangements in industrial relations was continually put forward in the shape of the annual demand of the Trades Union Congress for the enforcement of trade union rates and conditions. Six months after the passage of the Resolution, in its annual meeting of 1909, the T.U.C. agreed to the resolution:

> That this Congress protests against the unnecessary delay of the Postmaster General in dealing with the complaint of the Amalgamated Society of Farriers against firms which do not pay the farriers in their employ the recognized Trade Union rate of wages and do not observe the recognized hours of the trade; and instructs the Parliamentary Committee to request the Government to strike off the list of Government contractors all firms which do not comply with the fair wage resolution adopted by the House of Commons.

The mover of the resolution complained that one firm of contractors for the government paid its employees wages between 6s. and 9s. per week below the London rate of wages and made them work six hours a week above the regulation time in the trade. The same Congress deplored the decision of the 1908 Committee declining to recognize trade union rates in all contracts, and this same resolution was reiterated the following year.

The departments' position during these years was consistently ambiguous. In an exchange in the House of Commons in 1911 a War

For notes see p. 156

Office representative stated flatly that, 'Our rule is to pay the district rate'. On a subsequent occasion, however, he revealed that what the War Office meant by this was by no means the trade union agreed rate, but rather 'the rates of wages paid by private employers for labour of the same class employed under analogous conditions in the districts in question'. Far from preventing wage competition, the department stated bluntly that, where 'the district rate is lower in one place than in another, we are not justified in departing from that information put before us'.[1] The trade unions made strenuous attempts to get the terms of the Fair Wages Resolution applied to the direct employees of the War Office. Following T.U.C. pressure, the War Office in 1912 issued a poster which substantially reproduced the 1909 Resolution and posted it in their factories. The problem of interpreting the terms of this notice, however, proved to be no less confusing that those involved in applying the Resolution to contractors. The obstinacy of government departments in refusing to require the payment of recognized rates by contractors was reinforced when it was sought to impose these rates on themselves—the attitudes of the Admiralty can only be described as feudal.

Cases arose where agreements were simply ignored as standards for compliance with the Resolution. In April 1913, an M.P. protested to the Office of Works over the award of a contract to a firm paying only 8d. and 8½d. to cabinet makers, 'while the rate of wages in London as per agreement between the master cabinet makers and the furnishing trade unions is 11½d. for the class of work named'. It was pointed out that four out of five London firms who had been required to tender for the work paid this trade union rate. Consequently, he demanded that 'steps be taken to omit those firms who do not comply with the signed agreement between employers and workmen's organizations, so that the Fair Wages Clause may be carried into effect'. The Office of Works rejected the complaint, stating that it was satisfied that the Fair Wages Clause was being observed. All this seemed to mean, however, was that 'if it is shown that an employer is a notoriously bad employer we should take that into consideration in deciding a contract'.[2] At the Trades Union Congress later that year, a resolution moved by the Sheet Metal Workers was carried unanimously protesting against the departments' 'ignoring the rates and conditions agreed to between employers and Trade Unions and arrogating to themselves the right of determining what should be accepted as fair rates and conditions, a policy adopted solely with the object of reintroducing on the list of contractors some of the very worst sweating firms'. In anticipation of future developments, that same Congress passed a resolution calling for the inclusion in the Fair Wages Clause of a 'provision that the terms and conditions of employment contained in agreements as between federated employers and workmen's unions be considered binding on all Government contractors'. The ambit of agreements setting the standards for contractors was thereby widened from single employer-union contracts to those made between federations.

Attempts at Administrative Reform: The Fair Wages Advisory Committee

These fundamental disagreements as to the meaning of the Resolution continued despite the administrative reforms which were carried out during these years—a striking contrast to the inaction following the first Fair Wages Resolution. After the passage of the new Resolution on 10 March 1909, the Treasury, on the 24 March, directed that a copy of the Resolution be transmitted to each contracting department, together with the suggestion:

> that you should act upon the Resolution, and also upon the administrative proposals mentioned in the Postmaster General's (Sydney Buxton) speech, namely (1) that contractors should keep records of the time worked by pieceworkers in cases where a comparison with time rates of wages is likely to be required; (2) that the Fair Wages Clauses of Contracts should, where it is considered necessary, be prominently exhibited on the Contractor's premises, for the information of the workpeople; (3) that, where practicable, the names and addresses of all firms obtaining Government contracts should be published in the 'Board of Trade Journal' or the 'Board of Trade Labour Gazette'; and (4) that there should be uniformity among Public Departments in the wording of all clauses dealing with the conditions of labour affecting the same trades.

The Treasury went on to suggest that the departments should make arrangements for the appointment of the Advisory Committee recommended by the 1908 Committee, and this committee, called the 'Fair Wages Advisory Committee' was duly appointed by the Treasury Minute of 22 June 1909.

On 3 September 1909, this departmental Committee submitted a six-page Memorandum of Recommendations to the various government departments dealing with contractors, who were concerned mainly with the implementation of the measures referred to in the Treasury letter quoted above. Some confusion is noticeable immediately in the first recommendation that 'it is desirable that in future, before any firm is admitted to a Department's list of contractors, to whom invitations to tender are sent, it should be notified of the exact terms of the Fair Wages Resolutions passed by the House of Commons on February 13th, 1891, and March 10th, 1909, and required to give an undertaking to comply therewith'. The contractors were to be circularized with copies of the *two* Resolutions, with an 'intimation' that they be strictly observed, and required to sign and return an undertaking to that effect. This undertaking by contractors: 'that we accept and will fully discharge the obligations which the Resolutions impose upon Government Contractors', evinced the failure by the Committee to appreciate or accept that a change had occurred in Fair Wages policy between the 1891 Resolution and that of 1909, and that the obligations imposed by the two were different, if not contradictory. When it came to the clauses to be inserted into the contracts themselves, the Committee recommended the insertion *only* of the Resolution of 1909.

Other uniform clauses recommended concerned the exhibition of a notice at the contractor's works regarding his Fair Wages obligations for the information of his workers. Another clause required the contractor to keep proper wage books and time sheets of employees working on the contract and to allow for their inspection by any officer authorized by the department. Notes prepared by the Committee for departmental use only and circulated in March 1911 explained that these inspections 'will be limited strictly to the time and wages books or sheets necessary for the settlement of any dispute that may arise, and that any figures that may be furnished to the departmental inspectors will be treated as solely for the confidential information of the Department'. The notes also made it clear that enforcement of the Fair Wages policy obligations on sub-contractors was the responsibility of the main contractor, and 'the departmental investigation of Sub-contractors' books, &c., will ordinarily take place only where the main contractor's efforts seem unlikely to lead to early settlement'. These clauses show that departmental enforcement policy was not to change from passive reliance on the complaint mechanism. Other clauses prohibiting home-work, and requiring the direct payment of wages 'not through a foreman, or others supervising, or taking part in, the operations on which the workers are engaged' were stated to be desirable in certain unorganized trades only: uniform clothing, caps, head-dresses, water-proofs, harness, saddlery, accoutrements, and tents. The departmental tendency towards the exercise of discretion is evinced in the Committee's opinion that, as regards all these clauses, including the 1909 Resolution: 'it is unnecessary to insert any of these conditions in contracts for collieries for the supply of coal'. Again, although accepting that there should be monthly publication of the contracts let, with the name and address of the contractor: 'The Committee are of opinion that as a general rule contracts exceeding £500 in value should be published at present and that each Department should exercise its own discretion in including contracts of less value, when special circumstances render such a course desirable'. They did recommend, however, that information regarding contracts of less than £500 be given to bona fide enquirers, without indicating how inquiries could be made about unpublished contracts.

A major deficiency was revealed in the uncertainty which reigned over the imposition of penalties on defaulting contractors. The 1909 Resolution obliged the contractor to comply 'under the penalty of a fine or otherwise'. Yet the Fair Wages Clause proposed by the Committee for inclusion in contracts omitted this phrase. Indeed, the Committee went on to say, in discussing the exhibition of a notice containing the Fair Wages Clause at the workplace, 'that in no case should any reference be made in the notice to any penalty clauses which may have been included in the contract'. The Committee did in fact propose a penalty clause in its Memorandum, as follows:

> Any infringement of the conditions specified in (clauses ———), if proved to the satisfaction of ——— (whereof a certificate under his hand shall be sufficient evidence), shall render the Contractor liable to pay by way of liquidated damages and not as a penalty the sum of £———, which may be recovered by ———. In addition thereto the Department may, upon any such infringement, whether of (clauses ———), or of the corresponding clauses in any other contract forthwith terminate this contract and any other existing contract between the Department and the Contractor, and may recover from the Contractor any loss resulting from such termination.

To this proposal, however, the Committee attached the following note:

> There are certain difficulties in regard to the infliction of penalties for breaches of the Fair Wages Clauses of contracts, and the Committee propose to seek the opinion of the Law Officers of the Crown on the question. In the meantime they give above a form of clause which was drawn up by high legal authority to deal with breaches of the Factory clause (prohibition of home-work), and they leave it to the discretion of each Department to determine whether it will adopt the clause in connection with the Factory clause or any of the remaining Fair Wages Clauses.

The request of the Committee for legal advice was transmitted to the Law Officers of both England and Scotland, and their replies amply justified the Committee's suspicions as to legal difficulties. The view stated by the English Law Officers was as follows:

> In our opinion it is not possible in the present state of the law to provide effectively for payment by the contractor of a sum of money for failure on his part to comply with the Fair Wages Clause.
>
> A breach of that clause by the contractor would not occasion any legal damage to the department concerned.
>
> Accordingly, any sum made payable in respect of such a breach must necessarily have been made payable with a view to secure the performance of the contract and not with a view to compensate the department for any damage sustained. It would therefore be a penalty in the strict sense of the term and irrecoverable at law.
>
> We are further of opinion that a sum of money made payable for breach of the other clauses referred to would equally be held to be a penalty and irrecoverable.
>
> On the other hand, it would, we think, be possible to provide that a percentage of the price should only become payable if the Fair Wages Clause and the other clauses were duly observed and performed.
>
> The insertion of such a provision might possibly occasion difficulties of a practical character, but, in our opinion, it is the only method valid in law by which to provide in effect for the payment of a sum of money for a breach of the various clauses referred to.
>
> A provision giving the department liberty to terminate the contract in the event of the Fair Wages Clause, or any of the other clauses, not being observed would, in our opinion, be valid and binding and we think that, in any view, such a provision should be inserted in the contracts.
>
> We also think that it will be necessary to insert a clause giving power to some specified person to decide the various matters mentioned in the Fair Wages Clause upon which the question whether the wages paid are fair, or not, depends and making the certificate of such a person conclusive upon the question of whether a breach of any of the clauses has been committed.

The Scottish Legal Officers' opinion was in full concurrence with that quoted above. It also adverted, however, to problems particular to the substance of the Fair Wages Resolution as drafted:

In regard to the Fair Wages Clause it is difficult to see what loss the department could suffer by the breach of the clause. We can suggest no other course than that proposed, namely, to insert the clause for what it is worth and trust to a forfeiture clause as a means of enforcing it. The difficulty of enforcing a forfeiture clause is obvious: On the one hand the forfeiture may be out of all proportion to the question in dispute, and might be very disadvantageous to the department; on the other hand if the right of the department to forfeit is contested who is to say what are the 'rates of wages, &c., commonly recognized,' or who are the 'good employers,' or whose practice is to be followed? What constitutes a district? What is the nearest district with corresponding industrial circumstances? And finally, what are the 'conditions of employment' which are to be taken into account?

The effect of this legal advice was to move the Fair Wages Advisory Committee to issue their Memorandum of Recommendations (No. 2) on 1 December 1910. In the light of the Law Officers' opinions, the Committee considered that it was 'unable to recommend that any attempt should be made in Government contracts to provide for the payment by the contractor of a sum of money for failure on his part to comply with any of the clauses . . . relating to labour conditions'. As to the only valid legal method suggested, that a percentage of the price should only become payable if the Fair Wages clauses were duly observed: 'in the opinion of the Committee it would not be practicable to insert a provision to this effect in the contracts'.

It light of these legal problems, since something had to be done to enforce the will of the House of Commons on Fair Wages policy, the departmental policy proposed by the Committee was summed up as follows: 'On the whole question of the Fair Wages Resolution the Committee incline to the view that reliance should be placed on administrative rather than legal action'. In their Memorandum the Committee went on to justify this policy with various arguments. The enforcement by legal process of any punishment for breach of the Fair Wages clauses was difficult, it said, because of 'the lack of legal precision which to some extent appears to be unavoidable in such clauses'. This could be circumvented 'if the clauses be regarded as a declaration of policy governing the Department in placing its orders or withdrawing its custom rather than as a precise statement of legal obligations to be enforced in the courts'. A policy of enforcement via the courts would, they thought, lead contractors not to accept the results of Departmental investigation. Such a policy would actually decrease opportunities of enforcement 'as the Departments would only

take legal action where they had a strong case'. Departmental administration would be more effective if the motivating factor was the spirit
of the Resolution rather than the mere letter of contract clauses, for
'the policy of the Departments will in that case the more readily
respond to public opinion'. Finally, the Committee expressly emphasized that the application of sanctions was in practice at the
discretion of the departments regardless of which policy of enforcement was adopted: 'speaking generally, it is the power to withdraw
its custom which ultimately gives the Department its authority in
dealing with contractors and this power of course depends on no
contract clause, and whether a cancellation clause is adopted or not
the hands of the contracting Department are free to apply administrative action varying according to the circumstances of the case from
a serious warning to a restriction of business or removal from the list'.

Having laid down the principles of the enforcement policy proposed
for departments, the Committee went on to consider the possibilities
left after the Law Officers' opinions were taken into account. These
consisted of a provision giving the department liberty to terminate the
contract in the event of breach of the Fair Wages Clause by the contractor, with a complementary clause giving power to some specified
person to decide upon disputes as to whether wages paid were fair,
etc. The Committee conceded that many existing contracts contained
powers of cancellation and prescribed persons to determine disputed
points. Nonetheless, the Committee preferred to emphasize the problems
surrounding the application of such clauses. It was asserted that where
the trade was unaccustomed to cancellation provisions 'it may be
difficult to persuade contractors that the clause will be equitably
administered and enforced only in cases of serious and flagrant breach'.
If the promise of an easy-going enforcement policy was not enough,
it was further pointed out that 'the termination of a contract may be
a punishment out of proportion to the offence, and may involve the
contractor in loss and subject the Department to grave inconvenience'.
To protect workers as required by the policy of Fair Wages, 'somewhat
complex provisions as to completion of work, assignment of benefit of
sub-contracts, return of Government materials, &c., might be necessary
in certain cases'. Finally, the very need for a cancellation clause was
dubious: 'The experience of the departments may possibly show that
in the great majority of trades there is little difficulty in making the
Resolution effective without (it)'. The Committee's preference for the
utmost in departmental discretion was again reiterated: 'The end in
view, viz., the enforcement of the Wages Clauses, is essential, but the
methods adopted to secure that end are best left to the discretion of
the Departments, according to their experience of whether existing

contract clauses and administrative methods are sufficient to secure the carrying out of the intentions of the House of Commons'. It is not surprising to find in the conclusion to the Memorandum that '*the Committee do not propose to recommend any definite form of clauses for general adoption*' (My italics). The 'essential' end of enforcement of the Fair Wages Resolution, already burdened by lack of definition and uncertainty, was left to the uncoordinated efforts of individual contracting departments. The most the Committee would do was to put forward two draft clauses on cancellation and dispute settlement, which were, as reiterated in Notes circulated for departmental use in March 1911, only 'suggestions in those cases where the Departments consider that additional contract provisions are necessary on the points in question'.

The Fair Wages Advisory Committee thus abjured a co-ordinating role in the enforcement of the Fair Wages policy by departments. It was, nevertheless, fairly active in the implementation of the policy during its first few years. Set up in June 1909, it met for the eighteenth time in August 1911, and had another fifteen meetings over the following thirty months. As was mentioned in chapter 1, the First World War put an end to this activity, and it led only a marginal existence after 1914. During its active years it issued a number of reports on wages matters—for example, in the hosiery trade in Leicester (1910), in the iron and steel works of South Wales and Monmouth (1911), and of printers in London (1913)—and took a number of initiatives: in March 1911 it proposed the extension of the Fair Wages policy to contracts not actually entered into by departments, but which required the expenditure of public money or other consideration granted by departments, or required departmental approval. Its influence was apparent, for instance, in a circular dated 2 September 1911 from the Secretary of the Local Government Board to local authorities adopting and recommending policies advocated by the Committee, suggesting that Fair Wages clauses should be introduced into all contracts involving expenditure of public money or other consideration granted by a government department or which required the approval of the department. It appears that the Committee did not limit its interest to Fair Wages matters but undertook extensive enquiries into questions affecting government contracts which had nothing to do with wages— witness a 26-page report of January 1911 on Fire Insurance of Government Property in the Hands of Contractors, undertaken for the Treasury on its request in December 1909.

Given the abdication of responsibility by the Fair Wages Advisory Committee, the problems of laissez-faire administration of the policy were not slow to reveal themselves. Indeed they had been evident during the Committee's active years. For example, in November 1910,

at the instance of Dr. Addison, M.P., the Post Office made an investigation at the works of Messrs. Priddy and Hale, Ltd., London, W.,
makers of packing boxes, etc., as to the wages paid by them under
Post Office contracts. The conclusion was formed that certain of their
workpeople were underpaid, and as the firm would not undertake to
grant an increase it was decided that they should not be invited to
tender again. The decision was not communicated to other government
departments. On 26 April 1911, Dr. Addison asked in the House of
Commons about wages paid by this same firm under contracts let by
the Local Government Board and the War Office. The upshot of the
affair was that the Office of Works and the Local Government Board
defended the contractor's rates of wages whilst the Post Office regarded
them as unsatisfactory. In another case, the Victoria Rubber Company
of Edinburgh holding Post Office contracts was shown in a report from
an investigating officer to be working some of their men for exceptionally long periods, ranging from 76 to 104 hours per week. The company
explained itself by referring to the necessity of the work being done
after ordinary work hours. So, in the words of the report: 'It was
decided not to pursue the matter, as no complaints had been received
from or on behalf of the men concerned, and the Department had no
direct hold over the firm under the conditions of contract' (12 October
1909). In May 1914, an official of the War Office responsible for
seeing that the Fair Wages Clause in Army contracts was carried out,
testified that upon complaint the department would satisfy itself,
'either that the recognized rate in the district is being paid or that it
is not being paid. In the latter case we take steps to see that it is paid.'
He did not specify what he meant by recognized rates.

That is not to say that implementation of the policy was totally
anarchic or unsuccessful. For instance, after some debate within the
department, the Post Office referred to the Fair Wages Advisory
Committee the question as to how far, if at all, the Department should
actually initiate investigation respecting the wages paid to people who
could only be regarded as very indirectly employed in relation to its
contracts (March 1911). The inclination of the department in one
case—a stoker in the employ of Messrs. Abbott, Anderson and Company,
contractors for waterproof garments had his wages raised from $4\frac{1}{2}$d.
to 6d. an hour as a result of representations made—was towards a
liberal interpretation of the policy: 'It is a part of the duty of the
Investigating Officer to inspect the works of firms who apply to be
placed on our list with the view of tendering for contracts; and such
an inspection can hardly be regarded as adequate unless the conditions of labour throughout the factory are ascertained'. Unfortunately,
it seemed that this thoroughness applied only to new contractors, and

not those already on the list: 'A contractor who observes all the conditions of his contract may nevertheless be a bad employer, but under an inspection limited strictly to the Post Office work he would be retained on our list unless complaint happened to be made by the workers themselves or by a Trade Union on their behalf' (December 1910). Nevertheless, in the period up to beginning of the First World War, the policy's occasional successes were far short of what might have been achieved by a vigorous lead from the Fair Wages Advisory Committee enforcing a clear set of standards through the adoption of collective agreements.

Departmental Attitudes During the War Years: 1914–1918

The outbreak of the First World War appears to have released many departmental inhibitions as regards the recognition of collective agreements. On the 13 April 1915, a deputation from the Parliamentary Committee of the T.U.C. complained to the Financial Secretary to the War Office that the Fair Wages Clause was being evaded by certain contractors to that Department. They were told that War Office officials had been seriously handicapped in investigating complaints through the great pressure in connection with the war, 'but that the officials in the Contracts Department were every bit as anxious as he was to make the firms follow, nor merely the letter, but the spirit, of the Fair Wages resolution'. Following the interview he was sent a copy of the Green Book, a schedule of prices agreed between the National Union of Boot and Shoe Operatives and the employers. His acknowledgment on receiving this document contrasts sharply with pre-war attitudes:

> Dear Mr. Bowerman, – Many thanks for your letter of April 16th. We already have a copy of the Green Book which you enclosed. As I indicated in my reply to the deputation, the Committee on Production have already advised us that the rates laid down in this book shall be those payable by Army boot contractors. We have lost no time in putting into operation the advice of the Committee, and all firms against whom complaints have been made in Great Britain, to whom this finding is considered to apply, have been required to give an assurance that they will pay in accordance therewith. We have written to this effect to over a dozen firms, and I expect you will find that Mr. Richards knows what we have done in this connection. As I said, if you make any complaints which can be substantiated, the firms concerned will find themselves in an awkward position. Yours, etc.

Despite these promises, however, complaints continued to arrive as to shoe manufacturers refusing to 'pay up to the conditions' of the agreements, principally because the War Office would not send the contractors copies of the agreement when letting out the contracts. And a discussion on a resolution at the 1915 Trades Union Congress referred to widespread arrangements in the printing industry and complained of the violations by contractors of, and refusals by departments to implement, provisions in agreements relating to equal pay for women workers.

The debate over utilizing collective bargaining agreements as standards for observance of the Fair Wages Resolution was suspended under war-time emergency conditions. As explained in a T.U.C. pamphlet of 1922, during the war the situation was such that the Resolution was disregarded, at first because of the national necessities, and later because government control of work done for the State led to the fixing of wages by arbitration or by mutual agreement. Even where strict governmental regulation of contractors' labour policies was not in force, the scarcity of labour, the growth of collective bargaining, and the general rise in wages resulted in such an accession of strength to the workers that the Fair Wages Clause had to be invoked in few cases.

This did not prevent certain trade unions from complaining bitterly of the attitudes of government departments in carrying out their responsibilities under the 1909 Resolution. At the Annual Congresses of 1916 and 1917, identical resolutions were carried: 'That this Congress strongly protests against the manner in which the Fair Wages Resolution of the House of Commons has been administered'. The fault was seen as resting 'mainly with the permanent officials of the Departments . . . they seem to be the real masters of the situation'. The speaker, a representative of the Tinplate and Sheet Metal Workers, who moved the composite resolution in both years, protested in 1917:

> The trouble is that the permanent officials of the Government Departments have no sympathy with the workers, and they place all sorts of difficulties in our way instead of helping us. . . . What is required is a strong Minister, who will tell the officials of his Department to carry out the Fair Wages Resolution in the letter and the spirit; and if they will not do so, then they should be sent about their business. We visited the Minister of Labour on this question some time back; and while we were there the officials wanted to know what were the Trade Union rates of wages and who would define them. Well, I say that when the employers and the employed have arrived at an agreed rate that should be sufficient for the Government.

The occasion referred to in this statement, a visit to the Minister of Labour by a deputation from the Parliamentary Committee of the T.U.C. on 17 July 1917, affords a good illustration of the inter-action between trade unions, the Fair Wages Advisory Committee and the contracting departments during this period.

The Parliamentary Committee submitted to the Minister the T.U.C. Resolution strongly protesting the administration of the Fair Wages Resolutions together with a number of proposals designed to ameliorate the situation. These included the long-standing demand that 'all Government Departments shall supply to all authorized Trade Unions a list of firms invited to tender'; that 'no firm proved to be paying less than the Trade Union rate of wages to all its employees in any of its establishments, or not observing the working conditions general in the trade or calling, or agreed on with employers in all its establishments, shall be allowed to tender'; that 'where the bona fides of any firm to be considered a fair firm be challenged, the onus shall rest upon the Government Department concerned to bring together the Trade Union and contractor's representatives to allow of both sides stating their case directly to the heads of such Department'; and that 'contractors shall furnish to the several Departments names and addresses of all sub-contractors, the same to be supplied to all authorized Trade Unions and published in the "Board of Trade Journal". Contractors failing to supply such information shall be struck off the list of firms allowed to tender.' In addition, the complaint was made that even when a contractor was found to be in breach of the Resolution, the penalty imposed was merely that for the remainder of the contract the employer was required to increase his wages to the fair rate.

Following the reiteration of the T.U.C. protest at the 1917 Annual Congress, the Minister of Labour submitted a memorandum to the Fair Wages Advisory Committee in December 1917 asking it to consider and report on the T.U.C.'s submissions. He specifically asked for the views of the Committee upon the proposition: 'that if an employer is found not to have paid in accordance with the Fair Wages Clause in the contract he should be liable to be sued in the civil Court by the workmen for the difference throughout the whole period of the contract between the rate paid and the rate shown to have been due, the latter rate being assumed to be the rate due to the workpeople as part of the Contract between the Contracting Departments and the employer, and between the employer and the workpeople'. The Committee's Report of 1 March 1918 responded in detail to each of the T.U.C.'s proposals. As to the request that unions be supplied with a list of firms invited to tender, the Committee conceded that even the pre-war practice of monthly publication of successful contractors had been discontinued 'owing to war conditions'. It asserted that it would be 'impracticable', as a result of the enormous clerical labour involved, and 'undesirable, for reasons of public policy that the names of firms tendering for a particular piece of work should be known to anyone but the officials of the Department concerned'. Nevertheless, it declared that the departments were prepared to answer inquiries as to whether a particular firm was on the approved list or held a contract, and expressed its support for 'the practice of some Departments to furnish annually to the Secretary of the Parliamentary Committee of the Trades Union Congress a list of firms to whom invitations to tender are issued by the Department, revisions of the list being notified at intervals'.

To the demand that government contractors be required to pay fair wages to all their employees, including those engaged in private work, the Committee responded:

> The Fair Wages Clause is, in terms, limited to the fulfilment of the particular contract, and the Departments have no definite status in regard to any work except that concerned with the contract in question, but in practice the Departments would view with severe disfavour firms who endeavoured to evade the spirit of the Fair Wages Clause by paying low rates on their private work. If in the course of investigating a complaint it appeared that the rates generally paid, or the conditions observed, on private work were so unsatisfactory as to constitute the firm a 'bad employer' this would be regarded as a ground for removing the firm from the list of contractors, although, of course, no action could be taken for breach of the Fair Wages Clause.

The Committee confirmed the departmental practice that a contractor listed among those approved was presumed to be 'fair' until there was 'reasonably conclusive evidence furnished to the contrary': 'It would appear to be the business of the Trade Unions themselves to call attention to "unfair" firms if any are found to be among the list of contractors'. Yet where such a challenge was made, the Committee refused to be drawn on the proposal that the departments should bring together the complainant Trade Union and the contractor complained of: 'The matter is one in regard to which practice must necessarily vary according to the particular circumstances of each case, and for this reason the Committee feel unable to recommend any definite instruction to the Departments'.

The Committee regarded the T.U.C.'s proposal for the publication of information relating to sub-contractors as raising difficult questions of definition. Where it was known that important portions of the contract would be sub-contracted by the main contractor, there was no difficulty. But beyond this, it would be impracticable to frame a satisfactory definition of 'sub-contract', for: 'there is no logical ground for limiting the proposal to sub-contractors in the first degree; the same principle would apply to the sub-contractors of those sub-contractors, and so on indefinitely'. The Committee referred to the main contractor's duty to enforce observance of the Fair Wages Clause by sub-contractors, and concluded that it was, therefore 'not considered possible to adopt this proposal as a general obligation'.

Finally, the Committee considered the suggestion that employers found not to have paid in accordance with the Fair Wages Clause should be liable to be sued by the workers for the amount underpaid during the whole contract period. They concluded that they were 'unable to recommend this as a practicable proposal'. They pointed out that it would require a method of determining approved rates, probably by a special tribunal. They emphasized the difficulty of making such determinations in light of the extremely vague terms of the Fair Wages Clause—invoking the opinion of the Scottish Legal Officers quoted above. The departments' self-confidence in their ability to detect and exclude employers paying 'unfair' rates seemed to evaporate at the prospect of a judicial tribunal which might be used to challenge their view. They raised with alarm the prospect that a tribunal might decide upon a higher rate than that fixed by a department: 'which might encourage workmen to be dissatisfied with other decisions of the Department and to take every case they could to the courts; and it might also tend to increase the prices in tenders. Again, different courts might give different decisions, and so embarrass the Department in its dealings with employers.' The Committee asserted that in practice the departments did secure payment of arrears dating from the date of complaint, which did not seem to them to be unfair, since 'the onus of raising a complaint of unfair rates seems to rest upon the worker'. The only suggestion the Committee would propose was that where a contractor was debarred for breach of the Fair Wages Clause: 'restitution of back wages due to workpeople on the particular contract concerned could be made one of the conditions of reinstatement on the list of contractors'.

The Fair Wages Advisory Committee's defensive refutation of the T.U.C.'s proposals was aimed at retaining to the fullest extent possible the ability of individual departments to independently administer the Fair Wages policy. Being composed exclusively of departmental representatives, the Committee reflected the disparate policies of the departments and struggled to balance the unrelieved negativism of the majority with the enlightened attitudes of a few. The conflict within the Committee emerged openly after its report reached the Minister of Labour. After considering it, he concluded that given the abnormal pressure of work on departments, it was not necessary to adopt the T.U.C.'s suggestions as a whole. Nonetheless, he conceded that there were good reasons for adopting that part of the T.U.C. Resolution relating to 'fair' wages on private work of contractors. To the Committee's pleas that the departments were limited in this respect by the terms of the Resolution itself he stated: 'It appears desirable that the position of the Contracting Departments should be strengthened in this respect and that it should be an instruction to them that firms should be removed from the list of approved contractors if they have been shown not to be "fair" employers in regard to both their Government work and their private work'. In a memorandum of 6 June 1918, he proposed to put forward to the War Cabinet a suggested amendment to the Fair Wages Resolution so as to ensure this result. The proposed amendment read as follows:

> that, in the opinion of the House, with a view to carrying out the objects of the Fair Wages Resolution of the House of Commons of 10th March 1909, the Government Contracting Departments should exclude from the list of approved contractors firms which have been shown to the satisfaction of the Departments concerned not to observe the principles of the Resolution as regards rates of wages or hours of labour in respect of either Government work or private work.

The War Cabinet had the Minister's proposal before it at its meeting of 8 July 1918 and referred it to the Committee on Home Affairs, which considered it on 1 August 1918. The deliberations of the Committee and the responses of the departments are of interest for the light they cast on the attitudes towards the Fair Wages policy during this period. A memorandum by Lord Milner, Secretary of State for War, unequivocally opposed the amendment proposed:

> This would be a definite extension of the policy hitherto followed by the War Department, which has not gone further as regards private work than (a) to ascertain, as far as possible, before placing a firm on the list, that its labour conditions were generally satisfactory and (b) in the case of a firm already on the list, to take disciplinary action, by removal or suspension, where it appeared that the amount paid or hours worked on private work were such as to amount practically to 'sweating' or to constitute the firm a 'notoriously bad employer'.

The Secretary of State invoked the aid of Sydney Buxton who in introducing the 1909 Resolution had expressly restricted its application to contract work. He emphasized that the Fair Wages Advisory Committee had not recommended any change in policy. As to the Labour Minister's statement as to the desirability of strengthening the position of the contracting departments, this was specifically denied:

> there is no evidence that there is any general desire on the part of Contracting Departments for such an extension of the scope of the Fair Wages Resolution. Certainly, so far as the War Office is concerned, nothing has occurred to suggest that the proposed change is necessary or desirable, or that the present practice has encouraged the existence of any serious or widespread abuses.

Commenting on Lord Milner's memorandum, the Secretary of the Fair Wages Advisory Committee observed that it 'appears somewhat to exaggerate the effect which the adoption of the proposed amendment to the Fair Wages Clause would have upon the Contracting Departments'. He hastened to reassure in the following words:

> The Departments are not called upon themselves to take the initiative any more than they do at present in securing that firms pay fair rates upon their private work. The amendment merely provides that the Departments shall exclude from the list of private contractors firms who 'have been shown to the satisfaction of the Departments concerned not to observe the principles of the Resolution'.

To Lord Milner, however, the amendment posed a 'serious danger' which might 'prejudicially affect the execution of Government contracts'. This was not because the department's contractors' labour conditions on their private work were unsatisfactory, but 'because they prefer not to expose themselves to the liability of having their whole business and factory arrangements investigated by a Government enquiry whenever a disaffected workman chooses to lodge a complaint'. To the argument that this process of complaint and investigation was precisely that envisaged and currently used in enforcing the Fair Wages policy, he replied:

> but it is one thing for a Department to have a policy of striking off its list at its own discretion a firm which is shown to be definitely 'bad' on its private work; it is quite another for the Department to place all the firms on its list in the position of being liable to be arraigned at any moment on the charge of

failing in some particular respect to observe the standard district conditions on their private work, and to bind itself to black-list any firm against whom such a charge is held to have been proved.

The War Department conceded, without a hint of embarrassment, that its enforcement of the Fair Wages policy would differ substantially from that of an independent agency. It spoke with horror of how an independent tribunal adjudicating on complaints might 'be a source of considerable embarrassment' if its decisions led to the black-listing of 'important, and perhaps indispensable, contractors'. G. R. Askwith, a member of the Fair Wages Advisory Committee wryly observed that this view: 'is not very complimentary to the administration of the Fair Wages Advisory Committee to whom it would fall, without any new tribunal'. But even he admitted that: 'The Fair Wages Clause has been scarcely used during the war. If an amendment meant it would be, and that all awards would apply to private work, although in practice they largely do, the obligation for it so to apply might be difficult'. To these apprehensions, the Secretary of the Committee replied reassuringly:

> the advantage of the word 'principles' in the proposed amendment is that that term leaves to the Government Departments concerned as much latitude as is possible consistently with the object of the amendment. The term 'obligation' (the word which is used in the present Fair Wages Resolution) cannot very well be used in regard to the private work since there can be no obligations except under specific contracts.

He reiterated Askwith's point that in practice the same rates were likely to be paid by contractors on government and private work, otherwise recruitment for the latter was rendered impossible.

The Minister of Reconstruction and the Postmaster-General took directly conflicting views on the proposed amendment. In a memorandum of 4 July 1918, the former came out strongly in favour of the proposal and urged its adoption by the War Cabinet: 'I feel that Contracting Departments of State indirectly employing labour through the placing of Government orders are placed in a position of peculiar responsibility, as it is generally recognized that the Government should be a model employer'. To the contrary, in a memorandum of 9 July 1918, the Postmaster-General argued that adoption of the proposal 'will have very disastrous results for the Government and the taxpayer': 'The result of the Fair Wages Resolution is that the contractor, as a rule, pays more than the market price for labour. If—when the economic world becomes normal some years after the war—a firm becomes a Government contractor, he will either be shut out from other markets on account of his high cost of production as compared with his competitor, who does no Government work and only pays the market price for labour, or be forced not to undertake any Government work.' Some twenty-seven years after its introduction, the Fair Wages policy was still under fundamental challenge.

An unusually enlightened approach was evinced by the First Commissioner of Works, Sir Alfred Mond. In a memorandum of 9 July 1918 he described the proposed amendment as essential if the spirit of the recent Whitley Report was to prevail: 'Neither the original Resolution nor the proposed amendment sets a high standard but merely a reasonable one'. He expressed himself to be totally dissatisfied with the existing policy: 'I can state from personal experience since I took Office that the Fair Wages Resolution as it stands at present is difficult to administer and leads to endless disputes with the Unions ... it is a case of recognizing frankly that a grave defect exists in a formal Resolution of the House of Commons which does not express what most of its members undoubtedly intended it to mean at the time'. His own view was that 'fair' rates were 'only such rates as have been agreed upon between representative Associations of Masters and Men, in essence the recognized Trade Union rate'. He concluded:

> I have found the whole question of this Resolution most unsatisfactory, leading to distrust and disputes, and compelling Government Departments to go on dealing with firms whose general rate of wages is anything but fair on their own work. It is high time that the Government became a 'Model Employer' leading private enterprise, rather than a laggard timidly following behind progressive private capitalists.

The Parliamentary Secretary to the Ministry of Munitions, headed by Winston Churchill, objected to the proposed amendment on grounds specific to the war situation: that the proposal would either cause contractors to withdraw from war work or raise their prices to compensate themselves for their increased wage costs; that it would remove the inducement to labour to work in the higher-paid munitions industries; that these higher rates were to compensate for labour's loss of the right to strike and freedom of movement in those industries: 'Labour engaged on private work makes no such sacrifices, and I see no justification for conferring on such labour the privileges of munition workers without their liabilities'. In a note commenting on this memorandum, G. R. Askwith refuted the 'assumption that employers have found it possible to give advances to their workpeople upon munitions work and to withhold the advances from those on private work. I know of no evidence which supports such an assumption.' The Ministry again revived the old argument that: 'It might be necessary for the State to face these disadvantages if labour engaged on private work had any sufficient grievance to make the change necessary on grounds of policy, but in fact, it is difficult to establish any such grievance'. To which Askwith again replied reassuringly that the amendment proposed:

> does not contemplate that the Government Departments should themselves take the initiative in seeing that their contractors pay 'fair' rates on their private work. Action by the Departments will be necessary only in cases where the Trade Unions or the representatives of the workpeople put forward a bona fide complaint with sufficient evidence to warrant an enquiry being made.

The Committee on Home Affairs met on 1 August 1918 to consider the Ministry of Labour's proposals and had in front of them the above memoranda. The Ministry of Labour pointed to the 'good deal of irritation among the workmen and a growing pressure from the Trade Union leaders in favour of an obligation being legally put upon such (government) firms to observe fair conditions in their private contracts'. He was prepared to put off the amendment until the war was over: 'but, inasmuch as he was advised that the Trade Unions, taking advantage of war conditions, might seek to force the Government's hand, would it not be advisable to anticipate such pressure?' The representatives of the Post Office, the War Office, the Admiralty and the Ministry of Munitions all reiterated their opposition. A representative of the India Office reported that complaints to his department arose 'not from differences in rates paid to Government and private work, but because it was alleged that the particular firm did not pay the district rate'. Sir Alfred Mond repeated that at the Office of Works: 'they were constantly hampered because they had no legal power of ascertaining what rates were being paid on private work. They had no power of investigation, and could only resort to moral persuasion, which was very unsatisfactory.' In conclusion: 'The Committee were generally agreed that, while the proposal of the Ministry of Labour was in itself desirable, nothing ought to be done at present which might tend to send up the cost of Government contracts'. The Minister of Labour undertook to consider the matter further.

In an interesting post-mortem note, the Controller at the Ministry of Food submitted a memorandum on the proposed amendment dated 13 August 1918. Declaring himself in favour of the proposal, J. R. Clynes suggested the setting up a tribunal to secure uniformity where conflicts occurred between departmental determinations of fair rates or fair firms. He proposed that the Ministry of Labour was the 'natural authority' to settle such disputes. An anonymous memorandum written subsequently firmly suppressed any such initiative. Commenting on Clynes' proposal, it stated:

> Apart from the fact that there is already in existence the Fair Wages Advisory Committee, to which reference can be made by any of the departments if they are in doubt as to the course they should pursue, there is a more important point, that it is undesirable that the authority of the individual contracting departments over their contractors should in any way be weakened by the transfer to an outside body of the power conferred upon the departments by the Fair Wages clause.

Not until after the Second World War was it to prove possible to release the grip of the contracting departments on the Fair Wages policy. Having been ceded administrative control in 1891, they successfully resisted every attempt to wrest it from them.

Anti-Fair Wages Policy: Government Contracts as an Instrument of Curbing Labour's Post-War Power

The end of the First World War saw labour in a very powerful position and the ruling class correspondingly worried. A letter in the archives of the Department of Employment, dated 4 October 1918 from Stephenson Kent to the Minister of Labour warned him that:

> without some pronouncement that will go far to reassure labour that there is no danger of peace bringing in its train the old pre-war conditions against certain of which labour has for so long struggled, we must, I think, anticipate labour troubles, not only of a more complex but perhaps of a more revolutionary character than any hitherto experienced. In my view labour unrest in this country at the present moment is more acute and more dangerous than at any period of the war.

A Paper on Measures for Dealing with Unrest, also dated 4 October 1918 declares that: 'The authority of the Government, the provisions of the Munitions of War Act, and perhaps above all the authority of the official Trade Union organizations, are being increasingly flouted by the extreme Shop Steward movement, the rank and file, and by the pacifist, defeatist, and all the other groups of malcontents'. The paper urges the Government to make a declaration at the earliest possible moment 'announcing clearly their intention unswervingly to support the accredited leaders of Trade Unions and to assist with all their power in maintaining their authority within their organizations'. Additionally:

> the Government should take their courage in their hands and tell the Trade Unions that they no longer intend to tolerate a recurrence of the unconstitutional strikes from which we have suffered in the past; that the whole forces at the disposal of the State will be brought into action to end this lawlessness. The Military Service Acts, the Defence of the Realm Regulations, and what other powers may be thought necessary will be used to the utmost.

In addition to such draconian proposals, other more modest ways of dealing with labour's demands were suggested. Unavoidably, because of government involvement in war production, the use of pressure through its contracting policies was considered. In a memorandum on Wages in Munitions Industries, dated 6 July 1918, by Gordon Campbell, a paragraph headed 'Dangers of the Position' spells out the possibilities:

> The present chaos in the wages position involves a tremendous and increasing strain on the financial resources of the country. If not dealt with promptly it may have disastrous consequences. Labour still inclines to regard extravagant wages, extravagant in relation to the value of output given, and to the national income, as the fortunate exception. But the exception is becoming so rapidly the rule that in a short time munitions work will only be produced at a cost no nation could afford. The discipline of labour is deteriorating while its economic reserves are expanding, and it is falling into an attitude of doubtful value in the prosecution of the war. Administrative devices can only check these tendencies. Employers and Trade Unions are becoming partners in a conspiracy of profiteering against the State. *The chief prospect of controlling the situation lies in a rigid limitation of the amount of money which employers can obtain from the State.* (My italics.)

The memorandum goes on to prescribe measures necessary to achieve this end, in particular: (para. 4)

> *Contracts in a form where the contractor's profit depends to any substantial degree on the wages paid must be stopped.* No contract on the cost and percentage basis should in future be placed without requiring from the contractor a statement as to the wages he proposes to pay to each grade of labour employed on it. These wages should

then be submitted to the Labour Department for approval; once approved the labour costs on which he is to be paid profit should be reckoned only on these rates of wages. (para. 4) (Italics in text.)

The author described in detail how contractors exploited the machinery which imposed compulsory wage increases on them, via Orders and Awards, to inflate their wages costs. They were entitled to automatic reimbursement of these compulsory extra wages costs, and contractors would use the Awards as the reason for increasing these costs more than was actually warranted. Accordingly, the memorandum stated that '*contractors should never receive profit on compulsory wage advances*' (italics in text). This memorandum exposes the willingness of departmental officials to invoke measures of control to restrict wage increases which were never considered acceptable when the Fair Wages policy was introduced to safeguard them.

Despite these ambitious proposals, a subsequent memorandum by the same official, dated 3 October 1918, on 'The Administration of Wages in the Munition Industries', concluded that departmental powers to regulate wages and restrict increases were inadequate. The method of control via contracts could not withstand the pressures of increased bargaining power of labour:

> The question whether wages could be regulated through contract prices and conditions has been carefully examined. It is clear, however, that so many factors enter into the question of what each firm could afford to pay in wages on contracts placed at a standard price and that the allocation of contracts on any rigid basis will be so difficult while the needs of the Army are constantly varying, as to make it impossible to maintain control over wages by such means. Such stipulations in a contract as that standard wages only should be paid in its execution are useless where standards are in a state of flux. In short, regulation of wages through contracts is a method too clumsy, dilatory, and indirect to be at all effective. . . . Contract stipulations can only be used as auxiliary to other means for stabilizing wages. A very great deal could however be done by a system of allocation of contracts which took closer regard of wages and other labour conditions in particular manpower employed in relation to contracts to be placed than has hitherto been attained.
>
> Without clear principles generally accepted and loyally adhered to by the parties concerned, departmental control of wages will always be evaded by interested persons. It is impossible to have an official watching the wages paid in each establishment on

munitions work. Yet the State cannot give up control in a central-
ized form. In effect wages on munitions work are now paid by the
State which is the real employer and private firms cannot be left
to settle with their workpeople what amount of the State's money
the latter shall receive. Employers and workpeople must recognize
that in this matter they are trustees for the nation, the former
particularly in their dealings with Supply Departments. Supply
Departments must take part in the regulation of wages for wages
in their relation to contract prices are an integral part of supply.
Labour on munitions work, just as material, has under war
conditions a market price and just as the prices of material have
had in many cases to be fixed, it is inevitable that, if stability is
to be maintained, the war prices of labour should also be fixed.
Without stability there will be incessant labour unrest. (paras. 9
and 10)

The influence of these considerations on contracting departments is
indicated by a question asked in the House of Commons in 1920:

Mr. Doyle asked the Prime Minister whether, in cases where contractors to Government Departments were compelled to grant
increases of wages to their workers by Statutory Rules and Orders
made subsequently to the date or dates when the contracts were
entered into, by the Minister of Munitions acting in pursuance of
the Munitions of War Acts, the amount of the increased manufacturing charges resulting therefrom is allowed and paid by the
Government to the contractors in addition to the contract price,
and if not what allowance, if any, is made; and whether, in
regard to claims for such allowances, increases of wages paid in
conformity with such Orders are regarded as in the same category
as *increases of wages granted as a result of agreements between representatives
of employers and representatives of workers*?[3] (My italics.)

In the response to the first part of the question relating to Statutory
Rules and Orders increasing wages of contractors' employees, contracts
placed prior to the Armistice were divided into three categories: the
first two contained those where explicit provision was made throwing
the risk of such increases either on the Government, which became
obliged to increase the contract price, or the contractor, who bore the
loss accompanying the risk. Where no explicit provision was made,
the reply stated: 'It is the practice to grant ex gratia on application
such additional sums . . . as shall allow a contractor a reasonable
profit'. In sharp contrast to this charitable attitude with regard to
official increases, where these were the result of collective bargaining

arrangements: 'The answer to the last part of the question is generally in the negative, but the matter is one that depends upon the terms of the particular contract'. Where no express provision determined the question, therefore, the government was refusing to support collective bargaining arrangements which increased wages. Departmental recognition was reserved exclusively for the emergency, and thus temporary, institutional arrangements. Departments were not concerned that contractors should enter into voluntary agreements with their employees—quite the contrary. In circumstances where these led to wage increases, they were to be actively discouraged. But the end of the post-war boom in 1921 and the beginning of continuous high rates of unemployment led to the dismantling of the institutional forms of protection. The departments did not seek to ensure that voluntary arrangements replaced them. Already in November and December of 1920, complaints of breach of the Fair Wages Resolution appeared in Parliament.[4] They heralded the consequences of this failure.[5]

NOTES

1. Parl. Deb., H. of C. (Fifth Series); 15 March 1911, vol. XXII, col. 2335; 27 March 1911, vol. XXIII, col. 1091.

2. Parl. Deb., H. or C. (Fifth Series); 29 April 1913, vol. LII, cols. 983–4.

3. Parl. Deb., H. of C. (Fifth Series); 28 June 1920, vol. 131, cols. 33–4.

4. See Parl. Deb., H. of C. (Fifth Series); 8 November 1920, vol. 134, cols. 848–9; 13 December 1920, vol. 136, cols. 61–2; and see the complaint lodged with the Admiralty by the National Union of Gold, Silver and Allied Trades that certain silversmiths' contractors 'declined to be governed by the agreements made between the associations of employers and employees covering the industry in the Sheffield district'. Parl. Deb., H. of C. (Fifth Series); 10 November 1921, vol. 148, cols. 644–5.

5. The above account is principally derived from the following sources:
—E. Colston Shepherd, *The Fixing of Wages in Government Employment*, London, 1923.
—Report of the 42nd Annual Trades Union Congress, Ipswich, 1909, pp. 158–9.
—Fifth Quarterly Report of the Trades Union Congress Parliamentary Committee, March 1910, at p. 48.

—Report of the 46th Annual Trades Union Congress, Manchester, 1913, pp. 216; 218.
—Report of the 47th Annual Trades Union Congress, Bristol, 1915, pp. 205–7; 394–5.
—Report of the 48th Annual Trades Union Congress, Birmingham, 1916, pp. 335–7.
—Report of the 49th Annual Trades Union Congress, Blackpool, 1917, pp. 244–5.
—*The Fair Wages Clause*, pamphlet issued by the T.U.C., 1922. (15 pp.)
—Minutes of Evidence taken before the Select Committee on Estimates, House of Commons Papers of 1914, No. 429 (14 May 1914), at Q. 2579.
—Papers of the Fair Wages Advisory Committee, Department of Employment Library, Box GP.331.215:
—Papers Relating to Inquiry Relative to Wages in the Hosiery Trade in Leicester and Neighbourhood: (A) Report of Special Inquiry (9 August 1910) (8 pp.); (B) Letter and Enclosures from the War Office Referring the Matter to the Committee (7 August 1910) (2 pp.).
—Report: Wages in the Hosiery Trade

in Leicester and District, with Special Reference to Army Contracts (1 December 1910) (2 pp.).
—Report: Fire Insurance of Government Property in the Hands of Contractors (30 January 1911) (26 pp.).
—Memorandum of Recommendations (3 September 1909) (6 pp.).
—Opinion of the Law Officers on the Enforcement of Fair Wages Clauses in Government Contracts (12 May 1910) (8 pp.).
—Memorandum of Recommendations (No. 2) (1 December 1910) (3 pp.).
—Notes on Fair Wages Clauses, for Departmental Use Only (March 1911) (1 p.).
—Coordination Among Departments in Dealing with Contractors (12 June 1911) (2 pp.).
—Scope of Fair Wages Clauses (31 March 1911) (5 pp.).
—Report of Investigators: Report on Wages in the Iron and Steel Works of South Wales and Monmouth (6 December 1911) (24 pp.).
—Wages of Printers, London (December 1913) (19 pp.).
—Record of Minutes of Evidence taken on May 1, 1914; from representatives of the National Union of Bookbinders and Machine Rulers (20+pp.).
—Department of Employment Library: Report of Joint Admiralty and War Office Enquiry into Complaints of Infringement of the Fair Wages Clause in Admiralty and War Office Tinware Contracts (29 December 1910) (47 pp.).
—Department of Employment Library: Circular, dated 2 September 1911, from Secretary of the Local Government Board to Local Authorities (also papers relating to Clause recommended by the Fair Wages Advisory Committee; and other Committee proposals on Semi-Government Contracts).
—Department of Employment Library, Folder on Stabilisation of Wages, File No. 331.2, Box GP.331.18–331.2:
—Letter from Stephenson Kent, Council Member 'L', dated 4 October 1918 to Minister of Labour.

—Paper on Measures for Dealing with Unrest, dated 4 October 1918.
—Memorandum by Gordon Campbell, dated 3 October 1918, on The Administration of Wages in the Munition Industries (11 pp.).
—Gordon Campbell, Memo on Wages in Munitions Industries, dated 6 July 1918 (2 pp.).
—Large File containing papers in Department of Employment Library: Fair Wages Advisory Committee: Report on Certain Questions submitted by the Minister of Labour for the consideration of the Fair Wages Advisory Committee (4 pp.) (1 March 1918). Folder includes:
—Paper G.T. 4805: Memo to War Cabinet from Minister of Labour, dated 10 June 1918. (1 p.).
—Paper G.T. 4998: Memo by Lord Milner, Secretary of State for War, dated 29 June 1918 (2 pp.).
—Hand-written note from G. R. Askwith to H. J. Wilson, Secretary of the Fair Wages Advisory Committee, dated 10 July 1918.
—Reply by H. J. Wilson to G. R. Askwith, re Milner's memo, dated 16 July 1918.
—Paper G.T. 5023: Note by Minister of Reconstruction, C. Addison, dated 4 July 1918.
—Paper G.T. 4805: Memo by First Commissioner of Works, Sir Alfred Mond, dated 9 July 1918.
—Paper G.T. 5078: Memo by the Postmaster - General, Albert H. Illingworth, dated 9 July 1918.
—Paper G.T. 5201: Memo by Parliamentary Secretary to Ministry of Munitions, F. Kellaway, dated 22 July 1918.
—Reply to Memo from Ministry of Munitions by G. R. Askwith, dated 31 July 1918.
—Extract from Minutes of Meeting of the Committee on Home Affairs, held 1 August 1918.
—Memo by the Food Controller, J. R. Clynes, dated 13 August 1918.
—Anonymous Memo on Food Controller's proposal.

9

The Continuing Conflict: 1922–1931

A definitive statement of the conflict inherent in the view of the nature of the Fair Wages Resolution held by the trade union movement on the one hand and the government departments on the other was contained in a pamphlet published by the Trades Union Congress in 1922:

> In one respect the progress made during the war and post-war periods should have simplified the administration of the Fair Wages Clause and put an end to former troubles, for there is now a much higher degree of organization among the workers concerned while collective agreements are more numerous and more important. There should therefore be less dispute about recognized rates in these cases. It seems obvious that if in any trade employers and workers have agreed upon rates and conditions either by national or by district agreement, no dispute need occur; the agreed rate and conditions should be observed by the Government Departments and by contractors. Experience has shown that this is not so. The Departments have in a number of cases refused to recognize the rates which have been agreed upon by Trade Unions and Employers' Associations. (pp. 7–9.)

To illustrate their point, the T.U.C. pointed to the building industry, the arrangements of which were described briefly in chapter 7. The National Wages and Conditions Council divided the country into ten areas, each having its own rates for various classes of labour. These rates, however, were not being paid in all cases by contractors under the War Office and the Board of Works. In some districts groups of employers had been formed separately from, and in some ways antagonistic to, the national organization. These isolated groups paid wages which were lower than those recognized by the Council's

For notes see p. 166

national agreements. The Departments, however, accepted these lower rates as conforming to the requirements of the Fair Wages Clause. A chart was presented in the pamphlet to indicate the scale of the difference between the rates 'recognized' by the War Office, and those 'recognized' by the trade unions and employers; these are shown in Table 3.

TABLE 3

		Rate paid per hour	Area rate (national agreement) per hour
Aldershot	Painters	1s. 3½d. and 1s. 2½d.	1s. 5½d.
	Labourers	1s. 1d.	1s. 2½d.
	Brush Hands	1s. 2½d.	—
Bury St. Edmunds	Painters	1s. 4½d.	1s. 6½d.
	Labourers	1s. 2d.	1s. 2½d.
Devizes	Painters	1s. 5½d.	1s. 7d.
	Labourers	1s. 3½d.	1s. 3d.
Sheerness	Painters	1s. 6½d.	1s. 7½d.
	Labourers	1s. 3½d.	—
Salisbury	Painters and Grainers	1s. 6d.	1s. 7d.
	Painters	1s. 5d.	—
	Labourers	1s. 3d.	—
Warminster	Painters	1s. 5d.	1s. 8½d.
	Labourers	1s. 3d.	1s. 4d.

The pamphlet continued the argument as follows:

> The Departments contend that they are not bound by the wording of the Fair Wages Clause to pay rates which have been nationally agreed, but only the rates which prevail in the district. The resolution is quite explicit, however; the contractor is bound to pay 'rates of wages ... not less favourable than those commonly recognized by employers and trade societies'. Even if a local group has secured the agreement of its operatives to pay a lower rate this cannot be said to be the rate recognized by 'employers and trade societies' so long as there is an agreement between a national association of employers and a Trade Union to pay a higher rate in the district. ... If the official view is allowed to stand it will mean that the Departments will be able to define a district as they please and to accept the rate paid by a bare majority of employers (even though they may employ a minority

of operatives in the district) notwithstanding any national agreements between Trade Unions and Employers' Associations which would give a higher rate.

Although maintaining that their interpretation of the Resolution was the only valid one, the T.U.C. was prepared to suggest an amendment with a view to avoiding such different interpretations in the future. They proposed to amend the appropriate part of the Clause so as to lay down the following standards: 'not less favourable than those laid down in collective agreements concluded by national associations of employers and workers, or, where such do not exist, than those commonly recognized, etc.' The Annual Trades Union Congress held in Southport in September 1922 endorsed this view when the mover of the 'hardy annual' resolution condemning the administration of the Fair Wages Resolution accepted an amendment standing in the name of the House and Ship Painters so that the amended resolution read:

> That this Congress strongly protests against the manner in which the Fair Wages Resolution of the House of Commons has been administered, both in respect to contracts accepted and direct employment by Government Departments, and instructs the Parliamentary Committee to endeavour to get the following conditions carried out by all Government Departments:—...
> (2) That no firm proved to be paying less than the Trade Union rate of wages *as agreed to on a national basis in any industry* to all its employés in any of its establishments, or not observing the working conditions general in the trade or calling, or agreed on with employers in all its establishments, shall be allowed to tender. (Amendment in italics.)

The following year's Congress carried a resolution stating that, in light of fourteen years of continuous complaint against the 1909 Resolution and the changed industrial circumstances, an inquiry was warranted by a special Government Committee into the inadequate terms of the Clause 'with a view to a more satisfactory code of regulations controlling work for the public services and *direct recognition of industrial agreements with their inclusive terms of working conditions, wages, and hours*'. (My italics.) This call went unheeded.

The decline of the trade union movement during the remainder of the decade and the adverse economic conditions which affected workers appear to have prevented organized labour from advancing its viewpoint even so far as to successfully influence departmental action, let alone Parliamentary reform. For example, in their 1922 pamphlet, the T.U.C. were able to state that, despite some recent complaints against uniform clothing manufacturers, 'generally speaking the existence of national agreements and the operation of Trade Board rates has eliminated much of the difficulty in the clothing industry' (p. 9). Yet only two years later, a representative of the Tailors and Garment Workers' Trade Union was complaining bitterly that the Fair Wages Clause in Government contracts was 'very often ignored by contractors'. As explained to the 1924 Congress, the reason was because the unorganized conditions of the mass of women workers in the industry made it difficult for unions to challenge contractors or investigate them to see if they were paying the recognized or even the Trade Board rates. The result was that Government uniforms were manufactured under the most intense division of labour—twenty to forty operations—which allowed employers to employ girls between the ages of 14 and 18. In his particular town, one-third of the people employed in the wholesale tailoring trade were under the age of 18. The contractors exploited them by fixing piece rates which would give them only the Trade Board learners' rate of wages, instead of fixing them at what would enable adult workers to be engaged on the work. The departments appeared to regard this with equanimity.

During the decade of the 1920s, Parliament considered legislation extending the Fair Wages policy to areas where it previously had no application. Parliament was not, however, prepared to acknowledge the T.U.C.'s view of the possible amendments to the Clause. Section 2 of the Housing (Financial Provisions) Act, 1924, provided that when, in pursuance of proposals approved by the Minister of Health, or the Scottish Board of Health, houses were provided by local authorities, or by societies, bodies of trustees or companies, the Government contributions, payable under the Housing Act, 1923, should be increased if the houses were subject to the observance of special conditions specified in the Act. One of these conditions stated simply: '(d) that a fair wages clause which complies with the requirements of any resolution of the House of Commons applicable to contracts of Government departments and for the time being in force shall be inserted in all contracts for the construction of houses'. A Local Authorities (Contracts) Bill, 1925, which was not enacted had for its object to require the insertion of a Fair Wages clause in all local authorities' contracts and sub-contracts which involve the employment of labour.

A rather feeble gesture of recognition of collective bargaining developments was made by the British Sugar (Subsidy) Act, 1925, which provided for the payment of a subsidy in respect of sugar or molasses manufactured in Great Britain during a period of ten years beginning on 1 October 1924 from beet grown in Great Britain. It contained the following Fair Wages provision:

> 3. – (1) The wages paid by any employer to persons employed by him in connection with the manufacture of sugar or molasses in respect of which a subsidy is payable under this Act shall, except where paid at a rate agreed upon by a joint industrial council representing the employer and the persons employed, not be less than would be payable if the manufacture were carried on under a contract made between the Minister and the employer containing a fair wage clause which complied with the requirements of any resolution of the House of Commons for the time being in force applicable to contracts of Government departments, and if any dispute arises as to what wages ought to be paid in accordance with this section it shall be referred by the Minister to the Industrial Court for settlement.

This in effect negated the T.U.C.'s position on Fair Wages policy. The implication was that rates applicable under the Resolution were in sharp contrast to those fixed by collective arrangements. Far from Fair Wages standards being identified with negotiated rates, they were to be used as a fall-back standard in the absence of rates agreed in a joint industrial council. The substance of the Fair Wages standard, apart from the implied exclusion of collectively agreed rates, was not specified. Commenting on this provision, O. Kahn-Freund stated that 'the most serious shortcoming of the Sugar Act, 1925, was its failure to give sufficient guidance to the Industrial Court as to the considerations it ought to have in mind when making its award'. The Industrial Court was to specify the rates required by the Resolution; but, for example, in an early reference under section 3(1), Case No. 1140 of 13 November 1925, it spelled out the history of the rate of wages involved, but then fixed them without referring to any standard at all.

Despite the refusal to incorporate its view of the Fair Wages policy in these provisions, the T.U.C. supported similar legislation. During the British Empire Exhibition in 1924 workers had been imported to Wembley from all over Great Britain and Ireland to work and the result was termed: 'a disgrace to the trades concerned'. Consequently, the Annual Congress of 1924 passed a resolution whereby the government was urged to make it a condition of the granting of financial assistance or guarantee against loss to any exhibition, industry or commercial concern, that Fair Wages standards should apply in connection with the undertaking so assisted or guaranteed, 'so that working conditions and wages such as were in existence at the British Empire Exhibition shall not recur'. The T.U.C. was successful in its efforts and the British Empire Exhibition (Guarantee) Act, 1925, which authorized the Board of Trade to guarantee up to a specified amount any loss that might result from the re-opening in 1925 of the 1924 British Empire Exhibition, contained Fair Wages provisions applicable to persons employed in connection with the exhibition.

Throughout the decade there was a constant litany of complaints in which the trade unions' interpretation of the Resolution was continually pressed although the departments' opposing view prevailed. A few of those instances which were actually taken as far as questions in the House of Commons may be mentioned. In May 1923, the Prime Minister was asked whether he was aware that some contractors undertaking government work had refused to pay their workers the terms agreed upon by interim and joint industrial councils. In view of this, he was requested to issue instructions to all contracting departments, when accepting tenders, that agreements of these councils were to be construed as though such agreements were the Fair Wages Clause and applicable to all contracts where no Fair Wages Clause could be said to exist. In reply, Mr. Baldwin refused to issue any further instructions beyond reiterating the terms of the Resolution of 1909.

In a more specific complaint in February 1924 concerning joint industrial council rates, the Minister of Labour was asked if he was aware that the firm of T. and J. Tinkers, Ltd., Holmforth, who were contractors for cloth for the government, were continually breaking the regulations of the Joint Industrial Council for the wool and allied textile industry, regarding the 48-hours working week and labour conditions generally. When asked if he would take steps to see that the firm carried out the regulations, or else have them removed from the list of eligible contractors, the Minister of Labour replied that it was none of his business but was solely the concern of the contracting department. Satisfaction was hardly forthcoming from that quarter.

In another case of April 1924, the Minister of Labour was again appealed to in this last resort. This time he was informed that the employees of certain government contractors, Messrs. Cochrane and Company, who had iron-works at Middlesbrough, had ceased work in consequence of the firm not observing the working agreements of the North-East Coast Engineering Federation. The Company had paid wages as low as 33s. 2d. and were now advertising for non-union labour. When asked if he would take action to ensure that the conditions of the Fair Wages Clause were maintained, the Minister, while acknowledging that he knew of the dispute, asserted that his department could not usefully interfere, the question being one for the contracting department alone. In 1925, complaints were lodged that the firm of Messrs. Steel, Peech and Tozers, of Sheffield and Rotherham, contractors to the Colonial Office, were not observing the Fair Wages Clause as regards rates of pay and conditions of labour recognized in the district to the builders' labourers in their employ. In 1927 there was even a question concerning a Staffordshire firm of Admiralty contractors who had declined to conform to the terms of an Arbitration Award of the Industrial Court on the Fair Wages Resolution's application. The Admiralty's strong backing of the firm's interpretation of the Award by refusing to consider requests to strike them off the list of contractors indicates where their sympathies lay.[1]

The controversy over the opposing views of the Fair Wages Resolution was once again raised after the general election of May 1929 had produced the second Labour Government. The Labour Party emerged for the first time as the largest party in Parliament and formed a government with the support of the Liberals. There were six trade union sponsored Ministers in the Cabinet, including Margaret Bondfield of the General and Municipal Workers, who became Minister of Labour. Over the next year representations were made to the General Council of the T.U.C. with regard to various difficulties experienced by unions, particularly in the building industry, in securing the enforcement of the principles of the Resolution in government contracts. These difficulties were said to be due to departmental interpretations, or to differences of interpretation and practice between one department and another, and also to ambiguities in the wording of the Resolution itself. As the General Council put it in its 1930 Report: 'The Fair Wages Resolution was drafted in 1909, and it has been pointed out that its wording is quite ineffective to deal with modern conditions'.

The first approach to the new government was made by the National Federation of Building Trade Operatives in a deputation to the Minister of Labour in July 1929. A Labour Department memorandum records that the deputation urged that the rates of wages and conditions laid down in the agreements of the National Joint Council for the Building Industry should be recognized as determining fair rates and conditions, despite the fact that the national agreement rates and conditions might not be those prevailing in the district concerned. The matter was referred to the Fair Wages Advisory Committee and, at a meeting held on 17 October 1929, the departments concerned agreed to examine the Federation's proposals in the light of difficulties encountered and the experience gained in the administration of the existing clause.

The views obtained were embodied in a memorandum prepared by the Ministry of Labour and circulated to departments on 25 August

1930. The general conclusions of the Fair Wages Advisory Committee as stated in this memorandum were: (1) That the existing Fair Wages Clause worked equitably as between employers and workers; (2) that the present basis of administration conformed to the principles upon which the clause was founded; (3) that the amendment of the clause on the basis of the recognition of collective agreements would involve the introduction of a new principle foreign to the purpose of the clause; (4) that apart from the question of principle, any such amendment as proposed was open on general grounds to substantial objections that did not exist under the present clause; and (5) that a clause on the lines of the suggested amendment would involve departments in serious difficulties of administration. The Committee accordingly recommended that the Fair Wages Clause should be retained in its present form and continue to be administered on the same basis as hitherto. Considering that the Fair Wages Advisory Committee consisted solely of departmental representatives who had consistently opposed the T.U.C.'s interpretation of the Resolution since its inception, an 'expert' inquiry by them into the proposals of the building trades' unions could hardly have been expected to produce any other result.

There the question might have remained decently buried. It was, however, disinterred shortly thereafter when the General Council of the T.U.C., having collected a good deal of evidence, made representations to the Minister of Labour in October 1930, in regard both to departmental practice and to the possibility of revising the terms of the Resolution. The General Council submitted proposals to Bondfield and made enquiries as to the government's attitude to them. The suggested redraft of the Fair Wages Resolution, as amended and approved by the Finance and General Purposes Committee of the General Council, and adopted as a model by the General Council on 28 May 1930, contained the following clauses:

1. The Contractor shall, under penalty of a fine or otherwise, pay rates of wages and observe hours *and conditions* of labour not less favourable than *those established for the trade or industry by national agreements* made between associations of employers and workers or in the absence of such national agreements, *by district or local agreements*, made between associations of employers and workers for the district or locality in which the work is carried out.
2. Where there is no recognized agreement in the district the wages, hours and conditions adopted shall be not less favourable than those recognized by *agreements prevailing in the nearest district*.

3. Further the conditions of employment generally accepted in the district in the trade *or industry* concerned shall be taken into account in considering how far the terms of the fair wages clauses are being observed. (New wording italicized.)

These proposals were taken by the Ministry of Labour to be substantially identical to those previously submitted by the Building Trades' Operatives, i.e., that wages and conditions should be those fixed by an *agreement*, national, district or local, irrespective of the extent to which the agreement was, in fact, operative and even where there was no agreement covering the locality. It seems that Bondfield felt 'that as the Fair Wages Advisory Committee had already reached conclusions on the most important aspect of the proposals, the questions of policy involved should be considered by the various Ministers concerned'. A meeting of Ministers was accordingly convened by Bondfield in July 1931, at which it was agreed to appoint a small sub-committee of Ministers to consider and focus discussions that had taken place. The sub-committee of Ministers held its first and only meeting on 30 July 1931, when discussions took place on a suggestion put forward by the First Commissioner of Works, Mr. Lansbury, that contractors should be specially notified that the requirements of the Fair Wages Clause placed on them an obligation to have special regard to the terms of collective agreements. Preliminary consideration was given to a suggestion for dealing with the difficulty by means of the following notice to tenderers: 'Special attention is invited to the Fair Wages Clause of the Contract and tenderers are notified that in general its requirements demand adherence to any National or other wage or working rule agreement, commonly recognized by organized employers and trade societies in the district'. Bondfield also suggested that the National Federation of Building Trade Operatives should be asked for specific examples of cases in which difficulties had risen in connection with the present Fair Wages Clause. Shortly after this meeting and before any definite action had been taken, Ramsay McDonald resigned office on 23 August 1931, the Labour Government fell and was replaced by the National Government. The Committee of Ministers ceased to exist, the matter remaining in abeyance.[2]

NOTES

1. These complaints may be found in the order mentioned above in Parl. Deb., H. of C. (Fifth Series); 8 May 1923, vol. 163, col. 2193; 22 February 1924, vol. 169, col. 2167; 7 April 1924, vol. 172, col. 78; 25 March 1925, vol. 182, cols. 452–3; 14 February 1927, vol. 202, col. 557.

2. The above account is principally derived from the following sources:

—O. Kahn-Freund, 'Legislation Through

Adjudication. The Legal Aspect of Fair Wages Clauses and Recognised Conditions', in *Modern Law Review*, **11** (1948), at p. 286.

—*The Fair Wages Clause*, pamphlet issued by the T.U.C., 1922 (15 pp.).

—*The Fair Wages Clause—An Explanatory Statement*, pamphlet published by the General Council of the T.U.C. (ref. No. 4 F.W. 3/35). For the information of Officers and Members of Trade Unions and Trades Councils (March 1935), (15 pp.)

—Report of the 53rd Annual Trades Union Congress, Cardiff, 1921, at pp. 282–3.

—Report of the 54th Annual Trades Union Congress, Southport, 1922, p. 477.

—Report of the 55th Annual T.U.C., Plymouth, 1923, pp. 408–9.

—Report of the 56th Annual T.U.C., Hull, 1924, pp. 462–3.

—Report of the General Council to the 57th Annual T.U.C., Scarborough, 1925, p. 340 (Section O, para. 235).

—Report of the General Council to the 62nd Annual T.U.C., Nottingham, 1930, p. 224; pp. 377–8.

—Local Authorities (Contracts) Bill, 1925. Bill 105; 15 Geo. 5; House of Commons Papers of 1924–5, vol. ii, p. 957.

—Industrial Court Case No. 1140 (13 November 1925): The National Union of General and Municipal Workers and the English Beet Sugar Corporation, Ltd., vol. VII, pp. 283–5.

—Document dated 1 March 1934, which appears to be a memorandum by officials in the Labour Department, entitled 'Fair Wages Resolution—Re-Draft Suggested by the General Council of the Trades Union Congress'. This document may be found in the Public Record Office, Files of the Ministry of Labour: LAB 10/12; I.R. 1080 (1935).

—Document, undated: Draft 'A' of the Memorandum on Fair Wages Policy by the Minister of Labour, Appendix B. And generally paragraph 4. Public Record Office, Files of the Ministry of Labour: LAB 10/12 (1935–7); I.R. 1080/1935.

10

The Impact of the Depression: Steps
Towards Parliamentary Recognition
of Collective Agreements

Although the attitudes of department officials were unswervingly
opposed to the T.U.C.'s ideas for altering the implementation of the
Fair Wages Resolution, the political atmosphere, under the devastating
impact of depression and mass unemployment, was changing. The
report of the Balfour Committee on Trade and Industry published in
1929 rejected the idea of the compulsory enforcement of voluntary
agreements. It commented:

> to accept the proposal put forward would involve the risk of
> fastening compulsorily on certain organized industries methods
> and principles of industrial relations and even of business manage-
> ment, to which a minority of employers or workpeople may be
> strongly opposed. The problem of defining the precise scope,
> geographically and industrially, of compulsory enforcement is a
> minor, though in practice very real, difficulty. A much greater
> difficulty is the reaction which the application of compulsion
> with regard to principles and methods of industrial relations
> must have on the working of the voluntary machinery for the
> actual fixing of wages and hours in the industry.

In 1930, however, the Housing Act and Housing (Scotland) Act each
included in Part III provisions that made contributions by the Department of Health to local authorities subject to special conditions, one
of which was a Fair Wages provision similar to that which appeared
in the 1924 Housing Act quoted above. Again, during the Committee
stage of the Road Traffic Bill in the House of Commons, a new clause
was inserted and passed without a division, making the Fair Wages
Clause applicable to persons employed in connection with public
service vehicles. A condition attaching to any road service licence
was that the person operating the service should pay wages and

For notes see p. 180

observe conditions of employment not less favourable than those laid down by the Resolution. Any organization representing the workers would be entitled to make representations to the Traffic Commissioners if the clause was not carried out, and eventually might take the matter to the Industrial Court for settlement. Any person found guilty of not observing this condition would be dealt with as failing to comply with a condition of his road service licence. The clause was also accepted without a division on the report stage of the Bill in the House of Commons.

The House of Lords on 25 July 1930 struck out the Fair Wages Clause, Viscount Brentford opposing it because it was enforcing the clause on a private undertaking. When the Bill was returned to the House of Commons, the Commons decided, without a division, on 28 July 1930, to reinsert the clause. On the grounds of public safety, efficiency and fair competition between operators of public service vehicles it was necessary to have fair wages and conditions in the industry, and the application of the Fair Wages Resolution was the most suitable and effective means of attaining the end. Colonel Ashley, the former Conservative Minister of Transport, in supporting the motion of the House of Commons, said: 'Undoubtedly, there has been in the past, and still is, a great deal of labour engaged in this transportation work which is underpaid, and this amendment will not harm the good employer but simply bring up the bad employer'. The provisions became law in section 93 of the Road Traffic Act, 1930.

Section 32(2) of the Road and Rail Traffic Act, 1933, applied these provisions of the 1930 Act to persons employed as drivers or attendants of vehicles holding certain mandatory licences for the carriage of goods. Section 32(1) of the Act, however, went beyond this to provide that where any matter was referred to the Industrial Court under section 93 of the 1930 Act, the Court, in arriving at its decision, should have regard to any determination which might be brought to its notice relating to the wages or conditions of service of persons employed in a capacity similar to that of the persons to whom the reference related and contained in a decision of a Joint Industrial Council, Conciliation Board or other similar body, or in an agreement between organizations representative of employers and workers. This formula begins to approach the T.U.C.'s view on what constitutes Fair Wages standards, but a Minute circulated within the Ministry of Labour, dated 10 October 1936, questions: 'Is it quite correct to say that Parliament approved the principle of the statutory recognition of agreements in the Road Traffic Acts? They were not asked to do so, I think'.

More radical steps in the same direction were evidenced in a number of Bills introduced into Parliament during the first years of the economic depression. Almost annually during the early 1930s, an Industrial Councils' Bill was put forward which made it the duty of the Minister of Labour to promote the establishment of an Industrial Council for every industry deemed appropriate, representative of employers and workers, to be recognized as the official channel of communication between the Government and the employers and workers of that industry. The primary object of an Industrial Council, according to the 1930 Bill, was to be the consideration of matters specified in the attached Schedule (clause 3(1)). This included the settlement of the 'general principles governing the conditions of employment, including the methods of fixing, paying and readjusting wages, having regard to the need for securing to the workpeople a share in the increasing prosperity of the industry' (Schedule, section iii). An indication of the seriousness of the problem of wage-cutting may be gauged by the fact that the 1933 Bill had changed this primary objective of an Industrial Council rather to be 'to provide for the sanctioning and enforcement of rates of wages' (clause 3(1) of the 1933 Bill). The crucial aspect of these Councils was that their decisions might be confirmed by Orders of the Minister of Labour on application, and clause 3(2) provided:

(c) where any agreement relating to a minimum rate, time rate, or basic piece-work rate of wages, or to hours of labour or other matters within the scope of the constitution of a Joint Industrial Council or analogous thereto, arrived at or ratified by a J.I.C., has been made effective by an Order of the Minister, any evasion of, or non-compliance by an employer with such an Order shall be deemed to be an offence punishable on summary conviction by a fine not exceeding £50 for a first offence and by imprisonment without the option of a fine for a wilful continuance of such evasion or non-compliance.

(d) in the event of sufficient evidence of evasion of, or non-compliance with, any such Order by any person to whom the same applies, being laid before the Minister of Labour by any Industrial Council, or Employers' or Employees' Organization interested, it shall be the duty of the Minister of Labour, or the J.I.C. or the Employers' or Employees' Organization concerned, or any aggrieved person to take such proceedings against such person with a view to his conviction and punishment.

Another attempt at providing for the sanctioning and enforcement of rates of wages was introduced in June 1931. The Rates of Wages Bill would give the Minister of Labour power to issue Orders upon a joint written application by an association of employers and of employees in a trade sanctioning 'any arrangement for a rate or rates of wages agreed to by such association of employers and such association of employees and specified in such application' (clause 1(1)). Once the rate of wages had been thus sanctioned, 'every employee to whom such rate applies shall be entitled to receive from his employer wages at a rate not lower than the rate so sanctioned' (clause 2(1)). The employee was given the right to recover payment from his employer for any breach (clause 2(2)). In such civil proceedings 'it shall lie on the employer to prove by the production of such records of wages as aforesaid that he has not failed to pay to the employee the full wages to which such employee is entitled in pursuance of this Act' (clause 2(4)). To circumvent a possible contractual evasion, clause 2(6) rendered any agreement for the payment of wages in contravention of the provisions of the Bill void.

An attempt to incorporate the Fair Wages policy into legislation was made by the Living Wage Bill, introduced into Parliament by Mr. Maxton on 31 October 1931. The primary object of the Bill was to secure that the payment to every employed person of at least a minimum living wage was a first charge on industry, and to put the authority and resources of the State behind Trade Union and other efforts for the early attainment of this object. It was in no way to supplant the existing machinery of Trade Unions, Wage Boards, Trade Boards and Industrial Councils but was to supplement and assist them. Drawing on Australian and other precedents, the minimum living wage was defined in clause 1(1) as: 'a wage at least sufficient to meet the normal needs of the average worker regarded as a human being living in a civilized community, including the satisfaction of reasonable minimum requirements of health and efficiency and of cultural life and the provision of reasonable rest and recreation'. The Bill authorized the President of the Board of Trade to set up a Committee to interpret the definition in exact figures, having regard to the cost of living and the limits set by the actual amounts available for distribution in wages and other remuneration at any moment, proper provision being made for replacement and provision of capital. The Committee was to include representatives of housewives and of the Trade Union and Co-operative movements, as well as competent economists.

Clause 2 stipulated that after these figures had been determined, they were to be compulsory on all government departments, on local and other public authorities, and on railway, electricity supply, gas, water and other public utility companies working under Private Acts of Parliament, as minima below which all wages' scales were illegal.

There was no power or intention to limit the payment of wages above the minimum figures. Further, this principle was extended to contractors or others working on orders given out by government departments or other public authorities. The Fair Wages Clause was to be extended so as to include a stipulation of the payment to all workers of wages at least not lower than the minimum rate, and this stipulation was to be made statutory. The Bill carried the principle even further by requiring the conditions of such an extended Fair Wages Clause to be applied to all workers in industries protected or safeguarded by the State against foreign competition, e.g. the dyestuffs industry.

A final example of legislation resulting from the pressures of this period is the Cotton Manufacturing (Temporary Provisions) Act, 1934. As was mentioned in chapter 7, the severe economic depression in the industry led to ever more frequent evasion by both employers and workers of the terms of collective agreements. Richardson reported in 1938 that considerable numbers of employers in the industry had either not been members of employers' organizations or withdrew from them in order to be free to introduce lower conditions. Consequent on pressure from both sides of the weaving section of the industry, the 1934 Act was passed. It embodied the principle of compulsory extension of agreements if it could be shown that the organizations party to the agreements represented the employers controlling the majority of looms and the majority of workers affected by an Order imposing the agreement. This would prevent a minority of employers and workers from offering or accepting employment at wages lower than those provided for in the collective agreements. The first Order was issued in 1935. A Ministry of Labour memorandum of approximately April 1934 refers to the Act as temporary and experimental, but calls it 'the most noteworthy post-War experiment in State intervention in industrial relations'.

A Hint of Divergence in Administrative Policy: The Ministry of Labour's Response to the 1933 T.U.C. Initiative Contrasted with Departmental Attitudes

The issue of the relationship of collective agreements to the Fair Wages Resolution was specifically raised anew in a letter from the General Council of the T.U.C. to the then Minister of Labour, Sir Henry Betterton, of 27 February 1933. In the letter, the Minister was asked whether any opinion had yet been formed upon the proposals submitted in 1930 to the Labour Government. The letter, written by the General Council on behalf of the National Union of Stove, Grate and General Metal Workers, also raised the question of extending the Fair Wages Clause to cover the making and fixing of materials on government and municipal contracts, a proposal not previously raised in 1930. On 20 March 1933, the Minister of Labour invited government departments concerned to submit any observations they might wish to make with regard to the questions raised in this letter. In a memorandum dated 1 March 1934, the Ministry's officials stated that as regards the General Council's main proposal of 1930, i.e. to determine fair wages and conditions by reference to agreements, the general view of departments remained as summarized in the memorandum of 25 August 1930 described in chapter 9. This was completely negative. The only reference to the suggestion put forward by Mr. Lansbury in the Labour Government's sub-committee of Ministers' meeting of July 1931 was in the form of an objection to its adoption.

Despite this virtual unanimity of departmental views communicated individually to the Ministry of Labour, the Ministry decided nevertheless to refer the question for a collective view to the Fair Wages Advisory Committee. In a memorandum for the Committee, it set out some points for consideration. This memorandum hints for the first time at the possibility of change in departmental administration of the Fair Wages policy. It begins by stating that the Minister of Labour was being pressed by the General Council of the T.U.C. to state the government's attitude towards the amendment of the Resolution along the lines proposed by the T.U.C. The Committee was asked to express a view whether the reply should be a general negative, referring to the absence of evidence that the present Fair Wages Clause failed to carry out the principles underlying the existing Resolution and to the difficulties both general and administrative inherent in the acceptance of a new Clause on the lines suggested. Such a reply would reflect the attitudes of the departments expressed individually to the Ministry of Labour.

Alternatively, the memorandum proposed dealing with the various suggestions of the T.U.C.'s amendments in some detail. In proposing this more positive approach, the Ministry of Labour set out a few of its own underlying assumptions about the Fair Wages Resolution. First, it made the following general points: that the existing Resolution was intended to secure that the wages paid for government work were those ordinarily paid by good employers to competent workmen in each trade in the district where the work was carried out and to prevent government contracts from falling into the hands of employers who were able to quote lower prices by undercutting their competitors in the rate of wages paid. Thus, despite the seeming precedence in the Resolution itself of *recognized* rates and hours over those of *good* employers, it is evident that the latter standard was paramount in the

Ministry's conception of the policy. Referring to various administrative reforms adopted to secure the better operation of the Clause
since 1909, and the implementation of policies extending its application beyond the range of government contracts, the Ministry maintained that such actions had at all times been in conformity with the
general principles underlying the Resolution. Finally, the Ministry
revealed its own classic position: the T.U.C. view of the Resolution
was firmly rebuffed, while the pressures for reform were cautiously
recognized, subject to political considerations:

> (c) although the fact that the proposals submitted by the Council
> would require the authority of a further Resolution would not of
> itself prevent the acceptance of the Council's proposals in so far
> as they are otherwise practicable and desirable, it is essential that
> any amended Resolution submitted to Parliament is of such a
> character as to command general support.

The Ministry spelled out the practical implications of this position
in subsequent paragraphs. While noting the Fair Wages Advisory
Committee's previous rejection in 1930 of the T.U.C. proposals, it
pointed out that 'certain general considerations need to be borne in
mind'. Among these it mentioned the great increase in the number
of collective agreements since 1909, which had produced a situation
which seemed to require that greater weight should be given in the
Fair Wages Clause to the terms of collective agreements in the determination of fair wages and conditions. Again, it referred to some of
the Fair Wages Clauses operated by public and local authorities as
being 'more favourable to the interests of workers' than the government clause, and stated that 'without evidence it ought not to be
assumed that these more advanced clauses are regarded unfavourably
by good employers'. It might be thought, let it be said, that such an
assumption could be more rigorously challenged. Particular attention
was directed to the requirement in the Road and Rail Traffic Act, 1933,
that the Industrial Court have regard to decisions of or agreements
between various bodies. The Ministry was extremely cautious regarding the possible implications of these considerations. Any amendment
would of necessity need careful examination by some form of committee. But the question arose whether this was an opportune moment
for such an inquiry. The main T.U.C. proposal was in effect for the
compulsory enforcement of joint agreements in a limited field, a policy
which would reverberate within the much wider field of wage regulation, upon which the policy of the government and industrial organizations remained to be defined. The Ministry hesitated before any
sort of commitment.

On the other hand, there were many considerations which militated against any positive approach to the Resolution's amendment by the Ministry. It asserted that the volume of complaints under the Clause was small and that there was certainly no widespread demand for its amendment. It even questioned whether the General Council of the T.U.C. would have raised the subject at all if it had not been for the action originally taken by the National Federation of Building Trade Operatives (this despite the perennial resolutions and complaints registered at every Annual Trades Union Congress by various unions). Furthermore, it claimed that the purpose of the Resolution was not to create new standards for workers, but to prevent the undercutting of good employers. Thus, on the one hand, there was no very definite evidence that the Resolution failed in present day conditions to serve its original purpose, and on the other, there were obvious objections to the Resolution being used as a device for the improvement of wages in substitution for the normal methods of securing such improvement. This would involve straining the principle underlying the Resolution to cover circumstances in which it was of doubtful application. Such a new policy would have to be considered not only in relation to government contracts, but to industrial relations generally.

In addition, the T.U.C.'s suggestion amounted to the enforcement of rates and conditions fixed by a particular body regardless of other considerations. Acceptance of this proposal would create many new administrative difficulties. The Ministry foresaw that claims would be made in respect of agreements that were not recognized or supported by large sections of an industry; that an indeterminate liability would be imposed on contractors who were not party to agreements and that there would be increased difficulty in requiring firms to adopt Fair Wages conditions on private as well as on contract works. Interpretation of agreements would be much more difficult, more uncertain and more litigious than the discovery of actual rates, and numerous cases would occur of conflicting agreements, national and local, and between large groups purporting to cover the same ground. Thus, government departments would become involved in disputes relating to the scope and applicability of agreements and questions of demarcation, and administration could no longer proceed by reference to ascertained facts. Finally, even if all these objections and difficulties were not necessarily insuperable, the whole question of compulsory extension of collective agreements was at the time being subjected to close examination by all sections of industry. Consequently, 'it would seem to be highly undesirable for the discussions to be prejudiced by an early application of the principle for the purposes of the Fair Wages Clause'.

The approach exhibited here by the Ministry of Labour was only too clearly one of extreme caution towards any seemingly liberal interpretation of the Fair Wages Resolution, even in industrial circumstances which appeared to have rendered the conservative view irrelevant to the needs of workers and even contractors. Despite this, it was unmistakably an advance from the previous stone-wall denials of government departments that any alternative view of the Fair Wages policy was desirable, or even possible. The Ministry of Labour was at least prepared to recognize the changes in the industrial relations scene which warranted a more relevant approach to implementation of the Fair Wages Resolution, though it was also aware of the practical problems which would arise from the confused and unstable situation. The furthest it was prepared to go was to propose a lengthy inquiry into the whole question of amendment of the 1909 Resolution at some time in the future when the policy of the government and various industrial organizations materialized on the wider question of compulsorily extending collective agreements.

The sharply contrasting attitude displayed by the Fair Wages Advisory Committee to the T.U.C.'s proposals illustrated the magnitude of the advance contained in the Labour Department's memorandum. This had at least suggested that the proposals might be discussed in the light of certain general considerations and had then advanced serious and thoughtful objections to the proposals. The Committee, comprising representatives of the Ministry of Labour, War Office, Stationery Office, Office of Works, Ministry of Transport, Air Ministry, Ministry of Health, Admiralty, Treasury, Post Office, Scottish Office and Prisons' Department for Scotland, with Sir Thomas Phillips of the Ministry of Labour in the chair, considered the Labour Department memorandum at its fifty-ninth meeting on 23 March 1934. The minutes of the meeting record that it was 'agreed that in general the reply to the General Council should be as brief as possible and that it would not be advisable to attempt to enter into detailed arguments'. Consequently, their treatment of the whole question resolved itself into the following brief paragraph:

> As regards this section of the proposals of the General Council, which involves the introduction of a new principle for determining fair wages and conditions, the Committee agreed that there had been no change in the position to alter the conclusions reached by them when the similar proposals of the National Federation of Building Trade Operatives were considered in 1930. They decided, therefore, that any reply sent should be against acceptance of this proposal with reference to the lack of any substantial evidence that

the present Clause failed to operate satisfactorily or equitably. The question of also making reference to the general position with regard to the compulsory enforcement of voluntary agreements was left as a matter for consideration when the actual reply was being drafted.

It was agreed by the Committee that the Ministry of Labour should prepare a draft reply to the General Council based on these considerations and circulate it to all departments. When submitting the proposed reply to the Minister of Labour for his approval, Sir Thomas Phillips wrote as follows:

> The Fair Wages Resolution requires the observance of wages and hours 'commonly recognized' in the trade in the district in which the work is carried out. While this is often, or perhaps generally, the same thing as the hours and wages fixed in an agreement, the case is different if the agreement is only nominally in operation in a particular area and the wages and hours actually observed do not conform to it. In order to give effect to the T.U.C. request, the Fair Wages Resolution would have to be amended. Whatever may be said on the general question of making agreements compulsory, it is not thought to be right to make the Fair Wages requirement an instrument for this purpose in the partial and limited way in which alone it could apply.

A reply was finally sent from the Ministry of Labour to the General Council on 26 June 1934. Its style and substance were determined by the complacent attitude of the Fair Wages Advisory Committee. Thus, the second paragraph stated: 'that on a broad survey of the information available it appears that the existing clause operates equitably as between employers and workpeople and does not present undue difficulties in administration'. As regards the T.U.C.'s proposals, the letter concluded abruptly: 'The present Fair Wages Clause, as administered, ensures generally that wages and conditions recognized in any particular district either by agreement or by customary practice, are observed on Government contracts and a Fair Wages Clause is not an appropriate instrument for the enforcement of agreements irrespective of the question whether they are in fact recognized or put into operation in the particular district'.

This complacent attitude of the Fair Wages Advisory Committee is exemplified by its treatment of a complaint which it considered at the same meeting when its position on the T.U.C. proposals was formulated. The complaint was lodged by the Inverness Branch of the Scottish Union of Bakers and asserted that Messrs. Telford (Inverness)

Ltd., Wholesale Bakers and Confectioners, were in breach of the Fair Wages Clause. The facts, which were not in dispute, were that: (a) the Inverness District Bakery Agreement provided, *inter alia*: early men not to start earlier than 4 o'clock on the first five days and 3 o'clock on Saturday; general body of the men to start not earlier than 5 o'clock on the first five days and 4 o'clock on Saturday; allowance payable to early men to be 5/– per week; (b) Telford's worked a shift of bakers starting at 12 midnight; (c) the minimum wage under the district agreement was 63/6d. per week for a working week of forty-eight hours; (d) the wages paid by Telford's were 65/– per week, also understood to be for forty-eight hours, plus National Health and Unemployment contributions, value 1/7d.

The Scottish Office examined the complaint and came to the conclusion in view of the terms of the district agreement that, by working a full night shift, Telford's were working hours less favourable than those commonly recognized in the district and were not therefore employing their bakers under conditions which satisfied the terms of the Fair Wages Resolution. The War Office, it appears, were unaware of the position taken by the Scottish Office, and a contract was placed by the local military authorities with Telford's after the Scottish Office had decided to place the firm on their ineligible list. When the Inverness Branch of the Scottish Union of Bakers complained to the War Office, the War Office did not form the same view of the Fair Wages position as the Scottish Office. Broadly, their view was that (a) in deciding whether a firm was 'fair', it was not necessary to consider wages and hours independently; (b) though Telford's hours were different, they were not longer and were not necessarily 'less favourable'; and (c) even if it was held that Telford's hours were 'less favourable', the extra payment made by them could be regarded as adequate compensation. In subsequent discussion in the Fair Wages Advisory Committee, the War Office representative put this sum at 3/1d. per week above the minimum district agreement rate. The Scottish Office representative pointed out, however, that early men under the district agreement received 5/– extra. Extra payments were always made for early starting, increasing in amount as the starting hours became earlier.

The War Office representative also reported that the journeymen bakers on night-shift had the option of going on day shift upon alternate weeks, but that they seemed to prefer to remain continuously on night-shift. On this point, the Admiralty representative expressed the view that Telford's men with the option of doing day shifts in alternate weeks were really getting more than the district rate. He thought that there was a tendency to try to read too much into the Fair Wages

Clause, which had been invented to deal with a particular evil and was not meant to be a precise or comprehensive code. Instead of trying to interpret the clause as though it were an Act of Parliament, he thought it was better to ask whether the workers were in fact being exploited. In his view, Telford's men were not.

After general discussion, the opinion of the Committee appeared to be that the local agreement amounted to a method of baking on a one-shift system which was something different from the system employed by Telford's who worked two shifts, and that it was difficult to declare that Telford's should be stopped from working a two-shift system because of an agreement which was drawn up to provide for a single shift system and without considering the possibility of or need for a two-shift system. Unfortunately, as the Chairman put it, 'it would be very awkward from a general point of view if any decision was given by a Government Department at the moment which appeared to endorse the practice of night baking'. His solution to this difficulty was that the War Office and the Scottish Office should look into the case together and see whether they could reach an agreed view on the question whether the rate paid by Telford's was adequate for night work. In the meantime, the answer to enquiries on the subject would need to be that the matter was still under consideration.

The most appropriate comment on this treatment was voiced by a representative of the Scottish Bakers six months later at the Annual Trades Union Congress in September 1934. Reviewing the history of the dispute, he related that Telford's had unilaterally imposed night-baking on their men, although it was hardly known in Scotland outside Glasgow and the trade unions had constantly and consistently opposed any introduction of it. The men had protested this violation of their district agreement, but could make no headway. The Conciliation Department of the Ministry of Labour was brought in, but the employer refused to discuss it. The men were brought out on strike, but their places were filled with scab labour. Despite representations made to the War Office, the employer was still a government contractor. He concluded:

> Eight months have passed, and that firm are still contractors to the army. I hold that this is a direct violation of the whole spirit which inspired the fair wage clause. If we allow violations of this character to be carried on, then it becomes a misnomer, and no value to the worker at all. We feel the time has come when something might be done to strengthen it so that employers of this type may be brought to heel.[1]

NOTES

1. The above account is principally derived from the following sources:

—J. H. Richardson, *Industrial Relations in Great Britain*, I.L.O. Studies and Reports, Series A (Industrial Relations), No. 36, Geneva, 1938; pp. 128–9.

—*Labour Bulletin*, edited by the Labour Party Research Department, of July 1931, p. 156.

—*The Fair Wages Clause—An Explanatory Statement*, pamphlet published by the General Council of the T.U.C. (ref. No. 4 F.W. 3/35). For the information of Officers and Members of Trade Unions and Trades Councils (March 1935.) (15 pp.)

—Report of the 63rd Annual Trades Union Congress, Bristol, 1931, p. 253.

—Report of the 66th Annual Trades Union Congress, Weymouth, 1934, pp. 352–3.

—Memorandum on the Living Wage Bill, Bill 12 of 31st October 1931, presented by Mr. Maxton (21 Geo. 5). In the T.U.C. Library, Box HD 5016, 1931.

—Letters dated 22nd March and 27th March 1933, re application of Fair Wages policy. Also Memo on Rates of Wages on State-Associated Schemes, dated approximately 31st March 1930. In Department of Employment Library, Box G.P.331.18–331.2, File 405.

—Documents dated 27 November 1943: 'Note on the Compulsory Extension of Agreements to Cover (a) Firms in Organised Districts, and (b) Isolated Firms', attached to a letter dated 19 January 1945, from I. M. Vincent Smith to G. Moat. Public Record Office, Files of the Ministry of Labour: LAB 10/439 (1944).

—Committee Paper No. 1 of the Committee on the Regulation of Road Transport Wages entitled: 'State Intervention in Industrial Relations'. Public Record Office, Files of the Ministry of Labour: LAB 10/73; I.R. 538/1934.

—Memorandum on the Extension of the Fair Wages Clause to Materials Used by Contractors and Sub-contractors. Public Record Office, Files of the Ministry of Labour: LAB 10/23; I.R. 692/1935.

—Document dated 1 March 1934, which appears to be a memorandum by officials in the Labour Department, entitled 'Fair Wages Resolution—Re-Draft Suggested by the General Council of the Trades Union Congress'. Public Record Office, Files of the Ministry of Labour: LAB 10/12; I.R. 1080 (1935).

—Fair Wages Advisory Committee, Minutes of the 59th Meeting of the Committee held at Montagu House, Whitehall, S.W.1, on Friday, 23 March 1934. Public Record Office, Files of the Ministry of Labour: LAB 10/12 (1935–7); I.R. 1080/1935.

—Minute from F.W.L. to F. A. Norman, officials in the Ministry of Labour, dated 10 October 1936. Files of the Ministry of Labour: LAB 10/12 (1935–7); I.R. 1080/1935.

—Minute of 17 July 1935, from M. A. Bevan of the Ministry of Labour, Secretary to the Fair Wages Advisory Committee. Public Record Office, Files of the Ministry of Labour: LAB 10/12 (1935–7); I.R. 1080/1935.

—Industrial Councils Bills, No. 216, printed 24 June 1930, in House of Commons Papers of 1929–30, vol. ii, p. 363; Bill of 30 November 1932, House of Commons Papers of 1932–3, vol. i, p. 891; Bill of 24 November 1933, House of Commons Papers of 1933–4, vol. ii, p. 599, (see debate in Parl. Deb., H. of C. (Fifth Series); vol. 286, cols. 647–732); Bill of 26 February 1935, in House of Commons Papers of 1934–5, vol. iii, p. 193.

—Rates of Wages Bill, Bill 180 printed 25 June 1931, in House of Commons Papers of 1930–1, vol. iv, p. 201.

11

Agitation for Fair Wages Policy Reform

Despite the rebuff to the T.U.C.'s proposals contained in the Ministry of Labour's letter of June 1934, at the Annual Congress the following September, a resolution was moved by a representative of the Construction Engineering Union which in effect requested the General Council to draw up a model Fair Wages Clause to be submitted for acceptance by the government. In response to this, the General Council, in its Report for the year 1934–5, stated that it had appeared from communications received from unions that officials of unions were placed at a disadvantage because no precise information was readily available, first, of the operation and implications of the Fair Wages Clause, secondly, of government administrative practices in regard to the same, and thirdly, of the action already taken by the General Council. The Council therefore decided to issue a report dealing with the past history and present position of the Fair Wages Clause and embodying the Model Clause adopted by the General Council in 1930. The report in pamphlet form, entitled *The Fair Wages Clause An Explanatory Statement*, was issued to affiliated unions and trades councils in March 1935.

The pamphlet pointed out that the terms of the Fair Wages Clause, drafted so long ago, were quite inapplicable to modern industry. For instance, 'when the Resolution was drafted, agreements held by Trade Unions were very largely local agreements, whereas national agreements have now been established in many industries, and the phrase applying rates "recognized" or "prevailing" in the district is quite inapplicable'. Moreover, the pamphlet continued, the interpretation by departmental officials of even phrases such as 'commonly recognized' or 'prevailing' may well be something quite different from that meant by trade unionists. It had been alleged that government departments refused to enforce rates which had been agreed or scheduled by Trade

For notes see p. 206

Unions and Employers' Associations, even those scheduled by Joint Industrial Councils, on the ground that they were not being paid by the majority of the employers in the district in which the work is done. Thus, it was said that where an isolated group of employers was paying a lower rate than the agreed rate, the departments had been known to regard them as 'good employers', or the rate they paid as the 'recognized rate', and had refused to insist upon the rate agreed by the Trade Unions. The complaint applied particularly to the building industry. The departments maintained that they were not obliged to enforce the national rate but only the rate which prevailed in the district. It was alleged that the departments abused the definition of the word 'district' to expand or contract it according as best suited their purpose of allowing a lower rate: 'It is clear that so long as this view is allowed to stand, and so long as Departments can define a "district" as they please, they can accept a rate paid by a majority of employers in that district without regard to any Trade Union or Joint Industrial Council agreements'.

The pamphlet presented examples of local authority Fair Wages provisions which were more favourable than the government's. Thus, the London County Council stipulated in its contracts wages and hours 'recognized by associations of employers and Trade Unions in the district', or prevailing amongst 'good employers', but further required the contractor to 'perform and observe all and singular the terms, stipulations and provisions of agreements between associations of employers and Trade Unions or awards affecting any trade or trades'. The Fair Wages Clause of the Birmingham Corporation required the contractor to pay to the whole of his work-force 'not less than the Trade Union or standard rates of wages in the several districts' and observe 'hours and conditions recognized by associations of employers and the local organized bodies of workers in the several districts'. Again, in the case of Housing Schemes involving government grants, it was stated to be the habit of the Ministry of Health to require any local authority which had no Fair Wages Clause in its standing orders to use an amplified form of the government's clause, as follows:

> The contractor and all sub-contractors executing the works shall at all times, during the execution, pay to the whole of their work-people not less than the standard rate of wages (including any subsistence allowance, lodging money or recompense for lost time) in the several districts where their workpeople are actually engaged in the execution of the works, and shall observe the standard hours and conditions of labour in the district, that is

to say, such rates of wages and such hours and conditions of labour as may from time to time be fixed as applicable in the district to the class of labour concerned by any working rule agreement made by a body representative of persons employing that class of labour in the district and of persons employed in that class of labour in the district and as may be generally paid and observed in the district in respect of that class of labour, or if there is no such agreement or if the rate and conditions fixed by any such agreement are not those generally paid and observed in the district in respect of that class of labour, then the rates and conditions shall be those so paid and observed as aforesaid.

This clause spells out the 1909 Resolution to the extent that it makes explicit reference to the standards set by collective agreements as being 'fair' standards, while still excluding them where they are not in practice observed universally, this conforming to central government practice.

The pamphlet also referred to the Scottish T.U.C.'s Model Fair Wages Clause, intended particularly for local authorities, which put district agreements first and national agreements second:

The contractor and the local authority shall pay rates of wages and observe conditions of labour not less favourable to all employees than those commonly recognized by employers and Trade Unions in the trade in the district where the work is carried out. In the absence of any generally recognized rules as to wages and conditions of labour, those rules fixed by national agreements between employers and employees' organizations shall be adopted, but where no such district or national rules prevail the rules recognized in the nearest district where the general industrial circumstances are similar, shall be observed. Further, where within the foregoing provisions there are no recognized wages and conditions, those which prevail among good employers shall be adopted.

In contrast, the Irish T.U.C. Model Clause recognized first 'any agreement, national or general', and secondly, any 'working arrangement' in the industrial area. It defined an 'industrial area' as any district, large or small, covered by a working arrangement. It too retained the reference to 'good employers'.

The mid-1930s evinced a growing disparity between the Fair Wages policy implemented by a number of progressive local authorities and that of the central contracting departments and the majority of local authorities influenced by it. Evidence suggests that the policy was at any rate much more effective at the local level. A pamphlet entitled *Distributive Workers and the Fair Wages Clause* published in 1935 by the Research Department of the National Amalgamated Union of Shop Assistants, Warehousemen and Clerks began by asserting: 'It is becoming more and more recognized that the Fair Wages Clause in local government contracts provides a valuable instrument with which the Trade Unionist can ensure that all dealings which a Local Authority may have with its contractors are on the basis of the payment of fair wages and the observance of fair conditions of labour to the workers employed by the contracting firm'. The pamphlet encouraged distributive workers to invoke the Fair Wages Clause wherever they considered that the contractor was not conforming with its requirements. As to the problem of ascertaining that there was non-compliance with 'fair' wages and conditions, it was stated: 'Agreements are in existence between the Union and employers in different parts of the country which can be used for the purpose of determining compliance or otherwise with the Fair Wages Clause'. Indeed, the pamphlet went on to urge union members to regard even such agreed rates as minima, and not sufficient for compliance with the Fair Wages Clause, since: 'It is quite probable, and in practice a certainty that in some cases agreements with individual Co-operative Societies and private employers will prescribe higher rates and better conditions than obtain in Sectional Agreements. In such cases the more favourable wages and conditions will, of course, be regarded as "fair" for this particular district where they operate'.

The Scottish Model Fair Wages Clause quoted above was approved by the Scottish T.U.C. in 1932. It contained, apart from the provisions on wages and conditions, requirements as to observance of fair wages and conditions on private business, prohibition on trade union membership bans, on sub-contracting, insurance of workmen, keeping of wages books and inspection, penalties, exhibition of the Clause, and application to the supply of goods, materials or services. This Clause was circulated to all County and Town Councils in Scotland and subsequently, in October 1934, a report was published by the General Council showing in detail the Clause operated by the authorities. A second report was issued in October 1937 because, as it was stated: 'the requests by the Trade Unions for copies of this (first) Report clearly indicated that it was of practical value to their full-time and other officials'. A summary in the second Report dealt with information supplied by thirty-one of the thirty-three County Councils in Scotland, and sixty-seven of the seventy-two Burghs having a population of more than 5,000. It showed that the Fair Wages Clause generally operated was either the House of Commons Resolution of

1909 or one similar thereto. Of the thirty-one counties, only one, Lanark, had adopted the Scottish T.U.C.'s Model Clause. But the rest had Clauses similar or identical to that of the House of Commons. Of the sixty-seven Burghs, sixty-six had Fair Wages Clauses, of which eleven, including Glasgow, had accepted the Congress wording—the most important difference being the reference therein to National Agreements. The Report emphasized that the effect of the practices of Scottish Local Authorities relative to the Fair Wages Clause extended wider than Scotland itself, for they placed considerable contracts with firms outside Scotland. The Model Clause contained provisions relating to Foreign Manufacturers and Agents.

At the opposite extreme to these progressive authorities were others, characterized in a pamphlet published by the National Union of Public Employees in 1940 as 'die-hard Counties' who 'cared naught for this expressed wish of Parliament, and have contemptuously disregarded it'. Bryn Roberts, the General Secretary of N.U.P.E., lamented: 'Despite the most reasonable appeals which we have addressed to them, they have remained unmoved. They are indifferent to the plight of their miserably low-paid employees, and their anti-trade union attitude is shown by their constant refusal to enter into any form of negotiation or collective bargaining.' Since these authorities received substantial grants from the central departments, for example, for the maintenance of roads, the intervention of the government was solicited in a campaign stretching over many months. The result of this was an equivocal statement issued by the Minister of Transport in December 1939 supporting the Fair Wages policy in general terms. But the attitude of the central departments is more clearly evinced by a paragraph in the N.U.P.E. pamphlet which reads as follows:

> Had these same (local) authorities paid wages in *excess* of the Fair Wages standard the Government Auditor would have quickly intervened. Upon the receipt of his report the Ministry concerned would take very prompt action. It would refuse to sanction any further loans unless the excess wages were reduced to the Fair Wages standard, and it would not hesitate to impose surcharges upon the councillors responsible if, in defiance of this, they continued to pay such wages which the Government Auditors deemed to be excessive' (Italics in text.)

N.U.P.E.'s appeal to the central government was based in part on the argument that 'a Ministry which could take action when wages exceeded the Fair Wages standard could not justly refuse to take similar action when local authorities continued to pay wages considerably less than this standard'.

Another campaign began when notice was given on 9 June 1936 by Mr. Mainwaring, M.P., of a question to be asked in the House of Commons on 13 July 1936 as to whether in legislation promoting certain businesses in designated Special Areas 'proper provisions existed, or would be made, to safeguard trade union rates of wages for those engaged in any of the establishments'. A Minute considering government policy was set out by an official on 11 July 1936:

> Although it was considered that it would be difficult to avoid a fair wage requirement in the case of employers whose operations were encouraged or facilitated by assistance from State funds, it was pointed out that the Minister of Labour could in no circumstances undertake to 'safeguard Trade Union rates of wages' irrespective of whether such rates were fair in the sense that they were commonly recognized or generally observed by good employers in the trade in the district in which the employer was operating; and that it was, therefore, impossible to give a plain negative answer to the question.

Despite this degree of inhibition, a negative answer was given: businesses established on government sponsored trading estates were to be treated no differently from the renters of ordinary government-owned premises. They would be charged commercial rents and could not be differentiated by being subject to Fair Wages policy requirements. The pressure was renewed by the Labour Party on 1 February 1937. But a further departmental Minute of 17 February 1937 delimited the most advanced position the departments would take:

> Whatever may be the argument for requiring the observance of fair conditions I have been unable, on further consideration, to see how such a condition can be administered. It is one thing to refuse to continue to contract; it is another to refuse to allow a business to continue. If the lease or agreement contained a fair wages clause and this was not carried out, the Government would be placed in a very difficult position. ... It is possible, however, to take reasonable precautions to see that the tenants accepted are of a type who would be likely to be fair employers.

Administrative control was assured when on 22 February 1937, the Cabinet Committee decided that on balance it would be preferable not to put a Fair Wages clause in the Bill as introduced. Even a subsequent letter from the National Federation of Hoisery *Manufacturers* Associations enquiring if such a policy was possible was too late.

Despite this appearance of departmental intransigence, the two years following the publication of the T.U.C.'s pamphlet of 1935 produced a gradual shift in the attitudes of a key department in Fair Wages policy administration—the Ministry of Labour. The internal memoranda of the Ministry's officials supply a fascinating series of indications of the growing realization that the incongruity between an out-dated Resolution and the current collective bargaining system must be remedied. This development may be traced in some detail.

On 24 July 1935, a small deputation from the General Council of the T.U.C., consisting of Messrs. Bevin, Hicks, Sherwood and Tewson, was received by the Minister of Labour. They raised certain points with reference to the Fair Wages Clause. Thus, Bevin referred first to the fact that when the Fair Wages Resolution was passed joint agreements were usually of a local or district character. Since then there had been a considerable growth in agreements which were national in scope, so that the basis of the Resolution might be said to have been altered. Further, as a result of motor transportation and electrification, it was now possible for town contractors to go into country districts and to operate at considerable distances. This fact caused difficulties to arise in connection with the interpretation of the word 'district' in the Clause. It did not seem reasonable that, after organizations had entered into national agreements with each other, individuals should be able to evade the effect of those agreements merely because the agreements were not fully observed in certain districts. He pointed out that the Fair Wages section of the Road Traffic Act 1930, as amended, required the Industrial Court to pay regard to national agreements. Mr. Hicks emphasized the necessity, particularly in the building trades, of having such matters as the conditions under which work was carried out away from home, the rules governing travelling, and the payment of lodging allowances settled by responsible negotiators on a national basis. A somewhat different point was raised by Mr. Sherwood, who referred to the difficulty which arose when the Fair Wages Clause was interpreted as allowing the payment of the rate appropriate to some other industry, e.g., agriculture, in a particular district notwithstanding the fact that a properly constituted Joint Industrial Council had fixed a rate for the work. Such a case had occurred in the Quarrying Industry in Cornwall. The deputation accordingly asked for a short Bill, which they hoped would be regarded as non-contentious, to be introduced into the House of Commons at an early date with a view to securing that in the interpretation of the Fair Wages Clause regard should first be had to national agreements if such existed, and only in default of them to local or district practice.

The Ministry of Labour officials, having had the opportunity to read the pamphlet of March 1935, obviously knew what to expect from the deputation, and, prior to the meeting of 24 July, they prepared a note for the Minister briefing him on the points likely to be raised and the suggested proper response. In it, the progressive approach registered in the memorandum of 1 March 1934, described in chapter 10, was reiterated. The note stated that, as the general government policy was to encourage the regulation of working conditions by voluntary collective agreements, the T.U.C.'s representations could be viewed with sympathy. The increased desire of the trade unions to use the Fair Wages Clause to compel the observance of agreements, and similarly the prominence of proposals to legalize agreements, were the results of weakened organization. The unions expected the government to take every reasonable step to support agreements.

On the other hand, it was objected, the T.U.C. wished the contracting departments to use the Fair Wages Clause as if it was legislation to compel the observance of agreements. Even if all the other employers in a district were observing other conditions, an employer who happened to get a contract would have to operate different conditions, even if neither he nor his workers were party to an agreement. Since the T.U.C.'s proposal took no account of the representative character of the organizations making the national or local agreements, the contracting departments might be placed in the position of imposing conditions settled by a small minority. They might even be placed in the anomalous position of having to choose between two agreements without regard to the actual conditions in operation in a particular district. They concluded, therefore, that it was not, in fact, possible to ignore local agreements.

Instead of simply rejecting the T.U.C.'s proposals as in the past, however, the Ministry officials offered a counter proposal which sought to accommodate the pressures being exerted. They stated that, if government contracts were to be confined to employers observing agreements, some authority would have to be established to examine the validity of those agreements. The obvious precedent was the Cotton Manufacturing Industry (Temporary Provisions) Act of 1934. This Act enabled an organization of employers controlling the majority of looms in the industry, and an organization representative of the majority of workers concerned to make a joint application to the Minister of Labour for the making of an Order to give statutory effect to a voluntary collective agreement made between such organizations as to the rate of wages to be paid in the industry. On receiving such an application, the Minister was required to appoint an independent Board to consider the application. The Board was to consist of an impartial chairman and two other impartial members, and each organization party to the application was entitled to appoint six of its members as assessors. The Minister was precluded from making the Order unless and until the Board had unanimously recommended that it was expedient that the Order should be made. The terms of the agreement could not be modified in any way and, if the Order was made, the agreed rates became part of the terms of contract of every person employed in the industry to whom the rates were applicable.

The Ministry's position was that the House of Commons, in considering an amendment of the Fair Wages Clause, was unlikely to regard it as possible to accept all agreements blindly, as the T.U.C. apparently desired. It would be necessary to provide some satisfactory method of establishing the validity of agreements sought to be imposed. The officials were aware, however, that the government in at least two definite pieces of legislation, the 1934 Cotton Manufacturing Industry Act and the 1933 Road and Rail Traffic Act, had shown its desire to explore the possibility of giving the greatest possible effect to voluntary agreements. These experiments had been and were still providing experience that could be acted upon. The Ministry concluded that the issues involved were important both for the future of voluntary organizations and for the government. The mere amendment of the Fair Wages Clause would not in itself resolve these wider questions. For the moment, therefore, the officials prescribed a classic bureaucratic response: 'In the meantime the T.U.C. can be assured that their desires are viewed with the greatest sympathy and that cases in which agreed conditions appear to be wrongly put aside will always be carefully examined'.

The seven months following the meeting of 24 July 1935 between the General Council representatives and the Minister of Labour saw the development of a campaign by officials of the Ministry to have the whole question of the amendment of the Fair Wages Resolution thrown open to a full-scale inquiry. It seems that when the Minister met the T.U.C. deputation he promised to examine the suggestions put forward by them. In a Minute dated 30 July, an official of the department, Mr. F. W. Norman, stated that he presumed this involved circulating the points in question for the consideration of the contracting departments. Following such consideration, a meeting of the Fair Wages Advisory Committee would be held in order to prepare a line of reply to the T.U.C. This official went on, however, to advocate 'a general review of Fair Wages policy and practice' to be undertaken by a Committee of Inquiry appointed by the government 'to take stock of the position and to make recommendations'. He conceded that a similar proposal in March 1934 had been rejected, but noted the 'since then we have had a good deal of experience of the Road and Rail Traffic Acts in relation to Fair Wages questions and it may be that the situation has ripened towards a thorough overhaul of the whole question'.

Replying to this suggestion in a Minute of 3 August, another official of the department, a Mr. F.W.L., stated that at bottom the desire of the T.U.C. was to secure the wider observance of agreements and that there was now much more support for this from organized employers. The question was whether more could be expected from a Fair Wages Clause. In his view it was possible to over-estimate the importance of the Road Transport experience: 'The real question there is whether the principle of using the Fair Wages Clause as a basis of enforcement of proper conditions is a satisfactory method'.

In a Minute of 27 September, the Ministry of Labour official who was Secretary to the Fair Wages Advisory Committee, Mr M. A. Bevan, declared his dissatisfaction with the attitudes of other contracting departments as expressed in the Committee. In his view, the attitude of the Committee towards the 1930 proposals of the General Council for the revision of the Resolution 'was largely destructive and no serious consideration was given to the possibility of bringing this 26 year old Resolution more into harmony with the present day conditions'. He recognized the difficulty of extracting from the departments any of the jealously guarded authority to act on this delicate matter for the Labour Department: 'This department's position in the matter is not altogether easy. We have no direct responsibility for the administration of the Clause and must be guided in the main by the views of the Treasury and the contracting Departments as to the desirability and practicability of any revised Clause.' As a result he did not think it was the Labour Department's business to make any definite recommendations with regard to the Minister's promised review of the T.U.C.'s representations. Having thus excluded the Labour Department from any role, however, he went on to say that he was 'also in some doubt whether the committee itself is a very suitable body to decide the issue. The various Directors of Contracts, who largely influence the discussions, are almost necessarily concerned chiefly with the financial and administrative aspects of any change and hardly appreciate, as we do, the value and importance attaching to the general observance of collective agreements in industry.'

The first attempt to break through the authority of the contracting departments over the Fair Wages Resolution was made by another official of the Ministry of Labour in a long Minute dated 4 October. This official, Mr. Hodges, stated that with regard to the question whether the Resolution should be amended to require specifically that regard should be had to collective agreements, notwithstanding the views expressed by the Fair Wages Advisory Committee, it deserved serious consideration for various reasons. First, he asserted categorically that 'the present administration of the Resolution is out of sympathy with the intentions of its framers'. He castigated as 'seriously open to question' the following statement made in the letter sent by the Labour Department to the T.U.C. on 26 June 1934: 'The existing clause is designed to secure conformity with standards of wages and conditions generally observed in the district concerned'. This phrase had been based on the words adopted by the Fair Wages Advisory Committee— 'the rates actually found to prevail'—which are in substance indistinguishable from the words used in the 1891 Resolution. Yet in 1909 emphasis was deliberately laid on the practice of *good* employers, and the Resolution marked a deliberate departure from the requirement of the 1891 Resolution to pay 'such wages as are generally accepted as current'.

In addition to this fact that effect was not being given by the contracting departments to the intention underlying the Fair Wages Resolution, the Minute asserts, secondly, that 'the resolution in its present form fails to take account of the state of present opinion with regard to collective bargaining'. It was observed that 'collective bargaining stands in much higher regard than it did when the Resolution was passed', and claimed that it was the case that government policy now was to encourage the regulation of working conditions by voluntary collective agreements. As indications, the Balfour Committee on Industry and Trade's endorsement of this policy in their 1929 Report was cited, as was the statutory recognition accorded it in the Road and Rail Traffic Act of 1933 and the Cotton Manufacturing Industry Act of 1934.

Returning to the Fair Wages Advisory Committee, Hodges concluded that it was 'not a proper body to determine the issue'. Its composition was of a chairman provided by the Ministry of Labour, one Treasury officer and some ten representatives of the contracts or stores departments of the principal contracting government departments. Of these he commented: 'On civil servants in such departments, considerations of economy and ease of administration necessarily and rightly weigh heavily'. Moreover, the terms of reference of the Committee, laid down by Parliament, were only '*to advise as to the form of clauses in contracts* by which the Resolution of the House of Commons of the 10th March, 1909, can best be carried into effect, and as to the *methods of securing observance* of such clauses, and generally *to make such recommendations* as they may deem advisable *to promote uniformity of administration and co-operation* between Departments in dealing with the question of the payment of Fair Wages by Government contractors'.[1] (My italics.)

For the above reasons, this Labour Department official went on to make his two complementary suggestions: (a) that the Fair Wages Advisory Committee was not competent to determine the question whether the main principle of the Resolution needed amendment; and (b) that the method of determination of that question was a matter for which the Minister of Labour was responsible by virtue of his own office. Since the contracting departments were, of course, vitally interested parties, there was no harm in sounding them at the meeting of which they would be given warning. But subject to further consideration of the position after that meeting, the Minister should move independently to secure the appointment of a committee of inquiry and advice composed of representatives of employers, workers, contracting departments, the Treasury and some independents, one of whom should be the chairman.

This proposal appeared at first to have received a ready welcome from other officials concerned with the problem in the Ministry of Labour. A Minute dated 7 October, three days later, from F. W. Norman concurred with the suggestion. In expressing his agreement, this official referred to the previous reluctance to set up a committee of inquiry, but suggested that the question had entered into another phase, since the action being undertaken at the time to strengthen the defence forces of the country, and the prospective increased expenditures, would certainly enlarge very much the area of government contracting in fields where wages questions were likely to crop up very frequently. In such circumstances the question of Fair Wages was likely to be of increasing importance, and consequently it would be helpful to have in existence an up-to-date and authoritative body of doctrine in regard to Fair Wages together with a suitable procedure for the application of such doctrine:

> It may be true that few people are worrying very much about Fair Wages questions at present but I feel that once the rearmament programme is in full swing, in dealing with the wages paid by Government contractors, we shall need a sheet anchor in the shape of a well thought out and generally acceptable scheme of Fair Wages administration. We have no such scheme at present but on the basis of a report of a Committee of Enquiry representative of all interests I see no reason why one could not be devised.

Another official, Mr. F.W.L., agreed in a Minute of 19 October that such a scheme of administration was needed, but added that, 'The subject, of course, raises the question of the compulsory extension of agreements and cannot be easily divorced from that wider consideration'.

The misgivings aroused by the introduction of the latter question into the problem of amendment of the Fair Wages Resolution are evidenced by a lengthy Minute written by Mr. M. A. Bevan, Secretary of the Fair Wages Advisory Committee, dated 13 January 1936. In it he discussed a request by Ernest Bevin that the wages and conditions laid down in the Agreements of the National Joint Conciliation Board for the Road Transport Industry (Goods) should be prescribed as the fair wages and conditions required by the Fair Wages Clause applicable to government contracts. The Secretary asserted that Bevin knew perfectly well that under the present clause a National Agreement did not establish fair wages and conditions regardless of those prevailing in the district concerned. Bevin himself was the chief speaker at the T.U.C. deputation's meeting with the Minister of Labour in July 1935 when this interpretation of the Clause had been advanced as a proposed amendment. Bevin's proposal, therefore, was regarded as part of the much wider proposal to give effect to National Agreements generally for fair wages purposes, not only for road transport. This latter proposition gave rise to some further considerations.

The Secretary expressed the view that, if a National Agreement was to be recognized for the purposes of the Fair Wages Clause, it was essential that it should be a National Agreement not only in name but also in practice. It was asserted that the arguments for the recognition of National Agreements in relation to the Fair Wages Clause had been built up mainly on the basis of the National Agreement for the Building Industry, which was commonly recognized and observed by organized employers over a large part of England and Wales. This, the Secretary claimed, was not the position with regard to the Road Transport Agreements. While it was true that the Agreements had been reached by a national board, nonetheless, the employers' representatives of the board had in some parts of the country failed to carry with them even a majority of their own members leaving aside altogether a large body of unorganized employers. Even the most enthusiastic advocates of the legalisation of voluntary agreements recognized that before such agreements could have statutory effect they must be supported by a majority.

The public policy was seen by the Secretary as follows: although the government had helped to set up a joint body to assist the Road Haulage Industry in bringing order out of chaos as regards its industrial conditions, it did not seem to follow that the government was called upon to implement decisions reached by that body which were not accepted by employers as a whole in the industry. The Department of Labour would certainly support the Joint Board, but not to the extent of ignoring the views of large bodies of presumably responsible employers throughout the country. As he saw it, the responsibility rested with the employers' side of the Board either to satisfy their constituents that the terms of the present agreements were such as could be operated by reasonable employers without hardship or to endeavour to secure modifications of the agreements which their constituents would accept. The responsibility for saying that the agreement as it stood was a right and proper agreement and must be enforced ought not to be shifted on to the government and certainly not at the request of one side. If there seemed to be a danger of the Board's agreements falling to the ground, it was for the Board as a whole to present a proper case as to the nature of the assistance they needed to secure the observance of fair rates and conditions throughout the industry.

These misgivings did not augur well for the T.U.C.'s proposals for amendment of the Fair Wages policy, even if such an enquiry into amendment of the Resolution was held. In any event the momentum continued to grow, and in a Minute dated 17 January 1936, Mr. F. W. Norman was asked to put the case for a committee of inquiry in the form of a Cabinet memorandum for consideration. In the weeks that followed, doubts were again raised by the Secretary of the Fair Wages Advisory Committee. He pointed out that the responsibility of the Ministry of Labour was limited to giving advice when needed. In this Minute, dated 4 February, he conceded that problems existed: 'There can be no doubt that we have found great difficulty in giving advice based on a strict interpretation of the existing Resolution, having regard to our general knowledge of the circumstances prevailing in industry as a whole, and I think that we have felt that many of the questions raised could only be satisfactorily settled by an independent tribunal after hearing evidence'. Nevertheless, he felt that, as the Ministry only got the most difficult cases, the contracting departments as a whole might still take the view that generally speaking the existing clause and its administration worked equitably as between employers and workers and to themselves as contractors. He added, however: 'The contracting Departments and the Treasury are of course concerned with financial aspects of the matter'.

Taking his cue from this last sentence, Mr. Hodges, the author of the original suggestion for an independent initiative by the Ministry of Labour, pointed out in a Minute of 12 February, that while it was true that the Minister of Labour had no responsibility for the administration of the Resolution, 'he is the only Minister outside the Treasury who is in a position to review the working of the Resolution impartially and with official knowledge of the relevant circumstances prevailing in industry as a whole'. The formation of the Ministry in 1916 and its development since then gave him that position. To add some urgency to his argument, he mentioned that the 'T.U.C. are now pressing to know how this matter stands'. And a Minute from Mr. F. W. Norman on the following day, 13 February, referred to a letter from Sir Walter Citrine of the T.U.C. and mentioned 'that the T.U.C. are getting concerned about this matter I can well believe since on a recent occasion when Mr. Bevin saw the Permanent Secretary he gave expression to rather strong opinions on the whole question of fair wages policy'.

Despite these arguments and pressures, the suggestion for an independent initiative by the Minister of Labour seems to have faltered. A note of 15 February from Mr. F.W.L. states strangely enough: 'It seems to me that the proposal for a Committee of Inquiry, while right in normal circumstances, becomes impracticable in face of the circumstances created by the new Government rearmament programme'—strange because in a Minute of 19 October 1935 he had previously concurred in supporting the proposal for this same reason. By 19 February, the originator of the suggestion, Mr. Hodges, was already writing that, if 'the proposal to set up a committee is dead so far as the Ministry of Labour is concerned, the Minister is still in the position that last July he promised the T.U.C. that he would at once consider their views and consult with the Departments concerned'. Accordingly he reverted to the original response of putting the proposals to a meeting of the Fair Wages Advisory Committee.

The Committee held its sixtieth meeting on 16 June 1936 to consider the renewed proposals by the General Council of the T.U.C. for the revision of the Fair Wages Clause. The arguments canvassed above had been circulated earlier for the consideration of Committee members in a memorandum dated 9 June. After recounting the history of the dispute since its last treatment in 1934, the memorandum made this blunt confession:

> It may be admitted that when wages and conditions are not based upon the terms of a collective agreement between organized employers and workers it is sometimes difficult satisfactorily to define any standard of wages and conditions in accordance with the requirements of the Fair Wages Clause. Previous discussions on the subject, as shown in the memorandum summarizing the views of the Departments circulated by the Ministry of Labour on the 25th August, 1930, have been concerned more to show

that the existing Clause offers no very substantial ground for complaint than to attempt to devise some amendment of the Clause and/or its administration which would relate more closely to the present day position in regard to collective agreements.

In order to redress this unbalanced approach, the memorandum went on to point out how since 1909 there had been a progressive increase in the extent to which wages and other conditions of employment were settled by voluntary collective agreements between organizations of employers and workers and that at the present time over a large part of industry collective bargaining was the normal and established method of settling working conditions.

The not surprising result of this increase was 'that there has developed a movement not confined to trade unions in favour of the compulsory enforcement of agreements reached by collective bargaining'. At the central government level, the memorandum gave as examples the Road and Rail Traffic Act, 1933, and the Cotton Manufacturing Industry Act of 1934. At the local authority level it quoted as an example the following provision adopted by the Stoke City Council, a Labour body, in June 1935:

(a) The contractors and tradesmen tendering for the supply of any goods to the local authority shall pay rates of wages and observe conditions of labour not less favourable to all employees than those commonly recognized by employers and Trade Unions in the trade in the district where the work is carried out. In the absence of any generally recognized rules as to wages and the conditions of labour those rules fixed by National Agreements between employers' and employees' organizations shall be adopted, but where no District or National Rules prevail the rules recognized in the nearest district where the general industrial conditions are similar shall be observed.

In a schedule attached to the memorandum extracts were given from the Fair Wages Clauses adopted by various local authorities. Unlike the Stoke City clause, none of these made mention of National Agreements, though it was pointed out that a number of London Boroughs required the observance of trade union conditions and made no reference to district. Thus, the Hammersmith clause required the payment of 'the Trade Union or Standard rate of wages, as agreed upon by the Association or Associations of Employers and Employees in the Trade Unions concerned'. In Bradford, municipal contractors were required to pay not less than the standard rate of wages:

such standard rate of wages to be deemed to be the rate mutually
agreed upon by the Masters' Association and the Trade Unions
respectively concerned, or in case there should at any relevant
time be no such rate as aforesaid, then such rate of wages to be
deemed to be the last mutually agreed upon by the Masters'
Association and the Trade Unions respectively concerned. Provided that in the case of engineers, founders, and metal workers,
the rate of wages and conditions of employment last agreed upon
as between the Federated Engineering Employers and the Allied
Trade Unions shall be observed.

Other local authorities, the London County Council, Dundee, Birmingham, Portsmouth and Swindon, all referred to district rates or arrangements, though often explicit reference was made to collective bargaining
arrangements between associations of employers and employees.

There appears to have been some confusion among the authors
of the memorandum as to what conclusions to draw from this evidence.
An earlier draft of the memorandum stated:

The position seems to be that a decision must first be reached on
the question whether there is a case for applying the Fair Wages
principle on the basis of wages and conditions determined by
collective agreements in the industry generally, rather than by
reference to prevailing local conditions regardless of outside agreements. When this has been done, the form in which to express
such decision may arise.

This draft took the idea so far as to consider that, if the new principle
was introduced and administration of the Fair Wages policy no longer
proceeded on the basis of 'fact', it would be necessary to submit any
disputes as to agreements applicable to the judgment of an independent
and impartial tribunal. The final memorandum, however, carefully
avoided this rather sharp confrontation with principle. Rather, it
posed the problem in a form thought likely to be more acceptable to
departmental officials:

The position, therefore, is that Parliament has to some extent
and subject to certain safeguards approved of the principle of
giving statutory recognition to joint collective industrial agreements. Having regard to the very considerable volume of work
executed under contract (a) by Government, (b) by local authorities on State-aided work, and (c) by local authorities without
State aid, the general circumstances make it increasingly difficult
satisfactorily to maintain and defend the present Fair Wages
Clause against the contentions of the T.U.C.

Continuing in this somewhat indecisive vein, the memorandum explained that the subject was difficult and contentious and one in which employers and workers, as well as central and local government were concerned. It mentioned rather perfunctorily that one suggestion had been made that a committee, representative of these interests under an independent chairman should be appointed to enquire into the provisions and working of the Fair Wages Resolution and consider what changes, if any, ought to be made. It quickly dismissed this suggestion, however, by stating that, while it might have been appropriate in normal circumstances, 'it appears to be open to doubt whether it is opportune to set up such a committee in view of the circumstances created by the Government's new armament programme'. It concluded, therefore, that if the contracting departments were of this opinion then it would be necessary to submit a proposal to Ministers that no action should be taken at the present time and to send a reply to the General Council on this basis. It ended on the following abrupt if decisive note: 'Without in any way prejudging the issue on this point, there is attached a draft letter that might be sent to the General Council if it is decided that the appointment of a Committee to enquire into the position would be inopportune at present'.

It seems that this indirect rejection of the T.U.C.'s proposals was insufficiently robust for the departmental representatives. For at their meeting on 16 June 1936 the Fair Wages Advisory Committee amended and approved the draft letter and proposed instead that the Ministry of Labour send the following reply to the General Council:

I am to say that in consultation with other Ministers concerned the Minister has given most careful consideration to (the T.U.C. proposals). As the General Council will be aware, it is the policy of the Government to encourage the regulation of working conditions by voluntary collective agreements and practical evidence of this policy appears in the statutory recognition of collective agreements in the Road Traffic Act, 1930, as extended by the Road and Rail Traffic Act, 1933, and in the Cotton Manufacturing Industry Act, 1934. At the same time, the Minister is bound to recognize that even the strongest advocates of the statutory enforcement of voluntary agreements realize that certain conditions must be satisfied before such action is taken. It does not appear to be practicable, even if it were desirable, to embody these conditions in the Fair Wages Clause, and I am to say therefore, that he is unable to depart from the view previously expressed that the clause is not an appropriate instrument for the enforcement of agreements irrespective of the circumstances in which the various agreements were made or of the fact whether they are recognized or put into operation in the trade in the district in which the work is carried out.

This peremptory rejection of the T.U.C.'s proposals did not please the Ministry of Labour officials subject to continuing trade union pressure. In a Minute of 17 September, the Secretary of the Committee himself characterized the draft reply as 'purely negative' and stated that it would 'not satisfy the General Council of the T.U.C., and we shall have to deal with further representations'. On 5 October, he wrote a further lengthy Minute contrasting the attitudes of the Ministry of Labour and of the contracting departments to the amendment of the Resolution. He pointed out that the contracting departments felt that as a whole the existing clause worked equitably as between employers and workers, that the amendment on the basis of the recognition of collective agreements involved the introduction of a foreign principle, and that such a new clause would produce greater administrative difficulties. In the Ministry of Labour, however, 'we have more in mind the developments in industrial organization, the extent to which working conditions are determined by collective agreements and the increasing tendency among organized employers and workers to support the idea of some form of wages regulation'. The difficulty was that the government policy regarding such regulation had not yet been clearly defined, and amendment of the Resolution could not be considered apart from this broader question. Consequently, 'both the contracting Departments and ourselves hesitate to proceed with the amendment of the resolution, but for different reasons'. He objected, therefore, to the conveying to the General Council of 'a purely negative reply'; for while he thought there were good reasons for refusing to adopt the proposals at the moment, 'I do not feel that it is wise to give the impression that the Government is satisfied with the existing clause or that it is the best that can be devised in the light of present day conditions'. His own view, indeed, was that 'the existing fair wages resolution is not altogether in line with present day conditions, and that some amendment is desirable'. He elaborated his position further in two draft memoranda which he prepared for consideration.

One memorandum contained the assertion that the development of collective bargaining had proceeded for many years past with the encouragement of successive governments, and its advantages and those of securing the widespread observance of agreements reached by joint representative bodies had been welcomed by responsible leaders on both sides of industry. The other stated that the system of regulating working conditions by collective bargaining was now normal throughout industry and there was an increasing tendency to make national agreements or at least settlements which cover a wide area. Consequently, there had developed a feeling, not entirely confined to trade unions, that Fair Wages Clauses based on conditions 'recognized' or 'prevailing' in the district were inappropriate to the circumstances of modern industry. This draft detailed the origins and development of the T.U.C. proposals from the Building Trades deputation of 1929 up to the meeting with the Minister of Labour in July 1935.

Citing the Cotton Manufacturing Industry Act of 1934 as evidence, the Secretary stated the current position to be that Parliament had to some extent and subject to safeguarding qualifications already approved of the principle of giving statutory recognition to joint collective industrial agreements. As a result of the 1934 Act, a number of applications had been received from various industries (such as electrical contracting, quarrying, pottery, hosiery, glove-making, heating and domestic engineering) for enabling legislation which would give them powers for the compulsory enforcement throughout their industry of joint agreements. These applications had been deferred with the reply that the Act of 1934 was experimental and no further action was contemplated until experience of its workings had been gained. On the one hand, therefore, the Ministry maintained that this 'considerable expression of opinion in favour of the regulated compulsory enforcement of voluntary agreements' did not fully appreciate the difficulties and implications of such proposals. Yet it also asserted: 'At the same time, it is the policy of the Government to encourage the regulation of working conditions by voluntary collective agreements'.

In addition to these pressures, and concurrently with the representations of the General Council, the Secretary's memorandum also cited considerable sporadic and uncoordinated activities displayed by joint bodies in a number of trades with a view to inducing government departments and local authorities to recognize agreed wages and conditions as 'fair' within the meaning of the Fair Wages Clause. While, so far as contracts directly placed and thus controlled by government departments were concerned, these activities were characterized as 'merely troublesome'; as regards the contracts placed by local authorities, there was reason to believe that some diversity of practice existed among authorities in the interpretation of the clause, *even where the contracts were for works specifically aided by government grants.* At attempt to establish uniform practices among local authorities had been made through section 266 of the Local Government Act, 1933.

This stipulated that all contracts entered into by a local authority should be made in accordance with the Standing Orders of the authority. This meant that any local authority which had not already done so was obliged, on the coming into force of the Act, to adopt Standing Orders regulating the granting of their contracts. The Ministry of Health, in Circular 1388 of 28 March 1934 addressed to local authorities, offered a set of draft model Standing Orders and recommended their adoption. These model Standing Orders included a Fair Wages Clause in the same terms as the Clause in the Fair Wages Resolution. The T.U.C. pamphlet of March 1935 commented on this recommendation that 'there is no compulsion on the local authority to adopt the Government's Fair Wages Clause or any Fair Wages Clause'. And the Secretary's conclusion in his memorandum was that in the case of contracts for their own works, not only was there diversity of interpretation among local authorities, but also a diversity of the terms of the Fair Wages Clauses contained in the contracts. In some cases, the contractors were required to observe the terms contained in collective agreements in general or in certain specified agreements.

The Secretary of the Fair Wages Advisory Committee characterized the above situation as being 'indefensibly chaotic', and asserted that it was increasingly difficult to defend the existing clause against the contentions of the T.U.C. and in the face of the movement towards the legalization of collective agreements. His final conclusions were circulated in the Ministry of Labour and read as follows:

> I am not suggesting that the time has yet arrived for further legislation designed to give statutory force to voluntary agreements. *I find myself, however, in some doubt whether the existing Fair Wages Resolution and its administration secure that wages and working conditions on Government and Government aided contracts are in line with the standards generally accepted by the good employers in various trades.* Apart from anything else, the development of the national defence programme is likely to enlarge the field of Government contracting and to make fair wages questions assume increasing importance. I have therefore come to the conclusion that the time has arrived for the question of the need for the amendment of the Fair Wages Resolution and its general administration to be more fully examined. (My italics.)

The aftermath of this memorandum was a period of hesitancy and uncertainty. Sections of the memorandum were subjected to challenge by other officials of the Ministry of Labour. Meanwhile, the T.U.C. maintained pressure by raising the question again in a letter from

Sir Walter Citrine to the Minister dated 2 December. A note of 8 December by an official of the Ministry, Mr. F.W.L., refers to the T.U.C. inquiries as being merely designed to keep interest alive and to provide evidence of having done so. Nevertheless, there was great reluctance to send a purely negative reply: 'It seems to me to be impossible to give a finally negative reply to the General Council or, on the other hand, to do nothing'. His proposal was tentatively made to send the T.U.C. proposals to the Confederation of Employers' Organizations for consultation.

In the meantime, the question had been forcefully raised in the House of Commons. On 19 November, Mr. Mander asked the Financial Secretary to the Treasury whether it was the practice to insist that all firms receiving government contracts should officially recognize collective bargaining through the medium of trade unions. On receiving a direct and unequivocal answer in the negative, the Member asked whether the Treasury considered 'that this is one condition that certainly ought to be laid down before any Government contracts are given'. The answer was that this could only be as far as the Fair Wages Resolution allowed. In a supplementary question, another M.P. demanded that, 'As this Fair Wages Clause is ineffective to secure decent wages in many industries, will the Government consider making it a reality instead of a farce?' The Treasury denied that it was a farce.[2] A somewhat exasperated official of the Ministry of Labour, Mr. F. W. Norman, expressed himself as follows in a Minute of 23 December:

> The first Fair Wages Clause was adopted in 1891 and the second in 1909. The administration of the latter is fraught with considerable difficulty and the industrial outlook is now very different from 1909. It therefore seems reasonable that consideration should be given to the desirability of framing a third Fair Wages Clause in consonance with current conditions. Otherwise we only go on with the interminable debate with the T.U.C.

Consideration of these arguments appears to have led the Minister of Labour, Ernest Brown, to finally put the above view to the Chancellor of the Exchequer, Neville Chamberlain, in a letter of 28 January 1937. On 9 February, the Treasury stated in the House of Commons that the T.U.C. representations were being given active consideration. It had been asked again by Mr. Mander 'to bear in mind that there are several aspects in which the Fair Wages Resolution is not up-to-date, and will (the Treasury) consider the advisability of appointing a committee to look into the matter.[3] The result was that a departmental conference was convened in the Treasury on 11 February to consider the proposal to set up a committee to advise on the amendment of the Fair Wages Resolution. Representatives of the Admiralty, War Office, Air Ministry, Post Office, Stationery Office, Ministry of Health, Office of Works and Ministry of Transport were present, with Sir James Rae of the Treasury in the chair. The Minutes of the meeting record that the chairman 'referred to the fact that more than a quarter of a century had elapsed since the Fair Wages Resolution in its present form was adopted by the House of Commons and that there had been various developments in the industrial world in the meantime'. The attitude of the departmental representatives appears to have been one of unwavering hostility to the T.U.C. proposals. On the question of the observance of national agreements, the objection was raised that the contract might be placed in an area very remote from any district where a national agreement was in actual operation. Despite this, the representative of the Ministry of Labour, Mr. Leggett, succeeded in swaying the others to his Minister's point of view. He used the tactic of concurring with the others as to the administrative non-feasibility of the proposals, but added that 'he felt it would be better to appoint a Committee to examine the matter than to adopt a purely negative attitude. The sting would be taken out of the attack if all the facts were publicly considered.' Consequently, in a letter of 15 February, the Chancellor of the Exchequer wrote to the Minister of Labour expressing his agreement with the proposal to appoint a Committee.

It remained for the Minister of Labour to seek Cabinet approval for the proposal, and to this end a memorandum was drafted setting out the arguments in full once again. Two drafts of this memorandum are to be found and the differences between them indicate certain changes in emphasis desired by the Ministry's officials. The first draft related how over a long period the General Council of the T.U.C. had been pressing for an amendment of the Fair Wages Clause. The nature of these amendments was explained and the reasons for their rejection by the Fair Wages Advisory Committee in 1934 were reviewed. The same process occurred following the T.U.C. deputation of July 1935. The memorandum also mentioned that at that time the opinion of the Committee 'was invited on the desirability of setting up a committee to enquire into the provisions and working of the Fair Wages Resolution, and to consider what changes, if any, ought to be made'. Here again the reply had been in the negative. Then came the crucial passage concerning the changes in industrial relations which had precipitated the calls for reform (the last sentence of the following quotation was missing from this first draft, but was added on in the second draft):

Since 1909, there has been a progressive increase in the extent to which wages and other conditions of employment are settled by voluntary collective agreements between organizations of employers and workpeople, and at the present time over a large part of industry, collective bargaining is the normal and established method of settling working conditions. At the same time, the reduction in the membership of organizations and other circumstances have tended to weaken the effectiveness of agreements so that the wages generally operative in a district may not be on an agreed basis.

At this point came the inevitable reference to Parliament's seeming approval of the principle of statutory recognition of collective agreements in the Cotton Manufacturing Industry Act 1934, the result of which experiment still remained to be defined. In addition, the operation of the Fair Wages principle in the Road Traffic Acts 1930 and 1933, was mentioned. As a result of some criticism of its implementation by both employers' and employees' organizations, a Committee of Inquiry had been set up by the Ministry of Labour jointly with the Ministry of Transport. It was hoped this would throw further light on the matter. The second draft also mentioned the old doubt as to 'whether it is desirable to introduce any alteration in fair wages policy at a time when there is a wide extension of Government contracts in connection with the defence programme'.

A subtle change of emphasis is apparent in the differences between the following two paragraphs in the First and Second Drafts respectively:

I do not think there is any doubt that there is a case for the amendment of the existing Fair Wages Resolution although it may be open to question whether the moment has yet arrived to deal with the matter, which cannot be divorced from the wider question of the compulsory extension of voluntary agreements and wages regulation in general.

I do not think there is any doubt that sooner or later the existing Fair Wages Resolution will have to be amended, although when this is done the view of Local Government authorities and organized employers will have to be taken into account, as well as those of workers.

The First Draft assumes the need for immediate revision, but questions the timing. The Second Draft assumes the need for revision some time in the future. The implications of this difference are apparent in the recommendations that follow. The Second Draft's hesitancy led to the following paragraph:

In view of these considerations I do not wish to propose that we should institute at present the examination which in my opinion will later on be necessary, but they also make me reluctant to return a purely negative answer to the T.U.C. on the present occasion. Such an answer would invite criticism which would have a considerable appearance of justification.

The First Draft took the more positive approach which eventually prevailed:

In all the circumstances I have come to the conclusion that a further public review of the position by a Committee is desirable and when recently I saw Mr. Bevin, the Chairman of the General Council of the T.U.C., he indicated his personal view that such action would be acceptable. This is important, as if the Government are not prepared to make any move the General Council intend, I understand, to take steps with a view to having a new Resolution moved in the House. This would not be a satisfactory way of dealing with the matter and I think it is desirable to appoint a Committee now and not to do so as a result of pressure from the Opposition.

Accordingly, the Minister proposed formally to proceed forthwith with the appointment of a Committee including representatives of the Treasury and the contracting departments, together with representatives of employers' and workers' organizations and an independent chairman. The suggested terms of reference were to be: 'To consider the working of the Fair Wages Resolution of the House of Commons of the 10th March, 1909, as embodied in Government Contracts and to advise whether any changes are desirable and practicable'. He mentioned that the Chancellor of the Exchequer had agreed with this proposal and with the view that the Committee should be appointed by the Minister of Labour. A Cabinet meeting on 3 March approved the Committee with the terms of reference suggested, but left the composition to be determined after inter-departmental discussion.

Two weeks after the Cabinet had approved the setting up of a Committee, on 18 March 1937 the General Council of the T.U.C., which had evidently been kept completely in the dark, sent a deputation to meet the Minister of Labour. The deputation pointed out that representations on the subject of the desirability of redrafting the Fair Wages Resolution had been made over a period of by then nine years. Although they learned of the Cabinet's decision when the appointment of the Committee was announced in the House of

Commons by the Minister of Labour on 25 March, the General Council only received a formal reply on 9 April. This pointed out that the General Council's proposals were of a far-reaching character, and if put into operation would have considerable reaction on industry outside the field of government contracts. As there had been no public review of the subject since 1908, the Minister had come to the conclusion that it was desirable to appoint a Committee to examine the position in association with employers' and workers' representatives. The terms of reference were to be those quoted above.[4]

NOTES

1. Parl. Deb., H. of C. (Fifth Series); 14 March 1910, vol. XV, col. 9.

2. See Parl. Deb., H. of C. (Fifth Series); 19 November 1936, vol. 317, col. 1915.

3. Parl. Deb., H. of C. (Fifth Series); 9 February 1937, vol. 320, col. 216.

4. The above account is principally derived from the following sources:

—Report of the 66th Annual Trades Union Congress, Weymouth, 1934, pp. 351–2.

—Report of the General Council to the 67th Annual Trades Union Congress, Margate, 1935, at p. 225.

—Report of the General Council to the 69th Annual Trades Union Congress, Norwich, 1937, at p. 208.

—*The Fair Wages Clause—An Explanatory Statement*, pamphlet published by the General Council of the T.U.C. (ref. No. 4 F.W. 3/35). For the information of Officers and Members of Trade Unions and Trades Councils (March 1935). (15 pp.)

—*Distributive Workers and the Fair Wages Clause*, pamphlet published by the Research Department, National Amalgamated Union of Shop Assistants, Warehousemen and Clerks. In the Library of the T.U.C., ref. HD 5015 (1935).

—*Observance of the Fair Wages Clause by Scottish Local Authorities* (Second Report, October 1937); published by the Scottish T.U.C. In the Library of the T.U.C., ref. HD 5015 (1937).

—*Trade Union Recognition and the Fair Wages Clause—Our Fight*, pamphlet by Bryn Roberts, General Secretary, National Union of Public Employees. In the Library of the T.U.C., ref. JS 3175 (1940).

—In the Department of Employment Library, Box GP.331.18–331.2, File 405:

—Letter, dated 22 December 1937, concerning a complaint by Will Thorne, M.P. re Fair Wages policy application.

—Memo on Special and Approved Areas, Associated Undertakings and Fair Wages. Doc. No. E.M. 1227/37.

—Letter from E. W. Leggett to Somervell, dated 11 July 1938 (I.R. 359/1938) in connection with possible extension of Fair Wages policy to employers protected by tariffs. Negative reply.

—Memo on Extension of Fair Wages principle to work not subject to a government contract.

—Letters dated 22 March and 27 March 1933 re application of Fair Wages policy.

—Memo on Rates of Wages on State Associated Schemes, dated approximately 31 March 1930, Unemployment measures.

—Public Record Office, Files of the Ministry of Labour: LAB 10/12 (1935–37); I.R. 1080/1935:

—Note taken by the Secretary of the T.U.C. deputation meeting the Minister of Labour on 24th July 1935.

—Note for T.U.C. Deputation: Fair Wages Clause.

—Minute containing a note from Mr. F. W. Norman to Mr. Leggett, dated 30 July 1935.

—Minute from F.W.L., dated 3 August 1935.

—Minute from M. A. Bevan to Mr. Hodges, dated 27 September 1935.

—Minute from H. R. Hodges to Mr. Norman, dated 4 October 1935.

—Minute from F. W. Norman to Mr. Leggett, dated 7 October 1935.

—Minute from F.W.L. to Secretary, dated 19 October 1935.

—Minute from M. A. Bevan to Mr. Hodges, dated 13 January 1936.

—Note to Mr. Norman, dated 17 January 1936.

—Minute from M. A. Bevan to Mr. Hodges, dated 4 February 1936.

—Minute from Mr. H. R. Hodges to Mr. Norman, dated 12 February 1936.

—Note from F. W. Norman to Mr. Leggett, dated 13 February 1936.

—Note from F.W.L. to Secretary, dated 15 February 1936.

—Note from Hodges to Norman, dated 19 February 1936.

—Fair Wages Advisory Committee Memorandum—Renewed Proposals by the General Council of the T.U.C. for the Revision of the Fair Wages Clause, dated 9 June 1936.

—Another Draft of the Fair Wages Advisory Committee Memorandum— Renewed Proposals by the General Council of the T.U.C. for the Revision of the Fair Wages Clause.

—Draft of a Suggested Reply to the General Council of the T.U.C., as amended and approved by the Fair Wages Advisory Committee— Appendix to the Memorandum on Fair Wages Policy of the Ministry of Labour.

—Minute from M. A. Bevan to Mr. Norman, dated 17 September 1936.

—Minute from M. A. Bevan to Mr. Norman, dated 5 October 1936.

—Draft Memorandum 'B' on Fair Wages Policy by the Ministry of Labour.

—Draft Memorandum 'A' on Fair Wages Policy by the Ministry of Labour.

—Minute from F.W.L. commenting on the draft addressed to Norman, dated 10 October 1936.

—Note from F. W. L. to Secretary, dated 8 December 1936.

—Minute from F. W. Norman to Mr. Leggett, dated 23 December 1936.

—Copy, dated 12 February 1937, of the Minutes of the Meeting held in the Treasury on Thursday, 11 February 1937, to consider the proposal to set up a committee to advise on the amendment of the Fair Wages Resolution.

—Letter from Neville Chamberlain to the Rt. Hon. Ernest Brown, M.P., dated 15 February 1937.

—First Draft of a Memorandum on Fair Wages Policy by the Minister of Labour.

—Second Draft of a Memorandum on Fair Wages Policy by the Minister of Labour.

—Minute of 10 March 1937.

—Letter from C. C. Cunningham of the Scottish Office to T. S. Chegwidden of the Ministry of Labour, dated 4 March 1937.

12

Origins of the Fair Wages Resolution of 1946

Legislation Promoting Fair Wages Policy: 1935–1938

The debate among the government departments which culminated in the decision to appoint a committee to examine the Fair Wages policy had at its core the question of compulsory enforcement or statutory recognition of collective agreements. Were these to be designated as standards to be observed by employers in circumstances where the public interest was involved? The most frequently mentioned examples were the Road and Rail Traffic Act of 1933 and the Cotton Manufacturing Industry Act of 1934. These statutes were cited time and again as evidence that the trend was towards explicit recognition and enforcement of collective agreements by the government. Given the significance of this key issue, other enactments along these lines during this period should be examined. They were contemporary manifestations of the ideas which led to the new Fair Wages Resolution of 1946.

The London Passenger Transport (Agreement) Act, 1935, authorized the Treasury to guarantee securities issued in accordance with an Agreement between the Treasury, the London Passenger Transport Board, and certain railway companies, for providing passenger transport facilities by the construction of certain works specified in the Agreement. Section 19(b) of the Act gave the full quotation of the Fair Wages Resolution of 1909 and required that all contracts connected with the carrying out of these works were to contain a clause along those lines. A similar enactment of the same year, the Railways (Agreement) Act, 1935, contained the full statement of the 1909 Resolution in its section 16(b). The Housing Act, 1936, continued this traditional approach by following the precedents set by previous Housing Acts of 1924 and 1930: section 72(3) required the insertion of the current Fair Wages Clause in all contracts for the erection of houses.

For notes see p. 226

The Sugar Industry (Reorganisation) Act, 1936, continued the experiment introduced by the Road and Rail Traffic Act of 1933. In adjudicating over disputes, the Industrial Court was to refer to 'any determination that may be brought to its notice relating to the wages or conditions of service of persons employed in a capacity similar to that of the persons to whom the reference relates, being a determination contained in a decision of a joint industrial council, conciliation board, or other similar body, or in an agreement between organizations representative of employers and workpeople'. This provision, in section 23(2) of the Act, like that in another statute passed later in the year— section 27(2) of the Air Navigation Act—was identical to that contained in section 32(1) of the 1933 Act. The Sugar Industry Act of 1936 granted financial assistance to the British Sugar Corporation which was set up and charged with the duties of keeping under review the development of the industry. The attitude of the Corporation towards its Fair Wages obligation is worth noting. It was declared in Case 1713 which came before the Industrial Court on 25 October 1938:

> It was stated to be the wish of the Corporation to comply with its statutory duties both in the letter and in the spirit and that the wages paid should be fair and the conditions of employment beyond criticism. It was pointed out that in view of the financial assistance received from the State the Corporation cannot approach questions affecting wages and conditions of employment in exactly the same way as an ordinary employer of labour and that unless satisfied beyond doubt that any increase in wages asked for by its employees can properly be granted without prejudice to the interests of the State or to its own shareholders, the Corporation conceives itself to be under a duty to refer the matter to the (Industrial) Court. (para. 7)

So far as the Sugar Corporation was concerned, therefore, the position of the Industrial Court was crucial in its determination of fair wages. How did the Industrial Court, then, regard the Fair Wages obligation?

In Case 1659 of 22 September 1936, the Court, in an unusual lapse from its predominantly reticent attitude, gave a glimpse into its conception of the Fair Wages policy. The case before it concerned a complaint under the Road Traffic legislation. The Union involved complained, and the company concerned admitted, 'that the rates paid are lower than those laid down by the East Midland Area Joint Conciliation Board for the City of Oxford'. The company claimed, however, that these rates 'had never become operative and the rates paid by the firm are those commonly paid by all other firms in the Road Haulage Industry in the City of Oxford'. The Court gave the following account of its view of the Fair Wages policy embodied in section 32 of the Road and Rail Traffic Act, 1933:

> The issue in the present case is as to whether the firm concerned are or are not complying with the provisions of the Fair Wages Resolution and for this purpose the Court have to determine as regards rates of wages, for example, what are the rates paid in the trade in the district concerned. It is no part of the duty of the Court to determine under the present reference what those rates should be. The rates having been determined, the question of whether the firm concerned are or are not paying them is merely one of comparison.
>
> The question as to how far a decision of a Joint Conciliation Board as to rates of wages, etc., such as that to which the attention of the Court was directed in the present case, should be regarded as determining the rate of wages and conditions of employment proper to be observed in the localities which they purport to cover is not a matter which comes within the scope of the present reference and the decision of the Court in the present case is not to be regarded as being in any way indicative of the views of the Court in respect of this matter. (para. 8)

Upholding the contention of the company, therefore, the Court held that 'the rates of wages and conditions of employment of the employees of (the Company) are those commonly paid to and observed in respect of the employees of all the firms engaged in the Road Haulage Industry in the City of Oxford'.

What the Industrial Court in effect decided in this case was to reject the trade unions' interpretation of the Fair Wages policy—that it should support and encourage adherence to negotiated agreements. Instead, the Court followed the contracting departments' line that only the rates and conditions actually prevailing in the district concerned were relevant. The provisions of the Resolution itself, applicable under section 93(1) of the 1930 Act, that primacy was to be given to rates 'commonly recognized by employers and trade societies', and only in their absence were prevailing rates to be adopted, and then only those prevailing among good employers—all this was ignored by the Court as it had been by the departments. Even the express reference to rates contained in a decision of a Conciliation Board, made in section 32(1) of the 1933 Act, did not move the Court. Its view was that rates 'commonly recognized', or those contained in a decision of a Conciliation Board, were only relevant when they were actually being paid and observed by firms in the district. Their existence when not implemented in practice did not permit for them to be taken into account in fixing 'fair' rates. In circumstances where they were not paid or observed, as in this case, the provisions of the Resolution and the statutes were irrelevant. The Court could assert that they were not 'a matter which comes within the scope of the present reference'. Writing at about this time, the Committee on the Regulation of Road Transport Wages commented: 'It must, however, be borne in mind that the Industrial Court is an independent authority; that the National Joint Conciliation Boards are autonomous and voluntary bodies; that the force of the words "shall have regard to" has not been defined; and that, for reasons which will, no doubt, be submitted to the Committee in evidence, only two cases in the industry have in fact been referred to the Industrial Court under the provisions'. Given that the Court would only uphold negotiated rates where these were in fact adhered to by employers in the district, and would not where they were not, it is hardly surprising that trade unions did not regard the Court as a useful instrument. It would only uphold the *status quo*.

The significance of the Court's affirmation of departmental attitudes was not lost on the officials of the Ministry of Labour who were considering the future of the Fair Wages policy. A departmental Minute of 24 September 1936 refers to the decision in Case 1659 just two days before. The development of solutions to the problems posed by non-observance of collective agreements in the road haulage industry was doubtless of considerable interest to them. In 1936 the Ministers of Transport and Labour had appointed a Committee under the chairmanship of Sir James Baillie which recommended the institution of a Central Board for the industry consisting of representatives of the two sides with three independent members. It also proposed that the determinations of this Board be given statutory force. This scheme, however, would apply only to holders of 'A' and 'B' licences. As to the 'C' licence category, which covered about 67 per cent of all vehicles in the industry, where conditions were at their most chaotic, the Committee recommended a trade board for some, and for others, that the Fair Wages Clause should be applied, with disputes to be referred to the Industrial Court. The substance of these recommendations was embodied in the provisions of the Road Haulage Wages Act, 1938. The Act repealed section 32 of the Road and Rail Traffic Act, 1933, which applied the Fair Wages provisions of section 93 of the Road Traffic Act, 1930, to persons employed as drivers or statutory attendants of 'A' or 'B' licensed vehicles. Instead, machinery for the regulation of their wages was provided.

The position with regard to 'C' licensed vehicles was more complicated. Kahn-Freund described it in an article in 1948: because of the isolation of road haulage workers in those industries where it served a subsidiary purpose, it was very difficult to organize the scattered pockets of workers. As a result, collective agreements as a standard of 'fairness' were practically non-existent. No single agreement was possible. The different circumstances of workers in different industries doing the same job of road haulage prevented the application of the ordinary minimum wage machinery—Trade Boards—as this too presupposes uniformity of conditions to a certain extent. As Kahn-Freund put it:

> The puzzle was how to find a measuring rod, if neither a voluntary standard nor a statutory minimum rule could in the nature of things be available. Who could be capable of bringing to bear upon a multitude of contracts of employment made by firms of the most varying types and sizes a standard of adequacy which so obviously defied exact formulation?

The answer given by the Act he called the system of 'legislation by adjudication'. Part II of the Act provided for a complaints procedure against 'unfair' remuneration through the Minister to the Industrial Court. Remuneration was not unfair if it was: (i) equivalent to the remuneration payable in respect of corresponding work in connection with an 'A' or 'B' licensed vehicle and fixed by a Minister's Order made under Part I of the Act; or (ii) in accordance with an agreement in force between a trade union and the particular employer concerned, or an employers' organization of which he is a member; or (iii) equivalent to the remuneration payable in respect of corresponding work by employers in the same trade or industry in the same district in pursuance of an agreement between a trade union and an organization of employers which represents a substantial number of employers in the trade or industry; or (iv) equivalent to the remuneration payable in respect of corresponding work by an employer in the same trade or industry in the same district in pursuance of a decision given by the Industrial Court; or (v) equivalent to the remuneration payable in respect of corresponding work by similar employers in the same trade or industry in the same district in pursuance of a decision of a Joint Industrial Council, Conciliation Board, or similar body. If, in any case referred to it under Part II of the Act, the Industrial Court found that the remuneration paid was unfair, it was the duty of the Court to fix the remuneration to be paid. Remuneration thus fixed was known as statutory remuneration. In determining cases before it, the Court was required to have regard not only to the five provisions summarized above, but also to any collective agreements concerning the remuneration of similar workers in comparable trades or industries, and to the general level of remuneration of other classes of workers in the trade or industry to which the reference relates. Statutory remuneration fixed by the Court came into force as between the worker and his employer, and the Court was empowered to make its decision retrospective for a period not exceeding six months. In addition, statutory remuneration applied to all other workers employed by that employer on the same work. It remained in force, subject to review, for a period of three years from the beginning of the week following the date of the Court's decision.

The numerous references to collective agreements and arrangements were clearly intended to induce employers to escape the charge of 'unfairness' by adhering to them. With regard to the Industrial Court's own policy, however, it was intended that, while employers who failed to adhere to collective standards might be declared unfair, the Court would still have the option of upholding the employer's standards as fair despite this failure. As Kahn-Freund saw it:

> If the employer can show that the remuneration paid by him was 'fair' in the technical sense defined above, the complaint will be dismissed, and in so far, it might seem, at first sight, as if the task of the court was judicial in the traditional sense. But the statute clearly shows that the court may come to the same conclusion although not one of the alternative standards which serve as 'measuring rods' had in fact been complied with. It may and must have regard to all 'further circumstances' it considers relevant (s. 5(3)). . . . In other words, the court must formulate its own standard of 'fairness'. In defining what is 'fair' it gives effect to a policy, not to a crystallized legal norm.

While chaotic conditions in the industry might require some such latitude, the views of the Industrial Court expressed in Case 1659 above could not have inspired much confidence in its role as regards promoting collective agreements. It was for this reason, perhaps, that another crucial provision was included in the Act. Part II provided that, if there was in existence, by agreement between organizations of employers and workers representative of substantial proportions of employers and workers in the trade or industry concerned, joint machinery for settling disputes, any complaint concerning an employer whose organization is a party to the joint machinery must be referred to that machinery for settlement and can only be referred to the Industrial Court at the request of both sides.

Here, then, is a deliberate withdrawal of policy-making power from the Industrial Court where voluntary machinery exists. Kahn-Freund interpreted this provision in the following way:

> The whole body of legal principles designed to safeguard fairness of remuneration, the whole policy of using cases of unfairness as so many 'pegs' for the establishment of enforceable standards by a State-created agency falls to the ground if there is a collective agreement providing voluntary settlement machinery and the employer's organization is a party to it. If that is the case, the law insists that the further destiny of the matter should rest in the hands of the contracting organizations. Neither the individual employers nor the workers nor any outside union can then invoke the Industrial Court. Not even the contracting union or employers' organization can do so alone. They can do it only together as a matter of common policy for their industry. Where voluntary conciliation machinery exists, the State refuses to enforce 'fairness' unless invited to do so by the combined organizations on both sides.

It may be questioned whether this really was a refusal by the State to enforce 'fairness'. On the contrary, far from being a retreat from 'fair' standards, these were reinforced by excluding the Court from situations where collective arrangements existed. The Court's conception of 'fairness' did not manifest itself in the active support and encouragement of collective arrangements. Insofar as the policy expressed in the Act saw the essence of 'fairness' expressed in various collective arrangements, the latitude given the Court to diverge from these made it desirable to limit its intervention to those situations where no voluntarily agreed alternative existed.

The new policy initiative of the Road Haulage Wages Act to encourage collectively agreed standards in the road transport industry was not repeated in other enactments of 1938: the Cinematograph Films Act, the Bacon Industry Act and the Air Navigation (Licensing of Public Transport) Order. These merely provided that the wages and conditions of persons employed in these industries should comply with the requirements of any Fair Wages Resolution of the House of Commons applicable to government contracts. It may be wondered what this obligation to observe 'fair' standards implied to employers in these industries. They would look to the practices of government contractors and to the compliance procedures enforced by departments or various licensing inspectors. They would note that the observance of ordinary Trade Board rates would be held by government departments and municipalities to be compliance with the

Resolution. Thus, as a representative of the Tailors and Garment Workers complained in 1935: 'It therefore becomes a penalty for an employer of labour to observe trade union conditions against the Trade Board rates as fixed at present'. They would note that, in the year between April 1934–April 1935, only two firms had been struck off the lists of government contractors for non-observance of the Fair Wages Clause. In neither case had any question arisen of a wages agreement of a Joint Industrial Council and its non-observance. They would hear the Financial Secretary to the Treasury declare unequivocally in the House of Commons in December 1937: 'There is nothing in the fair wages clause which involved the recognition of this principle (of collective bargaining)'.[1] They would soon conclude that the Fair Wages policy was to be reckoned with only in situations such as the one described by a representative of the Building Trade Workers in 1937 as follows:

> The Council were asked to enforce their fair wages clause upon a contractor carrying out a large hospital contract. The council were not prepared to do this. They contended they had no right to do it, and they said they would approach the Ministry of Health to ask whether they would be in order in insisting upon the contractor's carrying out the terms of our national agreement. You will be pleased to know that in spite of the opposition of that council, as a result of efforts made by the Federation itself, having placed the firm concerned on the unfair list and withdrawn members from all jobs on that contract right throughout the London Division, we have been able to bring that firm to book. They have now given a written undertaking to observe the working rules on all their jobs, and consequently we have got through with that little difficulty.

Writing at this time, the Committee on the Regulation of Road Transport Wages had commented that standing by itself, a provision imposing a bare Fair Wages obligation involved but a small measure of 'statutory regulation' of wages and conditions of service: 'Certainly, having regard for the interpretation given to the Clause by the Government, this provision, by itself, could not be regarded as "State intervention" in the voluntary negotiation of wages and conditions in the industry'. At that late date, the Committee summed up the government's attitude as follows:

> Generally, therefore, it may be said that Government Wage Policy is a 'fair wage' policy, i.e. to take wages as they are in outside industry, to take no responsibility for fixing wages and,

in the expenditure of public money, to do nothing calculated to disturb the level, or influence the course of wages in outside industry.

Great Expectations: The Fair Wages Committee of 1937–1939

This was the background against which, in early 1937, the proposal for a Committee of Inquiry into Fair Wages policy was approved. The terms of reference suggested by the Treasury and accepted by the Cabinet at its meeting of 3 March were more restrictive than the Ministry of Labour would have liked. In a Minute of 16 February, the Ministry official who was the Secretary to the Fair Wages Advisory Committee had suggested that the terms of reference would 'need to be considered from the point of view of covering the wider application of the principle of the Resolution to undertakings and works aided by Government subsidy, grant or guarantee and the need for the establishment of special machinery to decide disputes as to what wages and conditions ought to be observed under a Clause based on the Resolution'. Last attempts, in Minutes of 25 February and 2 March, to revise the Treasury's terms in this direction, or even to extend them to encompass an inquiry into the wages policy for government employees, were unsuccessful. The final direction to the Committee was simply: 'to consider the working of the Fair Wages Resolution of the House of Commons of 10th March, 1909, as embodied in Government contracts, and to advise whether any changes are desirable and practicable'.

The Committee was to consist of one representative each from the Treasury, Admiralty, War Office, Air Ministry, Ministry of Health and the General Post Office, five representatives nominated by the National Confederation of Employers' Organisations, five nominated by the Trades Union Congress, and a chairman. There was some slight difficulty with the nomination of employers' representatives, the Confederation having suggested mostly employers from the Metal Industries, while the Ministry of Labour preferred representatives from 'badly organized industries, which cause most of the difficulties in respect of fair wages. For example, there are the Furniture industry, the Clay industries, and others.' A further embarassing episode occurred when Sir Norman Raeburn, who had been approached for the job of chairman, and had actually accepted the post, despite his confessed 'entirely judicial ignorance' of the subject, resigned the position upon learning that one of the T.U.C. nominees was to be Ernest Bevin. The grounds of his resignation were a strong repugnance to Bevin's 'activities in connection with the attempt to blackmail the public which is at present being made by the London busmen'. His resignation letter of 18 May continued: 'I am not prepared to sit on any body, in which he is a member. I recognize his ability but should find it difficult in the present circumstances even to be reasonably civil to him.' The busmen's strike had aroused hostility because it took place during the Coronation celebrations. The chairmanship was thereupon taken up by Dr. W. D. Ross, Provost of Oriel College, Oxford, and President of the Classical Association as well as of several Trade Boards.

Despite the limited terms of reference, the Secretary of the new Committee, Mr. M. A. Bevan, who had also been Secretary of the Fair Wages Advisory Committee, clearly intended that the review of the policy to be undertaken by the Committee would be extensive. This is evident from a paper, dated 14 April 1937, which he prepared to advise Sir Norman Raeburn, before his resignation, on the possible length of the investigation. He enumerated a long list of various points to which the Committee would have to decide whether to direct their attention. These were: (a) the basis upon which fair wages should be determined; (b) the observance of fair wages on both public and private work; (c) the position of sub-contractors; (d) the extension of the Fair Wages principle to materials used by contractors; (e) the machinery of administration; (f) the question of penalties; and (g) other miscellaneous matters. He presumed that statements would be invited from each of the principal government contracting departments on: (1) the number and character of Fair Wages complaints received; (2) the method of investigating and deciding complaints; and (3) examples of cases (a) where there is no difficulty in deciding under the existing clause, and (b) in respect of which the existing clause does not seem adequate. In addition, statements from five or six local authorities whose Fair Wages Clauses were different from and more severe than the government's clause would be invited. He proposed the preparation and discussion of documents on such subjects as: (i) the present position with regard to the compulsory enforcement of statutory agreements; (ii) the application of the Fair Wages principle to undertakings or works assisted by State grant, subsidy or guarantee; and (iii) information with regard to collective agreements in various industries from the point of view of their application as the basis of fair wages. In brief, the Ministry of Labour envisaged a detailed and comprehensive investigation stretching to the limit, if not going beyond, the Committee's terms of reference as prescribed by the Treasury. Furthermore, the preparation of special documents concerning topics (i) and (iii) just mentioned, indicate that the interpretation of the Fair Wages Resolution advocated by the T.U.C. was to become the focal point of the Committee's investigation and ultimately, of their decision.

The new Fair Wages Committee was to hold only three meetings, despite this rather grand agenda. Its first meeting was on 21 September 1937. Just two weeks earlier, at the annual Trades Union Congress, a representative of the General and Municipal Workers had successfully proposed the amendment of the 1909 Resolution, of which he stated: 'Its vagueness, its ambiguities and its omissions are patent to every impartial examiner, and it has never been able to safeguard the worker effectively or to penalize the exploiter'. The essence of his motion he declared to be as follows:

> In the first place it asks definitely for a fair wage clause that shall state simply and without ambiguity that all contractors shall observe trade union rates and conditions as agreed upon between employers and trade unions. It challenges the Government— who invariably seek to sabotage every progressive action of the International Labour Conference at Geneva on the ground of their faith in collective agreements existing at home—it challenges them to recognize those agreements and to show their genuineness in this direction by insisting on the strict observations of the fair wage clause by everyone concerned. We are just about getting tired of lip service.[2]

A memorandum of evidence putting the case for revision of the 1909 Resolution was submitted by the General Council, and oral evidence on behalf of the Council was given at the second meeting of the new Committee on 8 November 1937 by Ernest Bevin, among others. The main points put forward by the Council in their evidence were, *inter alia*, (i) owing to the increase in trade union organization and the development of collective bargaining, the clause adopted in 1909 was out of date; and (ii) that the district basis of the clause was inapplicable to industries in which agreements were mainly national. At its third meeting, the Committee heard evidence from several other organizations 'dealing largely with the need for the recognition of their agreements as the basis of "fair" conditions in their various industries. In general, the evidence of these bodies dealt with one of the principal points of revision suggested by the T.U.C.'—so wrote the Committee's Secretary on 6 January 1939. The National Confederation of Employers' Organisations (N.C.E.O.) did not give evidence, and the Secretary of the Committee noted in a Minute of 8 April 1938 that, 'Unofficially we are aware that there is a considerable divergence of view within the Confederation on the whole matter'.

The development which fundamentally changed the course of the otherwise straightforward business of a Committee of Inquiry was mentioned in the Report of the General Council to the Trades Union Congress in September 1938. It noted that in its evidence to the Committee in the previous November it had laid emphasis upon the use which might be made of an adequate Fair Wages Clause in strengthening the principle of collective bargaining. Arising out of that suggestion, an approach was made by the General Council to the N.C.E.O., as a body interested in maintaining the principle. Referring to this approach, in a Minute of 8 April 1938, the Secretary of the Fair Wages Committee stated that, after much hesitation, the N.C.E.O. had agreed to meet to examine the possibility of 'reaching a measure of agreement on the general lines of a revised Fair Wages Clause'. Arrangements were then being made for the meeting. As regards the Fair Wages Committee, he asserted that it 'must wait': 'Sir David (Ross's) personal view, with which I am in agreement, is that this effort on the part of the employers and workers to reach a basis of agreement is to be encouraged rather than otherwise, and that if it is successful, it will considerably shorten and simplify the work of the Committee'. To this statement of willingness that employers' and workers' organizations be permitted to consult each other independently with a view to formulating government policy on Fair Wages, the Secretary added the comment: 'I have reason to suppose that while the General Council hope to secure a revised and improved Fair Wages Clause, the matter is no longer regarded as one of particular urgency, especially as other and more important matters hold the stage'.

This prediction appears to have been borne out by subsequent non-developments. The Trades Union Congress of September 1938 heard that 'further consultations on this subject will take place', and a Minute of 11 October from the Secretary stated that the Fair Wages Committee was still in suspended animation: 'Unofficially I am told that not much progress has been made, chiefly because, owing to the holiday season and the recent crisis, it has been difficult to arrange meetings'. In December Sir David Ross left for America on other business for several months, as no particular progress in the T.U.C.– N.C.E.O. negotiations was expected quickly. It had been decided following the third meeting of the Committee in January 1938 that 'no useful purpose would be served by meeting until these discussions have reached a definite conclusion'. In March 1939, the Secretary of the Committee had been informed that discussions were practically complete and that he might expect to receive a report on them fairly soon. The report did not materialize and as late as June arrangements were being made for still another meeting, though the Secretary stated he was not sure whether it actually took place. His view, expressed in a Minute of 19 September 1939, was that 'No doubt the heavy pressure on both bodies of emergency work of all kinds may have held the matter up'. The General Council reported to the Trades Union Congress, which met on the day of the outbreak of the Second World War, that the negotiations had been completed, but added somewhat anomalously that it was 'anticipated that the hearing of the evidence by the Departmental Committee on the Fair Wages Clause will also be completed in the near future'.

The outbreak of the war put paid to this hope. The position of the Committee was expressed in a Minute of 19 September written by its Secretary. Two points of view were possible:

> One is that such a tremendous amount of work is being done on Government account that it is desirable that 'fair wages' standards should be defined as clearly as possible. The other is that in war conditions contractors will not be able to avoid paying rates and observing conditions such as fully satisfy 'fair wages' requirements.

He continued that since the pressure for revision came from the T.U.C., and as it was they who had initiated the bilateral discussions which had in effect delayed the Committee from proceeding, 'In a sense, therefore, the next move rests with them'. He then expressed a view which is difficult to understand given his familiarity with the previous decade of agitation: 'My impression, as the result of the examination of the subject that has already taken place, is that nearly everyone feels that there is nothing much wrong with the present Fair Wages Clause if it is administered effectively and that it will be difficult to devise a new and better clause to meet all points of view'. In any event, he felt sure, as experience certainly vouchsafed, that the contracting departments would be very averse to any alteration, especially during the present pressure of work. On balance, therefore, he suggested that, unless and until the question was raised elsewhere, no further action be taken in connection with the work of the Committee. He received a chorus of assent from all departmental officials. A letter from him, dated 19 March 1942, confirmed that the Committee, 'although not formally dissolved, has ceased to function and it is clear that if anything further were done, it would have to be reconstituted'.

World War II Produces a New Fair Wages Resolution

On this quietist note the efforts of a decade's agitation might have ended. The T.U.C., however, after two years of negotiations, were not prepared to let it go that easily. The matter was brought forward when Bevin, by then Minister of Labour and National Service, addressed a special conference of trade union executives at the Central Hall, Westminster, on 25 May 1940. His suggestion on that occasion was that the restoration of pre-war practices might be made one of the conditions of a new Fair Wages Clause. Armed with this new demand, Bevin placed before the Joint Consultative Committee on 26 June 1940 the proposals which had been agreed by the Joint Committee of the T.U.C. and the N.C.E.O. before the outbreak of war, with one or two modifications due to statutory enactments during the war period. During the following months a series of drafts were prepared. Final agreement was eventually reached between the General Council of the T.U.C. and the British Employers' Confederation (which the N.C.E.O. had become), and the agreed proposals were remitted to the Treasury by the Ministry of Labour for a draft to be prepared for the House of Commons. At this point in time, the T.U.C. optimistically described the new clause as 'a very decided advance on the present Clause' and the 'culmination of several years of difficult negotiations'. Mr. J. Hallsworth of the General Council declared to the 1941 Trades Union Congress: 'Those of you who know how long and arduous has been the agitation to secure Fair Wages Clauses far more effective than that embodied in the House of Commons resolution of March 9, 1939 [*sic*] will be glad to know that at long last a substantial measure of progress has attended our activity'. All he would say of the new clause, however, was that it would provide for the payment of recognized rates and conditions to *all* employees of a government contractor, and that the main contractor would be responsible for the same conditions applying to any of his sub-contractors.

The T.U.C.–N.C.E.O. negotiations over a new Resolution had begun in early 1938 and continued up to the outbreak of the war. In October 1939 there was established a National Joint Advisory Council of fifteen representatives of both the British Employers' Confederation and the T.U.C. The new war-time Government of May 1940 led to its being replaced by a Joint Consultative Committee, with seven representatives from each side. It was before this Committee that Bevin placed his proposals for a new Resolution on 26 June 1940.

At the same time, the Joint Consultative Committee was considering the problem of wage regulation in war-time. The T.U.C. reported in July 1940 that the Committee had sent its recommendations to Bevin. Chapter 14 analyses the result of these recommendations— Conditions of Employment and National Arbitration Order, No. 1305 which came into force on 25 July 1940. Briefly, this established a National Arbitration Tribunal, to which cases would be brought by either party to a dispute. It could make awards which were enforce-able at law. Part III embodied an obligation on employers to observe *recognized* terms and conditions where such conditions are in force. Recognized terms and conditions were those settled by machinery of negotiation or arbitration to which the parties are organizations of employers and trade unions representative respectively of substantial proportions of the employers and workers engaged in the trade in the district.

The origins of these recommendations are clearly to be found in the pre-war T.U.C.–N.C.E.O. discussions on Fair Wages policy. For example, in evidence to the Fair Wages Committee in November 1937, the T.U.C. had urged that an Advisory Council be set up, representing employers' organizations, trade unions and the State. It would give guidance on the Resolution to government departments, hear appeals against departmental decisions, investigate cases and report to the Government. The T.U.C.'s view was that national agreements should be generally observed, but that in their absence district or local agreements would set the standards.

Both the proposals for the new Fair Wages Resolution and the substance of the war-time Order rested on the same two principles: respect for existing collective bargaining arrangements, and a tribunal for the arbitration of disputes.

The Treasury appears to have taken an active part in the formula-tion of the new amended Resolution. A draft letter, dated 17 July 1940, addressed to Sir Alan Barlow of the Treasury refers to a list of points raised at a meeting of departmental representatives which discussed the proposed new clause. Commenting on one of the points, the author of the letter stated:

> The new clause says, in effect, that the fairness of wages and working conditions shall be tested by reference to wages and conditions established for a trade by agreement between organ-izations substantially representative of both employers and workers. It seems to me that such conditions are certainly not established 'if they are not recognized'. I am satisfied that the words 'established for' were deliberately chosen to carry out the intentions of the British Employers' Confederation and the T.U.C. and since they are agreed words we do not want to alter them unless it can be shown that they are really defective.

It is here evident that the long-standing pre-occupation of the contract-ing departments with the T.U.C.'s attempts to make them recognize collectively agreed standards that were not 'prevailing' was alive and well. They were highly suspicious that the use of the untested word 'established' might undermine their position, and consequently the letter went on to reassure them that 'in our view, the clause cannot be used to bolster up paper agreements'.

Despite the early optimism of the General Council, the Treasury raised several points for discussion and representatives of both sides of the T.U.C.–B.E.C. joint committee met Sir Alan Barlow of the Treasury on 21 November 1941. Little progress was made in these discussions and the General Council reported that, 'The view of the Treasury, which is not shared by the General Council, is that the new Fair Wages Resolution should wait until the end of the war, the present position being adequately safeguarded by the Conditions of Employment and National Arbitration Order'. Consequently, in September 1942, the Council reported that it had informed the Minister of Labour (Bevin) that, having given consideration to the points raised by the Treasury, they had decided to re-affirm the draft agreed upon with the B.E.C. and requested an early introduction of a new Fair Wages Resolution into the House of Commons.

In October 1942, the agreed new Resolution was published by the government as a White Paper. The intention was to submit the new Resolution to Parliament at the end of the war and any amendments in the meantime were to be subject to mutual agreement between the B.E.C., the Treasury and the T.U.C. The White Paper stated that, 'It has long been recognized that the existing Fair Wages Resolution of the House of Commons, which was passed in 1909, is not entirely appropriate in the changed circumstances of the present day, and the question of a new Resolution has been under consideration for some time'. Of the changes to the policy introduced by the new Resolution, the White Paper asserted:

> The standard of fair wages will no longer be solely the practice of 'good employers' in the district. The employer will be required to observe such conditions as have been established for the trade or industry in the district by representative joint machinery of negotiation or by arbitration.

So even at this late date the illusion persisted that the sole standard of the 1909 Resolution was the 'good employer' standard when in fact it was only the secondary standard to be utilized if no commonly recognized standard existed. Further, the power of the departments to determine disputes was to be removed to the Minister of Labour and thence to arbitration:

> Under the old Resolution the Minister of the Contracting Department had, if called upon, to decide whether or not fair

wages were being paid. Under the new Resolution any such questions will be reported to the Minister of Labour and National Service and, if not disposed of by negotiation, will be referred to arbitration.

This latter amendment was certainly welcome to trade unions who had too often encountered the indifferent politeness of departmental officials considering their complaints of breach of the Resolution by contractors.

To appreciate the full inadequacy of the new proposed Fair Wages standard, however, it must be recalled that the rallying cry of those who had struggled for an amendment to the Resolution since the T.U.C. pamphlet of 1922 had been the primacy of nationally agreed standards. The use of a formula: 'established for the trade or industry in the district' seemed at best a dangerously ambiguous conclusion to the years of effort. It was hardly to be compensated for by a reference to 'representative joint machinery of negotiation'. Yet in commenting on the draft clause in September 1943, the General Council could only reiterate its 'opinion that the maximum amount of agreement with respect to the introduction of a new Fair Wages Resolution had been reached and that the General Council had gone as far as ever they could in the exploration of the question'.

In January 1946, in answer to a Parliamentary Question, the Chancellor of the Exchequer said that the new Fair Wages Resolution would 'soon' be brought before the House of Commons; and, in March, at a meeting of the Joint Consultative Committee, the representatives of the B.E.C. and the T.U.C. were asked to confirm that it was their wish that the Resolution should be introduced without delay. Both sides of the Committee agreed that this should be done and neither side wished to amend the draft Resolution. The T.U.C. side, however, put forward the view that the reference to 'wages' appeared unduly restrictive as the term was intended to include all wages, salaries and remuneration of every description. They suggested that reference ought to be to 'remuneration' as in the Wages Councils Act 1945, so that not only wage earners, but salaried and otherwise remunerated employees would be covered by the Resolution. They asked that the Minister of Labour and National Service should bear this in mind when the Resolution was brought before the House. The Minister replied that he had noted these remarks, but that the Minister responsible for presenting the Resolution to the House would have to decide his course of action in the light of the debate.

On 14 October 1946, the Minister of Labour, George A. Isaacs of the Operative Printers and Assistants, who had been Chairman of the T.U.C. prior to his appointment to the new Labour Government, introduced the third Fair Wages Resolution:

1. (a) The Contractor shall pay rates of wages, and observe hours and conditions of labour, not less favourable than those established for the trade or industry, in the district where the work is carried out, by machinery of negotiation or arbitration to which the parties are organizations of employers and trade unions representative, respectively, of substantial proportions of the employers and workers engaged in the trade or industry in the district.

(b) In the absence of any rates of wages, hours or conditions of labour so established the contractor shall pay rates of wages, and observe hours and conditions of labour, which are not less favourable than the general level of wages, hours and conditions observed by other employers whose general circumstances in the trade or industry in which the contractor is engaged are similar.

2. The Contractor shall in respect of all persons employed by him (whether in execution of the contract or otherwise) in every factory, workshop or place occupied or used by him for the execution of the contract comply with the general conditions required by this Resolution. Before a contractor is placed upon a department's list of firms to be invited to tender, the department shall obtain from him an assurance that to the best of his knowledge and belief he has complied with the general conditions required by this Resolution for at least the previous three months.

3. In the event of any question arising as to whether the requirements of this Resolution are being observed, the question shall, if not otherwise disposed of, be referred by the Minister of Labour to an independent Tribunal for decision.

4. The contractor shall recognise the freedom of his workpeople to be members of Trade Unions.

5. The contractor shall at all times during the continuance of a contract display, for the information of his workpeople, in every factory, workshop, or place occupied or used by him for the execution of the contract, a copy of this Resolution.

6. The contractor shall be responsible for the observance of this Resolution by sub-contractors employed in the execution of the contract and shall if required notify the department of the names and addresses of all such sub-contractors.[3]

In a rather strange and misplaced attempt to link his Government's philosophy with that of the other sponsors of previous Resolutions, the Minister quoted the words of Mr. Plunkett, the Commissioner of Works who had introduced the 1891 Resolution, and who was reported to have said: 'We must not interfere with the full play of the labour market. It will not do for the State in any way to fix the rate of wages.' To this precept the Minister indicated his concurrence: 'This holds true today, as it held true 55 years ago. Wages are open to negotiation between employers and workers, and it has proved quite satisfactory.'[4]

NOTES

1. See for the statement on firms struck off during 1934–5, Parl. Deb., H. of C. (Fifth Series); 8 April 1935, vol. 300, cols. 817–18. For the declaration of the Financial Secretary to the Treasury, see Parl. Deb., H. of C. (Fifth Series); 21 December 1937, vol. 330, col. 1772.

2. In 1936 the International Labour Conference adopted the Reduction of Hours of Work (Public Works) Convention, which applied to 'persons directly employed on building or civil engineering works financed or subsidized by central Governments', and provided for a normal work week of 40 hours, overtime work up to a limit of 100 hours in any year and overtime wage rates of not less than 25 per cent in excess of normal rates. In the Public Works (National Planning) Recommendation, 1937, the Conference stated minimum standards of wage rates as follows: '9. The rates of wages of workers on public works should be not less favourable than those commonly recognised by workers organizations and employers for work of the same character in the district where the work is carried out; where there are no such rates recognized or prevailing in the nearest district, those recognized or prevailing in the nearest district in which the general industrial circumstances are similar should be adopted, subject to the condition that the rates should in any case be such as to ensure to the workers a reasonable standard of life as this is understood in their time and country'. See the *International Labour Conference*, 31st Session, San Francisco, 1948, Report VI (b)(1) – 'Wages – (b) Fair Wages Clauses in Public Contracts'. I.L.O., Geneva, 1947, at pp. 2–3.

3. Parl. Deb. H. of C. (Fifth Series); 14 October 1946, vol. 427, col. 619.

4. The above account is principally derived from the following sources:
—J. H. Richardson, *Industrial Relations in Great Britain*, I.L.O. Studies and Reports, Series A (Industrial Relations), No. 36, Geneva, 1938, pp. 120–1.
—O. Kahn-Freund, 'Legislation Through Adjudication. The Legal Aspect of Fair Wages Clauses and Recognised Conditions', *Modern Law Review*, **11** (1948), at pp. 437–41.
—Report of the 67th Annual Trades Union Congress, Margate, 1935, p. 433.
—Report of the 69th Annual T.U.C., Norwich, 1937, pp. 393–4, 396.
—Report of the General Council to the 70th Annual T.U.C., Blackpool, 1938, para. 273, pp. 237–8.
—Report of the General Council to the 71st Annual T.U.C., Bridlington, 1939, para. 307, p. 269.
—Report of the General Council to the 72nd Annual T.U.C., Southport, 1940, para. 228, p. 214.
—Report of the General Council to the 73rd Annual T.U.C., Edinburgh, 1941, para. 123, p. 147; p. 272.
—Report of the General Council to the 74th Annual T.U.C., Blackpool, 1942, para. 158, p. 95; p. 195.
—Report of the General Council to the 75th Annual T.U.C., Southport, 1943, para. 188, p. 120.
—*Fair Wages Resolution*, Cmd. 6399, October 1942.
—Industrial Court Case No. 1713, 25 October 1938, in *Industrial Court Case Reports*, 1938, pp. 60–6.
—Industrial Court Case No. 1659, 22 September 1936, in *Industrial Court Case Reports*, XVIII, pp. 93–6.
—Public Record Office, Files of the Ministry of Labour: LAB 10/73; I.R. 538/1934. Committee on the Regulation of Road Transport Wages, Committee Paper No. 2: 'Existing Statutory Regulation of Wages and Conditions of Employment in the Road Haulage Industry'.

—Public Record Office, Files of the Ministry of Labour: LAB 10/439 (1944): 'Note on the Compulsory Extension of Agreements to Cover (a) Firms in organized districts and (b) Isolated firms'. Also, document: 'The Fair Wages Clause', in the File on the Application of a Fair Wages Clause in the Special Areas.

—Public Record Office, Files of the Ministry of Labour: LAB 10/12 (1935–37); I.R. 1080/1935:

—Minute from F.W.L. to Secretary, dated 24 September 1936.

—Minute from M. A. Bevan to Mr. Leggett, dated 16 February 1937.

—Minutes of 25 February 1937, from M. A. Bevan and F. W. Norman.

—Letter from H. W. Moggridge of the Contracts Department of the War Office to F. W. Leggett, dated 2 March 1937.

—Minute from F.W.L. to Secretary, dated 13 July 1937.

—Letter from Sir W. Norman Raeburn to the Rt. Hon. Ernest Brown, M.P., dated 20 April 1937.

—Letter from Sir W. Norman Raeburn to the Secretary, Ministry of Labour, dated 18 May 1937.

—Paper prepared by M. A. Bevan, dated 14 April 1937.

—Letter from M. A. Bevan to the National Confederation of Employers' Organisations, dated 6 January 1939.

—Minute from M. A. Bevan to Mr. Ince and Secretary, dated 8 April 1938.

—Minute from M. A. Bevan to Mr. Ince, dated 11 October 1938.

—Minute from M. A. Bevan to Mr. Myrddin Evans, dated 7 December 1938.

—Minute from M. A. Bevan to Mr. Wiles, dated 19 September 1939.

—Letter from M. A. Bevan to the Secretary, Ministry of Supply, dated 19 March 1942.

—Draft letter to Sir Alan Barlow, dated 17 July 1940.

—Department of Employment Library, Box GP.33.18–331.2, File No. 405: Fair Wages Advisory Committee—Fair Wages Clause—Relation to semi-Government and State Associated Contracts. Extension of Fair Wages Principle to work which is not the subject of a Government Contract.

—*Labour—The Workers' Magazine*, published by the T.U.C., **2**, No. 11 (N.S.), p. 521 (July 1940).

13

The New Fair Wages Policy:
Ambiguity and Confusion

To what extent did the new Fair Wages Resolution of 1946 achieve the aims which had been fought for by the trade union movement over the previous decades? As was mentioned above, the wording of the Resolution was comparable to the terms of the Conditions of Employment and National Arbitration Order of 1940. Both referred to standards established for the trade or industry in the district by machinery of negotiation or arbitration to which the parties were organizations of employers and trade unions representative respectively of substantial proportions of the employers and workers engaged in the trade or industry in the district. The adoption of this wording was particularly unfortunate. In a debate on the moves to amend the 1909 Resolution at the annual Trade Union Congress of 1942, a representative of the Electrical Trades Union pointed out that the terms of the Order of 1940 had been interpreted by the National Arbitration Tribunal in such a way that it did not even go as far as the old Fair Wages Clause. The explanatory memorandum issued by the Ministry of Labour and National Service had stated: 'The Order requires the observance by all employers of terms and conditions not less favourable than recognized terms and conditions'. Those were defined as terms and conditions of employment which had been settled by machinery of negotiation or arbitration, to which organizations of employers and trade unions were parties. The E.T.U. representative pointed out to the Congress, however, that 'The National Arbitration Tribunal's interpretation of that was that if there was a single union which had a single agreement with a single employer, then the terms of that agreement could not be imposed upon an employer in the same district employing the same type of workpeople on the same kind of work'. He castigated this interpretation as entirely wrong. When the unions had accepted compulsory arbitration and gave up the

For notes see p. 236

right to strike, the least they had thought they would get in return was a statutory obligation on employers to observe terms no less favourable than those negotiated for similar workers in a given district. He specifically brought the point to the attention of the General Council currently negotiating for a new Fair Wages Clause, and expressed the hope that they would go into it and contest it.

The passage of the 1946 Resolution showed that they did not. Instead, by adopting the practically identical wording, what the T.U.C. appeared to have done was effectively to exclude all agreements other than those negotiated by 'organizations of employers and trade unions'. This might even be construed to refer to machinery to which both parties were federations of organizations on both sides, e.g., the T.U.C. and the (then) B.E.C.—who in practice did not negotiate agreements at all. Perhaps the T.U.C. intended by this limitation to agreements negotiated by organizations of employers to ensure that national agreements, which were the ones most commonly negotiated by organizations of employers, would become the sole standards of fair wages and conditions. In this unfortunate and cumbersome manner, the objective of securing national standards was to be attained.

In direct contradiction to this aim, however, was the express reference to 'the district' which appeared twice in clause 1(a) of the Resolution (though not at all in clause 1(b)). The first reference required that the wages, hours and conditions established by negotiations be those 'in the district where the work is carried out'. The second required that the organizations of employers and trade unions negotiating be representative respectively of employers and workers 'in the trade or industry in the district'. Read in its entirety, what clause 1(a) seemed to produce as the Fair Wages standard was the following: *a collective agreement negotiated between organizations of employers and (possibly organizations of) trade unions representative respectively of employers and workers in the district concerned which fixed wages, hours and conditions in that district.* The introduction of the national element by limiting agreements to those negotiated by organizations, as opposed to single employers and trade unions, was severely curtailed by demanding a strict district emphasis. National agreements would only be applicable where they established district rates and satisfied the criterion of representativeness in the district. *In was a fact, however, that where the trade unions did represent substantial proportions of workers in a trade or industry in a district, and had negotiated national agreements which determined rates for that district, they would have little need for a Fair Wages policy.* It was the recognition and enforcement of nationally agreed standards, held to be 'fair' standards, on government contractors that were sought, regardless of district rates or representativeness. In practice, therefore, it seemed unlikely that clause 1(a) of the Resolution would be of much use. In its absence, the secondary standard in clause 1(b) could be invoked as a fall-back. Yet even the most superficial reading indicates that its lack of precision was equal, if not inferior to the long outmoded and heavily criticized Resolution of 1891. In sum, the T.U.C.'s long campaign had again been effectively frustrated.

Evidence indicates that the T.U.C.'s views of Fair Wages policy succumbed to the departments' interpretation on other occasions. During the latter years of the war the old problem of the isolated factory arose once again. Advice was sought on the case of firms leaving London where they were tied down to a joint agreement and starting a factory in an area where there was no agreement and where they might be the only firm engaged in the particular line of business. It was suggested that, where the government gave assistance to firms to set themselves up, it should insist on a Fair Wages Clause. Again, the problem was connected with certain proposals then being prepared for legislation on the enforcement of voluntary agreements. These provided that the agreements should apply only in the districts where it could be shown that the parties to the agreement were organizations representing a substantial proportion of both employers and workers. In connection with these proposals, a departmental Minute of 13 May 1944 stated that 'the T.U.C. will press for something more than enforcement on a district basis'. Replying to the request for advice, a Ministry of Labour official asserted that the Fair Wages formula 'ensures that local circumstances are taken into account if an industry is started up in a new district apart from the main centres of the trade'. This assertion, in a Minute of 1 June, was supplemented by another from a second official, dated 8 June, stating: 'It is obviously most difficult to have any general power to apply the terms of a national agreement. There can rarely be an assurance that such an agreement is not only national in scope but is observed nationally.' A Minute of some six months later, dated 22 December 1944, indicates that the matter remained unresolved. The T.U.C. once again failed to impress its position upon the government.

As described above, the T.U.C. and the employers' organization (the N.C.E.O. followed by the B.E.C.) effectively negotiated between them the terms of the new Fair Wages policy. The clear intent of the T.U.C., manifested in innumerable statements and resolutions, was that nationally agreed standards should be those stipulated as 'fair'. The wording of the Fair Wages Resolution of 1946 as passed, however, was extremely ambiguous in the standards it prescribed. It seemed to be influenced considerably by the view of the Fair Wages policy upheld by the contracting departments during the inter-war period.

That the defects of the 1946 Resolution in achieving the T.U.C.'s goals were not foreseen by Ministry of Labour officials is not credible. The evidence to this effect is provided by a series of documents in the Public Record Office: an exchange of letters between Sir Harold Morris, President of the Industrial Court, and certain high officials in the Ministry of Labour. The subject of the exchange was the Wages Councils Bill, introduced into Parliament in December 1944, which provided for the establishment of wages councils and otherwise for the regulation of the remuneration and conditions of employment of workers in certain circumstances. Sir Harold was concerned with phrases in the Bill which were substantially identical, as it turned out, with the wording of the Resolution of 1946. As President of the Tribunal which was to adjudicate, in the words of clause 3, 'in the event of any question arising as to whether the requirements of this Resolution are being observed', his interpretation of these key phrases are of the utmost importance. In a letter to Sir Godfrey Ince of the Ministry of Labour and National Service, dated 11 December 1944, he stated:

The next thing I want to turn to is paragraph I(1) of the Third Schedule which repeats word for word paragraph 5(1) of Order 1305. There are two points about which I am not very happy. The first is 'organizations of employers and trade unions' in the fourth line. It seems to me that this phrase is equivocal and is open to one or more constructions. I think in the ordinary and natural signification of the words it means 'organizations of employers and organizations of trade unions'. *Most terms and conditions of employment which have been settled by machinery of negotiation or arbitration have been reached between an organization of employers and a trade union or possibly two or more trade unions. They are seldom, if ever, settled by more than one organization of employers and so far as my experience goes never by an organization of trade unions;* the trade union nearly always acting independently. Just as an instance, in, I suppose, the biggest industry in the country—the engineering— the terms and conditions of employment are established under machinery of negotiation between the Engineering and Allied Employers' Federation—an organization of employers, and the Amalgamated Engineering Union—a trade union. I think the words used are not happy and I would suggest that a revision should be made in them in the Act of Parliament.

The other point about which I am not happy are the words 'in the district' which appear in line 25 of the Bill. The words read 'substantial proportions of the employers and workers engaged in that trade or industry in that district'. *This confines the settlement by machinery of negotiation or arbitration to a district, and in nine cases out of ten the machinery of negotiation or arbitration is national,* and I would suggest that instead of having the phrase 'in that district', the words should read 'substantial proportions of the employers and workers engaged in that trade or industry either in that district or in the trade or industry nationally'. (My italics.)

Each of these two points may be considered separately.

Regarding the first point as to the interpretation of the phrase 'organizations of employers and trade unions', the Permanent Secretary to the Ministry of Labour replied to Sir Harold Morris in a letter of 13 December; he stated that certain Joint Industrial Councils consisted on the employers' side of more than one organization of employers, and that generally the phrase had never given rise to any question and was well understood by those concerned. He promised, however, to have the point further examined by experts. Other officials of the Ministry were not so sanguine; and, on writing away for a legal opinion, one mentioned, in a Minute of 14 December, that he had 'never felt very happy about this form of words as it seems to me that where the parties to an agreement were a single organization of employers or a single trade union it might be argued that the provision was not satisfied'. Thus, although they had not given rise to difficulty in the few cases dealt with under the Order, he thought it wise to clarify the intention of the Bill.

The opinion of counsel on the point raised distinguished the possibility of the phrase referring to 'organizations of trade unions' from the other question of whether only confederations of employers' organizations were included by the wording. In a letter of 19 December he stated:

> I cannot agree with Sir Harold Morris that, in the natural signification of the words in question, organizations of trade unions would be meant; in order to produce that result correct grammar would require the repetition of the word 'of' before 'trade union'. Further, that construction is an exceedingly unlikely one, and no reasonable person ought to adopt it unless driven to it by the grammar or context.

He went on to detail how the context of the Bill was against that construction generally. As to the second point, he admitted that he was 'not altogether happy about it, because, if the single organization case is the common one, it seems rather perverse to draft it in the plural'.

Despite this opinion, the Ministry's officials continued to express doubt, despite the fact that the wording had been adopted from the 1940 Order. As to that, a Minute of 22 December stated: 'The Order was drafted in an emergency and although no question has been raised in the comparatively few cases reported under Part III it is obviously desirable that the legislation should be drafted in the best possible manner'. Another official put the case for an amendment of the ambiguity in a Minute of 9 January:

> It is absolutely essential in my view that there should be no possible doubt of the position in the case of an agreement concluded between a single Trade Union and a single Employers' Association. The Trade Union may be concerned with workers in a number of industries and it may be part of its policy to retain within its own exclusive jurisdiction the negotiation and settlement of wages and terms and conditions of employment of its members. A serious situation would arise if it transpired that it was denied the protection of Part III of the Bill for maintaining the standard set by its agreement. I think, therefore, that we should press for an amendment.

On 24 January, another letter was received by the Ministry from Sir Harold Morris. He mentioned that he had consulted with judges on the National Arbitration Tribunal about the points he had raised, and had found that they had experienced similar difficulties in regard to the interpretation of the phrases in question. He reiterated his previously expressed view:

> The primary interpretation of 'organizations of employers and trade unions' is organizations of employers and organizations of trade unions.
>
> There are organizations of trade unions but there are not many of them and in the majority of cases the terms and conditions of employment have been settled by agreement between an employers' organization and a trade union or trade unions. We thought that to avoid any ambiguity the words should read either:— (a) employers' organizations and trade unions, or (b) trades unions and organizations of employers. . . .
>
> The secondary interpretation of the phrase is organizations of employers on the one hand and trade unions on the other.
>
> The words are in any case equivocal and I can find nothing in Order 1305 which shows expressly that the secondary meaning should be given to them.

In his official reply of 29 January, the Permanent Secretary to the Ministry referred to the opinion of counsel that the context of the Bill was generally against the construction of the phrase advanced by Sir Harold Morris. Nevertheless, he added, the matter had been discussed with the Minister and he had agreed to insert an amendment into the Bill to meet Sir Harold's objections. The amendment did not affect the part of the Bill which reproduced the vital section of Order 1305, but merely defined 'trade union' so as to meet the problem of associations of trade unions.

Why, it may be asked, was the same consideration not given to the problem when it arose in the context of the identical wording of the Fair Wages Resolution of 1946? There was absolutely nothing in the context of the Resolution itself, unlike the wording of the lengthy Wages Councils Bill of 1944, which might have indicated that the primary interpretation advanced by Sir Harold Morris was inapplicable. As his tribunal was to be the authoritative interpreter of the Resolution, his view would effectively render clause 1(a) of the Resolution valueless. Virtually all relevant agreements would be excluded on the grounds that they were made by a single trade union or a single employer, rather than organizations on both sides. Nor is the excuse available that Ministry officials were unaware of the parallel situation in the proposed wording of the Fair Wages Resolution. For, in his letter to Sir Harold Morris of 13 December 1944, the Permanent Secretary, Sir Godfrey Ince specifically referred to it. One must deduce that the Ministry's officials, aware of the potentially fatal ambiguity, were either satisfied that it could be dealt with in the exercise of departmental discretion, or were cynically prepared to allow the defective Resolution to go forward without amendment.

The reference by the Permanent Secretary to the Fair Wages policy arose with regard to Sir Harold Morris' second point concerning the *district* basis underlying the Wages Councils Bill. This was implicit in the use of the phrase: 'substantial proportions of the employers and workers engaged in that trade or industry in that district'. He suggested, in the above quoted letter of 11 December 1944, that at least an alternative *national* basis be inserted. This was, of course, precisely the crux of the T.U.C.'s long campaign for reform of the Fair Wages policy. The issue was, therefore, no longer one of legal interpretation, but became one of policy differences, and the Permanent Secretary refused to compromise. In his reply of 13 December, Sir Godfrey Ince stated categorically:

With regard to the words 'substantial proportions of the employers and workers engaged in that trade or industry in that district',

I am afraid that your alternative form of words would not meet the case. It is not the intention, for example, that if employers in a trade in a well-defined district, e.g. East Anglia, deliberately choose to stand outside machinery of negotiation which is otherwise national, agreements reached by such machinery should be imposed on them. If this were the case I doubt whether the proposal would be generally acceptable and it is certainly not our intention. A well-defined formula applicable to the many and varied circumstances of wages agreements negotiated by different types of machinery over the whole range of industry seems to be an almost impossible feat of draftsmanship. I realise that the interpretation of the word 'district' in this connection, as in the Fair Wages Clause, may present difficulty. Our feeling is, however, that by and large it is best to leave such questions to be decided by mutual acceptance, or if needs be, by the independent tribunal, which can take into account all the relevant circumstances of the particular case.

In a subsequent letter dated 24 January 1945, Sir Harold Morris again attempted to raise the issue by pointing to difficulties encountered by himself and the National Arbitration Tribunal in cases where the workers coming before them relied upon national agreements. The only way they could apply those agreements was by inferring that England, Scotland and Wales were 'a district', or England or Scotland is 'a district'. As he put it: 'I shouldn't care to hear the language of any Scot, if you told him that Scotland was a district'. Taking up the example referred to by the Permanent Secretary, if East Anglian employers were outside national machinery, he pointed out that if there were an agreement between the organized employers and the trade unions in that district to that effect, the employers in East Anglia would be amply protected: 'We have always thought that the whole principle of Article V of 1305 was to secure the observance of the "recognized terms and conditions" throughout the area where they are established whether nationwide or in a district'. The problem posed by the reference to 'district' was that it appeared to exclude all national agreements. Consequently, he reiterated his proposed amendment, and stated that he personally would have liked to see the abolition of the word 'district' completely. Although he recognized the 'great difficulty in getting any revision of the clause through', he noted that the words in Article 5(1) of Order 1305: 'there are in force terms and conditions of employment', had been revised and changed to 'terms and conditions of employment are established'. He welcomed this change since the old words had given rise to difficulties of proof. These arguments were unavailing. In his letter of 29 January, the Permanent Secretary replied as follows:

> We appreciate the difficulties but the Minister is not prepared to amend the Schedule by the substitution of the words 'either in that district or nationally'. The Minister feels that any such amendment might be regarded as a serious departure from the principles of Order 1305, which has now been in operation for over four years; also the change might have far-reaching consequences and would almost certainly arouse opposition. It may well be that the interpretation of the words 'in this district' will depend upon the varying circumstances of different industries but I am afraid that, notwithstanding the difficulties of the Schedule as it stands, the Minister is unable to act on your suggestion.

The departments' interpretation of Fair Wages policy was, therefore, to prevail. National agreements were to be discounted in favour of district practice. In those districts where trade unions had not succeeded in obtaining agreements with unorganized employers, no collectively agreed standards were specified as 'fair' standards to be observed. The conception of Fair Wages policy for which the trade union movement had been struggling since the beginnings in 1891 was successfully resisted. In the case of the 1946 Resolution, to justify their refusal to enforce national agreements as fair standards, the departments invoked the emergency policy of Order 1305 and the political authority of a war-time government. Neither of these was valid in the post-war period with the election of a Labour government. Nevertheless, in the 1946 Resolution national agreements were again subordinated to local considerations. While later developments were to inject new life into this anachronism, the Fair Wages Resolution of 1946 remains within the outmoded conception of policy and industrial relations to this day.[1]

NOTES

1. The above account is principally derived from the following sources:
—Report of the 74th Annual Trades Union Congress, Blackpool, 1942, pp. 194–5.
—Public Record Office, Files of the Ministry of Labour: LAB 10/439 (1944). File on the Application of a Fair Wages Clause in the Special Areas:

—Minute from H.A.E. to Mr. Gould, dated 13 May 1944.
—Minute from M. A. Bevan to Mr. Gould, dated 1 June 1944.
—Minute from King to C.I.C., dated 8 June 1944.
—Minute from H.A.E. to Mr. Gould, dated 22 December 1944.
—Public Record Office, Files of the

Ministry of Labour (Department of Employment and Productivity): LAB 10/527; I.R. 438/1945. File on 'Wages Councils' Bill: Proper Interpretation of Phrase "Organizations of Employers and Trade Unions" as Used in the Third Schedule: Question Raised by Sir Harold Morris':

—Letter from Sir Harold Morris, K.C., President of the Industrial Court, to Sir Godfrey Ince, K.B.E., C.B., Ministry of Labour and National Service, dated 11 December 1944.

—Letter from Sir G. H. Ince to Sir Harold Morris, dated 13 December 1944.

—Minute from H. Emmerson to Solicitor, dated 14 December 1944.

—Letter from Alan Ellis, Office of the Parliamentary Counsel, to C. L. M. Langham, Ministry of Labour and National Service, dated 19 December 1944.

—Minute from H. Emmerson to Mr. Gould, dated 22 December 1944.

—Minute from K.M.G. to D.G.M.P., dated 9 January 1945.

—Letter from Sir Harold Morris to Sir G. H. Ince, dated 24 January 1945.

—Letter from Sir G. H. Ince to Sir Harold Morris, dated 25 January 1945.

PART III

The Third Fair Wages Policy
1946–1976

14

The New Instruments of Fair Wages Policy

The Expansion of the Fair Wages Policy

The investigation of the origins of the Fair Wages Resolution of 1946 presented in chapter 12 noted the common sources of the Resolution and of the Conditions of Employment and National Arbitration Order, No. 1305, of 1940. Clause 1(a) of the new Resolution, which read as follows:

> 1. (a) The contractor shall pay rates of wages and observe hours and conditions of labour not less favourable than those established for the trade or industry in the district where the work is carried out by machinery of negotiation or arbitration to which the parties are organizations of employers and trade unions representative respectively of substantial proportions of the employers and workers engaged in the trade or industry in the district,

was substantially identical to the formula embodied in Order 1305. That Order, which came into force on 25 July 1940, established a new body, the National Arbitration Tribunal, to which cases could be brought at the instance of one party to a dispute, even though the consent of the other party was not forthcoming. The Tribunal consisted of five members, three of whom were appointed while the others represented employers and workers respectively. An award of the Tribunal was binding upon the parties and its terms became implied terms of the contracts between the employers and workers concerned. Part III of the Order contained the substance of the new Fair Wages policy subsequently stated in similar terms in clause 1(a) of the 1946 Resolution. It provided that:

> Where in any trade or industry in any district there are in force terms and conditions of employment which have been settled by

For notes see p. 256

machinery of negotiation or arbitration to which the parties are organizations of employers and trade unions representative respectively of substantial proportions of the employers and workers engaged in that trade or industry in that district (hereinafter referred to as 'recognized terms and conditions') all employers in that trade or industry in that district shall observe the recognized terms and conditions or such terms and conditions of employment as are not less favourable than the recognized terms and conditions. (Section 5(1))

Section 5(2) of the Order went on to define in somewhat greater detail than was subsequently done in the 1946 Resolution what were the requisite 'fair' standards. It provided that employers would be deemed to be in compliance with 'recognized terms and conditions' if their terms were 'in accordance with the terms and conditions relating to workers engaged in similar work' which were embodied in certain specified instruments:

(a) any agreement to which the parties are organizations of employers and trade unions which are representative respectively of substantial proportions of the employers and workers engaged or employed in the trade or industry in the district in which the employer is engaged; or

(b) any decision of a joint industrial council, conciliation board or other similar body constituted by organizations of employers and trade unions which are representative respectively of substantial proportions of the employers and workers engaged or employed in the trade or industry in the district in which the employer is engaged; or

(c) in the absence of any such agreement or decision as is mentioned in the foregoing provisions of this paragraph, any agreement between the particular employer concerned and a trade union which is representative of a substantial proportion of workers employed in the trade or industry in which the employer is engaged; or

(d) any award made by the National Arbitration Tribunal, the Industrial Court or any other body or person acting in the capacity of arbitrator relating to the terms and conditions of employment observable by an employer in the same trade or industry in the same district; or

(e) any statutory provision relating to remuneration, rates of wages, hours or working conditions, unless those provisions are themselves less favourable than the provisions of any such agreement, decision or award as is mentioned in the foregoing provisions of this paragraph, being an agreement, decision or award relating to the particular employer concerned or any employers' organization of which he is a member or to which such an employer or such an organization is a party.

Moreover, in deciding questions of whether an employer was complying with the requisite terms and conditions, section 5(3) instructed the National Arbitration Tribunal to 'have regard' not only to the five standards stipulated above, 'but also to any collective agreements concerning the terms and conditions of similar workers in comparable trades or industries'. Only an organization of employers or a trade union which habitually took part in the settlement of wages and working conditions in the trade or industry concerned could raise a question for referral to the Tribunal.

The origins of the standards just described which were to be applied by the Tribunal are obvious: the legislation of the 1930s, the Road and Rail Traffic Act, 1933, the Cotton Manufacturing Industry (Temporary Provisions) Act, 1934, the Sugar Industry (Reorganisation) Act, 1936, and particularly the Road Haulage Wages Act, 1938, embody similar standards. This legislation was, as noted in chapter 12, part of Parliament's response to the chaotic situation of collective bargaining during the mass unemployment of the period. The Order of 1940 can be seen as the culmination of this policy, adapted to the particular conditions of war-time. The connection between this policy and that embodied in the Fair Wages Resolutions is clear. Both were intended to stabilize wage rates and control wage competition; to prevent the undercutting of standards which were 'generally accepted as current for a competent workmen in his trade' (in the words of 1891), or 'commonly recognized by employers and trade societies (or, in the absence of such recognized wages and hours those which in practice prevail amongst good employers) in the trade in the district where the work is carried out' (in the words of 1909). Others have noticed the links in this chain of development. Thus, in 1950 I. A. Sharp commented on Part III of Order 1305: 'It is obvious that this Part has taken its form from the labour provisions of the 'fair wages' Acts. ... Part III was intended to accomplish throughout industry what those Acts were designed to effect in individual trades.' And in 1962, J. W. Grove stated: 'During the Second World War, when strikes and lock-outs were forbidden by law, the practice (of Fair Wages clauses in legislation) was extended to cover all kinds of employment.'

For the years 1940–6, therefore, there was in operation a procedure by which employers across British industry could be required to adhere to employment standards which had previously been applicable only to specific industries and to government contractors. The new and vastly extended standards were a development and refinement of the old standard prescribed for government contractors. An anomalous position was reached: the supposedly special protection accorded to employees of government contractors by the 1909 Resolution was surpassed by the new standards of Order 1305 from 1940 onwards. Only with the passage of the Fair Wages Resolution of 1946 were the new standards made formally applicable to the employees of government contractors as well.

The wholesale coverage of British industry by Fair Wages standards embodied in Order 1305 of 1940 did not cease with the end of the war. The provisions of Order 1305 continued in effect until 1951. In February 1951, however, seven dockers were prosecuted for conspiracy to incite strike action contrary to the provisions of Part II of the Order. Scenes not unfamiliar to observers of similar legal actions consequential on enforcement of the Industrial Relations Act 1971 followed, and eventually led to the revocation, in August 1951, some six years after the event, of the war-time emergency regulations. Unlike the ban on strikes, however, the comprehensive coverage of the Fair Wages standards was immediately renewed in a new Order, No. 1376, entitled 'The Industrial Disputes Order', which replaced Order 1305 in August 1951. The National Arbitration Tribunal was abolished, but its place was taken by the Industrial Disputes Tribunal with a similar composition and only slightly modified functions. The Fair Wages standards continued to be applied to the whole of British industry. Thus, section 2 of Order 1376 provided that where

> in any trade or industry or section of trade or industry in any district terms and conditions of employment are established which have been settled by machinery of negotiation or arbitration to which the parties are organizations of employers and trade unions representative respectively of substantial proportions of the employers and workers engaged in that trade or industry or section of trade or industry in that district (hereinafter referred to as 'recognized terms and conditions')

and an issue arises as to whether an employer in that district should observe the recognized terms and conditions, the issue could be referred to the Industrial Disputes Tribunal. And where:

> the Tribunal is of opinion that there are recognized terms and conditions applicable to the case and that the employer concerned is not observing those terms and conditions or terms and condi-

tions of employment which, in the opinion of the Tribunal, are not less favourable than those terms and conditions, it may by its award require the employer to observe the recognized terms and conditions or such terms and conditions of employment as may be determined by it to be not less favourable than the recognized terms and conditions. (Section 9(2))

Order 1376 continued in effect until superseded by the enactment, in February 1959, of similar provisions in section 8 of the Terms and Conditions of Employment Act 1959. In the by now familiar language, section 8(1) provided:

Where a claim is duly reported to the Minister under this section—
(a) that terms or conditions of employment are established in any trade or industry, or section of a trade or industry, either generally or in any district, which have been settled by an agreement or award, and
(b) that the parties to the agreement, or to the proceedings in which the award was made, are or represent organizations of employers and organizations of workers or associations of such organizations, and represent (generally or in the district in question, as the case may be) a substantial proportion of the employers and of the workers in the trade, industry or section, being workers of the description (hereinafter referred to as 'the relevant description') to which the agreement or award relates, and
(c) that as respects any worker of the relevant description an employer engaged in the trade, industry or section (or, where the operation of the agreement or award is limited to a district, an employer so engaged in that district), whether represented as aforesaid or not, is not observing the terms or conditions (hereinafter referred to as 'the recognized terms or conditions'),
the Minister may take any steps which seem to him expedient to settle, or to secure the use of appropriate machinery to settle, the claim and shall, if the claim is not otherwise settled, refer it to the Industrial Court.

The Industrial Court later became the Industrial Arbitration Board, and still later, the Central Arbitration Committee.

The latest reincarnation of the Fair Wages policy is in the provisions of the Employment Protection Act 1975. Section 98 of that Act stipulates: 'The provisions of Schedule 11 to this Act shall have effect in place of section 8 of the Terms and Conditions of Employment

Act 1959 and that Act in hereby repealed'. But the 1959 Act is not merely replaced; as confirmed by Eric Wigham in *The Times* of 22 April 1975: 'The proposal combines principles embodied in Section 8 of the Terms and Conditions of Employment Act, 1959, with those of the Fair Wages Resolution'. The first two paragraphs of Schedule 11 complete the incorporation of clause 1(a) and 1(b) of the 1946 Resolution into statute law applicable to all employers:

> 1. A claim may be reported to the Service, in accordance with and subject to the following provisions of this Part of this Schedule, that as respects any worker an employer is, in respect of any matter, observing terms and conditions of employment less favourable than the recognized terms and conditions or, where, or so far as, there are no recognized terms and conditions, the general level of terms and conditions.
>
> 2. In this Part of this Schedule—
>
> (a) the 'recognized terms and conditions' means terms and conditions of workers in comparable employment in the trade or industry, or section of a trade or industry, in which the employer in question is engaged, either generally or in the district in which he is so engaged, which have been settled by an agreement or award, to which the parties are employers' associations and independent trade unions which represent (generally or in the district in question, as the case may be) a substantial proportion of the employers and of the workers in the trade, industry or section, being workers of the description to which the agreement or award relates; and
>
> (b) the 'general level of terms and conditions' means the general level of terms and conditions observed for comparable workers by employers—
>
>> (i) in the trade, industry or section in which the employer in question is engaged in the district in which he is so engaged; and
>>
>> (ii) whose circumstances are similar to those of the employer in question,
>
> and for the purposes of sub-paragraph (a) above the reference to terms and conditions, in a case where minimum terms and conditions have been settled as mentioned in that sub-paragraph, is a reference to those minimum terms and conditions.

Not only has clause 1(a) of the Fair Wages Resolution been transmitted from the 1959 Act into paragraph 2(a) of Schedule 11, but for the first time clause 1(b) of the Resolution is substantially reproduced in paragraph 2(b) of the Schedule. A detailed analysis of this latest manifestation of Fair Wages policy will be presented in chapter 20.

To sum up the position: for the entire period since the Fair Wages Resolution of 1946 was passed by the House of Commons, there has been in operation at the same time a procedure whereby workers could enforce on their employers adherence to Fair Wages standards which were substantially identical to those imposed on government contractors by the Resolution. Employers, whether government contractors or not, were liable to be summoned before an idependent arbitration tribunal (the National Arbitration Tribunal, the Industrial Disputes Tribunal, the Industrial Court, the Industrial Arbitration Board and now the Central Arbitration Committee) and charged with non-compliance with 'fair' standards: terms of employment established for the trade or industry in the district where the work is carried out by machinery of negotiation or arbitration to which the parties arc organizations of employers and trade unions representative respectively of substantial proportions of the employers and workers engaged in the trade or industry in the district. The Fair Wages policy, originally intended for the benefit only of employees of government contractors, has been embodied in statute and expanded to cover the whole of British industry.

Harmonization of the Fair Wages Policy Instruments

Harmonization of the Fair Wages policy expressed in variously Order 1305, the 1946 Resolution, Order 1376 and the 1959 Act was gradually reflected in their administration. Thus, I. A. Sharp calculated that some 1,253 cases were referred to arbitration under Order 1305 up to the end of 1946. Of these, 83 were referred to the Industrial Court and 1,060 to the National Arbitration Tribunal. At the same time the Industrial Court was continuing to adjudicate in disputes involving the Fair Wages policy contained in various instruments, as shown in Table 4.

The Industrial Court during these years was interpreting and applying the Fair Wages policy as manifested in each of the six situations appearing in Table 4, as well as through Order 1305. For example, Award 1949 of 29 February 1944 (*Amalgamated Society of Woodworkers and Messrs. J. & N. Miller*), concerned government contracts for the construction of boats. The Union claimed that the rates applicable were building trade rates while the company insisted on paying shipbuilding rates. The Industrial Court held that 'the rates proper to be paid to the men are those obtaining in the shipbuilding industry'

TABLE 4

Year	Fair Wages Resolution	Claims by Government's Industrial Employees	Road Traffic Act, 1930 (amended)	Sugar Industry Legis.	Cinematograph Films Act, 1938	Road Haulage Wages Act, 1938
1939	—	1	8	1	—	—
1940	—	9	—	1+1 int.	1	—
1941	—	3	—	—	—	—
1942	—	2	—	—	—	—
1943	—	1	—	1	—	—
1944	1	3	1	—	—	—
1945	—	2	1 withd.	1	—	1
Total	1	21	10	5	1	1

int. = interpretation of a previous award.
withd. = withdrawn before decision.

Source: Published Awards of the Industrial Court.

(para. 4), and back-dated its award to 1940 when the firm was first engaged by the government.

I. A. Sharp goes so far as to suggest that the long-range policy of the government was to secure the gradual merger of the Industrial Court with the National Arbitration Tribunal. He notes that Sir John Forster, who had been chairman of the Tribunal since May 1944 was appointed President of the Industrial Court on 1 January 1946, but remained an 'appointed member' of the Tribunal, sitting as its chairman whenever present. From 1948 on the chairman of both the National Arbitration Tribunal and the Industrial Disputes Tribunal was Lord Terrington. Reference has been made in chapter 13 to an occasion when Sir Harold Morris, then President of the Industrial Court, mentions in a letter of 24 January 1945 having consulted judges of the National Arbitration Tribunal on a point of great significance for the interpretation of the Fair Wages policy. In cases referred to the Industrial Court under section 8 of the Terms and Conditions of Employment Act 1959, both employers and trade unions have invoked precedents decided by the Industrial Disputes Tribunal on Order 1376 to support their cases.[1] Finally, in a very important recent case on the Fair Wages Resolution of 1946 (Award 3290 of 24 April 1974; *Crittall-Hope Ltd. and Pay Board*), the Industrial Arbitration Board, in seeking to interpret clause 1(a) of the Resolution, resorted to clues provided by the Orders of 1940 and 1951, and the Act of 1959.

TABLE 5

Year	Fair Wages Resolution of 1946	Road Traffic Acts, 1930–60	Road Haulage Wages Act, 1938	Terms and Conditions of Employment Act, 1959	Civil Aviation Legislation 1946–49 (Air Corps. Act, 1949)
1946	—	—	—	—	—
1947	—	—	1	—	—
1948	2	3	—	—	4
1949	2	4	1	—	—
1950	2	2	—	—	1
1951	2	—	—	—	2
1952	1	3	—	—	2
1953	1	1+1 int.	2	—	—
1954	2+1 int.	—	2	—	—
1955	—	—	—	—	—
1956	2	—	1	—	—
1957	4	—	1	—	—
1958	1	—	1	—	—
1959	—	—	1	5+1 withd.	3
1960	3+1 withd.	—	3+1 withd.	14+1 withd.	—
1961	3	—	—	20	—
1962	1	—	3	10+3 withd.	—
1963	—	—	—	13	—
1964	2	—	2	9+1 int.	1 withd.
1965	1	—	—	5+ {1 int. / 3 withd.	—
1966	—	—	—	19+3 withd.	—
1967	—	—	1	22+1 withd.	—
1968	1	1	—	11	—
1969	—	—	—	5	—
1970	6	2	1	7+ {1 int. / 4 withd.	1
1971	2	1 withd.	—	7+ {1 int. / 1 withd.	—
1972	2	—	—	5	—
1973	4	—	1 withd.	—	—
1974	10	2	1	1 withd.	—
1975	3	1	—	11	—
1976	13	—	—	32+1 int.	—
May 20, 1977	18	—	—	15	—
Total	90	21	23	233	14

int.= interpretation of a previous award.
withd.= withdrawn before decision.

SOURCE: Published Awards of the Industrial Court, Industrial Arbitration Board and Central Arbitration Committee.

Utilization of the Fair Wages Policy

An indication of the activity of the Industrial Court in deciding cases involving Fair Wages policy during the period since the Resolution of 1946 was passed is given in Table 5.[2] A sprinkling of other cases involving Fair Wages policy, decided mainly during the 1940s, is not included in Table 5. These were determined by the Industrial Court in the exercise of its function under other instruments: in arbitration under the Industrial Courts Act 1919 on disputes concerning the government's industrial employees, under Order 1305, under legislation concerning the sugar industry and one case under the Cinematograph Films Act 1938.[3] Two other cases under similar statutory jurisdictions were decided in 1976—under the Independent Broadcasting Authority Act 1973, and under the Films Act 1960.[4]

But it is of primary significance that up to the end of 1975—a period including its first thirty-years—only fifty-nine complaints of violation of the Fair Wages Resolution of October 1946 have come before the Industrial Court or its successors—an average of about two per year. In eight of these thirty years, there were no cases at all concerning disputes over wage rates or conditions on government contracts which came before the Court. Yet it will be recalled that under clause 3 of the 1946 Resolution the function of resolving disputes was removed from the government departments and transferred to this independent tribunal.

Table 6 was compiled by the section of the Department of Employment which deals with questions raised under the Fair Wages Resolution. It gives the numbers of questions formally raised with the Department since 1957.

The trend since 1946 is consistent with the low number of reported complaints to government departments in previous years. The dissatisfaction formerly expressed by trade unionists with departmental action on their complaints under the Resolutions of 1891 and 1909 had led to their despairing of enforcement of the Resolutions, which nullified most of their impact. The dissatisfaction stemmed from the conviction that the contracting departments were applying the Fair Wages standard incorrectly, as well as a basic distrust of the departments' sympathies. It was thought that a transfer of the power to resolve disputes over interpretation of the Fair Wages policy to an independent tribunal would dispel some of this suspicion, and its attendent consequences in terms of enforcement success. This hopeful forecast is not borne out by the figures in Table 5. Enforcement of the Fair Wages Resolution through the Industrial Court was rarely

TABLE 6

Year	Awards[1]	(Award Numbers)	Withdrawn	Total
1957	3	(2641, 2651, 2672)	—	3
1958	1	(2694)	—	1
1959	—		—	—
1960	4	(2793, 2815, 2816, 2821)	1	5
1961	2	(2856, 2887)		2
1962	1	(2937)	—	1
1963	—		—	—
1964	2	(3009, 3039)	2	4
1965	1	(3071)	—	1
1966	—		1	1
1967	1	(3161)	3	4
1968	—		—	—
1969	1	(3206)	3	4
1970	5	(3212, 3216–19 inc.)	1	6
1971	2	(3242, 3243)	—	2
1972	3	(3267, 3275, 3285)	4	7
1973	10	(3280, 3281, 3282, 3283, 3286, 3288, 3291, 3292, 3293, 3296)	22	32
1974	5	(3300, 3302, 3307, 3308, 3314)	15	20
1975	3	(3327, CAC Nos. 2 and 6)	6	9
1976[2]	5	(CAC—14, 23, 30, 33, 36)	13	72[3]

NOTES:

1. Cases are given by year in which the claim was first registered with the Department, and *not* by year of award or withdrawal.
2. Up to 31 October 1976.
3. Includes 54 cases as yet unresolved.

SOURCE: Department of Employment.

attempted by trade unionists working on government contracts. The tiny numbers of complaints under the Road Traffic Acts 1930–60, the Road Haulage Wages Act 1938, the Civil Aviation Legislation 1946–9, and others confirm that workers covered by the Fair Wages policy did not regard it as a useful tool for their protection. This conclusion too is consistent with the experience under previous Resolutions.

Why was this so? Why did the new Resolution accepted by the T.U.C. not fulfil the stated goals of the long campaign which preceded its passage? One explanation might be derived from what has been said above about the expansion of the Fair Wages policy. The standard laid down by the 1946 Resolution was essentially identical to that contained in Order 1305 of 1940, Order 1376 of 1951 and section 8 of the 1959 Act. This Fair Wages standard became available, therefore, for the protection of workers generally, not only of those employed on government contracts. It may be possible to understand the absence of attempts to utilize the procedures of the Fair Wages Resolution of 1946 by reference to the substitution of the generalized protection for that specific to employees of government contractors. Workers on government contracts benefited from the Fair Wages policy not through the Resolution, but through the other substantially identical procedures. It is difficult to either confirm or deny this possibility. An attempt to assess it may be made by looking at the degree of utilization of these alternative instruments of Fair Wages policy. In this way, some idea may be obtained not only of whether the Resolution was supplanted by these other instruments, but also of the extent to which the expansion of the Fair Wages policy had an effect on industry as a whole.

In a book published in 1950, I. A. Sharp gives a very brief description of the disposition of cases arising from Order 1305. Of some 2,599 cases reported to the Minister up to the end of 1946, approximately half were withdrawn or settled by the parties. Of the other half, nearly 90 per cent went to the National Arbitration Tribunal. Most of the cases were brought on behalf of workers rather than employers, and the nature of the questions before the Tribunal changed after the end of the war from those of production and manning to terms and conditions of employment. Of the greatest interest to this study of the Fair Wages policy, however, is his unequivocal statement that: 'Only a small proportion at any time has been concerned with the observance by employers of recognized terms and conditions of employment under Part III of the Order'. The N.A.T. was primarily an ordinary arbitration tribunal for the settlement of disputes, not for the implementation of Fair Wages policy.

Under Order 1376 of 1951 two sorts of adjudications were undertaken by the Industrial Disputes Tribunal—'disputes' and 'issues'. 'Disputes' covered disagreements between an employer and his workers connected with their terms and conditions of employment. 'Issues' contained the Fair Wages policy element: an organization of employers or a trade union 'habitually' taking part in collective bargaining in the trade could claim that the employer was not observing 'recognized terms and conditions'. W. E. J. McCarthy estimated in his 1968 study that during its period of operation, the

Industrial Disputes Tribunal made over 1,270 awards, and less than a quarter of these concerned the observance of 'recognized' terms and conditions. The majority involved the settlement of national or local disputes. C. W. Guillebaud refines this figure still further: of the 1,270 awards made, 1,070 dealt with the settlement of 'disputes' and 200 with the settlement of 'issues' under the procedure for the observance of recognized terms and conditions of employment. K. W. Wedderburn and P. L. Davies went further and analysed the substance of each award of the I.D.T. and only subsequently considered whether it was rightly classified as a 'dispute' or an 'issue'. Their analysis concluded that in addition to the official number of classified 'issues' (201), there were 121 'disputes' which might well be regarded as 'issues'.

On this basis, it may be calculated that a maximum of 322 awards were classifiable as resolving 'issues', though only some 200 were formally accepted as such. Over the eight year period of operation of Order 1376 this comes to some forty (or twenty-five) awards annually— hardly a massive number, but a considerably greater use of the procedure than that evinced under the Fair Wages Resolution during those years. How many of these awards trespassed on the territory of the Resolution and thus effectively supplanted it is impossible to know without reviewing every award. The breakdown of cases given by McCarthy is not much help though it is likely that the large block of awards concerned with local authority services (238) and health services (105) were irrelevant to the Resolution. McCarthy does conclude that the great majority of references to the I.D.T. 'probably concerned comparatively weak groups' of workers in industry. On the other hand, the requirement that a reference come from a trade union which 'habitually' took part in existing voluntary machinery excluded industries with no such arrangements and low levels of organization. Reasons for the low utilization of the procedure were cited by McCarthy: some unions avoided the I.D.T. because they had their own arbitration machinery or because 'there was a feeling that negotiation, backed by the threat of possible strike action, was a more suitable method'. In any event, those who did choose to go before the I.D.T. did not do so with great expectations. He confirmed that the I.D.T.'s awards were generally slightly below those arrived at by other methods, though not substantially so. Guillebaud states that 'during the eight years of its existence the I.D.T., in its wage awards, followed on the whole the pattern set by voluntary agreements in general. It certainly did not act as a pace-maker, sparking off fresh rounds of demand for higher wages'.

The overlap with the Fair Wages Resolution, or degree of substitution for it, emerges more clearly through examination of the usage to which the procedure under section 8 of the Terms and Conditions of Employment Act 1959 was put. This procedure was concerned exclusively with the resolution of 'issues'—whether an employer was observing 'recognized' terms and conditions. As may be seen from Table 5, in the period 1959–72, 173 cases were brought before the Industrial Court (or Industrial Arbitration Board) under the 1959 Act. Due to the restriction on access to the Court to registered unions, following enactment of section 152 of the Industrial Relations Act 1971, no cases were decided in 1973 and only one in 1974. The normal flow was resumed in 1975. Of the 173 cases during the first fourteen years (an annual average of twelve to thirteen cases), seventeen were withdrawn before any award was made and four were simply interpretations of previous awards. While the total is some three times greater than the number of awards made since 1946 under the Fair Wages Resolution, and is seven times greater over the same period 1959–72, it is only half the average annual intake of 'issues' resolved by the I.D.T. (only one third or less if Wedderburn and Davies' calculations are taken). There appears to have been a decided decrease since 1959 in the number of claims made to the Industrial Court that employers were not observing 'recognized' terms and conditions. As the number was never very great, this merely evinced further decline.

In his study of section 8 of the 1959 Act, Geoff Latta confirms that the Fair Wages policy embodied in the Act was evident: many firms which were the object of claims were, according to him, small and unsophisticated employers. The effect on them was 'merely to provide a statutory means of bringing "undercutting" firms up to the level of the national agreement although it was a fairly long-winded and very piece-meal means of achieving this end'. Its efficacy frequently depended on 'the chance factor that a union member happens to go to work in the firm'. This critique is confirmation of the similar conclusion reached in the above study of the mechanism of enforcement by complaint of the Fair Wages Resolutions. Examination of all the cases decided during the first fourteen years of the 1959 Act produces only seven which involved the employees of government contractors, or which otherwise could have involved the 1946 Resolution.[5] This is some indication that the 1959 Act did not become a major channel of protest and redress in substitution for the inadequacies of the Resolution for workers on government contracts. Even seven cases, however, is still about one-third of all those brought under the Resolution between 1959 and 1972. The conclusion is, therefore, that the 1959 Act did not supplant the operation of the 1946 Resolution. The vast majority of the claims made under the Act, while concerned with the Fair Wages policy in its general application, did not trespass on the territory marked out for the Resolution. The only counter-indication is the sudden rise in the number or claims under the Resolution in the years 1973–4, when claims were restricted under the 1959 Act. This might be construed as indicating that previously the 1959 Act had usurped the function now being resumed of the Resolution. An alternative explanation having to do with the particular circumstances of the time—a pay freeze—is, as will later be seen in greater detail, the more likely one.

To summarize: the question was whether the expansion of the Fair Wages policy through Orders 1305 and 1376, and the Act of 1959, had led to the abandonment of the Fair Wages Resolution as a means of enforcing the policy. Examination of the experience under the new instruments indicates some increase in the utilization of the policy via enforcement of 'recognized' terms and conditions of employment on employers. This was only to be expected, however, since the coverage of the policy was vastly extended from government contracts only to the whole of British industry. It must be said that the increase in the number of claims to the National Arbitration Tribunal, the Industrial Disputes Tribunal and the Industrial Court did not parallel this enormous extension in coverage. As shown above, only a small proportion of claims to the N.A.T. involved the Fair Wages policy, the numbers to the I.D.T. were few and there was a further decrease after 1959. Measured by this infrequency or absence of enforcement measures, the impact of the policy cannot be considered to have been widespread. Furthermore, examination of the cases decided under the 1959 Act produces only a handful which might have been raised under the Resolution. The conclusion is, then, that the explanation for the rarity of complaint under the 1946 Resolution was not its replacement by other instruments of Fair Wages policy. The reasons for its apparent lack of impact, and that of the other new instruments of Fair Wages policy, must be sought elsewhere.

A Note on Interpretation by the Industrial Court

One explanation of the failure to utilize the enforcement mechanism provided for the Fair Wages policy might be that the independent tribunals were as inhospitable as adjudicators of complaints under the policy as the contracting departments had been found to be under earlier Fair Wages Resolutions. The equivocation which marked the decisions of the Industrial Court involving the policy during the inter-war period did not inspire confidence in its ability to adhere to a firm view consistent with the objects of the policy as perceived by trade unionists. The Court's attitude was described in the Introduction. So, in Award 967 of 1 August 1924, it took the view that: 'It would not therefore seem inequitable if, in time of falling wages, the reductions outside should be reflected in similar decreases inside the Admiralty establishments'. It added that 'due observance' of the Resolution 'does not necessitate following faithfully and minutely every change either upwards or downwards that occurs in private employment'. Almost two decades later, in Award 1943 of 18 February 1944, the Court could still say:

> there may be circumstances in which the payment of different rates for similar work done in different establishments operated by the same employer in the same district, may not be altogether inconsistent with the provisions of the Fair Wages Resolution.[6]

Following the promulgation of Order 1305 of 1940, the Industrial Court did not fail to comprehend its significance for issues involving Fair Wages policy. The Order was invoked together with the Resolution in some cases which came before the Court during the war; for example, in Award 1775 of 29 November 1940, the Court stated:

> In coming to their decision the Court have not only had regard to the principle of the Fair Wages Resolution, but in addition take the view that a relevant matter for consideration in the present case is the principle to be found in the provisions of Article 5(1) of Statutory Rules and Orders, 1940, No. 1305.[7]

In a previous section of this chapter, a tendency towards harmonization of the interpretations of the new Fair Wages policy instruments was traced. As the Industrial Court persisted in its practice of handing down awards without giving reasons (except on extremely rare occasions), it is difficult to establish any official interpretation of the policy. It may be deduced from the statistics produced above that the interpretations of the arbitration tribunals did not stimulate the trade unions to seek widespread implementation and enforcement of the Fair Wages policy through them. A more detailed review of the Industrial Court's interpretation of the Fair Wages formula will be undertaken in subsequent chapters.[8]

NOTES

1. See Award 3147 of 30 June 1967, *Woodhall-Duckham Ltd. and D.A.T.A.*, para. 7; Award 3160 of 29 January 1968, *Black Clawson International Ltd. and C.A.W.U.*, para. 23; and Award 3164 of 17 April 1968, para. 20.

2. A similar table is presented in K. W. Wedderburn and P. L. Davies, *Employment*

Grievances and Disputes Procedures in Britain, University of California Press, Berkeley, 1969, at p. 193 (Table 23). That table gives figures up to 1966, but, as will be noticed in comparing the two tables, Table 5 here traces four additional cases decided under the Civil Aviation legislation (three more in 1948 and one more in 1950) and one additional case decided under each of the Fair Wages Resolution (in 1960), the Road Traffic Act (in 1953) and the Road Haulage Wages Act (in 1947).

3. For cases on the government's industrial employees, see, for example, Award 1746 of 24 January 1940, *Trade Union Side of the Shipbuilding Trade Joint Council for Government Departments and Official Side;* Award 1852 of 26 February, 1942, *Trade Union Side of the Miscellaneous Trades Joint Council for Government Industrial Establishments and Official Side;* Award 2036 of 7 December 1945, *Trade Union Side of the Shipbuilding Trade Joint Council for Government Departments and Official Side;* and Award 2106 of 12 August 1947, *Trade Union Side of the Miscellaneous Trades Joint Council for Government Industrial Establishments and Official Side*. For cases under Order 1305, see, for example, Award 1770 of 22 October 1940, *N.U.G.M.W. and Tynemouth County Borough Council;* Award 1931 of 13 December 1943, *N.U.V.B. and R. Y. Pickering & Co.;* Award 2055 of 27 May 1946, *N.U.G.M.W. and Pitwood Association of Scotland;* and Award 2124 of 29 January 1948, *Amalgamated Union of Operative Bakers, Confectioners and Allied Workers and The South Wales Federation of Master Bakers' Associations*. For cases under the sugar industry legislation, see, for example, Award 1909 of 18 May 1943, *A.E.U. and British Sugar Corp.;* and Award 1996 of 12 January 1945. For the case on the Cinematograph Films Act 1938, see Award 1767 of 3 October 1940, *Association of Cine-Technicians and British Instructional Films, Ltd.*

4. See respectively Award 21 of 11 August 1976, *Radio Trent Ltd. and National Union of Journalists;* and Award 68 of 31 December 1976, *Clyde Leisure Pastimes Ltd. and the National Association of Theatrical, Television and Kine Employees*.

5. Award 2765 of 11 March 1960, *Hermit Industries (Dudley) Ltd. and Amalgamated Union of Foundry Workers;* Award 2822 of 13 February 1961; Award 2827 of 6 March 1961; Award 2872 of 28 September 1961; Award 2877 of 16 November 1961 (the Union claimed that 'The Company, in failing fully to implement the terms of the National Agreement were acting not only in violation of the Terms and Conditions of Employment Act, 1959, but also of the Fair Wages Clause implicit in all Government Contracts' (para. 4(d)); Award 3107 of 25 July 1966; and Award 3133 of 13 March 1967.

6. *Trade Union Side of the Engineering Trades Joint Council for Government Industrial Establishments and Official Side*, at para. 9. This sentence was quoted again, apparently with approval, in Award 1958 of 12 April 1944, which interpreted Award 1943.

7. *Trade Union Side, Miscellaneous Trades Joint Council for Government Industrial Establishments and Official Side*, para. 5. See also Award 1773 of 18 November 1940, *Trade Union Side, Shipbuilding Trade Joint Council for Government Departments and Official Side*, para. 5.

8. In compiling the account given in this chapter, use has been made of the following sources:

—B. C. Roberts, *National Wages Policy in War and Peace*, George Allen & Unwin, London, 1958; chapter 2: 'British Wage Policy in Wartime'.

—I. A. Sharp, *Industrial Conciliation and Arbitration in Great Britain*, George Allen & Unwin, London, 1950; chapter VII: 'State Action Arising out of World War II'; pp. 425–8.

—J. W. Grove, *Government and Industry in Britain*, 1962; p. 205.

—W. E. J, McCarthy, *Compulsory Arbitration in Britain: The Work of the Industrial Disputes Tribunal*, Royal Commission on Trade Unions and Employers' Associations, Research Paper No. 8, H.M.S.O., 1968.

—K. W. Wedderburn and P. L. Davies, *Employment Grievances and Disputes Procedures in Britain*, University of California Press, Berkeley, 1969; pp. 204–13.

—Geoff Latta, 'The Legal Extension of Collective Bargaining: A Study of Section 8 of the Terms and Conditions of Employment Act, 1959', *Industrial Law Journal*, **4** (March 1975), p. 215.

—C. W. Guillebaud, *The Role of the Arbitrator in Industrial Wage Disputes*, James Nisbet & Co., 1970, pp. 19, 22.

15

Fair Wages Policy and Collective Bargaining
after 1946

Collective Bargaining After 1946

The post-war economic situation has been marked by a factor of inestimable significance for the strength of the trade unions and the economic position of workers generally. For the two decades after the end of the Second World War, the percentage of the work-force unemployed has averaged about 1.8 per cent. Since the late 1960s it has risen dramatically, but still does not approximate the pre-war figure which averaged about 10.5 per cent. The debate on the effect this has had has revolved largely around Phillips's proposition in 1958 that there was a statistically significant relationship between the level and rate of change of unemployment and the rate of change of money wage rates, which has been remarkably stable since 1862. Others have argued that other variables, such as the rate of change of unionization offer a better explanation of the data. The years immediately preceding the Second World War and onwards have witnessed a massive increase in trade union membership, from 4,392,000 in 1933 to 6,053,000 in 1938 to 9,362,000 in 1948. Though not increasing substantially since then, the decades since the end of the war have not seen any such disastrous fall as was experienced after the First World War. Whatever the disagreements over the effects of the changed atmosphere engendered by the relatively low level of unemployment and the increased level of unionization, there has been little controversy over the existence of one undeniable phenomenon of post-war years—wage drift.

Wage drift was defined by E. H. Phelps Brown in 1962 as having as its essence 'that the effective rate of pay per unit of labour input is raised by arrangements that lie outside the control of the recognized procedures for scheduling rates'. The contrast between such a phenomenon and the pre-war experience is clear. Then the struggle was to

For notes see p. 307

ensure that rates negotiated through recognized procedures of collective bargaining were adhered to by employers. The difficulties of achieving this in the circumstances of economic depression and mass unemployment were evident in the widespread evasion or blatant disregard of negotiated rates. Rates actually paid were, if anything, below the negotiated rate for the industry, not above it as the phenomenon of wages drift implies. Thus, in an article in 1956, H. A. Turner states: 'It can be deduced from reported 1938 earnings that "workplace" rates did not, on the average, vary greatly from the "industry" rates then in force'. The Donovan Commission Report noted that: 'in 1938 there was only a modest "gap" between the rates which (industry-wide agreements) laid down for a normal working week and the average earnings which men actually received. By 1967, the two sets of figures had moved far apart' (para. 57). While the range of the gap between earnings and wage rates had undergone considerable fluctuations, detailed examination indicates a steady increase. The *Department of Employment Gazette* regularly charts the progress of this widening gap. In 1954, according to Turner's calculations, average workplace wage-rates exceeded those laid down in industry agreements by up to 15 per cent. According to another estimate by J. Marquand, between the years 1948–55, the overall earnings' drift in Britain was 17 per cent, made up of about 10 per cent attributable to increased overtime and a wage-drift of about 7 per cent. Earnings drift has vastly increased since then. According to the Donovan Commission Report, in the period 1962–7 alone the average earnings drift for all industries increased by an additional 13.3 per cent. Table 7 (given as Table B on p. 15 of the Report) illustrates the difference between the earnings and time rates of men in certain industries in October 1967.

The economic phenomenon of wage drift is implemented largely through the industrial relations mechanism of work-place collective bargaining. This mechanism is based on the growth, since 1945, of what has since achieved the status of a movement—the shop stewards. In the inter-war period, shop-floor activity by workers' representatives seems to have been minimal. Union organization was badly hit by the onset of economic depression and massive unemployment which followed the brief boom after the First World War, 1919–21. The overwhelming power of employers made it dangerous, if not fatal, for any worker to attempt to do more than defend minimum standards and conditions. Even these defensive actions could lead to victimization of shop floor leadership. The more favourable economic conditions following the Second World War and the increased numbers and density of trade union membership led to a resurgence of the leadership on the shop floor. One study suggests that the increase was about

TABLE 7.

Earnings and Time Rates of Men in certain Industries in October 1967

Industry	Time rates for normal week of 40 hours (national or provincial rate)	Average weekly earnings of adult male manual workers for industry (Second pay-week in Oct. 67)
Engineering Fitter: Labourer: (Minimum earnings levels: Fitter: £12.17. 8 Labourer: £10.17. 4)	£11. 1. 8 £ 9. 7. 4	*Engineering and electrical goods* £21. 7. 9 *Vehicles* £24. 8. 5
Building Craftsmen: Labourer:	£14.13. 4 £12.11. 8	*Construction* £21.13. 8
Shipbuilding and repairing: Fully skilled: Labourer: (Minimum earnings levels: Skilled: £12.17. 4 Labourer: £11. 3. 6)	£11. 1. 4 £ 9. 6. 0	*Shipbuilding and marine engineering* £21.17. 8
Dock labourers	(Guaranteed minimum weekly pay) £15. 0. 0	*Dock labour** £22.16. 6
Cocoa, chocolate and sugar confectionery	£10.15. 6	*Cocoa, chocolate and sugar confectionery* £21. 7. 5
Electrical cable making	£11. 8. 4½ to £13. 5. 6	*Insulated wires and cables* £23. 9. 4
Furniture manufacturing	£13. 0. 0 to £14. 3. 4	*Furniture and upholstery* £22. 5. 4
Motor vehicle retail and repairing trade	£11. 0. 0 to £13.10. 0	*Motor repairers, garages, etc.* £18.10. 4
Soap, candle and edible fat manufacturing	£10. 6. 6 to £11. 7. 0	*Vegetable and animal oils, fats, soap and detergents* £23.10. 5
Footwear manufacturing	£11.12. 6	*Footwear* £19.14. 4

SOURCE: Ministry of Labour.   * April 1967 figure.

50 per cent between 1947 and 1961. Research by Marsh and Coker on the records of the Amalgamated Engineering Union shows that the number of A.E.U. shop stewards in federated establishments increased three times faster than that of manual workers in such establishments between 1947 and 1961. In a most detailed study of the numbers, composition, functions and activities of shop stewards, McCarthy and Parker estimated that the total of stewards might be about 175,000. The system of workplace collective bargaining which has developed from the growth of numbers and strength of the shop stewards has been described by Goodman and Whittingham as follows:

> Workplace bargaining is diffuse, it has evolved spontaneously, and prior to the Donovan Report its nature and characteristics were largely unknown. The Report confirmed that it is pragmatic, continuous and often intensive, although its stage of development varies between and within industries. In some firms workplace representatives have successfully challenged basic rates, while in others bargaining is confined to non-monetary topics, though both have implications for production costs. Workplace bargaining may be partially measured by the extent of wage drift, the continuation of which in unfavourable economic conditions suggests that it has now developed its own institutional momentum.

This last conclusion, as to the institutional character of wage drift based on workplace bargaining, is of the greatest importance. As early as 1956, Turner had noted the systematic character of wage drift. Writing in 1973, Phelps Brown confirmed the change in the balance of class forces symbolized by the continuance of wage drift:

> It is very doubtful, moreover, whether the genie of expectations having once escaped from the bottle, a reversion to a harder market environment can of itself ever get it back again; and whether employees who have gained so much personally in confidence, independence and resources will revert to an older view of what is and is not within their power to control.

The phenomenon of wage drift has not gone unnoticed by the authorities concerned with expenditure on government contracts. A Report of the Comptroller and Auditor-General for 1965–6 contained this review of the situation:

> 81. As a direct result of full employment firms have found it necessary, under local pressure, to concede increases in wages, additional to those agreed nationally, in order to retain and attract labour. In so far as these increases are not accompanied

by an increase in productivity they are know as 'wages drift'. . . .
82. Information published by the Ministry of Labour shows that
between 1 January 1963 and 1 June 1966 the actual average
earnings of skilled pieceworkers (excluding overtime premium)
increased as follows:

Units in Pence per hour	1 January 1963	1 June 1966	Increase
Aircraft Engineering	100.7	130.1	29.4
Electrical Engineering	93.9	118.4	24.5
Mechanical Engineering	91.3	117.6	26.3

During the same period the national minimum earnings level for
workers of this type rose from 61.58 pence per hour to 70.4 pence
per hour, i.e. an increase of 8.82 pence per hour. The Ministry
of Labour figures show that the increases in actual earnings which
took place in these fields were approximately three times the
increases which could be attributed to national awards . . .
83. Wages drift affects all purchases whether in the public or
private sector. . . .

The Report went on to discuss the impact of wage drift on the tendering process for government contracts, on the control by the government
of contractors' wages costs, and the implications of this impact for the
Fair Wages Resolution of the House of Commons—topics which will
be discussed in a later chapter.[1]

The Effect on Fair Wages Policy

The relationship between the Fair Wages policy and the system of
collective bargaining is reflected in the experience of the Industrial
Court. This was the tribunal charged, from 1946, with the duty of
adjudicating upon disputes arising under the Resolution. The paucity
in number of decisions under this jurisdiction which were handed
down by the Court reflects, on the one hand, the improvement in the
economic position and industrial power of workers which vitiated the
need for Fair Wages protection, but also on the other hand, the
familiar problems in enforcement of the Resolution via the mechanism
of individual complaint by employees of government contractors. An
examination of the published awards of the Industrial Court proves
both valuable and inconclusive. The awards do outline the facts of the
disputes to be resolved concerning the application of the Fair Wages
policy, and also provide a detailed summary of the arguments put on
behalf of the parties to the dispute. Thus, an idea may be obtained

of the interpretation put on the policy and the Resolution itself by trade unions, employers and government departments. However, in adjudicating upon these disputes the Industrial Court has steadfastly maintained its long-standing refusal to give reasons for its decisions, or even to discuss the merits of the rival submissions of the parties.

Despite the optimistic outlook of the first President of the Court, Sir William MacKenzie, that the body of Court awards would comprise reasoned decisions gradually constituting an industrial jurisprudence, the initial endeavours of the Court to state reasoned grounds for decisions soon faded away. Guillebaud states bluntly that Mac-Kenzie's hopes were illusory, for 'there are no general principles of universal application in this field of industrial arbitration'. While the Fair Wages Resolution purports to contain such a general principle applicable to the employees of government contractors, the Court's awards in cases concerning it maintained this negative attitude to reasoned decisions. The position was reaffirmed by the last President of the Industrial Court. In his written evidence to the Donovan Commission, Sir Roy Wilson did claim that reasons are given 'where the Court feel that this would help to make clear the real meaning and intention of the award or to prevent misunderstanding or any unintended chain reaction'. On balance, however, in the great majority of cases it was felt that factors of finality, flexibility, unanimity and ease of decision justified the absence of reasons. Despite Sir Roy Wilson's later assertion in his oral evidence that the Court has been increasingly giving reasons for its awards, these remain few and far between.[2]

Those few decisions on the Fair Wages policy where reasons have been given do cast some light on the approach adopted by the Court, and will be examined in detail. But until 1959, relatively few cases came before the Industrial Court for a decision based on the new Fair Wages policy first embodied in Order 1305 of 1940 and later translated into the Fair Wages Resolution of 1946. Some of these fell directly within the jurisdiction conferred by Order 1305; others were concerned with the determination of rates payable to employees of the government in its industrial establishments; and still others arose under various statutes containing a reference to Fair Wages policy. Only twenty cases, however, came up specifically on the Fair Wages Resolution of 1946 as applicable to government contracts during the first dozen years of its existence.

1940–1946

The vast extension of Fair Wages policy embodied in Order 1305 came into force on 25 July 1940. Prior to this, naturally, the Industrial

Court did not advert to any development having occurred. Thus, in Awards 1757, 1759 and 1760 of June and early July 1940, cases concerning government ship-building employees, there was no mention of any new Fair Wages policy. The criteria invoked were the old standards of rates paid in other establishments in the engineering and ship-building industries.[3] Less expected was the absence in Awards 1764 and 1765 of 13 September 1940 (*N.U.G.M.W. and T.G.W.U. and Ministry of Supply*) of any reference to Fair Wages policy among the factors which determined the claim. And Award 1768 of 7 October 1940 (*Trade Union Side of the Shipbuilding Trade Joint Council for Government Departments and Official Side*) was identical in all respects to Award 1759 of 10 July 1940 which preceded the coming into force of the new policy. It was only in Award 1773 of 18 November 1940 (*Trade Union Side of the Shipbuilding Trade Joint Council for Government Departments and Official Side*) that the Industrial Court declared:

> The issue between the parties falls to be determined in the light of the provisions of the Fair Wages Resolution, under which the wages of Admiralty employees are determinable, and the provisions of Statutory Rules and Orders, 1940, No. 1305, 'Conditions of Employment and National Arbitration Order, 1940, para. 5(1)'. (para. 5)

This recognition of a new Fair Wages policy was reiterated in Award 1775 of 29 November 1940 (*Trade Union Side of the Miscellaneous Trades Joint Council for Government Industrial Establishments and Official Side*). In an extraordinary conflict of principle, however, the Court there applied both Order 1305 (quoted in full in para. 5) and the Fair Wages Resolution of 1909 (quoted in full in para. 4). In deciding this claim, the Industrial Court was simultaneously invoking the supposedly different principles of the Resolutions of 1909 and 1946 (as embodied in Order 1305). The Court seemed untroubled by this apparent contradiction. The failure to realize that the policy of the 1909 Resolution had been effectively superseded continued. In Award 2004 of 28 February 1945 (*Trade Union Side of the Engineering Trades Joint Council for Government Industrial Establishments and Official Side*), the Court again quoted the 1909 Resolution and added: 'The provisions of this Resolution are observed in all Government establishments'.

The Fair Wages policy being implemented up to 1946 and its relationship to the system of collective bargaining may be perceived through a perusal of the cases decided by the Industrial Court up to the passage of the new Fair Wages Resolution on 13 October 1946. For example, in several cases during these years, the National Union of Public Employees and the National Union of General and Municipal

Workers attempted, with a fair degree of success, to require various local authorities to adhere to terms and conditions of employment, mainly wage rates, arrived at by collective negotiating machinery—principally National Joint Industrial Councils.[4] Thus, in Award 1823 of 26 August 1941, in a claim by N.U.P.E. relying on Order 1305, the Industrial Court chaired by Sir Harold Morris required the Morley Town Council Waterworks Committee to adhere to the provisions recognized by the National Joint Industrial Council; and in Award 1866 of 10 July 1942, the N.U.G.M.W. brought the Aberystwyth Town Council to heel on the same terms. In a few other cases, trade unions attempted to require private employers to adhere to the terms of collective agreements, with varying success.[5] Some indication of the minimal standards invoked before, and sometimes by the Court, is evidenced by the occasional citation of Trade Board rates: in Award 1886 of 3 December 1942 the Court refused to allow a claim regarding some employees who were being paid Trade Board rates. In contrast, in Awards 1884 of 18 November 1942 and 1932 of 5 January 1944, workers were awarded rates which exceeded those fixed by the Trade Board.

In a number of cases relating to the terms of employment of the government's industrial employees, as determined by the Fair Wages Resolution, the emphasis was firmly placed on the district or local basis of the wages standard. Thus, in Award 1803 of 21 May 1941 (*Trade Union Side of the Shipbuilding Trade Joint Council for Government Departments and Official Side*) the government invoked the Resolution to oppose the claim, arguing that wage rates should be those prevailing in the district where the depot was situated, not those of other Admiralty establishments. This approach was repeated in Award 1843 of 21 November 1941, which was in turn cited in Award 1951 of 8 March 1944, and again appeared in Award 2072 of 27 November 1946. In another claim involving the Miscellaneous Trades Joint Council for Government Industrial Establishments, the Trade Union Side invoked the Resolution, but the Official Side, in opposing the claim, stated on behalf of the Air Ministry that the method adopted in determining the rates of wages of labourers in all Ministry establishments was as follows:

This method is to ascertain the general level of labourers' wages in the various localities in which the Air Ministry establishments are situated, and is based upon an average of the recognized rates for labourers in various trades in the district concerned. The rate so ascertained is then co-related to a scale agreed upon by the parties and is subject to review at six-monthly periods. In districts, however, in which another Government Department is the dominant employer the rates paid by that Department are also paid by the Air Ministry. In the present case it was submitted that the rates to be paid should be based on the general level of labourers' wages in the district, and not upon those paid at an Air Ministry establishment in a neighbouring dockyard town, at which, the Admirality being the dominant employer, the Admiralty rates are paid. (Award 1861 of 16 June 1942, para. 4.)

The principle of district rates led to the Air Ministry paying different rates for the same work in different districts. Award 2004 of 28 February 1945 was another instance of government departments endeavouring to evade a claim by invoking the district basis: the Official Side of the Engineering Trades Joint Council for Government Industrial Establishments argued that the district in which the factory was situated was not within the area covered by the collective agreement which the Trade Union Side wished to apply (para. 4). Government departments were not prepared to adopt the wider basis of wage determination embodied in the new Fair Wages policy formula contained in Order 1305 of 1940.

Yet already towards the end of this period there is visible a disparity between rates actually being paid in industry and those stipulated in collective agreements. And this disparity is giving rise to conflict before the Industrial Court: in Award 2022 of 6 September 1945 the attention of the Court was directed by one of the parties before it 'to the fact that the minimum rates contained in the agreements are rates for the least skilled workers and many, if not the majority of the employees, are paid higher rates in acknowledgment of skill or long service' (para. 4). In Award 2055 of 27 May 1946 (*N.U.G.M.W. and T.G.W.U. and Pitwood Association of Scotland*), a further reason put forward in a claim for raising the existing minimum time rates was that 'the introduction of a system of payment by results has resulted in the present time rate bearing little relation to the earnings under the payment by results system' (para. 3). Finally, in Award 2036 of 7 December 1945, involving the Shipbuilding Trade Joint Council for Government Departments, the Official Side contended that they had paid rates consistent with previous decisions of the Industrial Court 'and that in the case of craftsmen recruited locally at war-time Admiralty Industrial Establishments the practice had been followed of paying "local" rates in accordance with the agreements current in the appropriate industries, which practice, it was submitted, is in accord with the provisions of the Fair Wages Resolution of the House of Commons'. To the contrary, the Trade Union Side claimed 'that in outside industry systems of payment by result and piece work are operative to a much greater extent than in Admiralty establishments, and in consequence the basic day work rates in outside industry are on the low side' (para. 3). By the end of 1945, therefore, the national minimum base rates officially negotiated by trade unions were losing their efficacy in adequately safeguarding workers' wage standards.

To summarize: by the time of the passage of the Fair Wages Resolution of 1946, the Industrial Court was not evincing an appreciation of the change in Fair Wages policy manifested by Order 1305 of 1940. Although the Order was invoked by the Court as a basis for decision, its principle was not seen as contradicting that of the Fair Wages policy of 1909: the district basis of the policy remained unchallenged. Yet already towards the end of the war, it can be perceived that rates laid down in agreements of national or district application were inadequate reflections of economic changes which were producing rates far above those stipulated. This is the beginning of the growth which threatened to stifle the Fair Wages policy.

1946–1959

In the dozen years following the passage of the 1946 Resolution, up to the enactment of the Terms and Conditions of Employment Act 1959, relatively few cases involving Fair Wages policy came up for decision before the Industrial Court. Only twenty invoked the Resolution as it applied to government contractors, and of these over one-third were concerned with matters other than wage rates (e.g. trade union rights and liability for sub-contractors). Other cases arose under different Fair Wages policy jurisdictions of the Industrial Court—involving the industrial employees of the government—or under the Civil Aviation legislation 1946–9, the Road Traffic Acts 1930–60, or the Road Haulage Wages Act 1938. A review of the Industrial Court's activity during these years shows how the old 'district' basis of the Fair Wages policy, which persisted in the first few years after 1946, was gradually replaced by a readiness to recognize collectively agreed standards. More and more the Court found itself simply requiring adherence to collective agreements, instead of engaging in arithmetic exercises to determine the average of varying rates in a locality. The Fair Wages policy which the trade union movement and its sympathizers had envisaged at its inception in 1891 was finally being implemented over a half-century later.

Several cases concerning the Government's industrial employees illustrate the transitional period following the passage of the new

Resolution on 14 October 1946. Award 2072 of 27 November 1946 confirmed that government departments did not regard it as introducing any novel principle. This followed a claim by the Trade Union Side of the Shipbuilding Trade Joint Council for Government Departments which stated that the rates in Admiralty shipyards had fallen below those of workers in comparable situations, and contained a demand for a minimum base rate of 57s. 6d. for all workers concerned. The Official Side's response was blank denial of any discrepancy. They reasserted the traditional modes of assessment utilized in Award 1843 of 21 November 1941:

> In the view of the Official Side, Industrial Court Award No. 1843 established three clear principles, first that the rates of pay of labourers in Admirality industrial establishments set up just prior to the last war or later should fluctuate only with Admirality Industrial bonus, unless some general change is approved, second that basic rates fall to be determined by the principles of the Fair Wages Resolution of the House of Commons and third that the total rates first assessed for labourers at these establishments should conform to those payable locally by other Government Departments represented on the Miscellaneous Trades Joint Council subject to an overriding minimum basic rate at present 53s. 6d. The effect of the Award has been to ensure adherence to 'Fair Wages' in the various localities by means of a convenient general system for adjustment to suit national wage movements and there are as yet no signs of divergence between Admiralty and local rates which would warrant a revision of these rates resulting from that Award.

The Industrial Court disallowed the Trade Union Side's claim, but did raise the minima somewhat.

The minimum basic rate for adult unskilled labourers (or 'M' rate as it was known) began to appear frequently in the cases. Thus, in Award 2090 of 8 May 1947, the Trade Union Side of the Miscellaneous Trades Joint Council for Government Industrial Establishments attempted to widen the basis for the calculation of the 'M' rate as applied in the district around Wivenhoe. They pointed out that most workers in Wivenhoe (pop. 2,000) were employed in Colchester (pop. 44,000) and received Colchester rates of wages. Consequently, the cost of living in Wivenhoe was dictated by Colchester. To the contrary, the Official Side stated:

> that, so long as 'M' rates are fixed as they are under the present agreement on a broad 'fair wage' basis which takes into account

local rates in other industries, the concession of the present claim would be in defiance of the facts. The present formula for determining the 'M' rates is applied with a certain flexibility by consent of both sides of the Council. For example, if a depot is established in a stretch of purely agricultural land, and labour has to be obtained from the nearest town, the rates paid in the town are taken into account in fixing the 'M' rate for the depot; also, if two or more depots are situated fairly close together so that it is convenient to transfer labour from one to the other to meet pressure at either, then the fact of interchangeability of labour would be an influence towards uniformity of rates between the depots concerned. There are not special circumstances at Wivenhoe to justify going to Colchester for rates on which to base the 'M' rate. Wivenhoe is a small place but it has a distinct and separate industrial life of its own. (para. 4)

The Industrial Court denied the Trade Union Side's claim. Two other cases involving the Miscellaneous Trades Joint Council for Government Industrial Establishments, both decided on 12 August 1947, indicate that government departments were prepared to utilize different methods of determining rates of wages for different categories of workers. Award 2105 reiterated the district method of calculation of 'M' rates: they 'are fixed on the basis of an average of agreed rates paid for comparable employment in the locality concerned by both public and private employers' (para. 3). In Award 2106, however, another claim for a rise in the 'M' rate, the Official Side conceded that 'in determining the rates of pay at engineering units it is the practice to adopt the rates for the District as agreed between the appropriate unions and the Engineering and Allied Employers' National Federation, or where there are no agreed rates in the District, those of the nearest federated district'. In contrast: 'The agreed method of fixing the labourers' rate of pay at non-engineering Air Ministry establishments is to adopt the average of agreed rates paid to the unskilled labourer in comparable industrial employment in the vicinity of the station' (para. 5).

The traditional method of wage-fixing—by averaging out a number of local rates—was becoming less satisfactory than ever. In Award 2108 of 10 September 1947 the Trade Union Side of the Shipbuilding Trade Joint Council for Government Departments protested at the principles invoked in Awards 1843 and 2072 quoted above: 'Both these Awards provided for the payment of rates in a number of Admiralty Establishments lower than those in operation in the Dockyards and in other Government Industrial Establishments and it was submitted that on the basis of the Fair Wages Resolution of the House of Commons such lower rates were unjustified' (para. 4). But the new method invoked threatened to be no better. Their protests could not mask the growing dilemma facing the trade unions.

This dilemma is perfectly illustrated by Award 2130 of 6 February 1948. In argument, it was openly admitted that, without abandoning the old and customary basis of calculation ('the normal procedure for fixing the rate of pay of male adult unskilled labourers covered by the Miscellaneous Trades Joint Council is to ascertain the simple average of agreed minimum weekly rates being paid in the locality of the particular establishment in both public and private employment'), the London rate (in fact identical to the 'M' rate) was in practice fixed by following the rates agreed in the engineering industry. Surprisingly enough, in its first explicit appearance before the Industrial Court, the 1946 Resolution was referred to by the Trade Union Side as having been breached by this practice: 'In support of the claim it was contended by the Trade Union Side of the Joint Council that the present rate of 91s. does not comply with the requirements of the Fair Wages Resolution passed by the House of Commons on the 14th October, 1946'. Evidence was produced showing that higher rates were paid in London. The Trade Union Side contended that to rely on engineering rates was inadequate because they were fixed by export industries where piece-rates were common, unlike establishments under the Miscellaneous Trades Joint Council. They expressed their distaste for the 'very tedious method of assessing fair wages in accordance with the average of a large number of rates', but were nevertheless prepared to adopt it if it was the only alternative to the existing practice 'because the need of the workpeople concerned is so great and the agitation for an improvement in the rate so intense'.

For its part the Official Side pleaded the complexity and difficulty of fixing differing rates for and within London and advocated the practice of parallelling the engineering rates. They alleged that a new wage claim now being put forward in the engineering industry would redress any grievance of the Trade Union Side. This last factor seems to have influenced the Industrial Court. After going over all the considerations, it held that the engineering rate should continue to prevail, but if not redressed adequately by the new claim, the normal method of assessment should be used despite its practical difficulties. The case highlights the problem facing trade unions wishing to enforce the Fair Wages policy. On the one hand the old method of averaging out various local rates was unacceptable in principle since it ignored collectively agreed rates. On the other hand, these latter were rapidly being overtaken and exceeded as local bargainers exploited the favourable economic circumstances to increase rates paid. The government departments were prepared to abandon the customary principle if they could thereby ensure lower wage costs, and the Industrial Court was sufficiently malleable to allow this.

During the period between the passage of the Fair Wages Resolution of 1946 and the enactment of the Terms and Conditions of Employment Act 1959, cases involving the Fair Wages policy which came before the Industrial Court under various jurisdictions differed widely in the attitudes displayed towards collective agreements. Of nine cases under the Road Haulage Wages Act 1938, only one, Award 2443 of 20 April 1953 (*T.G.W.U. and J. Johnson & Son, Ltd.*), specifically referred to a collective agreement in fixing the statutory remuneration (para. 10). One other, Award 2549 of 20 December 1954 (*United Road Transport Workers Association of England and Messrs. G. H. Kime & Co. Ltd.*), referred to a Wages Council Order for the road haulage industry. In the seven other cases, the Court, in deciding whether or not the remuneration paid was unfair, did not advert to collectively agreed standards.[6] In the nine cases under the Civil Aviation legislation, 1946–9, the Court seemed a trifle readier to impose collectively agreed standards reached in the National Joint Council for Civil Air Transport.[7] In four of the cases, however, the Court simply declared that the firms complained of were or were not complying with the Fair Wages requirements of the legislation.[8]

In the first of the fourteen cases under the Road Traffic Act 1930, as amended, the Industrial Court manifested an awareness of the new Fair Wages policy formula, but in the application of that formula displayed once again a talent for disappointing complainants before it. In a trilogy of cases (Awards 2176, 2177 and 2178 of 30 August 1948), The Transport and General Workers' Union failed to substantiate complaints against three different employers—Messrs. Gibson Bros., Mr. L. D. Brown and Robinson & Son (Burbage) Ltd.—despite the Court's resort to collective standards. In Award 2176, the employer was a member of the Midlands Coach and Transport Association and observed agreements negotiated by that Association with a union affiliated to the T.U.C., the United Road Transport Workers Association of England (U.R.T.W.A.E.). Evidence was adduced as to the rates and conditions of workers employed by other operators of public service vehicles in the district concerned, and the membership of the T.G.W.U. in those undertakings, and the extent to which members of the Midlands Area Coach and Transport Association operated public service vehicles in that district. Despite the allegation by the T.G.W.U. that the employer was in breach of his Fair Wages obligations under section 93(1) of the Act, the complaint was dismissed.

The Industrial Court, chaired by Sir John Forster, found:

> that Messrs. Gibson Bros. are paying rates of wages and observing
> hours and conditions of labour established by machinery of
> negotiation to which the parties are an organization of employers
> and a trade union. The Court is of opinion that the organization
> of employers concerned is representative of a substantial pro-
> portion of the employers engaged in the trade or industry in the
> district. The Court is unable to say on the evidence adduced
> that the trade union concerned (the U.R.T.W.A.E.) is not
> representative of a substantial proportion of the workers engaged
> in the trade or industry in the district.
>
>   The Court therefore decide that the complaint to the effect
> that the wages paid . . . are not in accordance with the require-
> ments of Section 93(1) of the Road Traffic Act, 1930, has not
> been substantiated and award accordingly.

In a majority of the fourteen cases under this jurisdiction, however,
the complaints by trade unions were upheld.[9] In only one other case,
besides the initial trilogy, was a complaint by the T.G.W.U. rejected
by the Court. In Award 2245 of 6 December 1949, the union complained that certain companies were not observing an Agreement
between it and the London Transport Passenger Board. The companies
claimed that they were in a different business and the union initially
accepted their view and entered into negotiations with them. When
these failed to produce any agreement, the union proceeded with its
complaint, which was, however, dismissed by the Court. In another
case, Award 2228 of 5 August 1949, the Court upheld the complaint,
but chose to phrase its award in terms which deviated disturbingly
from the 1946 Fair Wages formula:

> (The Court) find that in the district in which the undertaking is
> carried on the rates of wages and conditions of employment of
> drivers which in practice prevail amongst good employers are: . . .
> (para. 6)

This is a reversion to the standard laid down in the Fair Wages
Resolution of 1909. It is unexpected and incomprehensible awards of
this kind that make systematic analysis of the Court's decisions a
discouraging exercise.

   Of the twenty awards involving the Fair Wages Resolution and
government contractors in the period 1946–59, twelve raised questions
concerning the applicability of collectively agreed standards. Some
idea of the Industrial Court's conciliatory attitude to enforcement of
the new Fair Wages policy may be gained from two cases decided

under Order 1305 one month before the first case on the Resolution itself. Awards 2124 and 2125 of 29 January 1948 concerned complaints by the Amalgamated Union of Operative Bakers, Confectioners and Allied Workers against the The South (and West) Wales Federation of Master Bakers' Associations. The Union demanded: 'that the sickness clause already embodied in the existing local agreements operating in South (and West) Wales shall be included in the award'. The Court, in the clearest possible circumstances, declined to intervene. Its attitude was manifested in the award which simply stated: 'The Court note that the parties have now agreed that as and when a new area agreement is concluded between them it shall contain a sickness clause in the terms of the clause already embodied in existing local agreements operating in South (and West) Wales'. The record of the twelve awards on collective standards under the Fair Wages Resolution does not evince any stricter enforcement of employers' Fair Wages obligations.

Of these twelve awards, in six the Industrial Court agreed to apply the terms of a collective agreement and in six it declined to do so. But of the six cases where the Court did accept a collective standard, three were in fact concerned with situations where the Court was faced with alternative collective arrangements being advocated by the opposing parties. Thus, Award 2236 of 13 October 1949 concerned Stationery Office contracts for the supply of loose-leaf binders. The National Union of Printing, Bookbinding and Paper Workers contended that the work concerned was bookbinding work and subject to an agreement negotiated by it and the wages fixed therein. The contractor, Pike Bros. & Co. Ltd., contended to the contrary that the work was governed by the Paper Box Wages Council Wages Regulation Orders, not being bookbinding work at all. The complaint was upheld and the Court required the contractor to adhere to the terms of the agreement. Again, in Award 2278 of 14 November 1950, the Scottish Painters' Society claimed that the rates applicable to workers on the contract were those prescribed by the National Working Rules for the Painting Trade in Scotland, which were laid down by the Scottish Painting Council comprising members of the union and of the Scottish Master Painters' Federation. The contractor, Structural Painters Ltd., claimed that it was observing the terms of an agreement negotiated by it with the T.G.W.U. covering the work and 'it was contended that by so doing the company was complying with the requirements of the Fair Wages Resolution'. The Court held that insofar as the company was paying less than the rates in the Working Rules, 'which was the only Collective Agreement within the meaning of Clause 1A of the Fair Wages Resolution applicable to the work carried out under the contract', it was in breach. Finally, in Award 2672 of 21 November 1957, the Amalgamated Society of Woodcutting Machinists claimed that the rates payable for workers making pallets for the Ministry of Supply under a government contract were those laid down by the National Joint Industrial Council for the Wood Box, Packing Case and Wooden Container Industry. The contractor, Messrs. Bartlett Materials Handling Ltd., claimed the rates payable were those of the Joint Industrial Council for the Home-Grown Timber Trade. The Court upheld the union's complaint.

In only two of all the twenty awards handed down under the Fair Wages Resolution did the Industrial Court actually impose a collective agreement on an employer in a situation where the employer was refusing to comply with any collective arrangement. In Award 2200 of 20 January 1949 (*Typographical Association and Jennings, The Printers*), the Court imposed an agreement between the British Federation of Master Printers and Newspaper Society and the Printing and Kindred Trades Federation on a contractor who, having been informed of the complaint, wrote to the Court of his refusal to be 'dictated to by any body whatsoever in the running of my business and I resent your interference'. And in Award 2651 of 24 May 1957 (*National Conciliation Board for the Mattress Making Industry and Chapman's of Trowbridge, Ltd.*), the Court applied the National Labour Agreement for the Bedding and Mattress Making Industry of Great Britain when the contractor failed to appear at the hearing. In the sixth case where the Court applied a collective agreement, the main question concerned the failure of a subcontractor to affix holiday stamps. The Court held that a collective agreement imposed an obligation on the main contractor which, together with clause 6 of the Resolution, was enough to make him liable (Award 2279 of 14 November 1950, *A.U.B.T.W. and Geo. Wright & Co. (Contractors, Wolverhampton) Ltd.*).

The six cases where the Industrial Court refused to apply any collective standards are good illustrations of the attitudes of employers, their organizations, trade unions and the Court itself. The first two awards of the Court under the 1946 Resolution concerned complaints that J. D. Robertson, a theatrical producer who had contracts with the War Office to entertain troops, was underpaying his chorus dancers. In Award 2140 of 3 March 1948, the union, the British Actors' Equity Association, claimed that he paid the dancers 10s. weekly 'below the established negotiated minimum rate' in contravention of clause 1(b) of the Resolution. A number of contracts negotiated were submitted in evidence. The contractor asserted that none of the contracts submitted had been negotiated with a representative employers' organization, so that the terms of such contracts did not constitute recognized terms within the meaning of clause 1(a) of the Resolution. Nor did they represent the general level of wages for the purposes of clause 1(b). Even if they did, he claimed that his terms were not less favourable. In its award, the Industrial Court simply held that there was no breach of the Resolution. In Award 2141, also of 3 March 1948, it was the employers' association, the Variety Artistes' Federation, which complained against this contractor. It was contended 'that the "Equity/V.A.F. Standard Contract for the Continent of Europe negotiated between the employers, the V.A.F. and the British Actors' Equity Association, was the appropriate form of contract to be entered into between Mr. J. D. Robertson and the chorus dancers he engaged'. It was asserted that Robertson paid below this 'established negotiated minimum rate'. Robertson simply reiterated his arguments set out above and again was upheld by the Court. As no reasons were offered by the Court in its award, it is impossible to say which of his arguments prevailed.

Another pair of cases (Awards 2353 and 2354 of 7 December 1951) concerned the question of whether contractors training pilots for military aircraft were covered by agreements negotiated for civil air transport. The complainant, the National Joint Council for Civil Air Transport, contended, 'that in the Aviation Industry the only fair "rate for the job" is that which is negotiated in the N.J.C. for Civil Air Transport . . . they apply nationally and they are obligatory upon the industry in all districts'. The contractors complained of (Marshall's Flying School, Ltd., Cambridge and Short Bros. & Harland Ltd., Kent) asserted that the military nature of their work took it outside the ambit of Agreements negotiated in the N.J.C. for Civil Air Transport. The Industrial Court upheld them, stating that they were not engaged in the trade or industry for which terms were negotiated by the N.J.C. and thus there was no breach of the Resolution in the fact that they were not observing those terms. One of the arguments put forward in the alternative by the contractors was, however, that the N.J.C. 'had not shown that they or any of their members are operating or that they had negotiated any rates of wages on behalf of any employers in the district or districts in which (the contractors) are operating'. In refusing to apply the N.J.C. Agreements, the Court did not address itself to this argument. But employers were obviously willing to avail themselves of the long-outmoded district basis of the Resolution in order to evade the impact of the new Fair Wages policy.

In Award 2370 of 7 April 1952, the National Union of Vehicle Builders claimed that the rates paid by the contractor were below those in the agreement negotiated by the National Joint Industrial Council for the relevant trade. It also submitted that the contractor was bound by a Procedure Agreement for Settling Differences Relating to Wages and Conditions of Employment being part of the general conditions of the N.J.I.C. agreement. The contractor, Drake Motors Ltd., claimed he was observing the agreement and paying the rates. He denied any obligation to discuss terms and conditions in accordance with the Procedure Agreement. In the award, the Court felt 'unable to say that (the contractors) are not complying with the requirements of the Fair Wages Resolution of the House of Commons'. Again, the failure to give reasons frustrates analysis.

Finally, in Award 2637 of 11 January 1957, the respondent, the St. Andrew's and Red Cross Scottish Ambulance Service, was a voluntary organization authorized by the Secretary of State to run an ambulance service either directly or by sub-contract. The pay and conditions of direct employees were negotiated by the Scottish Ambulance Service, Pay and Conditions of Service Committee. The National Union of Public Employees claimed that the terms negotiated for direct employees should apply to sub-contractors' employees working full-time on ambulance service. A sub-contractor who ran a garage claimed to observe rates for garage employees, not the higher ambulance service rates. The Industrial Court found that although the first claim on the employee's time was his ambulance duties, he was not exclusively employed on these duties. Consequently:

> The Court caused the Parties to obtain and furnish them with information as to the wages and conditions of service operated by other sub-contractors. This information indicated that varying rates of wages and other conditions of service were operative by other sub-contractors.
>
> On the evidence adduced the Court are unable to say that the A.P. & S. Engineering Co. did not comply with the requirements of Clause 1(a) and Clause 1(b) of the Fair Wages Resolution. (para. 6)

The Court here not only refused to accept the collectively agreed conditions negotiated for direct employees, it also rejected those paid to garage workers. Instead, it created an extremely artificial basis of comparison—that of the employees of other sub-contractors. Given this artificial basis of comparison, it is not surprising that little uniformity in rates could be ascertained. The Court's conclusion left the workers concerned where the Court found them—unprotected by the Fair Wages policy.

Apart from the six cases applying collective agreements, and the six others declining to do so, there were eight other awards under the Resolution during this period up to 1959. Three of these involved claims by individual workers, all of which were rejected by the Court. In Award 2605 of 3 April 1956 (*Mr. F. W. H. Luck and Decca Radar Ltd.*) the complainant, who had begun work in February 1950, stated that 'the reason why he had not lodged a claim earlier was because it was not until 1953 that he became aware of the significance of the Fair Wages Resolution' (para. 4). In Award 2616 of 18 July 1956 (*W. Kearns and George Wimpey & Co. Ltd.*), the complainant 'admitted to the Court that he could not establish a claim under either Clause 1(a) or 1(b) of the Fair Wages Resolution' (para. 4). And in Award 2694 of 2 June 1958 (*D. Broomhall and Parkinson Howard Ltd.*), the complainant failed to appear at all. Four other awards concerned liability for sub-contractors and one other, a question of breach of clause 4 of the Resolution concerning trade union rights. These will be subjects for more detailed discussion in later chapters.

In sum, the cases on the Fair Wages Resolution during 1946–59 fail to evince any great usage of the policy by trade unions or workers. The results of those complaints that were adjudicated upon by the Industrial Court may, to some extent, explain their lack of enthusiasm. The Court tended to impose collective agreements in cases where it was a question not of forcing a recalcitrant contractor to adhere to collective standards, but simply of deciding which of the alternative standards applied. In cases where attempts were made to bring such contractors into line, the complainant received little help or encouragement from the Court. But most important, the extreme rarity of utilization of the procedure designated by the Resolution is the factor which over-shadows any other generalization about the success or failure of the Fair Wages policy during these years. Thousands of contracts worth millions of pounds in wages generated fewer than twenty complaints of underpayment.

1959–1974

The Terms and Conditions of Employment Act 1959. With the replacement of Order 1376 of 1951 by section 8 of the Terms and Conditions of Employment Act 1959, many more cases with a Fair Wages policy element began appearing before the body charged with implementing section 8: the Industrial Court. But the years after 1959 nonetheless witnessed a considerable decline in numbers of cases on Fair Wages policy, when comparison is made with the numbers brought before the Industrial Disputes Tribunal under Order 1376. In a recent study of the 1959 Act in the *Industrial Law Journal*, Geoff Latta examined in detail the cases under the Act. He concluded that:

The economic effect of section 8 was very small. Not only were few workers directly involved—around 18,000 were the subject of claims and about 8,000 of those were involved in a successful decision, but where pay was directly involved the amounts of money were usually small. ... Section 8's effect was minimal and it did not even serve as an efficient means of bringing 'under-cutting' rogue employers into line.[10]

Table 5 above indicates that there was little change in the minimal numbers of Fair Wages policy cases under other jurisdictions of the Industrial Court.

Why were Fair Wages cases so few in number and the policy so minimal in impact? Without specifically addressing the question, Latta devotes most of his study to reasons why this might be so. Thus, he notes that certain areas (Wages Council industries and parts of the public sector) were simply excluded from coverage under the 1959 Act (p. 217). He analyses the interpretations of the Industrial Court in detail, and although he characterizes it as initially flexible and liberal, it later adopted a less favourable attitude to union claims (pp. 216, 224, 218). On the whole, the procedure under section 8 is described as 'slow, cumbersome and piecemeal' (p. 231). But it is only in the penultimate paragraph of his study that there is to be found an insight into why the 1959 Act was so under-utilized and thus insignificant. Latta there hints at the principal weaknesses of the Fair Wages policy which have been described in detail above. Focusing on the failures of a mechanism of enforcement by complaint, he points to the Wages Council Inspectorate as a possible remedy for this defect. He concedes, however:

> The experience of the latter however does not inspire confidence in the effectiveness of this type of approach. It is widely accepted that the present Inspectorate staff which comprises 142 people is inadequate for its task. ... If 142 people are ineffective in policing $3\frac{1}{2}$ million workers, the size of inspectorate to look after effectively over 20 million would probably by politically un-acceptable. (pp. 231–2)

Again, he notes that the standards of national agreements do not provide a satisfactory basis for determining fair wages: 'the weakness of most national agreements makes it arguable that for many terms and conditions the standards would be far too low' (p. 232). This point is, of course, the crux of this study of the 1946 Resolution. It is the current manifestation of a phenomenon traced back to 1891— the implementation of a policy on Fair Wages is subject to the overwhelming influence of the existing system of collective bargaining.

Thus, Latta devoted a major part of his study to 'the effect of section 8 on bargaining structure'. Yet his analysis is replete with indications that section 8's policy was completely dominated by this structure. He begins by saying:

> In its original conception section 8 was based heavily on the existing structure of industry-wide negotiations. To make a claim a union had to have some multi-employer agreement to quote, and in practice this usually meant a national agreement. As such the procedure proved a conservative force at a time when the trend was towards plant and company agreements. Its whole approach was to maintain industrial agreements, and the bargaining system on which they were based. (p. 226)

Many claims based on section 8 were precisely those 'where the court had to weigh up the advantages of a situation where both sides agreed the company were not observing one (or more) terms, but where other conditions exceeded the levels set by the national agreement' (p. 228). Rather than discovering that section 8 affected the bargaining structure, Latta eventually concluded that:

> The section 8 procedure was, and could only be, a mirror of the existing structure of collective bargaining. It could enforce parity of basic rates and conditions within one industry. It broke down in failing to relate company agreements to the industry-wide structure, where it clearly found it difficult to assess what was 'less favourable' than the national agreement. (p. 231)

The significance of this disparity between Fair Wages policy standards, embodied in national agreements, and local standards frequently superior to them due to local bargaining strength, cannot be overestimated. It is reflected in the numbers and types of cases which came before the Industrial Court. According to the calculations in Latta's study, only one in eight cases (twenty-two) during this period was concerned exclusively with the failure by an employer to observe minimum remuneration. In another thirty-one cases it was one of several issues in dispute. But in two out of every three cases which came before the Court, there was no question that the employer was observing the minimum (Fair Wages policy) remuneration. Most of the cases involved employers who were failing to observe some other term of the agreement: holiday pay, overtime rates or the length of the working week. In thirty-four cases the employer had failed to pass on a nationally negotiated increase. As Latta states:

The situations of complete failure to observe minimum rates were not very common and were as one might expect concentrated in white-collar employment were pay scales corresponded more closely to earnings than for manual workers. Elsewhere in those areas where the company was paying below minimum rates it was often when there was a dispute over which agreement should be followed. It must be emphasized that not all these cases involved firms in which workers were actually earning less than the rates. The importance of minimum rates to overtime pay, shift premia etc. was often the cause of the dispute. (p. 225)

For example, in Award 2754 of 2 December 1959, the National Society of Painters complained that Burns Shopfitters were not stamping the holiday cards of their employees, as provided in the Agreement for Holidays with Pay Scheme for the Building and Civil Engineering Contracting Industries: 'The Society argued that the fact that the Employers paid wages above the London Grade A rate for building craftsmen . . . did not absolve them from observing the other conditions of the Building Industry'. The Court upheld the complaint. In Award 2808 of 25 October 1960, the dispute was over a reduction in working hours negotiated nationally. On behalf of the Association of Engineering and Shipbuilding Draughtsmen 'it was pointed out that the National Agreements merely determined minimum conditions of employment and that quite a number of firms in membership of the National Federation employed draughtsmen on basic conditions superior to those offered by the Company'. Nevertheless, 'any bargain entered into by an employer and employees which, although on the one hand was designed to establish a condition better than that provided by a National Agreement, but on the other hand sought to establish other conditions of employment less favourable than the minimum terms of another National Agreement, was considered to be in violation of the terms of the latter Agreement'. The Court upheld the complaint against the Ford Motor Co. Award 3179 of 16 August 1968 concerned a claim that Cableform Ltd. was not observing the rates fixed in an Overtime Agreement. The union, D.A.T.A., submitted 'that the Company's claim that their overall conditions of employment were better than those generally afforded to draughtsmen in the Engineering Industry was irrelevant to the issue before the Court'. The complaint was again upheld.

During the period 1959–74 the failure rate for claims under the Act seems to have averaged roughly 50 per cent. The absence of the usual flow of claims during 1973–4 did not make the Industrial Arbitration Board's heart grow fonder: the last thirteen claims heard by the Board in 1975 and up to the end of January 1976 recorded a series of twelve defeats with only one successful claimant—in Award 3311 of April 14, 1975 (*National Union of the Footwear, Leather and Allied Trades and Michael Products Ltd.*) where the employer concerned did not attend the hearing. It is interesting to contrast the record of its successor, the Central Arbitration Committee: from February 1976 up to the end of 1976, of thirty claims under the 1959 Act twenty have been successful.

It is difficult to assess how much this high rate of failure of claims during 1959–74 reflects the disparity between the standards in national agreements and the higher rates often paid in practice. An award of the Industrial Court could turn on questions of whether the agreement sought to be enforced was the appropriate one for an employer in a particular industry, whether the organizations making the agreement were representative, or whether the agreement 'established terms and conditions' within the meaning of the Fair Wages formula contained in the 1959 Act. There were numerous cases, however, where the outmoded conception of collective bargaining embedded in the Fair Wages formula was clearly the reason for the failure of claims. In the third case brought under the 1959 Act (Award 2755 of 3 December 1959), the Industrial Court agreed with the claimant, the National Union of Vehicle Builders, that the National Agreement was applicable to the employer. It nonetheless held 'that the evidence before the Court is not such as to show that the rates which are being paid by Airflow Streamlines Ltd. are less favourable than those provided in the National Agreement and they Award that the claim has not been established' (para. 6). In Award 2829 of 10 March 1961, the Society of Lithographic Artists, Designers, Engravers and Process Workers succeeded in persuading the Court that the terms of a National Agreement between Engraving Unions and employers applied to an employer, Thames Board Mills Ltd., who claimed he was primarily a manufacturer of paperboard. But in the end the Court held that the actual wages paid were not less favourable than those in the Engraving Agreement. This was hardly surprising as the union itself had stated that the national rates were a minimum and that it was normal and expected for engravers to obtain a 'merit' level of wages which 'varied substantially, but currently ranged between £4 and £12 per week over the minimum'. The particular employer concerned had specifically stated that 'the gross earnings of the Society's members were well above the minimum rates in the Engraving Agreement' (para. 4). In Award 2854 of 6 July 1961, the Sign and Display Trades Union 'claimed that the Company should apply to the workers concerned, as a minimum, the terms and conditions of employment contained in the National Agreement: any bonus or extra payments should be paid after the agreed basic rate of pay had been applied'. The Company, Formica Ltd., 'submitted that the Union's claim had no basis because the Company were paying the workers concerned rates in excess of those provided in Clause 2(g)(ii) of the National Agreement'. And the Industrial Court found that the terms applicable were those in the National Agreement, but that the Company was not failing to observe them.[11]

Award 3181 of 7 November 1968 concerned a claim by the National Union of Hosiery and Knitwear Workers that Starwood Fabrics Ltd. was operating 168 hours a week in contravention of a national agreement which prohibited 7-day working. In its defence, the company even quoted the Donovan Commission's Report advocating the increased use of plant bargaining as opposed to industry-wide bargaining:

> The Royal Commission had also said, in paragraph 275 of their Report, that it would be necessary to insure that the use of Section 8 of the Terms and Conditions of Employment Act, 1959, did not 'hamper the development of company and plant bargaining', and that this could happen 'if an employer was compelled to comply with a particular term or condition laid down in an industry-wide agreement, although a company or plant agreement had varied that particular term or condition in return for other advantages granted to employees'. (para. 34)

The Industrial Court held that the National Agreement was applicable, that the company was not observing it, but that its terms were not less favourable and consequently, the complaint failed.

Finally, a classic illustration of the conflict of national and local standards is provided by Award 3193 of 28 July 1969. The Association of Patternmakers and Allied Craftsmen claimed that the company, Birmingham Refractories (Castings) Ltd., was not paying overtime rates as established in the 1968 National Agreement. In its submissions, the union conceded:

> that the terms and conditions on which the Association relied were in all cases minimum terms and conditions. Reference was made to the section of the 1968 Agreement dealing with minimum pay levels, the terms of which clearly indicated, in the Association's submission, that terms in excess of the minimum standards were current and recognized in the Engineering Industry. In fact the general level of wages had very little relationship with the established minimum rates. For example, it was common for semi-skilled operatives, especially those in mechanized foundries in the

Midlands, to have normal earnings in the region of £40 a week, whereas their minimum rate was between £13 and £14. Very few employers would be able under present conditions to employ workers strictly on the basis of minimum conditions. (para. 10)

The Company did not deny that they were not paying for overtime in accordance with the provisions of the Overtime Agreement, but:

In their submission it was clear from the wording of Section 8(1) of the Act that 'recognized terms or conditions' meant such terms and conditions of employment as had been settled, either generally or in any district by an agreement or award. It followed, therefore, that the recognized terms and conditions as respects the workers concerned were those settled by the agreements on which the Association relied. In the case of patternmakers the minimum time rate so provided was £15 13s. 4d. a week, to which was added a special supplement of 30s., making a total of £17 3s. 4d. It was that minimum time rate which represented recognized terms and conditions for the purposes of the Act, and the Association could not claim that the various wage rates shown in the Table which they had produced, (showing actual rates) which ranged from £15 to £34 a week, represented recognized terms and conditions.

The Company's contention that their terms and conditions were not less favourable than the recognized terms and conditions was illustrated by a comparison of the total earnings of a pattern-maker on the Company's contractual basis with what his earnings would be under the agreements on which the Association relied. For the purposes of the comparison it was assumed that the worker worked three hours evening overtime and four hours Saturday overtime, Sunday overtime being ignored because it was in fact very rarely worked. It was shown that the worker's earnings on the Company's contractual basis would amount to £29 15s. 3d., and on the basis of the relevant agreements to £21 6s. 10d., so that he would be better off to the extent of more than £8 on the former basis. (paras. 22–3)

The Industrial Court's Award was in the following terms:

(1) The terms and conditions on which the Association rely are recognized terms and conditions applicable to the workers concerned in the claim.

(2) The Company are not observing the recognized terms and conditions in that they are not paying the premium rates for overtime provided by the Overtime Agreement.

(3) The Court are satisfied, however, that the terms and conditions which the Company are observing are not less favourable than the recognized terms and conditions.

(4) The Court accordingly Award against the claim. (para. 27)

The embarrassing position in which the Industrial Court was placed by being urged to accept as Fair Wages standards minimum rates far below those actually paid led to conflicting and ambiguous results. This is particularly evident in cases concerning wage increases negotiated at the national level which still left the national rate below that prevailing locally in many cases. Trade unions attempted occasionally to force recalcitrant employers to add the nationally negotiated increase to the local rate. For example, Awards 2862 of 28 July 1961 and 2855 of 11 July 1961 (*Pianoforte Supplies Ltd. and A.E.U.*) concerned a new National Agreement providing for a negotiated increase, which stated in paragraph 2:

> The increase shall be paid as follows:—
> (a) In the case of timeworkers it shall be added to the consolidated rates.
> (b) In respect of workers on payment by results it shall be added to the existing supplements.
> (c) As regards workers in receipt of additional emoluments such as lieu rates, compensatory rates or other bonuses, their remuneration shall be increased according to their class by the above amounts, but not more, per week of 42 hours.

Nonetheless, the employer argued:

> that the basic rates that were being paid were so far in excess of the national minima which operated before (the new National Agreement), that even though under the Agreement the minimum was raised by the amounts therein provided, nevertheless the rates that were at present being paid exceeded the new national minimum consolidated time rates in the Agreement. It was submitted, therefore, that the Employer was not required to increase the pay of the workers concerned in order to observe the terms and conditions of that Agreement.

The union's argument was, it submitted, that:

> employees in the Industry as a whole were paid well in excess of what might be described as the national minimum rate and that there was no firm in the country in the Industry which paid all its members on the minimum basic rate: very few of the union's members were, in fact, employed at that rate. . . . It was customary

for all firms to give increases from time to time, e.g. bonuses, merit rates and the like, which were granted in addition to national agreements.

In both these cases, the Industrial Court upheld the union's claim in part. But in others, the Court rejected claims for increases which still left the national minimum rate below the employer's actual wages. For example, in Award 3116 of 5 September 1966, the employer stated 'that they were concerned more with the total earnings at the end of the week than with the constitution of piecework supplements or "additions". They reiterated that the additions they were paying to the piecework earnings (although not called piecework supplements) were in excess of those payable under the 1964 (National) Agreement.' The Court agreed that the 1964 Agreement contained the applicable terms and that the Company was not observing them. But it declared itself satisfied that the Company's terms were not less favourable and denied the claim. In a few cases this problem was anticipated by express provisions in agreements that domestic increases might be set off against national increases. But these contradictory decisions of the Industrial Court could not but confirm the questionable value of the 1959 Act in the eyes of the trade unions. The credibility of the Fair Wages policy suffered in this form as it had in its predecessors.[12]

The Fair Wages Resolution 1946. How did the conflict between national agreements and local standards, manifested in cases decided under the 1959 Act, affect the Fair Wages Resolution itself in its original function of regulating the wages paid by government contractors? A previous section of this chapter traced the gradual acceptance after 1946 by the Industrial Court of collective agreements as the basis of the new Fair Wages policy. By 1959, the cases decided by the Court on Fair Wages policy showed an increasing inclination to resort to collective agreements as the Fair Wages standard, although this generalization is limited by the scarcity of cases actually decided. The transfer to the Industrial Court from the Industrial Disputes Tribunal of the jurisdiction involving the extension of collective agreements under the 1959 Act made adherence to such agreements much more a matter of course, as the number of Fair Wages policy cases coming before it greatly increased. The major problem then became the conflict between the collective agreements cited as Fair Wages standards, containing the national minimum terms, and the employment standards actually prevailing at local level, the terms and conditions observed in practice. It is the cases under the Fair Wages Resolution of 1946 that provide the clearest indication that this conflict was a crucial factor in dissuading trade unions from seeking enforcement of the Fair Wages policy. For why should they bother if the standards sought to be enforced were so minimal as to make it virtually certain that the delinquent employer complained of could hardly help but exceed them?

The evidence is to be found in the abnormally large number of cases which suddenly arose under the Fair Wages Resolution in 1974. Up to then there were only faint hints in the Industrial Court as to the underlying defect of the Fair Wages policy. Very few cases arose on the policy as embodied in Fair Wages legislation. Thus, in the sixteen years 1959–74 only fourteen cases arose under the Road Haulage Wages Act 1938, of which two were withdrawn before decision. All these complaints were brought by individual workers and fewer than half succeeded. Only the last, Award 3305 of 10 December 1974 (*R. J. Seaman and M. J. Geraghty*), contains a reference to the fundamental problem: 'In response to a question by the (Industrial Arbitration Board), it was admitted that the weekly remuneration to which (the complainant) would have been entitled under the current road haulage wages regulation order was about £25 or a little more and that for the purposes of Part II of the Act his weekly remuneration of £50 for 50 hours could not be deemed to be unfair' (para. 5). The exceeding of the Fair Wages standard stipulated by the statute by the actual wages being paid rendered the claim futile.

Again, over this sixteen-year period only five cases arose under the Fair Wages policy governing the civil aviation industry. As it was put in Award 2725 of 30 April 1959 (*B.A.L.P.A. and Starways Ltd.*), in the Terms of Reference issued to the Air Transport Advisory Council by the Minister of Transport and Civil Aviation it was clearly indicated that 'one of the ways in which the Minister intended to stop unfair competition was in the field of wages and conditions of service. He introduced what was, in effect, a fair wages clause' (paras. 2–3). Of the few cases which attempted to implement the policy, the unions won two, lost two and had one referred to conciliation.

The year 1968 witnessed the first case under the Road Traffic legislation after a lapse of fourteen years without a complaint being made to the Court. Up to 1974 another five cases were heard, though one of these, Award 3287 of 5 February 1974 (*T.G.W.U. and Passenger Transport Executives of Glasgow, Tyneside and Merseyside*), resulted from the union being barred under the Industrial Relations Act 1971 from bringing a claim under the 1959 Act. These cases were brought under section 152(1) of the Road Traffic Act 1960, as amended, which referred to the Resolution of the House of Commons for the time being in force applicable to contracts with government departments—that is, the 1946 Resolution. The pattern of success for the unions in these cases was very uneven. A few of them stipulated national agreements in the omnibus industry as the standards to be enforced, with indifferent results: in Award 3163 of 2 April 1968 (*T.G.W.U. and T. D. Alexander, Greyhound Luxury Coaches, Arbroath*) the union won, while in Awards 3223 and 3224 of 6 August 1970 (*G.M.W.U. and G. R. A. Anderson, A. E. and J. A. Wilson—Economic Bus Co., Co. Durham*) the union lost.

The evidence of the critical factor in the failure of the new Fair Wages policy—the gap between national and local standards due to the incongruence between the collective bargaining structure envisaged by the 1946 Resolution and that which in fact developed—is to be found in the cases decided by the Industrial Court and later the Industrial Arbitration Board on the Resolution of 1946, most particularly, those of the year 1974. But before reviewing these cases in detail, a brief statistical summary is in order. During the period 1959–74, thirty-six cases came before the Industrial Court (or Board) based on the Resolution of 1946, two-thirds of these during the last five years, 1970–4 (twenty-four cases), and ten in the year 1974 itself. Of the first eleven years, 1959–69, there were five when none at all came before the Court (1959, 1963, 1966, 1967 and 1969), and three others with only one instance (1962, 1965 and 1968). In the first six-year period, 1959–64, there were ten cases; in the next five years, 1965–9, there were only two, in contrast to twenty-four in the final five year period, 1970–4. (See Table 5 on p. 249 for details.) It is difficult to discern any pattern in this uneven flow of cases.

Of the twelve cases brought to the Court in the first eleven years, 1959–69, nine were unsuccessful, one was withdrawn before decision and in another two the Court decided in favour of the complainant on one issue and against him on the other. Of the twenty-four cases in the last five years, 1970–4, nine were unsuccessful, thirteen succeeded and another two were split. Of the thirteen successful complaints, however, nine arose out of and were directly and vitally concerned with the circumstances of the wage freeze imposed by the Conservative government in 1973. Of the thirteen successes, therefore, only four were bona fide consequences of the Fair Wages policy affecting government contracts. In sum: of the thirty-six cases during the period 1946–74, eighteen failed outright to redress complaints, another four were split decisions and one was withdrawn, nine were successful in the peculiar circumstances of the wage freeze, and only four of the thirty-six cases can be counted as bona fide successful claims where workers benefited from the Fair Wages policy. Table 8 illustrates these figures, with Award numbers given in the appropriate columns.

TABLE 8

Year	Lost	Won	Split	Withdrawn	Wage Freeze
1959	—	—	—	—	—
1960	2793	—	—	2815	—
	2812				
	2816				
1961	2821	—	—	—	—
	2856				
	2887				
1962	2937	—	—	—	—
1963	—	—	—	—	—
1964	3009	—	3039	—	—
1965	—	—	3071	—	—
1966	—	—	—	—	—
1967	—	—	—	—	—
1968	3161	—	—	—	—
1969	—	—	—	—	—
1970	3216	3206	3212	—	—
	3217	3219			
	3218				
1971	—	3242	—	—	—
		3243			
1972	3267	—	—	—	—
	3275				
1973	3285	—	—	—	3281
					3282
					3283
1974	3286	—	3300	—	3290
	3288				3291
	3302				3292
					3293
					3294
					3296

SOURCE: Published Awards of the Industrial Court and the Industrial Arbitration Board

The three unsuccessful complaints of 1960 effectively illustrate the fundamental weakness of the Fair Wages policy described above. Award 2793 of 28 July 1960 is a classic example of a claim affected by wage drift. The union, A.S.S.E.T., claimed that rates being paid to aircraft staff inspectors were below those paid elsewhere: 'There was no nationally negotiated agreement for wages in the Aircraft

Industry as a whole but agreements had been made individually with Companies'. To the contrary, the English Electric Co. Ltd. of Preston, Lancs., claimed membership in the Engineering and Allied Employers' National Federation and asserted: 'A condition of Federation membership was that every firm observed the minimum rates and conditions laid down by Industrial Agreement or Recommendation'. The company referred to a National Agreement of 1942 which laid down the earnings of workers, including inspectors, and argued that these 'minimum wage conditions of the 1942 Agreement were still applicable to all skilled inspectors'. The employers were outraged by the challenge to their view of the Resolution as a minimum wage policy: 'The use of the procedure contained in that Resolution for progressing what was, in effect, a claim against a Federated employer for increased salaries, was a matter on which both the Federation and the Company held the strongest views. . . . Membership of the Federation was . . . in itself prima facie evidence that the terms of the Fair Wages Resolution were being met'. The Industrial Court rejected the complaint.

Another classic illustration is Award 2812 of 7 November 1960, which concerned a contract between Norwich Corporation and the Wroxham Dairies to supply milk to schools. Paragraph 23(a) of the municipal contract contained Clause 1(a) and (b) of the Fair Wages Resolution of 1946. When the contract was first entered into the Corporation informed the Company that since in their view the equivalent of Clause 1(a) of the Resolution did not apply, the rates payable to workers on the contract fell to be determined under Clause 1(b). They then specified various rates of wages and these were paid by the contractor. During 1960 the Corporation informed the Company that due to a general rise in wages in the trade, new rates were payable which were specified. In reply, the Company stated that it no longer accepted the view that there were no rates of wages meeting the requirements of the clause of their contract equivalent to Clause 1(a), but rather 'contended that observance of the minimum rates prescribed in the (Wages Regulation (Milk Distributive) (England and Wales)) Order, 1960, was adequate compliance with that part of the Clause' (para. 2). In complaining to the Industrial Court, the Corporation argued that the requirements of Clause 1(a) were not fulfilled by the Order 'and particularly that the proceedings of the Wages Council could not properly be regarded as negotiation or arbitration as visualised in the Clause' (para. 3). Arguing that there was no other wage negotiating organization for the Milk Distributive Industry, the Company described at length the proceedings of the Wages Council. In conclusion:

It was stated that the National Dairymen's Association (Incorporated), of which the Contractors were members and who were supporting them in the present reference, understood that at no time had any Government Department or Local Authority operating the House of Commons' Fair Wages Resolution claimed that compliance with a Wages Council Order was not compliance with that Resolution. (para. 4)

The Industrial Court held that the Company was complying with the provisions of its contract.

In the final case of 1960, Award 2816 of 20 December, the Amalgamated Society of Woodworkers claimed that W. & J. Tod, Ltd. was not observing wages and hours laid down in the National Shipbuilding and Engineering Agreement for employees engaged on Admiralty contracts. The Company argued, *inter alia*, that it was 'complying with the Fair Wages Resolution in that the total weekly earnings of their workers . . . amounted to more than they would receive if the pay and conditions of the National Agreement were strictly observed'. They admitted that they were not complying with the Resolution in precisely the way the union wished, but contended that, taken as a whole, their terms were more favourable than those of the National Agreements. The Court rejected the union's complaint.

The precedents established by these cases would have discouraged any hopes of utilizing the Fair Wages Resolution as a tool for the protection of prevailing wages standards. The nationally negotiated minimum rates accepted by the Industrial Court as satisfying the Resolution's requirements made it pointless for unions or workers to attempt to achieve more than these long-surpassed standards. The cases since 1960, other than those on non-wage aspects of the 1946 Resolution which will be analysed later, are a *mélange* of misfits—odd cases thrown up by peculiar circumstances. There is no evidence to suggest a regular or consistent supervision over whether government contractors maintained fair wages.

Of the three cases in 1961, Award 2821 of 13 February concerned the only instance discovered where a union sought to oppose an application by an emloyer to be included in the list of firms eligible to tender for government contracts. A.S.S.E.T. charged Walter MacFarlane & Co. Ltd. of Glasgow with breach of clause 4 of the Resolution—infringement of the freedom to belong to a trade union. Award 2856 of 12 July 1961 (*Autax Ltd., Manchester and Radio Cabs* (*Man.*)) was another unique case of one employer complaining that a competitor for government contracts was not observing the Resolution.

In Award 2887 of 29 December 1961 (*Association of Scientific Workers and Birmetals Ltd. of Birmingham*), a claim on behalf of seven women workers, the union scraped the bottom of the barrel: 'On the general question of equal pay it was mentioned that all the countries of the Common Market were pledged by the Treaty of Rome to concede, between 1962 and 1964, equal pay for equal work done, and it was stated that unskilled women in the Engineering Industry in the Paris region now received 94.5 per cent of the unskilled men's rate' (para. 4). The claim put by the union was for only 75–81 per cent of the men's rate. All three complaints of 1961 were unsuccessful.

Award 2937 of 5 November 1962 (*G. C. Harrison and Holophone Ltd.*) was an unsuccessful complaint by an individual worker. Opposing the claim, the employer submitted that as engineering labour was normally paid hourly, while the complainant was paid weekly, no national agreement existed which applied to workers on weekly rates (para. 11). The complaints of breach of clause 4 of the Resolution in Awards 3009 of 8 April 1964 (*National Association of Toolmakers and Pressed Steel Co. Ltd., Cowley, Oxford*) and 3039 of 28 August 1964 (*A.S.S.E.T. and M. Wiseman & Co. Ltd.*) were both dismissed. The employer in the latter case, however, was held not to have complied with clause 5 of the Resolution requiring the display of the Resolution at his works. In Award 3071 of 3 June 1965, the National Union of Dyers, Bleachers and Textile Workers satisfied the Court that the Company, William Denby & Sons Ltd., Yorkshire, was in breach of clause 1(a) of the Resolution, but failed in its complaint on clause 4.

Award 3161 of 30 January 1968 (*N.U.P.E. and Industrial Contract Cleaners*) involved another local authority contract including the following startling formulation: the contractors undertook to observe the Council's 'General Conditions of Tender and Contract', which included the 1946 Resolution, 'so far as the same were not inconsistent with the Contractor's Tender referred to in the said contract'. This was the first in a series of ten cases in the period 1968–72 which concerned the problems facing the employees of contract cleaning firms (Awards 3161, 3206, 3212, 3216–19, 3242, 3243 and 3275). These will be discussed in detail in chapter 19. Award 3267 of 26 July 1972 (*A.U.E.W. and Multiplex Designs Ltd.*) arose from a complaint that a company engaged in producing technical publications for the Ministry of Defence was paying sub-standard wages and also interfering with the freedom of its employees to belong to a trade union. In denying these allegations the Company advanced the following statement, which is quoted in full because of the light it sheds on some employers' and departmental attitudes towards enforcement of the Fair Wages policy:

Bearing in mind that, since the dispute had first arisen between the Parties, the Company had improved their provisions as to wages and holidays it was their contention that the wording of the Terms of Reference was such as to preclude consideration of evidence as to matters of the past which had been overtaken by more recent events. It might be argued, though the Company did not concede it, that when the dispute first arose the Company could have been regarded in some respects as having failed to observe the requirements of the Resolution; but if they had subsequently mended their ways it was reasonable that the Board should find at the date of the hearing the Company were complying with the Resolution. Furthermore, as the result of the findings of the Board the Government would take certain decisions as to future allocation of contracts and it would therefore be unfair to take account of events prior to the 25th May, 1972, on which date reference was made to the Board. (para. 22)

The Industrial Arbitration Board rejected the complaint.

Four other awards during 1973–4 were unexceptional in terms of the theme being pursued in this study. In Award 3285 of 17 December 1973 (*A.U.E.W. and Hiatt & Co. Ltd.*) the union failed to establish a breach of either clause 1(a) or (b); and in Award 3286 of 2 January 1974 (*S. B. Etweria and Fidelity Instrument Co. Ltd.*) a complaint by an individual worker was rejected, the Board holding he was being remunerated reasonably. In Award 3288 of 19 March 1974, the Board ignored pleas by the Association of Professional, Executive, Clerical and Computer Staff to distinguish the minimum rate negotiated generally from the minimum rate actually paid by the employer, G.E.C. Turbine Generators Ltd. Despite the union's statement that the Company's low rates gave it an unfair advantage over its main U.K. competitors when tendering for government contracts, the Board held that there was no breach of clause 1(a) or (b) of the Resolution (para. 11). Finally, in Award 3302 of 16 October 1974 (*Wickman Wimet Ltd. and A.S.T.M.S.*), the Board refused to extend the benefit conferred by a previous award on employees in a factory used for government contract purposes, to employees in another factory of the same employer who were employed on commercial work. The contrast between this award and the previous one was startling; it arose out of the peculiar circumstances engendered by the Conservative Government's pay policy of 1972–4. The Industrial Arbitration Board's role in these circumstances led to the most promising development to date in the history of the Fair Wages policy.

The Revival of the Fair Wages Policy: 1973–1974

The year 1973 saw the first cases which were to force the Industrial Arbitration Board to confront directly the contradiction described above as fundamentally undermining the Fair Wages policy. The discrepancy between national agreements and local standards was suddenly thrust into prominence as a result of developments in the implementation of the incomes policy of the Conservative Government of 1970–4. The Counter-Inflation (Temporary Provisions) Act 1972 caused wages paid by contractors to be 'frozen' in November 1972. Subsequently, the Counter-Inflation Act 1973 established the Pay Board, provided for the preparation by the Treasury of a Price and Pay Code, charged the Pay Board with the duty of ensuring that the provisions of the Code relating to pay were implemented and for that purpose empowered the Pay Board to restrict pay increases by an order (sections 1, 2 and 7). By section 17, the contravention of any such order was made an offence punishable by a fine. The Price and Pay Code was brought into effect by the Counter-Inflation (Price and Pay Code) Order 1973 (S.I. 1973, No. 658) on 1 April 1973, The freeze on wages was lifted and increases were allowed up to a maximum of £1 plus 4 per cent (paragraph 109). Certain exceptions to this limit were provided for, however, and thus paragraph 134 stated:

> The cost of increases to meet the purposes of section 8 of the Terms and Conditions of Employment Act, 1959, the Road Haulage Wages Act, 1938 and similar legislation, and the Fair Wages Resolution of 1946 will not count against the pay limit.[13]

The position was, therefore, that contractors could not raise wages (whether voluntarily or under pressure from unions) save by invoking the Fair Wages policy and the exception contained in paragraph 134 of the Code. Some contractors did raise wages using that authority and these were challenged as being in breach of the incomes policy. The resulting disputes came before the Industrial Arbitration Board for disposal. The question was still whether the company was in breach of the Fair Wages policy, but the complaint was argued in an unprecedented way. As it was put in Award 3281 of 29 October 1973 (*Desborough Engineering Co. and Mrs. I. Farral*), the first case of this nature to come before the I.A.B.: 'The Company considered that they were putting a case not only for themselves but also on behalf of their employees: they believed that the present was the first occasion on which a company had themselves questioned whether they were complying with the Resolution' (para. 5). The process of arrival at this point is described in detail in the case. The Company submitted that it had encountered difficulties in recruiting workers and had actually begun losing some of their employees. This was the result of sudden boom conditions in the town which had led to rising wages. As government contractors, they wrote to the Ministry of Defence for advice. The Ministry replied that they had 'no authority to over-rule the Government legislation or the Price and Pay Code of the 6th November 1972. They accordingly suggested that the Company should apply to the Pay Board for approval of the proposed wage increases' (para. 13). The Company wrote to the Pay Board and the result of the correspondence was that the Pay Board stated that the Company could submit an appeal to the Industrial Arbitration Board through the Department of Employment. The Pay Board would approve increases outside the pay limit only on the basis of an Award of the I.A.B. (paras. 14–15). Thus, the 'complaint' arrived before the Industrial Arbitration Board.

Two other such cases (Awards 3282, *Wickman Wimet and A.S.T.M.S.*, and 3283, *Wickman Wimet and The Workers*) arrived almost simultaneously with this first one and were decided on the following day, 30 October 1973. In all three, the I.A.B. upheld the wage increase. That is to say, they found that the Company had been in breach of the Fair Wages Resolution and the pay increases were needed to bring the workers concerned up to the fair standards. In each case, the basis of the I.A.B.'s decision perfectly illustrates the underlying contradiction of Fair Wages policy described above. In Award 3281, the first of the three:

> On the question whether rates of wages and hours and conditions of labour could be said to be 'established' in the district as provided by Clause 1(a) of the Resolution, the Company said that they knew of no employers who were observing the rates and conditions laid down by the National Engineering Agreement or who would dream of trying to engage people on that basis. . . . The Company acted on the basis that Clause 1(b) was the relevant provision of the Resolution. *The Board accepted that in all the circumstances this was right.* (para. 7) (My italics.)

Similarly, in Award 3283, the Company submitted that there were no local or domestic agreements in existence, and as to the National Engineering Agreement:

> its provisions were not now being observed either in the district or, it was thought, anywhere in the country. In the circumstances it could not be said that rates of wages or hours or conditions of labour were established in the district by machinery or negotiation or arbitration within the meaning of Clause 1(a) of the

Resolution. The Company, therefore, submitted that the question under reference had to be decided under Clause 1(b) of the Resolution. *The Board accepted this submission.* (para. 26) (My italics.)

In Award 3282 it was generally agreed by the Company, the Union and the I.A.B. that no national or district agreement covered the workers concerned.

What is astonishing about these cases is that the Industrial Arbitration Board appears to have accepted the inapplicability of national agreements establishing minimum wages and conditions as a matter of course. Equally amazing is that the Board should suddenly reverse the pattern of denying complaints which had been so firmly established over previous years. With the exception of four cases involved with the contract cleaning trade in 1970–1, complainants had lost all or part of every case brought since 1959. Suddenly, the Board found in quick succession a series of cases (three in 1973 and another six in 1974—all connected with the incomes policy) where the companies concerned were in breach of their obligations under the Fair Wages Resolution, and required them (albeit the companies themselves requested this) to grant wage increases.

The anomaly is highlighted by the contrast with the four other 'ordinary' cases during 1973–4 discussed in the previous section. Without exception all four complaints were rejected. Yet Award 3302 of 16 October 1974, where the complaint was rejected, involved the same company as Awards 3282 and 3283 of 30 October 1973, where the complaint had been upheld. The Wickman Wimet Co. Ltd. had premises at Featherstone, Wolverhampton, which were owned by the Ministry of Defence. One part of the premises was leased by the Company from the Ministry and run commercially by the Company (the commercial premises); another part was managed by the Company on behalf of the Ministry (the agency premises). Awards 3282 and 3283 were concerned with the agency premises. The Board held the company to be in breach of the Resolution and prescribed a wage increase. In Award 3302 the Association of Scientific, Technical and Managerial Staffs wanted the agency premises' terms applied to the commercial premises. A.S.T.M.S. claimed that the Resolution applied to the commercial premises as well: the agency and commercial premises were one factory, and so fell within clause 2 of the Fair Wages Resolution which reads: 'The contractor shall in respect of all persons employed by him (whether in execution of the contract or otherwise) in every factory, workshop or place occupied or used by him for the execution of the contract comply with the general conditions required by this Resolution':

The Association submitted that it was clear, if the history of the Fair Wages Resolutions of the House of Commons was examined, that the intention was to prevent a situation arising where a Government contractor, whilst paying a fair wage to those of his workpeople specifically engaged on Government contracts, paid substantially lower wages to other employees, not so engaged. To allow such a situation to arise was quite unreasonable, bearing in mind that (as the Association interpreted the Resolution) any employer invited to tender for Government contracts was required to give an assurance that he had observed the general conditions of the Resolution in respect of all his employees. In the Association's view, that requirement applied regardless of where any particular employee worked or on what work he was engaged. (para. 10)

In its Award, the Board simply denied that the workers concerned were employed in a factory used by the Company for the execution of the contract. Thus, no breach of the Resolution had been established. The flexibility which allowed for wage increases in Awards 3282 and 3283 was replaced by a rigid interpretation of 'factory' sufficient to deny the claim here.

But a principal theme of this study requires going beyond noting the simple, if significant, revival of the Fair Wages policy heralded by the success of the pay policy cases. It is necessary to ascertain the rationale of the Industrial Arbitration Board for the change in its application of the Fair Wages Resolution. By 1974 the challenge to the pay policy engendered by the Board's decisions in Awards 3281–3 was clear to the main instrument of the government—the Pay Board. The confrontation took place in Award 3290 of 24 April 1974 (*Crittall-Hope Ltd. and Pay Board*). The Company, sub-contractors to the Department of the Environment, asserted that the restrictions on pay increases led to their having fallen behind their competitors for labour and as a result they were losing workers and were unable to replace them (para. 6). Their attempt to increase wages, purporting to comply with the Fair Wages Resolution under the exemption granted by paragraph 134 of the Pay Code Order, had been prevented by the Pay Board's issuing a prohibition order (para. 7). The dispute was then referred to the Industrial Arbitration Board in accordance with previous practice (para. 8). In a cautious challenge at the outset of the hearing, the Pay Board stated, in contrast to the view which they had taken earlier, that although they would treat with respect any decision made by the I.A.B., the ultimate decision lay with them. The I.A.B. declined to accept that proposition and the hearing proceeded (para. 4).

The Company's argument is a concise affirmation of the fundamental weakness of the Fair Wages policy as described above in this
chapter:

The Company stated that it was necessary to consider whether
the case fell to be considered under Clause 1(a) or Clause 1(b)
of the Resolution. In their view Clause 1(a) could not apply in
the present case, because there was no agreement which conformed
to the criteria laid down in the Clause. The Pay Board, on the
other hand, clearly took the view that the Agreement between the
Engineering Employers' Federation and the Confederation of
Shipbuilding and Engineering Unions dated the 18th August
1972 (hereinafter referred to as 'the National Agreement')
applied. . . .
   The National Agreement referred to national minimum rates
of wages, holidays and related matters. It could not have anything
to do with the present questions because it did not establish rates
of wages and was not concerned with the general level of wages;
and even if it had done so at some time in the past, it was now
out of date for that purpose. It was a matter of common sense
when ascertaining what were fair wages to look first for an agreement which effectively determined what the workers were actually
paid in the district; and if such an agreement had been made
between representative bodies there was no need to look further—
the agreement would determine the rates of wages for the district.
If however no company in the district paid any attention to an
agreement it could not be said that it had established what were
regarded as fair wages in the district. An agreement could only
be treated as conclusive evidence of what was fair if it actually
represented what was going on, that is if it was being honoured,
observed or given effect to. In point of fact the National Agreement did not influence wage rates at all, because it established
minimum rates of wages only and the rates actually being paid
were well above the minimum. If, as the Pay Board appeared to
argue, it was right to treat a minimum wages agreement as
establishing the standard for the district, then it was implicit in
that argument that the fair employer need only pay the minimum
wage—a wage that in practice no one else was paying. A situation
like that would not make sense. . . .
   The National Agreement in certain circumstances could come
within the scope of Clause 1(a), as for example in a question
concerning minimum wages, holidays or the standard working
week. The present reference however was concerned with actual

wages. In those circumstances the National Agreement could not be regarded as having 'established' rates of wages for the district. The Company accordingly submitted that the case did not fall to be considered under Clause 1(a) but under Clause 1(b). (paras. 10–12)

The rest of the Company's submissions presented evidence as to how the 'general level of wages' stipulated by Clause 1(b) justified the wage increases.

The Pay Board opened its submissions with the novel assertion that:

> Although (the Resolution) was not an Act of Parliament the Pay Board suggested that it should be construed in the same way as an Act; and hence it was necessary to see what the legislature intended without inferring from the words something that might not have been considered by Parliament. That was particularly important because the situation in 1946, when the Resolution was passed, was that there was generally little difference between the rates laid down in an agreement and the actual rates paid, whereas by 1974 actual wages had leapt ahead because of the growth of plant bargaining. (para. 23)

As a guide to the intention of Parliament expressed in the Resolution of 1946, the Pay Board summarized the history of the Resolutions from 1891 to 1946 as follows: the 1891 Resolution accepted 'that any rate of wages agreed with a trade union was not regarded as unfair to workmen although it might well be unreasonable to ask an employer to pay so high a rate' (para. 24); the 1909 Resolution accepted 'without actually stating as much, that the minimum standard rate of wages recognized by a trade union was a fair wage' (para. 25); the 1946 Resolution imposed a new standard: 'in effect, it stated that a contractor had to abide by trade union agreements. It did not, however, state that contractors had to pay rates equal to the best' (para. 26).

Even as a capsule summary of the Fair Wages Resolutions of 1891 and 1909, the above quotations are a travesty. They imply attitudes of benevolence towards trade union standards, 'without actually stating as much', and 'unreasonable' though these standards might be, which are completely untrue of administration of the Resolutions by the departmental bureaucracies. There is even a blatant contradiction in the Pay Board's assertion that the 1909 Resolution's 'minimum standard rate of wages' was changed in 1946 and its subsequent statement that the 1946 Resolution 'quite clearly could not have been intended to deal with agreements other than those providing for minimum wages'. This latter statement is taken from the heart of the Pay Board's case, which was contained in paras. 27–9:

> The Pay Board contended that the Resolution, by expressly providing that rates fixed by negotiations were to be regarded as the standard, recognized that there had been, by 1946, a large development in collective bargaining which would ensure that workers were paid proper wages. They argued that it would be totally wrong, simply because circumstances had again changed, to put a construction on the words of the Resolution which would meet the current situation or to infer from them intentions which the House of Commons might not have considered. . . .
>
> An employer who was in the situation that he was obliged to comply with Clause 1(a) might well be paying rates of wages less favourable than if he were obliged to comply with Clause 1(b); that situation would arise because of the effect of plant bargaining, which did not really exist when the Resolution was passed in 1946. . . . It was submitted that, by and large, it was not the practice to have collective agreements which fixed actual wages: most national agreements fixed only minimum wages. Furthermore, it could not have been foreseen in 1946 that plant bargaining would become so widespread, and therefore the Resolution quite clearly could not have been intended to deal with agreements other than those providing for minimum wages.
>
> The Pay Board quoted a number of authorities in support of their submissions . . . that since 1946 it was no longer relevant whether a collective agreement was commonly recognized; and that it was the agreement as such that was the criterion and not whether it was observed.

There is here a remarkable reversal of departmental attitudes. The last sentence of this quotation is the complete negation of the oft-stated position of the contracting departments on Fair Wages policy. A constant theme of the departments' opposition to the T.U.C.'s proposals prior to 1946 was their determination not to accept national agreements which were not being effectively implemented due to the appalling economic circumstances of the 1930s. Yet here the Pay Board calmly asserted the converse: 'that it was the agreement as such that was the criterion and not whether it was observed'. For the remainder of their submissions, in case their view as to the applicability of Clause 1(a) was not accepted, the Pay Board went on to contradict the evidence of the Company as to the 'general level of wages' under Clause 1(b).

The Industrial Arbitration Board began its Award with the declaration that it had chosen this time to give if not reasons, then 'the views as to these matters by which they have been guided in reaching their decision in the present case' (para. 42). For the first time it gave a general statement of perspective on the Fair Wages Resolution of 1946:

> The general purpose of the Resolution, as of its predecessors, was to ensure that workers employed by the contractors concerned should have wages and hours and conditions of labour which are fair. It appears to have been thought, with some justification when the Resolution was passed, that terms and conditions established as the result of agreements or awards arrived at between representative organizations of employers and workers would be likely to be more favourable to the workers than would the general level of wages, hours and conditions observed by employers whose general circumstances in the trade or industry were similar to those of the contractor concerned; but in the event of that assumption turning out to be wrong at any given time *the general purpose of the Resolution would appear to be frustrated if the effect of Clause 1(a) were to confine the workers concerned to wages, hours or conditions which are less favourable to them than the general level referred to in Clause 1(b).* Clause 1(a) should not, therefore, be construed so as to give it that effect unless the wording of the Clause makes that construction unavoidable. (para. 43) (My italics.)

The I.A.B. then went on to discuss the Pay Board's contention 'that wage rates are "established" in a district by the mere fact of their being provided for in the national agreement in question'. It denied that proposition, and turning to the 1909 Resolution, Orders 1305 and 1376 and the 1959 Act for clues, it concluded 'that a term or condition of service is properly to be regarded as "established" in a district if in that district it is generally recognized there as the standard by which the adequacy of terms or conditions observed by employers in the district has to be judged' (para. 44(2)). The generality of this formula is not much advance over previous vague Fair Wages formulations. However, more concretely, the Pay Board's argument as to the meaning of 'established' was met by the I.A.B.'s accepting that the rates contained in a national agreement:

> may be 'established' in a district, in the sense indicated in paragraph 44(2) above, but established only as minimum rates and not as setting any standard of what an employer will be

expected actually to pay to his workers. When that sort of position occurs, Clause 1(a) of the Resolution will in the Board's view be applicable only in relation to minimum rates and any other matters covered by the agreement. In relation to other aspects of the workers' employment, including the rates of pay which the employer will be expected actually to pay to his workers, Clause 1(a) will not be applicable and the question whether in relation to such matters the employer is complying with the Resolution will have to be decided under Clause 1(b). (para. 45)

In the end, the I.A.B. held that the Company were in breach of Clause 1(b) and stipulated wage increases which would enable the Company to comply with the Resolution. These increases were in fact below those requested by the Company. Interestingly enough, the Company had proposed increases of £3.00 per week for both their male and their female production workers (para. 20). But in its Award, in the fourth year after the passage of the Equal Pay Act 1970, the Industrial Arbitration Board granted increases of £3.00 per week to male production workers, but only £2.50 per week to female production workers (para. 49).

This Award signifies the formal recognition of the inadequacies of the Fair Wages policy since 1946. The policy is regarded as having become irrelevant to the needs of workers following the development of plant bargaining which has led to wages actually paid exceeding the standards of national agreements. For the first time, the Industrial Arbitration Board took a vital and significant step in adapting the policy of the Fair Wages Resolution to the industrial relations system. The Fair Wages standard of Clause 1(a) having effectively become a minimum wage standard has been recognized as such and replaced by one which will fulfil the perceived purposes of the policy. A sequence of five Awards handed down by the I.A.B. following *Crittall-Hope* sustained the position adopted there.[14]

Neither employers nor the government, however, appear to have taken to heart the I.A.B.'s direction as to the general purpose of the Fair Wages Resolution quoted in para. 43 of Crittall-Hope—'to ensure that workers employed by the contractors concerned should have wages and hours and conditions of labour which are fair'. Thus, in Award 3291 of 25 April 1974, the company justified its claim by contending 'that the Resolution was intended in part to protect the interests of a contracting Government Department when there was a labour movement of the kind the Company had experienced, and in part to protect the contractors' employees' (para. 7). In Award 3292 of 1 May 1974, it was opined that 'the intention of the Fair Wages

Resolution was to enable any company undertaking a Government contract to obtain workers in the district in order to complete the contract, and for that reason the rates of wages could not be limited to the minimum rate laid down in the National Agreement' (para. 11). And in Award 3296 of 20 May 1974, the Pay Board attempted to evade the policy of Fair Wages by contending 'that the contract referred to in the Terms of Reference was a contract for the supply of standard products produced by the Company, and that for that reason it was not one in respect of which a contractor was required to observe the requirements of the Resolution' (para. 5). The Industrial Arbitration Board did not share this view, and has persisted in its new position on the Fair Wages policy. It remains to be seen whether this was an aberration developed under the pressure of circumstances of an incomes policy, to disappear when it had passed, or if it signifies the beginning of a revival of the Fair Wages policy.

Will the Courts Obstruct the Revival of the Fair Wages Policy ?

The revival of the Fair Wages policy by the Industrial Arbitration Board may be hampered by the decision of the Chancery Division of the High Court in the case of *Racal Communications Ltd.* v. *Pay Board* [1974] I.C.R. 590, handed down on 9 May 1974. The Pay Board challenged the I.A.B.'s new position by applying to the High Court for declarations that: (a) adherence to a 1972 national agreement in the engineering industry was compliance with the 1946 Resolution; and (b) in such or similar circumstances, resort to Clause 1(b) of the Resolution was unnecessary. The Pay Board's action was a counterclaim to the request by Racal Communications Ltd. for declarations that: (a) Clause 1(a) of the Resolution referred to district machinery of collective bargaining, not national machinery; (b) where district rates were not established by such machinery, Clause 1(b) applied; and (c) compliance with national minimum rates was a breach of the Resolution where the general level of wages was higher than these minima. The case was argued less than a week after the I.A.B. made its Award in *Crittall-Hope*, and the Award was referred to in the judgment. The decision itself was handed down two weeks after the *Crittall-Hope* Award, by which time the I.A.B. had maintained its view in four other Awards: 3291–4. Nevertheless, Griffiths J. announced, 'naturally with great regret that I feel unable to follow the decision of the Industrial Arbitration Board, conscious as I am of the wealth of legal and industrial expertise which their decisions represent' (p. 602 B). He granted the declarations requested by the Pay Board, thus in effect accepting the submissions rejected five times in succession by the I.A.B.

The basis of the judge's decision was his acceptance of the submission of counsel that in construing the Resolution he 'should approach the task applying the same principles as govern the construction of statutory legislation' (p. 596 A). This, it will be recollected, was also the basis of the Pay Board's argument in *Crittall-Hope* (para. 23). The Industrial Arbitration Board did not accede to this reasoning. It relied for clues to the meaning of the 1946 Resolution not on a parallel with statute, but on materials pertinent to Fair Wages policy: previous Resolutions, Orders 1305 of 1940 and 1376 of 1951, and section 8 of the 1959 Act (para. 44(2)). The parallel with statute is an extremely artificial construction to impose on the Fair Wages Resolution. It contradicts the ruling in the ancient case of *Stockdale* v. *Hansard* (1839) 9 A. & E. 1, that a resolution of one House of Parliament is not law. It also ignores the view expressed by Kahn-Freund in his classic study in the *Modern Law Review* of 1948 of the legal aspect of the Fair Wages clauses that they are not comparable to statutes. This is apparent from the procedure of the passage of the Fair Wages Resolution—a resolution passed by a simple majority in the House of Commons; and from its intended function—an administrative direction to government departments.

It may be noted here that by foreclosing discussion of this issue, Griffiths J. left unresolved some fascinating legal questions: if a resolution is not 'law' in its pure form, does it acquire legal quality when embodied in statutes, as has been the regular practice with the Fair Wages clauses over the last few decades? Kahn-Freund thought they thereby changed their legal quality. What their new legal qualities were, however, was a very difficult question. They might vary according to the sanctions envisaged by the statutes in which they were embodied—withdrawal of subsidies to local government housing projects, revocation of road haulage licences, or the imposition of wage rates by the Industrial Court or I.A.B. In *Racal*, Griffiths J. did not consider whether the legal quality of the Fair Wages Resolution was affected by its inclusion, as was the case in the matter before him, in a statutory instrument (the Counter-Inflation (Price and Pay Code) Order, 1973, para. 134). For the purposes of construction it was all the same to him.

Having taken this fundamental step, Griffiths J. proceeded to apply the rules of statutory construction. He insisted that he must 'give to the words of the resolution the meaning to be attached to them in the year 1946, and, in so far as industrial conditions differed in 1946 from those of the present day, it is against the 1946 background that the resolution must be construed' (p. 596 B). This approach eliminates certain qualities of the Resolution as a direction by the House of Commons to government departments—flexibility and the exercise of administrative discretion as industrial conditions change. It ignores the fact that the Resolution in question was incorporated into a statutory instrument of 1973, not 1946. The judge even adverted to past practice inconsistent with this approach to construing the Resolution: 'although the resolution of 1891 did not refer to a rate of wages paid in a district, it had been interpreted by government departments as obliging the contractor to pay the rate of wages current in the district' (p. 597 G). In other words, the departments exercised discretion to adapt the Resolution to prevailing industrial conditions with a view to achieving the object of securing Fair Wages. That approach had been expressly approved on a number of occasions— notably in the Reports of the Committee on Government Contracts 1897 (p. iv) and of the Fair Wages Committee 1908 (para. 8).

The judge was advised by Professors H. A. Clegg and R. W. Rideout as to the general circumstances in industry which surrounded the passing of the Fair Wages Resolution of 1946 (p. 595 C). He noted the shift from district to national negotiations which occurred between 1909 and 1942 (p. 598 E). He referred to the gap between the standards of national agreements and the earnings of workers which had developed since then (p. 599 G–H). He acknowledged the attempt by the Industrial Arbitration Board to accommodate this development in the Award in *Crittall-Hope*. Nevertheless, he did not feel able to adopt it. Instead, he felt himself bound by the canons of statutory construction:

> I must nevertheless give to the words of the resolution the meaning to be attached to them in the year 1946, and, in so far as industrial conditions differed in 1946 from those of the present day, it is against the 1946 background that the resolution must be construed. If there be ambiguity, I must ask myself which meaning fits more naturally with conditions as they must have been known to the members of the House at the time when they passed the resolution. (p. 596 B–C).

His decision, therefore, was to accept the view advocated by the Pay Board in *Crittall-Hope* and other cases, that the minimum rates embodied in national agreements were the standards prescribed by Clause 1(a) of the Resolution. In conclusion, he stated:

> The reality of the matter is that the passage of time has rendered the Fair Wages Resolution of 1946 out of date. If it became necessary to invoke it to secure its original objectives, it would

in many cases be an ineffective instrument. It is the increased bargaining power of organised labour that provides today's principal safeguard against exploitation by would-be unscrupulous government contractors and no doubt accounts for the fact that no attempt has been made to re-draft the resolution. But the fact that the wording of the resolution is no longer appropriate to present-day bargaining procedures must not deter me from giving the resolution the meaning which I believe the language plainly conveyed to all who were concerned with its implementation in 1946. (p. 602 C–D)

This is an admirable appreciation of the reality of industrial relations but does little to enhance the reputation for creativity of the English judiciary.

The question is whether the lifeline thrown to the Fair Wages policy by the Industrial Arbitration Board is to be cut off by the Court's proclamation that the Resolution is a dead letter. In Award 3296 of 20 May 1974 (*Sheffield Rolling Mills Ltd. and Pay Board*), a case substantially identical to *Crittall-Hope* some eleven days after Griffiths J.'s judgment, the Board following its own line of reasoning without adverting to the *Racal* case. More significant, however, was Award 3300 of 29 August 1974, an ordinary case on the Fair Wages Resolution not concerned with incomes policy and not involving the Pay Board— *Electrical, Electronic, Telecommunications and Plumbing Trades Union and Clarke & Smith Manufacturing Co. Ltd.* Some three months after *Racal*, the question was once again posed unequivocally whether Clause 1(a), and thus the Resolution's requirements, were satisfied by adherence to national agreements in the engineering industry. The Company submitted that that was adequate compliance and:

> also placed before the Board a copy of the decision of the High Court in the Racal case and submitted that in the light of that decision some at least of the views set out by the Board in paragraphs 43–48 of their Award No. 3290 (in which Crittall-Hope Ltd. and the Pay Board were concerned) were no longer tenable. If that were so, it followed that the Company's obligation under the Resolution was to pay rates of wages not less favourable than those laid down under the May 1974 Agreement. It followed that the Union could not rely on Clause 1(b) of the Resolution. (para. 17)

To the contrary, the Union, while asking the Board to take account of the implications of *Racal*, 'took the view that despite that decision it was for the Board to determine the application of Clauses 1(a) and 1(b)' (para. 8).

There would appear to be some legal authority for the Union's submission. In *R*. v. *Industrial Court, ex parte A.S.S.E.T.* [1965] 1 Q.B. 377, the Divisional Court held that the Fair Wages jurisdiction of the then Industrial Court derived from the reference to it by the Minister as a private tribunal for arbitration, not under any statutory jurisdiction (e.g. the Industrial Courts Act 1919). Consequently, the Court could not compel it to sit. Similarly, in *B.B.C.* v. *A.C.T.A.T.*, *The Times*, 30 November 1966, Megaw J. refused to grant a declaration to stop the Industrial Court exceeding its jurisdiction, as only a question of interpretation of the Resolution was raised, which the Industrial Court could decide for itself. *Racal* itself, as Griffiths J. conceded, was 'the first occasion on which a court has been called upon to construe a resolution of the House of Commons' (p. 595 H). In its submissions, however, the Union chose to stress:

> It was a reality of industrial life that wages levels were in practice determined at district or local level and that the national Agreement merely constituted a safety net. The main purpose of the minimum rates prescribed by the national Agreement was for the compilation of the holiday and overtime payments. Accordingly the Union submitted that the present case fell to be considered in relation to Clause 1(b) of the Resolution. (para. 8)

The Industrial Arbitration Board came out firmly in support of its previous position in *Crittall-Hope*:

> There was at the hearing some discussion as to whether the question referred to the Board fell to be decided in the light of Clause 1(a) or of Clause 1(b) of the Resolution. The Board think it right to say that they have made their decision in accordance with the guide-lines pronounced by them in paragraphs 43–48 of their Award No. 3290 (in which Crittall-Hope Limited and the Pay Board were concerned). In the present case it was submitted by the Company that in the light of the High Court decision in the Racal case some at least of those guide-lines were no longer tenable. The Board do not accept this submission and do not consider that there is anything in the decision in the Racal case which invalidates the decisions made by the Board in their Award No. 3290 and a number of other Awards similar to that Award. (para. 25(2))

Accordingly, the Board maintained that Clause 1(a) accepted the applicability of the national Agreements, but only as minimum wage standards:

and there is nothing to preclude the Board from considering and deciding, under Clause 1(b) of the Resolution, the questions whether at any material time there has been a general level of actual wages paid by similarly-circumstanced employers which was higher than the minimum wage rates prescribed by one or another of the above-mentioned Agreements and, if so, whether the Company has at any material time been in breach of the Resolution by paying below that general level. (para. 25(3))

Disturbingly enough, however, the Board, while requiring adherence to the minimum rates, decided that: 'Insufficient evidence was placed before the Board to enable them to decide whether or not there was at the date of the hearing a general level of wages paid by similarly circumstanced employers which was higher than the minimum rates prescribed by the May 1974 Agreement' (para. 25(5)(c)). This left the workers concerned in the application little better off than before their call for protection by the Fair Wages policy. It is not clear whether more efficient research or presentation of its evidence by the Union would have fulfilled the Board's requirements (a request for additional written evidence had been made by the Board during the hearing—para. 1). This is an ominous turn of events after the Board had avoided the dead-end interpretation in *Racal*. For the practical result in both cases was substantially the same.

The *Crittall-Hope* doctrine and its aftermath provide both an important insight into and a remedy for the fundamental contradiction of the Fair Wages Resolution of 1946. The necessity for the Fair Wages policy to come to terms with the industrial relations system in which it operates is apparent if it is to achieve the aims it was designed for some eighty-six years ago. Whether a successful adjustment to the system will be sufficient is by no means obvious. But it is a vital first step.

NOTES

1. The above account is principally derived from the following sources:
—R. C. O. Matthews, 'Why has Britain had Full Employment Since the War?', *Economic Journal*, **78** (September 1968), 555.
—A. G. Hines, 'Unemployment and the Rate of Change of Money Wage Rates in the U.K. 1862–1963—A Reappraisal', *Review of Economic Statistics*, **50** (February 1958), 60.
—G. S. Bain, *Trade Union Growth and Recognition*, Royal Commission on Trade Unions and Employers' Associations, Research Paper No. 6, London, H.M.S.O., 1967; especially chapter III.
—E. H. Phelps Brown, 'Wage Drift', *Economica*, **29** (1962), at p. 340.
—E. H. Phelps Brown, 'New Wine in Old Bottles: Reflections on the Changed Working of Collective Bargaining in Great Britain', *British Journal of Industrial Relations*, **11** (1973), at p. 335.
—H. A. Turner, 'Wages: Industry Rates,

Workplace Rates and the Wage-Drift', *The Manchester School of Economic and Social Studies*, **XXIV** (1956), at p. 101.
—Royal Commission on Trade Unions and Employers' Associations, 1965–8, *Report*, H.M.S.O., London, June 1968, Cmnd. 3623; para. 57, Table B, p. 15, Table C, p. 16.
—G. Perrice, 'Earnings and Wage Rates since 1938', *London and Cambridge Economic Bulletin*, September 1952, p. IV.
—G. Perrice, 'Earnings and Wage Rates 1948–1955', *London and Cambridge Economic Bulletin*, December 1955, p. XI.
—J. Marquand, 'Earnings-Drift in the U.K., 1948–1957', *Oxford Economic Papers* (N.S.), **12** (1960), at p. 79.
—J. F. B. Goodman, and T. G. Whittingham, *Shop Stewards*, Pan Books Ltd., London, 1973; chapter 2; p. 183.
—A. I. Marsh and E. E. Coker, 'Shop Steward Organisation in the Engineering Industry', *British Journal of Industrial Relations*, **1** (June 1963), p. 170.
—W. E. J. McCarthy and S. R. Parker, *Shop Stewards and Workshop Relations*, Royal Commission on Trade Unions and Employers' Associations, Research Paper No. 10, H.M.S.O., London, 1968; para. 56.
—Report of the Comptroller and Auditor General, Civil Appropriation Accounts (Classes I–V) 1965–6; H.C. 270 of 1966–7, paras. 81–3.

2. For these statements by Sir Roy Wilson, see Royal Commission on Trade Unions and Employers' Associations, *Minutes of Evidence*, No. 45, Written Memorandum of Evidence Submitted by Sir Roy Wilson, Q.C., dated 16 March 1966, pp. 1934–6, at para. 4; and the Examination of Sir Roy Wilson, 26 July 1966, at Q. 7223, p. 1957.

3. Award 1757 of 14 June 1940, *Trade Union Side of the Shipbuilding Trade Joint Council for Government Departments and Official Side;* Award 1759 of 10 July 1940; Award 1760 of 18 July 1940. See para. 2 of Award 1757: 'Evidence was submitted in regard to the number of employees, the nature of the work upon which the men concerned are engaged, their rates of wages and the rates of men similarly employed in private shipyards and ship-repairing establishments, the basis upon which wages are fixed by the Admiralty, having regard to the provisions of the Fair Wages Clause, and other relevant considerations'.

4. See Awards: 1823 of 26 August 1941, *N.U.P.E. and Morley Town Council Waterworks Committee;* 1842 of 21 November 1941, *N.U.G.M.W. and Monmouth Town Council;* 1847 of 9 December 1941, *N.U.P.E. and Lewes Borough Council;* 1850 of 19 December 1941, *N.U.G.M.W. and Lanark Town Council;* 1855 of 15 April 1942, *N.U.G.M.W. and Caernarvon Corporation;* 1856 of 23 April 1942, *N.U.P.E. and Surbiton Borough Council;* and 1866 of 10 July 1942, *N.U.G.M.W. and Aberystwyth Borough Council.* Others were also active, e.g. Awards 1781 of 13 January 1941 and 1808 of 13 June 1941, for similar attempts by the Electrical Power Engineers' Association.

5. See, e.g. Awards 1826 of 15 September 1941, *National Union of Cokemen and Bye-Product Workers and Brancepeth Gas and Coke Ltd.;* 1869 of 22 July 1942, *N.U.G.M.W. and Candy & Co. Ltd.;* 1931 of 13 December 1943, *N.U.V.B. and P. Y. Pickering & Co.;* and 1938 of 3 February 1944, *N.U.G.M.W. and A. Wooton & Sons Ltd.*

6. Awards 2111 of 1 October 1947, *T.G.W.U. and Messrs. A. & R. Brownlie;* 2221 of 22 June 1949 (claim won by the Scottish Horse and Motormen's Association); 2467 of 17 August 1953 (claim lost by an individual worker), *R. E. Mahoney and The Octagon Brewery Ltd.;* 2538 of 25 October 1954 (claim by individual worker; won £9 13s. 4d. accrued holiday pay), *C. N. Hamilton and Messrs. Cotterell Bros. Ltd.;* 2593 of 31 January 1956 (claim lost by individual worker), *W. Nield and J. Billig & Sons Ltd.;* 2675 of 19 December 1957 (claim won by individual worker, aided by a T.G.W.U. member), *R. J. Duncan and R. C. Cessford;* 2685 of 24 March 1958 (claim lost by individual worker, aided by a T.G.W.U. member), *R. C. Jones and Burgess Webb and Squire Ltd.*

7. See Awards 2161 of 10 June 1948, *A.S.S.E.T. and Skyways Ltd.* (claim upheld); 2164 of 30 June 1948, *Aeronautical Engineers' Association and Olley Air Service Ltd.* (claim upheld) (both cases under the Civil Aviation Act, 1946, s. 41); 2288 of 29 December 1950, *A.S.S.E.T. and Field Aircraft Services, Ltd.* (claim upheld, but see the amazing sequel in Award 2319 of 4 May 1951, when the company succeeded in totally evading the Court's Award by simply amending its Memorandum of Association. The Industrial

Court thereupon reversed its former decision by accepting the company's self-definition as not being concerned in the business of providing air transport services, and thus no longer bound by the J.I.C. agreements); and 2386 of 13 June 1952, *Aeronautical Engineers' Association and Morton Air Services Ltd.* (claim upheld) (these cases under the Civil Aviation Act, 1949, s. 15(1)).

8. Awards 2157 of 31 May 1948, *Aeronautical Engineers' Association and London Aero & Motor Services Ltd.* (claim upheld under the Civil Aviation Act, 1946, s. 41); 2351 of 19 November 1951, *A.S.S.E.T. and Reid & Sigrist Ltd.* (claim upheld in part); 2390 of 17 June 1952, *Aeronautical Engineers' Association and Air Trade Ltd.* (claim dismissed) (both cases under the Civil Aviation Act, 1949, s. 15(1)). In the ninth case, Award 2190 of 24 November 1948, *Aeronautical Engineers' Association and Olley Air Service Ltd.*, the trade union did not attend the hearing and thus the claim failed.

9. Awards 2222 of 22 June 1949; 2240 of 27 October 1949; 2265 of 16 June 1950; 2275 of 17 October 1950; 2384 of 13 June 1952; 2393 of 25 June 1952; 2403 of 3 September 1952; 2454 of 27 May 1953; 2458 of 3 July 1953.

10. Geoff Latta, 'The Legal Extension of Collective Bargaining: A Study of Section 8 of the Terms and Conditions of Employment Act, 1959', *Industrial Law Journal*, **4** (March 1975), p. 217. References to this article will be accompanied by the page number where they are to be found.

11. Award 2854 of 6 July 1961, *Formica Ltd. and Sign and Display Trades Union.* For other cases where the Court found Agreements applicable but held that employers were already observing terms not less favourable, see e.g. Awards 2879 of 30 November 1961 (involving a district agreement on top of the National Agreement, with the North Staffs. Tile Fireplace Association); 3121 of 29 November 1966, *W. H. Paul Ltd. and National Society of Metal Mechanics* (a compli-

cated case involving the translation of piece rates into the hourly rates fixed by the Agreement); 3151 of 17 August 1967 (another district agreement between the *Henry Miller and Company (Timber) Limited and Amalgamated Society of Wood-Cutting and Machinists*); and 3160 of 29 January 1968, *Black Clawson International and C.A.W.U.* (company not complying with agreement, but, except for five workers, its terms were not less favourable).

12. For other instances where the Court upheld unions' claims for national increases to be added to local rates, see Awards 2990 of 4 October 1963, *Hudswell, Clarke & Co. Ltd. and D.A.T.A.;* and 3123 of 29 November 1966, *Crawley Engineering Developments Ltd. and C.A.W.U.* For instances where these claims were denied, see Awards 3003 of 3 February 1964 and 2877 of 16 November 1961. For instances where the national agreement anticipated the problem, see Awards 3197 of 5 September 1969, *Black Clawson International Ltd. and C.A.W.U.;* 3204 of 3 February 1970, *Scot Meat Products and T.G.W.U.;* 3230 of 13 October 1970, *Coulthurst Ltd. and C.A.W.U.* (interpreted in Award 3241 of 11 May 1971).

13. An identical exception was contained in paragraph 155 of the Counter-Inflation (Price and Pay Code) (No. 2) Order, 1973 (S.I. 1973, No. 1785). In Award 3287 of 5 February 1974, *T.G.W.U. and Passenger Transport Executives of Glasgow, Tyneside & Merseyside*, the Industrial Arbitration Board held section 152 of the Road Traffic Act 1960 to constitute 'similar legislation' within the meaning of that paragraph (see para. 24).

14. Awards 3291 of 25 April 1974, *F. Bamford & Co. and Pay Board;* 3292 of 1 May 1974, *Sanderson Kayser Ltd. and Pay Board;* 3293 of 3 May 1974, *Rank Precision Industries Ltd. and Pay Board;* 3294 of 6 May 1974, *Crittall-Hope Double Glazing Ltd. and Pay Board;* and 3296 of 20 May 1974, *Sheffield Rolling Mills Ltd. and Pay Board.*

16

The Interpretation and Application of the Fair Wages Policy Formula

It has been shown above that the incompatibility of the Fair Wages Resolution of 1946 with the industrial relations system in which it operated was a principal reason for its lack of effect. But analysis of cases which came before the Industrial Court indicates other deficiencies in its implementation. The interpretation of the new Fair Wages policy formula by the Industrial Court was no less subject to criticism than that of the government departments which had previously resolved disputes arising out of the policy. Much dissatisfaction was registered with regard to the Industrial Court's interpretation of the parts of the new formula setting up the new Fair Wages standards: clause 1(a)

> not less favourable than those established for the trade or industry, in the district where the work is carried out, by machinery of negotiation or arbitration to which the parties are organisations of employers and trade unions representative, respectively, of substantial proportions of the employers and workers engaged in the trade or industry in the district;

and clause 1(b)

> not less favourable than the general level of wages, hours and conditions observed by other employers whose general circumstances in the trade or industry in which the contractor is engaged are similar.

The resolution of disputes by the Industrial Court which arose from differing interpretations of the new formula has not found favour in the eyes of trade unions. Thus, the General Council reported to the 1970 Trades Union Congress that: 'N.U.P.E. had also written to mention the "perversity" of Industrial Court decisions in determining

For notes see p. 339

issues that N.U.P.E. had been concerned with in trying to get an equitable interpretation of the Fair Wages Resolution' (p. 191). A number of key phrases in this new Fair Wages policy formula will be analysed to illustrate the obstacles that still faced workers and unions who decided to formally complain under the procedure for enforcement of the policy.

'Trade or Industry'

Perhaps the most frequent source of contention before the Industrial Court in the context of the new Fair Wages policy has been the interpretation and application of the phrase 'trade or industry' which appears three times in clause 1 of the Resolution of 1946. Such problems could have been anticipated: in her book, *Arbitration Principles and the Industrial Court*, published in 1931 (P. S. King & Son Ltd., London), M. T. Rankin exposed the difficulties experienced by the Court in applying such a phrase during the first ten years of its existence. Up to the end of 1974, some sixty-five cases concerned with the application of the new Fair Wages policy of 1946 contained some disagreement on this matter: thirty-four were brought under the Terms and Conditions of Employment Act 1959, fifteen under the Resolution itself, and sixteen under other instruments of the policy.

In line with its general practice of rendering opaque decisions, the Industrial Court did not offer any guidance as to its views on the interpretation of this phrase. In only one case did it even hint at the existence of a distinction between trade and industry. In Award 3140 of 8 May 1967, the Court held that the company complained of under the 1959 Act was 'not engaged in the Process Engraving Trade (or in other words the process engraving section of the Printing Industry), and that the workers in the claim are not employed in the said Trade or section' (para. 24).[1] Occasionally, respondent employers before the Court would seek to exclude their activities entirely from the ambit of 'trade or industry'—for example, Caernarvon Corporation in 1942, Eton House School in 1960 and the City of Leicester Working Men's Club in 1961.[2] Most of the cases, however, were concerned with one of two problems: (i) whether an agreement negotiated in a particular 'trade or industry' applied to an employer who claimed he was engaged in a different 'trade or industry'; or (ii) which 'trade or industry' was the employer engaged in when a number of possibilities occurred. Illustrations of these problems abound in all three periods: 1940–6, 1946–59 and 1959–74. The following are a few examples.

In Award 1767 of 3 October 1940 under section 34(1) of the Cinematograph Films Act 1938 (*Association of Cine-Technicians and British Instructional Films, Ltd.*), the Court accepted the company's submission that it did 'not carry on in Great Britain the business of making films to which the 1938 Act applies' (para. 7). Cases under Order 1305 involved disputes over whether the North Riding County Council's maintenance workers were in the building industry or not, whether a company using 80 per cent imported hickory was governed by an agreement in the Home-Grown Timber Trade and whether another company engaged in general vehicle repairs was governed by an agreement negotiated by the National Federation of Vehicle Trades, as the Union claimed, or by the Motor Agents Association Ltd., as the company claimed.[3] In Award 1852 of 26 February 1942 concerning the Miscellaneous Trades Joint Council for Government Industrial Establishments, the Court upheld the Official Side's contention that the workers concerned were not in the printing trade and thus not covered by agreements invoked by the Trade Union Side. Award 1949 of 29 February 1944, the only case on the Fair Wages Resolution during the War, was mainly concerned with whether shipbuilding or building trade rates applied. In other cases on the Resolution between 1946–59, the Court had to decide between the bookbinding and paper box industries, the box-making and the home-grown timber trade, agreements for each of which were advocated; whether companies training pilots for military aircraft were covered by agreements negotiated for civil air transport, and what industry described a garage providing ambulance services.[4] In two cases under the Road Haulage Wages Act 1938, the Court had to decide whether the workers concerned were employed in road transport or agricultural work, and in a case under the Road Traffic Act 1930, the respondent employers succeeded in their defence that the agreement produced by the Union did not cover their business.[5]

A dispute over the application of section 15(1) of the Civil Aviation Act 1949 indicates the legalistic approach of the Industrial Court to the problems of interpreting the phrase 'trade or industry'. In Award 2288 of 29 December 1950, the Court upheld the claim of the Union, A.S.S.E.T., that the respondent company, Field Aircraft Services Ltd., was constituted for the purpose of providing air transport services or performing other aerial work, was therefore subject to section 15(1) of the 1949 Act, and was thereby obliged to observe the current Agreement negotiated by the National Joint Council for Civil Air Transport. At the hearing which preceded the Award, the company had contended that they were not and never had been engaged on air transport services or other aerial work. On 25 January 1951, the company convened an Extraordinary General Meeting at which a Special Resolution was passed amending their Memorandum of Association deleting some articles and inserting others. They thereupon invited the Union, A.S.S.E.T., to enter into negotiations outside the provisions of section 15(1) of the Act. When the dispute that subsequently arose arrived before the Industrial Court once again, the company made bold to state that:

> as the Company have not been constituted since the 25th January, 1951, for the purpose of providing air transport services or carrying out other forms of aerial work it was now contended that the provisions of Section 15(1) of the Civil Aviation Act, 1949, have not since the 25th January, 1951, applied and that Industrial Court Award 2288, dated 29th December, 1950, should not apply to the Company and should be revoked. (Award 2319 of 4 May 1951, para. 5)

The Union, of course, did not hesitate to submit 'that this fresh Reference to the Court was merely a device to avoid observance of Award No. 2288 which is now four months old and has not yet been honoured'. It reiterated its arguments as to the nature of the Company's work made at that hearing and stressed that 'all the physical and organisational elements of the situation then still remain'. It repeated its previous contention that 'an unfavourable decision on its claim would have meant legal encouragement being given to any charter company to lapse from the agreements carefully built up within the National Joint Council for Civil Air Transport by disestablishing its maintenance and repair, and controlling it through a subsidiary company'. In conclusion:

> It was therefore contended that the Company has been in breach of the Fair Wages Resolution, and it was submitted that if the Company's plea, viz. that since 25th January, 1951, the Company has not been constituted for the purpose of providing air transport services or carrying out other forms of aerial work, is allowed, an incentive will be provided for firms to disregard the patiently created standards of the organized employer and trades union bodies in the industry, thus placing an unduly heavy liability upon the employer seeking to have good relationships and maintain fair standards. (para. 6)

In a single short paragraph, the Court upheld the Company's contention. By simply amending its Articles of Association, the Company succeeded in removing the protection of the Fair Wages policy from its employees and even in revoking a prior Award of the Industrial

Court (para. 7). The Union was clearly aware of the disastrous implications of such a decision. One can scarcely imagine a more deadly blow being struck against the Fair Wages policy.[6]

The same sorts of disputes, as to the applicability of agreements to, and as to the 'trade or industry' of, employers summoned under section 8 of the 1959 Act arose frequently in the period following its enactment. Thus, to give a few illustrations, the Court had to decide whether a builders agreement applied to shopfitters, whether engineering draughtsmen in a rubber products factory were covered by an engineering agreement, whether eighteen Forest Keepers employed at Epping Forest were covered by agreements between the two sides of the National Joint Council for Local Authorities Services (Manual Workers), whether off-site bar-benders were covered by building industry agreements, and again whether draughtsmen employed by companies in the pottery and building industries respectively, were covered by an engineering agreement.[7] In other cases, the Court had to decide whether the workers and employer concerned were engaged in road haulage or local authority service, cotton or worsted textiles, engineering or iron and steel, engineering or vehicle building, engineering or construction, footwear or rubber manufacture.[8] In Award 2994 of 1 November 1963, the B.B.C. even succeeded in avoiding a collective agreement negotiated between the Variety Artistes Federation and the I.T.A. by claiming, *inter alia*, that 'the television industry really consisted of two industries (or sections) or two distinct parts of an industry (or section), as to which quite different considerations applied' (para. 10(3)).

A number of disputes concerned whether only a small proportion of the employees of the respondent employer should be covered by the collective agreement invoked. Or, what sometimes amounted to the same thing, whether the employer who was only partly engaged in a particular industry should be covered, wholly or in part, by the collective agreement for that industry. Thus, in Award 3151 of 17 August 1967, the Amalgamated Society of Woodworkers succeeded in getting an agreement applied to two of the respondent company's seventeen employees, despite the argument that considerably less than ten per cent of the company's total activities was in that side of the business. But although the Union succeeded in persuading the Court that the Agreement applied, they still lost their claim, as the Court held that the company was observing terms not less favourable. In another case, a company's clerical employees were allocated to each of their various departments, including the accounting, buying, sales and typing departments, as well as the production and engineering departments. The substance of the Union's claim was that inasmuch as the company in relation to part of their business was engaged in engineering activities (albeit only a minor part), the terms and conditions laid down in an engineering Agreement of 1967 were applicable to the whole of the company's clerical staff. The Court did not accept this proposition.[9]

In his article in the *Industrial Law Journal* of March 1975, Geoff Latta points out how such cases could undermine a large company's internal wage structure 'by allowing a small group of employees within a plant to have their wages fixed in relation to a national agreement different from the one which applied to the majority of the firm's employees', or 'by forcing one plant in a multi-plant company to follow a different agreement' (p. 227). This is exemplified by Award 2829 of 10 March 1961 where the Union, S.L.A.D.E., sought to have the terms of a National Agreement between Engraving Unions and employers applied. The employers, Thames Board Mills Ltd., claimed that the men involved in the work in question numbered eleven: they represented 0.59 per cent of the total employment force and the cost of their work as a percentage of the total cost of production of the employer's factory was 0.18 per cent. They were primarily manufacturers of paper board and packing cases. The reason why the employer fought was candidly stated—it was necessary to maintain relativities: 'Any interference with the current relationship between the rate of wages paid for the different occupations, could, it was submitted, have serious consequences and would be industrially undesirable'. The Court nonetheless held that the agreement was applicable. The claim failed, however, because it also found that the minimum standards set out in the agreement were exceeded by the employer.

While the Court's refusal to give reasons prevents any definitive judgment, it appears that it was generally inclined to look to the nature of the work actually being performed by the workers concerned in determining whether an Agreement was applicable. Thus, in Award 2818 of 16 January 1961, the Union claimed the workers concerned were engaged not only in delivering asphalt, but also helped out regularly in road construction, and so should be paid rates laid down in the Building and Civil Engineering National Agreements. The company claimed their help in construction activities was negligible. The Court held that the Agreements applied, but only to the workers employed 'otherwise than for the delivery of asphalt for customers' own use' (para. 6). Another dispute between the A.E.U. and Aston Martin Lagonda Ltd. was over whether the company was covered by agreements for the engineering or vehicle building industries. In Award 3102 of 18 May 1966, the Court decided 'having had regard to the nature of the work carried out at the present time by the workers concerned in the claim' (para. 30). Latta agrees that the central issue was 'the nature of the work performed by the occupational group', but adds 'and no account was taken of the overall end-product of the company's operations' (p. 227). Award 3192 of 15 July 1969 tends to contradict this, as the Court held 'that it has not been established that the terms and conditions contained in the Agreement on which the Union rely (between the N.U.V.B. and the U.K. Joint Wages Board of Employers for the Vehicle Building Industry) are the recognized terms and conditions applicable to the workers concerned in the claim, who constitute a mixed labour force engaged, irrespective of trades, in the production of various products only a minority of which can be described as vehicle building products'. Finally, an instance of the at times Solomonic judgment of the Court is Award 3244 of 5 July 1971 (*Martin & Son, Edinburgh Ltd. and National Union of Furniture Trade Operatives*). The Court resolved the dispute between a firm claiming it was engaged in retailing furniture, and a Union which said it was engaged in furniture manufacture, by stating: 'Retailers who carry out these operations are for the sake of convenience hereafter referred to as retail furniture manufacturers' (para. 38(2)). The Union still lost the claim.

Of the nine cases under the Fair Wages Resolution of 1946 in which the question of interpreting 'trade or industry' arose between 1959–74, seven were concerned with the position of women cleaners employed by contractors to the government. Their difficulties over this question will be discussed separately in chapter 19. Of the remaining two, Award 3267 of 26 July 1972 concerned a dispute over whether Multiplex Designs Ltd. was engaged in producing technical publications or in engineering; Award 3285 of 17 December 1973, whether Hiatt & Co. Ltd., a plastics manufacturer, was governed by engineering rates. The A.U.E.W. failed to established a breach of the Resolution in either case.

It is difficult to assess the significance for the success of the Fair Wages policy of the Industrial Court's approach to the question of determining the meaning and application of the phrase 'trade or industry', even if a consistent one could be definitely established. Of the more than thirty cases involving this question brought under instruments other than the 1959 Act, approximately half were successful. Of the thirty-four cases under the 1959 Act in which it was ascertained that a dispute existed over this phrase and its application, two-thirds were unsuccessful. Perhaps a preliminary assessment can be made that the Industrial Court's interpretation and application of the phrase had some negative effect. Certainly, some individual cases must have been highly discouraging.

'Organizations of Employers and Trade Unions'

Another phrase which aroused disputation in cases arising out of the Fair Wages policy was that requiring the parties to the machinery of negotiation or arbitration establishing the 'fair' standards to be 'organizations of employers and trade unions'. The difficulties anticipated by Sir Harold Morris, the President of the Industrial Court, should a strict interpretation of this phrase be adopted—that described in chapter 13—did not arise in the cases published by the Industrial Court. Questions were forthcoming, however, on what was and what was not an organization of employers, and what was the position of an employer not federated to the employers' organization which had negotiated the fair standards.

As might be expected, the Court did not seek to lay down a definition of 'organization of employers'. In three cases in 1941, local authorities tried to avoid the Fair Wages formula contained in the terms of Order 1305 by claiming that employers on the National Joint Board of the Electricity Supply Industry and on the National Joint Industrial Council of the water supply industry were not 'organizations of employers', and thus these were excluded from consideration in determining fair standards. The Court simply rejected the contention in all three cases.[10] Some twenty years later, however, in Award 2847 of 8 June 1961, the City of Leicester Working Men's Club contended against the Variety Artistes' Federation that the Midland Counties Entertainment Secretaries' Council was not and did not represent an organization of employers. This argument, among others, led to the Court holding the claim not to fall within the terms of the formula in section 8(1) of the 1959 Act (para. 5). In a recent case, Award 3177 of 13 August 1968, the Greater London Council Staff Association tried to impose an agreement made between themselves and the London County Council on to the London Borough of Tower Hamlets. Denying the claim under the 1959 Act, the Industrial Court specifically upheld the contention of the Borough 'that it has not been established that the agreement on which the Association rely is a current agreement one of the parties to which is, or represents, an organization of employers or an association of such organisations' (para. 34).

Employers affiliated to organizations could be expected to adhere to agreements negotiated by them, though Geoff Latta calculated that over forty claims under the 1959 Act involved federated firms. He adds that a majority of cases, however, was provided by non-federated firms (p. 220). The Court seems to have wavered somewhat in its attitude. For example, in early cases, such as Award 2806 of 11 October

1960, the Association of Engineering and Shipbuilding Draughtsmen claimed that the Ford Motor Company should observe an agreement reducing hours negotiated between the Union and the Engineering and Allied Employers' National Federation, although Ford was not a member of the Federation and the Union negotiated with them separately. In argument opposing the claim, the Company pointed out that in the Engineering Industry a number of large organizations were not in membership of the Federation. Nonetheless, the Court accepted the Union's claim. Again, in Award 2879 of 30 November 1961, a non-member of the North Staffs Tile Fireplace Association was held to be subject to an agreement negotiated with it (though in the end the claim failed as his terms were held to be not less favourable).

But in three cases during the mid-1960s the Court inexplicably abandoned this view. In Award 3059 of 1 March 1965, the Union attempted to impose the provisions of a grievance procedure agreement on the employer. In denying the claim, the Court stated: 'The terms of those provisions are, moreover, such that they are inapplicable where, as in this case, the workers concerned are not employed in an establishment by a member of one of the Employers' Organizations parties to the Agreement' (para. 28(2)). The excuse provided by the particularity of the grievance machinery was not available in two other cases which were concerned with a guarantee of employment. In both Award 3110 of 3 August 1966 (*N.S.M.M. and Dawes Cycle Co. Ltd.*, at para. 15(2)) and Award 3168 of 7 May 1968 (*T.G.W.U. and Brooks Motor Ltd.*, at para. 21(2)), the Court held in identical terms that the guarantee 'by its terms relates only to hourly rated manual workers employed by federated firms. The provisions of that Agreement are accordingly not applicable to the workers employed by the Company, who are not a federated firm.' Inexplicably, the Court seemed to single out this term as not being applicable, for it stated, in paragraph 15(1) of Award 3110, that 'subject to what is said in (2) below, the recognized terms and conditions of employment applicable to the workers concerned in the claim are those contained in the Engineering Agreements'. Geoff Latta concludes that 'the decisions probably contradicted the Act itself since the clear intent of the statute was that employers could be made to observe agreements to which they were originally not party, and this was the essence of the position of non-federated firms' (p. 220).

It is obvious that the agreements or awards stipulated by the Fair Wages policy formula as setting 'fair' standards will of necessity refer expressly to the parties involved in them and not others. The function of the Fair Wages policy instrument is to require those other employers to adhere to the 'fair' standards. To take the words of the agreement as establishing the scope of its intended coverage is accurate; but to impose that limited scope on the Fair Wages policy is absurd. An interpretation which effectively excludes other employers from coverage is a contraduction of the Fair Wages policy. The new policy in Schedule 11 to the Employment Protection Act 1975 avoids this pitfall—as will be seen later.

Finally, it may be noted that the Industrial Relations Act 1971 retained the Fair Wages standards prescribed in the 1959 Act: those agreed by 'organizations of employers and organizations of workers, or associations of such organizations'. Schedule 7 to that Act, however, changed the provisions relating to use of the procedure—claims could be made by one of the parties to the agreement or award only if it was 'registered as a trade union or an employers' association under the Industrial Relations Act 1971'. The position was restored by paragraph 8 of Schedule 3 to the Trade Union and Labour Relations Act 1974.

'Representative'

Where it was established that the parties were organizations of employers and trade unions, it was still necessary to show that these were 'representative, respectively, of substantial proportions of the employers and workers engaged in the trade or industry in the district'. In the first cases in which the question of the 'representative' character of the parties to an agreement was raised, the Industrial Court did not offer any clues as to what it regarded as satisfying this requirement. Thus, Awards 2176–8 of 30 August 1948 concerned complaints by the T.G.W.U. against three small employers under the Road Traffic Act 1930. The Industrial Court simply heard evidence as to the membership and activities of, on the one hand, the Midlands Area Coach and Transport Association, of which the respondent employers were members, and on the other, of a number of employers, mainly local Borough Corporations, who undertook to provide similar services. It then baldly declared its view that the organization of employers was representative. Equally, the Court found itself 'unable to say on the evidence adduced that the trade union concerned (the United Road Transport Workers Association of England) is not representative' (para. 6). The complaints were rejected.

Under section 8(1)(c) of the 1959 Act, the position was further clarified by the express stipulation that employers might be bound by collective agreements negotiated by bodies on which they were not represented at all. The question arose in the first cases decided under the Act: Awards 2744–5 of 16 October 1959 (*South Western Fire Area Joint Board and National Association of Fire Officers and Chief Fire Officers' Association*). Responding to a complaint that he was not observing terms established by the appropriate National Joint Council, the employer claimed that he was not directly represented on the N.J.C., but only indirectly through the Association of County Councils in Scotland. Further, of fifteen members on the N.J.C., only one was from that Association. He asserted that terms negotiated by a predominantly English body should not apply to Scotland where 'conditions and sometimes living standards tended to be quite different' (para. 5). Despite this argument, this time the Court upheld the claim.

The first substantial discussion of the issue of representativeness was in Award 2779 of 11 May 1960, a claim by the N.U.G.M.W. that Eton House School was in breach of the 1959 Act. The Union, accepting the burden of proof, contended that:

> in construing what was a substantial proportion of Employers for the purpose of Section 8(1)(b) it was permissible to have regard to the size of the enterprise which the Employers, parties to the Agreement relied upon, were conducting and to the number of their employees. Something like 80 per cent of the education in the country was undertaken by the Local Education Authorities and not by Proprietors of private schools.

The Union then submitted that there were thirteen L.E.A.s in the district concerned, but unfortunately were unable to say how many private schools there were, either nationally or in that district. In the event, this was to prove fatal to the claim, for the Court held:

> In the absence of any sufficient evidence as to the number of employers engaged in the school catering or School Meals Service in education either nationally or in the area . . . the Court are unable to say that Section 8(1)(b) of the (Act) is satisfied. They accordingly Find, and so Award, that the claim has not been established.

In the result, it seems that the Court tends to a strict and mechanical interpretation of representativeness. All employers are equal in the eyes of the Court. Although a few may employ a disproportionate number of workers in the industry, if several others employ the remainder, the Union representing the workers employed by a few large employers may not be able to use the agreement negotiated with those employers who do not constitute a substantial proportion of employers in the relevant trade and district. This was the problem in the Eton House School case, where 80 per cent of the 'trade' was carried on by only about a dozen employers.

Similar results were reached in other early cases. In Award 2915 of 29 June 1962 (*T.G.W.U. and Road Services (Forth) Ltd.*), the Court refused to apply an agreement between the T.G.W.U. and British Road Services, accepting the employer's contention that B.R.S. did not represent a substantial proportion of employers—at most they constituted thirteen out of 17,000 in the industry, though this thirteen supplied 8–10 per cent of the lorries used in the industry. Again, assumption of the burden of proof by the E.T.U. in Award 2949 of 12 February 1963 (*E.T.U. and H. Bernard & Co. (Electrical) Ltd.*), led to the failure of its attempt to apply its agreement with the Electrical Contractors Association to the radio and television industry. The Court stated: 'No evidence is before the Court as to what are, actually or approximately, the numbers of employers and of workers in the industry or the numbers represented as aforesaid'.

Yet it might have been anticipated that the Court would recognize that the requirement of representativeness could be satisfied in less rigidly arithmetical ways. The history of the new Fair Wages policy is against the view that even a large number of small employers should preclude the establishment as 'fair' standards of those agreed over a substantial proportion of the industry. So if a relatively small number of employers do represent a substantial proportion of the industry—measured in employment, production, etc., it might be said that they were 'representative' within the meaning of the Fair Wages policy formula.

Such considerations may account for the otherwise inexplicable contradictions apparent in decisions of the Industrial Court on this question. Two cases of 1966 illustrate these contradictory results. In Award 3109 of 28 July 1966, the members of the Lowestoft Fishing Vessel Owners' Association were held not bound by Agreements negotiated by the National Joint Industrial Council for the Trawler Fishing Industry, which they had claimed was not representative. Yet in Award 3123 of 29 November 1966 (*Crawley Engineering Developments Ltd. and C.A.W.U.*), a member of the Welsh Engineers' and Founders' Association, which claimed with a membership of fifty-two employers to be the largest employers' organization in South West Wales, was nevertheless held bound by agreements negotiated by the Engineering Employers' Federation, which had, it was claimed, only three members in the area.

The most starting result on the issue of representativeness arose in Award 3285 of 17 December 1973 on the Fair Wages Resolution (*A.U.E.W. and Hiatt & Co. Ltd.*). The employer, a plastics manufacturer, sought to avoid engineering rates by proving that the Engineering Employers' Federation was not a representative employers' organization. He submitted first that Clause 1(a) of the Resolution was not satisfied because there was no evidence to show that the E.E.F. represented a substantial proportion of employers in the industry in the district, and produced figures showing that of sixty to seventy manufacturing companies in the relevant district, only thirteen were members, and of these only one was in plastics (para. 19). He went on to claim, moreover, that 'only a small proportion of engineering and plastics firms in the district, however defined, were members of the E.E.F.' (para. 27). The Appendix to the Award provided the figures shown in Table 9 to substantiate the claim. The Industrial Arbitration Board upheld the employer's contention; however the district was defined: 'it has not been established that rates of wages or hours and conditions of labour have been established in such district by machinery of negotiation conforming to the requirements of said Clause (1(a))' (para. 32).

TABLE 9

	No. of known		No. in Membership of E.E.F.	
	Engineering Companies	*Plastics Companies*	*Engineering Companies*	*Plastics Companies*
West Midlands	10,644	147	850	11
East Midlands and Coventry	5,837	74	537	4
Total	16,481	211	1,388	15

This result is logically contiguous with previous interpretations requiring substantial numbers of employers, regardless of size, to be represented by the organization of employers. But although the Award concerned only the representation by the E.E.F. of plastics manufacturers (5.40 per cent in the East Midlands and 7.48 per cent in the West Midlands), it may be questioned whether the representativeness of the E.E.F. in the engineering industry (9.19 per cent in the East Midlands and 7.98 per cent in the West Midlands) is any less subject to contradiction. The proportion of engineering companies represented by the E.E.F. in the West Midlands is only 0.5 per cent higher than the proportion of plastics companies it represents. However absurd this would be in light of the widespread acceptance of standards negotiated by the E.E.F., the Board's rigid interpretation would seem to require that they be disregarded.

Not surprisingly, perhaps, the Board has declined to take this course in subsequent cases on the Resolution. In the very next case, Award 3286 of 2 January 1974 (*S. B. Etweria and Fidelity Instrument Co. Ltd.*), it accepted the parties' common contention that the 1972 Agreement in Engineering established terms within Clause 1(a) of the Resolution (para. 17(1)); and found similarly in Award 3300 of 29 August 1974 (*E.E.T.P.U. and Clarke & Smith Manufacturing Ltd.*) (para. 25(3)). In *Crittall-Hope* (Award 3290 of 24 April 1974) the Board found expressly that the parties to the National Engineering Agreement were representative organizations within the meaning of Clause 1(a) (para. 46). And in Award 3292 of 1 May 1974 (*Sanderson Kayser Ltd. and The Pay Board*) the company conceded that the E.E.F. and the C.S.E.U. were representative of substantial proportions of employers and workers (para. 11). In Award 3294 of 6 May 1974 (*Crittall-Hope Double Glazing Ltd.*) the company itself claimed that plastics workers were the same as engineering workers as regards skills, recruitment, pay, etc., and this was accepted by the Board without demurrer (para. 7). In conclusion, one can only wonder if the Board was aware of these divergences in its application of the requirement of representativeness. The later cases may indicate that an interpretation which led to the rejection of widely accepted standards will not prevail.

'Established'—'Settled'

There are slight differences in the terminology employed by the various Fair Wages policy instruments to define the standards that were held to be applicable. Clause 1(a) of the 1946 Resolution referred to 'established' terms. Those specified by Order 1305 of 1940, Order 1376 of 1951 and the 1959 Act were referred to as 'recognized' terms, and were defined respectively as those 'in force' and 'settled' (Order 1305), 'established' and 'settled' (Order 1376) and again 'established' and 'settled' (the 1959 Act). The new Fair Wages policy in Schedule 11 to the Employment Protection Act 1975 also refers, in paragraph 2(a), to 'recognized' terms, and these are defined simply as those 'settled'. These slight differences were homogenized in meaning through the practice of the arbitration tribunals which enforced the Fair Wages policy instruments. Thus, for example, in one of the early cases under the 1959 Act, the Industrial Court in Award 2808 of 25 October 1960 referred to a Court of Appeal interpretation of Order 1376 in *R. v. Industrial Disputes Tribunal, ex parte Technaloy Ltd.* [1954] 2 All E.R. 75. Similarly, the Industrial Arbitration Board in the key case of *Crittall-*

Hope (Award 3290 of 24 April 1974) referred to preceding Fair Wages policy instruments (para. 44(2)).

A major problem involving these phrases concerned arrangements in industry which were so informal as to cause the Industrial Court to hesitate in declaring them the Fair Wages standards stipulated by the various instruments of the policy. Thus, the first two cases under the 1959 Act. Awards 2744–5 of 16 October 1959, involved standards embodied in recommendations made by a National Joint Council which were subsequently approved by the Secretary of State. Were these agreements or awards? The Court appeared to affirm that they were by upholding the claim. It found 'that the Joint Board is not observing the terms and conditions of employment as recommended by the N.J.C. for Local Authorities' Fire Brigades and approved by the Secretary of State for Scotland' (para. 6). In another context, where the Fair Wages Clause was also invoked, an employer claimed that the fact that the Engineering Employers' Federation only recommended the payment of increases denied it the character of an agreement under the 1959 Act. In Award 2877 of 16 November 1961, he asserted that 'an agreement, within the meaning of the Act, meant more than an agreement to recommend the payment of increases' (para. 5). The Court impliedly overruled this contention, though no reasons were given, by accepting the National Agreement. In Award 3086 of 18 January 1966, the applicable Agreement was described as follows:

> The 1965 Agreement ... was reached on an informal basis and its provisions are not specifically set out in any formal document. The proposals on which agreement was reached are, however, contained in a letter from the (Engineering Employers') Federation dated 9th February, 1965, and addressed to one of the unions concerned (the Association of Scientific Workers). (para. 4)

The Court accepted the terms of that Agreement as applying.

The Court was not always so flexible. In Award 3229 of 8 October 1970, the Textile Officials Association claimed that Joshua Hoyle & Sons Ltd. was not observing 'terms and conditions of employment which have been settled by an understanding and agreement between the Textile Officials Association and the Federation of Master Cotton Spinners' Association Ltd. (now the British Textile Employers' Association), issued in the form of a recommendation by the Federation' (para. 1). The union pointed to the preamble to the Recommendations, which urged all employers to observe them, and stated that they were accepted as the standard code of practice in the industry. The union argued that the fact that the Federation had not entered into signed agreements did not invalidate their submission (para. 9). The company claimed that 'the Recommendations were indeed only recommendations or guidelines to the drawing up of contracts of employment', and pointed to a statement in the Preamble which re-iterated the refusal to enter into signed agreements (para. 14). The Court held:

> that the Recommendations were not settled by an agreement or award as required by Section 8 of the Act. The Court are further not satisfied that, having regard to the wording of the Recom-mendations, they were intended to establish or did establish recognized terms and conditions for the Industry. (para. 17(1))

In the very different context of a complaint of anti-trade union bias under Clause 4 of the Fair Wages Resolution, in Award 2481 of 4 November 1953, the Court had ignored certain 'understandings' put forward by the A.E.U., which it claimed were about to be included in a new agreement with the employer, the Medical Supply Association Ltd.

It was still questionable, therefore, even where an agreement had been acknowledged, whether its terms had been 'established'. By upholding a claim by the Association of Engineering and Shipbuilding Draughtsmen in Award 2806 of 11 October 1960, the Court impliedly rejected the contention in that case of the Ford Motor Company 'that only terms and conditions which had been generally accepted for some time could be said to be "established"'. Newly negotiated terms were held to be binding. On the other hand, in two cases brought by the G.M.W.U. under the Road Traffic Act 1960, Awards 3223–4 of 6 August 1970, the Court upheld an employer's refusal to pay even where, the Union claimed:

> It has become general practice throughout the country that where the trade union members were willing to concede the principle, the 10s. bonus had been paid even by employers who did not intend to introduce one-man operation; and the Union had not been able to discover any other case where the employer had refused to make the payment in such circumstances. (para. 11)

The Court here followed a strict interpretation of the relevant clause of the Agreement, even though the employer concerned was not a member of the National Council for the Omnibus Industry which negotiated it!

Two curious cases seemed to imply that for terms to be applicable under the Fair Wages formula, they had to be legally binding on the employers concerned. The first, Award 3213 of 11 May 1970, found A.C.T.A.T. arguing that 'wage dividends' and other benefits paid by Kodak Ltd. to employees should not be considered in the calculation of pay as they were discretionary and could be withdrawn unilaterally (para. 12). Kodak Ltd. argued against such a strict construction of terms and conditions as referring only to those legally enforceable:

> There were all sorts of benefits which were in fact enjoyed, and which were in fact not precarious, but which were not in strict law enforceable; and it would be unfortunate, in the Company's view, if the Court were to be precluded by some sort of strict construction of the relevant provision from taking into account the reality of the situation. (para. 44)

The Court, inscrutable as ever, upheld the Union's claim under the 1959 Act. (See the sequel to this case in Award 3234 of 7 December 1970). The attitude of the Court here may be contrasted with its earlier decision in Award 3197 of 5 September 1969, where it refused to accept the Union's argument that a unilateral increase (albeit legally enforceable) should not be taken into account. In the second case, under the Civil Aviation Act 1949, the Court held, in Award 3225 of 10 August 1970 (*B.A.L.P.A. and B.U.A. Ltd.*), on the one hand that ' "Terms and conditions" must be such as to be of binding force under the contract of employment', but on the other, that the Fair Wages formula:

> has at any rate the effect of excluding from the comparison any provision which, although it continues to be set out in a written contract, has by agreement between the Parties, whether express or tacit, been treated either as being completely inoperative or as being in abeyance during the period relevant to the dispute. (para. 152(c))

The somewhat confusing situation which emerges from the cases described in the previous two paragraphs may be summarized as follows: the Court has held that terms, to be established: (a) need not have been implemented for long (Award 2806), but (b) that having been generally implemented may not be enough (Awards 3223–4); (c) even if implemented, they may have to be legally enforceable (Award 3213), but (d) being legally enforceable will not be enough if they are not implemented (Award 3225). It appeared that if the Union could show that the specified terms and conditions embodied in the Agreement in question were both legally enforceable as between the employer and his employees, and were being implemented in practice, the Court would be satisfied that the terms were 'established'.

The meaning of the word 'established', with regard to the need for such terms to be implemented in practice, became the focus of the objections by the Pay Board to the use of the Fair Wages Resolution of 1946 to breach the government's incomes policy of 1972–4. In Awards 3281 of 29 October 1973 and 3282 and 3283 of 30 October 1973, there was no dispute over the companies' contention that the National Agreement concerned did not 'establish' rates within the meaning of Clause 1(a). In 1974, however, the companies' interpretation was directly challenged. In the first and decisive case, Award 3290 of 24 April 1974 (*Crittall-Hope and Pay Board*), the company had contended:

> that 'established' should be interpreted as 'practically enforced' as distinct from 'fixed'; the interpretation should be consistent with the social intention of the Resolution. If the good employers in the district were not paying the National Agreement rate, or regarding the Agreement as operative to determine wage levels in practice, then that rate would have to be disregarded. (para. 12)

The Pay Board countered:

> that Clause 1(a) would not make sense if it were not accepted that machinery of negotiation could in itself establish rates of wages and conditions of labour; the Clause assumed that they could be established in that way. There was nothing in the Clause to support the argument that rates of wages were only to be regarded as fixed or determined by agreement when they were thereafter observed: 'established' simply meant fixed or determined in the sense of forming part of an agreement, because there was no other way by which something could be established by negotiation. (para. 29)

The Industrial Arbitration Board could not accept the Pay Board's formalist proposition, but recognized that to ignore national agreements would appear rather transparently to evade the intention of the Resolution of 1946. For clues to a solution, it turned to other instruments of Fair Wages policy—the 1909 Resolution, Orders 1305 and 1376 and the 1959 Act:

> In the Resolution of 1909 the 'recognized' wages and hours, as contrasted with the 'prevailing' wages and hours, are those which are commonly recognized by employers and trade societies; and in the two Orders and the Act the term 'recognized terms and conditions' are those the creation of which is described in words closely similar to those of Clause 1(a) of the Resolution but which

have in addition to be 'in force' or 'established' in a district. With these indications in mind, the Board have come to the conclusion that a term or condition of service is properly to be regarded as 'established' in a district if in that district it is generally recognized there as the standard by which the adequacy of terms or conditions observed by employers in the district has to be judged. (para. 44(2))

The vagueness of this formula still leaves doubt as to whether it is formal recognition or practical implementation which is the critical element in the meaning of 'established'. Thus, the I.A.B. did not 'consider that, in order to be "established", rates of pay, hours or conditions of labour must be universally or even generally paid or observed'. But this, perhaps deliberate, vagueness enabled it to reach its subtle compromise in *Crittall-Hope:*

> the rates contained in such an (national) agreement may be 'established' in a district, in the sense indicated in paragraph 44(2) above, but established only as minimum rates and not as settling any standard of what an employer will be expected actually to pay to his workers. (para. 45)

Counsel for the plaintiffs in *Racal Communications Ltd.* v. *Pay Board* [1974] I.C.R. 590 argued that 'established' should be 'construed as "fixed or settled by negotiation or arbitration and in fact paid in the district" ' (p. 559D). But in the view of Griffiths J., this was 'to strain the meaning of the language beyond permissible limits in an attempt to deal with a situation which did not exist in 1946' (p. 599E). Instead, he accepted the Pay Board's contention that 'established' meant 'fixed', arguing that to allow the element of practical implementation to enter into the meaning of 'establish' would confuse the standards of Clause 1(a) and 1(b):

> If the word 'established' is to be construed as 'fixed and in fact paid' it is difficult to see any real difference between the two clauses, for in each case it would be necessary to investigate the current level of wages being paid by other employers in like circumstances. If, on the other hand, 'established' is construed as 'fixed', the new test becomes meaningful for it sets as the standard of fairness those rates of wages set by relevant collective bargaining. (p. 600D)

He further remarked on the appearance of the word in the Agreement between the E.E.F. and the C.S.E.U. as showing it in this, 'its natural sense' (p. 600F). Yet at the hearing before the I.A.B. in Award 3293 of 3 May 1974 (*Rank Precision Industries Ltd. and The Pay Board*), a Trade Union representative submitted, as regards the 1973 National Agreement, that 'during the discussions leading up to the adoption in August 1973 of the £25 national minimum rate it had been stated that that rate was not for the purpose of the general bulk of trade union members but was only a means to raise premium payments on overtime, holidays, and the like, and that independent domestic arrangements for wage increases were to go ahead' (para. 11). Nevertheless, the judge dismissed the I.A.B.'s interpretation in *Crittall-Hope* as allowing the element of practical implementation to contaminate this 'natural' meaning (pp. 610E–602B).

In the result, the current interpretation of 'established' is subject to the conflicting views of the Industrial Arbitration Board and the Chancery Division of the High Court. The Board has adopted a pragmatic meaning, allowing for elements of both formal recognition and practical implementation. The Court has adopted a legalistic approach, insisting that only the former is relevant. One may ask whether the decision of the Board, an expert industrial arbitration tribunal with some decades of experience in applying the Fair Wages policy, ought not to be preferred to that of the Court which, on the first occasion when it was called upon to interpret the Fair Wages Resolution, has rendered it a dead letter.

Schedule 11 to the Employment Protection Act 1975 will be discussed in detail later. But it is worth noting here that while the 1946 Resolution remains in effect, the word 'established' has been omitted from the new Fair Wages policy formula contained in paragraph 2(a) of Schedule 11 (Extension of Terms and Conditions). This should avoid any further legalistic wrangling over this particular term. The substance of the dispute, however, is likely to remain in the forefront of the argument over Fair Wages policy. Thus, the *Industrial Relations Legal Information Bulletin* (No. 105 of 4 June 1975) has stated that the omission of the word 'established' was deliberate to decide the controversy between the High Court and the I.A.B. in favour of the former. If, indeed, the term was omitted for that reason, such a change appears to have been superfluous. Paragraph 2(a) of Schedule 11 replaces the provisions of section 8 of the 1959 Act, which is repealed by the 1975 Act (section 98). The terms and conditions of employment to be extended under paragraph 2(a) are those 'settled', whereas under section 8 of the 1959 Act they were those both 'established' and 'settled'. But since the terms of employment in both cases are to be decided by the same kinds of parties in the same kind of agreement or award, it is clear that the terms to be extended will not differ under the new law from those extended under the old. The only other distinction is introduced by the additional qualification made at the end of paragraph 2 of the Schedule that the terms so settled may be minimum terms. But since it is notorious that agreements negotiated between unions and organizations of employers on the national or regional level almost always settle only minimum terms and conditions, this is a statement of the obvious.

Schedule 11, however, goes beyond the policy of extension of terms and conditions formerly contained in section 8 of the 1959 Act. It also introduces elements of the Fair Wages Resolution of 1946. Under Schedule 11, a claim may be reported to A.C.A.S. that an employer is observing terms and conditions of employment less favourable than the 'general level of terms and conditions' (paragraph 2(b)). The origins of this provision lie in clause 1(b) of the 1946 Resolution. Clause 1(b) was intended to provide protection for workers not covered by the terms of collective arrangements (called 'recognized' terms under the 1959 Act). Consequently, '*In the absence of any rates of wages, hours or conditions of labour so established*' by such arrangements, a complaint was allowed under clause 1(b) of the Resolution for non-compliance with the 'general level'.

In *Crittall-Hope*, the I.A.B. held that the company's adherence to the collective arrangements specified in clause 1(a) of the Resolution *did not preclude* the application of clause 1(b). A complaint based on clause 1(b) was allowed on the grounds that, although the terms specified by clause 1(a) were 'established', they were so 'established' *only as minimum* terms and conditions of employment. The Fair Wages policy is intended to require 'fair' terms and conditions, not minima. Since there were no such fair terms 'established', clause 1(b) was applicable.

Under paragraph 1 of Schedule 11, a claim may be based on the 'general level', '*where, or so far as, there are no recognized terms and conditions*'. Following the I.A.B.'s lead, it is open to the Central Arbitration Committee to decide that where an employer is adhering only to minimum standards, it is not precluded from allowing a claim based on the 'general level'. The Committee may indeed decide that minimum terms have been settled by collective arrangements—that is are 'recognized'. But where *only* minimum terms are 'recognized', and the collective arrangements do not settle 'fair' terms, it may be held that there are no 'recognized' fair terms. Accordingly, a claim may be allowed under Schedule 11 based on the 'general level'.

Clause 1[b] and the 'District' Element

Heretofore, it is problems in the application of the primary Fair Wages standard—clause 1(a) of the 1946 Resolution—which have been discussed. The evolution of collective bargaining was described which led to national agreements being overtaken by locally agreed rates. As a result, employers were able to invoke the rates actually paid by them to show compliance with the 'Fair' Wages standard which was often much lower. Other difficulties faced by complainants were found in the determination of the appropriate 'trade or industry', in demonstrating that the organizations of employers and trade unions were representative, and that the terms concerned were duly 'established'. In the event of failure to satisfy the Industrial Court that the employer was in breach of clause 1(a), for whichever of these reasons, the complainant came to rely on the alternative and secondary Fair Wages standard of clause 1(b):

> In the absence of any rates of wages, hours or conditions of labour so established the contractor shall pay rates of wages, and observe hours and conditions of labour, which are not less favourable than the general level of wages, hours and conditions observed by other employers whose general circumstances in the trade or industry in which the contractor is engaged are similar.

The most obvious difference between the standards in clause 1(a) and clause 1(b) was the former's emphasis on the 'district' element: the standards for the relevant industry had to be established 'in the district', and they had to be created by machinery representative of workers and employers 'in the district'. In contrast, clause 1(b) made no reference whatever to a 'district' element. As has been described in detail above, this emphasis on 'district' in the Fair Wages standard was something which the trade union movement had sought to oust in the campaign to reform the Resolution which preceded the Second World War. Opposing them, the government departments were equally determined that the national agreements promoted by the unions as embodying fair standards should only be accepted where these were actually implemented in practice. The outcome of the controversy, the 1946 Resolution, saw the triumph of the departments. Clause 1(a) of the Resolution produced as a Fair Wages standard a collective arrangement between organizations of employers and trade unions representative respectively of employers and workers in the district concerned, which fixed wages, hours and conditions in that district. The national element, introduced by restricting the qualification 'fair' to standards arranged between organizations, as opposed to individual employers and trade unions, was severely curtailed by the insistence on a narrow 'district' element as well. National agreements could only be invoked where they established district rates and satisfied the criterion of representativeness in the district. In practice, however, where unions did represent substantial proportions of workers in a trade or industry in a district, and had national agreements which determined rates for that district, there was rarely a need for a Fair Wages standard. The policy was needed *wherever* government contractors evaded the national standards negotiated by the unions, regardless of local rates or representativeness. The policy was intended to eliminate inequalities in terms of employment arising due to the weakness of workers' organization and the wage-cutting competition of local entrepreneurs. It seemed unlikely that the standards specified in clause 1(a) would be of much use to that end. Consequently, in their absence, clause 1(b) became applicable.

The district emphasis of the primary Fair Wages standard of clause 1(a) appears to have led to the blurring of any distinction between 1(a) and 1(b). Frequently, the Fair Wages policy would be invoked without any reference being made to either 1(a) or 1(b) and no acknowledgment of any difference between the two. This attitude was particularly apparent in the government's application of the Fair Wages policy to its own industrial employees. In cases before the Industrial Court during the 1940s, the departments tended to invoke the Fair Wages Resolution, but reduced it to a simple and none too precise formula: 'wage rates prevailing in the district'; 'the general level of labourers' wages in the various localities . . . based upon an average of the recognized rates for labourers in various trades in the district concerned'; 'local rates in other industries'; and 'an average of agreed rates paid for comparable employment in the locality concerned by both public and private employers'.[11] The first two of these formulations preceded the 1946 Resolution, whereas the latter two were decided in 1947. The virtual identity between them indicates a degree of inattentiveness to changes in Fair Wages policy dictated by the House of Commons. This is further illustrated by Award 2004 of 28 February 1945 which concerned the Engineering Trades Joint Council for Government Industrial Establishments. Here the 1909 Resolution was invoked, although Order 1305 of 1940 had long since superseded it.

Eventually, the departments did begin to appreciate the subtleties introduced by the 1946 Resolution into their previous Fair Wages policy. This was evident in Award 2106 of 12 August 1947 which concerned the Miscellaneous Trades Joint Council for Government Industrial Establishments. Here, albeit never explicitly, the different standards of clause 1(a) and 1(b) were applied respectively to skilled and unskilled workers:

in determining the rates of pay at engineering units it is the practice to adopt the rates for the District agreed between the appropriate unions and the Engineering and Allied Employers' National Federation, or where there are no agreed rates in the District, those of the nearest distict. . . . The agreed method for fixing the labourers' rate of pay at non-engineering Air Ministry establishments is to adopt the average of agreed rates paid to the unskilled labourer in comparable industrial employment in the vicinity of the station.[12] (para. 5)

This adherence by the Official Side to agreed rates in engineering was rather disingenuous. Subsequently, in Award 2130 of 6 February 1948, the Trade Union Side decried the use of this parallel. It produced much lower wages in practice since piece-rates were common in private industry, unlike government factories. Nonetheless, the Industrial Court, somewhat reluctantly, allowed the practice to continue.

Following the passage of the 1946 Resolution, the 'district' element was apparent in the Industrial Court's willingness to enforce district agreements.[13] When it came to national agreements, however, employers charged with breach of the Resolution would defend themselves by arguing that the agreements concerned did not apply to the districts in which they operated.[14] This tendency was particularly evident in the many more cases under section 8 of the 1959 Act. That Act had apparently broadened the restrictive 'district' emphasis of the Fair Wages policy up to then. Henceforth, it was to be required only that the terms be established 'either generally or in any district' (s. 8(1)(a)), that representativeness be 'generally or in the district in question, as the case may be' (s. 8(1)(b)), and that the employer against whom the claim was made be engaged in the trade, industry or section '(or, where the operation of the agreement or award is limited to a district, an employer so engaged in that district)' (s. 8(1)(c)). Nevertheless, there persisted a tendency to invoke a 'district' element as a requirement of the policy being implemented by the Act. For example, in three of the earliest cases, Awards 2744–5 of 16 October 1959 and 2756 of 8 December 1959, employers asserted that nationally negotiated agreements were inapplicable to Scotland. They were unsuccessful in that event, but later, in Award 3244 of 5 July 1971 (*Martin & Son, Edinburgh Ltd. and National Union of Furniture Trade Operatives*), the Court was to declare that 'Scotland is properly to be regarded as a "district" for the purposes of Section 8 of the Act' (para. 38(1)). In a number of cases, district agreements were accepted as applicable by the Court, as for example, one between the T.G.W.U. and the Delivery Agents Association (Luton and Dunstable Area).[15] In other cases, the district element was introduced through the national agreement itself, which referred to local agreements.[16]

This tendency to emphasize the district element of the Fair Wages policy had the effect of attaching to clause 1(b) of the Resolution a strong district bias by no means justified by its wording. This district emphasis imposed uniformly on both Fair Wages standards could be regarded as just another blow to the T.U.C.'s pre-war ambition of utilizing national agreements as the standards of fair wages. However, it soon became apparent that the primary Fair Wages standard of national agreements, to the extent that it was embodied in clause 1(a), was becoming less and less effective. National agreements were taking on the character of minimum standards and were being gradually exceeded by locally negotiated rates. Award 2130 of 6 February 1948, a claim by the Trade Union Side of the Miscellaneous Trades Joint Council for Government Industrial Establishments, indicates how soon this development was realized by the unions. The realization was apparent in a large proportion of the cases on the Fair Wages Resolution which were concerned with wages issues. For example, in Award 2793 of 28 July 1960 (*A.S.S.E.T. and English Electric Co. Ltd., of Preston, Lancs.*) the union tried implicitly, and in Award 2812 of 7 November 1960 (*Norwich Corp. and Wroxham Dairies Ltd.*), explicitly, to avoid the national minimum standards prescribed by clause 1(a) by invoking the formula in clause 1(b). Ironically enough, therefore, perhaps the principal value of this second Fair Wages standard was in its use in tactical avoidance of the primary Fair Wages standard which had turned out to have minimal value.

This did not mean that resort to clause 1(b) was solely in the course of a tactical manoeuvre by complainants trying to avoid the minimum standards of clause 1(a). The very first case on the Fair Wages Resolution of 1946, Award 2140 of 3 March 1948 (*British Actors' Equity Association and J. D. Robertson*) was brought on clause 1(b). In cases where negotiated agreements did not exist, attempts to require government contractors to adhere to fair standards were forced to invoke clause 1(b). The best illustration is the contract cleaning industry, ten complaints concerning which came before the Industrial Court based on clause 1(b) of the Resolution.[17] Clause 1(b) appears strangely akin, in the vagueness of its language, to the amorphous standard of the 1891 Resolution. Its deficiencies, as illustrated by the contract cleaning cases, discussed later in chapter 19, bring to mind those of that first Fair Wages Resolution. They also show that in some spheres of industrial life, relationships have not fundamentally changed since the end of the last century.

The best illustration of the tactical use of clause 1(b) to avoid clause 1(a) is in the cases arising from the 1972–4 pay policy. There, applicants to the Industrial Arbitration Board expressly pointed to the minimal character of clause 1(a) standards to argue that it was clause 1(b) which was the appropriate Fair Wages standard. The sudden influx of cases drew from the Board a more sophisticated approach to the content of clause 1(b) than their previous simple averaging out of a number of local rates. Here again, Award 3290 of 24 April 1974, *Crittall-Hope and Pay Board*, is the principal case, the first few having simply accepted the applicability of clause 1(b).

An aspect of major importance to the Board's decision in *Crittall-Hope* concerns the concept of clauses 1(a) and 1(b) as equal and alternative Fair Wages standards. The company argued that clauses 1(a) and 1(b) were equal and alternative standards, that 1(a) was not fulfilled as the National Agreement had been superseded by locally negotiated rates, and that consequently 1(b) was applicable (paras. 11–12). The Pay Board argued that 1(a) and 1(b) should be considered as applying in a strictly hierarchical order:

> Discussing whether the case fell to be considered under Clause 1(a) or Clause 1(b), the Pay Board submitted that the onus was on the Company to show that Clause 1(a) was not applicable before they could ask that Clause 1(b) should be applied. If there was an appropriate agreement which governed rates of wages then there could be no question of having the case considered under Clause 1(b): the intention of the Resolution was to ensure that the trade union rate, if there was one, was paid. (para. 28)

(A similar view of clause 1(b) as a 'fall-back' standard was presented by Griffiths J. in *Racal Communications Ltd.* v. *Pay Board* [1974] I.C.R. 590, at page 600C.) As described above, the I.A.B.'s decision was a subtle compromise of these two positions: where a collective agreement fixed rates, if these turned out to be minimum rates in practice, then clause 1(a) would apply to these only as such, and clause 1(b) would apply to other aspects of the employees' terms and conditions, including rates actually paid (para. 45). Hints of this approach were visible in the company's submissions (para. 12). The reasoning behind the I.A.B.'s compromise was given in paragraph 43:

> the general purpose of the Resolution would appear to be frustrated if the effect of Clause 1(a) were to confine the workers concerned to wages, hours or conditions which are less favourable to them than the general level referred to in Clause 1(b).

Clause 1(b) had thus become of equal status to clause 1(a) in the eyes of the Industrial Arbitration Board. The applicability of the standards laid down in the Fair Wages Resolution is to be determined by the extent to which they implement the Fair Wages policy in a given context. A similar principle could well guide the Central Arbitration Committee in its application of the new Fair Wages policy in Schedule 11 to the Employment Protection Act 1975.

Two other points emerge from *Crittall-Hope* as distinguishing characteristics of clause 1(b). The case provided further definition of the district element in clause 1(b) and of the method of calculating the 'fair' rate of wages. In *Crittall-Hope*, the Company duly advanced the 'district' element explicit in clause 1(a) as excluding that clause from consideration where the national agreement in question did not have any relevance to wages paid in the district (para. 11). Consequently, as the case fell to be considered under clause 1(b), questions of comparable wage rates arose, and thus 'from what geographical area should the comparators be sought, and from what section of industry?' (para. 13). Whilst opposing the Company, the Pay Board adopted broadly the same approach in their submissions 'as to the question of the district in which the Company was located' (para. 30). The I.A.B. confirmed in its Award that the district element was critical in clause 1(a)—in para. 44(1) the words 'in the district' are underlined. But in the part of the Award concerned with applying clause 1(b), the I.A.B. was careful to distinguish the district element in clause 1(a) from that in clause 1(b). In the latter:

> the comparison between the rates of wages, hours and conditions observed by the contractor concerned and the general level of wages, hours and conditions observed by other employers is not limited to any district, although geographical propinquity may have to be taken into account in deciding whether the general circumstances of the other employers are similar. (para. 48)

The Board was careful to note that as clause 1(b) made no express reference to district rates, the introduction of a local element was only by way of the mandated comparison with 'employers whose general circumstances in the trade or industry in which the contractor is engaged are similar'.

The meticulousness of this distinction was not maintained unambiguously throughout the I.A.B.'s subsequent application of clause 1(b). Later, in para. 48, the Board referred to the standard observed by 'similarly circumstanced employers in the district', though it subsequently reverted to the precise wording of clause 1(b) (para. 49(2)). In Award 3296 of 20 May 1974 (*Sheffield Rolling Mills Ltd. and Pay Board*), the company concerned submitted that clause 1(b) meant 'the typical wages paid in the district' (para. 15). But in its Award the I.A.B. adhered to the precise wording of the clause (para. 23(3)).

Again, in Award 3300 of 29 August 1974 (*E.E.T.P.U. and Clarke &
Smith Manufacturing Co. Ltd.*), the union and the company referred
numerous times to the district element in their submissions (paras. 7,
9, 10, 24). In its determination of the relevant district, the Board
this time failed to distinguish clause 1(a) from 1(b) (para. 25(1)).
But again in its application of 1(b), it did not mention the district
element at all (paras. 25(4) and 25(5)(c)). The result is slightly
ambiguous, due to the laconic nature of the Board's Awards, but it
seems reasonably safe to say that the Board has regarded clause 1(b)
as containing a district element, to the extent that geography may
affect the comparability of similarly circumstanced employers. The
assimilation of a district element into clause 1(b) may have led to its
explicit recognition in the equivalent to clause 1(b) in the new Fair
Wages policy in Schedule 11 to the Employment Protection Act 1975.
The 'general level' is there defined as meaning that 'in the trade,
industry or section in which the employer in question is engaged in
the district in which he is so engaged' (para. 2(b)(i)).

The handling of the vital question of the district element in clause
1(b) by the Industrial Arbitration Board may be contrasted with its
treatment by the High Court in *Racal Communications Ltd.* v. *Pay Board.*
Griffiths J. simply asserted:

> When the wording of the resolution was changed in 1946 it
> introduced ... a delicate dichotomy between clause 1(a) and
> clause 1(b). The old test of practice in the district is now a fall-
> back clause contained in 1(b); the primary test is to be the rate
> fixed by collective bargaining, which it is reasonable to suppose
> would be applicable in the great majority of cases. (p. 600C)

In so far as he locates the district element primarily in clause 1(b)
and not in clause 1(a), Griffiths J. would appear to be mistaken. The
opposite is the case.

As should be clear by now, the significance of the district element
in clause 1(b) cannot be overestimated. In the Fair Wages Resolution
of 1891, the standard stipulated was 'the rate of wages generally
accepted as current for a competent workman in his trade'. That
amorphous formula was useless to trade unionists seeking to enforce
locally negotiated rates. It was impossible to establish to the satisfaction of government departments that such a trade rate existed. The
contractors were able to evade the strictures of this vague and unenforceable obligation. It was the importation of a district element
by some departments, thus changing the formula in their contracts,
which made the standard more concrete and capable of implementation. The significance of the I.A.B.'s interpretation in *Crittall-Hope* is

similarly apparent: it not only avoids the imposition of exclusively minimal terms and conditions through clause 1(a), it also creates a standard of wages, hours and conditions negotiated locally as the applicable standard.

In this development there lies a substantial danger which was already visible in previous Awards. The Board has creatively opened a path along which trade unions may go to enforce actually paid locally negotiated rates. The Board has not, however, given any clues as to the method by which it calculates the Fair Wages standard applicable—the 'general level'. The method of ascertaining the standard of wages required was subject to conflicting views in *Crittall-Hope*. In the company's opinion 'any exercise to determine a general level could not be expected to produce a precise figure; at best it could be only a "broad brush" exercise':

> The Company suggested that where statistics showed that wages clustered around the median or arithmetical average it would be permissible to judge that the general level was also near to those points. It could not be an accurately determined figure but one arrived at by the Board using their collective and perhaps intuitive judgment. (para. 20)

Arguing to the contrary, the Pay Board rejected the concepts of 'clusters' and 'medians':

> In the Pay Board's opinion statisticians would not accept such a concept: they would think it was far too imprecise. The Pay Board suggested that the use of quartiles would provide a useful yardstick: if the first and fourth quartiles (the highest and the lowest) was ignored, the second and third, which comprised the middle 50 per cent of employers, would provide the general level of wages. It was contended that an employer paying a rate within that middle band or even at the lower end of it was complying with the requirement of the Resolution. (para. 35)

The I.A.B., unfortunately, said nothing that would enlighten one as to its calculation of Fair Wage rates in its Award. It gave no indication of which of the two, or any other, methods it preferred. It simply reiterated its dedication to 'a general comparison' in the broadest terms (para. 48). The Award itself allowed some of the specified wage increases, but not others requested. Subsequent cases have done nothing to enlighten potential applicants to the Board as to how to go about proving that clause 1(b) is being infringed. The Awards provide no guidance to future applicants under Schedule 11 to the

Employment Protection Act 1975 as to what constitutes a 'general level of terms and conditions'.

Moreover, in a number of complaints based on clause 1(b) which preceded *Crittall-Hope*, the I.A.B. denied the complainants any satisfaction at all. The reason was the failure of the complainant to demonstrate to the satisfaction of the Board, in the words of the last of them 'that in relation to the industry concerned there is any ascertainable level of wages, hours or conditions of labour observed by other employers whose general circumstances in the industry are similar, or if so what that level is'.[18] Ominously, even after *Crittall-Hope*, the Board was prepared to deny the claim in Award 3300 of 29 August 1974 (*E.E.T.P.U. and Clarke & Smith Manufacturing Co. Ltd.*) on the basis that 'insufficient evidence was placed before the Board to enable them to decide whether or not there was at the date of the hearing a general level of wages paid by similarly-circumstanced employers which was higher than the minimum rates prescribed by the May 1974 Agreement' (para. 25(5)(c)). So the Board's revival of the Fair Wages policy may be for naught in the face of its reluctance to specify the proper method of calculating the 'general level' it will enforce. The implications for the successful utilization of Schedule 11 to the Employment Protection Act 1975 are clear. On the vital issue of what evidence is necessary to convince the Central Arbitration Committee that an ascertainable general level of terms and conditions exists which employers must observe, trade unions are left guessing.[19]

NOTES

1. Another recent case concerned with elaborating the phrase 'section of a trade or industry' was Award 3213 of 11 May 1970 (*Kodak Ltd. and A.C.T.A.T.*), in which a High Court case attempting to decipher similar language in the Industrial Disputes Order (Order 1376 of 1951) was cited: *R. v. Industrial Disputes Tribunal, ex parte Courage & Co. Ltd.* [1956] 3 All E.R. 411.

2. Award 1855 of 15 April 1942, *N.U.G.M.W. and Caernarvon Corp.* (claim under the Industrial Courts Act 1919 succeeded); Award 2779 of 11 May 1960, *Eton House School and N.U.G.M.W.* (claim under the 1959 Act failed); and Award 2847 of 8 June 1961, *City of Leicester Working Men's Club and Variety Artistes Federation* (claim under the 1959 Act failed).

3. Award 1802 of 9 May 1941, *N.U.P.E.*

and *North Riding County Council* (claim succeeded); Award 1938 of 3 February 1944, *N.U.G.M.W. and A. Wooton & Sons Ltd.* (claim succeeded); Award 1944 of 28 February 1944 (claim failed).

4. See Awards 2236 of 13 October 1949; 2672 of 21 November 1957; 2353-4 of 7 December 1951; and 2637 of 11 January 1957.

5. See Awards 2549 of 20 December 1954; 2675 of 19 December 1957; and 2245 of 6 December 1949.

6. For a case similar in substance many years later, where the company concerned tried to use section 15(1) of the Civil Aviation Act 1949 to avoid the claim under section 8 of the 1959 Act, see Award 3157 of 28 December 1967, *Manchester Airport Agencies and T.G.W.U.* The Court rejected

the complaint on the ground simply that the company were not engaged in the industry to which the agreements negotiated in the N.J.C. for Civil Air Transport applied.

7. Award 2754 of 2 December 1959, *National Society of Painters and Burns Shopfitters* (it did; complaint upheld); Award 2808 of 25 October 1960 (it did; complaint upheld); Award 2987 of 27 August 1963, *Corp. of London and N.U.G.M.W.* (complaint rejected); Award 3044 of 30 October 1964 (complaint rejected); Awards 3124 of 5 December 1966 and 3203 of 27 November 1969 (both complaints rejected).

8. Award 2872 of 28 September 1961 (complaint upheld); Award 3063 of 12 April 1965, *Haigh & Heppenstall Ltd. and Yorkshire Cotton Operatives Association* (complaint rejected); Award 3099 of 26 April 1966 (complaint rejected); Award 3102 of 18 May 1966, *Aston Martin Lagonda Ltd. and A.E.U.* (complaint rejected); Award 3233 of 7 December 1970, *Atcost (Northern) Ltd. and D.A.T.A.* (complaint failed even though the company actually agreed at the hearing to observe the engineering Agreement for the future); Award 3269 of 2 August 1972, *Futura Rubber Co. Ltd. and National Union of Footwear, Leather & Allied Trades* (complaint upheld).

9. Award 3169 of 31 May 1968. For other examples, see Award 2788 of 5 July 1960 (complaint upheld); Awards 2804 and 2805 of 27 September 1960 (complaints rejected); Award 2924 of 7 August 1962, *Parnall & Sons Ltd. and National Union of Furniture Trade Operatives* (complaint upheld); Award 3084 of 10 January 1966 (complaint rejected); and Award 3147 of 30 June 1967, *Woodhall-Duckham Ltd. and D.A.T.A.* (complaint rejected).

10. Award 1781 of 13 January 1941, *Electrical Power Engineers' Association and Stockton-on-Tees Corp.;* Award 1808 of 13 June 1941, *Electrical Power Engineers' Association and Worthing Corp.;* and Award 1823 of 26 August 1941, *N.U.P.E. and Morley Town Council Waterworks Committee.*

11. Respectively: Award 1803 of 21 May 1941, *Trade Union Side of the Shipbuilding Trade Joint Council for Government Departments and Official Side;* Award 1861 of 16 June 1942, *Trade Union Side of the Miscellaneous Trades Joint Council for Government Industrial Establishments and Official Side,* at para. 4; Award 2090 of 8 May 1947, *Trade Union Side of the Mis-*cellaneous Trades Joint Council for Government Industrial Establishments and Official Side, at para. 4; and Award 2105 of 12 August 1947, *Trade Union Side of the Miscellaneous Trades J.C. for Government Industrial Establishments and Official Side,* at para. 4.

12. See also the statements by Treasury Officials in their Evidence to the Royal Commission on Trade Unions and Employers' Associations, *Minutes of Evidence* No. 10, H.M. Treasury, Oral Evidence, 14 December 1965, at Q. 1595.

13. For example, Awards 2176–8 of 30 August 1948 (under the Road Traffic Act 1930, as amended), *T.G.W.U. and Messrs. Gibson Bros.; T.G.W.U. and L. D. Brown; T.G.W.U. and Robinson & Son (Burbage) Ltd.* Award 2278 of 14 November 1950, *Scottish Painters' Society and Structural Painters Ltd.*

14. For example, Awards 2353 and 2354 of 7 December 1951, *N.J.C. for Civil Air Transport and Short Bros. & Harland Ltd., Kent; N.J.C. for Civil Air Transport and Marshall's Flying School Ltd., Cambridge.* For a later case, see Award 3206 of 24 March 1970, *C.S.U. and Cleaners Ltd.,* at para. 20.

15. Award 3127 of 23 January 1967. See also, for example, Award 2879 fo 30 November 1961; Award 3109 of 28 July 1966; Award 3123 of 29 November 1966; and Award 3151 of 17 August 1967.

16. See, for example, Award 2779 of 11 May 1960 (referring to District Joint Councils for Local Authorities (Manual Workers)); Award 2800 of 29 August 1960 (referring to Regional Joint Committees for the Building Industry); Award 3230 of 13 October 1970 and Award 3204 of 3 February 1970.

17. The ten cases between 1968 and 1973 were Awards 3161, 3212, 3216–19, 3242–3 and 3275. All were claims based, in part, on clause 1(b) of the Resolution except for Award 3206 of 24 March 1970, *C.S.U. and Cleaners Ltd.,* in which the complainant union stated: 'Although the Union considered that Clause 1(a) of the Fair Wages Resolution could be said to be applicable in the present reference, they believed that their case was good under Clause 1(b)' (para. 9). The Court held the company to be in breach of Clause 1(b) (para. 29(1)).

18. Award 3288 of 19 March 1974, *Association of Professional, Executive, Clerical and Computer Staff and G.E.C. Turbine Generators Ltd.,* at para. 35(2). See also Awards 2637 of 11 January 1957, *N.U.P.E. and St.*

Andrew's & Red Cross Scottish Ambulance Service, at para. 6; 3267 of 26 July 1972, *A.U.E.W. and Multiplex Designs Ltd.*, at para. 34(1)(c); and Award 3285 of 17 December 1973, *A.U.E.W. and Hiatt & Co. Ltd.*, at para. 32(c).

19. A study of the policy of the Industrial Disputes Tribunal in its wage awards could only conclude that it settled claims at 'the going rate'. It sought to give 'about as much as that which was generally available elsewhere'. See W. E. J. McCarthy, *Compulsory Arbitration in Britain: The Work of the Industrial Disputes Tribunal*, Royal Commission on Trade Unions and Employers' Associations, Research Paper No. 8, H.M.S.O., 1968, at paras. 25ff.

I7

Clause 4 and Trade Union Protection

Clause 4 of the Fair Wages Resolution of 1946 stipulates that:

> The contractor shall recognize the freedom of his workpeople to be members of trade unions.

It might suffice, as an assessment of this provision, to state simply that in not one of the eight cases brought by trade unions complaining of breach of this clause was the contractor held blameworthy by the Industrial Court or the Industrial Arbitration Board.[1] But there are some lessons to be learned from an analysis of the effects of the clause and its deficiencies. Three aspects of an employer's relationship to organized labour will be covered, each of which aroused controversy during the period after 1946: the freedom of workers to join trade unions, the bargaining rights of the unions, and the closed shop and inter-union conflicts. Finally, an aspect will be examined which is indirectly related to these problems: the position adopted by the Industrial Court regarding the enforcement of disputes procedure agreements between trade unions and employers.

Freedom to Belong to a Trade Union

Little dissent was to be found amongst employers, trade unions or government departments as to the prescribed formula of freedom to belong to trade unions. The problems arose in attempts to define more precisely whether this formula granted trade union demands. Thus, in 1963 the Minister of Labour could uphold in the House of Commons the freedom of contractors' employees to be trade union members, but could also maintain that: 'It does not require them to recognize trade unions'.[2] Or in the following year, the General Council of the T.U.C.,

For notes see p. 353

in response to a query, could confirm to the 1964 Annual Congress the freedom declared in clause 4, but go on to deny that it meant 'that all employees must be union members'.

The substance of the freedom to belong to a trade union, as it emerged from the cases before the Industrial Court, was tenuous indeed. In each of the eight cases, the Court limited itself to a very brief statement to the effect, as in Award 3212 of 1 May 1970 (*C.S.U. and General Cleaning Contractors (Northern) Ltd.*), that: 'It has not been established that the Company have failed to comply with the require-ment of Clause 4 of the Resolution' (para. 38(3)). The varied circum-stances which gave rise to this uniform conclusion belie the promise of protection made in clause 4. The employers concerned were anti-union, some of them virulently so. Thus, in Award 2821 of 13 February 1961 (*A.S.S.E.T. and Walter MacFarlane & Co. Ltd. of Glasgow*) the company claimed they allowed their employees the freedom to belong to the union, but refused to recognize the union for negotiating purposes, arguing that this was not obligatory under the Resolution. Award 3039 of 28 August 1964 records the story of the long and unsuccessful struggle by the Association of Supervisory Staffs, Executives and Technicians for recognition by M. Wiseman & Co. Ltd. The Industrial Court accepted the employer's evidence, though he had even attempted to prevent the union from being present as a party before the Court, asserting that the dispute concerned the contract between the Ministry and the contractor only (para. 6). At the Annual Trades Union Congress later in 1964, the General Secretary of A.S.S.E.T. charac-terized the Resolution as 'weakly worded and with flimsy text': 'The protection of the Fair Wages Resolution now is absolutely inadequate'. Yet again in Award 3071 of 3 June 1965 (*National Union of Dyers, Bleachers and Textile Workers and William Denby & Sons Ltd., Yorkshire*), a company which refused to recognize any right on the part of the union to negotiate with them was held to comply with clause 4.

Other blatant examples exist of animus by employers towards trade unions which were regarded as acceptable by the Court and the government departments. In Award 3212 of 1 May 1970 (*C.S.U. and General Cleaning Contractors (Northern) Ltd.*) the company had taken over a previous cleaning contract, but had refused to engage trade unionists working there on the grounds of unsatisfactory work. In its defence, the company also submitted that in any event, 'Clause 4 of the Resolution was related by its terms to people in the employment of the employer in question and not to workpeople who were not yet employed by him' (para. 36). The government department concerned refused to do anything about it, so the Civil Service Union reported to the Annual Trades Union Congress in September 1970. The Union complained that 'the Civil Service Department and the Post Office could not care less whether or not trade unionists are barred from employment in Government contracts'. At the same Congress, the Post Office Engineering Union condemned anti-trade union contractors who played 'some sort of game of finding loopholes and avoiding responsibilities'; and the National Union of Public Employees referred to examples of 'the failure of some of the public authorities to provide adequate safeguards against this Tolpuddle type of tyranny'. But in Award 3267 of 26 July 1972 (*A.U.E.W. and Multiplex Designs Ltd.*), a contractor dismissed some shop stewards for 'insubordination', 'not fitting in', and generally being against the company's interests (paras. 16–17). Other unionists struck in support and were dismissed as well. The I.A.B. awarded as follows:

> The Board are of the opinion that at the time of the events referred to in paragraphs 16 and 17 above trade union activities were unwelcome to the Company. They also find that when the witness referred to in paragraph 16 was dismissed by the Company on the 23rd December 1971 they were aware that he was a member of the Union. The Board are however inclined to think that when they dismissed this worker, and also when on the 3rd January 1972 they dismissed the workers who had staged a stoppage of work they did so because of their view of these workers' conduct as employees rather than because they were members of the Union. (para. 34(2))

There was, consequently, no breach of clause 4.[3]

Anti-union bias by employers was exposed in other Fair Wages policy cases where clause 4 protection was not available. In cases under the 1959 Act, for example, as in the successful claim in Award 3119 of 3 November 1966 (*Worden Printers and N.G.A.*), the company simply refused to have anything to do with the Union. Or, in Award 3234 of 7 December 1970, A.C.T.A.T. had previously won a claim on behalf of the employees of Kodak Ltd., but were unsuccessful in claiming that 'the Company were determined to discriminate against the workers concerned, to make the Award unpopular and to discredit the Association' (para. 8). In other cases under the Fair Wages Resolution, from very early on—Award 2370 of 7 April 1952 (*N.U.V.B. and Drake Motors Ltd.*) where the employer refused to discuss terms with union representatives, to much later—Award 3300 of 29 August 1974 (*E.E.T.P.U. and Clarke & Smith Manufacturing Co. Ltd.*) where the company declared that 'they did not recognize any trade union for the purposes of collective bargaining' (para.15), the I.A.B. did not see fit to report this attitude as at all inconsistent with government policy on contractors' relationships with organized labour. In sum: in the eyes of the Industrial Court and government departments, anti-union attitudes and behaviour, even when openly exhibited, did not render employers in breach of the Fair Wages Resolution. In terms of the protection of trade union rights, clause 4 has been useless.

Recognition of Trade Unions

Many of the above-mentioned cases concerned employers who, while paying lip-service to their obligation to allow their employees to join unions, effectively nullified that freedom by refusing to allow unions to fulfil any function. In the face of continual rejection of their complaints, the unions resigned themselves to the fact that the Industrial Court was not going to pierce the facade of an employer's verbal acceptance of trade union rights. Thus, in Awards 3039 of 28 August 1964 (*A.S.S.E.T. and M. Wiseman & Co. Ltd.*) and 3071 of 3 June 1965 (*National Union of Dyers, Bleachers & Textile Workers and W. Denby & Sons Ltd., Yorkshire*), the unions conceded that they were not claiming breach of clause 4 because of the employers' refusal to negotiate: 'The Association appreciated that recognition was not one of the matters covered by the Resolution'. Nonetheless, in the latter Award, the Union went on to protest:

> Although that Clause (4) did not expressly state that employers should recognize trade unions, the Union believed that such recognition was implicit in its terms. In their view the freedom of a worker to belong to a union was pointless unless his union was enabled to carry out effectively the functions of representing their members and negotiating on their behalf. (para. 9)

A great deal of dissatisfaction was manifested during the early 1960s. Questions were raised in the House of Commons in 1962–3 about Securicor's dismissal of trade unionists who had refused to sign a yellow-dog contract. Only after the intervention of the Ministry of Labour would the firm retract, but it still did not recognize the union and would not negotiate with it. In June 1964 Julius Silverman, M.P., introduced a Bill on the Fair Wages Clause to enable the Industrial Court to deal with discrimination against trade unions, specifically the Foremen and Staff Mutual Benefit Society. This attempt to extend the protection beyond the existing clause 4 came to nothing.[4] At the Annual Trades Union Congress in September 1964, Clive Jenkins castigated this Benefit Society as an 'anti-trade union organization'. He gave the Congress a detailed account of an employer who was a public contractor and had refused to reinstate the chairman, the secretary, a negotiating committee member and the man who had started the union organization in the factory after a strike. At the same Congress, the General Council reported on a request from A.C.T.A.T. that an amendment should be sought to clause 4 to strengthen it by providing that a contractor should also be obliged not to deny employees facilities for trade union negotiation and representation. The General Council demurred, arguing that where the unions were insufficiently strong, the employer could not be compelled to negotiate. Also, a legislative definition of 'trade union' might lead to the recognition of non-bona fide organizations. Still, in 1966, Clive Jenkins was to be found protesting to the Donovan Commission of the disgraceful situations resulting from the fact that:

> as long as the employer does not discriminate against the fact of trade union membership he does not have to recognize the union. . . . The Fair Wages Resolution was a rudimentary attempt to set up a code. What we need to do is to develop and extend it.

Efforts continued during the early 1970s. Further to a resolution passed at the 1970 Trades Union Congress, the General Council considered a letter from the Post Office Engineering Union which proposed the insertion of clauses in the Fair Wages Resolution as to: (a) the production of proof that the contractor recognized and negotiated with the appropriate union; (b) making non-observance of the Resolution grounds for terminating the contract; and (c) making it obligatory on the main contractor to notify the Civil Service Department of the names and addresses of all sub-contractors so that they should be required to give the same assurances to the departments as those required from the main contractor. At a meeting on 26 May 1971, the Chief Secretary to the Treasury had these points put to him. He replied that the Government was unable to accept the changes, though the departments 'would ensure that the spirit as well as the letter of the Fair Wages Resolution was observed in all cases'. Further questions were raised in the House of Commons in 1971 and 1972 about the refusal of contractors in the insurance and contract cleaning industries to recognize trade unions. The Government's reply was that clause 4 covered only freedom to belong; the new Industrial Relations Act 1971 covered recognition by employers of trade unions.[5] Yet precisely at this time, the eleven largest employers in contract cleaning (represented by the Contract Cleaning and Maintenance Association) had rejected the suggestion of the Department of Employment that a joint meeting with the four unions principally concerned in the industry (C.S.U., N.U.G.M.W., N.U.P.E. and the T.G.W.U.)

be held under the Department's chairmanship. The evidence appears to be that neither the government departments nor the Industrial Court regarded the trade union freedom in the Fair Wages Resolution as granting trade unions any role as representatives of their members—employees of government contractors.

Union Security

Two cases on clause 4 of the Resolution concerned inter-union disputes: Award 2672 of 21 November 1957 (*Amalgamated Society of Woodcutting Machinists and Messrs. Bartlett Materials-Handling Ltd.*, in which the rival union was the T.G.W.U.) and Award 3009 of 8 April 1964 (*N.A.T. and The Pressed Steel Co. Ltd., Cowley, Oxford*, in which the rival union was the A.E.U.). The companies refused to negotiate with the complainant union, and in one case made a speech threatening sackings and in the other actually sacked the workers concerned. In both cases the Industrial Court held that neither the threats nor the sackings amounted to a breach of clause 4. One is hard put to think what an employer has to do in order to breach the requirement of the Resolution. If the Court was following a policy of single-union representation, it should have done so explicitly. Otherwise, the most anti-union actions of an employer are made to appear legitimate.

In cases under the 1959 Act, the Industrial Court has intervened in questions concerned with union security. In Award 2787 of 4 July 1960 the union and the employers' association had agreed that new machinery was to be introduced and operated by women only in certain cases. One employer defied this arrangement. The union complained and the Court awarded that the company 'shall employ males only'. One is somewhat baffled at how the Court intended its Award to 'have effect as an implied term of the contract of employment', as required by section 8(4) of the 1959 Act. In Award 2870 of 21 September 1961 an attempt by the National Society of Metal Mechanics to safeguard its membership from the A.E.U. by forcing an employer, Rolls-Royce Ltd., to register them failed. And again in a previous Award 2801 of 29 August 1960 the Court had refused to force the employer to register his apprentices. But in eight other cases between 1961–4 (Awards 2880, 2882–3, 2981, 2997, 3000, 3023 and 3047) the Union succeeded in its attempt.

Individual trade unions attempted a number of times to raise the question of a closed shop on government contracts. At the Annual Trades Union Congress of 1963, the Variety Artistes' Federation moved that in the spirit of the Fair Wages Resolution local government authorities should ensure that their contractors engage members of trade unions. The Union pointed to agreements with the Lambeth Borough Council and the Corporation of Liverpool which had undertaken to engage only performers 'who are members of a trade union affiliated to Congress'. The London County Council, on the other hand, would not 'wear it at any price'. In reply to this motion, the General Council reported back to the Congress of 1964 that the Variety Artistes' Federation had been informed 'that the Fair Wages Resolution was not as comprehensive as they believed'.

At the 1970 Congress, a resolution moved by the Post Office Engineering Union and seconded by the Civil Service Union called upon the Government 'to ensure that, when contract work has to be carried out for the any Government Department or nationalized industry, a prerequisite is that the "contractor" employs "organized labour" '. In a follow-up letter, the P.O.E.U. suggested that the T.U.C. might maintain a register of approved contractors to the public sector who recognized and negotiated with unions affiliated to the T.U.C. This time the General Council's reply took the view that this suggestion would raise a number of practical difficulties and that the nature and scale of the complaints about contractors would not justify embarking on such a scheme. The P.O.E.U. further suggested the insertion of a new clause in the Resolution making it obligatory on contractors to provide facilities to the appropriate union or unions for their organizers to visit sites. Again, the General Council reported back to the 1971 Congress in the negative: any difficulties concerning access to sites could best be dealt with on the basis of direct approaches by unions to the contractors concerned.

The right to trade union recognition is now enshrined in the Employment Protection Act 1975 and the legitimacy of the closed shop has been sustained by the provisions for union membership agreements in the Trade Union and Labour Relations Act 1974 (as amended). It is by no means inconceivable that government contractors and others should be compelled both to recognize and negotiate with trade unions, and to ensure that their employees become trade union members. A precedent exists: in Award 1826 of 15 September 1941, Brancepeth Gas and Coke Ltd. had refused to adhere, with regard to twenty-five key workers, to an agreement between the Durham Coke Owners Association and the National Union of Cokemen and Bye-Product Workers, that it be a condition of employment that all workers join the union. The Industrial Court, under the chairmanship of Sir Harold Morris, held, following Article 5(1) of Order 1305 of 1940, that the above condition was one of the 'recognized terms and conditions' in that industry in that district:

The Court accordingly award that for the period of the war (as stated in the agreement) membership of the appropriate trade union shall be a condition of employment of all workers employed by the Company. (para. 9)

There is no reason why what was done then could not be done now.

Enforcement of Procedure Agreements

Finally, a question related to the clause 4 protection of trade union freedom was whether the Industrial Court would enforce agreements requiring a degree of recognition by employers of trade unions— disputes procedure agreements. In Award 2370 of 7 April 1952 the Court rejected a complaint based on the Fair Wages Resolution that Drake Motors Ltd. was refusing to meet the N.U.V.B. in breach of the agreed Procedure for Settling Differences Relating to Wages and Conditions of Employment, being part of the general conditions of the relevant National Joint Industrial Council Agreement. And the following year, in Award 2481 of 4 November 1953, the Court rejected an A.E.U. complaint based on clause 4 where the employer, the Medical Supply Association Ltd., had ignored certain 'understandings' which laid out consultative procedures to occur in the event of redundancy. But the principal debate centred on trade union claims under the 1959 Act: that if the employer failed to adhere to the agreed procedures, the Industrial Court should 'make an award requiring the employer to observe the recognized terms and conditions' (section 8(3)).

First indications were that the Court would look favourably on such claims. In Award 2875 of 8 November 1961 Northampton City Council refused to accept the award of a tribunal designated by the grievance procedure provided for in the Medical Whitley Council Agreement establishing terms and conditions of employment of County Medical Officers of Health. In a claim by the British Medical Association under the 1959 Act, the Court held, *inter alia*, that the terms and conditions applicable to the case were those laid down in the Whitley Council Agreements 'and in the Agreed Procedure which is incorporated in those Agreements'. Accordingly, Northampton City Council was bound by the award of the tribunal under the Procedure. Similarly, in Awards 2950 and 2951 of 12 February 1963, a salary dispute was submitted to a 'Disputes Panel' in accordance with a disputes procedure agreement. The Panel's decision supported the Unions—the Chief Fire Officers' Association and the National Association of Fire Officers—but the employer, the South Western Fire Area

Joint Board, refused to implement the award. In a claim to the Industrial Court, it was held that the employer was bound by the National Joint Council Agreements, and insofar as these provide for adherence to the decision of the Disputes Panel, the employer must comply with it. Again, in Award 3026 of 20 July 1964, the National Society of Metal Mechanics attempted to obtain enforcement of three agreements in the engineering industry, including one dated 2 June 1922: 'which recognized the right of trade unions to function and emphasized the value of consultation' (para. 4). The employer, Newtown Polishing Co. Ltd., professed not to understand this contention of the Union (para. 13). In its Award, the Industrial Court held that all three agreements contained applicable terms (para. 14). Although this presumably included the 1922 Procedure Agreement, it was ominous that nothing was said specifically about the problem of union recognition.

The turning point came in Award 3059 of 1 March 1965. Reference was made during the hearing of that case to the decision some ten years earlier of the Court of Appeal in *R.* v. *Industrial Disputes Tribunal, ex parte Portland U.D.C.* [1955] 3 All E.R. 18. In that case, Lord Justice Romer had said of certain procedural provisions:

> I do not regard paragraph 25(2) as forming part of the 'recognized terms and conditions' within the purview of that phrase as used in article 2 of the Order of 1951. The scheme admittedly formulates a complete code of terms and conditions, but that is not to say that a term or condition of employment emerges from every paragraph of the scheme. No such term or condition emerges from paragraph 25(2) which does no more than provide administrative machinery for the purpose of settling questions. (p. 28)

Lord Justice Denning agreed: 'Furthermore paragraph 25(2) is not, properly speaking, one of the "terms and conditions of employment" at all. It is only machinery for settling a difference' (p. 23). The influence of an interpretation of the Court of Appeal narrowing down the scope of the Fair Wages formula in Order 1376 overcame the independent judgment of the Industrial Court. Both the Lords Justices of Appeal were quoted in paragraph 27 of the Court's Awards. And in paragraph 28(2), the Court held that certain provisions relating to procedures for the avoidance of disputes, and the appointment and functions of shop stewards, were 'not terms or conditions of employment, or recognized terms or conditions, within the meaning of Section 8 of the Act'. The decision of the Courts overwhelmed the better judgment of the Industrial Court here, as it failed to do almost a decade later, when the Industrial Arbitration Board refused to follow *Racal*.

Thus, the Industrial Court's application of the agreements in Award 3026 of 20 July 1964 was refined in a retrospective interpretation in Award 3069 of 12 May 1965: 'The Court's view was and is that none of the provisions of the Procedure Agreement referred to ... constitute terms or conditions of employment or, consequently, recognized terms or conditions within the meaning of Section 8' (para. 10). In Award 3105 of 20 June 1966, the Court, following Award 3059, held that a provision in a National Agreement relating to the appointment of a shop steward was not a term or condition within the meaning of Section 8. And in Award 3127 of 23 January 1967, it was already being conceded that:

> While the Union would have preferred that the Court require the Company to observe all the provisions of the Luton Agreement, including those relating to the procedure for the avoidance of disputes, they recognized that in Award(s) (3026 and 3069) the Court had taken the view that similar provisions relating to such procedure were not recognized terms or conditions of employment within the meaning of the Act. (para. 6)

There is some evidence, however, that the Industrial Court did not regard itself as irrevocably wedded to this restrictive interpretation of 'recognized terms and conditions'. Two cases in 1969 and 1970 concerned a procedure laid down by the National Joint Council for Local Authorities' Administrative, Professional, Technical and Clerical Services. It provided for the determination of 'any question as to the rights of an officer under the Scheme', first, by the employing authority, with an appeal to the Provincial Council. Despite its previous decisions that procedural provisions were not recognized terms and conditions, the Industrial Court held in Award 3190 of 24 April 1969 that:

> The provisions of the National Scheme, including the obligation on Local Authorities to abide by the decision of the appropriate Council, constitute recognized terms and conditions of employment applicable to the officer concerned in the claim. (para. 27(1))

(The claim nonetheless failed as the Council concerned had not yet come to a 'firm decision' (paras. 20–1).) And in Award 3227 of 25 August 1970, the Court held that the failure of the Local Authority to implement the decision of the Provincial Council meant that they were not observing the recognized terms and conditions: 'the recognized terms and conditions include provision for the hearing of grading appeals by a Provincial Council and by the National Joint Council' (para. 21(1)).

Another indication of flexibility is to be found in Award 3225 of 10 August 1970 (*B.A.L.P.A. and B.U.A. Ltd.*), a claim based on the Fair Wages formula in Section 15 of the Civil Aviation Act 1949. Here the Industrial Court affirmed the view expressed in Awards 3026, 3059, 3069 and 3105, following Lords Justices Denning and Romer in the *Portland* case, that certain disputes procedure provisions did not come within the scope of the formula: 'They do not think that employers or employees would regard provisions of the kind in question as, in ordinary parlance, terms or conditions of employment' (para. 152(c)(iii)). To this, however, the Court attached the following addendum:

> What is said in (iii) above is not to be taken as meaning that what is truly a term or condition of employment ceases to be properly so described because it lays down procedures or 'machinery' for determining an employee's rights in relation to the term or condition. Examples of such provisions are those contained in the B.E.A. contract of service which relate to promotions and transfers and to redundancy. (para. 152(c)(iv))

The potential of the Fair Wages policy being used for the enforcement of procedure agreements is, therefore, rather ambiguous. On the one hand, it seems clear that the Industrial Court would not require employers to adhere to all procedures laid down in agreements with trade unions. In Award 3234 of 7 December 1970, the Court cited the series of Awards following the *Portland* case as justifying its refusal to enforce clauses in agreements which dealt with recognition by employers of union representatives and with disputes procedures. In further justification it cited Award 3225 on the Civil Aviation Act 1949 and added 'also because the said provisions are in the main concerned with the mutual rights and obligations of the parties to the said Agreement and not with the mutual rights and obligations of employers and employees' (para. 15(4)). On the other hand, it also seems that once an employer had entered into the procedures agreed upon, the Court would not permit him to withdraw. He was bound to implement the resulting award. Further, the Court was prepared to consider the enforcement of some disputes settlement machinery defined in a procedure agreement, if it fell within the terms of paragraph 152(c)(iv) of Award 3225 quoted above: if 'it lays down procedures or "machinery" for determining an employee's rights'. This could cover cases where terms of employment are subject to joint determination following a procedure laid down in the Agreement, should disputes as to the interpretation or application of agreed terms arise. In sum, the restrictive view adopted by the Court of Appeal in

1955 no longer holds sway. Certainly, a contrary view would accord much better with the increasing tendency towards joint decision-making in industry. An interpretation which encourages the spread of agreed machinery for resolving disputes is clearly to be preferred.[6]

NOTES

1. Awards 2481, 2672, 2821, 3009, 3039, 3071, 3212 and 3267. In one other case, a complaint of breach of clause 4 was withdrawn before any decision: Award 2815 of 13 December 1960, *Association of Scientific Workers and Park Foundry (Belper) Ltd., Derby.*

2. Parl. Deb., H. of C. (Fifth Series); 8 July 1963, vol. 650, cols. 840–2, per Mr. Hare.

3. The Company specifically requested the Board to consider if the Union concerned, the A.U.E.W., qualified as a trade union for the protection of clause 4, as it was not registered, and thus not a trade union for the purposes of the Industrial Relations Act 1971 (para. 31). The Board stated that it had no power to decide on such a question of law, but expressed the opinion that clause 4 should not be cut down by the restrictive definition of 'trade union' in the Act of 1971 (para. 34(2)).

4. For references to these events, see Parl. Deb., H. of C. (Fifth Series); 18 December 1962, vol. 669, cols. 1077–9; 8 July 1963, vol. 680, cols. 840–2; 10 June 1964, vol. 696, cols. 454–6.

5. See Parl. Deb., H. of C. (Fifth Series); 25 November 1971, vol. 826, col. 452 (Written Answers), per Mr. Patrick Jenkin; and 20 April 1972, vol. 835, cols. 145–6 (Written Answers), per Mr. Kenneth Baker.

6. In this chapter, reference has been made to the following sources:

—Royal Commission on Trade Unions and Employers' Associations, *Minutes of Evidence* No. 53; A.S.S.E.T., Oral Evidence given 25 October 1966, at Q. 8514, p. 2285.

—Report of the 95th Annual Trades Union Congress, Brighton, 1963, at pp. 312–13.

—Report of the General Council to the 96th Annual T.U.C., Blackpool, 1964, para. 46, p. 125 and para. 100, p. 152.

—Report of the 96th Annual T.U.C., Blackpool, 1964, pp. 527–8.

—Report of the 102nd Annual T.U.C., Brighton, 1970, at pp. 555–7.

—Report of the General Council to the 103rd Annual T.U.C., Blackpool, 1971, para. 67 at pp. 51–2.

—Report of the General Council to the 104th Annual T.U.C., Brighton, 1972, para. 63, at pp. 47–8.

18

Clause 6 and the Control of Sub-contractors

Sub-contracting

As Hepple and O'Higgins have put it: 'sub-contracting is older than the industrial revolution'. In 1888 and 1890 the Trades Union Congress passed resolutions requesting government departments to prevent any contract 'being carried out by sub-contractors or sweaters' and 'to secure the insertion of a clause in all contracts prohibiting subletting'. The original Fair Wages Resolution proposed by Sydney Buxton in the House of Commons on 13 February 1891 required:

> that the contractor should, under penalty, be prohibited from sub-letting any portion of his contract, except where the Department concerned specifically allows the sub-letting of such special portions of the work as would not be produced or carried out by the contractor in the ordinary course of his business.

The Government sponsored Resolution of 1891 which was eventually passed by the House of Commons, however, simply required the departments 'to insert such conditions as may prevent the abuses arising from subletting'. Dissatisfaction with the enforcement of this policy led to a substantial tightening up of the provisions regulating sub-contracting in the Fair Wages Resolution of 1909:

> The contractor shall be prohibited from transferring or assigning directly or indirectly, to any person or persons whatever, any portion of his contract without the written permission of the department. Sub-letting, other than that which may be customary in the trade concerned, shall be prohibited. The contractor shall be responsible for the observance of the fair wages clauses by the sub-contractor instead thereof.

For notes see p. 363

It is instructive to contrast this advance with the provisions on sub-contracting contained in the Resolution of 1946. Clause 6 reads:

> The contractor shall be responsible for the observance of this Resolution by sub-contractors employed in the execution of the contract, and shall if required notify the Department of the names and addresses of all such sub-contractors.[1]

The contractor continues to be responsible for the observance of the policy by his sub-contractors. But instead of the requirement of written departmental permission when seeking to sub-let, and this only being granted where customary in the trade, the contractor under the new Resolution was not even required to notify the department of any sub-contracting, unless specifically asked to do so. The progress of the Fair Wages policy in the area of sub-contracting has been of the nature of one step forward, two steps back.

It is not within the province of this book to discuss in detail the many issues of concern in the field of sub-contracting. It should be noted, however, that the Committee of Inquiry into the subject under Professor E. H. Phelps Brown found that of the 1,850,000 workers in construction in 1966, some 147,000 were self-employed workers, an increase of 60 per cent over 1961. Up to 200,000 operatives worked under 'labour-only' sub-contracts. During this period, the late 1960s, the Government was responsible for about 60 per cent of all construction work in the country and about 90 per cent of the civil engineering work. It purchased half the products of the building industry, and the estimated expenditure by the Ministry of Works on contracts in 1967–8 was about £200 million. Of the 14,000 or so contracts placed annually by the Ministry, a great many were very small, of £1,000 or less.

On 23 January 1967 the Minister of Public Building and Works was questioned about the relation of the Fair Wages Clause to labour-only sub-contracting. Mr. Prentice would only reply that the responsibility for sub-contractors lay on the principal contractor. He himself was unaware of any cases of non-observance by sub-contractors of the Fair Wages policy: 'Labour-only sub-contracting, and in particular self-employed operatives, are only used in exceptional circumstances on Government contracts'.[2] But by 1969 the estimate of construction workers supplied under various types of 'labour-only' contracts had risen to 250,000 in the industry. When asked what government contractors used labour-only sub-contracting, the Secretary of State for the environment replied on 17 November 1970 that the information was not readily available and would involve disproportionate staff costs and time to obtain. He reassured the questioner:

Contracts let on Government form CCC/Wks./1 require contractors to observe the working rules of their industry. In the building sector this includes National Working Rule 8 which sets out agreed conditions to be observed in the employment of a labour-only sub-contractor.[3]

It is, perhaps, not surprising that government departments confess ignorance of the dimensions of the problem of sub-contracting as it affects their own contracting requirements. A Public Accounts Committee Report of 1943 criticized a department when a ship repair firm obtained by means of inflated claims payment of some £750,000 more than was due. This was the result, *inter alia*, of charging for fictitious employees' wages and for wages in excess of those actually paid. The firm concerned was a sub-contractor. The department concerned claimed that due to limited staff, reliance had been placed on the main contractor to check the sub-contractor's expenditure.

Eighteen years later, another Public Accounts Committee Report of 1961–2 noted that instructions issued by the Ministry of Aviation placed the responsibility upon the contractors of both fixing sub-contract prices and satisfying the Ministry that they were fair and reasonable. The Ministry informed the Committee that they put very great emphasis on the responsibility of the main contractor. They sought to ensure in their examination of the main contract that the contractor had an efficient system for securing tenders, for the examination of them and for the analysis of costs. The Ministry itself, however, only examined a proportion of sub-contracts and kept no records of the numbers actually examined. They relied primarily upon investigation by their technical costs officers to ensure that sub-contract prices were acceptable, rather than referring them for verification of actual costs by accountants after the event. The Public Accounts Committee concluded:

> But the small number of investigations made, and more particularly the small number of cases where actual costs are examined by the Ministry's accountants, have left Your Committee in doubt whether adequate checks are applied in this wide field. . . . Your Committee are not convinced that the interests of the main contractor are sufficiently at stake to justify such extensive reliance on the responsibility placed on him to secure fair and reasonable prices.

Following on from this, in 1968–9 the Committee was informed that of the allocated complement of 121 professional officers, the

Directorate of Accountancy Services was still 23 officers short. Work was proceeding on 750 cases of investigation of cost-plus contracts, but the Ministry stated that there were probably some 300 further cases on which they would have liked to have started if they had had the staff to deal with them. Consequently, because of the shortage of technical costs officers, the Ministry had temporarily reduced drastically the oversight of cost-plus expenditure. The Ministry informed the Public Accounts Committee that it had been unable to increase materially the number of investigations into sub-contracts as had been recommended by the Committee of Session 1961–2.

If the government fails properly to look after its own interests on contracts, it can hardly be expected effectively to protect those of the workers. The role of the Fair Wages Resolution in the field of sub-contracting was, therefore, exceedingly modest. It was far from being a preventative measure designed to exclude undesirable sub-contractors and protect workers from their practices. Instead, it became a retrospective remedy available where workers had suffered loss due to the main contractor's failure to select fair sub-contractors. An example is Award 2279 of 14 November 1950 (*A.U.B.T.W. and Geo. Wright & Co. (Contractors, Wolverhampton) Ltd.*). The contractor had engaged a labour-only sub-contractor to do part of the work. He failed to attach holiday stamps and eventually skipped without even returning their cards to the workers. The Union claimed that the contractor was liable under an agreement in the industry whereby employers were obliged to fix stamps and deliver cards on termination. The Industrial Court held that the agreement imposed this obligation on the employer which 'is a condition of labour in the industry concerned within the meaning of Clause 1 of the Fair Wages Resolution for which the contractor is responsible in respect of his sub-contractor under Clause 6 of the Resolution' (para. 9). Despite this successful result, the case illustrates the futility of a retrospective remedy. The contractor paid in advance damages to the Court in the amount of £2 14s. and another 8s. came from the employers' federation. Neither of them even bothered to appear before the Court. So while undeniably in breach of the Resolution, the consequences were minimal. There was no incentive for contractors to take their obligations seriously.

With the growth of labour-only sub-contracting, however, this unsatisfactory situation worsened. The representative of the Amalgamated Union of Building Trade Workers complained to the Annual Trades Union Congress of 1952 that since the end of the war:

> there have infiltrated into the building industry a great number of 'labour-only' subcontractors, men who have no background,

no financial standing, no business acumen, men of straw, as we term them, who are here today and gone tomorrow, leaving workmen short of wages, short of holiday credits, and national insurance credits.

He conceded that using the Fair Wages Resolution, the unions 'in many, many cases . . . have got main contractors to meet the defaults of their subcontractors'. But eventually a contractor had refused to pay up. Though this initial challenge had been defeated by Award 2279 just described, yet another challenge had arisen. Although this too was settled out of court, a case had finally come to court. And in the case of *Hughes* v. *Rose* in January 1952, the judge held there was no action under the Fair Wages Resolution whereby damages were recoverable from the main contractor.[4] The Resolution, said the A.U.B.T.W. delegate, 'on which we had placed such faith and . . . such reliance (the judge said) had not the force of law, (but) was merely a pious expression in the form of a resolution in the House of Commons'.

Following this judgment, the A.U.B.T.W. had immediately proposed to the General Council of the T.U.C. that legislation should be brought in to make public contractors liable for financial default on the part of sub-contractors. In reply, the General Council had expressed itself considerably less surprised than the A.U.B.T.W. and had stated that it considered the proposal impracticable. The A.U.B.T.W. declared itself dissatisfied with this conclusion and moved the following resolution at the 1952 Annual Congress:

> This Congress, in view of a recent Court decision that the Fair Wages Resolution is not legally enforceable, demands that legislation be passed to give effective statutory force to the Resolution in order to secure that any worker may recover, by the normal processes of law, any remuneration negotiated jointly by and for industry.

The resolution was eventually remitted to the General Council for consideration. During the subsequent discussion of it in the Council 'doubt was expressed on the desirability of making a wide extension of statutory wage-fixing without fuller consideration by Congress of all its implications upon trade union membership'. That effectively signalled the end of the proposal.

The need for remedial measures became even more apparent after three cases in 1954 where the Industrial Court interpreted clause 6 as making any liability of the main contractor dependent on some 'fault' on his part. Award 2495 of 27 January 1954 (*A.U.B.T.W. and*

Drury & Co. Ltd.) concerned the usual case of a labour-only sub-contractor having skipped owing wages and without having stamped holiday cards. In a claim based on clause 6, the Industrial Court held:

> In the view of the Court the duty of a main contractor under the Fair Wages Resolution or under the provisions of a contract embodying its requirements is to take reasonable steps to ensure that a contractor pays wages and observes conditions which, if he were executing works for a Government Department, would satisfy the appropriate requirements of the Fair Wages Resolution of the House of Commons. (para. 9)

The Court stated that by including a clause in the sub-contract requiring payment of the negotiated rates, the main contractor had fulfilled his duty as regards payment of wages. It stressed that no employee of the sub-contractor had ever complained. Consequently, 'there was no step which in the circumstances the main contractor could reasonably have been expected to take to prevent his sub-contractor's default in this respect'. The Court contrasted this with the position as regards the stamping of holiday cards. The workers do not see the cards as they are given to the employer, so they are not able to complain:

> It is, however, open to a main contractor with whom a sub-contractor has contracted . . . to demand a sight of the holiday cards of the sub-contractor's employees and so to satisfy himself whether or not the sub-contractor is honouring his contractual obligation. For the main contractor to take such a step would be no more than was reasonable and prudent.

In the result, the contractor was held in breach of the Resolution as regards the holiday cards, but not as regards the wages lost when the sub-contractor skipped.

It may be objected to this interpretation that the obligation in clause 6 appears to be absolute, not subject to a test of reasonableness on the part of the contractor. If he hires an unfair sub-contractor, he is responsible for the damage caused to the workers concerned. This is not for any imprudence in the hiring or supervision of the sub-contractor, but because his absolute obligation to ensure that the workers are fairly paid has been broken. A test of reasonableness would hardly be acceptable in the event of breach of other clauses of the Resolution. To introduce it into clause 6 waters down the obligation considerably. Application of it becomes dependent on proof of circumstances which may be difficult to establish. Further, to make the contractor's liability dependent on the workers' ability to complain, let alone their actual complaints, would have the legal obligation turn on certain practicalities of industrial relations which are dangerously subject to mis-interpretation. Such a view is perilously close to the complacent conclusion that absence of complaint signifies compliance with the Resolution. For in Award 2495 itself the Industrial Court overlooked the fact that the workers could hardly have complained of the *impending* disappearance of the sub-contractor. It was the loss of the last days' wages which they were claiming was a breach of the Resolution.

The hazards of such a circumstantial lottery were well illustrtaed by the second case of 1954. In Award 2526 of 27 July 1954 (*A.U.B.T.W. and D. C. Heard & Co. Ltd.*) the main contractor had entered into a verbal agreement with a labour-only sub-contractor. He claimed that he had asked whether the sub-contractor observed the Resolution and had been answered in the affirmative. He believed the sub-contractor's financial standard to have been good. He had never asked to see the holiday cards, but did ask if they were being stamped and was reassured on this point. The sub-contractor was then discovered to have been remiss on both wages paid and holiday cards stamped. The basis of the Court's Award was its finding that the verbal agreement did not suffice even to place the Fair Wages obligation on the sub-contractor. Consequently, the main contractor was undoubtedly responsible for the default. The Court went on to say:

> The Court would add that even had the main Contractors, by the terms of their sub-contract, placed the Sub-contractor under obligation to observe the Fair Wages Resolution, steps taken by them to satisfy themselves that the provisions of the Holidays with Pay Scheme were being complied with by the Sub-contractor would not in the circumstances have been held to be reasonable. (para. 9)

This view of the main contractor's liability was clearly spelled out again in the third case of 1954, Award 2544 of 13 November 1954, which was an interpretation of Award 2526.

The Court thus indicated that every case of liability of a main contractor was to depend on the proven unreasonableness of his behaviour in all the circumstances. In the event, and perhaps as a consequence, it was never again to be called upon to exercise its judgment in such circumstances. Only one other case came before the Court concerning the responsibility of a contractor under clause 6 of the Resolution. And that case, Award 2641 of 30 January 1957 (*National Union of Packing Case Makers (Wood & Tin), Box Makers, Sawyers and Mill Workers and A. V. Roe & Co. Ltd.*) was brought mainly because the sub-contractor concerned was alleged to be merely a 'supplier'.

The absence of cases brought to the Industrial Court does not mean that the problem has disappeared. In 1970 the Post Office Engineering Union complained to the Annual Trades Union Congress of the 'formal position' of the Post Office. The department maintained that it was their practice to seek assurances from prime contractors that they will in turn exercise proper control over their sub-contractors. The Union commented:

> But anybody who is acquainted at all with this field will know what difficulties arise, and it is clear from the experience of our members that control exercised over sub-contractors is, in many cases, quite inadequate.

To remedy the deficiency, the Union proposed the insertion of a clause in the Resolution making it obligatory on the main contractor to notify the Civil Service Department of the names and addresses of all sub-contractors so that they should be required to give the same assurances to the Department as those required from the main contractor. Following up this initiative, the General Council of the T.U.C. put this proposal to the Chief Secretary to the Treasury. It was rejected, although a similar provision had been included in Fair Wages Clauses between 1909 and 1946. Nothing has since occurred to indicate that sub-contracting practices on government contracts have changed.

Self-employment

A problem related to those discussed above arises where workers are said not to be in a relationship of employment with an employer, so as to be covered by the Fair Wages policy. Nor are they related to him through a sub-contractor, so as to be safeguarded by clause 6. Instead, they are held to be 'independent contractors'. The spectre of 'self-employment' haunting labour law, to use Wedderburn's evocative phrase, has not yet revealed itself in cases on the Fair Wages Resolution. But in two cases under the Terms and Conditions of Employment Act 1959, the status of workers in the entertainment industry was questioned. In Award 2847 of 8 June 1961 the City of Leicester Working Men's Club claimed it was not an employer of members of the Variety Artistes' Federation within the meaning of section 8(1)(c) of the Act. The Union lost its claim. In Award 2994 of 1 November 1963 (*B.B.C. and A.C.T.A.T.*), the Court 'assumed, without deciding the point, that a Variety Artiste engaged in television can properly be regarded as a worker and the Corporation or an Independent Television Company as his employer, and the relationship between them as one of employment, within the meaning of the Act' (para. 12(a)). The Union still lost the claim.

In Award 3107 of 25 July 1966, however, the question was confronted directly whether the workers concerned—roof tilers and tilers' labourers—were 'self-employed' or 'employees'. The Union claimed they were employees: 'The Company were able to control their workers effectively since they secured the initial contracts, directed the workers where to go, controlled the flow of materials to the site and satisfied themselves as to the quality of the work done' (para. 5). The Company claimed the men were self-employed: there was no written contract, they were on piece-work, the money was paid to a group leader who shared it out, and there was no supervision (paras. 27–8). In a robust judgment evincing an appreciation of industrial realities, the Court held that:

> on the facts, the relationship between the Company and the workers concerned in the claim is by way of contract of service and not by way of contract for services; that the expression 'self-employed' is a misdescription of the true position of the said workers in relation to the Company; and that the Company are employers and the workers concerned are employees within the meaning of Section 8. (para. 44(1))

The significance of this decision for the Fair Wages policy was apparent from the Union's submission that:

> the Company's present system of engaging labour gave them very substantial financial advantages over other roofing contractors who observed the conditions laid down by the N.J.C. as well as their legal obligations as employers. This enabled the Company to enter into unfair competition with those other employers, contrary to the terms of the Fair Wages Resolution. (para. 21)

Unfortunately, in the more recent Award 3256 of 15 March 1972 (*C. E. Borden & Sons Ltd. and Amalgamated Society of Woodworkers, Painters & Builders*), the Industrial Arbitration Board retreated from this forthright position. The Union, contending that 'at times people needed to be protected from the consequences of their actions', submitted that the lump workers in question were in a similar position to those in Award 3107, and that here too the expression 'self-employed' was a misdescription (para. 12). The Board was overcome by a list of High Court decisions on the question of 'self-employment', all of which were argued in the Company's lengthy submission (paras. 21–5). The Company even threw in *Hill* v, *Parsons* [1971] 1 All E.R. 1345 for good measure as prospectively banning the now de-registered Union from appearing in the case (para. 19). The claim was dismissed: 'it has not been established that the relationship between the Company and those workers is an employer–employee relationship' (para. 34). It remains to be seen whether the future Fair Wages policy protection of workers in employment will be reduced by legalistic interpretation of the scope of 'employment'.[5]

NOTES

1. The provisions on sub-contracting quoted above from the Resolutions of 1891, 1909 and 1946 may be found in Parl. Deb., H. of C. (Third Series); 13 February 1891, vol. CCCL, at cols. 626 and 642; (Fourth Series); 10 March 1909, vol. II, col. 425; and (Fifth Series); 14 October 1946, vol. 427, col. 619.

2. Parl. Deb., H. of C. (Fifth Series); 23 January 1967, vol. 739, col. 168 (Written Answers).

3. Parl. Deb., H. of C. (Fifth Series); 17 November 1970, vol. 806, cols. 379–80 (Written Answers).

4. I have not been able to find any official report of this case. The name is given in the Report of the General Council to the 85th Annual Trades Union Congress, Douglas, Isle of Man, 1953, at pp. 221–2.

5. In this chapter, reference has been made to the following sources:

—P. O'Higgins and B. A. Hepple, *Individual Employment Law*, Sweet & Maxwell, London, 1971, at p. 18.

—K. W. Wedderburn, *The Worker and the Law*, (2nd ed.) Penguin Books, 1971, at pp. 61–7.

—Report of the Committee of Inquiry under Professor E. H. Phelps Brown, Cmnd. 3714, H.M.S.O. 1968.

—Parl. Deb., H. of C. (Fifth Series); 19 June 1967, vol. 748, col. 1094, per Mr. Prentice, Minister of Public Building and Works.

—Fourth Report from the Estimates Committee, 1967–8, 'The Public Build-ing Programme in the U.K.', H.C. 351; Minutes of Evidence, Memorandum Submitted on Behalf of the Ministry of Public Building and Works, at para. 1.2, and at Q. 365.

—Epitome of the Reports from the Committees of Public Accounts, vol. II (1938–1969), H.C. 187 of 1970: at

—pp. 67–8 (P.A.C. Report, 1943, H.C. 116 (Treasury Minute, 12 February 1944), paras. 18–19).

—pp. 409–10 (P.A.C. Third Report, 1961–2, H.C. 251 (Treasury Minute, 13 November 1962), paras. 54, 55, 57).

—pp. 548–9 (P.A.C. Third Report, 1968–9, H.C. 362 (Treasury Minute, 5 November 1969), paras. 44, 48).

—Report of the 21st Annual Trades Union Congress, Bradford, 1888, at p. 39.

—Report of the 23rd Annual T.U.C., Liverpool, 1890, at p. 39.

—Report of the General Council to the 84th Annual T.U.C., Margate, 1952, at pp. 223–4.

—Report of the 84th Annual T.U.C., Margate, 1952, at pp. 398–400.

—Report of the General Council to the 85th Annual T.U.C., Douglas, Isle of Man, 1953, at pp. 221–2.

—Report of the 102nd Annual T.U.C., Brighton, 1970, at p. 555.

—Report of the General Council to the 103rd Annual T.U.C., Blackpool, 1971, at para. 67, p. 52.

19

A Case History of the Fair Wages Policy in Action: The Contract Cleaners

This chapter deals with an area of operation of the Fair Wages Resolution of 1946 which aroused great controversy in recent years—the contract cleaning trade. During the decade up to 1975 there were, amongst other symptoms of unrest, numerous protests from trade unions and resolutions from the Trades Union Congress, ten Industrial Court cases, a Report by the National Board for Prices and Incomes, a Fabian pamphlet and even a full-length feature film. The material collected in the N.B.P.I. Report and the Fabian pamphlet make it unnecessary to reiterate the information contained in them. The N.B.P.I. Report described at length the nature and workings of the industry—employers and the work-force, pay and conditions, collective bargaining or the lack of it, and the position of the government and its influence on the trade. The Fabian pamphlet is on the Fair Wages Resolution generally, but throughout it the experience of the contract cleaners is used to illustrate the workings of the Resolution. This can be very deceptive, as is indicated by the wholly disproportionate volume of Industrial Court cases concerned with contract cleaning. The pamphlet itself notes that one-third of the Industrial Court cases brought by trade unions since 1946 were heard between 1968–72: 'an indication of the pressure exerted by the Civil Service Union during that period on behalf of cleaners. The outcome has been that complaints against contract cleaning firms dominate the scene from 1968 onwards.'

The use of the contract cleaning trade to illustrate the application of the Resolution should not obscure the general discounting, or even total unawareness, of the Fair Wages policy by government contractors, their employees and the unions. Yet the experience of the contract cleaning trade is illuminating in that it shows how even the maximal utilization of the Resolution of 1946 could yield only such

For notes see p. 381

meagre results. Investigation discloses in intimate detail the workings of the Fair Wages policy, affected to varying degrees by departmental perceptions, trade union pressures, Industrial Court Awards and competing government policies. The workings of the Resolution itself are best perceived through an analysis of the interaction between the T.U.C. and the government departments, and of the Industrial Court cases.

But concurrently with these, other more realistic struggles were being undertaken, particularly by the women cleaners who form some 88 per cent of the work-force in the industry. A number of strikes took place: the Fabian pamphlet refers to a successful strike by women cleaners employed on all night cleaning at the Fulham site of the Ministry of Defence. Another long and bitter strike was fought by women of the Cleaners Action Group. A full-length feature film, *The Night Cleaners*, was made portraying this latter struggle. It reproduces the anomie in which these women work—with families to care for during the day, isolated at night, faced with employers hostile to any union organization. The Fabian pamphlet noted that anti-union behaviour is known to occur and is widespread. The Fair Wages policy, as in decades past, was meaningless at this level of struggle. Its only use was to the T.U.C. in its battle with the departments, and to the trade unions complaining to the Industrial Court.

Origins

Anxiety was already being voiced about the position of women cleaners in government offices in 1950 when a wage claim was rejected.[1] But, according to leaders of the Civil Service Union, it was the Conservative victory in 1951 that led to pressure being put on departments to get rid of their directly employed cleaners. The C.S.U. representative reported to the 1964 Annual Trades Union Congress that as a result 'literally thousands of women trade unionists were made redundant and the work was given to the contract cleaning firms'. Dissatisfaction was expressed on numerous occasions both in Parliament and in the Whitley Councils. But by 1955, a written answer in Parliament stated that government departments employed seventeen firms of cleaning contractors employing about 1,000 women. According to the N.B.P.I. Report, cleaning of government offices was still normally carried out by directly employed cleaners during the 1950s, but in 1959 experiments undertaken showed that savings of up to 30 per cent could be made by going over to contract cleaning, and departments were asked to further review their arrangements (para. 59). Later, at the

Trades Union Congress of 1968, union spokesmen were to refer to Selwyn Lloyd's 'obsessional Tory fetish for private enterprise' and Treasury 'economics running amok', but if anything the trend was accelerated after the arrival of the Labour Government in 1964. As an economy measure following devaluation, the Government decided in January 1968 to accelerate the transfer from direct to contract cleaning in order to reduce costs. As a result, many of the government's own cleaners became redundant. By October 1970, the government directly employed about 1,000 full-time and 5,200 part-time cleaners, compared with 1,200 full-time and 8,100 part-time cleaners in October 1967. Some two-thirds of the total area of government offices was cleaned under contract (42 million square feet v. $21\frac{1}{2}$ million square feet by directly employed cleaners) compared with one-third in 1967.

That the impact of this new central government policy was substantial is evident from an illustration of its implementation by a local authority in early 1968. In Award 3161 of 30 January 1968 (*N.U.P.E. and Industrial Contract Cleaners Ltd.*) the contractor was charged with breach of the Fair Wages Resolution. The contractor explained that his contracts with the local authority concerned normally did incorporate a provision that he must observe the rates paid by the authority, which were those laid down by the appropriate N.J.C. He even submitted that if the Council had made such a stipulation in the present contract of 31 July 1967, he would readily have complied with it: 'The Council had, however, told the Company on this occasion that as the workers concerned would no longer be Council employees the Company were not required to pay them local authority rates' (para. 16). The Industrial Court rejected the complaint.

The First Trade Union Campaign: 1964–1969

A major campaign of protest got underway with a formal resolution proposed and carried at the Annual Trades Union Congress in 1964:

> This Congress notes with concern the increasing use of private contract firms to clean Government buildings. Congress deplores this policy which results in sub-standard cleaning and which is often carried out by unorganized labour paid below the trade union rate negotiated for direct cleaning of Government buildings. It considers that a properly managed Government direct labour force could provide a better service at an economical cost, and urges the General Council to give all support to the opposition to contract cleaning.

The proposer of the resolution, the representative of the Civil Service Union, condemned the Treasury. Despite the Fair Wages Resolution, there was no fair list of contract cleaners who paid a reasonable rate and consequently contracts were being given to firms paying substantially below the direct cleaners' rate. He contrasted the substandard rates and sweated conditions of the cleaners with the fat profits of the principal cleaning firms. The Union put forward to the Treasury a 'practical, detailed, constructive proposal' for direct cleaning of a number of departments. As the Treasury agreed to discuss it, no subsequent action was taken on the resolution by the General Council of the T.U.C.

Following the decision in January 1968 to transfer one-third of existing direct cleaning to contract work, however, representatives of the General Council and of the unions concerned met the Chancellor of the Exchequer on 27 June 1968. The union representatives challenged the economics of the proposed transfer and 'concern was also expressed that the level of wages paid to contract cleaners was much lower than those paid to directly employed cleaners who were themselves among the very low-paid workers'. In his reply, the Chancellor declined to reverse the Treasury decision, but reassured the unions that the contractors were bound by the Fair Wages Clause. Any disputes, he added in a subsequent letter, could be referred to an independent tribunal. In its reply to this, the General Council continued to express dissatisfaction.

But this was tame stuff beside the language of the unions concerned at the Annual Trades Union Congress in September 1968. One spoke of the Government's 'Operation Eyewash' in thus reducing the number of public servants on paper; another of the 'philosophy of equality of misery' of the 'stop-go incumbents of 11 Downing Street'. The appalling conditions of cleaners employed by government contractors were described in detail—one minute's notice, no sick pay, no legal entitlement to holidays, and the anti-trade union activities of contractors specified: to sack unionists, to fail to answer letters or 'to kick you around from one aspect of this organization to another'. These workers were 'still in the dark days of the fight for basic trade union recognition and organization'. The Union of Post Office Workers 'had considerable research made in many areas of the wages paid by these contract firms, and the difference in the wages paid was astounding. In the unorganized labour fields some of them were as low as half-a-crown per hour'. Only one brief reference was made to the Fair Wages Resolution. Rather, the C.S.U. moved and the Congress carried the following resolution:

This Congress considers that the Government should take immediate steps to ensure that contracts in the Civil Service should be restricted to firms undertaking to pay rates and conditions not less favourable than those established by negotiations or arbitration *in the appropriate part of the public service.* (My italics.)

That the unions considered the Fair Wages Resolution to be inadequate is evident from the C.S.U.'s subsequent suggestion to the General Council. This was that in future, an additional paragraph should be inserted in all government contracts, after inclusion of the Resolution, to the effect that, where the contractor's work was similar to that carried out within the Civil Service, the contractor should be bound to pay rates and observe conditions of service not less favourable that the appropriate Civil Service rates where these were more favourable than those specified in clause 1(a) of the Resolution. In light of what were felt to be the general repercussions of this suggestion, the T.U.C. General Council circulated all affiliated unions in December 1968. A favourable response having been received, a letter was sent to the Chancellor of the Exchequer in February 1969 requesting action along the lines proposed. The government was asked to incorporate a clause into their contracts in addition to those of the Resolution, to read as follows:

Where the work carried out is similar to that done within the industrial or non-industrial Civil Service, the contractor shall pay the rates and observe hours and conditions of labour established in the appropriate part of the Civil Service where these are more favourable than those which would otherwise apply under paragraph (1) (of the Fair Wages Resolution).

The General Council went on to state expressly that some of the savings from the system of contracting-out were derived from the low wages paid to contractors' employees. The Resolution had not prevented this happening.

On 2 April 1969 the Chancellor replied in the negative: the proposed change was not considered necessary and would exceed the original intentions of the Resolution by making public service wage rates the *sole* criterion by which the terms of contractors' employees were measured. Any difficulties on the question of what were fair rates could be resolved by reference to the Industrial Court. Significantly, the Chancellor added that where government employees undertook similar work, their rates and conditions could be brought to the attention of the Industrial Court as *one of the factors* to be taken into account. Five unions directly concerned with contract cleaning, the

C.S.U., N.U.P.E., U.P.W., N.U.G.M.W. and T.G.W.U. were informed of the Chancellor's reply on 6 June 1969.[2]

The Campaign in the Industrial Court. 1970

The C.S.U., N.U.P.E. and the U.P.W. all stated that they found the Chancellor's letter unsatisfactory. But the correspondence, and particularly the Chancellor's reference to the Industrial Court, clearly affected their strategy in combatting the cleaning contractors. For in the first six months of 1970 no less than six cases were taken to the Industrial Court charging contractors with breach of the Fair Wages Resolution.

The suggestion by the Chancellor in his letter of 2 April 1969 of the Court as a possible remedial agency is all the more intriguing in light of a written answer given by his colleague, the Secretary of State for Employment, on 10 February 1969. The Secretary of State was asked how many questions as to whether the requirements of the Fair Wages Clause in Government contracts were being observed she had referred to an independent tribunal for decision in each of the last three years. Her answer was: 'None'.[3] It may have escaped the notice of the civil servant preparing that answer that the Minister *had* indeed referred a question on observance of the Resolution to the Industrial Court, and the Court had handed down its Award 3161 on 30 January 1968. Alternatively, the civil servant concerned may have considered that as the Fair Wages Clause in question in that case was that of a local authority contract, it did not fall within the terms of the Parliamentary question. Nevertheless, the case was considered important enough to be reported in *Knight's Industrial Reports* (vol. IV, p. 157).

Most interestingly, that Award concerned the complaint by N.U.P.E. that Industrial Contract Cleaners Ltd. was not paying fair wages nor observing fair conditions of labour in respect of six women cleaners employed by them in the execution of their contract. This was the first case of its kind, and the report of it preceded by more than a year the Chancellor's suggestion of 2 April 1969 that in their claims to the Industrial Court the unions might invoke the rates and conditions of government employees engaged on similar work as one of the factors to be considered. Yet in that Award 3161 of 30 January 1968, the principal contention of the contractor, *who was upheld by the Court*, directly contradicted the Chancellor's view:

> In the Company's submission they were engaged in the cleaning industry, and their employees could not be said to be employed

in local government service. There was no negotiating machinery for the cleaning industry, and in the absence of such machinery it was the Company's practice, in carrying out contracts which required compliance with the Fair Wages Resolution, but which did not stipulate any particular rate of pay, to observe terms and conditions of employment which were not less favourable than those observed by *other contract cleaners* whose general circumstances were similar to theirs (see Clause 1(b) of the Fair Wages Resolution).

It was conceded that the work carried out by the Company's cleaners was comparable with that carried out by cleaners in local government service, but it was submitted that *the general circumstances of local authorities were not the same as those of the Company*. Their respective employees worked different hours and carried out the work under different systems. The Company's cleaners could be asked to do work other than the cleaning of the Council's offices although in practice they were not required to. (paras. 17–18) (My italics.)

The question arises, then, whether the Chancellor intended to suggest to the unions an argument which, it would appear, had been previously rejected by the Industrial Court. And if so, why?

The argument suggested by the Chancellor became the basis of the dispute between the Civil Service Union and the six contractors it hailed before the Industrial Court during 1970. In all six cases the Union's position rested on one basic submission. As stated in the first Award 3206 of 24 March 1970 (*C.S.U. and Cleaners Ltd.*):

> that the trade or industry concerned in the present reference was the trade of cleaning and not the contract cleaning industry, as the Company were contending. Indeed, it was the Union's view irrelevant whether or not there was such a thing as a contract cleaning industry. All the rates they would quote in their evidence were rates for cleaners, and it would be clearly irrelevant to quote a rate for anybody who was not a cleaner. The Union accepted that the rates paid by contract cleaners were a relevant factor, but they denied the Company's contention that they were the only relevant factor. (para. 10)

The Union accepted that government departments and local authorities did not represent a substantial proportion of the employers engaged in the trade or industry concerned, and in fact had gathered evidence relating to eleven trade groups, only one of which was national and local government (para. 9).

In the second Award 3212 of 1 May 1970 (*C.S.U. and General Cleaning Contractors (Northern) Ltd.*), the Union submitted that the industry with which the Company was to be compared was the office and factory cleaning industry. This included two groups of employers of cleaners—contract cleaners, and firms engaged in various activities which used direct labour in cleaning their premises. To that extent they were also engaged in the office and factory cleaning industry. The fact that employers engaged in contract cleaning had formed a trade association did not establish the Company's contention that such employers constituted a separate industry (para. 7). Basing its compaint, as they all were, on breach of clause 1(b) of the Resolution, the Union 'submitted that Clause 1 gave the Industrial Court a very wide discretion in the matter of comparisons within the trade or industry in which the employer in question was engaged, requiring only that employers with whom a comparison was made should be in similar general circumstances' (para. 8).

In the last four cases as well (Awards 3216–19 of 12 June 1970, *C.S.U. and All England Cleaning Co. Ltd.*), the Union drew comparisons with employers who made use of direct labour in the cleaning of their own premises. In support of their contention that the rates paid by national and local government employers were among the factors to be taken into account when considering compliance with the Resolution, the Union at the hearing of these cases (and also in Award 3206 (para. 9)):

> placed before the Court a copy of a letter dated the 31 March 1969 from the Chancellor of the Exchequer to the T.U.C., in which this factor was stated to be relevant. No other factors were referred to in that letter but in the Union's submission it was reasonable to assume that other relevant factors would be the rates paid to cleaners employed in industries other than the cleaning industry, including public and private employers of cleaners.[4] (para. 6)

The position of the cleaning contractors in the six cases was identical to that quoted above from Award 3161 of 30 January 1968: that the relevant trade or industry was that of office cleaning contracting, and consequently the rates of cleaners employed directly by the owners of premises, including government departments and local authorities, were irrelevant. The Company in Award 3206 went so far as to argue that these two categories were not in fact engaged in trade or industry of any kind: 'The provision required comparison with an undertaking carrying out cleaning on a profit-making basis and not merely as a function ancillary to some other function' (para. 21). This point was not stressed in the Company's submissions in Award 3212; rather they stressed that 'although the work of that industry was not different from that of office and factory cleaning generally, the organization of the industry was entirely different. Cleaning contractors specialized in the cleaning of premises and they were constantly engaged in research. Where an undertaking employed cleaners direct to clean their own premises, the work was incidental to that undertaking's main activity. The contract cleaning industry had its own association' (para. 23). And in Awards 3216–19, the Company simply:

> asked the Court to ignore the bulk of the evidence in question on the ground that apart from the three cleaning contractors cited, all the employers referred to employed cleaners solely for the purpose of cleaning their own premises. . . . The Company therefore submitted that these examples were not representative of the contract cleaning industry as a whole and there was nothing in the Union's evidence to compare with the Company's contract cleaning activities. (para. 20)

The failure of the Industrial Court to give reasons for its Awards makes it impossible to ascertain precisely why it reached the decisions it did. But it seems reasonably clear that on the whole the Union's submissions were accepted. In both Awards 3206 and 3212, the Company concerned was held to be in breach of Clause 1(b) of the Resolution. In Awards 3216–19, one of the four different companies named was held to be in breach. It is not always useful to hypothesize, but it may be noted that in several cases decided by the Industrial Court in the early 1940s, it was held that various local authorities were engaged in a 'trade or industry' for the purposes of the Fair Wages formula contained in Order 1305 of 1940.[5] Perhaps the Court's long experience in applying the Fair Wages Resolution to the industrial employees of the government served to influence it here to accept comparisons between public and private employers.[6]

In the event, the victory earned by the C.S.U. turned out to be a strictly limited one. For unexpectedly, the Industrial Court did not content itself in these cases with its normal task of establishing whether or not the contractors were in compliance with the Resolution. Rather, in each case where it found the cleaning contractor to be in breach of Clause 1(b) of the Resolution, it went on to specify the *minimum* hourly rate of pay which would be consistent with observance of the Resolution. In Award 3206 this was 4s. 9d. (para. 29(2)); in Award 3212, 4s. 6d. (para. 38(2)), and in Awards (3216–19, the company in breach was required to pay a minimum rate of 4s. 9d. per hour (para. 23). So while in Award 3206 the Union had put forward as the fair current rate 5s. 1d. per hour (para. 12), although the complaint was upheld, it was awarded a minimum standard 4d. lower. In subsequent cases, the union itself specified the minimum rate it considered to be required by the Fair Wages Resolution, and when a breach was held to be established, this rate was awarded.

A process of enforcing the Fair Wages policy which was directed towards the determination of a minimum standard—but then fixed a different minimum standard for each individual contractor in breach —was scarcely the outcome required by the Union. It precluded the Court's Awards being used in a general campaign to eliminate the low pay of contract cleaners. It is not clear why the Industrial Court adopted this new approach to enforcement of the Fair Wages policy. There was no call for it in the Resolution and no precedent in previous cases. Indeed, in evidence before the Donovan Commission on 26 July 1966, the President of the Industrial Court, Sir Roy Wilson, had made the following statement:

> *Lord Tangley:* I think the duty of the Court is limited to a deter-
> mination of facts—in other words, you are limited to questions
> of full comparability.
>
> *Sir Roy Wilson:* Yes, and we do not, in my recollection, make a direct
> award in the form of a direction at all: we merely make a finding
> as to whether there has been a failure to observe the principle.

The establishment of a 'fair' standard according to clause 1(b)—a 'general level of wages, hours and conditions observed by other employers whose general circumstances in the trade or industry in which the contractor is engaged are similar'—might have been a useful precedent. But a minimum standard which differed for each individual contractor in breach was something very different.

Another obstacle confronted the C.S.U. following its victories in the Industrial Court. The Civil Service Department declared that they were unable to give an assurance that a contractor would be given four weeks' notice to terminate the contract in accordance with paragraph 15(iv) of same entitled 'Default of Contractor', even if the Industrial Court found that the contractor was in breach of the Fair Wages Resolution in not recognizing the freedom of his workpeople to be members of trade unions, as was alleged in Award 3212. The view of the legal advisors of the Civil Service Department was that if the contractor was in breach with regard to the quality of his work the contract could be terminated, but that this was not the position if his only breach was of the Fair Wages Resolution.

The C.S.U. informed the General Council of the T.U.C. that if this advice were correct, the Fair Wages Resolution would be unenforceable in government contracts until all existing contracts had been terminated and new forms of contract issued. The 'protection' so frequently invoked by the Treasury in previous exchanges thus appeared to be non-existent. This posed a serious problem for all organizations with an interest in government contracts. The C.S.U. representative bitterly summed up the year's campaign to the 1970 Annual Trades Union Congress:

> In the field of contract cleaning, we have had practical experience during this year of the value to be placed on the pledges given by previous Chancellors of the Exchequer about the value of the Fair Wages Resolution.

The C.S.U.'s experience was described as follows: the Union had had three separate complaints upheld by the Industrial Court. It had organized the whole staff of a small local contractor and obtained an agreement with him with an agreed renewal after twelve months. Before this could occur, the government department concerned let the contract out to tender once again. Despite the strong representations of the Union, it was given to a firm which had been charged with breach of the Resolution before the Industrial Court only one month earlier. The new contractor offered rates lower than those previously agreed and refused to employ trade unionists. Charged with breach of clause 4 of the Resolution, the contractor argued that the protection of clause 4 did not apply to workers not yet employed. As the outraged C.S.U. representative reported:

> In other words, if a contractor refuses to employ trade unionists he is not limiting the freedom of his workpeople because he has taken steps to see that people never become his workpeople as long as they remain trade unionists. It is bad enough that the employer should argue this. But when we took it up with the client, in the form of the Civil Service Department, this is the reply we received: 'The relationship with contractors is such that, except in very special circumstances relating primarily to national security a Government Department had no *locus* in the question of whom a contractor employed'.
>
> 'Having no *locus*' is Civil Service jargon for 'Couldn't care less'.

It was experience of this kind that led the C.S.U. to second the motion of the P.O.E.U. at the 1970 Congress demanding the closed shop on government contracts. The Union representative added somewhat acidly the hope that the General Council would implement the new resolution a little faster than the C.S.U.'s previous resolution of 1968: that was 'two years and three Chancellors of the Exchequer ago, but they still have not got a meeting with him. Could we have a bit of urgency on this one?'

The Second Trade Union Campaign: 1971–1973

When last seen in 1969 the General Council was indeed attempting to arrange a meeting with the Chancellor following his unsatisfactory response to the C.S.U. resolution contained in the letter of 2 April 1969. A letter to this effect was duly sent on 16 December 1969 and a reply duly received on 24 February 1970. The Chancellor said he could add little to his previous statement but was willing to meet members of the General Council to discuss the matter. The preparations were disrupted, however, by the announcement of the General Election of 1970 and the subsequent change of government. At the time of the 1970 Trades Union Congress, the General Council were still seeking a meeting, but the sharper resolution proposed by the P.O.E.U. and carried by the Congress necessitated further consultation and preparation which again caused the proposed meeting with the Chancellor to be deferred. Finally, some two years after the initial impetus, a meeting was arranged for 26 May 1971. Shortly before, however, the Chancellor informed the T.U.C. that pressing Ministerial business prevented his attendance, and the General Council had to make do with the Chief Secretary to the Treasury. This gentleman, however, was able to advise the General Council that its proposals were unacceptable, though naturally, 'the contracting Departments would ensure that the spirit as well as the letter of the Fair Wages Resolution was observed in all cases'. The Chief Secretary did appear to add one concession: 'that where there was difficulty in establishing fair wages in a particular locality, all factors, including Civil Service rates, would be taken into account'.

The travails of the contract cleaners did not pass entirely unnoticed by the Labour Government of 1964–70. About one month before its downfall, on 22 May 1970, the Secretary of State for Employment and Productivity referred to the National Board for Prices and Incomes for examination, with particular reference to the problem of low pay, the question of the pay and conditions of service and the principles for determining these of workers employed in the contract cleaning trade. The N.B.P.I. Report, No. 168, came out in April 1971. In Chapter 5 on the government's cleaning requirements, the Board noted that although government departments obtain a declaration of observance of the Resolution from a successful contractor, they:

do not attempt to determine themselves what a 'fair wage' is or to get information about the pay, hours and conditions of the contractors' employees on the site. Any disputes arising from the Resolution can be referred to the Department of Employment which may, if it cannot resolve the dispute itself, refer it to the Industrial Court.

In conventional fashion, the Board turned to the record of complaints as a gauge of the Resolution's effectiveness. It was calculated that since the beginning of 1969, fourteen complaints had reached the Department of Employment, of which six were settled by the Department and one was still under investigation at the time. Of the remaining seven, six were decided by the Industrial Court (as described above—three upheld and three dismissed), and the seventh was still under reference. The Resolution's efficacy was summed up in the following way:

the fourteen complaints which have reached the Department of Employment must be viewed against the background of the 2,300 Government cleaning contracts on which no complaint has been made and in light of our findings on general levels of pay prevailing in the trade. (paras. 63–4)

The Report had stated bluntly that 'It cannot be said this is a low paid trade as a whole; if weekly earnings are low it is because hours are short rather than because hourly earnings are low by standards found elsewhere' (para. 58). Their survey did however show that 'conditions of service are on the whole not generous' (para. 54).

The Board did take cognizance of the low rate of unionization of the trade—some 3 per cent—and blamed both the unions' lack of attention and the employers who 'have not made it easy for them to get a foothold'. This even-handedness was not reflected in their allocation of future responsibilities: 'The task of organizing the cleaners rests primarily with the trade unions themselves, but the attitude of employers is likely to be crucial to their success, since in such a trade as this so much depends on the facilities for organization which they are prepared to extend to trade unions' (para. 79). Given the previously noted employer attitudes, their prognosis was pessimistic in the absence of some special support. Of the T.U.C.'s proposed amendment to the Fair Wages Clause looking to comparability with Civil Service rates, the Board had this to say:

We understand that the Goverment has taken the view that the T.U.C. proposal would not be compatible with the principle of 'fair comparisons' on which Civil Service pay determination is itself based, and that it would be inflationary for the Government to bring pressure to bear on outside employers to bring their rates up to the Government rate, or to use Civil Service pay policy to further social and political objectives. (See Appendix C.) We agree. (para. 75)

This Report can hardly have given any encouragement to those trade unions seeking to remedy the deficiencies of the government's contracting policies through the Industrial Court. Nevertheless, the Civil Service Union did persist. In Awards 3242 and 3243 of 24 and 25 June 1971 (*C.S.U. and General Cleaning Contractors (Northern) Ltd.; and C.S.U. and Cleaners Ltd.*) both the companies complained of invoked the above quoted paragraph 75 of the N.B.P.I. Report in support of their claim of compliance with the Fair Wages Resolution. The Industrial Court still held them liable. But in Award 3275 of 23 October 1972 (*C.S.U. and 20th Century Cleaning & Maintenance Co. Ltd.*), the Industrial Arbitration Board held that there had been no breach of the Resolution. No reasons were given for any of these decisions.

The General Council of the T.U.C. considered the N.B.P.I. Report and duly noted the Board's view that the prime responsibility for organizing contract cleaners lay with the unions themselves. Accordingly, they wrote to the four unions principally concerned (the C.S.U., N.U.G.M.W., N.U.P.E. and T.G.W.U.) enquiring whether there was any way in which the T.U.C. might assist in improving trade union organization and in establishing collective bargaining machinery in the contract cleaning industry, and whether a meeting with the General Council's Organisation Committee would be useful. In the meanwhile, however, the C.S.U. together with representatives of the other unions, had held a meeting with officials of the Department of Employment and had pressed the Department to assist in the establishment of collective bargaining in the contract cleaning trade. As a result, the Department had undertaken to convene a meeting with the eleven largest employers in the trade (represented by their association, the Contract Cleaning and Maintenance Association—C.C.M.A.). When that meeting eventually took place late in 1971, the Department suggested that a joint meeting under their chairmanship should be held between the unions and the C.C.M.A. The Association rejected the proposal.

The unions then invoked the T.U.C.'s offer of aid, and the General Council wrote to the Secretary of State for Employment in January 1972 stressing its concern at the C.C.M.A.'s attitude. In reply, the Secretary of State said that the C.C.M.A. reiterated that they were not yet ready or mandated for joint discussions with trade unions at national level, and that in any case the very low level of union membership in the industry made such a national approach inappropriate. The Association considered that the best way forward lay in the development of relationships at company level where member firms were already recognizing unions which had appropriate membership. The Secretary of State added that in the circumstances he did not think he could take any further action at present to try to bring the parties together at national level, and he doubted whether there was much prospect of any real progress on an industry basis until the unions had improved their membership within the industry. However, the Department of Employment's Manpower Advisors would give the unions whatever help they could towards developing relationships at company level where it appeared likely that an approach by the Department could be of assistance.

The T.U.C. having drawn a blank, the unions concerned again met on 15 June 1972 and decided to make further efforts to get the two biggest employers in contract cleaning to meet them under Department of Employment chairmanship. Meanwhile, pressure was also being exerted through questions in Parliament. On 15 June 1971 the Minister for the Civil Service had been asked: 'what steps are taken to ensure that the conditions of work and rates of pay of the cleaners are satisfactory; and what change in expense to public funds arises from switching from direct employment to contract cleaning?' The substance of the reply to these two questions was respectively: the Fair Wages Resolution, and it was economical. Again on 20 April 1972 the Minister was questioned about the extent of contract cleaning, and in addition, whether he would make trade union recognition a condition of government agreements with contract firms. The answer was no, it was explained, since protection was provided both by clause 4 of the Resolution and by the new Industrial Relations Act 1971. The Minister stated that he was satisfied with the operation of the Resolution in government cleaning contracts and cited the low number of complaints recorded in the N.B.P.I. Report. Of four complaints upheld by the Industrial Court, 'in each case the contractor implemented the award and the contract was allowed to continue'. This appeared to him to be a satisfactory sanction for breach of the Resolution. Finally, a month before the unions' decision in 1972 to concentrate on the two biggest contractors, the Minister was asked on 18 May 1972 how many cleaners were employed by two specified firms, what the average weekly payment was by the Government to those firms, and whether any representations had been made by the Cleaners' Action Group. The Minister replied that there was no information available centrally, as contracts were negotiated locally by departmental representatives. Nothing had been heard from the C.A.G.[7]

None of this pressure produced the desired results, so in September 1972 the C.S.U. revealed its latest proposal to the Annual Trades Union Congress:

> Cleaning contracts in public sectors should be restricted to companies able to demonstrate that they recognize and negotiate with unions and contracts should provide that companies which agree to wages increases in order to practise fair wages policy should be entitled to corresponding increases in costs.

The Congress carried the motion after the C.S.U. representative had gone on to condemn the Government for not concerning itself with whether cleaners got a fair rate of wages:

> I have no doubt that the customary questions re fair wages and freedom to join unions are asked before a contract is given to the contract cleaning companies, and they of course agree to both. The Government then sit back and do absolutely nothing. They have done everything, according to them, that is required.

She commented sardonically on the urgings of the N.B.P.I. and the Secretary of State for Employment for the unions to increase their membership: 'How can we organize against such a background? The pay is so low that it takes most cleaners all their time to pay their bus fares backwards and forwards to work. They cannot afford union subs.' Accordingly, she proposed that the contractors' fixed contract provide for increases in pay.

Although the motion had been carried by the Congress, the General Council took the view that the proposition that any contractor observing the 'Fair Wage' should be entitled to automatic corresponding increases in contract payments, irrespective of the level of profitability of the company or its efficiency, was not one which the trade union movement itself could support. The Council did consider, however, that some special machinery was needed to deal with the problems of low-paid industries, including contract cleaning, and wrote to the C.S.U. to this effect. The C.S.U. replied supporting some such machinery, and in due course the T.U.C. recommended tripartite bodies representing unions, employers and the government to consider the question. It again wrote to the unions concerned asking their views. The unions expressed their satisfaction and appointed representatives to the proposed machinery. As for employers: 'the representation of the contract cleaning employers would be a matter for them to decide'. In April 1973 a letter was accordingly sent to the Lord Privy Seal as head of the Civil Service Department pressing for the establishment of special machinery. On 23 May 1973 a negative reply was duly received and duly condemned at the following Annual Trades Union Congress: 'This is a classic example of the Government's indifference to the disgraceful conditions that exist in this industry'.

A Concession At Last

The first indication that the return of a Labour Government in February 1974 might have the effect of thawing the frozen positions on this problem was in the reply of the Secretary of State for Employment to a question in Parliament as to whether he was satisfied with the operation of the Fair Wages Resolution. He replied on 21 May 1974:

> I realize that the circumstances in which the Fair Wages Resolution was passed by the House of Commons in 1946 were different from those which exist today. The Government would be prepared to discuss these arrangements with the T.U.C. and C.B.I. in the wider context of collective bargaining.[8]

The latest concession appears in a report that the Civil Service Union and the Civil Service Department have agreed that as from 1 May 1975 all contractors involved in cleaning government offices would provide at least local authority pay rates and holidays to their workers. The report continued that since local authority rates were similar to civil service ones, the undercutting of directly employed cleaners' pay rates by outside contractors would be prevented. While the implicit recognition by the Civil Service Department of the deficiencies in the employment conditions of contract cleaners has thus been made, this has been done only in the most indirect fashion and altogether too much room remains for the introduction of evasive comparisons.[9]

Conclusion

The history of the application of the Fair Wages policy to contract cleaners is a record of over two decades of delay in the recognition by the government of any problem, of the indifference of the Civil Service and the calculated hostility of the contractors. A strenuous campaign of over a decade by trade unions, through questions in Parliament, petitions to the government, approaches to the contracting departments and complaints to the Industrial Court has produced only the last-mentioned concession by the administration. It would be optimistic indeed to expect that this will be the salvation of the cleaners. The entire experience reflects no credit on either the Fair Wages Resolution or those charged with its implementation.[10]

NOTES

1. See Parl. Deb., H. of C. (Fifth Series); 12 December 1950, vol. 482, cols. 134–5 (Written Answers).

2. This information is contained in the Report of the General Council to the 101st Annual Trades Union Congress, Portsmouth, 1969, at para. 40, pp. 147–8. The Government's reply is described in rather different terms in Appendix C of the N.B.P.I. Report, p. 73.

3. Parl. Deb., H. of C. (Fifth Series); 10 February 1969, vol. 777, col. 304 (Written Answers).

4. This is probably the identical letter to that heretofore referred to as dated 2 April 1969. A discrepancy between the date of posting and the date of receipt may account for the difference. In any event, their import was the same.

5. See, e.g., Awards 1781, 1802, 1808, 1823, 1842, 1850, 1855–7, in 1941–2. Section 8(5) of the 1959 Act specifically provided that: 'For the purposes of this section the carrying on of the activities of public or local authorities shall be treated as the carrying on of a trade or industry'.

6. See, e.g., Awards 1773, 1775, 1803, 1861 and 2105, between 1940–7; and also the statement by the Chancellor in the House of Commons in 1952: the wages of the government's industrial employees are 'determined by reference to the approved rates for the individual trades concerned in outside industry'. Parl. Deb., H. of C. (Fifth Series); 21 October 1952, vol. 505, cols. 848–9.

7. For these Parliamentary exchanges see Parl. Deb., H. of C. (Fifth Series); 15 June 1971, vol. 819, col. 61 (Written Answers), per Mrs. Lena Jeger; 20 April 1972, vol. 835, cols. 145–6 (Written Answers), per Mr. Kenneth Baker, question from Mrs. Lena Jeger; 18 May 1972, vol. 837, col. 185 (Written Answers), per Mr. Kenneth Baker.

8. Parl. Deb., H. of C. (Fifth Series); 21 May 1974, vol. 874, col. 76; per Mr. Booth.

9. For the latest developments, see Jill Sullivan, *The Brush Off*, Low Pay Pamphlet No. 5, February 1977 (31 pp.), published by the Low Pay Unit.

10. Reference has been made to, and much of the above account is derived from the following sources:

—National Board for Prices and Incomes Report No. 168, *Pay and Conditions in the Contract Cleaning Trade*, Cmnd. 4637 (April 1971).

—Jim Skinner, *Fair Wages and Public Sector Contracts*, Fabian Research Series 310, June 1973.

—Royal Commission on Trade Unions and Employers' Associations, 1965–8; Evidence of Sir Roy Wilson, Q.C., *Minutes of Evidence* No. 45, Oral Evidence given on 26 July 1966, at Q. 7250.

—*Industrial Relations Review and Report*, No. 101 (April 1975), at p. 13.

—Parl. Deb., H. of C. (Fifth Series); 12 July 1955, vol. 543, col. 155 (Written Answers).

—Parl. Deb., H. of C. (Fifth Series); 15 June 1971, vol. 819, col. 61 (Written Answers).

—Report of the 96th Annual Trades Union Congress, Blackpool, 1964, speech by Mr. J. O. N. Vickers of the C.S.U., at p. 403.

—Report of the General Council to the 97th Annual T.U.C., Brighton, 1965, para. 407, at pp. 379–80.

—Report of the General Council to the 100th Annual T.U.C., Blackpool, 1968, para. 32, at p. 154.

—Report of the 100th Annual T.U.C., Blackpool, 1968, at pp. 433–5.

—Report of the General Council to the 101st Annual T.U.C., Portsmouth, 1969, para. 40, at pp. 147–8.

—Report of the General Council to the 102nd Annual T.U.C., Brighton, 1970, para. 87, pp. 190–1.

—Report of the 102nd Annual T.U.C., Brighton, 1970, at pp. 555–6.

—Report of the General Council to the 103rd Annual T.U.C., Blackpool, 1971, at pp. 51–3.

—Report of the General Council to the 104th Annual T.U.C., Brighton, 1972, para. 63, at pp. 47–8.

—Report of the 104th Annual T.U.C., Brighton, 1972, at p. 373.

—Report of the General Council to the 105th Annual T.U.C., Blackpool, 1973, para. 53, at pp. 48–9.

—Report of the 105th Annual T.U.C., Blackpool, 1973, at p. 456.

PART IV

Schedule 11 and the Future of Fair Wages Policy

20

The New Fair Wages Policy: Schedule 11 to the Employment Protection Act 1975

Apart from the occasional statutory embodiment of the Fair Wages Resolution (as in the Films Act 1960, and the Independent Broadcasting Authority Act 1973), the last major reincarnation of the Fair Wages policy was section 8 of the Terms and Conditions of Employment Act 1959. Its origins can be traced back through Order 1376 of 1951, the Fair Wages Resolution of 1946, Order 1305 of 1940 and the Fair Wages Resolutions of 1909 and 1891. However, as of 1 January 1977, yet another manifestation of Fair Wages policy has superseded the 1959 Act. Section 98 of the Employment Protection Act 1975 declares:

> The provisions of Schedule 11 to this Act shall have effect in place of section 8 of the Terms and Conditions of Employment Act 1959 and that Act is hereby repealed.

The essence of the new Fair Wages policy is contained in the first two paragraphs of Schedule 11:

> 1. A claim may be reported to the Service, in accordance with and subject to the following provisions of this part of this Schedule, that as respects any workers an employer is, in respect of any matter, observing terms and conditions of employment less favourable than the recognized terms and conditions or, where, or so far as, there are no recognized terms and conditions, the general level of terms and conditions.
> 2. In this Part of this Schedule—
> (a) the 'recognized terms and conditions' means terms and conditions of workers in comparable employment in the trade or industry, or section of a trade or industry, in which the employer in question is engaged, either generally or in the

For notes see p. 401

district in which he is so engaged, which have been settled by an agreement or award, to which the parties are employers' associations and independent trade unions which represent (generally or in the district in question, as the case may be) a substantial proportion of the employers and of the workers in the trade, industry or section, being workers of the description to which the agreement or award relates; and

(b) the 'general level of terms and conditions' means the general level of terms and conditions observed for comparable workers by employers—

   (i) in the trade, industry or section in which the employer in question is engaged in the district in which he is so engaged; and

   (ii) whose circumstances are similar to those of the employer in question,

and for the purposes of sub-paragraph (a) above the reference to terms and conditions, in a case where minimum terms and conditions have been settled as mentioned in that sub-paragraph, is a reference to those minimum terms and conditions.

These paragraphs contain elements of both section 8 of the 1959 Act and of clause 1(b) of the Resolution of 1946. The new Fair Wages policy of Schedule 11 thus contains phrases which are familiar from the old formula: *trade or industry, employers' associations* (defined now with particular care in section 126(2) of the Act) and trade unions, *representativeness* of these organizations of employers and workers, *settled* by agreements or awards, in the *district*; and perhaps the most important —the *general level* of terms and conditions. A detailed analysis of the meaning of each of these phrases, as elucidated from previous awards of the Industrial Court and the Industrial Arbitration Board, is to be found in chapter 16. That chapter provides a basis for understanding the same phrases which appear in Schedule 11. The Central Arbitration Committee, heir to the I.A.B., will in time establish its own interpretations. An indication of its attitude to these old problems, and its new approach during the first sixteen months of its existence (February 1976 to May 1977) is given in the following chapter. For now, it remains to review in more detail the provisions of Schedule 11.

'Recognized terms and conditions'

A claim under Schedule 11 may be based upon 'recognized terms and conditions' as defined in paragraph 2(a). Insofar as this claim was presumably to supersede section 8, few differences between the new claim and the old under the 1959 Act may be discerned:

(i) The terms of employment sought to be extended under section 8(1)(a) were those both 'established' and 'settled' by agreement or award, whereas those under Schedule 11 are only 'settled'. Since the terms in both claims are 'settled' by the same kinds of parties in the same kind of agreement or award (cf. section 8(1)(b)), it is clear that the terms to be extended will not differ under the new law from those extended under the old. The only distinction is introduced by the additional qualification made at the end of paragraph 2 that the terms settled may be minimum terms. But since it is notorious that agreements negotiated between unions and organizations of employers at the national or regional level almost always settle only minimum terms and conditions, this is a statement of the obvious. The supplementing of these agreements by local workplace bargaining is irrelevant here, as it was to claims under section 8. The 1959 Act developed as a marginal instrument for the extension of minimum terms and conditions—and that is all that can be expected from claims for 'recognized terms and conditions'.

It is worth reiterating here the point made earlier in chapter 16 that the omission of the word 'established' has, therefore, no significance in terms of the impact of these provisions. The relevant terms of employment for the purposes of these provisions of Schedule 11, as for those of section 8, are those settled by organizations of employers and trade unions which are usually minimum terms. The extension of minimum terms and conditions is a policy distinct from the policy of requiring Fair Wages to be paid.

(ii) The constipated draftsmanship of paragraph 2(a) (largely due to the meaningless omission of the word 'established' from the substance otherwise reproduced of section 8(1) of the 1959 Act) makes it difficult, but eventually possible to ascertain that the terms to be extended may be (settled) 'either generally or in the district' in question. This was the case under section 8(1)(a) of the 1959 Act.

(iii) A difference of some significance concerns which terms are to be extended. In Schedule 11, the workers whose terms are those 'recognized' are those in 'comparable employment' in the same industry. Under section 8, the workers whose terms are to be extended are those of 'the relevant description', defined in section 8(1)(b) as being those of the description to which the agreement relates. The effect is that workers who may be the subject of claims under Schedule 11 are not necessarily those of 'the relevant description' (as under section 8(1)(c)). They are instead those 'in comparable employment' in the same industry. Workers who may be affected need not be those to whom the agreement was intended to relate, but to 'comparable' employees.

So whereas section 8 was used to extend a collective agreement to cover employers refusing to comply with an agreement covering their employees who were of 'the relevant description', i.e. described under that agreement, Schedule 11 covers employers of all comparable workers in the industry. This change is of significance due to several Awards of the Industrial Arbitration Board. These held non-federated firms not to be bound as such by terms negotiated by an employers' association, which were stated in the agreement to be applicable to employees of federated firms (see Awards 3059, 3110 and 3168 discussed in chapter 16). Such findings appeared to contradict the clear intent of the 1959 Act. Any doubts raised by these Awards are now put to rest.

'General level of terms and conditions'

A claim under Schedule 11 may be based upon the 'general level of terms and conditions' as defined in paragraph 2(b), where, or so far as, there are no recognized terms and conditions. The grounds for such a claim are substantially similar to those for a complaint under clause 1(b) of the Fair Wages Resolution of 1946. Minor differences may be ascertained:

(i) Comparison is made not only with other employers whose circumstances are similar, but the workers whose terms are the standard to be complied with must also be 'comparable' with the workers the subject of the claim.

(ii) A degree of fragmentation is introduced by virtue of the words 'section' and 'district' which are not to be found in clause 1(b) of the 1946 Resolution. The 'general level' may be only that of a *section* of an industry in a particular *district*—both of which terms are subject to very elastic interpretation. The analysis in chapter 16 of Awards of the Industrial Court and Industrial Arbitration Board showed that despite the absence of a 'district' element in clause 1(b), this was in practice imported from clause 1(a). Consequently, the difference introduced in Schedule 11 may not be appreciable. The 'district' element is, of course, present in the definition of 'recognized terms and conditions' in paragraph 2(a). There it is not *necessarily* imported, but depends on whether the specified terms are relevant 'generally or in the district'.

(iii) The 'circumstances' of the employer compared need be similar, not the 'general circumstances'.

Who can claim?

A claim founded upon recognized terms and conditions may be reported by an employers' association or an independent trade union being one of the parties mentioned in paragraph 2(a) quoted above (para. 4 of Schedule 11). A claim founded upon the general level of terms and conditions may be reported by either an employers' association having members engaged in the trade, industry or section, in the district to which the claim relates, or by a trade union of which any worker concerned is a member (para. 5(1)). At the Committee Stage in the House of Lords, an amendment was inserted which had the effect of preventing non-recognized unions from reporting claims with respect to workers of a description in respect of which an employer recognizes an independent trade union (para. 5(2)).

A major difference is here obvious between those who can claim under the 'general level' provisions of Schedule 11 and those who can claim under clause 1(b) of the 1946 Resolution. Under Schedule 11, only a trade union or employers' association can claim. Under the Fair Wages Resolution, anybody can—workers, organized in trade unions or not, trade unions, individual employers or their associations. Since it is most frequently *unorganized* workers who are paid unfairly— below the 'general level'—it might seem desirable to allow them to lodge a claim under Schedule 11 to better their conditions. At present the Schedule does not permit claims to be made *by* unorganized workers. But it may be the case that claims could be made by trade unions *on their behalf.* Such a solution, if implemented, may, by illustrating the benefits of trade union organization, be considered more practical in the long run than claims by individual workers. This solution could be said to arise from the wording of paragraph 5(1)(b) of Schedule 11.

The right of a trade union to report a claim founded upon the general level of terms and conditions only arises when one of its members is a worker 'concerned'. Some ambiguity exists as to when a worker is deemed to be concerned in a claim. One view would be that the union reporting the claim must have at least one member employed by the employer subject to the claim. Such an interpretation would render paragraph 5 inconsistent with paragraph 4 which allows claims based on 'recognized terms and conditions' by unions having members in the trade, industry or section, in the district to which the claim relates, though not necessarily with the employer subject to the claim. Such a narrow view would certainly hinder claims against small employers who are generally perceived as the target of these provisions. A better view, therefore, would regard workers as 'concerned' in the claim not only if they are the subjects of a claim, but also if their wages and conditions are being undermined by the employer's low standards. Indeed, these workers will often be the ones concerned to the extent that it is their terms that are actually the basis of the comparison. If they are trade union members, their union should be given the right to make a claim based on the 'general level'. Thus, trade unions could lodge claims on behalf of unorganized workers where their members were concerned, in the broad sense of the word, with the unfair terms and conditions observed by the employer.

The Burden of Proof

Where the claim is founded on 'recognized terms and conditions', the burden of proving relevant terms should not be difficult. But in showing what the 'general level of terms and conditions' is, the party making the claim can anticipate greater difficulty. Unhelpfully, Schedule 11 does not specify in greater detail what is meant by the 'general level'. This is difficult enough to establish with regard to wages; when it comes to other terms and conditions it is next to impossible. The analysis in chapter 16 of the interpretation by the Industrial Arbitration Board of the substantially similar provisions of clause 1(b) of the 1946 Resolution offers little consolation. It may be recalled that in Award 3290 of 24 April 1974 (*Crittall-Hope Ltd. and Pay Board*), detailed submissions by the company and the Pay Board arguing on behalf of clusters around the median or arithmetical average or the use of quartiles sank without trace in the Award: the I.A.B. simply reiterated its dedication to 'a general comparison' in the broadest sense.

It will also be recollected that the reluctance of the I.A.B. to specify a method of calculating a 'general level' did not prevent it in a number of Awards from rejecting complaints based on clause 1(b) of the Resolution. It did this on the grounds of the failure of the complainant to demonstrate to the satisfaction of the Board, in the words of Award 3288 of 19 March 1974: 'that in relation to the industry concerned there is any ascertainable level of wages, hours or conditions of labour observed by other employers whose general circumstances in the industry are similar, or if so what that level is' (para. 35(2)). Schedule 11 does narrow down the scope of relevant terms to those 'in the district', and this may help, though it did not do so in the cases on clause 1(b). It is clear that claimants under Schedule 11 will have to be prepared to present sufficient information to substantiate the existence of a 'general level of terms and conditions' which is not being observed.

If the claimant does establish the existence of either 'recognized terms' or a 'general level', however, Schedule 11 provides that 'it shall be for the employer to satisfy the Committee that he is observing terms and conditions of employment not less favourable' (para. 8(b)). The significance of this shift in the burden of proof on the question of whether the employer's terms are not less favourable is increased by virtue of the explicit recognition that 'regard shall be had to the whole of the terms and conditions observed by the employer as respects the worker to whom the claim relates' (para. 9). Previously, an employer could defeat a claim by simply producing other superior terms alleged to balance out specified inferior terms so as to produce a 'general level' not less favourable. Now he must *prove* that this is the case. The claimant under Schedule 11 needs simply produce evidence establishing a 'general level' relating to one or more specific terms not observed by the employer. To rebut the claim, the employer will have to show that his failure is balanced out, not only with respect to his own other terms of employment, but having regard to the balance established by other employers. For example, it will not be enough for him to show that his terms as to holidays balance out his low pay. He will have to prove that his other terms are not matched by other employers, for otherwise his terms as a whole will still be less favourable than the 'general level'. With this explicit shift in the burden of proof, employers will have to maintain a much higher standard in the presentation of evidence in their defence than was formerly the case. It will not be overlooked that the accumulation of such comparative evidence may be of considerable interest to unions in their negotiations with employers.

Resolving the Claim

Paragraph 7 of Schedule 11 provides that: 'When a claim is reported to the Service under paragraph 1 above the Service shall take any steps which seem to it expedient to settle the claim or to secure the use of appropriate machinery to settle the claim and shall if the claim is not otherwise settled refer it to the (Central Arbitration) Committee'. The Committee, as the successor to the Industrial Arbitration Board and its predecessor the Industrial Court, is the independent tribunal which hears and determines the claim. So: 'If the Committee finds the claim wholly or partly well-founded it shall make an award that the employer shall observe the recognized terms and conditions or, as the case may be, terms and conditions conforming to the general level of terms and conditions' (para. 10). And: 'Any terms and conditions which by an award under paragraph 10 above the employer is required to observe in respect of employees of his shall have effect as part of the contract of employment of any such employee as from the date specified in the award' (para. 11).

Like its predecessors under the 1959 Act, the Committee's award is to have the effect of making the 'recognized terms and conditions' part of the contract of employment of any employee specified in the award. But, unlike the practice under clause 1(b) of the Fair Wages Resolution, the Committee, in deciding whether an employer is observing the 'general level of terms and conditions', is required to 'identify or specify . . . terms and conditions conforming to the general level of terms and conditions' (para. 10(a)). The traditional approach of simply upholding or denying a complaint of breach of the Resolution was abandoned in the contract cleaning cases, as described in chapter 19. There the Industrial Court specified *minimum* terms consistent with the observance of the Resolution. Under Schedule 11, the Committee is to specify not minimum terms and conditions, but those 'conforming to the general level'. These terms then have effect as part of the contracts of employment of the employees covered by the Award (para. 11).

That terms 'conforming to the general level' are *not* to be minimal would seem to be implied by paragraph 12 of the Schedule. This provides that where a contract of employment is affected *both* by an enactment providing for minimum remuneration or terms and conditions *and* by an award of the Committee under paragraph 10, that contract shall have effect in accordance with whichever of the two, the award or the enactment, is the more favourable to the employee. This paragraph might appear to consider that an award of the Committee could be more or less favourable in its terms and conditions than those minimum terms provided for by other enactments. But it can hardly be expected that the Committee would reward an employer's failure to conform to the 'general level' by, in effect, ordering him to observe sub-minimum standards. The logical inference is clear: the Committee is to specify standards 'conforming to the general level' which will be higher than minimum standards. The contract of employment will reflect this higher 'general level' even where it is subject also to minimum standards provided by virtue of an enactment. It may happen, through passage of time, that the Award's terms will be exceeded by statutory minima. Then the Award may be legally supplanted.

Low-Paid Workers in Certain Industries

The new Fair Wages policy of Schedule 11 contains, apart from the provisions described above, a number of special provisions relating to low-paid workers in certain industries. The new policy of enforcement of the 'recognized terms and conditions' or the 'general level of terms and conditions' is to apply even as respects workers whose remuneration or terms and conditions (or minimum remuneration or terms and conditions) is or are fixed in pursuance of the Agricultural Wages Act 1948 or the Agricultural Wages (Scotland) Act 1949, the Wages Councils Act 1959 or the provisions of the Employment Protection Act 1975 setting up statutory Joint Industrial Councils (sections 90–4).[1] But in addition, with regard to these low-paid workers, Schedule 11 goes on to provide that:

> 15. A claim may be reported to the Service under this paragraph by an independent trade union as respects any worker who is a member of that trade union and who falls within the field of operation of a wages council, a statutory joint industrial council, the Agricultural Wages Board or the Scottish Agricultural Wages Board—
>
> (a) that the union is a party to one or more collective agreements and that those agreements cover a significant number of establishments within the field of operation of that council or Board either generally or in the district in which the worker is employed; and
>
> (b) that in those establishments the circumstances of the employer are similar to those of the employer of the worker in question; and
>
> (c) that the employer is paying him less than the lowest current rate of remuneration (disregarding any rate agreed to more than 12 months before the date on which the claim was reported) payable to workers of his description under any of those agreements. (para. 15)

Independent trade unions in particularly low-paid industries are to be allowed, therefore, to claim the extension of collectively negotiated terms under different provisions in addition to those previously discussed. The only terms which can be extended under these new provisions, however, are those relating to rates of remuneration; and the 'lowest current rate of remuneration' payable to workers on whose behalf the union is claiming, at that. As the rate to be enforced by the Committee is the 'lowest current rate', it might be preferable for the union to proceed to claim rates of remuneration, and other terms and conditions, at the 'general level' envisaged by paragraph 2(b). The alternative procedure should be invoked only where such a 'general level' cannot be established by the trade union.

Where a 'general level' cannot be established, it may be easier for the union to proceed via this alternative procedure than to try to claim 'recognized terms and conditions'. For in order to claim the latter, the union must show that it represents a substantial proportion of the workers in the trade, industry or section, being workers of the description to which the agreement or award relates (para. 4) (as well as satisfying other criteria). To obtain the 'lowest current rate', the union claiming on behalf of its underpaid member need not be particularly representative, so long as it is a party to one or more agreements covering 'a significant number of establishments' within the field of operation of the joint machinery. And once it is shown that the employer is paying less than the lowest current rate under an agreement, it is not open to him to avoid this obligation even by showing that he is observing terms and conditions on the whole not less favourable (para. 16).

The Paradox of the New Fair Wages Policy

The provisions of Schedule 11 to the Employment Protection Act gave rise during their passage through Parliament to a great deal of controversy. John Elliott in the *Financial Times* (14 April 1975) branded them as 'potentially the most inflationary of the Bill's many provisions', a view which Eric Wigham in *The Times* (22 April 1975) characterized as 'needless worry'. Wigham in turn was accused of presenting an 'apologia . . . based on a fundamental misunderstanding of the Bill', since the provisions were, in fact, a 'bombshell', a view cited by the Conservative Opposition in the committee considering the Bill.[2]

The basis of the controversy rests on the assertion that the Fair Wages policy embodied in the Fair Wages Resolution of 1946 has been made applicable not only to government contractors, but to the whole of British industry. The policy laid down in that Resolution was substantially similar to that laid down in Order 1305 of 1940 and continued by Order 1376 of 1951 and embodied in section 8 of the 1959 Act. These enactments had in common with the 1946 Resolution the Fair Wages policy formula which had been agreed by the T.U.C. and the National Confederation of Employers' Organizations in negotiations prior to the Second World War. This formula required employers to adhere to terms of employment (in the words of clause 1(a) of the 1946 Resolution):

> not less favourable than those established for the trade or industry in the district where the work is carried out by machinery of negotiation or arbitration to which the parties are organizations of employers and trade unions representative respectively of substantial proportions of the employers and workers engaged in the trade or industry in the district.

The vital distinction which needs be drawn between the policy embodied in the 1946 Resolution and the legislation of 1940, 1951 and 1959 is that although the Fair Wages standard applied by the latter was substantially similar to the primary standard contained in clause 1(a) of the 1946 Resolution, the Resolution, albeit of more limited scope, had further effect. For where there were no agreements applicable which could be held to establish the standard stipulated in clause 1(a), there was another standard—that of clause 1(b)— which applied:

> In the absence of any rates of wages, hours or conditions of labour so established the contractor shall pay rates of wages, and observe hours and conditions of labour, which are not less favourable than the general level of wages, hours and conditions observed by other employers whose general circumstances in the trade or industry in which the contractor is engaged are similar.

Where no agreements applied as stipulated in the legislation of 1940, 1951 and 1959, there was no such secondary safeguard and workers had no protection from that quarter. That legislation, albeit adopting the standard of the Fair Wages policy, is often regarded, therefore, as merely providing for the extension of collective agreements.

It is this vital distinction between the Fair Wages policy of the legislation of 1940, 1951 and 1959, and that of the Resolution of 1946, which Schedule 11 to the Employment Protection Act both highlights and attempts to overcome. It seeks to achieve this by combining elements of both policies. This is done by reproducing provisions substantially similar first to those of section 8 of the 1959 Act, and secondly, to those of clause 1(b) of the 1946 Resolution. The end result is as if the policy of the 1946 Resolution had been reproduced, but made applicable to all of British industry instead of only to government contractors. The principal difference, however, is that for clause 1(a) of the 1946 Resolution there is substituted the provisions of section 8 of the 1959 Act. In sum, the provisions of Schedule 11 may be seen to approximate the following equation:

'*recognized terms*'

Schedule 11, para. 2(a) = Terms and Conditions of Employment Act, section 8. (Cf. clause 1(a) of the Fair Wages Resolution of 1946.)

'*general level*'

Schedule 11, para. 2(b) = Clause 1(b) of the Fair Wages Resolution of 1946.

The result of this combination of elements of the two policies is that a potentially paradoxical situation may occur. The effect of the substitution of the provisions of section 8 of the 1959 Act for clause 1(a) of the 1946 Resolution appears to change the impact of the Fair Wages policy as laid down by that Resolution. As interpreted by the Industrial Arbitration Board that policy requires government contractors to pay fair wages to their employees. Where collective agreements are made between organizations of employers and trade unions (as envisaged by both clause 1(a) of the 1946 Resolution and section 8 of the 1959 Act as reproduced in Schedule 11), these were to be the standard applicable, *to the extent that they established fair wages*. Where they merely established *minimum* rates, however, they obviously did not establish fair, but only minimum wages, and thus resort was to be had to clause 1(b) of the Resolution.

In Schedule 11 to the 1975 Act, however, the substitution of section 8 of the 1959 Act for clause 1(a) of the 1946 Resolution appears to produce a contrary result. For, far from disposing of minimum standards, it seems to embrace them—as in the last lines of paragraph 2 of Schedule 11. That this would be in contradiction of the *Fair* Wages policy has not prevented the insertion into the Schedule of additional provisions substantially similar to clause 1(b) of the 1946 Resolution. It would be misleading, however, to characterize this insertion as being the general introduction of a Fair Wages policy into British industry. So long as minimum standards are allowed to prevail over the 'general level' which is perceived as 'fair', it cannot be thus characterized. Rather, what appears to be produced by Schedule 11 is decidedly odd. Workers who have the protection of minimum standards, through the negotiation of collective agreements between employers' associations and their trade unions, retain the protection available to them previously through section 8 of the 1959 Act, but do not benefit from the 'fair' standards envisaged by the provisions of the Schedule adopted from clause 1(b) of the 1946 Resolution. On the other hand, workers who do not have the protection of minimum standards through such agreements, gain that of 'fair' standards provided by Schedule 11.

A Solution to the Paradox

In order to avoid this unsatisfactory and paradoxical result, the Central Arbitration Committee (heir to the Industrial Arbitration Board) may adopt the approach laid down by the Board in its Award 3290 of 24 April 1974 (*Crittall-Hope Ltd. and Pay Board*), described in detail in chapter 15 above. In applying the 1946 Resolution, the Board was faced with the question of which of the standards in clause 1(a) and 1(b) of the Resolution was appropriate. The complainant in that case argued that clauses 1(a) and 1(b) stipulated equal and alternative standards; that clause 1(a) was not appropriate as the National Agreement in question had been superseded by locally negotiated rates; and that consequently, clause 1(b) was applicable. The Pay Board argued that clauses 1(a) and 1(b) should be considered as applying in a strictly hierarchical order:

> Discussing whether the case fell to be considered under clause 1(a) or clause 1(b), the Pay Board submitted that the onus was on the Company to show that clause 1(a) was not applicable before they could ask that clause 1(b) should be applied. If there was an appropriate agreement which governed rates of wages then there could be no question of having the case considered under clause 1(b): the intention of the Resolution was to ensure that the trade union rate, if there was one, was paid. (para. 28)

The Board's decision was a subtle compromise of these two positions: where a collective agreement fixed rates, if these turned out to be minimum rates in practice, then clause 1(a) would apply to these, but only as such. Clause 1(b) would apply to other aspects of the employees' terms and conditions, including rates actually paid (para. 45). The reasoning behind the compromise was given in paragraph 43 of the Award:

> The general purpose of the Resolution would appear to be frustrated if the effect of clause 1(a) were to confine the workers concerned to wages, hours or conditions which are less favourable to them than the general level referred to in clause 1(b).

A similar policy argument may equally sway the Central Arbitration Committee in interpreting Schedule 11. To avoid the paradoxical result of awarding certain workers minimum wages under paragraph 2(a) of the Schedule, and others 'fair' wages under paragraph 2(b), the Committee may prefer to follow in the steps of its predecessor. Thus, where the 'recognized terms and conditions' were minimal, the Committee would enforce the 'general level' stipulated by the

Schedule. Its decision might run along the lines suggested in chapter 16: under paragraph 1 of Schedule 11, a claim may be based on the 'general level', 'where, or so far as, there are no recognized terms and conditions'. Following the I.A.B.'s lead, it is open to the Committee to decide that where an employer is adhering only to minimum standards, it is not precluded from allowing a claim based on the 'general level'. The Committee may indeed hold that minimum terms have been settled by collective arrangements—i.e. are 'recognized'. But where *only* minimum terms are 'recognized', and the collective arrangements do not settle 'fair' terms, it may be held that there are no 'recognized' *fair* terms. Accordingly, a claim may be allowed under Schedule 11 based on the 'general level'. The distinction between minimum terms laid down in a collective agreement, and terms actually observed, is commonplace. The Central Arbitration Committee could accept that recognized 'minimum' terms exist, but recognized 'actual' terms do not. Claims could then be put forward for the 'general level' of terms actually observed. The Committee's likely interpretation of 'recognized minimum terms and conditions' is discussed further in the following chapter.

The Future Potential of the New Fair Wages Policy

It is the possibility that workers might be enabled to claim 'fair' wages based on a 'general level' that has caused so much of the controversy provoked by these provisions. At the very least, even if the benefit of clause 1(b) of the 1946 Resolution is available through Schedule 11 only to workers *not* covered by collective agreements negotiated between employers' associations and trade unions, there is certainly potential for widespread utilization of the provisions. The procedure could be used to impose a 'general level of terms and conditions' across an industry untouched by such collective bargaining. Such an attempt was made using clause 1(b) of the Fair Wages Resolution in the contract cleaning industry, as described in chapter 19. Between 1968 and 1973 ten cases came before the Industrial Court concerning complaints that employers were not observing a 'general level' of terms and conditions.

In white collar employment, particularly in the private sector, collective agreements negotiated between employers' associations and trade unions are rare indeed. Unions are also inclined, perhaps more through necessity than choice, to use legal procedures rather than industrial strength. In these sectors, there is a clear possibility of implementing a concerted drive to eliminate low pay.

Paradoxically, low-paid workers in industries *covered* by such collective agreements might be left without such an opportunity. It is hoped that the Central Arbitration Committee will appreciate the industrial relations consequences of excluding such low-paid workers by a narrow interpretation of the phrase 'where, or so far as, there are no recognized terms'. If the Committee were to exclude workers covered by 'recognized minimum terms' from the benefits of Schedule 11, the trade unions negotiating such agreements might be tempted to remedy this. They could do so simply by excluding wholesale certain categories of workers from coverage by those agreements. They could then proceed to the Committee to claim terms and conditions based on the 'general level'. The Committee would do well to avoid such disruption of long-standing bargaining arrangements by adopting a broad interpretation of the Schedule which would accord with its intent to afford a remedy to the unfairly low paid workers.

But the real potential of the new Fair Wages policy is based on the recognition that the Fair Wages standard of national agreements, as embodied in clause 1(a) of the 1946 Resolution and section 8 of the 1959 Act, has become ineffective. As national agreements have taken on the character of minimum standards and have been gradually exceeded by locally negotiated rates, that 'Fair Wages' standard has come to represent a minimum standard. The value of the alternative Fair Wages standard embodied in clause 1(b) of the 1946 Resolution has thereby become enhanced. Particularly in recent years it has come to be used in tactical avoidance of the minimum standards set by national agreements.

It is by learning from experience of the Fair Wages Resolution of 1946 that trade unions may be able to derive the greatest benefit from the new Fair Wages policy in Schedule 11. So long as national agreements establish what are in practice only minimum terms and conditions of employment, superseded by locally negotiated rates, the procedure laid down by Schedule 11 for the extension of such agreements ('recognized terms and conditions') will have as little value as in the past. Using Schedule 11 to make claims based on the 'general level of terms and conditions', however, may be infinitely more productive. The 'general level' as interpreted by the Industrial Arbitration Board in cases on the Fair Wages Resolution of 1946 is different from the minimum level of terms and conditions. Should the Central Arbitration Committee similarly hold the 'general level' of Schedule 11 to be different from the minimal 'recognized terms and conditions', and follow the Board in holding that 'general level' to reflect terms of employment actually observed (e.g. rates actually paid), then Schedule 11 could become the instrument for a widespread campaign. Trade unions could use leading sectors of workers as the spear-head in establishing a high 'general level'. Pockets of low-paid workers which do not reflect the 'general level' could be eliminated.

The best illustrations of the tactical use of clause 1(b) of the Resolution to avoid clause 1(a) are in the nine cases concerning the 1972–4 pay policy, described in detail in chapter 15. There, applicants to the Industrial Arbitration Board expressly pointed to the minimal character of national agreements to argue that it was the 'general level' which was the applicable Fair Wages standard. The sudden influx of cases drew from the Board a more sophisticated approach to the content of clause 1(b) than the previous simple averaging out of a number of local wage rates. The submissions of the parties and the decisions of the Board interpreting the meaning of the 'general level' in these cases are, needless to say, of considerable interest in any attempt to assess the potential effect of the substantially similar provisions of Schedule 11. The results in themselves would seem to augur well for the similar use of Schedule 11. In the nine cases a 'general level' was established which allowed for increases in wages where national agreements settled only minimum rates. Looking at the overall record of complaints under the Resolution between 1959–74: out of thirty-six cases, eighteen failed outright to redress complaints; another four were split decisions and one was withdrawn. Only four of the thirty-six can be considered as bona fide successful claims where workers benefited from the Fair Wages Resolution. The nine successful cases under the pay policy constitute an omen for a future constructive role for the new Fair Wages policy. It is hoped the Central Arbitration Committee will consider it carefully.

A Note of Caution

Despite these possibilities, which have clearly fired the imaginations of some, others have remained determinedly unenthusiastic. Certainly the Government which produced the new law has taken a very conservative view of its potential impact. In shepherding the bill through the House of Commons Committee, Mr. A. Booth, then Minister of State at the Department of Employment concluded: 'The very fair experience of fair wages resolutions that this country has, from which it can judge the effects of Schedule 11, would not lead anyone to expect that there would be massive numbers of successful claims under its provisions'. Another Labour M.P. referred to the Resolution as 'ineffective', and to both section 8 of the 1959 Act and the Resolution as being 'quite derisory'.[3] The detailed study in preceding chapters

of the antecedents of Schedule 11—the 1946 Resolution and the enactments of 1940, 1951 and 1959—does tend to confirm these harsh
judgments. But the enormous number of claims which have been
lodged under Schedule 11 during the first few months of 1977 indicates
that the trade unions are prepared once again to hope that the Central
Arbitration Committee will breathe life into it. It remains to be seen
if the new Fair Wages policy can redeem the reputation of its predecessors.

NOTES

1. The existing position of low-paid workers in relation to the Fair Wages policy of the 1959 Act was described in the recent Award 3309 of 12 February 1975 (*Home Brewery Co. Ltd. and National Association of Licensed House Managers*):

> the Industrial Relations Act 1971 amended the original provisions of Section 8 by (inter alia) removing the bar therein contained upon the report- ing of claims as respects workers whose remuneration or minimum remunera- tion was fixed under the Wages Council legislation. The provisions of the Industrial Relations Act 1971 had, however, been repealed by the Trade Union and Labour Relations Act 1974 ... the effect of the Act of 1974 was to amend, in the single respect set out in paragraph 8 of its Schedule 3, the provisions of Section 8 as re-formulated

in Part II of Schedule 7 of the Act of 1971, and that accordingly it did not restore the bar, referred to above, which had been imposed by Section 8 in its original form and removed by the Act of 1971. Accordingly the existence of a Wages Regulation Order under the Wages Councils Act 1959 is not, as the law now stands, a bar to a reference under Section 8 (para. 17).

2. See *Industrial Relations Legal Information Bulletin* No. 105, 4 June 1975; cited in Standing Committee F on the Employment Protection Bill, 25th Sitting, 10 July 1975, col. 1324.

3. See comments by Mr. A. Booth and Mr. J. W. Rooker, in the Report of Standing Committee F on the Employment Protection Bill, 25th Sitting, 10 July 1975, at cols. 1311, 1314 and 1316.

21

The Central Arbitration Committee
and Fair Wages Policy

The Central Arbitration Committee, which is to determine claims made under Schedule 11 came into existence on 1 February 1976. Section 10(2) of the Employment Protection Act 1975 empowered the Committee to hear the outstanding cases of the Industrial Arbitration Board which it replaced. Since 1 February 1976, the Committee has determined these cases. Amongst others, the Committee has handed down awards on a number of references concerning the Fair Wages policy—under the Fair Wages Resolution of 1946, section 8 of the 1959 Act and other instruments.

Analysis of the activity of the Committee during the first sixteen months of its existence, up to Award 114 of 20 May 1977, reveals two significant trends in the implementation of Fair Wages policy. The first relates to the dramatic increase in the Fair Wages activity of the Committee; the second to the equally dramatic increase in the proportion of successful claims under the Fair Wages policy. Each of these will now be briefly reviewed.

The Increase in Fair Wages Activity

There has been a substantial increase in the Fair Wages activity of the Committee. With regard to the Fair Wages Resolution itself, it may be recalled that during the thirty years up to the end of 1975, the Industrial Arbitration Board and its predecessor, the Industrial Court, had produced an annual average of two awards. The peak year had been 1974 with ten awards on the Resolution, and three others on related statutes.

In 1976, however, the Industrial Arbitration Board (January) and Central Arbitration Committee (February–December) handed down

For note see p. 469

thirteen awards on the Resolution, and another two on related statutes. And in its *First Annual Report, 1976*, the Committee reported that it had received thirty-three references under the Resolution from the Secretary of State for Employment, of which at the end of the year nineteen were still awaiting a hearing (Appendix 2 of the *Report*).

In the first five months of 1977 (up to 20 May), another eighteen awards were published. And all the signs are that activity is likely to continue at this high level. Table 6 showed the number of questions raised formally with the Department of Employment to have risen from nine in the whole of 1975 to seventy-two in the first ten months of 1976 alone (up to 31 October). The Committee's timetable of cases to be heard indicated a total of eleven hearings of complaints under the Resolution in May, six in June and ten in July 1977.

With regard to section 8 of the 1959 Act, the year 1976 saw the Industrial Arbitration Board and Central Arbitration Committee handing down by far the largest number of awards in the history of the statute—thirty-three in all (the previous peak had been twenty-three in 1967—see Table 5). And in its *First Annual Report, 1976*, the Committee reported that it had received fifty references from the Secretary of State under the 1959 Act, of which at the end of the year fifteen were still awaiting hearing (Appendix 2).

As has been described in the preceding chapter, however, on 1 January 1977, section 8 of the 1959 Act was replaced by Schedule 11 to the Employment Protection Act 1975. Furthermore, paragraph 13(2) of Schedule 17 to that Act provided that:

> Any claim reported to the Secretary of State or referred to the Industrial Arbitration Board under the said section 8 which immediately before the commencement of the said Schedule was pending before the Board shall be treated on that commencement as if it had been reported to the Service or referred to the Committee under Part I of the said Schedule.

Up to the 20 May 1977, fifteen more awards had been published concerning claims originally submitted under the 1959 Act, but treated by the Committee as if reported under Schedule 11.

Yet even this greatly increased number of references and awards under the old Fair Wages policy instruments fades into insignificance when compared with the impending deluge of claims under Schedule 11— the new instrument of Fair Wages policy. Claims could be lodged under the Schedule as of 1 January 1977. Up to 28 January, A.C.A.S. was reported to have received seventy-nine formal claims under the Schedule, and up to 21 March, a total of 281 claims had been formally reported. Officials confirm that the flow of claims is being maintained at between three and four per day. The Committee's timetable of cases to be heard indicated a total of fourteen Schedule 11 case hearings in May, twenty-seven in June and twenty-nine in July. The first award on a claim under Schedule 11 was handed down on 20 April—Award 103—a successful claim by the Transport and General Workers' Union against I. E. White (Plastics) Ltd.

The New-Found Success of Fair Wages Claims

The second significant trend in the activity of the Committee is the increasing success of claims made under the various instruments of Fair Wages policy. During the last thirteen months of its existence, January 1975 to January 1976, the Industrial Arbitration Board handed down five awards concerned with the Fair Wages Resolution (three on the Resolution itself, one on the Road Traffic Act 1960, and one on a Greater London Council Fair Wages Clause). All five complaints were dismissed. During the same period, the Board also determined thirteen claims under the 1959 Act. Of these, twelve failed and only one was successful.

In contrast, during the first sixteen months of its existence (up to Award 114 of 20 May 1977), the Committee had upheld twenty-three of the thirty-one complaints made to it under the Fair Wages Resolution, and had upheld thirty-two of the forty-five claims made under the 1959 Act—an overall success rate of over two-thirds.

The difference in results between the Industrial Arbitration Board and the Committee is clear beyond doubt. The success of the Fair Wages policy in the Committee does not seem quite so secure, however, when the awards handed down are subjected to close analysis. For it is rather difficult to distinguish exactly where the difference in the Committee's approach to the policy lies. Caution is necessary when attempting to draw conclusions from such a short span of time and limited number of awards. But the following two points may be made with regard to the new-found success of the policy.

The Pattern of Success: 1976–1977

With regard to complaints under the Fair Wages Resolution, the pattern seems to be one of an initial burst of successful references, followed by an increasing degree of failure. The first months of the Committee's activity saw an uninterrupted flow of successful complaints under the Resolution. From February to December 1976, twelve awards were handed down upholding complaints (Awards 2,

6, 14, 23, 30, 33, 36, 37, 50, 53, 55 and 58). In addition, there were two successful complaints under statutory Fair Wages provisions—Award 21 under the Independent Broadcasting Authority Act 1973, and Award 68 under the Films Act 1960. December saw the first unsuccessful complaint—Award 67. Beginning with January 1977, the complaints under the Resolution began to receive a more mixed reception from the Committee. January had one award upholding a complaint (Award 71); but February had two failures (Awards 76 and 78) to five successes (Awards 79, 80, 81, 84 and 88); March, one failure (Award 86) and one success (Award 90); April, two successes (Awards 100 and 106); and May three failures (Awards 104, 111 and 114) and three successes (Awards 108, 112 and 113).

The pattern is much more even with regard to awards under the 1959 Act. The position is complicated by the fact that during 1976 the Committee treated claims as falling under the 1959 Act, while since 1 January 1977 they have been treated as falling under Schedule 11. Nonetheless, there do not appear to have been any substantial fluctuations. In 1976 the Committee made thirty awards of which twenty were successful (Awards 1, 3, 4 and 5, 12, 15, 16, 18, 24, 27, 28, 38, 42, 44, 45, 47, 52, 54, 59 and 66), seven failed (Awards 9, 10, 32, 35, 40, 41 and 56), and of the others, one was settled (Award 57), one postponed (Award 62) and one was an interpretation of a previous award (Award 63). Up to 20 May 1977, there were fifteen awards published, eleven successful claims (Awards 73, 75, 77, 82, 83, 85, 92, 94, 95, 97 and 102), and four failures (Awards 74, 89, 93 and 99).

The Influence of the Chairman

The second point concerns the pattern of success which appears to change as the sitting chairman of the Committee changes. The Chairmen of the Committee is John C. Wood, Professor of Law at Sheffield University. He has handed down forty-one awards on Fair Wages policy, more than all the other deputy chairmen combined. Of these forty-one awards, thirteen concerned complaints under the Fair Wages Resolution. All thirteen were upheld. An additional Fair Wages complaint under the Independent Broadcasting Authority Act 1973 was also upheld. Professor Wood also handed down twenty-seven awards under the 1959 Act, of which twenty-one were successful claims and three failed (the three others comprised one interpretation of a previous award, one interim decision and one settled). Not only has Professor Wood made more awards than any of his colleagues, but they also reflect a much higher ratio of success than the overall pattern:

in complaints under the Resolution—13 : 13 versus 23 : 31; in claims under the 1959 Act—21 : 27 versus 32 : 45.

The deputy chairman who sat the most frequently is Stuart McDowall, who teaches economics at the University of St. Andrews. He has handed down nineteen awards on Fair Wages policy. Of these, nine concerned complaints under the Resolution, of which six were upheld, two dismissed and one was split. Another complaint under the Films Act 1960 was upheld. Under the 1959 Act, Mr. McDowall has handed down another nine awards, of which five were successful claims and four failures. His ratio is thus just below the norm of successful awards: on the Fair Wages Resolution—6 : 9 versus 23 : 31; in claims under the 1959 Act—5 : 9 versus 32 : 45.

Mr. N. Singleton has handed down twelve awards: six on the Fair Wages Resolution and six on the 1959 Act. Of those on the Resolution, two complaints were upheld and four dismissed. Of those under the 1959 Act, three claims were successful and three failed. His ratio is thus well below the norm of successful awards: on the Resolution—2 : 6 versus 23 : 31; on the 1959 Act—3 : 3 versus 32 : 45.

Mr. J. S. Wordie, a barrister, has handed down six awards on Fair Wages policy, including the first successful claim under Schedule 11. Under the Resolution he has handed down two awards, one upholding a complaint and one dismissing a complaint. Under the 1959 Act, three claims were dealt with, two allowed and one rejected. The sample is too small to be of any significance.

Finally, Mr. N. S. Ross has, at the time of writing, made only one award, dismissing a complaint under the Fair Wages Resolution.

It would, at this early stage, be unwise to draw any definitive conclusions regarding the significance of the varying ratio of favourable and unfavourable awards from different chairmen. The fact remains, however, that the Chairman of the Committee has succeeded in giving substance to the Fair Wages policy to an extent greater than any of his fellows.

Leaving behind the above description of trends and patterns in the activity of the Committee, the remainder of this chapter will be concerned with an attempt to analyse the substance of its awards. From such analysis, certain conclusions may be drawn as to the Committee's attitude towards the new Fair Wages policy of Schedule 11. But first, a brief description of the Committee itself is warranted.

The Central Arbitration Committee

The Committee was brought into existence by section 10 of the Employment Protection Act 1975. But apart from its role in implementing the new Fair Wages policy of Schedule 11, it was given a number of other functions by that Act. Whereas the industrial tribunals are to be the instruments of settling disputes over individual rights, the Committee has the function of adjudicating on disputes over certain collective rights granted by the Act: recognition and disclosure of information. The Committee also has jurisdiction over certain equal pay disputes under the Equal Pay Act 1970, and a general arbitration function under section 3 of the Employment Protection Act 1975. It retains its old jurisdiction over the Fair Wages Resolutions as well.

Relation to A.C.A.S.

The Employment Protection Act 1975 assigned the primary role in dealing with the problems of arbitration, recognition, disclosure and Schedule 11 to A.C.A.S. The Committee was given the role of adjudicating in disputes where A.C.A.S. had failed to achieve a voluntary settlement. So effectively, the Committee emerges as the enforcement arm of A.C.A.S.

The close relationship of the Committee to A.C.A.S. is made abundantly clear in the provisions relating to its constitution in Schedule 1 to the Act. The Committee is to consist entirely, with the possible exception of its chairman and deputy chairmen (para. 14(1) and (3)) of members experienced in industrial relations, some of them as workers' representatives and some as employers' representatives (para. 14(2)). The constitution of its predecessor, the Industrial Arbitration Board, simply stipulated that some members should be representative and others independent (as well as a statutory woman) (Industrial Courts Act 1919, s. 1(1)). It is in the composition of its membership that the close relationship of the Committee to A.C.A.S. may best be perceived. For although appointed by the Secretary of State for Employment, its membership is composed of nominees of A.C.A.S. (para. 14(2)). In addition, its chairman and deputy chairmen may only be appointed after the Secretary of State has consulted A.C.A.S. Further, the Service provides the Committee's staff from among its own officers and servants, and controls as well their requisite accommodation, equipment and other facilities (para. 8). Certain of the Committee's most important functions are subject to the control of the Service. Thus, for example, it can only arbitrate in disputes referred to it by the Service under section 3(1)(b); the Committee only adjudicates on complaints of a failure to comply with a recommendation for trade union recognition (made by the Service) when the Service's conciliation has failed; and, not least, the Committee only adjudicates on a claim under Schedule 11 after the Service has first attempted settlement. The Committee even has to account annually to the Service for its activities (para. 25). Despite this formal dependence, the Committee does not seem to have been unduly influenced, let alone dominated, in its operations to date by A.C.A.S. In its *First Annual Report, 1976,* the Committee scarcely refers to A.C.A.S. at all; for example, merely expressing its gratitude for its assistance and co-operation (p. 14).

Codes of Practice

Perhaps the most substantial way in which A.C.A.S. may influence the workings of the Committee is through the Codes of Practice it issues, in accordance with section 6(1) of the Employment Protection Act: 'The Service may issue Codes of Practice containing such practical guidance as the Service thinks fit for the purpose of promoting the improvement of industrial relations'. The Service is obliged to issue Codes relating to the obligation of an employer to disclose information to trade union representatives (sections 17 and 18) and to allow time off to trade unions officials and members (sections 57 and 58). But ordinarily, Codes are to be prepared and issued at the discretion of the Service, subject to the approval of the Secretary of State for Employment. The significance of Codes of Practice to the Fair Wages policy and the Central Arbitration Committee emerges from the provisions of section 6(11) of the Employment Protection Act:

> A failure on the part of any person to observe any provision of a Code of Practice shall not of itself render him liable to any proceedings; but in any proceedings before an industrial tribunal or the Central Arbitration Committee any Code of Practice issued under this section shall be admissible in evidence, and if any provision of such a Code appears to the tribunal or Committee to be relevant to any question arising in the proceedings it shall be taken into account in determining that question.

It is clear, therefore, that in cases concerning Fair Wages policy which come before the Committee, relevant provisions of Codes of Practice may influence the Committee's decisions. Indeed, the possibility exists that a Code of Practice might be specially devised by A.C.A.S. to provide practical guidance to employers (or indeed to the Committee itself) on the application of Fair Wages policy. The opportunity exists for a Code on Fair Wages policy to be drawn up, relying on the experience of past decades and with a view to the scope of the new policy of the future.

It may be noted, however, that this potential is not entirely new. A similar provision existed in the Industrial Relations Act 1971 (section 4). Curiously enough, the possibility was extinguished when the 1971 Act was repealed by the Trade Union and Labour Relations Act 1974. Although Part I of Schedule 1 to the 1974 Act retained the Code of Practice issued under the Industrial Relations Act by the Commission on Industrial Relations, it only provided for its authority to extend to industrial tribunals, and omitted the Industrial Arbitration Board from the sphere of the Code's influence (paragraph 3 of the Schedule). The Employment Protection Act 1975 retains this curious refusal to allow the Central Arbitration Committee to consider the Code—paragraph 4(1) of Schedule 17 refers only to industrial tribunals taking it into account. But the 1975 Act has restored the old position as regards new Codes. In the section quoted above, the Committee must take the new Codes into account, including, oddly enough, those new Codes replacing parts of the old Code. Despite the fact that the Code could have been invoked during the existence of the 1971 Act before the I.A.B., there is no record of any reference to it in any proceedings involving the Fair Wages policy.

Despite its lack of impact in the past, the significance of the Codes of Practice before the Committee should not be underestimated. For example, the provisions of a Code of Practice relating to trade union recognition would seem to be very relevant to complaints by workers or a trade union under clause 4 of the Fair Wages Resolution. The heretofore restricted scope of clause 4 would seem to have been amplified enormously—A.C.A.S. in drawing up the Codes is bound by its duty stated in section 1(2): 'of encouraging the extension of collective bargaining'. Similarly, claims under Schedule 11 would be influenced by the employer's attitude to trade unions and collective agreements. The very definition of the 'general level of terms and conditions' considered to be 'fair' might be affected by standards of good industrial practice laid down by A.C.A.S. in the Codes. The policies of the Service may thus be reinforced through the Awards of the Committee, as the industrial tribunals have already enforced the standards relating to unfair dismissal. While still ignored, the potential for exploitation of the Codes of Practice awaits the hand of an imaginative Committee.

Independence

Whatever its relationship to A.C.A.S. will prove to be in the future, the Committee clearly wants to establish itself in the eyes of the public as an independent body—independent particularly from government influence. In the Introduction to its *First Annual Report, 1976*, it specifically points out:

> In relation to the Committee's independent approach to its tasks, attention may usefully be drawn to the terms of Clause 27 of Schedule 1 (to the Employment Protection Act 1975) which states:—
>
>> 'The functions of the Committee shall be performed on behalf of the Crown but the Committee shall not be subject to directions of any kind from any Ministers of the Crown as to the manner in which it is to exercise any of its functions under any enactment.'
>
> This important provision plainly secures the Committee's independence.[1] (para. 1.4)

The Committee exercises its powers in many politically sensitive areas, not least of which will be the Fair Wages policy. The degree to which it maintains its independence of government policy (e.g. on incomes) will only be ascertainable from the results of its activity—the Awards it hands down. It is greatly to be regretted, therefore, that the Committee was not required to publish the reasons for its decisions, though the decisions themselves must be published (para. 24). The same omission on the part of its predecessors rendered much of their activity opaque and misunderstood. As will shortly be indicated, the Committee has taken regularly to explaining its Awards by listing various 'General Considerations' it has had regard to. It is to be hoped that this practice will become more firmly established, and that the reasons for the Committee's actions will be systematically expounded. The Committee may wish to avoid public controversy, but it must make its policies known to the constituencies it serves.

A final point worth noticing is the extremely powerful position of the chairman of the Committee: he decides whether the Committee should discharge its function privately or publicly (para. 18); and if in any case the nominee members of A.C.A.S. disagree on an award, or even if they both agree but the chairman disagrees with them, then he decides the matter (para. 19).

The Last Cases of the Industrial Arbitration Board: 1975–1976

It is not difficult to understand the application of Fair Wages policy by the Industrial Arbitration Board during the last year of its existence: the awards were consistent with the ineffectual impression given

by the Fair Wages policy in previous decades. With the sole exception
of the cases concerned with the 1973–4 pay policy, the past record
of cases brought to the Board and its predecessor had been dismal.
So the five complaints of breach of the Fair Wages Resolution decided
between January 1975 and January 1976 were all rejected in predict-
able fashion.

In Award 3307 of 27 January 1975 (*A.U.E.W.* (*T.A.S.S.*) *and
British Nuclear Design and Construction Ltd.*), it was common ground
between the parties that clause 1(a) of the Resolution was inapplicable
—no terms were established by machinery of negotiation or arbitration. The dispute arose over which 'trade or industry' the contractor
was engaged in, so as to enable the I.A.B. to decide whether he was
complying with the 'general level' observed by other employers whose
general circumstances were similar, as required by clause 1(b). The
Union 'regarded the workers concerned as being engaged in a specialized section of the engineering industry, that section being the nuclear
power industry' (para. 8). The Union argued that:

> in past cases the Board had consistently taken account of the
> type of work actually being performed by the workers concerned
> in a Reference, rather than give weight to any loose industrial
> association that might exist. In the present case the Company
> were clearly not engaged in manufacturing: they provided a
> service for the nuclear power industry which was part of the
> general engineering industry and, while it was true that the
> functions of their employees were engineering functions, they
> were of a level well above those normally to be found in the
> engineering industry. (para. 9)

Accordingly, it was submitted that the only true comparison could be
with the wages levels of the Nuclear Power Group or of the C.E.G.B.
or of companies who were customers of the U.K. Atomic Energy
Authority—having regard to the special requirements called for and
the particular skills of the workers concerned. In contrast, the company stated that they were engaged 'in the design and construction
of industrial plant, which was part of the private sector of the engineering and the construction industry' (para. 17). As to the workers
concerned in the case: 'their work might be specialized but it was
certainly general engineering work' (para. 19). It was submitted
that according to a survey conducted by the East Midlands Engineering
Employers' Association in August 1974, 'the lower and upper quartile
and median salaries of the Company's draughtsmen aged 30 and over
were almost identical to those of similar workers employed in the
Company's locality' (para. 22). Although the Union's submissions

were not without substance, as evinced by previous interpretations of 'trade or industry' described in chapter 16 above, the Board did not give any reasons for its Award. It simply declared that: 'the relevant trade or industry is that which is concerned with the design and construction of industrial plant' (para. 29(1)). And without commenting on the adequacy of the Company's evidence, it concluded that its terms of employment were not established to be in breach of clause 1(b).

The next Award of the I.A.B., Award 3308 of 7 February 1975 (*A.U.E.W.* (*T.A.S.S.*) *and Marshall of Cambridge* (*Engineering*) *Ltd.*) also proceeded on the basis that clause 1(a) of the Resolution was inapplicable: a National Agreement dated 15 May 1974 made between the E.E.F. and the C.S.E.U. did exist, but the categories of workers concerned in the case did not appear among the grades listed in that Agreement. The Union based their case under clause 1(b) on a comparison with the terms of employment observed by one other employer only—the Ministry of Defence: 'The Union contended that the degree of skill required of their members in carrying out the duties involved in the contract was no lower than that required of Ministry of Defence employees' (para. 7). The Company's contention was simple: 'that there were no other similarly-circumstanced employers in the district in the relevant trade or industry. They stated that there was no other employer within 75 miles of Shawbury undertaking similar work. They therefore submitted that the wages paid to their employees should be compared with those paid by other commercial organizations undertaking similar work elsewhere in the country' (para. 13). The Civil Service was not, in the company's view 'a comparable trade or industry' (para. 14). The Company's submission indirectly conceded that the absence of similar employers in the *district* was not fatal—comparisons could be made with other organizations in the country at large. Clause 1(b) does not postulate a 'district' element, as emphasized in chapter 16. But the I.A.B. simply held again that an infringement of clause 1(b) had not been established. Also, that 'amongst other things the Board do not consider that the Ministry of Defence, the only employer put forward by the Union for the purposes of comparison, can properly be regarded as "employers whose general circumstances in the trade or industry in which the contractor is engaged are similar" ' (para. 18(2)). No indication was given, however, as to whether the Civil Service was considered a 'trade or industry', or whether the rejection was based on the Ministry of Defence being an employer whose general circumstances were dissimilar. Failure to give reasons renders the decision useless for the purpose of considering future claims.

Award 3314 of 22 July 1975 (*Association of Professional, Executive, Clerical and Computer Staff and The Beeston Boiler Co. Ltd.*) concerned the Fair Wages Clause in a contract let by the Greater London Council. The contract was unusual in that while it contained the equivalent of clause 1(a) of the 1946 Resolution, instead of clause 1(b), its alternative Fair Wages formula resembled more that contained in the Resolution of 1909:

14(i)(b) In the absence of any rates of wages, hours or conditions of labour so established the Contractor shall in respect of all persons employed by him as aforesaid pay rates of wages and observe hours and conditions of labour that are not less favourable to such persons than those in practice paid and observed by good employers in the district where the work is carried out whose general circumstances in the trade or industry in which the Contractor is engaged are similar. (para. 2)

It was never made clear, either in the submissions of the parties or the Award of the I.A.B., which of the two Fair Wages standards was being invoked. From the evidence submitted by the parties, it appears to have been their intention to satisfy the Board with regard to the clause quoted above. Thus, both the Company and the Union submitted tables of comparable salaries paid by other organizations to substantiate their claims. The Union made the following interesting submission:

The basis of the Union's case was thus that the rates paid by the comparator organizations were to be compared not with the actual rates paid by the Company but with the rates agreed between the Company and the Union as set out in paragraph 12 hereof. The maxima of the scales of pay of that structure were, in fact, lower in some instances than the salaries actually paid by the Company to staff concerned in the Reference. The Union, however, contended that that was irrelevant, since they objected to the Company paying their employees either more or less than the rates set out in agreements which had been made between the Company and the Union. (para. 13)

The Union went on to admit, moreover, that 'only one of the comparator organizations put forward by them was engaged in the same industry as the Company and that that organization was outside the district in which the Company was situated' (para. 14). Nonetheless, they argued that the comparisons were justified 'irrespective of the business of the firms concerned, because job values in clerical work did not vary'. The Company contended on the basis of the information submitted by it that 'the rates of wages actually paid to their employees were within the general range of the wage rates of the other companies . . . (they) were therefore reasonable and their was no foundation whatsoever for any suggestion that they were paying unfair wages' (para. 22). The I.A.B. simply held that it had not been established that the Company were failing to observe the requirements of the G.L.C.'s Fair Wages Clause (para. 26).

The Fair Wages Resolution was invoked in a claim under the Road Traffic Act 1960 in Award 3315 of 19 August 1975 (*T.G.W.U. and Rees & Williams Ltd.*). The Union contended that the National Council for the Omnibus Industry covered more than 90 per cent of company bus employees throughout the U.K. and that the majority of company bus employees working in South Wales were covered by the National Conditions Agreement of the Council. The Company complained of was not a member of the Council and did not consider itself bound by the Agreement. The Union also claimed that the majority of the bus companies, including the independent bus companies, which operated within South Wales followed the terms of the Agreement. Accordingly, the Company was in breach of clause 1(a) of the Resolution in not complying with terms established by the Agreement (para. 6). The Company denied that the majority of operators complied with the terms laid down in the Agreement (para. 16). They also queried the Union's evidence that the majority of company bus employees working in South Wales were covered by the Agreement—though they did not produce any evidence of their own (para. 17). But apart from the dispute over whether the Agreement established terms as required by clause 1(a), the Company contended that the Agreement was not an agreement made by an organization of employers representative of a substantial proportion of the employers engaged in the trade or industry in the district (para. 18). The Union conceded that the structure of the industry was such that the majority of employers were independent bus companies who were not covered by the Agreement. But the majority of employees were employed by the National Bus Company and its subsidiary firms who were parties to and observed the Agreement (along with a small number of independent companies). The Union claimed that the independent companies were not willing to set up a wage-fixing body, and there was no organization of such employers with whom the Union could undertake collective bargaining. As there was in the district no organization of employers representative of substantial proportions of employers within the industry the Union had been forced to rely on the fact that substantial numbers of workers were engaged in the industry to support their case under clause 1(a) of the Resolution (para. 9). The Union waived any possibility of claiming under clause 1(b) (para. 14). But they contended that the purpose of Section 152 of the Road Traffic Act was to protect the majority of workers against those employers who did not follow a national agreement (para. 9). This plea fell on deaf ears. As might have been anticipated from the analysis of previous interpretations of 'representative' given in chapter 16, the I.A.B. adopted a strict and mechanical view of representativeness: 'As to clause 1(a) of the Resolution, the two sides of the National Council for the Omnibus Industry are organizations of employers and workers within the meaning of the Clause. It has not however been established that the employers' side are representative of a substantial proportion of employers in the said district.' The Board went on to hold that it had also not been shown that the terms of the Agreement are established in the district. The complaint was dismissed.

The last complaint of breach of the Fair Wages Resolution of 1946 dealt with by the Industrial Arbitration Board was Award 3327 of 9 January 1976 (*A.S.T.M.S. and G.E.C. Ltd.*). The Union complained of breach of clause 1(b), in particular that the Company was not observing terms of employment on a par with those of similar employees of the Post Office. Three questions were raised. The first was whether the Post Office was engaged in the same industry as the Company. The Union contended that the relevant industry was the telecommunications industry, and, in particular, the part which related to the installation of telephone equipment. It invoked in support an interpretation of 'trade or industry' by the House of Lords in *N.A.L.G.O.* v. *Bolton Corporation* [1943] A.C. 166. The I.A.B. itself drew attention to its Award 3307, described above, as bearing on the Union's contention. The Company in Award 3307 were engaged in the trade or industry of designing and constructing industrial plant, while the Central Electricity Generating Board, with whom comparison had been made, while sometimes undertaking construction and installation of power stations themselves, were mainly engaged in the operation of power stations and the production and circulation of electricity. The Union submitted that there was a difference here, in that while the design and construction of nuclear power stations was a small and distinct part of the activities of those concerned with the supply of electricity, in the present case the Company was an integral part of the telecommunications industry (para. 9). Conversely, the Company argued that the Post Office was engaged in a different industry, that of planning the telecommunication network, procuring equipment to go into it, managing it, and generally maintaining it (para. 14). The Post Office carried out only a small amount of installation work themselves, which was in any case different from that undertaken by the Company (para. 15). Since the Company's installation work was to them not a separate activity but an integrated part of their entire business, and since, unlike the Post Office, their own purchasing of manufactured equipment was on a very small scale, their activities as a whole could not be compared with those of the Post Office, nor could they be said to be in the same industry as the Post Office (para. 18).

The second question raised was, if the Post Office was engaged in the same industry as the Company, whether it was an employer 'whose general circumstances in the trade or industry in which the contractor is engaged are similar', as required by clause 1(b). The Union's attention was again drawn to Award 3308, described above, where the I.A.B. held that the only employer put forward for the purposes of comparison, the Ministry of Defence, could not properly be regarded as 'employers whose general circumstances in the trade or industry in which the contractor is engaged are similar'. In reply:

> ASTMS pointed out that when the Resolution was passed in 1946 some of the problems currently arising as to its interpretation could not have been visualized. At that time there were a number of contractors undertaking the kind of work done by the Company, whereas there were currently only four main contractors for the supply and installation of telephone exchange equipment. . . . Each of the four contractors mentioned were moreover specialists dealing with particular items of equipment. Given that there was a limited number of contractors and that each of them was a specialist, it appeared to be very difficult to say that their rates of wages and other conditions constituted a general level of wages and other conditions among employers whose circumstances were similar to those of the Company. ASTMS had therefore concluded that the only comparator for the purpose of the present case must be the Post Office; and that was the only comparison which they sought to make. (para. 10)

The Company contended that the general circumstances of the four contractors, including itself, were not similar to those of the Post Office. The four companies were in the private sector of industry, whereas the Post Office was in the public sector. Furthermore the four companies were eligible for membership of the E.E.F.; they were members of the Telecommunications Engineering and Manufacturing Association; and they were subject to the Engineering Industry Training Board. The Post Office was none of those things (para. 19).

The third question arose if the answers to the first two questions were in the affirmative: whether the rates of wages paid and the hours and conditions of employment observed by a single employer, the Post Office, could properly be regarded as constituting a general level of wages and conditions observed by other employers within the meaning of clause 1(b). A.S.T.M.S. presented an activity chart which showed that the total number of Post Office employees engaged in installation work of a similar nature to that undertaken by the grades concerned in the present Reference was double that of employees of private companies in the industry engaged on similar work. It followed that the rates of pay and conditions of employment observed by the Post Office could rightly be regarded as representing the general level observed in the telecommunications industry in which the Company were also engaged (para. 13). The Company disputed the Union's interpretation of the chart (para. 20).

Despite these detailed and substantial submissions, the I.A.B. saw fit to give only its usual laconic Award in this its last case on the Resolution. The matter was decided by the Board's negativing the first question: 'The Post Office, the sole employer put forward by A.S.T.M.S. for the purposes of comparison, is not engaged in the same trade or industry as the Company'. Surprisingly, however, it went on to say that 'even if, contrary to the Board's view, it were right to regard the Post Office as being engaged in the same industry as the Company', the claim failed as the latter two questions were also answered in the negative: the Post Office's circumstances were not similar and its rates did not constitute a 'general level' within the meaning of clause 1(b). As if this was not enough, the Board preceded these determinations with the statement that it had 'not been established that the Company are in breach of that Clause for the following *among other reasons*' (para. 24(3)) (My italics). So, while the Union was given clear-cut rejections of its submissions, no explanations were forthcoming, and indeed, there were hints that other unspecified reasons operated to invalidate the claim.

In its last awards on the Fair Wages Resolution, the Industrial Arbitration Board retreated from the peak of imagination and boldness it had displayed in the awards on the pay policy of 1973–4. Instead of pursuing the path charted there—taking a broad view of the Resolution and seeking to adapt it to contemporary industrial realities—the Board lapsed into its old ways. Complaints brought before it were simply rejected without any explanation.

Claims brought to the Industrial Arbitration Board under section 8 of the 1959 Act during this period suffered the same fate. Of thirteen claims, only one was successful—Award 3311 of 14 April 1975 (*Michael Products Ltd. and National Union of the Footwear, Leather and Allied Trades*)— where the Company was not represented at the hearing and made no written submissions, so the Union won by default. In the other twelve cases, the Unions' claims failed. The reasons for the failure as expressed by the I.A.B. are familiar. In a majority of the failures, the Unions failed to show that the company concerned in the claim was in the 'trade or industry' covered by the collective agreement invoked. For example, in Awards 3318–23 of 13 November 1975, the T.G.W.U. confronted six road haulage firms and in each case the Board found:

> that it has not been established that in respect of the road haulage drivers referred to in the Terms of Reference the Company by whom they are employed are engaged in the building industry as claimed by the Union, or that the terms and conditions contained in the Building (Road Haulage Workers) Agreement are the recognized terms and conditions applicable at any time to the said drivers. The claim accordingly fails.

Similarly, in Award 3329 of 28 January 1976 (*Domestic Electrical Rentals Ltd. and Furniture, Timber & Allied Trades Union*), it was not established that the company was in the furniture manufacturing trade, and in Award 3330 of 28 January 1976 (*Spalding Sheepskin Co. Ltd. and National Union of the Footwear, Leather & Allied Trades*)—the last case on the 1959 Act before the Board—it was held that the company was not in the fellmongering industry.

Another decision was familiar from previous cases, described in chapter 16, on the question whether terms and conditions were established which had been settled by an agreement or award. In Award 3309 of 12 February 1975 (*Home Brewery Co. Ltd. and National Association of Licensed House Managers*), the Association claimed that terms were established in the licensed house trade as set out in the Code of Practice as agreed in October 1970 and issued by the Brewers Society, which related to payment of wives of managers. The Association also submitted extracts from the Minutes of the National Brewer/Manager Liaison Committee relating to agreed increases in such payments which had been recommended by the Brewers Society to their members. The Company rebutted this evidence by asserting, as regards the Code, that 'one only had to look at its provisions to see that it was not an agreement dealing with terms and conditions of employment'. Similarly, the extracts from the Minutes 'did not constitute evidence of the existence of an agreement or award within the meaning of the Act'. Furthermore, payments to wives of managers were alleged to be on a non-contractual basis, being only 'token payment' or 'honorarium' (para. 18). It is not clear which of these arguments found favour in the eyes of the Board which simply held: 'It has not been established in the present case that terms and conditions of employment have been established in licensed houses, either generally or in the relevant district, which have been settled by agreement or award as required by Section 8' (para. 25(2)).

The Industrial Arbitration Board, it appeared, had not lost its determination to adhere to a narrow interpretation of the terms of the Fair Wages policy of Section 8. Claims continued to be dismissed, even where it was openly acknowledged, for example, that the companies concerned were refusing to recognize the trade union—as in Award 3324 of 3 December 1975 (*Precision Dippings Ltd. and T.G.W.U.*) and Award 3325 of 22 December 1975 (*Rathdown Industries Ltd. and T.G.W.U.*). It is difficult to see how the Central Arbitration Committee could fail to improve upon a predecessor which had dismissed almost every claim for Fair Wages made to it. (The twelfth case lost, not yet mentioned, was Award 3326 of 22 December 1975 (*Anson Cast Products Ltd. and G.M.W.U.*).)

Fair Wages Policy in the Central Arbitration Committee

As the instruments of Fair Wages policy, the 1946 Resolution and section 8 of the 1959 Act, were unchanged, the transformation that appeared to overtake the fate of the policy when the first cases concerning it came before the Central Arbitration Committee after 1 February 1976 is all the more remarkable. As is recorded above, during its last thirteen months, the Industrial Arbitration Board had dismissed all five complaints made to it of non-compliance with the Resolution, and had rejected twelve of the thirteen claims made under the 1959 Act. In contrast, during the first sixteen months of its existence (up to Award 114 of 20 May 1977), the Committee had upheld twenty-three of the thirty-one complaints made to it under the Fair Wages Resolution of 1946 (plus two others under Fair Wages statutes), and had upheld thirty-two of the forty-five claims made under the 1959 Act.

The undoubted success of the Fair Wages policy in the Central Arbitration Committee is attributable to two principal factors. The first of these reflects a theme consistent with the historical experience of the Fair Wages policy since its beginnings in the late nineteenth century. A large proportion of the cases before the Committee have arisen as a consequence of a new development in the system of industrial relations—the intrusion of government incomes policy on collective bargaining. The cumulation of incomes policies over the past decade, particularly in its latter half, has severely disrupted the normal process of wage determination through collective bargaining. It has led to the creation of an increasing number of anomalies in pay structures affecting workers. These workers have fallen behind, or been caught out by the arbitrary vagaries of various wage restraint policies. The Fair Wages policy has offered a route by which these workers can catch up, a means whereby these anomalies can be rectified. The relationship of incomes policy to Fair Wages policy will be the subject of the next and final chapter of this study.

The second principal factor behind the new-found success of the Fair Wages policy is the approach of the Committee itself. This is clearly stated in the final paragraph of its *First Annual Report, 1976*:

> 5.4 The overriding philosophy of the Committee can be briefly stated. The Committee is not a court in the traditional sense. Its procedures and hearings are structured so as to achieve complete informality. The aim is to encourage the approach by way of problem solving rather than by emphasizing the aspects of conflict and verdict. Above all there is a commitment to the principles of sound industrial relations and workable solutions. Wherever, whether in interpretation of fact or application of rules, the Committee finds it is left with uncertainty or discretion, it is determined to exercise that discretion within this overriding commitment. That, it is hoped, will rapidly become its well known and distinctive characteristic.

This new approach will be reinforced should the Committee begin to invoke the guidance contained in the Codes of Industrial Relations Practice to be issued by A.C.A.S. It is already apparent in the new form of the awards themselves. Instead of proceeding directly from the submissions of Employer and Union to the Award, the Committee has inserted a section entitled 'General Considerations'. The Committee is not obliged by law to state the reasons for its decisions on Fair Wages policy, so its awards need not expressly be logically watertight. Nonetheless, the Committee seems willing to explain its awards in light of what it considers good industrial relations practice.

It is these 'General Considerations' that account in large part for the recent successes of the Fair Wages policy before the Committee. A careful reading of the Committee's awards does not reveal any radically new interpretations of the Fair Wages policy formula that would explain the startling change in results. It does not appear to be the adoption of new principles that has led to the transformation. Indeed, in many of its awards problems appear which are all too familiar from the past. The Committee's resolution of these problems has been only marginally more favourable to claimants than that of its predecessors. There have been no dramatic reversals of precedents or repudiation of previous applications of Fair Wages policy. It is the new approach of the Committee to its task which has transformed the policy.

The Committee has determined to attempt to resolve the problems brought before it in the form of Fair Wages policy cases. It will not seek merely to adjudicate in legalistic fashion whether a party is guilty of non-compliance with the policy. As it states in its *First Annual Report, 1976*:

> The Committee hopes to prevent the parties or witnesses from feeling that they are taking leading parts in a murder trial. They are encouraged to assist the Committee by evidence as to facts and opinions with, as far as possible, participation in the task of problem solving which, in the ultimate, lies with the Committee. (para. 3.6)

Within the limits of the Fair Wages policy jurisdiction, the Committee will seek to achieve what it believes are its primary objectives: 'a flexible procedure, a practice of acceding to the joint wishes of the parties, wherever possible and a major role in encouraging the growth and development of good industrial relations' (para. 3.8). An active, problem-solving approach by the Committee would mark a complete break from the tradition of its predecessors in enforcing the Fair Wages policy.

The remainder of this chapter will be concerned to illustrate these last points. First, the awards of the Committee will be used to indicate its new approach. Then its attitude to various old and worn phrases of the Fair Wages policy formula will be presented. Finally, the Committee's view of the key to the new Fair Wages policy—the 'general level of terms and conditions'—will be examined.

A New Approach

The most noticeable feature of the Committee's awards is the care with which it has regard to the industrial relations background of the cases which come before it. In its very first award under the Fair Wages Resolution of 1946, Award 2 of 16 March 1976 (*Bolton Gate Co. Ltd. and A.U.E.W.*), the Committee commenced with the statement: 'It was necessary for us to consider the process of wage fixing and the pattern of comparable wages to determine the exact way in which the Fair Wages Resolution should be applied to this Reference' (para. 19). It then went on to examine in detail the structure of national and local collective bargaining as it affected the types of workers concerned. Again, in Award 3 of 9 March 1976 (*John Lyle Carpets Ltd. and Scottish Carpet Workers' Union*), a claim under section 8 of the 1959 Act that the employer observe terms settled by the two sides of the National Joint Committee for the Carpet Industry:

> the Committee took into account the nature and construction of the industry and in particular the extensive bargaining arrangements at national level. Although local plant bargaining does take place the Committee is of the opinion that settlements at national level are of greater significance than in many industries. Rates of pay, including cost of living bonuses, established through NJC negotiations are therefore more meaningful in the carpet industry at both national and district levels. (para. 38)

This industrial relations background, having been carefully investigated, will often be a substantial influence on the shape of the final award. Thus, in Award 77 of 16 February 1977 (*Kitson's Sheet Metal Ltd. and the National Union of Sheet Metal Workers, Coppersmiths, Heating and Domestic Engineers*), the Committee noted that terms of employment were set out in a document drawn up by management alone, but observed: 'It has been the practice for the management to discuss pay issues with the shop steward and for minimum rates to be based on the minimum rates established by national agreement in the engineering industry' (para. 17). The Committee upheld the claim for the holiday provisions of the engineering agreement to be applied, stating:

> It is the Committee's view that the appropriate national agreement for determining issues regarding minimum pay and conditions in the Company is the engineering agreement which is already partially used for this purpose. There is of course nothing to prevent the Company and the Union from negotiating a comprehensive domestic agreement which would pay full regard to the circumstances of employment within the Company. It would in the Committee's view be desirable if relations between the Company and the Union were placed on a more formal basis and the terms and conditions of employment within the Company made the subject of a formal joint agreement. (para. 20)

Another illustration of the influence of the industrial relations background is provided by a complaint that a government contractor was not observing the 'general level' of salaries for certain staff employees. In Award 84 of 28 February 1977 (*Light-metal Forgings Ltd. and A.S.T.M.S.*), the Committee stated:

On the evidence before the Committee it appeared that the case for an increase might be stronger in some instances than others. The Committee is, however, mindful that there has fairly recently been introduced into the Company a jointly agreed job-evaluated salary structure. Moreover the evidence before the Committee was not sufficiently precise to provide a certain basis for awarding differential adjustments which would disturb the existing relativities. In these circumstances the Committee concluded that the best course was to make an award providing for an increase in the general level of wages without disturbing the existing structure. (para. 25)

Accordingly, the Committee awarded a 10 per cent increase.

Particularly good examples of the problem-solving approach of the Committee are Awards 82 and 83 of 23 February 1977 (*North Eastern Co-operative Society Ltd., Greater Nottingham Co-operative Society Ltd. and National Association of Co-operative Officials*). Reorganization of the business had led to the replacement of a nationally agreed payment system by a new job-evaluation scheme. Unforeseen developments had led to the rates under the new scheme falling behind those of the national agreement, which led the Union to submit a claim calling for observance of the latter's terms. Reviewing the problem, the Committee felt: 'it would be wrong for us not to consider these difficulties. It would be no service to either side to leave an impossible tangle to be sorted out "when free collective bargaining returns"—a somewhat imprecise date' (para. 36). This led it to propose the following solution:

These lines of thought led us to a difficult dilemma. Simple acceptance of the application of Section 8 . . . would destroy the recently agreed wages structure in each of the Societies. . . . Another alternative solution appears possible. It is not difficult to calculate that amount of money by which the current salaries fall below the entitlement under the national agreement. It might be possible to solve the dilemma by allocating this money within the current employment structure so as to achieve a package which could be said to provide a satisfactory equivalent solution. (para. 37)

On the urging of the Committee, an adjournment took place during which the parties agreed upon just such a package as suggested by the Committee. It formed the substance of the Committee's award.

Occasionally, employers would advert in their submissions to the Committee to the effect of the claim on their industrial relations.

Thus, in Award 35 of 27 September 1976 (*Norprint Ltd. and S.L.A.D.E.*), the company disputed the claim under the 1959 Act by arguing that it was not in the trade or industry covered by the Process Trade Agreement and to apply that agreement would have 'serious industrial relations consequences for the industry' (para. 29). And in Award 32 of 21 September 1976 (*Sunblest Bakeries (GLW) Ltd. and City Bakeries Ltd. Glasgow and T.G.W.U.*), two bakery companies argued against a claim on behalf of their vehicle maintenance workers for a fourth week of holiday in accordance with the N.J.I.C. Agreement for the Motor Vehicle Retail and Repair Industry. The companies alleged that: 'To grant an extra week's holiday to vehicle maintenance workers would cause fragmentation and induce friction and dissension amongst different groups' (para. 11). In both cases the claim failed, and in the latter the Committee expressly stated its view that various conditions of employment such as holidays 'should be uniform throughout all groups' (para. 13).

On the other hand, in Award 24 of 13 August 1976 (*W. Lovatt Transport and United Road Transport Union*), the Committee considered the 'poor trading conditions' and 'genuine financial problem' of the company concerned: 'We feel that our Award might prove to be a severe embarassment to the Company' (para. 19). In light of the good industrial relations in the company, the Committee expressed the hope that the arrears owed could be implemented over time: 'This we feel would contribute to the good industrial relations between them and would avoid any sudden commercial embarassment to the Firm on whose success the livelihood of the drivers in question depends'. The company's plight did not, of course, excuse it from its obligation—in its very first award, a claim under the 1959 Act (Award 1 of 19 February 1976, *James North Footwear Ltd. and National Union of the Footwear, Leather and Allied Trades*), the Committee had rejected a plea by the employer of financial hardship.

Along with its emphasis on problem-solving, and its consideration of industrial relations factors, the Committee stresses the virtues of voluntariness. Thus, part of the Committee's Award 18 of 4 August 1976 (*Cambion Electronic Products Ltd. and A.U.E.W.*) read as follows:

> There appears to be the possibility of future fruitful negotiations, when circumstances allow, on individual grading and on the introduction of an agreed incentive scheme, for example. We feel that that part of the claim, mainly that certain workers should, under Section 8, be said to merit a semi-skilled rate, is something we can properly leave to such future negotiations. (para. 27)

Again, in Award 23 of 9 August 1976 (*Effingham Steel Works Ltd. and A.S.T.M.S.*), the Committee noted that the reference concerned only five workers out of a staff complement of thirty-five and felt that 'alterations to a handful of employees (in terms of a fair wage) might lead to patent anomalies' (para. 20). But the complaint was upheld and the Committee, while admitting that it could only consider the instances referred to it by the Union, expressed the expectation that the company would look carefully at the salaries they pay to others to see if they require adjustment. The Committee accepted that this was a possible result of what they had decided.

Despite its commitment to a new approach to cases coming before it, there are obvious limits to the freedom of manoeuvre of the Committee. It has to ensure that its decisions are consistent with the instruments granting it jurisdiction. This is illustrated in three of its earliest cases. In Awards 4 and 5 of 14 March 1976 (*Kyle and Carrick District Council and N.A.L.G.O.*), the Committee made full allowance for the difficulties faced by a Council which had set high pay levels in ignorance of pay negotiations which were to lead to backdated increases in scales. But it went on to state: 'Despite this the legal position is clear. If the Council is to continue to participate in the collective bargaining machinery and implement its decisions then no discretion arises in relation to the salary increases of 1974 and 1975' (para. 33). Considerations of collective bargaining practice did not always suffice to overcome the restrictions of the legal framework. In Award 6 of 6 April 1976 (*Dowty Boulton Paul Ltd. and A.S.T.M.S.*), the Association had argued that by custom and practice the wage for rate-fixers in the company was linked to that paid to the company's senior foremen. The Committee was forced to ignore this argument:

> No doubt, in normal free collective bargaining, the Union would have a strong case for the restoration of parity with the foremen, but in applying the criteria of the Fair Wages Resolution we must look strictly to outside comparisons and our award is entirely based on such comparisons. (para. 26)

The Committee went on to say: 'We recognize that at a future date, when free to do so, the Company may wish to restore the previous parity between rate-fixers and foremen and the parties may think it desirable to have a common review date for the two groups' (para. 27).

Later cases also illustrate the conflict between the Committee's new approach and its limited powers under the new Fair Wages policy. In Award 89 of 8 March 1977 (*Eric Bemrose Ltd. and the National Graphical Association, The Society of Graphical and Allied Trades*), the parties had, after lengthy negotiations, reached agreement only to be blocked by the Department of Employment's veto on grounds of pay policy. The Committee recorded that: 'It was urged at the hearing by both parties that it could not be Government policy, as embodied in their White Papers on inflation to "frustrate an honourable agreement between the Company and Union, because to do so would create considerable resentment on the shop floor and do quite immense harm to industrial relations" (the words of Mr. Harvie, a Director of the Company)' (para. 19). In rejecting the claim, the Committee felt obliged to state:

> It is important to understand the function and power of the Central Arbitration Committee as set out in the legislation under which it operates. In relation to this claim, the relevant legislation is Schedule 11 of the Employment Protection Act 1975. This Committee is charged by Parliament with giving effect to the provisions of that Schedule; the Committee does not sit to approve or not as the case may be a perfectly honourable and sensible bargain struck by the parties: it does not sit to decide what is or is not in accordance with current pay policy. The Committee sits to decide whether or not the provisions of Schedule 11 apply to the facts put before it and, if it finds the claim wholly or partly well-founded, to make an award in appropriate terms. (para. 21)

Award 74 of 7 February 1977 (*Walter Somers (Materials Handling) Ltd. and G.M.W.U.*) involved another freely negotiated agreement. Again, the Committee felt constrained to say:

> It is clear to the Committee that, under free collective bargaining, the agreement reached by the Company and the Union in March 1976 would have been implemented. We believe that it was a good agreement and we fully endorse the standard 40-hour week which it established. In the absence of the Government's pay policy, no claim would have been made.
>
> The Committee, however, like the parties, is bound by the terms of Schedule 11 of the Employment Protection Act, 1975. (paras. 23–4)

Finally, the Committee's dilemma is encapsulated in its statement in a recent award on the Fair Wages Resolution (Award 112 of 10 May 1977, *The Hymatic Engineering Co. Ltd.*, para. 14):

> It is one of the problems of the process we have to undertake in cases of this sort that basic industrial relations considerations such as salary structures and internal differentials are strictly speaking

irrelevant to our concern. At least they represent a different approach to the problem to the one we are able to take under the Resolution.

In sum, the Committee's new approach aims at problem-solving with regard to the background of industrial relations in the cases coming before it. Consistently with this, it encourages voluntary settlements. This approach is occasionally at variance with the Fair Wages policy which it is required to enforce. Ideally, its Awards would take the form of the very first under Schedule 11—Award 103 of 20 April 1977 (*I. E. White (Plastics) Ltd. and T.G.W.U.*):

> We had no difficulty in concluding that there was a failure to observe the recognized terms and conditions as settled by agreement for the workers covered by the reference. The Committee has carefully considered the agreement by stages concluded between the parties, and conclude that it is a sound and sensible solution, which, in the main, the Committee would wish to endorse. (Para. 14.)

Within the limitations of the policy, the Committee has determined to exercise its discretion in pursuance of its aims. For the first time, it may be that the enforcement machinery of the Fair Wages policy will use it as a lever, rather than a brake.

Old Problems

The Committee has not been any more successful than its predecessors in laying down guidelines for defining the old familiar phrases of the Fair Wages policy formula. It probably would wish to avoid doing so, taking the view that such hard and fast propositions would reduce its flexibility and diminish the exercise of its discretion. The new approach of the Committee is evident in its interpretations of the Fair Wages policy formula.

Trade, industry or section

The standards adopted by Schedule 11 are those terms and conditions, whether recognized or the general level, in the 'trade, industry or section in which the employer in question is engaged'. In reviewing the Committee's attempts to define the relevant 'trade or industry' for the purposes of the Fair Wages Resolution or section 8 of the 1959 Act, the usual run of problems and solutions is encountered. The most common arises when one party before the Committee asserts that it is engaged in a particular section of a larger industry, and that consequently, the standards invoked by the other party are not applicable. Thus, in Award 3 of 9 March 1976 (*John Lyle Carpets Ltd. and Scottish Carpet Workers' Union*), the company submitted that it 'had severed its historical links with the weaving of carpets and was now a small, struggling, tufting firm engaged in the "Tufted Carpet Industry" which was an identifiable industry separate from the "Carpet Industry" ' (para. 34). Rejecting the submission, the Committee stated that it was 'satisfied that the Company is engaged in the carpet industry as generally understood by both sides of the National Joint Committee for the Carpet Industry' (para. 37). Under section 8 of the 1959 Act, therefore, the company was obliged to observe the terms specified in the N.J.C. Memorandum of Agreement.

Again, in Award 38 of 12 October 1976 (*Gillow Heath Mining Co. Ltd. and National Union of Mineworkers*), the Company claimed that the Agreement negotiated between the National Coal Board and the N.U.M. related exclusively to coal mining, which was only part of the mining industry. The Company, engaged in whetstone mining, was not comparable to the N.C.B. The mining of whetstone, used as an abrasive, made the Company part of the 'abrasive industry'. The Committee dealt with the problem as follows:

> It is obvious that the vast majority of miners in Britain are engaged in coal-mining and are employed by the N.C.B. Where significant numbers of miners are employed in a branch of mining where conditions are sufficiently different from those obtaining in coal-mining one would expect a separate wage agreement to have emerged. We are informed that such separate and distinct agreements exist between the N.U.M. and the employers in clay-mining and between other trade unions and the employers in quartz-mining. If no such separate agreement exists we think it fair to assume that general conditions in any section of the industry are sufficiently similar to those in coal-mining to justify the application of the N.U.M./N.C.B. agreement. The Union, indeed, confirmed that this is the case. There is no separate agreement for whetstone-mining. (para. 20)

The Company's argument was rejected.

In Award 35 of 27 September 1976 (*Norprint Ltd. and S.L.A.D.E.*), it was the Union which claimed that the company was in the Photo Engraving Trade and must observe the Process Trade Agreement negotiated for that industry. The Committee held that the company was part of the printing industry, but: 'The printing industry, when the term is used in its widest meaning, is a complicated collection of various trades' (para. 31). It concluded without more that the company was not within that part of the trade or industry to which the Process Trade Agreement could appropriately be applied. Accordingly, the claim failed.

In contrast, in Award 85 of 2 March 1977 (*Twyfords Ltd. and Union of Construction, Allied Trades and Technicians*), the company employed approximately 1,000 operatives, mainly pottery workers, but including twenty-three bricklayers and bricklayers' labourers who repair and rebuild kilns with refractory bricks. The Union 'accepted that the company was engaged in the Ceramics Industry but this particular kind of specialized work should be construed as a separate section of the industry. There was a national collective agreement governing the terms and conditions of employment for bricklayers and bricklayers labourers required to carry out refractory work as needed at this establishment' (para. 9). The Committee accepted the agreement as appropriate to be applied to the employer 'in that section of the industry concerned with refractory work' (para. 16). The employer had initially resisted the claim, but later conceded. The Committee was doubtless influenced by the stated fact that 'with the exception of Twyfords Limited, there is universal observance within the Ceramics Industry of the terms' (para. 16).

Finally, in Award 9 of 24 May 1976 (*National Bank of Pakistan and N.U.B.E.*), the Union sought to extend the terms of the national agreement between the Federation of London Clearing Bank Employers and the Banking Staff Council to an overseas bank in the U.K. The Committee stated that 'for historical, traditional and no doubt other reasons the London Clearing Banks are established as a special group. We do not feel entitled to hold that a negotiation for such a well known and separate group can be regarded as applying more widely to other types of bank' (para. 32). Consequently, its award was as follows:

> The claim is based on the banking industry regarded as a whole. The collective agreement, which applies to a section of the industry, is said to relate to a substantial proportion of employers and appropriate workers. At the present time, and in the present state of bargaining arrangements, we regard it as unrealistic to treat banking in the widest sense as a unity. We are forced to the conclusion that the collective agreement on which the union relies covers a section of the industry of which the Employer is not part. (para. 37)

The engineering industry, with its enormous variety of trades and products, has been subjected to numerous attempts to divide it into separate sections. Thus, in Award 2 of 16 March 1976 (*Bolton Gate Co. Ltd. and A.U.E.W.*), a gate manufacturer disputed comparisons advanced by the Union under clause 1(b) of the 1946 Resolution. The Committee rejected the Company's contention, stating:

> These rates applied to firms which may be said to fall into the category of general engineering. We had no evidence that the work involved in the Contractor's company differed so markedly as to form a separate entity. We asked the Door and Shutters Association whether this type of work could be regarded as a distinct and special category and were assured that this was not so. We feel, therefore, that the rates we were given were from firms which are in the main properly comparable. (para. 22)

Again, in Award 18 of 4 August 1976 (*Cambion Electronic Products Ltd. and A.U.E.W.*), the dispute under the 1959 Act centred on the question of whether the employer concerned was covered by the national engineering agreement. In support of its claim, the Union submitted that: 'The Company's sales brochures emphasized the "high quality of its engineering standards" and the Standard Industrial Classification published by H.M.S.O. placed the Company in the electrical engineering category as a manufacturer of radio and electronic components'. The Company had not questioned the appropriateness of the A.U.E.W. as a negotiating body and had previously undertaken in correspondence to observe the agreement (paras. 11–12). The Company rejected these arguments and pointed to its membership of the Radio and Electronic Components Manufacturers' Association, contending that the manufacture of passive electronic components was a separate industry (para. 17). They argued that:

> In determining which industry a firm was engaged in it was necessary to examine the type of work done by the employees. In this Company what engineering did exist, apart from the toolroom and maintenance work, was very light press work or fine wire coil winding. Most of the work was light assembly and injection moulding, The Committee were invited to visit the factory to examine the operations involved. (para. 18)

The Committee availed itself of this invitation. It stated:

> We considered the evidence and arguments put before us and at the request of the Company we visited their premises at Castleton. We can see why the Company felt that the operatives primarily concerned are not doing general engineering work. But the definition of the term engineering is very wide and we

must have regard to the operation of the Company as a whole. Its work is in the field of electronics, but we have no doubt that viewed as a whole it must properly be regarded as engineering. (para. 24)

Finally, in Award 77 of 16 February 1977 (*Kitson's Sheet Metal Ltd. and the National Union of Sheet Metal Workers, Coppersmiths, Heating and Domestic Engineers*) the Union's complaint of non-observance of the national engineering agreement was met by the Company's contention that, as a subsidiary company serving the Thermal Insulation Industry, it was not engaged in the engineering industry: 'The group's major activities placed the Company within the Thermal Insulation Industry and not the engineering industry' (para. 15). The Committee noted the past practice of the management to base rates on the engineering agreement; and had regard to the negotiating bodies involved in engineering (including the Union) and in thermal insulation (which did not include the Union). It concluded that the appropriate national agreement was the engineering agreement.

The engineering industry has not always survived undivided by the Committee. In Award 111 of 12 May 1977 (*Charles Richards Fasteners Ltd. and A.S.T.M.S.*), the Union claimed that the industry in which the Company was engaged was general engineering and not, as the Company contended, the specialized trade of fasteners (para. 7). The Company manufactured bolts and nuts and other industrial fasteners, cold and hot forgings and machined parts. Although the Company was a member of the West Midlands Engineering Employers' Association, the conclusion was that: 'In the Committee's view, the Company is engaged in the fasteners trade' (para. 20). The evidence was held not to substantiate a complaint under the Fair Wages Resolution.

The variations in approach exhibited by the Committee in dealing with the definition of 'trade, industry or section' can be illustrated by a series of cases concerning firms involved in aerospace. In Award 50 of 7 December 1976 (*Dowty Boulton Paul Ltd. and A.U.E.W. (T.A.S.S.)*), the Union invoked the Fair Wages Resolution against the Company, using as a comparison the only other company in the Wolverhampton area said to be in the same industry—Lucas Aerospace. But since a small proportion of the work of the Company was allied to Ship-building and Marine Engineering and Mechanical Engineering, the Union also provided similar comparisons to those industries. The Company challenged the use of only one Aerospace Employer in an attempt to ascertain the general level, and argued: 'Furthermore, similarity of product should not be the sole criterion in selecting firms for comparison. It was important to look at the type of work undertaken by the staff' (para. 14). Comparisons were produced from general engineering firms. Referring to the Union's evidence, the Committee concluded briefly: 'We do not consider it appropriate to take into account information relating to salaries paid by employers in industries other than the Aerospace Industry which is the main one in which Dowty Boulton Paul is engaged' (para. 18). And with regard to the Company's submission:

> The Company took the view during the hearing that too much emphasis was being placed on comparisons of the type of products produced by the companies which participated in its survey. The Company contended that if the work undertaken by the employees of the companies being compared was similar then comparisons could justifiably be made between the salaries paid to such staff by the comparator companies even if they were engaged in entirely different industries. We cannot accept this view. (para. 18)

In Award 76 of 9 February 1977 (*Bristol Aerojet Ltd. and A.S.T.M.S.*) the Association attempted to establish a general level in the Aerospace Industry, giving several reasons for the choice of that Industry. First, the Company had links with other companies in the industry and worked on common projects involving rockets. It also worked with government departments and establishments. Again, it was a member of the Society of British Aerospace Contractors (S.B.A.C.) and recruited from other companies in the industry. Finally: 'It was agreed that 78% of the Company's activities were in research and development and the Union maintained that general engineering companies differed markedly in that they did not undertake that amount of research and development' (para. 13). The Company rejected this contention, asserting that it was federated to the Engineering Employers' West of England Association. The Company: 'although an associate member of the S.B.A.C., was in common with other engineering Employers, a supplier of components to the Aerospace Industry, but was not a part of that industry' (para. 16). The Committee concluded that there is an Aerospace Industry 'consisting of a comparatively few large companies most, if not all, of whom are full Ordinary (as opposed to Associate) Members of the Society of British Aircraft Contractors. They are engaged in the design and construction of aircraft, engines and guided missiles' (para. 24); this paragraph continues:

> Bristol Aerojet Limited is not, in our view, part of that Aerospace

Industry: it is part of the Engineering Industry manufacturing and supplying components, accessories and equipment to the Aerospace Industry in the same way as many engineering firms supply components and equipment to the Motor Vehicle Manufacturing Industry. We therefore find that the Company is engaged in the Engineering Industry and not in the Aerospace Industry.

As to the manufacture of rockets by the Company, the Committee commented that these 'when filled with a propellant, are capable of being fired into the upper atmosphere but not into space'. In any event, they accounted only for about 8 per cent of the Company's sales. Consequently: 'We do not find that the manufacture of these rockets (complete except for the propellant) is sufficient to take the Company into the Aerospace Industry (para. 25).

In Awards 50 and 76, therefore, the decision of whether or not the company was in the aerospace industry—and hence the validity of comparators—appeared to turn on the company's products. This criterion may be contrasted with the grounds for the decision in two other cases.

In Award 104 of 2 May 1977 (*Hawker Siddeley Aviation Ltd., Hamble, and A.S.T.M.S.*), a complaint under the Fair Wages Resolution, the Union regarded the industry as 'Aerospace Equipment Manufacturing and Repairing; Aircraft and airframe manufacturing and repairing' as defined by the Standard Industrial Classification. It restricted its comparisons to firms covered by that description. The Company rejected this interpretation as too narrow. There were few similar establishments to its own:

> However, it was reasonable to make comparisons on the basis of the nature of the work undertaken. The Company pointed out that the nature of the Company's business clearly fell within the broad description 'precision engineering'. It emphasized the point by stating that Instructors and Assistant Foremen in its large machine shop were well able to take up similar posts in any engineering machine shop which produced quality precision products, even though it was not related to the aviation industry. (para. 15)

To this the Union's reply was that it 'considered the Company's definition of the relevant industry, precision engineering, to be too broad, although it did not dispute that precision engineering formed part of the jobs carried out by its members' (para. 9). This emphasis on the work performed by the employees rather than the products of the Company was reflected in the Committee's decision:

In the Committee's view the general language of the Fair Wages Resolution has to be interpreted in relation to the facts and circumstances of each particular case. The reference in the Resolution to 'the district where the work is carried out' would support an emphasis on *comparisons* in the locality where employment is normally sought and found within the local labour market *for the occupations under reference*. Labour market considerations are again often helpful in seeking appropriate comparisons within the broad industrial framework indicated by national negotiating. arrangements. *Some highly specialized skills may be closely related to particular products but other skills may be applied with some adaptation to a wider range of production. In such cases the critical considerations are not so much the particular product as the degree of skill and responsibility required.* (para. 26) (My italics.)

The emphasis on allowing comparators to be used where the occupations and skills of the workers are similar, although this means adopting a wider range of products to fall within an industry, was reiterated in Award 112 of 10 May 1977 (*The Hymatic Engineering Co. Ltd.*). The Company manufactured precision valves for the aerospace industry. In assessing the comparisons invoked to establish the general level of terms and conditions, the Committee looked at different categories of workers separately. For the purposes of technical staff, the Committee had this to say:

The comparisons chosen gave a double check. One list of companies compared were, *as the Resolution intends*, in the specialized industry—aerospace: the other was of local companies chiefly in more general engineering. The jobs were broken down into various grades and the comparisons naturally were not always absolutely identical but gave a good basis for our decision making. (para. 11) (My italics.)

For the purposes of clerical staff, the Committee followed the same procedure:

Here the Company chose local comparisons, most of which were general engineering rather than aerospace. *Despite the wording of the Resolution* we felt that for this category of staff, the *wider designation* of engineering—providing ample comparisons, *was preferable* to either geographically wide comparisons or a mere handful of local specialized firms. Again we thought that as far as possible the grades should be treated overall since precise comparison of some of the individual jobs could be difficult. (para. 12) (My italics.)

As for the category of other staff, the evidence produced was, the Committee stated, 'barely satisfactory'. Without specifying any category of industry, however, the Committee felt able to prescribe an increase to bring these workers up to the general level. This was justified in industrial relations terms, which, the Committee acknowledged 'are strictly speaking irrelevant to our concern' (para. 14).

It seems possible to state, therefore, that the Committee will exercise its discretion in interpreting the phrase 'trade, industry or section' to encompass a wider designation of industry where comparisons are chiefly available on the basis of similar occupations and skills.

The problem of designating a 'trade, industry or section' is particularly acute where the claim is lodged on behalf of a highly autonomous group of workers within a large enterprise. The occupations of this group of workers may be peripheral to the main activity of the enterprise. Indeed, so autonomous may the group be that it may be legally distinct in the form of a subsidiary company supplying services to the parent company. If a Fair Wages claim is lodged on behalf of the group of workers, the question becomes: is the 'trade or industry' to be designated according to the activity of the group, or subsidiary company, or the activity of the enterprise as a whole? Obviously the answer will determine the choice of comparators.

Characteristically, the Committee has so far refused to supply a definitive answer. In Award 32 of 21 September 1976 (*Sunblest Bakeries (GLW) Ltd. and City Bakeries Ltd. Glasgow and T.G.W.U.*), the companies employed 2,500 workers of whom thirty-eight were vehicle maintenance workers. The Union claimed under the 1959 Act for a fourth week of holidays in accordance with the N.J.I.C. Agreement for Motor Vehicle Retail and Repair Industry. It argued that the Companies 'although principally engaged in the Baking Industry, were in part also engaged in the Motor Vehicle Retail and Repairing Industry' (para. 8). The Companies warned that 'all groups of hourly paid employees in the two Companies had three weeks' holiday except shop workers, who under a Wages Council Order received an extra two days. To grant an extra week's holiday to vehicle maintenance workers would cause fragmentation and induce friction and dissension amongst different groups' (para. 11). The Committee held that: 'The two Companies are engaged in the Baking Industry and quite properly follow the Baking Industry Agreement's terms and conditions of employment for their production workers' (para. 13). That Agreement was of no use since it did not refer to vehicle repairers. To fill the gap, the Committee recommended that a domestic agreement be concluded. But it would not apply the N.J.I.C. agreement, because, it said: 'In the Committee's view other conditions of employment such as holidays, sickness arrangements and pensions should be uniform throughout all groups (of workers in the Companies)' (para. 13).

Again, in Award 10 of 2 June 1976 (*BE & HL Patternmaking Co. Ltd. and The Association of Patternmakers and Allied Craftsmen*), the Committee did accept that there was a section of the engineering industry with its own terms and conditions of employment settled by a district agreement covering the North East Coast—the Master Patternmaking Industry. The case concerned a group of workers in a subsidiary company which supplied patterns to its parent company which was in the general engineering industry. When these workers claimed under the 1959 Act for the subsidiary to observe the agreement, the Committee held it *not* to be engaged in the patternmaking section of the engineering industry. The Union had submitted that the Company, though not a party to the collective agreement, had followed the negotiated rates closely until re-organization in 1974. The Company even admitted this, but claimed it 'was largely coincidental and should not be taken to imply that the Company had recognized or intended to follow the district agreement' (para. 26). The Committee chose to emphasize that the 'Company's primary function is to provide a service to its own group' (para. 37); 'the Company's survival and prosperity are largely dependent on its associated companies, not on customers outside the group'. It concluded that 'the nature of the work the Company's patternmakers are engaged in firmly establishes the Company as a tied pattern shop and not a master pattern shop' (para. 38). It was in the general engineering industry, the agreement did not apply, and thus the claim was rejected.

In contrast to these two negative results, Award 27 of 31 August 1976 (*STD Services Ltd. and A.S.T.M.S.*) offers a positive ray of hope to autonomous and identifiable groups of workers submerged in large enterprises, who are being treated unfairly compared to similar workers in other enterprises. STD Services Ltd. was a wholly owned subsidiary of Tube Investments Ltd. The Company employed seven Engineer Surveyors, who carried out statutory inspections on various equipment for the parent company on a fee-paying basis. The work of Engineer Surveyors is ancillary to the normal business of insurance companies. National terms and conditions of employment for Engineer Surveyors are established by negotiation between the Engineer Surveyors' Association (now part of A.S.T.M.S.) and 'The Employers' Consortium' consisting of several large insurance companies. The Union submitted that the Company was bound by this agreement, being, together with the insurance companies, in a separate industry—the statutory certification on mechanical, electrical and industrial machinery. The

Company argued that it was an engineering company, part of a large engineering group, with no insurance interest, and was thus not in the same trade or industry as members of the Employers' Consortium. In stating its Award, the Committee made the following observations:

> The Union claims that there exists the statutory certification on mechanical, electrical and industrial machinery industry. We believe it was unnecessary for the Trade Union to choose such an unwieldy title. It would have simplified the issue to have claimed that there is a section of the insurance industry, the function of which is the statutory certification on mechanical, electrical and industrial machinery. It is perfectly clear that there is such a section. There is a collective agreement which relates exclusively to personnel who undertake no duties other than such certification. Approached this way it is only necessary now to consider whether the Company, STD Services Ltd., is engaged in that section. (para. 19)

The Committee went on to hold that:

> *It is perfectly possible, in our view, for a company to be engaged primarily in one industry and yet be engaged also in one or more other industries or sections of them.* An organization such as STD Services Ltd. will almost inevitably fall into this category. (para. 21) (My italics.)

Since the Company was engaged in 'that section of industry which deals with the statutory certification on mechanical, electrical and industrial machinery', it was bound to the terms of the Agreement.

A similarly successful result was achieved in Award 77 of 16 February 1977 (*Kitson's Sheet Metal Ltd. and the National Union of Sheet Metal Workers, Coppersmiths, Heating and Domestic Engineers*). The Company argued that it 'was one of the group controlled by Kitson's Insulation Limited and existed to serve the Thermal Insulation Industry' (para. 13). The applicable terms, it submitted, were to be found in the national agreements for that industry. The Union said 'that the Company, although serving the interests of the controlling company in the Thermal Insulation Industry, was nevertheless registered as a separate company and was wholly engaged in engineering work' (para. 12). The terms and conditions applicable, therefore, were those laid down in the national engineering agreement. The Committee upheld the Union's contention.

A final set of problems arises in cases where the employer concerned is undergoing a substantial change in the nature of his operations so as to allow him to cast doubt on the applicability of a collective agreement invoked by the Union. Thus, in Award 102 of 20 April 1977

(*Globe Petroleum Sales Ltd. and T.G.W.U.*), the issue was whether the Motor Vehicle Retail and Repair Industry Agreement was appropriate to the Company which asked the Committee to accept that its filling station was now concerned with the sale of groceries so as to cause the workers in question no longer to fall within the categories of workers covered by the agreement. As the Committee saw it, the matter was basically one of factual judgment:

> The question we have to determine is whether this has been so developed, with such separation as to enable us to say that certain workers fall outside the agreement. The evidence we regard as important is—the formal description of the workers, the way in which their duties combined shop and filling station work and the proportions devoted to each aspect in terms of functions and financial revenue' (para. 19)

The Committee's conclusion was that the functions were not yet separate and the workers still fell under the agreement. A similar conclusion was reached in Award 15 of 14 July 1976 (*Navy, Army and Air Force Institutes and U.S.D.A.W.*).

The general conclusion which can be advanced at the time of writing is that discretion, not principle, remains the Committee's must useful, and used, instrument in determining the appropriate 'trade, industry or section'. This can be simply illustrated using one of its more recent cases. In Award 95 of 22 March 1977 (*The Blackpool Tower Company Limited and A.U.E.W. (Construction Section)*) the Committee forthrightly declared that: 'The employers, the Blackpool Tower Co. Ltd., are engaged primarily in the entertainment industry' (para. 22). The workers concerned in the claim, however, were riggers, welders and chippers and painters, who maintain the structure of the Blackpool Tower. They sought the observance of the Mechanical Construction Engineering Agreement. The Committee was in doubt whether the agreement could appropriately be adopted: 'Certainly there is a marked difference between construction and maintenance work. We do not consider that it would be correct to regard the Mechanical Construction Engineering Agreement as constituting "recognized terms and conditions" under the Schedule (11)' (para. 24). Happily, however, this did not preclude resort to the 'general level', and the Committee felt able to say that 'the best approach to general level is to use the Mechanical Construction Engineering Agreement as the framework upon which a modified pay rate can be determined' (para. 26). Given this successful result, the Chairman, Professor John Wood was perhaps justified in ignoring the implications for the rest of the entertainment industry.

District

The awards handed down by the Central Arbitration Committee on clause 1(b) of the Fair Wages Resolution of 1946 have not been required, by the terms of that clause, to specify any district. The clause refers to a 'general level . . . in the trade or industry'. Hence, the Committee has for the most part not specified in its awards what it considers to be the parameters of a 'district' for the purposes of fair comparisons. In contrast, the 'general level' specified by Schedule 11 is to be that 'in the district' where the employer is engaged (paragraph 2(b)(i)).

It was pointed out in the discussion of the 'district' element in chapter 16 that locality was a consideration in choosing fair comparisons. This was imported by the Industrial Arbitration Board in a careful statement in Award 3290 of 24 April 1974 (*Crittall-Hope Ltd. and Pay Board*):

> the comparison between the rates of wages, hours and conditions observed by the contractor concerned and the general level of wages, hours and conditions observed by other employers is not limited to any district, although geographical propinquity may have to be taken into account in deciding whether the general circumstances of the other employers are similar. (para. 48)

The problem of defining a district has, therefore, cropped up in cases brought before the Committee under clause 1(b) of the Resolution. For the purposes of divining its intentions regarding the 'district' element in Schedule 11, a few of its comments in these cases may be noted.

The parties before the Committee have not hesitated to specify any number of different districts: Worcestershire (Award 90), Greater London north of the Thames (Award 78), the West Midlands (Award 88), a divisional area of the Union, A.U.E.W. (T.A.S.S.) (Award 86), the Greater Manchester area (Award 71), or the whole South West (Award 76). In its awards, however, the Committee has specifically referred only to few: e.g. the Bolton district (Award 2), a five or ten mile radius in the London area (Award 78), or the Bristol area (Award 76).

An indication of the Committee's thinking on this question may be found in Award 104 of 2 May 1977 (*Hawker Siddeley Aviation Ltd., Hamble, and A.S.T.M.S.*). The Union drew comparisons from the same geographical area as the Company (Hamble, Hampshire), and also ranged further afield for other comparators in aerospace in the Midlands, Lancashire, Yorkshire and Scotland (para. 11). The

Company's comparators were drawn from a much narrower area, its view being that 'it was important to take locality into account when determining the "general circumstances" of other employers to ensure that they were in the same labour market area' (para. 16). In its Award, the Committee, while emphasizing that 'the general language of the Fair Wages Resolution has to be interpreted in relation to the facts and circumstances of each particular case', addressed itself to the problem of defining the district as follows:

> The reference in the Resolution to 'the district where the work is carried out' would support an emphasis on comparisons in the locality where employment is normally sought and found within the local labour market for the occupations under reference. (para. 26)

While the words quoted by the Committee are from clause 1(a) of the Resolution, it appears to acquiesce in the importation of the district element into clause 1(b) in the form of emphasizing local labour market considerations. This approach was reiterated in Award 114 of 20 May 1977 (*AEI Semiconductors Ltd. and A.S.T.M.S.*). Commenting on the inadequacy of the comparisons produced by the parties, the Committee stated that it:

> has no doubt that more could be done in gathering information about the local labour market for many of the grades covered by this reference as well as information on a wider basis within the industry for more specialized employees for whom employment opportunities normally cover a wider area. (para. 20)

The wider the labour market for particular occupations, it seems, the wider is the district which the Committee is prepared to have regard to in considering comparisons, within the industry of course.

Such a pragmatic approach offers Unions the opportunity to extend the range of comparisons according to the type of employees concerned. Indeed, it would seem useful to propose a number of different ranges of comparisons for the Committee to consider. That the Committee encourages this approach may be deduced from its comments in Award 30 of 17 September 1976 (*Dobson Hydraulics Ltd. and A.U.E.W. (T.A.S.S.)*):

> Clearly, both sides had gone to some trouble to collect such information and the Committee was able to take into account data concerning:
> (a) salaries paid by other employers in the same industry in the immediate locality;

(b) salaries paid by other employers in the same industry in a somewhat wider area, and

(c) salaries, analysed by industry and by region, paid to comparable T.A.S.S. members. (para. 15)

It then went on to confirm that its view was that clause 1(b) of the Resolution was relevant, and stated:

> The Employer argued strongly that the words 'whose general circumstances in the trade or industry in which the contractor is engaged' in Clause 1(b) were of paramount importance and the 'general circumstances' should be interpreted to include such factors as size of firm and *locality*. The Union was of a similar view but wished the Committee to have regard also to prevailing *national* salary levels for the kind of work in which its members in Dobson Hydraulics were employed. *We are of the opinion that 'general circumstances' is a term sufficiently imprecise to allow the Committee to exercise its discretion in determining the relevance of evidence on wages, hours and conditions.* (para. 17) (My italics.)

The efforts of this same Union were again rewarded in Award 108 of 6 May 1977 (*Weldall Engineering Ltd. and A.U.E.W. (T.A.S.S.)*). The case presented some difficulty, and the Committee commented:

> the Company does not have a pay structure with staff grouped into categories. Obviously the type of job gives an indication of its ranking. Since, at the hearing, we were directed to the T.A.S.S. (i.e. A.U.E.W. (T.A.S.S.)) salary census we feel that as far as possible we must look at the staff along the lines of its categorization. (para. 17(a))

With regard to the appropriate comparisons:

> Again, the point is one of real difficulty. We were given several possible sets of figures. We have considered them all but first noted the type of Company we were dealing with and its location. On balance, whilst not entirely discounting the figures from firms selected nationally we feel that the proper comparison should be, as far as possible with local industry in the Stourbridge–Birmingham area. Both parties referred us to the T.A.S.S. survey and we found the figures for Birmingham and Stafford useful though not conclusive. (para. 19)

In conclusion, the problem-solving approach of the Committee once again comes to the fore. It will reserve to the utmost its discretion to determine the district from which comparisons may be drawn for the purpose of establishing a general level. In the interests of a workable solution, it is even prepared to have regard to national comparisons, though it obviously prefers those from the locality. In preparing their cases, the parties should bear in mind the openmindedness of the Committee on the question of 'district'.

Similar circumstances

For the purposes of establishing a 'general level', Schedule 11 requires comparators to be employers 'whose circumstances are similar to those of the employer in question' (para. 2(b)(ii)). The Committee has dealt with numerous cases under clause 1(b) of the Fair Wages Resolution, where the general level is that observed by other employers whose 'general circumstances . . . are similar'. When complaints are made under the Resolution, each side is keen to produce comparators that favour its own case, and dispute those produced by the other party.

For example, in Award 23 of 9 August 1976 (*Effingham Steel Works Ltd. and A.S.T.M.S.*) the Company submitted that 'comparison had to be made with employers of similar size, who were direct competitors', and 'rejected the Union's table of comparisons, because those companies were not direct competitors of similar size' (paras. 13–14). And in Award 108 of 6 May 1977 (*Weldall Engineering Ltd. and A.U.E.W. (T.A.S.S.)*), the Company submitted that: 'Comparisons made by the Union between the Company and 5 competitors was rejected as the 5 employers selected were not competitors but customers. Furthermore they were more sophisticated than Weldall Engineering and all employed between 1000 and 3000 staff whereas the Company had a total work force of less than 500' (para. 12). Again, in Award 88 of 28 February 1977 (*Hostess Furniture Ltd. and A.S.T.M.S.*) the Company was engaged in the manufacture of tubular chairs and tables, cupboards and mobiles for use mainly in educational establishments. It employed 225 workers, thirty of whom were staff:

> The Company questioned the validity of the comparisons made by the Union. One of the companies was a motor vehicle manufacturing firm employing over 9000 workers of whom 1600 were staff; another was a shopfitting firm paying amongst the highest wage rates in the area and there was another company employing 530 workers of whom 150 were staff. These companies were dissimilar in size and operations to Hostess Furniture Limited and could not therefore be validly used in a comparative exercise. (para. 17)

Despite these protests, the complaints were upheld in each case.

On the other side, in Award 86 of 8 March 1977 (*Grundy and Partners Ltd. and A.U.E.W. (T.A.S.S.)*), the Union submitted that:

> The work undertaken by the Company was of a high technical standard. It was therefore also appropriate to make comparisons with leading companies in the area. Information was provided showing details of salary structures within 2 large engineering companies in the district. ... It was accepted that these 2 companies were known in the district as relatively high payers but they had been used because of their close proximity. (para. 9)

The Company protested that this evidence was too select and narrowly based. The Union in Award 78 of 17 February 1977 (*Kelvin Hughes and A.U.E.W. (Engineering Section)*) submitted comparisons with twenty-eight other companies. The Committee dismissed the complaints in both cases, stating in the latter that 'we considered the evidence produced by the Union was of a very general character and, for comparative purposes, of limited value' (para. 20).

The inadequacy of the evidence produced by the parties has on occasion driven the Committee to conduct its own survey. In Award 33 of 22 September 1976 (*Newton Derby Ltd. and Association of Professional, Executive, Clerical and Computer Staff*): 'To support their case under paragraph 1(b) the Union produced an analysis of collective agreements in 25 engineering companies throughout Great Britain and Northern Ireland' (para. 14). On the other hand, the Company stated its view that:

> To compare with employers in the industry whose circumstances were similar it was necessary to select companies which were:
> (a) not vastly different in size;
> (b) in the Derby district where the work was carried out;
> (c) parties to the same organization and trade unions;
> (d) not completely or partly state-owned or government-subsidized;
> (e) engaged in the engineering industry carrying out mainly metal cutting and fabrication and assembly of an engineering product. (para. 18)

The Committee upheld the complaint, but stated:

> We met a serious difficulty in this case. It is essential, if the Committee is to produce a satisfactory answer, that it should have a sufficient number of appropriate wage rates for comparison. The trade union had done a great deal of research and cast their

net rather widely—both in type of Company and in geographical area. The Company gave less evidence, gathered on a much narrower basis. Its effectiveness was considerably reduced by a veil of secrecy over its source. The figures gave quite different pictures; there was no overlap. Plainly we could not reach a satisfactory decision on this evidence alone. We therefore made enquiries of various sources so that we had a clearer picture of the range of rates for the types of job we were considering. (para. 24)

Only rarely does the Committee specify its own views on the question of what does or does not constitute 'similar circumstances'. In Award 76 of 9 February 1977 (*Bristol Aerojet Ltd. and A.S.T.M.S.*) the Union put forward as comparators three large aerospace firms in Bristol. The Company objected that comparisons should be made only with engineering firms of similar size. Of this the Committee said:

> This contention we do not accept for in our view the comparison should be made with other engineering firms in the Bristol area whether large, small or medium-sized, and the employers with whom comparison is to be made should include the three large companies in the area who are part of the Aerospace Industry. (para. 26)

Apart from such rare statements of its view in a particular case the Committee clearly wants to reserve to itself the utmost freedom to decide whether comparators are appropriate. There has already been quoted the Committee's statement as to the extent to which the phrase 'general circumstances' will restrict comparators to the locality: (Award 30 of 17 September 1976, *Dobson Hydraulics Ltd. and A.U.E.W.* (*T.A.S.S.*)):

> We are of the opinion that 'general circumstances' is a term sufficiently imprecise to allow the Committee to exercise its discretion in determining the relevance of evidence on wages, hours and conditions. (para. 17)

The Committee's position is best illustrated by its Award 84 of 28 February 1977 (*Light-metal Forgings Ltd. and A.S.T.M.S.*). It summed up the parties' submissions as follows:

> Both parties were agreed that the claim fell for consideration under Clause 1(b) of the Fair Wages Resolution. There were, however, basic differences between the parties about the interpretation of the requirement in that paragraph that comparison

should be made with 'other employers whose general circumstances in the trade or industry in which the contractor is engaged are similar'. A different emphasis was placed by each party on the relevance of such factors as size of firm, the way production was organized, the technology required, the value of the materials used or the quality and importance of the product. (para. 22)

Its own view was stated carefully to be that:

Many of the factors mentioned by both parties contributed in the Committee's view towards finding an answer to the question posed by the terms of the Resolution. They were, however, indicators rather than decisive and exclusive criteria and their importance varied in relation to particular jobs. (para. 23)

The Committee's classic formula in its decisions remains precisely and clearly to spell out the maximum of discretion.

Employers

The comparators establishing the 'general level' must be 'employers'— a term now defined by section 30(1) of the Trade Union and Labour Relations Act 1974 (as amended by the Employment Protection Act 1975, Schedule 16, Part III, para. 7(2)) as follows: 'employer':

(a) where the reference is to an employer in relation to an employee, means the person by whom an employee is (or, in a case where the employment has ceased, was) employed, and
(b) in any other case, means a person regarded in that person's capacity as one for whom one or more workers work, or have worked or normally work or seek to work;

And section 30(2) of T.U.L.R.A. adds that:

'employer' includes any Area Health Authority, Family Practitioner Committee or Health Board in accordance with whose arrangements a person provides or has provided or normally provides or seeks to provide any such service as aforesaid.

According to the Fair Wages Resolution of 1946, the 'general level' with which employers must comply is that observed by 'other employers'. In Schedule 11, the 'general level' is defined as that observed by 'employers'. It is not clear, therefore, whether the general level is to be determined by reference also to the employer the object of a claim —are his terms to be considered in determining the general level? If they are, and he appears near or at the bottom of the scale, the result would be to lower the general level.

A parallel question arises in the case of an enterprise which maintains a number of establishments. Some of these may be 'associated employers' within the meaning of the definition of section 30(5) of TULRA:

> For the purposes of this Act any two employers are to be treated as associated if one is a company of which the other (directly or indirectly) has control; and in this Act 'associated employer' shall be construed accordingly.

There would not appear to be any obstacle to using associated employers as comparators to determine the general level applicable to a particular company.

But other establishments of a particular enterprise, though separate in most other ways, may yet belong to the same legal entity. The question is whether other establishments of the same employer can be invoked as comparators in determining the general level. If the employer himself is taken into account in determining the general level, obviously the question is answered in the affirmative. Other things being equal, there would have to be good reasons for excluding some but not others of the employer's establishments. The question was posed in Award 104 of 2 May 1977 (*Hawker Siddeley Aviation Ltd., Hamble, and A.S.T.M.S.*) when the Union submitted that 'the most relevant section of the industry from which to draw comparisons comprised other HSA companies. The Union understood that the duties and responsibilities of its members in the various plants of those companies were equivalent' (para. 9). The submission continued:

> The Union acknowledged that the point was arguable but nevertheless considered that it was appropriate for them to treat the HSA companies as being 'other employers' within the meaning of the Resolution. Whilst there was a holding company which covered the different companies, each company regarded itself as independent and conducted separate domestic negotiations on pay and conditions. (para. 10)

The Company simply stated that 'the Union's comparisons with other establishments of HSA were invalid, for the purposes of the Resolution, because such establishments were all part of the same company as a legal entity' (para. 14). The Committee repeated the Company's argument in its 'General considerations', but concluded:

> The Union argued that as each establishment had independent powers to settle terms and conditions of employment it was right to bring the resultant settlements within the scope of the com-

parisons. The Committee has proceeded on the view that it is right to take account of such independently reached settlements for the purpose of the Fair Wages Resolution but only to the extent that the general circumstances of the other establishments are similar. (para. 21)

Despite its apparent willingness to accept comparisons from other establishments of the same employer, the Committee does appear to draw the line at claims invoking internal differentials within a company as a basis for the claim. Thus, in Award 6 of 6 April 1976 (*Dowty Boulton Paul Ltd. and A.S.T.M.S.*), the Committee cited the terms of the Fair Wages Resolution and concluded:

We are therefore unable to consider further the Union's argument that by custom and practice the Company's ratefixers' wages have been linked to those of senior foremen. No doubt, in normal free collective bargaining, the Union would have a strong case for the restoration of parity with the foremen, but in applying the criteria of the Fair Wages Resolution we must look strictly to outside comparisons and our award is entirely based on such comparisons. (para. 26)

And again in Awards 36 of 5 October 1976 (*Ferranti Ltd.*), 113 of 20 May 1977 (*William E. Farrar Ltd. and A.U.E.W. (T.A.S.S.)*) and 114 of 20 May 1977 (*AEI Semiconductors Ltd. and A.S.T.M.S.*), the Committee reiterated the Resolution's requirement that it consider outside comparisons and not internal relativities. It should be remembered, however, that the word 'other' was omitted from the comparator 'employers' to be used in determining the general level under Schedule 11. It remains to be seen if the Committee will feel that it can have regard to internal relativities, so vital to good industrial relations, in making awards under that Schedule.

Employers' associations and independent trade unions

'Recognized terms and conditions', within the meaning of Schedule 11, can only be those agreed by employers' associations and independent trade unions. Only these parties, again, can report claims under Schedule 11, whether based on recognized terms or the general level. Individual employers and workers cannot. 'Employers' association' is defined in section 126(2) of the Employment Protection Act 1975 as 'any organization representing employers and any association of such organizations or of employers and such organizations'. This is the meaning of the term for the purposes of Schedule 11 (cf. the ordinary meaning in section 28(2) of T.U.L.R.A.). 'Trade union' is defined in s. 28(1) of TULRA, and 'independent trade union' in section 30(1) of that Act.

Settled by an agreement or award

'Recognized terms and conditions', as defined by Schedule 11, are those 'settled by an agreement or award'. The problem of what constitutes an agreement or award was one which occasionally arose under previous Fair Wages policy instruments, as described above in chapter 16. The Committee faced this problem in Award 24 of 13 August 1976 (*W. Lovatt Transport and United Road Transport Union*), which turned on the question of whether there was an 'Agreement' within the meaning of section 8 of the 1959 Act. The Agreement invoked was made between the Negotiating Committee of the Road Haulage Association and representatives of the Union. The Company argued that there was no Agreement: the R.H.A. merely reached a conclusion and then 'advised' their members to accept. Although the Negotiating Committee expect members to accept their proposals, there was no commitment to do so. Members were independent in contrast to other instances of bargaining by Employers' Associations. The Committee's response was as follows:

> We see the strength of the Employer's argument, but we do not accept it. The nature of bargaining and settlement of terms and conditions in the Road Transport Industry is in the process of considerable change. It seems to us that it is now beyond doubt that in certain areas . . . collective bargaining of the usual pattern is established. The fact that the individual employers may be more independently minded, or less disciplined, does not in our opinion disturb our conclusions. It follows that we find that W. Lovatt Transport should have 'accepted the RHA advice' to implement the terms of the agreement. (para. 18)

The Committee's interpretation of 'agreement' is not dissimilar from that of its predecessors—but the general considerations that led to the interpretation are now being made explicit.

Recognized . . . minimum terms and conditions

In the preceding chapter, I described how, paradoxically, Schedule 11 might be interpreted so as to set up two separate and different standards —a 'minimum' level of 'recognized terms and conditions', and a 'fair' 'general level'. All depended on how the Committee chose to interpret the wording of paragraph 1 of the Schedule: 'where, or so far as, there are no recognized terms and conditions'. An interpretation might be adopted which precluded a claim based on the 'fair' general level where recognized 'minimum' terms existed. Alternatively, the Committee might interpret the phrase so as to allow for a claim based on the general level where there were no recognized 'fair' terms—only minimum terms were settled. There are two indications that the Committee might be inclined to adopt the latter interpretation of Schedule 11.

The first, and more general, is the Committee's non-legalistic, problem-solving, industrial relations orientated approach. This approach can be illustrated by a case which raised precisely the question of whether national minimum terms precluded consideration of terms actually observed. In Awards 40 and 41 of 1 November 1976 (*University of Manchester, University of Manchester Institute of Science and Technology and A.U.T.*), counsel for the employers began his argument with the submission that section 8(1)(a) of the 1959 Act required the union to prove that terms and conditions were settled by national agreement and established. Awards 3290 (*Crittall-Hope Ltd. and Pay Board*) and 3300 of the Industrial Arbitration Board and Award 2 of the Committee were quoted as precedents to show that the necessary conditions of being *established* meant actually observed in practice in the industry. It was submitted that the union had failed to prove that the terms were 'established' (para. 12). The union contested this view. But the Committee stated clearly in its section on 'general considerations' that it would not determine claims in accordance with such legalistic arguments:

> The Committee ruled against deciding the issue on the narrow basis suggested by the University. It appeared to them to be necessary to examine what terms were settled by the agreement before considering, *if such consideration appeared to be useful*, whether or not there were in this case established terms and conditions which differed from or in some way defined the terms and conditions settled by agreement. In any event it would be the Committee's wish to hear all the submissions which both parties wished to put forward. (para. 21) (My italics.)

Another example of legalism rejected by the Committee is Award 16 of 14 July 1976 (*George Allinson (Transport) Ltd. and T.G.W.U.*). This concerned a claim that the employer comply with the Agreement as regards both a pay supplement and a subsistence allowance. The solicitor for the employer pointed out to the Committee that section 8 of the 1959 Act is couched in the present tense: 'where a claim is duly reported . . . that as respects any worker . . . an employer . . . *is* not observing the terms and conditions'. He drew the Committee's attention to the fact that at the date of the claim only the extra subsistence allowance was not being paid. To this the Committee replied:

> We do not think that our powers are limited to terms and conditions not being honoured on the formal date of the claim to the Secretary of State, but extend to any matters raised at the outset with the Employer. (para. 24)

Such a constructive approach to the legislation granting it jurisdiction augurs well for the future of Schedule 11.

Secondly, the indications are that the Committee favours a *Crittall-Hope* solution to the problem of minimum terms and conditions. In Award 2 of 16 March 1976 (*Bolton Gate Co. Ltd. and A.U.E.W. (Engineering Section), Amalgamated Society of Boilermakers, Shipwrights, Blacksmiths and Structural Workers*), the Company claimed compliance with the Resolution, clause 1(a): 'by ensuring that their Plant Rate did not fall below the NTR (National Time Rate) of the National Agreement' (para. 16). The Committee's award referred to that Agreement as setting 'a national minimum set of terms and conditions, observed by all assenting employers'. It continued:

> The position does not, however, stop there. It is well established that local negotiations will follow and the National Agreement is struck with this in mind. . . . Individual firms bargain, at various times of the year, and establish a plant rate.
>
> It follows that there are in the Bolton District a considerable number of plant rates. From these rates it is possible to see the pattern of rates for the district. The national rates are in effect a platform upon which these local rates are based. We were given a comprehensive list of individual rates paid by a large number of firms which we were able to use to determine the local pattern of wage rates. (paras. 20–1)

The Committee went on to require the Company to increase its rates. In this case, therefore, the Committee did not hesitate to use the Fair Wages policy to cut through the recognized minimum level and require adherence to a fair general level.

The issue was raised again in Award 78 of 17 February 1977 (*Kelvin Hughes and A.U.E.W. (Engineering Section)*). The Company again contended 'that as rates of pay and conditions of employment for manual workers were well above the minima laid down in the national agreement there was no question of a breach of the Fair Wages Resolution' (para. 10). In support they invoked the High Court decision in *Racal Communications Ltd.* v. *Pay Board* (see chapters 15 and 16). The Committee noted that in that decision:

> The contention briefly was that, as in this case, the national engineering agreement established minimum rates of wages which were below the general level obtaining in the district. Argument centered on the meaning of the word 'established' and whether or not national rates, unless specifically adopted and paid in the district, came within scope of Clause 1(a). (para. 17)

Its conclusion was as follows:

> We have studied the High Court decision and note the particular references selected for our attention by the Company. We also consider it of particular significance that the judgment stated 'The reality of the matter is that the passage of time has rendered the Fair Wages Resolution of 1946 out of date'. To assist us further in concluding whether this case should be considered under Clause 1(a) or 1(b) we examined Awards Numbers 3290, 3296 and 3300 of the Industrial Arbitration Board. Our conclusion is that the question should be pursued under Clause 1(b). (para. 18)

The Committee thus seems to favour the *Crittall-Hope* solution for the paradox of Fair Wages policy contained in Schedule 11: the existence of recognized minimum terms does not preclude resort to the general level of fair terms. The above decisions, however, have considered only the Fair Wages Resolution. Only one other decision appears to have been concerned with the question—Award 89 of 8 March 1977 (*Eric Bemrose Ltd. and The National Graphical Association, The Society of Graphical and Allied Trades*). In this Award, the Committee seems to have made what appears to be a statement contradicting the *Crittall-Hope* doctrine:

> The Committee was invited to make a comparison with the terms and conditions being observed in the 3 other major firms in the Photogravure Printing section of the Industry—namely Odhams and Sun Printers at Watford and Parnells at Bristol. We asked and were told that the only existing recognized terms and conditions are the nationally negotiated agreements covering the whole of the printing industry: and we were further told, in answer to our questions that it was these national agreements, all of which were put before us, to which reference is made in the preamble to the 1972 House Agreement, when it is stated that that House Agreement is 'supplementary to all national agreements'. The

Committee accordingly finds that it is unable under the provisions of Schedule 11 to make a 'favourability comparison' as between the Company's House Agreement and the respective House Agreements of the 3 other large firms in photogravure. Such a comparison is not within the powers of the Committee in relationship to this claim. (para. 27)

I have read a transcript of the proceedings in this case and it appears that the issue was not argued before the Committee. This was partly a consequence of the fact that the claim was originally submitted under section 8 of the 1959 Act, before Schedule 11 came into force. And as the Chairman, Mr. J. S. Wordie commented in his opening remarks, Schedule 11 allows a claim based on recognized terms and conditions:

It then goes on to deal with the general level of terms and conditions which is not applicable as I and my colleagues in a brief chapter have looked at beforehand. I do not think the case is put under that further wording of Schedule 11 which was not in the old Section 8. (Page 3 of the transcript.)

The issue, therefore, was not argued before the Committee. Moreover, the Award does not specify any reason for the proposition that the Committee is powerless to carry out a 'favourability comparison'. The issue still awaits an authoritative decision by the Committee.

Comparable employment—Comparable workers

In formulating a claim under Schedule 11, a basic determinant is the classification of the workers on whose behalf the claim is lodged. The workers whose terms of employment constitute the 'recognized terms' under Schedule 11 must be in 'in comparable employment' to those the subject of the claim; while the 'general level' is that observed 'for comparable workers'. The standards which can be invoked under the Schedule require, therefore, a degree of similarity between the workers seeking the benefit of that standard, and those who have already achieved it. Much turns on how great a latitude the Committee will allow to parties seeking to affirm or deny that a worker or group of workers is comparable to another, so as to be governed by their 'recognized terms', or be entitled to their 'general level'.

Parties before the Committee have submitted comparisons assembled with varying degrees of sophistication. Some seek simply to assert a three-tiered classification of skilled, semi-skilled and unskilled workers, and this was accepted by the Committee in Awards 2 of 16 March

1976 (*Bolton Gate Co. Ltd. and A.U.E.W.* (*Engineering Section*), *Amalgamated Society of Boilermakers, Shipwrights, Blacksmiths and Structural Workers*) and 71 of 21 January 1977 *J & E Arnfield Ltd.*). Such a broad approach has occasionally been contested. In Award 78 of 17 February 1977 (*Kelvin Hughes and A.U.E.W.* (*Engineering Section*)), the Company criticized this classification by the Union, asserting that it 'did not relate to any specific grades but merely stated rates for skilled workers' (para. 15). On its own behalf, the Company presented a 'survey related to 23 bench mark jobs in the engineering industry which spanned the 7 grades within the Company's wage structure' (para. 11). The Committee's verdict was that:

> the evidence produced by the Union was of a very general character and, for comparative purposes, of limited value. It covered a wide geographical area and the rates shown were not sufficiently specific. On the other hand the employer, in our view, had taken considerable care in the comparisons of specific jobs. Of the two sets of evidence, that submitted by the Company was of greater assistance to us in determining the general level'. (para. 20)

The bench mark system is one occasionally invoked, though with a varying number of bench marks whose acceptability is often disputed. In contrast to the Company's twenty-three submitted bench mark jobs in Award 78, in Award 76 of 9 February 1977 (*Bristol Aerojet Ltd. and A.S.T.M.S.*), the Union selected three bench mark jobs—project engineer, foreman and inspector. And in Award 37 of 12 October 1976 (*F. G. Miles Engineering Ltd., Part of Hunting Hivolt Ltd.*) the Company made its submission on the basis of rates of pay of seven key grades of manual workers: skilled machine operator, numerically-controlled machine operator, jig-borer, wirer (to drawings), fitter, storekeeper, inspector (para. 7). In determining what were the fair rates for the workers concerned, the Committee stated: 'In performing this task we have accepted the bench mark jobs selected by the Company for the purpose of comparison and we have slotted in comparable jobs' (para. 12). In Award 88 of 28 February 1977 (*Hostess Furniture Ltd. and A.S.T.M.S.*), the Union undertook a general survey of pay for clerical, typing and administrative grades, while in Awards 80 and 81 of 22 February 1977 (*ML Engineering Co. Ltd. and ML Aviation Co. Ltd.*), the Companies showed comparative hourly rates of pay for thirteen groups of occupations. Finally, in Award 108 of 6 May 1977 (*Weldall Engineering Ltd. and A.U.E.W.* (*T.A.S.S.*)) the Union produced statistics for categories of staff taken from the T.A.S.S. annual salary survey. The Company disputed the grade categories selected, stating, for example that 'the engineers at the Company were below the level of category 5, which was engineers of degree equivalent, and to introduce a figure which included higher qualified staff showed the Company at a disadvantage' (para. 13). Nonetheless, the Committee concluded, referring to the T.A.S.S. survey 'that as far as possible we must look at the staff along the lines of its categorization. We accept the Company's argument that this cannot be done with precision and we have taken account of several points and made adjustments accordingly' (para. 17(a)).

The claims which present the greatest difficulty are those where comparisons with particular workers are extremely difficult to draw. The Committee adopts an approach which focuses not on the titles of the workers concerned, but rather on their actual work descriptions. This is often an approach adopted by parties experiencing difficulties finding comparisons. For example, in Award 50 of 7 December 1976 (*Dowty Boulton Paul Ltd. and A.U.E.W. (T.A.S.S.)*), the employer argued that:

> The Company operated in a highly specialized field so as to make valid comparisons impossible or, at best, extremely difficult. It was misleading to use similar job titles when comparing the functions of its technical staff with other Companies since the content of the job was different and, therefore, not properly comparable. (para. 12)

Again, in Award 84 of 28 February 1977 (*Light-metal Forgings Ltd. and A.S.T.M.S.*), the Union 'concentrated on comparisons with the nature of the job and work content rather than exact occupational titles' (para. 10).

Illustrations of this approach can be found in Award 86 of 8 March 1977 (*Grundy and Partners Ltd. and A.U.E.W. (T.A.S.S.)*) where the Union, claiming on behalf of technicians in the quality department, argued that 'although these were responsible jobs carrying staff status the salaries were below those paid to less skilled inspectors employed by other companies within the district. In support of this, figures were provided showing wages paid to inspectors at 7 factories in the district' (para. 10). And in Award 76 of 9 February 1977 (*Bristol Aerojet Ltd. and A.S.T.M.S.*) the Union invoked the fact that the Company's project engineers had been 'employed under contract in place of permanent civil servants who were graded higher, had more responsibility and received higher salaries than those obtaining at the Company' (para. 13).

Disputes invariably arose over classification. In Award 23 of 9 August 1976 (*Effingham Steel Works Ltd. and A.S.T.M.S.*), the Company rejected the Union's table of comparisons arguing that the job descriptions of the five men involved were not accurate: 'the Union's descriptions overstated the extent and responsibility of the work' (para. 14). It admitted that there was no grading structure and no formal method of evaluating the particular type of work, and conceded that accurate comparisons with employees in direct competitor companies were difficult. The Committee's award favoured the Union's view in some cases, the Company's in others. It would form its own judgment, as in Award 113 of 20 May 1977 (*William E. Farrar Ltd. and A.U.E.W. (T.A.S.S.)*):

> The evidence of comparable rates relating to the clerical staff and the telephonists we found harder to evaluate. It must of necessity .be less certainly comparable since duties covered by the usual job titles vary considerably. We therefore scrutinized this evidence closely. (para. 21)

The Committee's approach is probably best indicated by Award 6 of 6 April 1976 (*Dowty Boulton Paul Ltd. and A.S.T.M.S.*). The Union argued:

> Furthermore, an examination of the job description of Dowty Boulton Paul's ratefixers showed that substantial elements of work study and negotiating skills were required. Other companies used different titles, for example, 'Work study engineer', for employees engaged on similar work. It was necessary, therefore, when trying to make useful comparisons with other companies, to look at the salaries of some work study engineers (para. 17)

To the contrary, the Company contended that:

> There was a fundamental difference between ratefixers and work study engineers. This difference was manifested in the required standards of education and training as well as in the demands of the job. It was true that ratefixers sometimes performed some of the functions of work study engineers, but they certainly did not perform the full range of duties and the two groups were not strictly comparable for wage purposes. (para. 23)

In awarding wages increases under the 'general level' clause of the Fair Wages Resolution, the Committee held:

> The Committee concluded that in many cases in the engineering industry, the duties of a ratefixer and of a work study engineer, while not identical, contain similar elements. Moreover, virtually identical jobs in different companies are frequently given different

job titles. Inevitably, therefore, accurate comparisons in this field across several companies are extremely hard to make.

The Committee felt therefore, that it must take a broad view of the statistics provided by the two parties, especially since there are elements in the work of the Company's ratefixers which would in other companies be performed by individuals with the title of work study engineers. (paras. 29–30)

The Committee, it is clear, will not respond readily to claims that the workers concerned cannot be compared. In Award 90 of 16 March 1977 (*H. W. Ward and Company Ltd. and A.U.E.W. (T.A.S.S.)*), the Company disputed the Union's case:

> on the grounds that it was not possible to make valid comparisons as the functions of the technical staff in question varied widely from company to company. The Committee was invited to agree that as logical comparisons were extremely difficult it was not possible to ascertain a general level. (para. 10)

The Committee rejected the Company's submissions:

> It is unreasonable to suggest that in a section of the engineering industry where specific skills and qualifications are widely recognized and freely transferable between employers, there is no general level. It may be difficult to discern, but we feel that a general level exists. (para. 13)

The Committee's positive approach to its task led it to uphold a wage increase where the Company itself admitted that:

> It was possible to make meaningful comparisons for clerical staff, but there was no possibility of obtaining direct comparisons with its executive and managerial staff. There were no comparable grades on Orkney and Caledonian MacBrayne was a bigger organization with executives employed purely as general managers, where the O.I.S.C. executives were additionally directly involved with ships. (Award 79 of 22 February 1977, *Orkney Islands Shipping Company Ltd.*) (para. 14)

Nonetheless, the Committee held:

> We feel the choice of Caledonian MacBrayne is an entirely reasonable one. The method used has been to adopt the Caledonian MacBrayne's grading scheme and to apply it to the Company's staff. We note that this had been done both with care and discretion and without any attempt to do other than tackle the fair wage problem. (para. 18)

So, although 'there are no appropriate comparable jobs in respect of the three most senior staff' (para. 19), an increase could still be granted.

Finally, an innovative method whereby the Committee has succeeded in overcoming the problem of jobs which defy comparison in particular circumstances is illustrated in two Awards in such cases. In Award 94 of 25 March 1977 (*Woodhouse Parish Council and N.U.P.E.*), the Union 'accepted that a village hall caretaker was not one of the occupational groups listed in national agreements' (para. 8), though it argued that 'comparisons could be made with comparable workers employed by the eight other Parish Councils in Leicestershire' (para. 11). The Committee noted that the employment of the worker concerned 'followed a pattern increasingly rare' and that 'as the Council saw it, this was a unique situation with the terms of the employment adapted to the special circumstances' (para. 19). The trade union's view, the Committee observed, was that 'taking a wider conspectus they regard Mr. Satterthwaite's job as part of the whole fabric of local government work. Thus it is to the national agreement they turn to find that appropriate terms and conditions for Mr. Satterthwaite's job' (para. 20). The Committee clearly adhered to this latter viewpoint. Although the worker's job did not fall within the scope of the agreement:

> This decision makes little practical difference. Mr. Satterthwaite's terms and conditions must be fixed in relation to the appropriate general level which can only be taken to mean in this context the structure established by the NJC for manual workers. Mr. Satterthwaite's job has no direct comparison so his terms and conditions must be determined by special consideration. . . .
>
> We have looked at the overall pay structure of local authorities, at the Group A jobs and rate of pay and at the Parish hall keeper's job and present rate. From these comparisons we arrived at the rate we feel appropriate bearing in mind the general level for workers of this general description. (paras. 24–5)

This method, whereby *a comparison was not sought with a directly comparable job, but with a structure of jobs into which the worker could be considered to fit somewhere, if at no specific grade*, was used again in Award 95 of 22 March 1977 (*The Blackpool Tower Company Ltd. and A.U.E.W. (Construction Section)*). The claim concerned sixteen workers (riggers, welders, painters, sprayers and chippers) employed on the maintenance of the structure of the Blackpool Tower. The Union argued that the Company must observe the terms of the Mechanical Construction Engineering Agreement. The Committee, however, accepted the Company's contention that it would not be correct to regard the Agreement as constituting 'recognized terms' under Schedule 11: 'Certainly there is a marked difference between construction and maintenance work' (para. 24). It went on, however:

> This decision does not, in this case, make as much difference as might first appear. Having found that there are no recognized terms and conditions means that we must consider whether there is a general level applicable here. The mere fact that the work in question has unique features does not mean that there is no general level. *The work plainly forms part of a pattern of similar or related jobs, involving recognized skills which, taken together, give indications of a general level.* The principal feature of those related jobs is, of course, the Agreement which we have decided is not precisely applicable. We were referred to other points of comparison—local government maintenance work and especially the Runcorn-Widnes Bridge. We have considered these and have evaluated the character, extent and nature of the work done by the Blackpool Tower workers we are considering.
>
> We accept that the best approach to general level is to use the Mechanical Construction Engineering Agreement as the framework upon which a modified pay rate can be determined. (paras. 25–6) (My italics.)

The Committee's ingenuity indicates that where it can be shown that a claim is justified, that the workers concerned are unfairly treated, it will use its discretion to find a remedy within the terms of Schedule 11.

A final word of caution: the problem of deciding whether workers or groups are in comparable employment is one often encountered in collective bargaining over grading or job evaluation schemes. If comparisons can be found, a claim for a higher rate of pay may be justified. It might be thought that Schedule 11 could enable workers to appeal to the Committee when faced with an employer's adamant refusal to re-grade where this is thought to be clearly justified. The Committee is understandably reluctant to become what would be in effect a grading court of appeal. Such claims, unless overwhelmingly indicative of a situation of blatant unfairness, are unlikely to succeed.

The whole of the terms and conditions observed by the employer

Paragraph 9 of Schedule 11 states:

> In ascertaining whether, in respect of any matter which is the subject of a claim under paragraph 1 above, the employer is

observing terms and conditions less favourable than the recognized terms and conditions, or as the case may be, the general level of terms and conditions regard shall be had to the whole of the terms and conditions òbserved by the employer as respects the worker to whom the claim relates.

The principle of considering the whole of the employer's terms and conditions in deciding whether he was unfair is familiar from previous cases on Fair Wages policy. On a number of occasions, employers have contested claims before the Committee by invoking their other terms and conditions. For example, in Award 30 of 17 September 1976 (*Dobson Hydraulics Ltd. and A.U.E.W. (T.A.S.S.)*), 'the Company pointed out that the Union had ignored the fact that hours and conditions of employment obtaining in the Company compared very favourably with those of other employers' (para. 13). And in Award 77 of 16 February 1977 (*Kitson's Sheet Metal Ltd. and The National Union of Sheet Metal Workers, Coppersmiths, Heating and Domestic Engineers*), the Union's claim for an increase in annual holidays with pay from eighteen days to twenty days to comply with the new National Engineering Agreement was met with the contention that: 'Company employees received more holiday pay for 18 days than they would receive for 20 days under the engineering agreement rules for calculations' (para. 14). The companies still lost both cases. On the other hand the Company was successful in Award 114 of 20 May 1977 (*AEI Semiconductors Ltd. and A.S.T.M.S.*) when its submissions included the argument that the Union's evidence 'was inconclusive as it took no account of peripheral benefits' (para. 17). And, in an interesting variation, two Companies seeking to increase their rates under the Fair Wages Resolution submitted 'information on terms and conditions of employment other than pay', and 'contended that their terms and conditions were below the district average' (para. 10). In Awards 80 and 81 of 22 February 1977 (*ML Engineering Co. Ltd. and ML Aviation Co. Ltd.*), the Committee granted the increase.

Naturally, trade unions would oppose any such attempts to justify inadequate terms with compensatory items. So in a claim for increased rates, the Company in Award 78 of 17 February 1977 (*Kelvin Hughes and A.U.E.W. (Engineering Section)*) submitted that the 'peripheral benefits offered to manual workers were still more favourable than those offered by most other companies. For example only 10 out of 35 companies used in the survey gave their manual employees staff conditions' (para. 14). The Union countered that 'traditionally the Company observed better secondary conditions of employment such as holidays, sickness pay and pension scheme but in recent years most other companies had improved secondary conditions for their manual workers so that the advantage enjoyed by Kelvin Hughes' employees had been eroded' (para. 8). The claim was still unsuccessful.

The Central Arbitration Committee may be expected in the future to reserve to itself the discretion which appears to be granted by the wording of paragraph 9 of Schedule 11. This only requires the Committee to look at the whole of the terms observed by the employer. It is not directed by the law to weigh up all the benefits precisely and compare the totals. The Committee has discretion to discount certain factors in light of particular circumstances of a case. It is to have regard, no more.

An analogy may be drawn with section 6(11) of the Employment Protection Act 1975. Codes of Practice are admissible in evidence before the Committee, and if relevant, 'shall be taken into account'. This does not mean that the Committee must strictly apply every provision of a Code. It has discretion. Industrial tribunals, which also take the Codes into account, have repeatedly asserted that while Codes must be considered, they may not always be applicable in every case. So the Committee should have regard to other terms, but it has the discretion to discount them if it feels it would be right in the circumstances.

Schedule 11 firmly places the burden on the *employer* to satisfy the Committee that he is observing terms not less favourable (paragraph 8(b)). It could be argued that in principle the Committee should not regard itself as satisfied where the employer falls below the standards set for important terms—wages and hours. With regard to insignificant terms, an employer may seek to compensate for a deficiency in one item by a compensatory item, e.g., a subsidized canteen may compensate for lack of prescribed luncheon vouchers. But vital terms should be strictly adhered to, save in exceptional circumstances.

The cases which illustrate these points have produced a variety of results. A contrast can be found between Awards 18 and 108. In Award 18 of 14 August 1976 (*Cambion Electronic Products Ltd. and A.U.E.W.*), the Company submitted that:

> Transport to and from work provided free by the Company had been evaluated. When this was added to basic rates, together with the weekly equivalent of the profit sharing scheme, the resultant figures in all cases were no less favourable than the national minimum rates laid down in the National Engineering Industry. (para. 21)

The Union contended that 'neither element could justifiably be construed as part of weekly emoluments since the value of free transport was not a taxable item and the profit sharing bonus was an *ex-gratia* payment' (para. 14). The Committee's view of the benefit of free transport was to say that 'while we accept readily that this is an important advantage to many workers, we do not feel that it is the type of payment that can be included in our calculation. It has a somewhat uncertain legal foundation and it is of variable advantage depending upon circumstances'. And as regards the profit sharing bonus, 'we feel that, since our task is to ensure that workers do not receive less than the rates established in the collective agreement, we have to take a strict view of the current entitlement. In its present form, with neither legal entitlement nor guaranteed minimum we feel that the profit sharing bonus does not fall to be considered in our matching exercise' (para. 26).

In Award 108 of 6 May 1977 (*Weldall Engineering Ltd. and A.U.E.W. (T.A.S.S.)*), the Union sought to exclude the Company's production bonus 'as this was variable and did not constitute part of the conditions of employment. The bonus had been unilaterally introduced by the Company and, in the Union's view, could be withdrawn at any time' (para. 8). The Company's submission included the bonus and in addition argued that 'secondary conditions of employment at the Company were generous' (para. 14). The Committee's view was that 'it appeared to be accepted that the Company provided average or above average fringe benefits. There was marked difference as to how the production bonus should be treated' (para. 17). Its conclusion was as follows:

> It appears to us that a fair wage relates to the likely pay in bad times as well as good. We accept the Company's contention that their productivity bonus, although not the outcome of collective bargaining, is a permanent feature of the payments system. It is so constructed as to yield an inevitable £2 per week. . . .We have no doubt that the Company intends the bonus to be permanent. Unilateral withdrawal seems most improbable. (para. 18)

A clear cut case was made out in Award 89 of 8 March 1977 (*Eric Bemrose Ltd. and The National Graphical Association, The Society of Graphical and Allied Trades*). The Committee concluded:

> There is no doubt that, apart from the single provision relating to a paid night shift meal-break, the terms of the 1972 House Agreement are more favourable than the terms and conditions of the national agreements. For example, there is at present a 5 week holiday entitlement under the House Agreement compared with a 4 week entitlement under the national agreements.

The hours of the night shift at the Company are presently 38½ hours as against the 40 hours of the night shift under the national agreements. And the House Agreement remuneration has historically been over 50% above the minimum remuneration of the national agreements and was still 40% higher as recently as 1975. Having regard to the totality of the terms and conditions being observed by the Company as respects the workers engaged on night shift production, and our belief that the parties freely negotiated the exclusion of payment for meal-breaks during night shifts in the 1972 House Agreement which has now been operating for over 4 years, the Committee is left in no doubt that the terms and conditions being observed are not less favourable than the recognized terms and conditions as contained in the national agreements. (para. 26)

The attempt to enforce adherence to the single provision relating to a paid night shift meal-break failed, being overwhelmed by the more favourable terms in other respects. A reading of the transcript of the hearing, however, and the Committee's statement in its award that 'the Schedule mandatorily requires' regard to be had to the whole of the terms (para. 22), does not reveal an awareness on the part of the Committee that it did possess some discretion in considering other terms in this case.

On the other hand, in Award 21 of 11 August 1976 (*Radio Trent Ltd. and N.U.J.*), the Union, commenting on the Company's submission that, as their journalists' basic working week was thirty-five hours instead of the thirty-seven and a half hours in the collective Agreement, their total terms and conditions were not less favourable despite lower salaries, contended:

> that the Agreement specified an annual minimum salary for any particular grade. Minimum salary levels were not dependent on the length of the working week, particularly in an industry where irregular and extensive overtime and shiftworking operated. The Company's submission, therefore, was irrelevant. (para. 17)

On the Company's submission that they be assessed on their hourly rates, the Committee concluded:

> It is exceedingly difficult to accept that this approach, by way of assessment of an hourly rate, can always be applied. The differential in hours must be considered, as must the availability of overtime. We find, however, that Radio Trent has not issued a statement of Contractual terms, as required by the Contracts of Employment Act 1972 and that it is not possible to assess with

certainty and accuracy a true comparative position. So we feel the clearest way of dealing with the matter is to determine both hours of work and rates of pay as under the 1975 Agreement' (para. 30)

In conclusion, the Committee seems inclined to revert to an arbitration position in the event of dispute involving secondary benefits. It will try to allow for some benefit and detriment to both sides. Thus, in fixing the 'lieu' bonus rate of the maintenance workers on the Blackpool Tower in Award 95 of 22 March 1977 (*The Blackpool Tower Co. Ltd. and A.U.E.W. (Construction Section)*), it stated 'that we have taken into account the present system by which all components of pay apply to these men throughout the year, irrespective of the type of work done in any particular week. This gives the men no doubt welcome consistency of earnings and the Company get a flexible workforce' (para. 28). And in Award 94 of 25 March 1977 (*Woodhouse Parish Council and N.U.P.E.*), the Committee did take into account 'the intermittent nature of Mr. Satterthwaite's job and his irregular hours', but with regard to the District Valuer's assessment of the residential accommodation supplied: 'We did not consider it right to take full account of the district valuation of his living accommodation' (para. 25).

General level of terms and conditions

At the end of chapter 16, an attempt was made to ascertain how the predecessors to the Central Arbitration Committee had sought to define the concept of the 'general level' in the Fair Wages Resolution of 1946. The conclusion was that trade unions seeking to enforce the Fair Wages policy were left guessing on the question of what evidence was necessary to convince the authorities that an ascertainable general level of terms and conditions exists which employers must observe. In Award 3290 of 24 April 1974 (*Crittall-Hope Ltd. and Pay Board*), for example, the Industrial Arbitration Board simply reiterated its dedication to 'a general comparison' in the broadest terms (para. 48).

As might have been anticipated, the Committee has also not proposed any precise definition. It can be said with some assurance that the Committee is not going to commit itself to a specific statistical definition of the general level. In a large number of cases, the parties have based their submissions on the average terms of a number of comparable employers (e.g., Awards 78, 84, 88 and 90). In others, argument has focused on whether or not the general level was to be determined by reference to the median terms of a number of comparators (e.g. Awards 76 and 86). In its decisions, the Committee has resolutely declined to commit itself as being in favour of one or the other of the potential statistical methods. Only rarely has it expressed a view on the question at all. For example, in Awards 80 and 81 of 22 February 1977 (*ML Engineering Co. Ltd. and ML Aviation Co. Ltd.*), the Committee stated:

> The argument was based on the average wage rates obtained from appropriate comparisons. The Committee does not base its approach upon average figures, but seeks to identify wage bands which indicate those rates which fall below the general level and so can be designated unfair. (para. 14)

The Committee does clearly affirm that the determination of a general level is not an exercise which can be carried out with a high degree of precision. For example, in Award 23 of 9 August 1976 (*Effingham Steel Works Ltd. and A.S.T.M.S.*), the Committee noted that 'the parties did not entirely agree upon the exact nature of the jobs. The comparables used by the Trade Union were challenged by the Company, which in turn emphasized the difficulty in discussing true comparables' (para. 17). The Committee confessed: 'We do not think that it is possible to achieve anything approaching mathematical certainty in our task' (para. 19). And again, in Award 33 of 22 September 1976 (*Newton Derby Ltd. and Association of Professional, Executive, Clerical and Computer Staff*), the Committee was unable to reach a satisfactory decision on the evidence submitted: 'We therefore made enquiries of various sources so that we had a clearer picture of the range of rates for the types of job we were considering' (para. 24). Even then, the Committee had to admit: 'It would be wrong to say that we had reached a statistically refined answer to our question' (para. 25).

The Committee's awards have, therefore, been expressed in rather vague statements, as the following examples show. Claims are rejected in various terms. In Award 76 of 9 February 1977 (*Bristol Aerojet Ltd. and A.S.T.M.S.*), the Company is 'paying wages lower than those paid by the 5 large firms but it is well in the top half of the other 15 firms of comparable size', and thus the Committee is left 'in no doubt that the rates being paid by the Company do not show unfairness and are not less favourable than the general level' (para. 27). In Award 100 of 19 April 1977 (*Calibration Systems Ltd.*), the Committee states: 'It is our task . . . to make a careful and objective assessment of the general level' (para. 10); but 'it is not our function to award increases in salaries which place the Company at or near the top of the table of district salaries' (para. 14). In Award 104 of 2 May 1977 (*Hawker Siddeley Aviation Ltd., Hamble, and A.S.T.M.S.*), the Company's payment levels were held to be 'relatively low. . . . They compared unfavourably with most of the other HSA establishments' (para. 27). There was, nonetheless, no breach of the Resolution. In Award 111 of 12 May 1977 (*Charles Richards Fasteners Ltd. and A.S.T.M.S.*), the Committee's view was that the evidence submitted by the parties indicated a range of annual leave entitlements 'in respect of which the Company's present arrangements could not be regarded as being conspicuously out of line' (para. 20). And in Award 113 of 20 May 1977 (*William E. Farrar Ltd. and A.U.E.W.* (*T.A.S.S.*)), with respect to one of the categories of staff involved in the claim: 'the evidence we were given did not indicate a really significant shortfall' (para. 22). Where a complaint was upheld, as in Award 88 of 28 February 1977 (*Hostess Furniture Ltd. and A.S.T.M.S.*), the Committee said: 'Having considered the evidence at length, we are satisfied that a "general level" is ascertainable and that the salaries of the employees in question are substantially below that level and require to be increased' (para. 20).

The only common denominator I have found to underlie the Committee's conception of the 'general level' is the elemental criterion of the Fair Wages policy—*fairness*. When faced with difficulty in determining the general level, the Committee almost invariably resorts to using fairness to justify its decision. Indeed, there seems to be almost an equivalence established between the 'general level' and the 'fair wage'. Thus, in Award 6 of 6 April 1976 (*Dowty Boulton Paul Ltd. and A.S.T.M.S.*), the Committee began its award with the statement:

> In the Committee's opinion the Fair Wages Resolution clearly states that to determine a *fair wage* rate *or general level* of wages it is necessary only to compare rates paid to workers employed by the contractor with those of workers employed by other employers in the trade or industry. (para. 25) (My italics.)

The degree to which the purpose of the Fair Wages policy dominates the Committee's view of the 'general level' was most evident in Award 14 of 25 June 1976 (*Wimet Ltd. and A.S.T.M.S.*). The Committee began by saying that to explain its decision it was necessary to consider in general terms the purpose of the Fair Wages Resolution:

> This resolution is virtually a directive to the Government not to contract with employers who are failing to pay fair wages. . . . This Committee has to determine the somewhat elusive concept of the appropriate fair wage and the Resolution in paras. 1(a) and 1(b) gives an *indication* of the comparisons to be made. (para. 26) (My italics.)

The Award was quite emphatic: 'The primary task of the Committee is then, again expressed in general terms, to satisfy itself that the wage rates to which its attention is drawn present a clear, unmistakable situation of unfairness' (para. 28). The Committee then proceeded to elaborate to an hitherto unprecedented degree its perception of the 'general level':

> This process involves two difficulties. The Committee must have an idea of the nature of the concept of unfairness and it must also base its decision upon proper, reliable evidence. It should now be readily appreciated why this task is an objective one for the Committee which cannot be left to the parties whose interests may well not spring from the same considerations. On the question of fairness it is only necessary to make two points. Wage rates are almost impossible to determine with precision, for a multitude of reasons. Exact comparisons are rare. The fixing of rates in different firms at different times of the year means a comparison at any particular time has an inevitable artificiality. In most situations the evidence will show a range of wage rates and the task of the Committee is to assess whether the rates in question appear, on comparison, to show real unfairness. It is not a matter of asking whether the rates are appropriate, or could with advantage be improved. It is a much more simple task of determining that the workers in question are being plainly unfairly treated. Once this is found the Committee can then go on to assessing what would be a fair wage. Again it must be emphasized that the Committee is not at this stage attempting to supplant a free collective bargain. Its task is to make sure that the rates fixed fall, without doubt, within the range that can be said to be fair.
>
> It is obvious that to perform its duties the Committee requires evidence of appropriate comparable wage rates. In common with a court, the Committee looks to the parties to provide such evidence which can be tested and supplemented at the hearing. Yet it cannot be expected in particular cases to rely solely on this evidence. Unlike a court this Committee is investigatory in nature and so more ready to seek out appropriate evidence so that it can ensure that its decision is soundly based. (paras. 29–30)

This emphasis on fairness has been repeated in almost every complaint that the 'general level' was not being observed. Thus, in Award 23 of 9 August 1976, described above, despite the admitted impossibility of 'anything approaching mathematical certainty', the Committee 'nevertheless found that the evidence indicated that the level of salaries in these instances fell below a fair wage by about 8 per cent' (para. 19). Again, in Award 33 of 22 September 1976, described above, the Committee began by declaring:

> Our task is to ensure that a fair wage is determined—not to establish the figure we feel would be produced by normal negotiations or even by arbitration. We take the view that we must identify the band of wage rates for the job in question and to ensure that the wage paid does not fall outside the range that can be described as fair. (para. 23)

And despite their admission that their answer was not 'statistically refined': 'We are, however, satisfied that we have obtained enough information to be clear of the point below which a wage for a particular grade of job becomes unfair' (para. 25). In Award 37 of 12 October 1976 (*F. G. Miles Engineering Ltd., Part of Hunting Hivolt Ltd.*), the Committee repeated: 'It is not our task to determine the precisely appropriate rate nor to achieve an ideal pay structure. It is our task to ensure that rates are paid which are properly regarded as fair' (para. 11). The purpose of the 1946 Fair Wages Resolution was thus re-affirmed almost thirty years to the day after it was passed by the House of Commons—14 October 1946.

Latterly, in Award 50 of 7 December 1976 (*Dowty Boulton Paul Ltd. and A.U.E.W. (T.A.S.S.)*), it was stated: 'We do not believe it possible to achieve a mathematically precise level, but we are satisfied that the evidence indicated that the level of salaries paid by the Company to employees covered by the Reference fall below a fair wage by the appropriate percentage indicated in the following awarding paragraph' (para. 20). In Award 106 of 29 April 1977 (*M. L. Engineering (Plymouth) Ltd.*) the Committee stated: 'We accept that the current rates are less than fair and make our Award accordingly' (para. 10). And in Award 112 of 10 May 1977 (*The Hymatic Engineering Company Ltd.*), increases were granted to three categories of employees. For the first: 'We feel that the correct method of approach is first to determine whether the rates paid by the company fell below what we could regard as fair. That we felt they did. To cure the unfairness we feel that an overall increase of 8% would be appropriate' (para. 11). For the second: 'We were satisfied that the rates for most grades were less than fair. To cure the unfairness we feel that in general an increase of 4% would be appropriate' (para. 12). And for the third and most difficult: 'The evidence in this area was barely satisfactory but we were able to say that at the lower levels there is evidence that the salaries fall below the standard we have used for assessing fairness' (para. 14)— 4 per cent was awarded.

In conclusion, two optimistic comments may be made about the future of claims based upon the 'general level' First, the Committee seems ready to reject assertions that a general level cannot be established or does not exist—this was the case in Awards 50 and 90. Commenting on the evidence in Award 108 of 6 May 1977 (*Weldall Engineering Ltd. and A.U.E.W.* (*T.A.S.S.*)), the Committee said:

> We are not trying in a fair wages case to establish the precisely correct salary for each individual concerned. Our duty is, perhaps fortunately in view of the difficulty and complexity, to establish a rate which is demonstrably not unfair. Our decision does not preclude, in a free bargaining climate a different figure being achieved. This case was one where the Committee considered mounting a detailed study of the firms salaries and local comparables. We felt, however, that we had been given enough information of adequate precision to discharge the task we have just described. (para. 20)

As indicated in Award 14, the Committee is prepared to, and in Award 33 actually did, undertake such enquiries as would enable it to perform its function in determining whether fair terms are being observed.

Secondly, it is clear beyond doubt that the 'general level' referred to in Schedule 11 is derived from the Fair Wages policy embodied in clause 1(b) of the 1946 Resolution. The Committee's decisions on claims based on the 'general level' in Schedule 11 must necessarily, therefore, strive for consistency with the parallel jurisdiction it exercises over complaints under the Resolution.

At the time of writing, four decisions have been handed down by the Committee which, while originating in claims under section 8 of the 1959 Act, were dealt with under Schedule 11, and affected by the 'general level' provisions. In the section of this chapter on 'comparable employment—comparable workers', I described how in two of them, Awards 94 and 95, the Committee resolved the claim not by seeking a comparison with a directly comparable job, but rather comparison was made with a structure of jobs into which the worker could be considered to fit. This structure was in each case a collective agreement considered by the Committee to be not directly applicable, but nonetheless directly relevant. In the other cases, Awards 82 and 83 of 23 February 1977 (*North Eastern Co-operative Society Ltd., Greater Nottingham Co-operative Society Ltd. and National Association of Co-operative Officials*), the Committee declined to deal with the claim by applying the collective agreement with destructive results. Instead, it stated: 'Another alternative solution appears possible. It is not difficult to calculate that amount of money by which the current salaries fall below the entitlement under the national agreement. It might be possible to solve the dilemma by allocating this money within the current employment structure so as to achieve a package which could be said to provide a satisfactory equivalent solution' (para. 37).

In sum: the Committee was prepared to resolve a claim using Schedule 11's 'general level' jurisdiction, in the context of existing collective bargaining arrangements. Where workers are not specifically covered by such arrangements, claims cannot be made based on 'recognized terms'. Nonetheless, where it can be shown that the workers concerned operate in a context where collective bargaining has some direct relevance, the Committee will look to those collective bargaining arrangements for the framework of a solution. Such an approach is securely based on good industrial relations, as enshrined in section 1(2) of the Employment Protection Act 1975: 'promoting the improvement of industrial relations, and in particular (of) encouraging the extension of collective bargaining and the development and, where necessary, reform of collective bargaining machinery'. If the Committee persists in this approach, it may at last achieve the successful integration of Fair Wages policy and collective bargaining.

NOTE

1. As the Fair Wages Resolution of 1946 is not an enactment, the question arises whether the Committee could safely ignore an instruction from the Government to have regard to criteria other than 'Fair Wages' in determining complaints against government contractors under that Resolution.

22

Fair Wages Policy and Incomes Policy:
The Future

The last chapter of this study analyses the problem of the relationship between Fair Wages policy and incomes policy. It serves as an appropriate concluding point, for it appears that for the foreseeable future the Fair Wages policy will be ever more closely affected by developments in incomes policy. A constantly reiterated theme of this study has been the significance of the interrelationship of legislative policy and the system of industrial relations. As the Fair Wages policy has sought to determine wages and conditions of employment, it has been affected by the growth of and structural changes in the system of collective bargaining. In recent years there has been increasing intervention by government in the field of collective bargaining through incomes policy. A centrally determined policy for regulating wages and conditions of employment has been implemented through various instruments, ranging from statements of policy, declarations of intent, White Papers, legislation and most recently, the Social Contract. It is, perhaps, not too early to assert that the intervention of government through incomes policy constitutes a fundamental change in the system of industrial relations—on a par with the growth of collective bargaining at the turn of the century, the development of national bargaining during and after the First World War, and the reversion to local bargaining with the advent of 'full' employment in the years after the Second World War.

Fundamental or not, there is no doubt that the influence of incomes policy has been felt in the sphere of Fair Wages policy implementation. The series of cases before the Industrial Arbitration Board in 1973–4 in which the Pay Board became actively involved is only one manifestation of the recent interaction of the two policies. The future of the new Fair Wages policy of Schedule 11 to the Employment Protection Act 1975 will depend on whether it can successfully adapt to this change in the system of industrial relations.

For notes see p. 496

To help assess the future prospects of the new Fair Wages policy, this chapter analyses one set of circumstances where the interaction between Fair Wages policy and incomes policy has raised significant questions in the past. The problem arose out of a contradiction between the growing awareness by government departments of the fact that control of contractors' wages costs was the logical corollary of incomes policy, and the desire to ensure, at a time of wage inflation, that contractors should produce the goods and survive profitably. The experience analysed indicates that government departments tend jealously to guard their interest in fulfilling their contracting requirements from the delays, difficulties and embarassments engendered by the intervention of governments' social or economic policies. The introduction of variation clauses into government contracts was one compromise solution to this problem.

Outside the important sector of government contracts, the contradiction between the Fair Wages and incomes policies was bound to have implications for the body concerned with enforcement of the Fair Wages policy. It is not insignificant that most of the lengthy questioning of Sir Roy Wilson, then President of the Industrial Court, by the Donovan Commission was concerned with the relationship of incomes policy to the Court's activities. The problem can be traced back to the Second World War when restraint was urged on workers claiming under the Fair Wages formula in Order 1305 and before. The cases show that tribunals have not been immune from pressure of government policies on incomes, whether introduced through submissions of the parties to a dispute, by intervention of government agencies in the proceedings, or even in the form of a letter from the Chancellor of the Exchequer, as in the contract cleaning cases described in chapter 19. The elusiveness of the concept of a 'Fair Wage' could be powerfully employed in the hands of a tribunal determined to carry out government policy. But such a course is strewn with hazards, some of which could be fatal to the Fair Wages policy and to the tribunal itself. The path through this minefield charted by the predecessors to the Central Arbitration Committee will be described.

Finally, the record of the Central Arbitration Committee itself will be examined. Many of the cases coming before the Committee have arisen as a direct result of the operation of incomes policy. The 'unfairness' that is alleged is a consequence of the arbitrary workings of different incomes policies over time. The path the Committee has taken during its first months may indicate its future role, and that of the Fair Wages policy, in a system of collective bargaining influenced, if not governed by, a centrally determined incomes policy.

The Problem in Government Contracts

The question faced by government departments in reconciling their contracting requirements with the government's policies on incomes control was easily appreciated: could they effectively restrain the wages paid by their contractors to the workers on the contract, and would this have adverse consequences on their ability to obtain the goods and services required?

It would seem that wages, as one of the contractor's costs, could have been subject to rigid control accounting procedures. As long ago as 1890, the Committee of Public Accounts had reported in detail on methods of checking wage rates of men engaged in ship-building in government dockyards. In 1920, the same Committee reported on a contract for shipbuilding 'in which, in addition to the contract price, £43,000 was paid to the contracting firm for bonuses to the men for good time-keeping'. It was explained that the payments secured acceleration of the work, and were regarded as matters within the discretion of the Admiralty. The Treasury stated that in their view permission was required, but that anyway the practice had since been abandoned on grounds of policy.[1]

The impact of the Fair Wages policy instituted in 1891 upon these procedures had been minimal. They were designed to ensure that wage costs were not inflated, not that workers should not be underpaid. With the advent of full employment after the Second World War, the problem dealt with by the Fair Wages policy—wage cutting and underpayment of workers—was replaced, if not actually reversed. The new problem perceived by the government was that of contractors first conceding wage increases to their workers, either willingly to attract workers in the full employment economy, or unwillingly due to pressure of powerful trade unions, and then demanding of the departments that they allow for these increases either in a *post hoc* reimbursement procedure or through the tendering process.

An illustration of the government's perception of the problem of anticipating wage increases is given in the Reports of the Public Accounts Committee of the early 1950s. In one instance, the Committee expressed surprise at learning that the Estimate for the National Health Service, England and Wales, for 1952–3 included a substantial amount for possible increases in salaries and wages. They had understood that no provision was made in Estimates for claims to increased remuneration which were merely under consideration at the time the Estimates were presented to Parliament. Indeed, the P.A.C. of 1950 had expressed satisfaction on learning that the Treasury could never accept the view that Departments should be encouraged or permitted to provide in their annual Estimates for liabilities which might not become due for payment in the year of estimate. While appreciating the need to enforce the discipline that no more could be spent in the year than was provided from the beginning, the Committee found it difficult to appreciate the value of this discipline where the sum provided included a substantial amount for undetermined claims to increased remuneration, as the Hospital Board were admittedly aware. The Committee recommended that the Treasury review this exceptional practice. In reply, the Treasury reiterated their principles dealing with over-estimating:

> Provision should properly be made in Estimates for sums in respect of salaries and wages awards which, so far as can be foreseen, will become due even though there may exist the possibility that they will not do so. On the other hand, no contingency provisions should be made in Estimates for such awards which cannot be foreseen. Supplementary or Revised Estimates should, where necessary, be presented to meet the cost of unforeseen salaries and wages awards.[2]

The controversy as it affected government contractors centred on the desirability of the insertion of variation clauses in contracts. The opposing aspects of the debate were aired, along with the initial position of the departments, in an exchange in the House of Commons on 24 March 1955.[3] The Chancellor of the Exchequer was asked if he would recommend to the appropriate departments that in the future, government contracts should be made firm contracts without escape clauses for increases in the cost of materials or labour. The reply affirmed that it was 'already the general policy for Government Departments to call for tenders at fixed prices and not to include variation of price clauses in their contracts'. There were exceptions, however, where this was not practicable, for example, in long-term contracts. The Chancellor was pressed to use his influence to spread this practice throughout industry 'to prevent wage increases, when they take place, from being immediately passed on to the consumer'. To the contrary, another speaker argued that 'at a time when wage rates and costs are constantly rising, a time of full employment, which results in long delivery dates, an escape clause which allows for the variation of a contract with variations in costs of wages and materials frequently provides the cheaper method and not the most expensive to the customer of obtaining the article'.

In 1956 the Ministry of Works announced its intention to carry out an experiment in inviting tenders on a fixed price basis, without cost variation clauses for labour and materials, for selected projects of values not exceeding £100,000. A year later the experiment was pronounced a success and, after discussions with representatives of the building and civil engineering industries, it was stated in the House of Commons on 30 April 1957:

> The Government have now decided that in future all Government Departments shall invite tenders on a fixed price basis for all works of building and civil engineering, irrespective of size, provided that they have been thoroughly planned in advance and that the estimated contract period is not more than two years. Local authorities and the nationalized industries will be invited by those of my right hon. Friends concerned to adopt a similar policy. The Government hope that these steps will be a real contribution to the stabilization of costs and prices.[4]

It appeared that most local authorities had followed the lead of the government in inviting tenders on a firm price basis, for between 1960–8 the percentage of housing schemes to which contracts with fluctuation clauses related had fallen from 12.6 to 8.6 per cent in England and Wales, and from 4.3 per cent to a negligible figure in Scotland. The policy was not received with total enthusiasm by contractors. Thus, for example, in 1968, the National Federation of Building Trade Employers submitted that if variations, particularly in the case of labour costs and taxation were allowed, contractors would find it helpful. In fact, local authorities in some cases did introduce a fluctuations clause into their standard R.I.B.A. contract which had previously been on a fixed price basis. This was a result of the introduction by the government of the Selective Employment Tax which increased contractors' costs considerably. In 1966, the Government also promised to reimburse contractors on fixed price contracts for the sudden imposition of S.E.T. on employees on construction sites and others.[5]

The tendency to exclude variation clauses was not welcomed in other spheres of government contracting. For example, in 1960 an association of film producers complained of the difficulties caused to its members contracting with the Central Office of Information by the failure to include a contingency or price variation clause in the contract: 'This is particularly unfair in view of the fact that a contractor may find his labour costs increased due to a revision of Trade Union Agreements to which all reputable contractors are a party'.[6]

Some insight into the implementation and workings of government policy for control of contractors' wages costs emerges from the Minutes of Evidence to and the Report of the Estimates Committee of 1967–8 on the government's construction programme.[7] According to the

Memorandum of Evidence submitted on behalf of the Ministry of Public Building and Works, a sub-committee chaired by the Ministry is responsible for all Government procurement in the building and civil engineering fields. The estimated expenditure of the Ministry on contracts in 1967–8 was about £200m. Direct works contracts placed are normally on the General Conditions of Contract for Government Building and Civil Engineering, known as CCC/Wks./1. A Memorandum submitted by representatives of the Royal Institute of Chartered Surveyors noted that the Ministry were responsible for the introduction of firm price tendering in 1957, and this, at that time, was a very significant contribution towards obtaining a degree of stabilization in building prices and was very widely adopted: 'It did, however, rest on the presumption that for the period stated the increases which contractors would have to bear were within reasonable limits. The recent effects of legislation, e.g. S.E.T., have put this system in jeopardy to the extent that the R.I.B.A. Form of Contract has been altered so that completely firm prices are becoming the exception and not the rule' (p. 76). The R.I.B.A. Form is negotiated by the Joint Contracts Tribunal, which consists of representatives of the Royal Institute of British Architects, the R.I.C.S., the National Federation of Building Trade Employers, of sub-contractors organizations, of the four Local Authority Associations and of the G.L.C. The Memorandum submitted to the Committee by the N.F.B.T.E. urged the Ministry to use the R.I.B.A. Form, adapted for use for government work, in place of CCC/Wks./1 (p. 87).

In the course of Oral Examination of officials of the Ministry, the Committee asked them: '*A propos* variations in a scheme, what usually causes variations that have, ultimately to be made? . . . What would you say is the general cause which leads to variations in a contract?' (Qs. 22ff.). Among the possibilities mentioned, there was nothing of changes in labour costs. It might be assumed from this that wage increases were not a significant factor. It was admitted that in a two and a half year period between 1965–7, seventeen claims over £50,000 had been settled with respect to contractors who had exceeded their tenders in fulfilling the contract. The annual total of claims of all types was about two hundred. The payments were only made when the contractor had made an overall loss on the contract, not to beef up a small profit: 'The reason given for *ex gratia* payments sometimes made to contractors who suffer unforeseen losses is justified on the ground that otherwise the contractor would insist on "rigged prices" and contingency allowances in order to safeguard himself against such an event' (Qs. 194, 203, 213). The officials later testified that the Superintending Officer on the site had plenty of power to run the contract on a day to day basis, including 'delegated powers from the Contracts Directorate for instance to order variations' (Q. 991). The procedure for dealing with variations was described as follows:

> Some of the variations are of a very minor nature and the normal drill is for our site staff to receive instructions, to confirm them to the Ministry in writing and following that, the Ministry usually issues a formal variation order which is handed to the surveyors for the purpose of valuing that operation. (Q. 762.)

The changes envisaged by the Ministry officials as giving rise to variation orders were primarily those resulting from structural alterations decided upon after the initial tender had been accepted. It is clear from other evidence, however, that changes in labour costs were by no means unknown, and could be substantial where disputes arose as to wage rates payable to the workers on the site (e.g. Qs. 767ff.). The position in road construction may be compared. It was estimated by the Ministry of Transport that price increases for contracts since 1962 were largely attributable to the higher costs of labour and materials: 'Between 1962 and 1968 while road construction prices rose by 22 per cent, labour earnings in construction increased by 43 per cent, S.E.T. added about 8 per cent to labour costs and the price of construction materials rose by 17 per cent.'[8]

To summarize: during this period it appears that on construction sites financed by the Ministry of Public Building and Works, the procedures for changes in wages costs were not stipulated in the formal terms of the contract. Variations might be issued, but if the wages cost changes resulted in the tender price being exceeded, it was a matter for the discretion of the Ministry, subject to Treasury approval, to allow an *ex gratia* payment.

A different approach is exemplified in the Minutes of Evidence to and Report of the Estimates Committee of 1969–70 on hospital building in the U.K., where the R.I.B.A. Form was used. Under the R.I.B.A. Form, the contract sum might be adjusted either (a) in respect of fluctuations, increases or decreases, in the cost of labour and materials and of new or changed Government imposts (e.g. S.E.T.) occurring during the currency of the contract; or (b) only in respect of new or changed Government imposts occurring during the currency of the contract. Type (a) was most frequently used, as contracts expected to take more than two years were common.[9] When giving Oral Evidence, officials of the Department of Health and Social Security testified on 20 January 1970 that estimates for a proposed scheme submitted to the Treasury were based on prices prevailing at the time of submission. Even with schemes of a probable length of three of four years duration, there was no attempt to build into the original estimate any figure or percentage for prospective increases in price of one kind or another. The officials were asked whether 'in the light of events since the war when we have had more or less steady inflation each year, would it not be more realistic in the case of a scheme that is going to last for four or five years to build into the original estimate some figure which seeks to take account of that inflation'. Their reply was that at most they would account for any increases in the current estimates which are produced annually throughout the term of the project (Report, H.C. 59(iii), Qs. 265–7).

It seems, therefore, that while provision for increases is made in the actual contract, the estimates from which those increases are to be paid are not calculated in advance to take account of them. This was confirmed in a Supplementary Memorandum submitted to the Committee by the D.H.S.S., dated 16 February 1970. It explained that the discrepancy between the original and current estimates of costs may occur because the original estimate may have been prepared up to eighteen months before the building scheme started and, in some instances, a substantially longer period beforehand. While the hospital authorities are asked to include in their estimates the assessed effect to the end of the contract of *known* fluctuations (i.e. amounts payable under the contract for increases in wages and costs of materials): 'The Department has become aware that some Hospital Boards have not observed this request'. The Memorandum contains details of a number of hospital building projects which had overrun their estimates, including the amounts attributable to increases in wage bills and materials costs. Many of these were very substantial in terms of the amount by which the eventual cost exceeded the original estimate (Report, H.C. 59(vii), pp. 163–74).

In the light of this apparent deficiency, the Department's officials were asked if they did not think their cost limits were on the low side, and perhaps their original estimates ought to be raised. The reply was as follows: 'The curious thing . . . is that our general experience is that there are not at the moment, and there have not been, a very large number of excessively high tenders . . . in the case of 36 out of 44 schemes . . . . tenders have been accepted within the design cost'. The reason why contractors felt able to tender at prices which experience indicated were very likely to be grossly exceeded before completion is apparent. It was stated by the officials themselves in an answer seeking to explain the excess costs: 'The reason why price rises occur frequently in the explanations you have been given is that all these are schemes which are in progress, and in the case of schemes which are in progress price rises, due to fluctuations in the cost of labour and materials, are allowed over and above the contract' (Qs. 913, 915). The introduction of a variation clause in his contract ensures that cost increases will be remimbursed to him.

The procedure under the R.I.B.A. contract for the control and authorization of contract variations was described as follows: the formal position under the contract is that the nominated architect issues the variations. However, the responsibility is that of the regional hospital board if the variation is a minor one and can be made within the contract sum, that is, from the contingency sum (usually one to two per cent) within the contract. If it increases the contract sum, there is a formal procedure whereby they must come to the Department. In addition to unexpected changes, the contractor is provided with a list of items where provisional figures only are included in the bill of quantities (price per unit of work). It is up to the quantity surveyor as the cost planner to ensure that whenever a provisional figure is firmed up he keeps a running total to see that this can be met within the cost. Changes in wages were not regarded as a major source of cost overruns: 'In so far as alterations are required in relation to fluctuations in wages and so on, it is, I assume, the quantity surveyor's responsibility to approve these. They would not normally come to (the Department) at that level. They would be dealt with at regional level.' Only larger variations which could not be contained within the contract sum would have to be approved (Qs. 219, 350–2, 696–8).

The above account, derived from the Committee Reports, leaves the impression that the contracting departments concerned neither perceived nor encountered a problem with respect to wage fluctuations during the term of a contract. Neither under the CCC/Wks./1 nor the R.I.B.A. Form of contract, whether for more than two years duration or less was anybody but the on-site official concerned with authorizing wage increases. Certainly there was no mention anywhere of a policy for wages, whether this be Fair Wages or incomes policy. The only mention of the former was found in the proposal by the National Federation of Building Trade Employers urging the adoption by the Ministry of Public Building and Works of the R.I.B.A. Form of contract. This required, they added, the addition of certain clauses, for example, the Fair Wages Clause. In the light of the above account, this was scarcely perceived as being of great significance—its addition to the ordinary commercial R.I.B.A. Form was not expected to have much effect on policies or procedures for the regulation of wages.[10]

The lack of concern expressed in the above Reports on the part of the Ministries concerned is in sharp contrast to a Report of 1965–6 by the Comptroller and Auditor General on the pricing of a contract for Buccaneer aircraft by the Ministry of Aviation.[11] The Report described the phenomenon of wage drift and went into details as to its extent and scale. Wage drift, it declared, affected all purchasers whether in the public or private sector. It had caused particular concern to the Ministry of Aviation, whose votes included each year contract expenditures amounting to over £500m. of which some 95 per cent arises from non-competitive contracts, in respect of which prices are fixed either by negotiation or by reference to actual costs. The standard conditions which are used in fixed-price government contracts of long duration provided for the reimbursement of extra costs resulting from national awards negotiated in industry: *they do not cover wages drift*. In estimating labour costs in such contracts the Ministry had sought to persuade contractors that increased earnings should be compensated by increased productivity. In recent years, however, contractors had maintained that they had to concede wages drift without any commensurate increase in productivity. They had 'felt unable to accept fixed prices for future work unless these assumed continuation of wages drift' (para. 83). Thus, for example, the fixed prices, valued at a total of approximately £110m., which were agreed early in 1966 for the Buccaneer Mk. 2 and the Maritime Comet aircraft for delivery in later years included contingencies in the labour cost estimates for future wages drift. For contracts without even varia-tion clauses allowing for national increases, but instead priced simply on actual costs, Departments had had to accept the labour costs actually incurred, including the element of wages drift 'so long as the rates were in line with those paid locally and the costs were also fair and reasonable and appropriate to the work required under the contract' (para. 84).

The Ministry of Aviation had become concerned at the particularly rapid rise in hourly earnings in the latter half of 1965 and, during 1966, had reviewed the problem of wages drift:

On the one hand they recognized a committment to pay prices which were fair and reasonable when judged against the labour costs which firms had to incur to do the work under the contract and, on the other, they were concerned at the possible conflict between allowing an element for wages drift in future prices and the Government's prices and incomes policy. They also had regard to the requirement that all Government contractors should observe the Fair Wages Resolution of the House of Commons and to the difficulties which might ensue if they insisted that differential and lower rates should be paid to workers employed on Government contracts. (para. 85)

The Ministry was unable to resolve the conflicting elements in the policies towards incomes control and that requiring Fair Wages. They simply decided to continue to price contracts on the best terms they could get. This involved making concessions to the effect of wages drift, while continuing to stress the importance of increasing productivity wherever possible. As regards future national wages awards, they issued instructions not to allow contingencies in prices in respect of such awards, but, where necessary, to cover these by price variation clauses provided in standard conditions of the contract.

In sum: running through this account of the Departments' regulation of the wages element in their contract costs is a thread clearly recognizable from the Fair Wages policy experience. The Departments' primary concern has been to ensure that the contractors were able to fulfil their contracts. While not overly sympathetic to contractors who found themselves in difficulties as a result of cost overruns, these were to be sustained so as to enable them to carry out the objective of fulfilling the Departments' requirements. Where the overruns were the result of the phenomenon of wages drift, notice was, on the rare occasion, taken of conflicting government policies—on incomes control and Fair Wages. But these were clearly secondary to the objective of completion of the contract.[12]

Incomes Policy in Fair Wages Policy Cases—Up to 1976

Recognition of the interaction between incomes policy and Fair Wages policy was evident in the reports of a number of cases coming before the predecessors of the Central Arbitration Committee. Government employees and workers paid from public funds indirectly through government contracts are particularly vulnerable to austerity measures based on policies of wage restraint. Most of the major efforts by government to impose such restraints on incomes had repercussions on the content, type and number of cases which came before the Industrial Court. Thus, Award 1754 of 12 April 1940 (*National Union of Operative Heating and Domestic Engineers—General Metal Workers and Association of Employers*), was a wage claim that went to arbitration before the Industrial Court in the first year of the Second World War. The Employer, whose work was almost entirely financed either directly or indirectly by government funds, argued that 'it is essential as regards wages costs, and similarly as regards in materials, to keep, as the Employers have been asked to do, any claims for increases on these accounts down to a minimum' (para. 7).

The incomes policy effectively implemented during the last years of the Labour Government of 1945 by the General Council of the T.U.C. had implications for Fair Wages policy. The policy was elaborated in a White Paper on Personal Incomes issued on 4 February 1948, and on the 26 February the Financial Secretary to the Treasury was asked what instructions had been given to the official side of Whitley Councils as to the application of the principles laid down in the White Paper in negotiations over claims for wage increases by government employees. His reply was: 'Claims for wage increases by Government employees will, of course, be dealt with in accordance with the principles laid down in the White Paper'.[13] The governing principle had been the Fair Wages Resolution, and the challenge was taken up some two weeks later by the trade unions in a claim by 2,550 watchmen employed by the government for a wage increase. In Award 2145 of 15 March 1948, the government's view was put by the Official Side of the Miscellaneous Trades Joint Council for Government Industrial Establishments: 'In conclusion it was submitted that the White Paper on Personal Incomes issued on 4 February, 1948, makes it clear, that apart from reasons not relevant to this claim, wages should not be increased except in consideration of an increase in production' (para. 4). Despite this, the Industrial Court granted the increase claimed. In a number of other cases before the Court during 1948, there was sharp contention over whether the Government's White Paper applied so as to deny the validity of a claim, but the Court appears to have taken little notice of the pay restraint policy in its awards.[14]

The Conservative Pay Pause of the late 1950s and early 1960s was also invoked to dispute a claim under section 8 of the 1959 Act. In Awards 2950 and 2951 of 12 February 1963 (*South Western Fire Area Joint Board and Chief Fire Officers' Association and National Association of Fire Officers*) an employer refused to apply agreements reached by the relevant National Joint Council because, *inter alia*, 'the proposed increase of salary was excessive having regard to the Government's policy which sought to relate increases in personal incomes to increases in national productivity'. In Award 2950 the employer went on to argue that 'the claim represented an increase of 14.3 per cent on the current scale, which the Board considered was excessive for an officer earning £2,360 a year at a time when the Government had specifically stated that it was necessary that the increase of wages and salaries, as of other incomes, should be kept within $2\frac{1}{2}$ per cent' (para 15.). Nevertheless, the Industrial Court ignored the incomes policy and allowed the claim. That the effects of the policy were still felt is indicated by a remark by Sir Roy Wilson, President of the Industrial

Court, in giving evidence on 26 July 1966 to the Donovan Commission. He stated that during the 1961 pay pause there was a period 'when all terms of reference coming to the Industrial Court had to include a form of words saying that the award if made in favour of the union would not be operated before 1st April 1962. That was an exercise of the Minister's residual power' (*Minutes of Evidence* No. 45, Q. 7239).

The Minister's residual power which allowed for the delay in implementation of a successful claim was eroded during the experience of the Labour Government's pay freeze of July 1966. The details are given in Award 3135 of 16 March 1967 (*S.L.A.D.E. and Littlewoods Pools, Ltd.*). The Union had reached a settlement with the employers which was confirmed by them in a letter dated 13 July 1966. But owing to the incidence of annual holidays it was not ratified by the Union until the 9 August 1966. Meanwhile, on the 20 July, the Government had imposed a standstill on prices and incomes. On 23 August the employers wrote to the Minister of Labour for advice as to the implementation of their Agreement with the Union. In their reply dated 30 August, the Ministry indicated that, in accordance with the White Paper on Prices and Incomes Standstill (Cmnd. 3073), increases under such commitments entered into on or before 20 July, but not implemented by that date, should be deferred for six months. The employers thereupon deferred implementation and notified the Union accordingly. In the Union's submission, they 'had never thought that the Government intended the standstill to apply to workers who were being paid less than a nationally accepted minimum, and they therefore sought the advice of the T.U.C. on this point'. In the light of that advice they wrote on the 6 December to the Ministry of Labour. The Ministry's reply of 22 December advised that cases arising under section 8 of the 1959 Act could be referred to the Industrial Court, and that if the Court made an award under that Act, it would not be subject to deferment during the standstill and the ensuing period of severe restraint. The Union accordingly made a claim under section 8 of the Act, and was upheld for the most part by the Court. Their example was quickly followed by a number of other Unions. At times the Union and Company concerned both agreed on the submission in order to circumvent the deferment in implementation called for by the standstill. Thus, in Award 3137 3 April 1967: 'It was further stated that the Company would not object if the Court were to require them to observe the provisions of the 1965 Agreement with effect from the 18 November 1966, which the Parties agreed was the date on which the Company had first been informed of the claim by the Association' (para. 5). The claim was successful.[15]

The loophole devised *ad hoc* by the Ministry of Labour in 1966 was formalized in the similar circumstances of the Conservative pay freeze of 1972. The Counter-Inflation (Price and Pay Code) Orders of 1973 expressly allowed for increases under statutory and other instruments of Fair Wages policy. The Government specifically suggested, through the Pay Board, that recourse be had to the Industrial Arbitration Board for an award allowing implementation of pay increases. Thus, Awards 3281, 3282, 3283 and 3287 of late 1973 and early 1974 were all cases where companies and unions co-operated to circumvent the pay freeze. The Orders of 1973 and these Awards of the Industrial Arbitration Board demonstrate conclusively that the contradiction between incomes policy and Fair Wages policy was initially resolved in favour of the latter. Subsequent events, however, might *suggest* that the Fair Wages policy is not considered as the paramount policy in the eyes of the *Government*. For in Award 3290 of 24 April 1974, the Pay Board challenged the results of what it had initially recommended. That Award, *Crittall-Hope and Pay Board*, and the developments leading up to it, have been described in detail in chapter 15. It is vital to appreciate that the Pay Board's challenge did not explicitly focus on the fundamental issue of incomes policy versus Fair Wages policy. The Pay Board did not confront the Fair Wages policy claim by asserting the paramountcy of incomes policy. To do this would be to fly in the face of the Orders of 1973. Instead, the Pay Board sought by a legalistic interpretation to render the Fair Wages policy useless: an impotent minimum wage standard. The Industrial Arbitration Board rejected this interpretation in *Crittall-Hope* and subsequent cases. But the only reference to the fundamental conflict of policy at stake is to be found in one of the subsequent cases. In Award 3291 of 25 April 1974 (*F. Bamford & Co. Ltd. and The Pay Board*), the company seeking to implement a wage increase adverted to it indirectly:

> In conclusion the Company stated that while the cost to them of implementing the Resolution would be about £250 weekly, the whole of the their order book comprised contracts negotiated on a fixed price basis and compliance with the Resolution in their case would not militate against the stabilization of prices which was the chief aim of the current Counter-Inflation legislation. (para. 14)

The Board itself did not advert to the fundamental questions of policy behind the legalistic argument.

Thus, the position of the Industrial Court and the Industrial Arbitration Board as regards the relationship of Fair Wages policy to incomes policy was extremely ambiguous. It is impossible, particularly in light of their refusal to give reasons for their Awards, to ascertain what their policy was in relating the two. For example, in Award 3160 of 29 January 1968 (*Black Clawson International Ltd. and C.A.W.U.*) under the 1959 Act, the Company was accused of not observing the pattern of increases granted by a national agreement of 1967. The Company submitted that 'it was clear that the settlement had been reached against the background of the Government's incomes policy. It has been fundamental to that policy that any increases granted during the period of the "freeze" should be offset against any increases awarded thereafter' (para. 32). Accordingly, they argued, certain increases were not due as the Union claimed. The Industrial Court held, inscrutably enough, that the Company was not complying with the Agreement, but, except for five workers, the terms observed by them were not less favourable. Again, in Awards 3242–3 of 24 and 25 June 1971, claims involving contract cleaners, the Company argued against using comparisons with Civil Service rates, citing paragraph 75 of the N.B.P.I. Report on the contract cleaning trade to the effect that 'it would be inflationary for the Government to bring pressure to bear on outside employers to bring their rates up to the Government rate, or to use Civil Service pay policy to further social and political objectives'. The Union still won both cases. When a similar argument was put forward in a later Award 3288 of 19 March 1974 (*Association of Professional, Executive, Clerical and Computer Staff and G.E.C. Turbine Generators Ltd.*), the Union countered that 'the question was whether the Company was complying with the terms of the Resolution and not whether any award of the Board might be inflationary' (para. 17). But although the Union complained that the rates of pay received by the workers 'did not provide for a decent standard of living . . . the take-home pay was often less than £20' (para. 4), the Industrial Arbitration Board dismissed the complaint. The result is that whether or not submissions putting forward government policy, or pointing to the potentially inflationary consequences of a successful claim do in fact influence awards remains a mystery.

There is some other evidence relating to the influence of incomes policies on the tribunals concerned with applying Fair Wages policy. In his book on *The Role of the Arbitrator in Industrial Wage Disputes*, C. W. Guillebaud, a member of the Industrial Disputes Tribunal which administered Order 1376 during the 1950s, states categorically that:

> on no occasion to my knowledge did Government attempt to influence the decisions of the Tribunal in cases that came before it. In the event of the issue of a White Paper setting out the views of Government on wages policy, and urging the need for wage

restraint, copies of this were sent to the Tribunal as well as to other bodies concerned with the determination of wages and conditions of employment, such as Wages Councils, the Industrial Court, etc. But it was left completely within the discretion of the body concerned to decide for itself the relevance of any such official pronouncement to the circumstances of a particular claim.

He quotes the chairman of the I.D.T. as saying, after having received an exceptionally strongly worded White Paper: 'if the Government wishes us to be bound by its official policy, it must legislate; short of that we use our own discretion'. For his own part, Guillebaud concludes that the I.D.T. did not operate as a direct instrument of Government wages policy, but that it was fully aware of its public responsibilities. W. E. J. McCarthy's study of the work of the I.D.T for the Donovan Commission cites findings that there was little evidence that I.D.T. awards could be correlated with variations in Government policy.[16]

Sir Roy Wilson, the President of the Industrial Court and subsequently of its successor, the Industrial Arbitration Board, testified as to the functions of these bodies before the Donovan Commission on 26 July 1966. In his evidence to the Commission, both written and oral, he discoursed at length on the problems concerned in arbitration which is subject to considerations of national interest, which he distinguished carefully from the incomes policy of the Government (*Minutes of Evidence* No. 45, Written Evidence, para. 12). His reason for carefully avoiding any contamination in arbitral standards from government policy was clear and unambiguous: 'any attempt to ensure that arbitrators should apply Government policy would have a probably fatal effect on the voluntary arbitration system' (para. 14). He was remarkably straightforward as to the relationship between incomes policy and Fair Wages policy, as the following exchange records:

> *Chairman:* Is the incomes policy something which you would take into account in that (deciding Fair Wages policy complaints)?
> *Lord Tangley:* On this type of jurisdiction I do not believe the Court would be entitled to go into the incomes policy at all?
> *Sir Roy Wilson:* Nor do I—if it is simply a question of our deciding are the terms and conditions observed by an employer unfavourable compared with those which constitute the standard to be complied with. (Oral Evidence, Q. 7257.)

But awkward questions about the relationship of the general arbitration system to the national interest, and particularly to incomes policy, produced a far more ambiguous line. Just one quotation should suffice:

> The incomes policy is one of the matters that we take into account and have in our minds when an arbitration comes before us at all, but we do not lay down any principle that we should conform to it, unless something comes within the exceptions. We simply consider the incomes policy as one of the factors relevant to any inquiry that we have to decide upon, and make our conclusions accordingly. (Q. 7143.)

As the recent pattern of Fair Wages policy cases has shown, it is unlikely that the issue of the relationship between incomes policy and Fair Wages policy can be avoided for much longer. The burden of resolving the problem has now descended upon the Central Arbitration Committee. It remains to describe how the Committee has dealt with it in the first months of its existence.

The Central Arbitration Committee, Incomes Policy and the Future of Fair Wages Policy

The change in the system of industrial relations entailed in the new influence of incomes policy on wage determination will significantly determine the success of the new Fair Wages policy of Schedule 11 to the Employment Protection Act 1975. Conversely, however, this new system of wage determination—collective bargaining subject to a centrally determined incomes policy—may be affected by the Fair Wages policy which requires all employers to adhere to the standards of Schedule 11: 'recognized terms and conditions' and the 'general level'. This interaction between Fair Wages policy and incomes policy was the subject of a long paragraph in the Conclusions to the *First Annual Report, 1976*, of the Central Arbitration Committee:

> 5.2 It is obvious that the volume of the work of the Committee is determined to a considerable extent by the current pay policy. A substantial proportion of the work undertaken during 1976 may have come to the Committee directly because of the constraints of pay policy. But the Committee is in no sense an 'appeals committee' against pay policy rulings. Awards made under the Committee's statutory powers—for example Fair Wages, Section 8, Terms and Conditions of Employment Act 1959 and Equal Pay issues, are exempt from the current pay policy limits. Decisions on these matters are governed by well-established considerations.

The parallel pay policy limitations are not the Committee's concern. Where its jurisdiction does not fall within these special provisions, pay policy considerations, as with all other forms of industrial arbitration, are inevitably an important element in shaping the issues which come before it. The Committee is constantly aware of the impact of pay policy on the industrial relations scene. That follows from its determination to reach informed and realistic decisions. It is not, however, nor does it seek to be, a body charged with interpretation of such policy. Although the implementation of Schedule 11 of the Employment Protection Act 1975 at the beginning of 1977 falls outside the period of this report, it seems certain that problems arising from the incidence of pay policy and the relation of statutory provisions to pay policy will be intensified. The Committee will continue to fulfil its functions bearing in mind its objective of securing, wherever it can, that its decisions are conducive to the maintenance and improvement of standards of industrial relations.

The Committee here states that in its statutory jurisdictions—including Fair Wages policy—its awards 'are exempt from the current pay policy limits'. Pay policy is 'not the Committee's concern'. Only in its other, non-statutory jurisdiction does the Committee admit to an awareness of the importance of pay policy considerations. So what of Schedule 11? Seemingly, it falls within the definition of a statutory jurisdiction where pay policy is not a concern. Nonetheless, the Committee does anticipate as a consequence of its implementation, 'that problems arising from the incidence of pay policy and the relation of statutory provisions to pay policy will be intensified'.

The questions confronting the Committee will be whether employers who fail to comply with one or the other of the new Fair Wages standards of Schedule 11 can invoke the incomes policy as a justification. If an employer is not observing, either at all or in some respect, the 'recognized terms' or the 'general level', can it be argued that to raise his standards to that level would breach the incomes policy? What will be the impact of current pay policy on the awards of the Committee?

The answers to these questions as regards the pre-Schedule 11 Fair Wages jurisdictions were presented forthrightly in the Committee's *First Annual Report, 1976,* quoted above. But the development of this clear-cut position was a gradual matter which stretched over a large number of early awards. An examination of how its pre-Schedule 11 position on Fair Wages policy and incomes policy developed may provide guidance on the answers the Committee will give to the questions posed above as regards Schedule 11.

Looking first at the Fair Wages Resolution of 1946, most of the early cases arising out of complaints of breach of the Resolution were a consequence of disputes or anomalies resulting from incomes policy. For example, in Award 36 of 5 October 1976 (*Ferranti Ltd.*), the Company explained that an anomaly had been created inadvertently, mainly as a result of a timing difference between their annual review dates of 1 April 1975 for staff and 1 July 1975 for manual workers. As a consequence, an overlap resulted between the pay of manual workers and of staff in lower grades, including those the subject of the complaint. Normally, the Company would have removed the anomaly making adjustments to staff salaries, but it was prevented from doing this under incomes policy restrictions. The Company agreed after joint discussions with the Union (T.A.S.S.) and the Department of Employment to proceed with a test case under the provisions of the Fair Wages Resolution. Again, in Award 14 of 25 June 1976 (*Wimet Ltd. and A.S.T.M.S.*), negotiations had broken down in later 1975 after the Company's offer of £6 per week in accordance with the maximum permitted by the White Paper, *Attack on Inflation* (Cmnd. 6151), was rejected. The Union referred the matter to the Secretary of State for Employment under the Fair Wages Resolution. On 15 May 1976, after the date for a hearing by the Committee had been arranged, another negotiating meeting was held at which a settlement was reached. This agreement was submitted to the Department of Employment for their approval, but the Department ruled that despite the agreement the question had not otherwise been disposed of and withheld approval of the agreement pending the Committee's decision.

The Department of Employment was instrumental in other cases which came before the Committee. In Award 2 of 16 March 1976 (*Bolton Gate Co. Ltd. and A.U.E.W.*), both the Company and the Union jointly asked the Department of Employment for an interpretation of how the Government's pay policy affected the Union's claim, after the Company had rejected it. The Department advised that the Company should not make an increase as claimed in October 1975 as this would breach the twelve-month rule. In Award 21 of 11 August 1976 (*Radio Trent Ltd. and N.U.J.*), brought under the Fair Wages Resolution implied by the Independent Broadcasting Authority Act 1973 (section 16), the Department of Employment were asked to declare whether the grading of staff and increases in pay and annual leave entitlement claimed were permissible under the existing pay policy. The parties were told that the Department were unable to approve such increases and the Union, therefore, brought the claim under section 16 of the Act.

In other cases, the companies concerned simply rejected the unions' claims on the grounds of pay policy restrictions; and because they were government contractors, the unions were able to summon them before the Committee. For example, in Award 6 of 6 April 1976 (*Dowty Boulton Paul Ltd. and A.S.T.M.S.*), the Company agreed that it would normally have conceded a rate of £64 per week, but as the Government's White Paper *Attack on Inflation* was published before the negotiations eventually took place on 8 October 1975, it offered only a £6 per week increase, which was rejected. In Award 23 of 9 August 1976 (*Effingham Steel Works Ltd. and A.S.T.M.S.*), the Company's board rejected the claim on the basis that it was a contravention of the pay policy in breaching the twelve-month rule and in exceeding the £6 limit. And in reply to the union's claim in Award 30 of 17 September 1976 (*Dobson Hydraulics Ltd. and A.U.E.W. (T.A.S.S.)*), the Company explained that it was prevented from exceeding the £6 maximum laid down in the Government's guidelines on incomes policy.

A consequence of these rejections of the Unions' claims was the reference of a complaint to the Committee—usually on the grounds of failure to observe the 'general level' stipulated by clause 1(b) of the Resolution. When it is realized that the scope of the Fair Wages policy is expanded by Schedule 11 from government contractors to employers generally, the enormous potential of the new policy stipulating observance of the 'general level' is all too clear. Unions whose members are aggrieved by the workings of incomes policy have a means of redress, within the limits of Schedule 11.

The degree to which the Fair Wages policy offers a means of redressing the anomalies created by the workings of incomes policies will depend largely on the Committee's view of the relationship between the two policies. It was not easy at first to establish a consistent attitude on the part of the Committee to this question in its early Awards. The first case in which this question came under consideration was Award 2 of 16 March 1976 (*Bolton Gate Co. Ltd. and A.U.E.W.*). The Joint Shop Stewards Committee had negotiated an increase with the Company in March 1975, with a promised further review in October 1975. Due to dissatisfaction among the membership, however, in July the J.S.S.C. asked the Company to bring forward the review date and requested an increase of £10 per week to bring the pay of the Company's employees into line with that of other workers in the Bolton area. Both requests were refused by the Company, with the backing of the Department of Employment ruling that to make an increase even in October 1975 would breach the twelve-month rule. The Award of the Committee began by considering the general collective bargaining circumstances of the parties. Having done so, it went on to confront the issue directly: 'It is necessary to consider the impact of the current Government's Pay Policy upon our decision' (para. 23). This was stated in the following paragraph:

> It is our understanding that once the year has elapsed from the last major settlement (which was operative from 4 April 1975) the Bolton Gate Company intends to negotiate with the appropriate trade unions for the new rate to be paid within the pay policy. We cannot anticipate this negotiation but would emphasize that our award *together* with any increase that may be negotiated in April should not altogether exceed the current £6 limit. (para. 24) (My italics.)

The Award of the Committee gave the workers concerned an extra £4.75 per week from October 1975. So the Award led to a clear breach of the pay policy, but it contained a warning about the £6 limit. This was to operate in the context of the parties' bargaining relationship—but it is not clear what force can be attached to the Committee's warning.

After this somewhat promising beginning, however, there were a number of Awards where the Committee itself did not advert to the pay policy at all. In Awards 6 of 6 April 1976, 23 of 9 August 1976 and 30 of 17 September 1976, the Committee upheld the complaints and granted increases despite the employer's invoking of the rules of government pay policy. In Award 21 of 11 August 1976, the Committee allowed that:

> pay policy has reduced to a very great extent the flexibility available to allow rationalization. It became clear to us at the hearing that the exceptionally strict interpretation of the rules of pay policy given in advice to the Contractor had served to make them appear to the trade union to be exceptionally difficult employers. Plainly this bad relationship will take time to improve, but we hope that our determination of the issues put to us will serve as a basis upon which good relations will be built. (para. 26)

In light of these considerations it upheld the complaint and awarded increases.

The Committee next attempted really to grapple with the problem of relating Fair Wages policy to incomes policy in Award 14 of 25 June 1976 (*Wimet Ltd. and A.S.T.M.S.*). The parties, after an initial impasse over the effect of pay policy, had reached agreement. The Department of Employment, however, would not approve the agreement and insisted on the case being heard by the Committee. The parties asked the Committee to endorse the agreement. The Committee addressed the problem at length:

> it is necessary to look at the impact of incomes policy upon the concept of a fair wage. Unless this is taken into account the existence of an agreement that the wages paid are unfair is hard to understand and the failure to implement the agreement has an almost Alice-in-Wonderland look about it. The explanation is simple. The employer finds himself challenged but constrained to act because of the effect of incomes policy. Were he to pay the agreed wage it could be that under current incomes policy he would suffer unacceptable disadvantages. If, however, the wage is determined by this Committee these disadvantages are avoided and payment of the sums set out fall within the rules of the pay policy. It is for these reasons that a case of this sort looks collusive.
> 28. None of these matters directly affects the task of this Committee other than to make it of paramount importance to ensure that the evidence truly substantiates the allegation of breach of the fair wages concept and that there is not a mere collusive attempt to avoid some of the unwelcome consequences of pay policy. The primary task of the Committee is then, again expressed in general terms, to satisfy itself that the wage rates to which its attention is drawn present a clear, unmistakable situation of unfairness. (paras. 27–8)

The Committee's conclusion was stated as follows:

> We do not think that we can ignore the existence of pay policy. ... It is not binding upon us but we feel it would be a different type of unfairness if wages determined by reference to us avoided disadvantages attached to comparable settlements. The effect of our view on this has determined the shape of our award. (para. 32)

The Award nonetheless upheld the complaint that the Company were in breach of clause 1(b)—not observing the general level—and granted increases which clearly exceeded the limits of pay policy as normally applied.

At this point, the Committee, in three cases under the Resolution, had upheld the complaints without adverting to the employer's assertion that pay policy precluded any increase being awarded (Awards 6, 23 and 30). In a fourth case, the Committee had commented on the adverse effects on industrial relations between the parties caused by the policy, but did not seem to regard it as affecting the decision (Award 21). In two other cases, however, the Committee specifically stated that it was necessary to look at the impact of the pay policy (Awards 2 and 14). The Committee nonetheless had granted increases outside the normal pay policy limits. Incomes policy did not, therefore, seem to have the effect of overruling Fair Wages policy, but it was not made clear what effect it did have.

It was only in Award 36 of 5 October 1976 that the Committee confronted the problem directly. The complaint was brought by Ferranti Ltd., with the Union, A.U.E.W. (T.A.S.S.) present only as observers. It arose out of anomalies that had grown up between staff and manual workers which could not be remedied due to pay policy restrictions. In reply to a question from the Chairman of the Committee the full time officials of T.A.S.S. explained at the hearing that their Union did not make a claim against Ferranti Ltd. under the Resolution because they considered that the Company had a distinct advantage over them in the collecting of comprehensive figures relating to the pay of workers in the area where trade union organization was not strong. Also, T.A.S.S. wished to indicate that there was no real dispute between them and Ferranti. The Committee began its Award by restating the aim of the Resolution—to ensure that contractors pay fair wages. It continued:

> The Committee is empowered to make an Award if it finds that the Government contractor is in breach of the Resolution. The Government has made it clear that such Awards are exempted from the limitations imposed by their incomes policy. *There is, therefore, a contradiction of objectives. On the one hand there is an incomes policy designed to control wage inflation by means of a universal pay limit and on the other hand there is a long standing Resolution aimed at ensuring that fair wages are paid to employees of Government contractors.* (para. 15) (My italics.)

Without saying more about the problem, the Committee went on to find and decide that the Company were in breach of clause 1(b) and granted the increases requested.

The Committee here faced the unavoidable contradiction between the two policies. It did not explain its proposed resolution of this conflict. But it emerged clearly from the Awards themselves—and has now been confirmed in the *First Annual Report, 1976*—that the pay policy itself is subject to considerations of 'fairness'. If the employer is not observing Fair Wages policy standards, the Committee will not allow the pay policy to hinder them from awarding increases up to those standards.

A similar position in resolving the problem emerged from the Awards of the Committee under section 8 of the 1959 Act. In two early cases, Awards 4 and 5 of 14 March 1976 (*Kyle and Carrick District Council and N.A.L.G.O.*), the Council had invoked in its defence to a claim a 'duty both to its ratepayers and to central government in accordance with the White Paper "Attack on Inflation" to contain expenditure and contribute towards curbing inflation' (para. 29). The Committee did not advert to this argument in upholding the claim.

In Award 9 of 24 May 1976 (*National Bank of Pakistan and N.U.B.E.*), the employer had been prepared to increase salaries substantially, but after the publication of the Government's White Paper had informed the Union on 30 July 1975 that it was limited to maximum pay increases of £6 per week. Hence the claim. The Committee this time dealt with the problem directly:

29. It was obvious to us that this reference had come before us because of the impact of pay policy upon the 1975 wages negotiation. Indeed, by way of background information for us, both parties told us that this was so. The imposition of the principles set out in the White Paper 'The Attack on Inflation' apparently means that the 1975 settlement must be restricted to £6 rather than to a sum in excess of 20%. The parties made it clear that if pay policy allowed there would be a settlement at the higher figure. It is not our function in a reference of this type to give a ruling on the impact of current incomes policy. We were told by the parties that the advice of the Department of Employment has been sought and there has also been the advantage of conciliation. It is safe to assume that the parties understanding of the impact of pay policy is ·correct. *No doubt this reference is an attempt to remedy what is seen, certainly by the Union, as an injustice by other means.*

30. *We do not feel that this background prevents, in any sense, a claim under Section 8. Any group of workers such as those concerned in this claim is entitled to the protection of that Section provided that they establish proper grounds. The exact position of the current incomes policy does not affect this issue and in coming to our decision we have paid no attention to the pressures that have caused them to be brought.* (paras. 29–30) (My italics.)

The claim was eventually dismissed on grounds that the Agreement invoked by the Union as the relevant standard was not applicable to the workers concerned. But the position taken by the Committee on the problem of relating Fair Wages policy to incomes policy was clear. It was reiterated in Award 18 of 4 August 1976 (*Cambion Electronic Products Ltd. and A.U.E.W.*). The Committee again acknowledged that the dispute had arisen due to the difficulties of pay policy, but went on to declare: '*An award under section 8 is meant to correct an injustice and so is directly unaffected by pay policy*' (para. 27) (My italics). This time the claim succeeded.

Finally, in Award 27 of 31 August 1976 (*STD Services Ltd. and A.S.T.M.S.*), the Committee again observed that it was only the contraints of Cmnd. 6151 which prevented the Company from increasing salaries in accordance with the National Agreement. It went on to state its position in terms very similar to those of Award 36 on the Fair Wages Resolution (quoted above):

> The Terms and Conditions of Employment Act 1959 lays down a clear and specific duty to make an Award if it finds the claim well founded. We recognize, that such Awards exemplify the *contradiction between the objectives of a blanket incomes policy designed to control wage inflation without favour and long standing legislation designed to secure observance of recognized terms and conditions of employment.* (para. 23) (My italics.)

Its very next words were: 'The claim is well founded'.

It appears, then, that the Central Arbitration Committee does acknowledge the contradiction between Fair Wages policy and incomes policy. But the questions posed above about the future of Schedule 11 in light of this contradiction remain to be answered. It is submitted that an historical perspective might aid the Committee in finding a way out of the impasse and, at the same time, to establish for itself a role in the evolving system of industrial relations.

Previous Fair Wages policies were designed to ameliorate the defects of the then existing systems of wage determination. They dealt with employers who failed to observe, in 1891, 'current' rates; in 1909, rates recognized on a district basis by employers and trade societies or those prevailing amongst good employers; and in 1946, rates settled by organizations of employers and trade unions or the general level observed by similar employers. The inadequacies of the autonomous working of the system of industrial relations were to be remedied by this means, albeit only in limited spheres, e.g., government contracts. That was the theory. The practice was very different. A changing system of industrial relations, and particularly developments in collective bargaining paralysed the outmoded Fair Wages formula. Employer opposition, bureaucratic indifference and trade union weakness all contributed to make the Fair Wages policy an ineffective instrument.

The new Fair Wages policy of Schedule 11 has adopted the standards of the old: 'recognized terms and conditions' and the 'general level'. But the system of collective bargaining in which the old standards were rendered useless is undergoing major changes. The system of wage determination is becoming ever more subject to policies laid down centrally by Government—in public declarations, White Papers, legislation or social compacts with the unions. As in the past, the system will inevitably have its deficiencies and anomalies. The main role in wage determination will continue to be played by the autonomous parties, but there will be an increasing degree of central control. These influences will inevitably overlook some groups of workers—those who are unorganized or otherwise vulnerable. The question is : do the Central Arbitration Committee and the new Fair Wages policy have a role to perform in such a system?

Its first Award under Schedule 11 indicates such a role. The Company concerned was engaged in the plastics industry, employing 145 workers. In September 1976, the Transport and General Workers' Union sought and were accorded recognition and negotiating rights for all hourly paid workers at the Company's factory. An agreement was concluded to provide minimum rates of pay up to the standards set out in the national agreement between the Engineering Employers' Federation and the Confederation of Shipbuilding and Engineering Unions. Permission to pay the agreed rates was sought from the Department of Employment but approval was withheld pending a decision by the Committee. The Union, therefore, submitted a claim under Schedule 11 to A.C.A.S. on 1 January 1977. In Award 103 of 20 April 1977 (*I. E. White (Plastics) Ltd. and T.G.W.U.*), the claim was upheld:

> The Committee is, therefore, satisfied that the appropriate terms and conditions to consider are those set out in the national engineering agreement.
>
> We had no difficulty in concluding that there was a failure to observe the recognized terms and conditions as settled by agreement for the workers covered by the reference. The Committee has carefully considered the agreement by stages concluded between the parties, and conclude that it is a sound and sensible solution, which, in the main, the Committee would wish to endorse. (paras. 13–14)

The Committee amended one point in the agreement relating to consolidation of the £6 supplement, but otherwise upheld the 'recognized terms and conditions'. Cases on the 'general level' will doubtless tax its ingenuity to a greater extent. But the fundamental questions remain: will Schedule 11 be interpreted by the Committee so that it can be used to remedy the anomalies and injustices that are bound to arise in the developing system of industrial relations? Will the Committee allow incomes policy to emasculate the new Fair Wages policy? Will employers resist and government departments obstruct the use of Schedule 11? Above all, will the trade unions undertake to exploit the new Fair Wages policy despite the disappointments of the previous policies?

Past experience does not augur success for the Fair Wages policy. It is a last resort for workers unable to obtain fair wages through their own efforts. But a Fair Wages policy is better than none at all. Better still is a useful last resort than one which is futile. Schedule 11 can be interpreted flexibly; the Committee has so far withstood the challenge of incomes policy; and the unions have submitted hundreds of claims in the few months since it came into force on 1 January 1977. There may yet be a future for Fair Wages policy.

NOTES

1. For these two Committee reports, see Epitome of the Reports from the Committees of Public Accounts, vol. I, 1857–1937, (H.C. 154 of 1938); at pp. 238–40, Fourth Report of the P.A.C., 1889, H.C. 259, Appendix, paras. 10–15 (Treasury Minutes of 11 December 1889 and 6 January 1890); and Epitome, vol. I, p. 284; Third Report of the P.A.C., 1891, H.C. 361, paras. 47–9 (T.M. 5 January 1892). And Epitome, vol. I, p. 593; Second Report of the P.A.C., 1919, H.C. 145, para. 21 (T.M.s of 29 November 1919 and 26 February 1920). See also the close supervision over wage rates paid on housing contracts placed by the Office of Works during World War One, Epitome, vol. I, p. 557; First Report of the P.A.C., 1916, H.C. 83, para. 5 (T.M. 1 September 1916).

2. These principles were set out previously in the Treasury Minute of 4 January 1951 on the Fourth Report from the Public Accounts Committee, Session 1950, paras. 11–13. See for the exposition, Epitome of the Reports from the Committees of Public Accounts, vol. II of 1938–69, (H.C. 187 of 1970), pp. 259–60; Third Report of the P.A.C., 1953–4, H.C. 231, para. 36 (T.M. of 31 January 1955).

3. Parl. Deb., H. of C. (Fifth Series); 24 March 1955, vol. 538, col. 2260.

4. Parl. Deb., H. of C. (Fifth Series); 30 April 1957, vol. 569, col. 6 (Written Answers), per Mr. Molson; and again, 9 July 1957, vol. 573, col. 25 (Written Answers), again per Mr. Molson.

5. These consequences of the government's initiative may be found in the Housing Statistics quoted in the Fourth Report of the Estimates Committee, Housing Subsidies, 1968–9, H.C. 473, vol. I, paras. 253, 255, and Evidence at Qs. 1745, 5635. Also, Parl. Deb., H. of C. (Fifth Series); 21 July 1966, vol. 732, cols. 980–1.

6. See Third Report of the Estimates Committee, The Central Office of Information, H.C. 259 of 1959–60; Evidence, p. 218, Memorandum submitted by the Association of Specialised Film Producers, at para. 6.

7. Fourth Report from the Estimates Committee, 1967–8, The Public Building Programme in the U.K., H.C. 351.

8. See Report of the Estimates Committee (Sub-Committee E), Session 1968–9, Motorways and Trunk Roads, H.C. 102(i); Minutes of Evidence, 28 January 1969, Introductory Memorandum by the Ministry of Transport, p. 20, para. 6.15.

9. See Report of the Estimates Committee (Sub-Committee B), Session 1969–70, Hospital Building in Great Britain, H.C. 59(i); Minutes of Evidence, 8 December

1969; Memorandum of the Department of Health and Social Security, p. 1, para. 49; also Report, H.C. 59(ii); Evidence of Officials of the D.H.S.S., 15 December 1969, at Qs. 169–70.

10. See Oral Evidence to the Estimates Committee, Fourth Report, 1967–8, on The Public Building Programme in the U.K., H.C. 351, at Q. 453. Similarly, Oral Evidence to the Estimates Committee Report on Hospital Building in Great Britain, ibid., on 16 February 1970, Qs. 945–52.

11. Report of the Comptroller and Auditor General, Civil Appropriation Accounts (Classes I–IV) 1965–6; H.C. 270 of 1966–1967, at paras. 73–85.

12. It remains to be seen whether government departments will change their attitudes as maintenance of the Government's incomes policy becomes more of a priority. That pressure is mounting is evidenced by a circular sent out in early August 1977 by the Department of Health and Social Security to all regional and area health authorities and hospital boards of governors. It names three firms which are alleged not to have complied with pay policy limits, and states:

Authorities having current contracts, or contemplating placing new contracts, or extensions to contracts, with any of the firms mentioned should inform the Department (Supply Division, HSSB 8) as soon as possible. No tender should be invited from, nor any contract or extension of any existing contract be awarded to, a firm in breach of the pay limit unless the prior approval of the Department has been obtained.

Existing contracts with firms in breach may be allowed to finish their term, but care must be taken, where contracts provide for price increases or reimbursement of cost increases under prime cost clauses, that payments of such increases do not contain any element of the pay settlement in excess of the limit. Where there is any doubt an assurance should be sought from the firm that the increase is claimed in accordance with the provisions of the Price Code.

Without the specific and prior approval of the Department, no *ex-gratia* assistance should be given to a firm which has breached the pay limit. Normally, the Department will be reluctant to approve *ex-gratia* assistance to a firm in breach even though there might otherwise be grounds for treating the case sympathetically.

Quoted in *The Sunday Times* of 21 August 1977, p. 45.

13. Parl. Deb., H. of C. (Fifth Series); 26 February 1948, vol. 447, col. 2123, per Mr. Glenvil Hall.

14. See Awards 2167 of 8 July 1948 (*U.S.D.A.W. and Navy, Army and Air Force Institutes Corp.*); 2173 of 16 August 1948 (*U.S.D.A.W. and White's Dairies (South Shields) Ltd.*) (claim succeeded); 2175 of 27 August 1948 (*British Sugar Industry National Trade Union Negotiating Committee and B.S.C. Ltd.*); and 2186 of 29 October 1948 (cement workers' claim succeeded).

15. See also Awards 3141 of 8 May 1967; 3143 of 26 May 1967, and 3145 of 19 June 1967.

16. The quotation from C. W. Guillebaud may be found in *The Role of the Arbitrator in Industrial Wage Disputes*, James Nisbet & Co., 1970, at pp. 21–2. W. E. J. McCarthy's findings are in *Compulsory Arbitration in in Britain: The Work of the I.D.T.*, Royal Commission on Trade Unions and Employers' Associations, Research Paper No. 8, London, H.M.S.O., 1968, at para. 26. But query his statement that: 'It is perhaps worth pointing out in this connection that throughout its life the Tribunal was never given directions by the Government, and that it was never even formally notified of their preferences and policy'.

Appendix
Text of Fair Wages Policy Instruments

The Fair Wages Resolution of 1891:

> That, in the opinion of this House it is the duty of the Government in all Government contracts to make provision against the evils which have recently been disclosed before the House of Lords' Sweating Committee, and to insert such conditions as may prevent the abuses arising from subletting, and make every effort to secure the payment of the rate of wages generally accepted as current for a competent workman in his trade.

The Fair Wages Resolution of 1909:

> Clauses in Government contracts should be so amended as to provide as follows: The contractor shall, under the penalty of a fine or otherwise, pay rates of wages and observe hours of labour not less favourable than those commonly recognized by employers and trade societies (or, in the absence of such recognized wages and hours those which in practice prevail amongst good employers) in the trade in the district where the work is carried out. Where there are no such wages and hours recognized or prevailing in the district, those recognized or prevailing in the nearest district in which the general industrial circumstances are similar shall be adopted. Further the conditions of employment generally accepted in the district in the trade concerned shall be taken into account in considering how far the terms of the fair wages clauses are being observed. The contractor shall be prohibited from transferring or assigning directly or indirectly, to any person or persons whatever, any portion of his contract without the written permission of the department. Sub-letting, other than that which may be customary in the trade concerned, shall be prohibited. The contractor shall be responsible for the observance of the fair wages clauses by the sub-contractor instead thereof.

498

The Fair Wages Resolution of 1946:

That, in the opinion of this House, the Fair Wages Clauses in Government Contracts should be so amended as to provide as follows:—

1. (*a*) The contractor shall pay rates of wages and observe hours and conditions of labour not less favourable than those established for the trade or industry in the district where the work is carried out by machinery of negotiation or arbitration to which the parties are organizations of employers and trade unions representative respectively of substantial proportions of the employers and workers engaged in the trade or industry in the district.

(*b*) In the absence of any rates of wages, hours or conditions of labour so established the contractor shall pay rates of wages and observe hours and conditions of labour which are not less favourable than the general level of wages, hours and conditions observed by other employers whose general circumstances in the trade or industry in which the contractor is engaged are similar.

2. The contractor shall in respect of all persons employed by him (whether in execution of the contract or otherwise) in every factory, workshop or place occupied or used by him for the execution of the contract comply with the general conditions required by this Resolution. Before a contractor is placed upon a department's list of firms to be invited to tender, the department shall obtain from him an assurance that to the best of his knowledge and belief he has complied with the general conditions required by this Resolution for at least the previous three months.

3. In the event of any question arising as to whether the requirements of this Resolution are being observed, the question shall, if not otherwise disposed of, be referred by the Minister of Labour and National Service to an independent tribunal for decision.

4. The contractor shall recognize the freedom of his workpeople to be members of trade unions.

5. The contractor shall at all times during the continuance of a contract display, for the information of his workpeople, in every factory, workshop or place occupied or used by him for the execution of the contract a copy of this Resolution.

6. The contractor shall be responsible for the observance of this Resolution by sub-contractors employed in the execution of the contract, and shall if required notify the department of the names and addresses of all such sub-contractors.

Conditions of Employment and National Arbitration Order No. 1305 of 1940, Part III:

5. (1) Where in any trade or industry in any district there are in force terms and conditions of employment which have been settled by machinery of negotiation or arbitration to which the parties are organizations of employers and trade unions representative respectively of substantial proportions of the employers and workers engaged in that trade or industry in that district (hereinafter referred to as 'recognized terms and conditions') all employers in that trade or industry in that district shall observe the recognized terms and conditions or such terms and conditions of employment as are not less favourable than the recognized terms and conditions.

(2) For the purposes of this Article, and subject to the provisions of paragraph (4) hereof terms and conditions of employment shall not be deemed to be less favourable than the recognized terms and conditions if they are in accordance with the terms and conditions relating to workers engaged in similar work which are applicable under—

(a) any agreement to which the parties are organizations of employers and trade unions which are representative respectively of substantial proportions of the employers and workers engaged or employed in the trade or industry in the district in which the employer is engaged; or

(b) any decision of a joint industrial council, conciliation board or other similar body constituted by organizations of employers and trade unions which are representative respectively of substantial proportions of the employers and workers engaged or employed in the trade or industry in the district in which the employer is engaged; or

(c) in the absence of any such agreement or decision as is mentioned in the foregoing provisions of this paragraph, any agreement between the particular employer concerned and a trade union which is representative of a substantial proportion of workers employed in the trade or industry in which the employer is engaged; or

(d) any award made by the National Arbitration Tribunal, the Industrial Court or any other body or person acting in the capacity of arbitrator relating to the terms and conditions of employment observable by an employer in the same trade or industry in the same district; or

(e) any statutory provisions relating to remuneration, rates of wages, hours or working conditions, unless those provisions are themselves less favourable than the provisions of any such agreement, decision or award as is mentioned in the foregoing provisions of this paragraph, being an agreement, decision or award relating to the particular employer concerned or any employers' organization of which he is a member or to which such an employer or such an organization is a party.

(3) If any question arises as to the nature, scope or effect of the recognized terms and conditions in any trade or industry in any district or as to whether an employer is observing the recognized terms and conditions or is observing terms and conditions which are not less favourable than the recognized terms and conditions, that question may be reported to the Minister by any organization of employers or any trade union which in the opinion of the Minister is an organization or trade union that habitually takes part in the settlement of wages and working conditions in the trade or industry concerned and if so reported the question shall thereupon be dealt with in the same manner as if it were a trade dispute reported to the Minister under the provisions of Article 2 of this Order and the provisions of that Article shall apply accordingly: so, however, that in making an award on any question referred by the Minister by virtue of the powers conferred by this paragraph the National Arbitration Tribunal shall have regard not only to the provisions of paragraph (2) of this Article, but also to any collective agreements concerning the terms and conditions of similar workers in comparable trades or industries.

(4) Where an award has been made by the National Arbitration Tribunal in consequence of a report made under the foregoing provisions of this Article then as from the date of the award or from such date as the Tribunal may direct, not being earlier than the date on which the question to which the award relates first arose, it shall be an implied term of the contract between the employer and workers to whom the award applies that the rates of wages to be paid and the conditions of employment to be observed under the contract shall, until varied by a subsequent agreement, decision or award such as is mentioned in the foregoing provisions of this Article, be in accordance with the award.

(5) Any reference in the foregoing provisions of this Article to an agreement, decision or award shall be construed as a reference to that agreement, decision or award as modified by any subsequent agreement, decision or award.

The Industrial Disputes Order No. 1376 of 1951, Sections 2, 7, 9 and 10:

2. Where—

(*a*) in any trade or industry or section of trade or industry in any district terms and conditions of employment are established which have been settled by machinery of negotiation or arbitration to which the parties are organizations of employers and trade unions representative respectively of substantial proportions of the employers and workers engaged in that trade or industry or section of trade or industry in that district (hereinafter referred to as 'recognized terms and conditions'); and

(*b*) an issue as to whether an employer in that district should observe the recognized terms and conditions (hereinafter referred to as 'an issue') is reported to the Minister in accordance with this Order by an organization of employers or a trade union; and

(*c*) the Minister is of opinion that the organization of employers or trade union reporting the issue habitually takes part in the settlement of terms and conditions of employment in the trade or industry or section of trade or industry concerned; that issue shall be dealt with in accordance with the subsequent provisions of this Order.

7. For the purpose of settling disputes referred to it by the Minister, there shall be constituted a Tribunal to be known as the Industrial Disputes Tribunal (hereinafter in this Order referred to as 'the Tribunal'), and the provisions of the First Schedule to this Order shall have effect with respect to the constitution and proceedings of the Tribunal.

9. (1) Where an issue has been reported to the Minister in accordance with this Order, that issue shall, if not otherwise settled, be referred by the Minister to the Tribunal.

(2) Where an issue has been referred by the Minister to the Tribunal and the Tribunal is of opinion that there are recognized terms and conditions applicable to the case and that the employer concerned is not observing those terms and conditions or terms and conditions of employment which, in the opinion of the Tribunal, are not less favourable than those terms and conditions, it may by its award require the employer to observe the recognized terms and conditions or such terms and conditions of employment as may be determined by it to be not less favourable than the recognized terms and conditions.

10. Where an award on a dispute or issue has been made by the Tribunal then as from the date of the award or from such other date, not being earlier than the date on which the dispute or issue to which the award relates first arose, as the Tribunal may direct, it shall be an implied term of the contract between the employer and workers to whom the award applies that the terms and conditions of employment to be observed under the contract shall be in accordance with the award until varied by agreement between the parties or by a subsequent award of the Tribunal or until different terms and conditions of employment in respect of the workers concerned are settled through the machinery of negotiation or arbitration for the settlement of terms and conditions of employment in the trade or industry or section of trade or industry or undertaking in which those workers are employed.

Terms and Conditions of Employment Act, 1959, Section 8:

8. (1) Where a claim is duly reported to the Minister under this section—

(a) that terms or conditions of employment are established in any trade or industry, or section of a trade or industry, either generally or in any district, which have been settled by an agreement or award, and

(b) that the parties to the agreement, or to the proceedings in which the award was made, are or represent organizations of employers and organizations of workers or associations of such organizations, and represent (generally or in the district in question, as the case may be) a substantial proportion of the employers and of the workers in the trade, industry or section, being workers of the description (hereinafter referred to as 'the relevant description') to which the agreement or award relates, and

(c) that as respects any worker of the relevant description an employer engaged in the trade, industry or section (or, where the operation of the agreement or award is limited to a district, an employer so engaged in that district), whether represented as aforesaid or not, is not observing the terms or conditions (hereinafter referred to as 'the recognized terms or conditions'),

the Minister may take any steps which seem to him expedient to settle, or to secure the use of appropriate machinery to settle, the claim and shall, if the claim is not otherwise settled, refer it to the Industrial Court constituted under Part I of the Industrial Courts Act, 1919:

Provided that—

    (i) no claim shall be reported under this section as respects workers whose remuneration or minimum remuneration is fixed (otherwise than by the employer, with or without the approval of any other person) in pursuance of any enactment other than this section or in the case of whom provision is made by or under any enactment other than this section for the settlement of questions as to remuneration or minimum remuneration;

    (ii) no claim shall be reported under this section as respects terms or conditions fixed as aforesaid.

(2) For the purposes of this section a claim, to be duly reported, must be reported to the Minister in writing by an organization or association being, or represented by, one of the parties mentioned in paragraph (*b*) of the foregoing subsection; and if in the opinion of the Minister the report of a claim does not contain sufficient particulars he may require further particulars to be given, and if he does so the report shall not be treated as having been duly made until the Minister is satisfied that the particulars required have been given.

(3) If on a reference under this section the Industrial Court is satisfied that the claim is well founded, then unless the Court is satisfied that the terms or conditions which the employer is observing are not less favourable than the recognized terms or conditions the Court shall make an award requiring the employer to observe the recognized terms or conditions as respects all workers of the relevant description from time to time employed by him.

(4) An award under this section shall have effect as an implied term of the contract of employment, and shall have effect from such date as the Industrial Court may determine, being a date not earlier than the date on which, in the opinion of the Court, the employer was first informed of the claim giving rise to the award by the organization or association which reported the claim to the Minister; and an award under this section shall cease to have effect on the coming into operation of an agreement or award varying or abrogating the recognized terms or conditions.

(5) For the purposes of this section the carrying on of the activities of public or local authorities shall be treated as the carrying on of a trade or industry.

Schedule 11 to the Employment Protection Act 1975:

SCHEDULE 11

EXTENSION OF TERMS AND CONDITIONS

PART I

RECOGNIZED TERMS AND CONDITIONS AND GENERAL LEVEL OF
TERMS AND CONDITIONS

1. A claim may be reported to the Service, in accordance with and subject to the following provisions of this Part of this Schedule, that as respects any worker an employer is, in respect of any matter, observing terms and conditions of employment less favourable than the recognized terms and conditions, or, where, or so far as, there are no recognized terms and conditions, the general level of terms and conditions.

2. In this Part of this Schedule—

(a) the 'recognized terms and conditions' means terms and conditions of workers in comparable employment in the trade or industry, or section of a trade or industry, in which the employer in question is engaged, either generally or in the district in which he is so engaged, which have been settled by an agreement or award, to which the parties are employers' associations and independent trade unions which represent (generally or in the district in question, as the case may be) a substantial proportion of the employers and of the workers in the trade, industry or section, being workers of the description to which the agreement or award relates; and

(b) the 'general level of terms and conditions' means the general level of terms and conditions observed for comparable workers by employers—

    (i) in the trade, industry or section in which the employer in question is engaged in the district in which he is so engaged; and

    (ii) whose circumstances are similar to those of the employer in question,

and for the purposes of sub-paragraph (a) above the reference to terms and conditions, in a case where minimum terms and conditions have been settled as mentioned in that sub-paragraph, is a reference to those minimum terms and conditions.

3. No claim shall be reported under paragraph 1 above as respects workers whose remuneration or terms and conditions, or minimum

remuneration or terms and conditions, is or are fixed (otherwise than by the employer, with or without the approval of any other person) in pursuance of any enactment other than—

(*a*) the Agricultural Wages Act 1948 or the Agricultural Wages (Scotland) Act 1949;

(*b*) the Wages Councils Act 1959;

(*c*) sections 90 to 94 above; or

(*d*) this Schedule;

or in the case of whom provision is made by or under any such enactment for the settlement of questions as to remuneration or terms and conditions or minimum remuneration or terms and conditions.

4. A claim may be reported under paragraph 1 above, where, or so far as, the claim is founded upon recognized terms and conditions, by an employers' association or an independent trade union being one of the parties mentioned in paragraph 2(*a*) above.

5. (1) A claim may be reported under paragraph 1 above, where, or so far as, the claim is founded upon the general level of terms and conditions, by—

(*a*) an employers' association having members engaged in the trade, industry or section, in the district to which the claim relates; or

(*b*) subject to sub-paragraph (2) below, a trade union of which any worker concerned is a member.

(2) Where any such worker is of a description in respect of which an employer recognizes one or more independent trade unions, such a claim may be reported by a trade union only if it is that recognized union or, as the case may be, one of those recognized unions.

6. A claim under paragraph 1 above shall be in writing and shall contain such particulars as the Service may require.

7. When a claim is reported to the Service under paragraph 1 above the Service shall take any steps which seem to it expedient to settle the claim or to secure the use of appropriate machinery to settle the claim and shall if the claim is not otherwise settled refer it to the Committee.

8. The Committee shall hear and determine the claim and it shall be for—

(*a*) the party making the claim to show that there are recognized terms and conditions and what those terms and conditions are, or, as the case may be, what the general level of terms and conditions is; and (*b*) the employer to satisfy the Committee that he is observing terms and conditions of employment not less favourable than the recognized terms and conditions or, as the case may be, the general level of terms and conditions.

9. In ascertaining whether, in respect of any matter which is the subject of a claim under paragraph 1 above, the employer is observing terms and conditions less favourable than the recognized terms and conditions, or as the case may be, the general level of terms and conditions regard shall be had to the whole of the terms and conditions observed by the employer as respects the worker to whom the claim relates.

10. If the Committee finds the claim wholly or partly well-founded it shall make an award that the employer shall observe the recognized terms and conditions or, as the case may be, terms and conditions conforming to the general level of terms and conditions and shall identify or specify—

(*a*) the recognized terms and conditions or, as the case may be, terms and conditions conforming to the general level of terms and conditions;

(*b*) the description or descriptions of employees in respect of which they are to be observed; and

(*c*) the date from which they are to be observed, being a date not earlier than the date on which the employer was first informed of the claim giving rise to the award by the union or association which reported the claim to the Service.

11. Any terms and conditions which by an award under paragraph 10 above the employer is required to observe in respect of employees of his shall have effect as part of the contract of employment of any such employee as from the date specified in the award, except in so far as they are superseded or varied—

(*a*) by a subsequent award under that paragraph;

(*b*) by a collective agreement between the employer and the trade union for the time being representing that employee; or

(*c*) by express or implied agreement between the employee and the employer so far as that agreement effects an improvement in any terms and conditions having effect by virtue of the award.

12. Where—

(*a*) by virtue of any enactment, other than one contained in this Part of this Schedule, providing for minimum remuneration or terms and conditions a contract of employment is to have effect as modified by an award, order or other instrument under that enactment; and (*b*) by virtue of an award under paragraph 10 above any terms and conditions are to have effect as part of that contract,

that contract shall have effect in accordance with that award, order or other instrument or in accordance with the award under paragraph 10 above, whichever is the more favourable, in respect of any terms and conditions of that contract, to the employee.

13. If in the course of determining a claim under this Schedule after the commencement of section 3 of the Equal Pay Act 1970, it appears to the Committee that a collective agreement or pay structure within the meaning of that section contains any provision applying specifically to men only or to women only so that it would, had it been referred to the Committee by the Secretary of State under that section, have required amendment in accordance with subsection (4) of that section so as to remove that discrimination between men and women—

(*a*) that provision shall not be regarded as part of the recognized terms and conditions or, as the case may be, shall not be taken into account in assessing the general level of terms and conditions; and

(*b*) the Committee shall report its opinion to the Secretary of State and, in the case of a collective agreement, to the parties to that agreement or, in the case of a pay structure, to the employer concerned.

14. For the purposes of this Schedule the carrying on of the activities of public or local authorities shall be treated as the carrying on of a trade or industry.

Part II

Collectively Negotiated Terms and Conditions in Certain Industries

15. A claim may be reported to the Service under this paragraph by an independent trade union as respects any worker who is a member of that trade union and who falls within the field of operation of a wages council, a statutory joint industrial council, the Agricultural Wages Board or the Scottish Agricultural Wages Board—

(*a*) that the union is a party to one or more collective agreements and that those agreements cover a significant number of establishments within the field of operation of that council or Board either generally or in the district in which the worker is employed; and (*b*) that in those establishments the circumstances of the employer are similar to those of the employer of the worker in question; and

(*c*) that the employer is paying him less than the lowest current rate of remuneration (disregarding any rate agreed to more than 12 months before the date on which the claim was reported) payable to workers of his description under any of those agreements.

16. The provisions of paragraphs 7, 8 and 10 to 14 above shall apply to a claim under paragraph 15 above—

(*a*) as if for any reference to the recognized terms and conditions there were substituted a reference to the rate of remuneration referred to in paragraph 15(*c*) above;

(*b*) as if references to the general level of terms and conditions were omitted; and

(*c*) as if the reference in paragraph 12(*a*) to Part I of this Schedule were a reference to Part II of this Schedule and so much of Part I as is thereby applied.

TABLE OF CASES

TABLE OF AWARDS

511

No.

1760	18 July 1940	Trade Union Side of the Shipbuilding Trade Joint Council for Government Departments and Official Side	264, 308n
1764–5	13 September 1940	N.U.G.M.W. and T.G.W.U. and Ministry of Supply	264
1767	3 October 1940	Association of Cine-Technicians and British Instructional Films, Ltd.	257n, 312
1768	7 October 1940	Trade Union Side of the Shipbuilding Trade Joint Council for Government Departments and Official Side	264
1770	22 October 1940	N.U.G.M.W. and Tynemouth County Borough Council	257n
1773	18 November 1940	Trade Union Side of the Shipbuilding Trade Joint Council for Government Departments and Official Side	257n, 264, 381n
1775	29 November 1940	Trade Union Side of the Miscellaneous Trades Joint Council for Government Industrial Establishments and Official Side	256, 257n, 264, 381n
1781	13 January 1941	Electrical Power Engineers' Association and Stockton-on-Tees Corporation	308n, 340n, 381n
1802	9 May 1941	N.U.P.E. and North Riding County Council	339n, 381n
1803	21 May 1941	Trade Union Side of the Shipbuilding Trade Joint Council for Government Departments and Official Side	265, 340n, 381n
1808	13 June 1941	Electrical Power Engineers' Association and Worthing Corporation	308n, 340n, 381n
1823	26 August 1941	N.U.P.E. and Morley Town Council Waterworks Committee	265, 308n, 340n, 381n
1826	15 September 1941	National Union of Cokemen and Bye-Product Workers and Brancepeth Gas and Coke Ltd.	308n, 348–9
1842	21 November 1941	N.U.G.M.W. and Monmouth Town Council	308n, 381n
1843	21 November 1941	Trade Union Side of the Shipbuilding Trade Joint Council for Government Departments and Official Side	265, 268, 269
1848	9 December 1941	N.U.P.E. and Lewes Borough Council	308n
1850	19 December 1941	N.U.G.M.W. and Lanark Town Council	308n, 381n
1852	26 February 1942	Trade Union Side of the Miscellaneous Trades Joint Council for Government Industrial Establishments and Official Side	257n, 312
1855	15 April 1942	N.U.G.M.W. and Caernarvon Corporation	308n, 339n, 381n
1856	23 April 1942	N.U.P.E. and Surbiton Borough Council	308n, 381n

No.

No.

2538	25 October 1954	C. N. Hamilton and Messrs. Cotterell Bros. Ltd.	308n
2544	13 November 1954	Interpretation of Award 2526	360
2549	20 December 1954	U.R.T.W.A.E. and Messrs. G. H. Kime & Co. Ltd.	271, 339n
2593	31 January 1956	W. Nield and J. Billig & Sons Ltd.	308n
2605	3 April 1956	Mr. F. W. H. Luck and Decca Radar Ltd.	277
2616	18 July 1956	W. Kearns and George Wimpey & Co. Ltd.	277
2637	11 January 1957	N.U.P.E. and St. Andrew's & Red Cross Scottish Ambulance Service	276, 339n, 340–1n
2641	30 January 1957	National Union of Packing Case Makers (Wood & Tin), Box Makers, Sawyers and Mill Workers and A. V. Roe & Co. Ltd.	360–1
2651	24 May 1957	National Conciliation Board for the Mattress Making Industry and Chapman's of Trowbridge, Ltd.	274
2672	21 November 1957	Amalgamated Society of Woodcutting Machinists and Messrs. Bartlett Materials Handling Ltd.	274, 339n, 347, 353n
2675	19 December 1957	R. J. Duncan and R. C. Cessford	308n, 339n
2685	24 March 1958	R. C. Jones and Burgess Webb and Squire Ltd.	308n
2694	2 June 1958	D. Broomhall and Parkinson Howard Ltd.	277
2725	30 April 1959	B.A.L.P.A. and Starways Ltd.	286
2744–5	16 October 1959	South Western Fire Area Joint Board and National Association of Fire Officers and Chief Fire Officers' Association	320, 324, 333
2754	2 December 1959	National Society of Painters and Burns Shopfitters	280, 340n
2755	3 December 1959	N.U.V.B. and Airflow Streamlines Ltd.	281
2756	8 December 1959	Proprietors of the Regal Cinema, Nairn and National Association of Theatrical and Kine Employees	333
2765	11 March 1960	Hermit Industries (Dudley) Ltd. and Amalgamated Union of Foundry Workers	257n
2779	11 May 1960	N.U.G.M.W. and Eton House School	320, 339n, 340n
2787	4 July 1960	Aston Hosiery Co. Ltd. and Hinckley and District Hosiery Warehouse-men's Association	347
2788	5 July 1960	Bibby and Baron (New Bridge) Ltd. and Society of Lithographic Artists, Designers, Engravers and Process Workers	340n

No.

No.			
2793	28 July 1960	A.S.S.E.T. and English Electric Co. Ltd. of Preston, Lancs.	288–9, 334
2800	29 August 1960	Hills of Leeds (Meyer Hill (Leeds) Ltd.) and The Amalgamated Society of Woodworkers and the Amalgamated Society of Woodcutting Machinists	340n
2801	29 August 1960	Mr. T. Cowie and Electrical Trades Union	347
2804–5	27 September 1960	Marshall and Brush, Ltd., Coates and Co. Ltd. and Scottish Carpet Trade and Factory Workers' Union	340n
2806	11 October 1960	Association of Engineering and Shipbuilding Draughtsmen and Ford Motor Co.	317–18, 325, 326
2808	25 October 1960	Association of Engineering and Shipbuilding Draughtsmen and Ford Motor Co.	280, 323, 340n
2812	7 November 1960	Norwich Corporation and Wroxham Dairies Ltd.	289–90, 334
2815	13 December 1960	Association of Scientific Workers and Park Foundry (Belper) Ltd., Derby	353n
2816	20 December 1960	Amalgamated Society of Woodworkers and W. & J. Tod, Ltd.	290
2818	16 January 1961	Ayton Asphalt Co. Ltd. and N.U.G.M.W.	315
2821	13 February 1961	A.S.S.E.T. and Walter MacFarlane & Co. Ltd. of Glasgow	290, 343, 353n
2822	13 February 1961	Messrs. P. F. McKerracher and The Scottish Painters' Society	257n
2827	6 March 1961	Kenex Coachwork Ltd. and N.U.V.B.	257n
2829	10 March 1961	S.L.A.D.E. and Thames Board Mills Ltd.	281, 315
2847	8 June 1961	Variety Artistes' Federation and City of Leicester Working Men's Club	317, 339n, 361
2854	6 July 1961	Sign and Display Trades Union and Formica Ltd.	281–2, 309n
2855	11 July 1961	Pianoforte Supplies Ltd. and A.E.U.	284–5
2856	12 July 1961	Autax Ltd., Manchester and Radio Cabs (Man.)	290
2862	28 July 1961	Springer Engineering and A.E.U.	284–5
2870	21 September 1961	National Society of Metal Mechanics and Rolls-Royce Ltd.	347
2872	28 September 1961	Robert Deards Ltd. and N.U.P.E.	257n, 340n
2875	8 November 1961	British Medical Association and Northampton City Council	349
2877	16 November 1961	Centrax Ltd. and The Association of Engineering and Shipbuilding Draughtsmen (since the 11 August 1961, re-named D.A.T.A.)	257n, 309n, 324

No.

3151	17 August 1967	Henry Miller and Co. (Timber) Ltd. and Amalgamated Society of Wood-cutting Machinists	309n, 314, 340n
3157	28 December 1967	Manchester Airport Agencies and T.G.W.U.	339n
3160	29 January 1968	Black Clawson International Ltd. and C.A.W.U.	256n, 309n, 484
3161	30 January 1968	N.U.P.E. and Industrial Contract Cleaners	291, 340n, 366, 369–70, 371
3163	2 April 1968	T.G.W.U. and T. D. Alexander, Greyhound Luxury Coaches, Arbroath	287
3164	17 April 1968	The Rt. Hon. Lord Newborough and National Federation of Building Trades Operatives	256n
3168	7 May 1968	T.G.W.U. and Brooks Motor Ltd.	318, 388
3169	31 May 1968	Morganite Carbon Ltd. and C.A.W.U.	340n
3177	13 August 1968	Greater London Council Staff Association and London Borough of Tower Hamlets	317
3179	16 August 1968	D.A.T.A. and Cableform Ltd.	280
3181	7 November 1968	National Union of Hosiery and Knitwear Workers and Starward Fabrics Ltd.	282
3190	24 April 1969	County Borough of Walsall and N.A.L.G.O.	351
3192	15 July 1969	Rollalong Ltd. and N.U.V.B.	316
3193	28 July 1969	Association of Patternmakers and Allied Craftsmen and Birmingham Refractories (Castings) Ltd.	282–3
3197	5 September 1969	Black Clawson International Ltd. and C.A.W.U.	309n, 326
3203	27 November 1969	Carrier Engineering Co. Ltd. and D.A.T.A.	340n
3204	3 February 1970	Scot Meat Products and C.A.W.U.	309n, 340n
3206	24 March 1970	C.S.U. and Cleaners Ltd.	340n, 370–3
3212	1 May 1970	C.S.U. and General Cleaning Contractors (Northern) Ltd.	340n, 343, 353n, 371–3
3213	11 May 1970	A.C.T.A.T. and Kodak Ltd.	326, 339n
3216–19	12 June 1970	C.S.U. and All England Cleaning Co. Ltd.	340n, 371, 372
3223–4	6 August 1970	G.M.W.U. and G. R. A. Anderson, A. E. and J. A. Wilson—Economic Bus Co., Co. Durham	287, 325–6
3225	10 August 1970	B.A.L.P.A. and B.U.A. Ltd.	326, 352
3227	25 August 1970	Dorchester Rural District Council and N.A.L.G.O.	351

No.

2	16 March 1976	Bolton Gate Co. Ltd. and A.U.E.W.	404, 421–2, 430, 439, 449–50, 452–3, 488–90, 492
3	9 March 1976	John Lyle Carpets Ltd. and Scottish Carpet Workers' Union	405, 422, 428
4–5	14 March 1976	Kyle and Carrick District Council and N.A.L.G.O.	405, 425, 493
6	6 April 1976	Dowty Boulton Paul Ltd. and A.S.T.M.S.	405, 425, 447, 455–6, 465, 489–91
9	24 May 1976	National Bank of Pakistan and N.U.B.E.	405, 429, 493
10	2 June 1976	BE & HL Patternmaking Co. Ltd. and The Association of Patternmakers and Allied Craftsmen	405, 436
12	21 June 1976	Frank Wilson (Filing) Ltd. and The Society of Graphical and Allied Trades	405
14	25 June 1976	Wimet Ltd. and A.S.T.M.S.	405, 465–6, 468, 488, 490–2
15	14 July 1976	Navy, Army and Air Force Institutes and U.S.D.A.W.	405, 438
16	14 July 1976	George Allinson (Transport) Ltd. and T.G.W.U.	405, 449–50
18	4 August 1976	Cambion Electronic Products Ltd. and A.U.E.W.	405, 424, 430–1, 460–1, 494
21	11 August 1976	Radio Trent Ltd. and N.U.J.	257n, 405, 462–3, 488–90, 492
23	9 August 1976	Effingham Steel Works Ltd. and A.S.T.M.S.	405, 425, 442, 454–5, 464, 466–7, 489–91
24	13 August 1976	W. Lovatt Transport and United Road Transport Union	405, 424, 448
27	31 August 1976	STD Services Ltd. and A.S.T.M.S.	405, 436–7, 494
28	6 September 1976	Willowbrook International Ltd. and T.G.W.U.	405

No.

30	17 September 1976	Dobson Hydraulics Ltd. and A.U.E.W. (T.A.S.S.)	405, 440–1, 444, 459, 489–91
32	21 September 1976	Sunblest Bakeries (GLW) Ltd. and City Bakeries Ltd., Glasgow and T.G.W.U.	405, 424, 435–6
33	22 September 1976	Newton Derby Ltd. and Association of Professional, Executive, Clerical and Computer Staff	405, 443–4, 464, 467–8
35	27 September 1976	Norprint Ltd. and S.L.A.D.E.	405, 424, 428–9
36	5 October 1976	Ferranti Ltd.	405, 447, 488, 492, 494
37	12 October 1976	F.G. Miles Engineering Ltd., Part of Hunting Hivolt Ltd.	405, 453, 467
38	12 October 1976	Gillow Heath Mining Co. Ltd. and National Union of Mineworkers	405, 428
40–1	1 November 1976	University of Manchester, University of Manchester Institute of Science and Technology and A.U.T.	405, 449
42	1 November 1976	John Dobson (Milnthorpe) Ltd. and T.G.W.U.	405
44	16 November 1976	Tropical Foods Ltd. and U.S.D.A.W.	405
45	1 November 1976	C. Compton Ltd. and T.G.W.U.	405
47	30 November 1976	Bristol Metal Spraying and Welding Co. Ltd. and G.M.W.U.	405
50	7 December 1976	Dowty Boulton Paul Ltd. and A.U.E.W. (T.A.S.S.)	405, 431–3, 454, 467–8
52	13 December 1976	Weyfringe Ltd. and T.G.W.U.	405
53	13 December 1976	Marconi Space and Defence Systems Ltd. and Association of Clerical, Technical and Supervisory Staffs, T.G.W.U.	405
54	21 December 1976	W & C Mercer and T.G.W.U.	405
55	30 December 1976	Wimet Ltd.	405
56	30 December 1976	Quinton and Kaines Ltd. and Furniture, Timber and Allied Trades Union	405
57	31 December 1976	Brewster Precision Instruments Ltd. and T.G.W.U.	405
58	31 December 1976	Rank Precision Industries Ltd. and A.U.E.W. (Engineering Section)	405
59	31 December 1976	The Open University and A.U.T.	405
62	13 December 1976	Gordon Ellis and Co. and Furniture, Timber and Allied Trades Union	405
63	31 December 1976	Interpretation of Award 28	405
66	31 December 1976	Allpak International Ltd. and The Fibreboard Packing Case Employers' Association	405

No.

67	31 December 1976	Dowty Mining Equipment Ltd. and A.S.T.M.S.	405
68	31 December 1976	Clyde Leisure Pastimes Ltd. and National Association of Theatrical, Television and Kine Employees	257n, 405
71	21 January 1977	J. & E. Arnfield Ltd.	405, 439, 453
73	3 February 1977	WH & EE Whitley (Concrete) Ltd. and G.M.W.U.	405
74	7 February 1977	Walter Somers (Materials Handling) Ltd. and G.M.W.U.	405, 426
75	9 February 1977	Doncaster Newspapers Ltd. and National Society of Operative Printers, Graphical and Media Personnel	405
76	9 February 1977	Bristol Aerojet Ltd. and A.S.T.M.S.	405, 432–3, 444, 453–4, 463–4
77	16 February 1977	Kitson's Sheet Metal Ltd. and the National Union of Sheet Metal Workers, Coppersmiths, Heating and Domestic Engineers	405, 422, 431, 437, 459
78	17 February 1977	Kelvin Hughes and A.U.E.W. (Engineering Section)	405, 439, 443, 450–1, 453, 459–60, 463
79	22 February 1977	Orkney Islands Shipping Co. Ltd.	405, 456–7
80–1	22 February 1977	ML Engineering Co. Ltd. and ML Aviation Co. Ltd.	405, 453, 459, 464
82–3	23 February 1977	North Eastern Co-operative Society Ltd., Greater Nottingham Co-operative Society Ltd. and National Association of Co-operative Officials	405, 423, 468–9
84	28 February 1977	Light-metal Forgings Ltd. and A.S.T.M.S.	405, 422–3, 444–5, 454, 463
85	2 March 1977	Twyfords Ltd. and Union of Construction, Allied Trades and Technicians	405, 429
86	8 March 1977	Grundy and Partners Ltd. and A.U.E.W. (T.A.S.S.)	405, 439, 443, 454, 463
88	28 February 1977	Hostess Furniture Ltd. and A.S.T.M.S.	405, 439, 442, 453, 463, 465
89	8 March 1977	Eric Bemrose Ltd. and the National Graphical Association, The Society of Graphical and Allied Trades	405, 425–6, 451–2, 461–2

No.

90	16 March 1977	H. W. Ward and Co. Ltd. and A.U.E.W. (T.A.S.S.)	405, 439, 456, 463, 468
92–3	23 March 1977	Tarantella (Edna Kirby Ltd.) and National Union of the Footwear, Leather and Allied Trades	405
94	25 March 1977	Woodhouse Parish Council and N.U.P.E.	405, 457, 463, 468
95	22 March 1977	The Blackpool Tower Co. Ltd. and A.U.E.W. (Construction Section)	405, 438, 457–8, 463, 468
97	29 March 1977	The Birmingham Box Co. Ltd. and Society of Graphical and Allied Trades	405
99	31 March 1977	Newalls Insulation Co. Ltd. and G.M.W.U.	405
100	19 April 1977	Calibration Systems Ltd.	405, 464
102	20 April 1977	Globe Petroleum Sales Ltd. and T.G.W.U.	405, 437–8
103	20 April 1977	I.E. White (Plastics) Ltd. and T.G.W.U.	404, 427, 495
104	2 May 1977	Hawker Siddeley Aviation Ltd., Hamble, and A.S.T.M.S.	405, 433–4, 439–40, 446–7, 464–5
106	29 April 1977	M.L. Engineering (Plymouth) Ltd.	405, 467
108	6 May 1977	Weldall Engineering Ltd. and A.U.E.W. (T.A.S.S.)	405, 441–2, 453–4, 460–1, 468
111	12 May 1977	Charles Richards Fasteners Ltd. and A.S.T.M.S.	405, 431, 465
112	10 May 1977	The Hymatic Engineering Co. Ltd.	405, 426–7, 434–5, 467
113	20 May 1977	William E. Farrar Ltd. and A.U.E.W. (T.A.S.S.)	405, 447, 455, 465
114	20 May 1977	AEI Semiconductors Ltd. and A.S.T.M.S.	404, 405, 440, 447, 459

TABLE OF STATUTES

INDEX